HUMAN DEVELOPMENT

Selected Readings

HUMAN DEVELOPMENT

Selected Readings

EDITED BY

MORRIS L. HAIMOWITZ

Director, Human Relations, Chicago Public Schools

AND

NATALIE READER HAIMOWITZ

Milwaukee Psychiatric Services

THOMAS Y. CROWELL COMPANY

New York · Established 1834

First Printing, April, 1960
Second Printing, July, 1960
Third Printing, April, 1961
Fourth Printing, August, 1962
Fifth Printing, June, 1963

Library of Congress Catalog Card Number 60-6060

Designed by Laurel Wagner
Cover design by Herbert S. Stoltz

Manufactured in the United States of America
By Vail-Ballou Press, Inc., Binghamton, N.Y.

To Our Parents
and to Our Children

PREFACE

The articles in this book have been selected because they were important, and because they were clear; important to us, the editors, and written clearly enough to be understood by college students.

Observations of children around the world and in our own city of Chicago show that a very wide variety of personalities is possible. Which kind do we want? The first section of the book presents articles identifying a number of conflicting values.

All right, suppose we could decide what kind of children—and adults —we would like; then, what would we have to know about our raw materials? What does scientific knowledge tell us about children, about how they grow and develop into various kinds of personalities? The major portion of this volume is composed of scientific studies, descriptive and theoretical, dealing with the psychological behavior of infants and children.

Once we know what we want, and we understand the nature of the human being we are working with, then we still have the problem of applying our knowledge to achieve the desired outcomes. We might call this the fine art of applied psychology. The materials in the section entitled "Planned Intervention" demonstrate some of the approaches in current use.

Thus in selecting materials we were guided by this outline:

What kind of children do we want?
What readings in science, philosophy, or fiction eloquently describe the nature of infants and children?
How can this knowledge be applied to help children grow?

We found many exciting readings and often could not place them according to our outline, so we often revised the outline and remained uncertain.

A good many issues in this area are controversial; many outstanding studies contradict the findings of other studies as equally outstanding. We may as well face it. Much of what we know to be true today may be found false tomorrow. Since we have faith in the scientific method, we present many kinds of scientific studies, but also great psychological insights by poets and writers have also been included. Because one may be led to believe that juvenile delinquency is a modern invention, we have selections from the Holy Bible which place the contemporary problem in perspective; thus the student can see how ancient and perhaps universal are some of the characteristic human problems, and how local and transitory are others which seem so urgent.

We are grateful to the authors and publishers who so graciously permitted us to use their materials, and to Herman Makler of the Thomas Y. Crowell Company for his indispensable suggestions in editing this book. We are also grateful to our many colleagues for their generous and valuable suggestions about the composition of this volume:

THERON ALEXANDER	GORDON L. LIPPITT
SISTER MARY AMATORA, O.S.F.	NER LITNER
BERNARD ARONOV	BOYD MC CANDLESS
EDYTH BARRY	WILLIS H. MC CANN
BRUNO BETTELHEIM	CARSON MC GUIRE
SIDNEY W. BIJOU	FRIEDA AND RALPH MERRY
CHARLOTTE BUHLER	ELIZABETH H. MORRIS
RUTH C. BUSSEY	NORMAN L. MUNN
HY CHAUSOW	HUGH V. PERKINS
JAMES M. DUNLAP	EDWARD REINFRANCK
HORACE ENGLISH	REUBEN SEGAL
CLIFFORD G. ERICKSON	OSCAR SHABAT
JACOB W. GETZELS	BEATRICE G. SHUTTLEWORTH
JACOB L. GEWIRTZ	MARVIN STEINBERG
JACK GIBB	RUTH STRANG
JOSEPH HARNEY	FLORENCE M. TEAGARDEN
SARA S. HAWK	GEORGE G. THOMPSON
MARJORIE P. HONZIK	HEINZ WERNER
PHILIP W. JACKSON	REGINA H. WESTCOTT
BARNEY KATZ	BEN WRIGHT
STANLEY LIPKIN	

CONTENTS

II. INFANCY

Satisfying Fundamental Needs: Some Dimensions of Love

III. CHILDHOOD

The Child Views His World

IV. DISTORTED VIEWS

V. PLANNED INTERVENTION

VI. ADOLESCENCE

HUMAN DEVELOPMENT

Selected Readings

PART I

GOALS

What Kind of People Do We Want?

INTRODUCTION

It is one thing to investigate the values of exotic cultures—commenting on how strange, primitive, or vulgar they are—and quite another to examine one's own standards critically in order to select them carefully. Men at all times have sought truth, beauty, and justice, but they have rarely agreed on exactly what these are. Each generation inherits the values of its fathers and adds some of its own. In one generation firm discipline is advocated, but in the next a thousand reasons for sparing the rod are manufactured. Should we be governed by fashion in such matters? Or should we study and re-evaluate our own cultural heritage?

What do we want in life? What do we want for our children? If it is pleasure that we seek, why do we work so hard? If "freedom," then, specifically, freedom from what and to do what? Wealth might be the goal, but it often appears that the rich are slaves to their riches. Courage? to thumb our noses at the law, or at our neighbors? Or perhaps we desire to love our neighbors as ourselves; child sacrifice is not advocated in our families, but we manage—in a land overflowing with milk and honey— to sacrifice many of our neighbor's children to poverty, ignorance, and delinquency. Do we believe that the meek shall inherit the earth? that the mourners shall be comforted? Or do we believe that might makes right? If we believe in democracy, why are we ruled by bureaucracy?

The articles in this Part deal with our rich heritage of values; they discuss, advocate, or condemn many different standards of behavior and attitudes. Cultural values in France, Israel, India, Ireland, and the

1

U.S.S.R. are described. Watson, Foote, and Cottrell state their more general points of view in wider scientific terms.

The articles here might be compared with standards and statements from other and previous cultures. For example, Machiavelli contended during the Italian Renaissance that the Prince must do anything—lie, cheat, steal, murder—in order to remain in power. Rousseau, in the eighteenth century, believed that man needed freedom to express himself, to do as *he* pleased, not as society demanded. Or Mussolini, in our time, felt that people are not born equal and should not be treated as such. To him some were born wise and forceful; others were born as sheep to be ruled. For himself, he declared, "Better one hour as a lion than a thousand years as a sheep!"; the contrast with the point of view expressed in, "The Lord is my shepherd," is obvious.

By contrasting some of the articles in this Part with those in later sections, the reader may notice the essential differences between methods which exhort, moralize, or philosophize and those which are descriptive, analytical, experimental, or therapeutic in intent.

1. WHAT PRICE VIRTUE?

MORRIS L. HAIMOWITZ

"Virtue" conveys many different meanings to different people. For one individual to be "virtuous" may mean to be a saint; for others it may mean to be a political leader, businessman, general, artist, or good mother. Each of these roles requires the cultivation of different and sometimes contradictory "virtues." No man can serve two masters; he is forced to choose the particular "virtues" appropriate to his way of life.

This article points out that many psychological troubles stem from the necessity of choosing one set of social values and thereby rejecting another. If one is to be free and independent, he cannot also be dutiful and obedient. A gentle and kindly individual cannot also be cold and uncompromising. The parent who wants his little boy to develop "masculine" self-confidence will have to let the child win a lot of family arguments. Aristotle's Golden Mean, unfortunately, does not seem to provide an easy solution to this problem.

Revised from "What Kind of Children Do We Want?" in *Teleclass Study Guide in Child Psychology*, (1958), 22–29, by permission of the Chicago Board of Education. The author thanks Kenneth Telford and Jerry Cohen for their help in preparing this article.

Two thousand years ago Pericles declared the secret of happiness to be freedom and the secret of freedom, a brave heart. Many parents today believe this, for when asked, "What kind of children do you want?" more replied, "bold and courageous" than gave any other answer. We wonder if parents wish for their children what the parents do not themselves have. If this is true, parents who are fearful therefore would wish for their children boldness and courage. Can the child be bold when his parents are afraid? Doesn't the child identify with his parents, become as they are rather than what they would like him to be? If the child really were bold, and the parents afraid, won't the parent envy his child, compete with him, and because of his greater strength, subdue the child—so that he could not be bold?

We assume that children grow up this way and that; no two are the same, but in one society there is more docility; in another society, more independence; in another, hunger and misery; in another, tyranny and sadism. The Nazis developed sado-masochistic characters, people who loved to obey orders and to give orders to their underlings. Medieval Jews developed pious and scholarly characters, who loved learning, who wanted to do nothing except study the Bible. The Ancient Greeks and Romans developed men of courage, who loved to prove their bravery in battle. Some Americans want children who are free, independent, honest and courageous. But such a child might be expected to talk back to his parents, to disagree with his teachers. How much of this freedom, independence, honesty and courage can adults take? The most common question parents bring to us is, "How can I get my child to behave, to do what I tell him to do?" This indicates that the parents want the child to be obedient, submissive. We suppose that a child can be both submissive and bold, but it would be impossible to be both at the same time.

Perhaps the parents want their children submissive to teachers, policemen, the clergy and to other adults; but to be bold with children their own age and size—submissive in some situations, bold in others.

In children's literature you often find the following theme: a few boys make a pledge to each other to perform some great obligation, which they carry out at considerable danger and pain to themselves and others, such a pledge might be to keep their gang name a secret; or to save some prisoner, as in *Huckleberry Finn;* or to guard a make-believe warehouse in a public park, as in *Word of Honor* (a short story in a 1957 Russian textbook, *Rodnaya Rech,* translated into English by Olga M. Beeks). In *Word of Honor* the little hero will not leave his guard post because he has given his word, even though it is getting dark and he is very hungry. In *Huckleberry Finn* the boys strenuously risk death in a dozen ways to fool the adults and to test themselves.

We showed *Word of Honor* to some parents. Here are their comments.

"You can really admire the courage of this little boy, bravely standing alone in the dark. His word means something to him." But Mrs. Smith said, "How foolish can a kid be! Standing alone in the dark! He doesn't know the difference between a game and the real thing! Is this courage that keeps him there? Or fear? Is he brave or submissive?"

Mrs. Gudensky felt very differently: "I think you are both wrong. He is just a cute kid. I admire his will; just as cute as he can be." This made Mrs. Smith angry. "Do you want children growing up like that, stubborn, foolish? Do we want kids cute, who will entertain us with their whimseys; or do we want them to be able to know the difference between what is important and what is just a game!" Mrs. Gudensky was offended at this. "This little boy was learning something I wish we could teach to our kids and that is *obedience*." Mr. F. (we did not get his name) was quiet all this time, but when he heard the word *obedience*, his ears turned red and he could not wait to shout, "We don't want slaves; we don't want passive obedience to stupid authority. This is America! We want our children to be independent, to think for themselves, to judge for themselves, not to stand in the dark and cry for some childish phantasy." Mrs. Smith agreed. She said, "The ancient Greeks used to say a *liberal* education is one befitting a free man. A free man must know how to make wise decisions in ruling himself and his government. It is a slave who does only what he is told. The Russians may be giving their children excellent technical training, but are they preparing a fine lot of slaves?"

Whenever we hear a discussion on freedom, we think of Kant's *Foundations of the Metaphysics of Morals* and John Stuart Mill's essay *On Liberty*. If we were to imagine a conversation between Kant and Mill on the meaning of freedom, with those two gentlemen sitting before the fireplace, Kant knocking the ashes out of his pipe, it might go like this:

MILL.   Freedom is the ability to do what you please. If you have to do something someone else wants you to do, then you are not free.

KANT.   You are absolutely wrong. Freedom is the ability to do what is *right* for you to do. A man is not free who must follow every fancy, who is a slave to his impulse. A free man is a moral man.

MILL.   That's what Buddha and Socrates said. A man must be free of his body if his soul is to soar. But to me body and soul are one. The man is a man, an individual. He must do what a man must do, not what a soul must do. I agree freedom is not license. There could be no freedom to anyone if there was license for one. If one man had license to go out and kill, there could be no freedom for anyone else. A man finds that some things are most pleasant; those are the things most truly befitting a man. He is most free who expresses his peculiar individuality, according to his own nature.

KANT.   When I knock the ashes out of my pipe, I am careful not to get them on your floor. I do this of my own free will, feeling it is the best thing for me to do.

MILL.   Of course, that would be obnoxious, and you are a gentleman.

We heard a more up-to-date conversation on the meanings of freedom recently in a corner drug store. Four ivy-leaguers were sitting around the table. One dropped his cigarette butt on the floor and squashed it with his toe.

I.L. 1.   That's what I like about this country. Freedom [*and he downed his soda*].

I.L. 2.   Yep, I drink to freedom, gentlemen.

I.L. 3.   You guys don't even know what freedom means.

I.L. 2.   You have a monopoly of knowledge, my friend? I know very well. It means the state of single blessedness. It means . . .

I.L. 3.   See, I told you, you don't know. A single man is not free. He is the slave of a constant longing. As a hungry man is free to do nothing except seek food.

I.L. 4.   Who has freedom? Are you free to be born or to die? You say you have freedom to think. What do you think about? Every thought you have, every action you take is determined by social or biological forces. Some of these forces were poured into you with your mother's milk. It used to be mother's; the social forces today make it cow's. You are conditioned in a thousand ways. Everything you feel, everything you want, everything you believe has been determined. You have no free will.

I.L. 2.   You mean the good Lord did not give us a brain to choose between good and evil?

I.L. 3.   Of course not. The only people who believe that use it as an excuse for cruelty. They say, "Johnny was a bad boy. He could have been a good boy like the rest of us. Let Johnny be punished." They don't wait for the good Lord to punish Johnny. They do it themselves, for they are full of hate. They were hated as children and grow up to be hateful. Their hate is as much determined as my pity for them. I have no freedom to love them or to kill them. I have been trained to believe I should understand them, and I really try.

I.L. 1.   You, my friend, are a supercilious fool and I will pray for you.

I.L. 3.   You must pray. I must not. Neither of us has freedom or free will.

I.L. 2.   Freedom means, nobody telling you what to do. Nobody pushing you around. We have a free country, we put in a government and if we don't like it, we throw it out. The government doesn't push anybody around in this country.

I.L. 3.   See. You just don't know. Look over the counter there. Six government licenses, to sell cigarettes, liquor, drugs, and what-not. Look over there by the cash register. While you have been yapping, I have been watching an interesting conversation. That man talking to the druggist works for the government. Just listen.

DRUGGIST.   You government people! Boy, every week it's somebody. Last week the man from the pure food and drug administration, the week before it was the man from the jewelry tax; examining my books, testing my bottles, getting everything all mixed up! Now you want to look at my books for 1951. If you find something wrong, you fine me $1,000 or $10,000. If you don't find anything wrong it costs me a days wages—two days wages to look after you instead of after my own business. In addition, I and other taxpayers have to pay your salary whether you find anything wrong or not. 1951! That's ancient history!

GOVERNMENT MAN [*wiping his glasses*].   You need a central government stronger than any business; otherwise the people of this country would be fleeced by business men who suddenly turn into crooks. Before the pure food laws, people were getting poisoned; even with inspectors, half the people falsify their tax returns. Show me your books.

DRUGGIST.   Maybe you are right, but every time I turn around, there are two government men (living off my taxes) telling me what to do.

I.L. 2.   A government man should not talk like that to a private citizen. We don't get pushed around by our servants, our employees.

I.L. 1.   A government man represents the common will, the conscience of the people. The big policeman. He represents our duty. We have a strong sense of duty. I used to be a Boy Scout: "On my honor, I will do my best to do my *duty* to God and my country, to obey the Scout laws at all times, to keep myself physically strong, mentally alert and morally straight."

I.L. 3.   There is a lot about duty and obedience in that oath, very little about courage or independent thinking. *Poor Richard's Almanac* was also full of duty and obedience. John Quincy Adams, one of our greatest presidents, the son of the second president, had a powerful sense of duty. Here are two letters he wrote at the age of 10 and 11, showing characteristics not too different from the story of honor above:

JOHN Q. ADAMS, AGED 10, TO HIS FATHER [1]

Braintree, June the 2nd, 1777

DEAR SIR, I love to receive letters very well; much better than I love to write them. I make but a poor figure at composition, my head is much too fickle, my thoughts are running after birds eggs play and trifles, till I get vexed with myself. Mamma has a troublesome task to keep me steady, and I own I am ashamed of myself. I have but just entered the 3d volume of

[1] C. F. Adams, *Memoirs of John Quincy Adams* (J. B. Lippincott, 1874), Vol. 1, pp. 7–9.

Smollet tho' I had designed to have got it half through by this time. I have determined this week to be more diligent, as Mr. Thaxter will be absent at Court, & I cannot persue my other studies. I have Set myself a Stent & determine to read the 3d volume Half out. If I can but keep my resolution, I will write again at the end of the week and give a better account of myself. I wish, Sir, you would give me some instructions, with regard to my time, & advise me how to proportion my Studies & my Play, in writing, & I will keep them by me, & endeavor to follow them. I am, dear Sir, with a present determination of growing better, yours.

P.S. if you will be so good as to favour me with a Blank Book, I will transcribe the most remarkable occurances I met with in my reading, which will serve to fix them upon my mind.

AGED 11, TO HIS MOTHER [2]

Passy, September the 27th, 1778

(He was in Paris with his father who was representing the Continental Congress at the French court during the Revolutionary War.)

HONOURED MAMMA, My Pappa enjoins it upon me to keep a journal, or a diary of the Events that happen to me, and of objects that I see, and of Characters that I converse with from day to day; and altho. I am convinced of the utility, importance & necessity of this Exercise, yet I have no patience and perseverance enough to do it so Constantly as I ought. My Pappa, who takes a great deal of Pains to put me in the right way, has also advised me to Preserve copies of all my letters, & has given me a Convenient Blank Book for this end; and altho I shall have the mortification a few years hence to read a great deal of my Childish nonsense, yet I shall have the Pleasure and advantage of Remarking the several steps by which I shall have advanced in taste judgment and knowledge. A journal Book & a letter Book of a Lad of Eleven years old Can not be expected to contain much of Science, Litterature, arts, wisdom, or wit, yet it may serve to perpetuate many observations that I may make, & may hereafter help me to recolect both persons & things that would other ways escape my memory. I have been to see the Palace & gardens of Versailles, the Military scholl at Paris, the hospital of Invalids, the hospital of Foundling Children, the Church of Notre Dame, the Heights of Calvare, of Montmartre, of Minemontan & other scenes of Magnificence in & about Paris, which, if I had written down in a diary or a letter Book, would give me at this time much pleasure to revise and would enable me hereafter to entertain my friends, but I have neglected it. & therefore can now only resolve to be more thoughtful and Industrious for the Future. & to encourage me in this resolution & enable me to keep it with more ease & advantage, my father has given me hopes of a Pencil and Pencil Book in which I can make notes upon the spot to be transfered afterwards in my Diary & my letters this will give me great pleasure both because it will be a sure means of improvement to myself & enable me to be more entertaining to you. I am my ever honoured and revered Mamma your Dutiful & affectionate Son

JOHN QUINCY ADAMS

[2] *Ibid.*

I.L. 2.   Johnny Adams sure got around a lot. Here he is eleven years old writing home letters from Paris.

I.L. 3.   There is another angle about freedom. It means footloose and fancy free to move from place to place, from country to country.

I.L. 1.   People move, up the ladder, away from guilt, away from constraint. That's why people move; some move down the ladder, into constraint.

I.L. 2.   Jefferson was against that. He said good citizens were farmers, bound to the land, not rootless wanderers.

I.L. 3.   He is out of date. He wrote a Constitution for farmers. We need a new Constitution for a country where everything is new.

I.L. 1.   Boy, are you a radical!

I.L. 3.   We need a Constitution based on today's realities. People are not tied to the family, to the church, to the community. City people won't repair their homes and schools, because they are afraid the government will come tear them down for a new highway or project, or because they want to move away.

I.L. 2.   But if people don't feel attached to anything, they won't feel any past or any future, and they will have a wishy-washy present, wavering between alcoholism and nothing at all. If they are not attached to their family and neighborhood, their children will get run over in unkept streets, their schools will fall down in decay or go up in smoke. . . . That's what's happening every day.

I.L. 3.   People are destined to move because of new inventions, floods and wars, so we need a bigger sense of community. Maybe people can't feel tied to their neighborhood because they just moved in last week and may be moving out again next week. That's why neighborhoods run down. Freedom to move runs down neighborhoods.

I.L. 1.   It isn't freedom that runs down neighborhoods; it's ignorance. People are ignorant of how to live, how to organize for today's civilization.

We had finished our business in the drug store and were filled up with notions of freedom and duty. We know that duty to one person means something quite different from what it means to another but that in all duty there is a general idea of responsibility to others.

In Plutarch's *Lives* the conception of duty which stands out is the desire for greatness. This might be achieved in a number of ways, but among the most prominent was by courage in battle. Among medieval and even some modern Jews the conception of duty was different: to achieve by learning, by knowledge. To show how the Jewish child developed such a conception we looked through the Jewish lore. Their prayer books, textbooks, songs and poetry ring with the importance of learning. Here are two prayers which illustrate this: "Make pleasant, therefore, we beseech thee, O Lord, the words of thy Torah (The Holy Bible and commentaries about it) in our mouth and in the mouth of thy people, so that we with our children and the children of thy people may all know thy name and thy Torah." This is a prayer which the children recited before going to school in the morning. Another daily prayer emphasized learning: " . . . and thou shalt teach them diligently unto thy children. . . ." Learning was not merely a duty; it was also a pleasure. To symbolize this pleasure the child's first day at school included an important ceremony:

On Pentecost, the feast commemorative of the giving of the Torah, the boy of five began his career at school. (Instances of three and four year old boys being taken are well known). Neatly attired, he was put in the care of a member of the community distinguished for piety and scholarship, with whom he went to the synagogue at the break of day. There he was met by the teacher, who took him in his charge and began to instruct him. He was handed a slate on which the Hebrew alphabet was written forward and backward. The first lesson consisted in asking the pupil to repeat the names of the letters after the teacher. The slate was smeared with honey which the child licked from the letters, to taste the sweetness of Torah, as it were. Then the boy was given a cake on which several verses from the Prophets and Psalms were traced. . . .[3]

From early infancy the Jewish woman soothed her child with the lullaby that expressed the wish for the child to learn Torah.

> What is the best reward?
> My baby will learn Torah.
> Sforim (Books) he will write for me.
> And a pious Jew—he'll always be.

Bialic, the Hebrew poet, expressed the pleasure and comfort in the Torah when he wrote:

> In my worn, moth eaten Talmud leaves,
> Dwell ancient legends, captivating tales,
> In you my soul finds soothing from its woes,
> To you I come whenever grief assails.[4]

Rabban Yochanan used to say, "If thou has learned much Torah, ascribe not any merit to thyself, for there unto wast thou created."[5]

To sum up, one may characterize this Jewish ideal as one who is scholarly and pious, both being part of a unified whole.

We in America have a problem primitive people did not have. Primitive people, living in an isolated area, out of communication with

---

[3] L. Ginsberg, *Students, Scholars, and Saints,* pp. 19–20.
[4] N. Bialic, "To the Aggadah," translated from Hebrew by Israel Efios in *Complete Works of H. N. Bialic.*
[5] *Sayings of the Fathers,* Chapter 2.

other peoples, never had to choose between rearing their children this way or that. They knew only one way; they had no choice. In this sense they had less freedom than we. But along with our freedom of choice comes responsibility. We have no real freedom to choose from the thousand and one varieties of cultures of which we are composed unless we understand what we are choosing. The problem of what we should do with our children leaves us in a quandary, or in a conflict with our neighbors.

One hundred and fifty years ago Jefferson and Madison brought forth a plan for a new kind of agrarian community. It was a remarkable plan, but today the United States is no longer agrarian; it is an industrial power where people live in megalopolitan aggregates facing space and time and TV. Today we are in the process of making a new plan. What kind of world do we want in the next 150 years? Before we can decide whether there is too much or too little pap in our curriculum, too much science or not enough math, we must decide what kind of people we want. The decisions on these questions will be made by the minds and acts of men. Whether we deal with these issues or not, whether we know what we are doing or not, we are making the decisions. Our decisions must begin to flow from a rational control of the situation we desire, not from the crises of the immediate circumstance we find ourselves in. Ernest J. Seeton once stated "Manhood, not scholarship, is the first aim of education." It is now time to begin to think about the type of manhood that is desirable and needed in our world. It would be wise to study this for our own benefit and for the good of our children.

SOME VIRTUES WE ADMIRE

Every parent wants a good child. The problem arises when we try to make more specific what we mean by "good."

Probably agreement on health, as meaning free from disease would be unanimous. But sometimes we hear the expression, "it's not healthy to let the child practice music too much, or to let him swim so much," and then the meaning of "healthy" becomes controversial too. What is "good"? Does it mean active, even boisterous? Some people like children quiet, so that they grow up quiet, with spontaneous outbursts of curiosity, friendship, hostility curbed.

Does "good" mean to work hard? Among some groups, working hard seems to be more important than producing.

Is a good child a popular child? Which means other children like him? For early Americans, popularity was not an essential trait. The conception of freedom was much more important; men were free to disagree with one another, free to be unpopular, to do what their conscience told them was right. Current research of adolescents shows a majority agree with such statements as these: "Want people to like me more." "Want to gain (or lose) weight." "I try very hard to do every-thing that will please my friends." [6] They feel a need to be popular, which often involves, giving up one's own taste, judgment, intelligence and wisdom for the whimsicalities of the mob.

Is a good child an "average" child? This means he has the abilities, tastes, interests and talents of the average person, with some people better, some less good no matter how these may be measured. This means to many that if he is not average he is a screwball. The men who developed immunization against small pox and polio, who developed TV and wrote symphonies and *The Grapes of Wrath* were not average children.

Well, then, is a good child a "great" child, one who hides in an ordinary body and behind an ordinary face a mysterious power of creativity? So that we might say a good child is a "creative" child? "Creativity" is again a slippery word. The creation of a fine meal is creativity but it is not the same as the creation of a cure for syphilis. Nor is it the same as the special kind of creativity of the mother or teacher who creates an atmosphere in which children can grow.

Then is the good child the one who grows, that is, who learns, who is studious? The scholar was held in high esteem in China and among Jews of recent centuries, yet what they learned and their mode of learning could not be considered creative. They did not use the scientific method. The Chinese scholar was meek, tremendously learned in the proper books, endowed with a great memory and had little or no effect in changing Chinese civilization. The Jewish scholar was not meek; a young man of ten might argue boldly with his teacher of sixty, and might even win the argument. And yet a basic precept among the Jews has been "To do justly, to love mercy and to walk humbly before God." (We should point out that to "do justice" may be opposed to "love mercy.")

Is a good child musical? or especially talented in chemistry or human relations? or in tearing apart old clocks? So that he misses other activities, perhaps misses school, perhaps misses a neighbor's birthday party or his grandmother's funeral. This seems to have been true for a number of inventors, musicians, great scientists. We don't know for certain whether Mozart or Irving Berlin if faced with the same hectic schedule a middle class child faces today would ever have written a note. Edison had trouble in school.

A good child is clean, neat, orderly. A child who is too meticulous will be a miserable adult. The Nazis had a great love for order. Every person and every thing was arranged in one grand order. Of course, no one had much freedom.

[6] H. H. Remmers and D. H. Radler, "Teenage Attitudes," *Scientific American,* June, 1958.

Then should the child be "free"? Free to do what? Anything he likes, to eat anything he likes, to hurt anybody he likes? There could be no health, no society in such chaos. Freedom involves understanding. One is free who can make an intelligent choice. The truth alone will not make one free. There is no freedom without a controversy—meaning persons are not free unless they are free to be different.

A good child is an honest child. It is clear for some people what honesty involves. There is a rule that one should be courteous, and this often conflicts with the need for honesty. The tattle tale is honest; he carries a message of doom, but he is disloyal to his peers. A good child is loyal. To what, to whom? Is he loyal to his own aspirations, to those of his parents, teachers or friends? Loyalty to one's country in some countries means supporting the administration; we enjoy a broader definition. Loyalty to our country means supporting the principles of liberty to all (except to criminals, idiots, children, the insane, Communists, Jehovah's Witnesses) and means freedom and justice to all (except Negroes, American Indians, Mexican-Americans; Japanese-Americans, Jews, Italians, Greeks, Catholics and Protestants). We believe in freedom and justice for all but sometimes fail to practice it because of the problems of political or economic power. Then should the child seek power, wealth? Some believe the meek shall inherit the earth. Did you ever see a meek politician, industrialist, or person of wealth or position?

The good child is happy, well adjusted. He sings, dances, plays, has fun, bubbles with good humor and is a joy to all who behold him. Is the child well adjusted to poverty, to prejudice, to ignorance, to starvation, to atomic fallout, to murder on the highways, to one million juvenile delinquents, to the imminence of hydrogen death, to millions suffering of alcoholism, drug addiction, and mental disease? What does "well-adjusted" mean?

The good child is sincere. Sincere means honest, genuine, saying what one thinks. For Germany Hitler was sincere. He said what he thought.

The good child is one who makes his parents happy. He does all the things the parents wish they might have done for themselves.

The good child loves beauty, hates dirt and ugliness. Some are so preoccupied with dirt that they spend all their lives looking for it, cleaning up things. Others are so squeamish that they can't stand cleaning their own dish or their own mess after they have made it. Many a lover of beauty in the abstract lives in filth in reality.

A good child is full of love, of compassion for his fellow man, helping unselfishly the poor and the sick. In order to help the crippled, the insane, the ex-convict, one must identify with such people. To help those who suffer one must identify with the suffering. It follows that the saint would suffer most of all. He appears to be completely preoccupied with the suffering of others, as if he personally were responsible. And if he could devote himself to others he could undo the harm he feels he has done them. Actually he has done others no harm, he may have helped many people, but his suffering is part of a grandiose delusion that he is responsible for all men. Some people feel we must be our brother's keepers, but others say that the most one can do is to realize his own potential growth. If we want our child to be a saint, let us keep in mind the cost to him. Or is the saint the happiest, the ideal?

A good child will be a great athlete, or musician, or business man, surgeon or actress. These are the highest-paid occupations in our land for a very few, and the lowest paid for the majority. Such occupations involve tremendous drive, as well as talent and opportunity for training, usually from an early age, though there is no guaranteed formula for success.

A good child knows the great cultural heritage from Plato to Plutonium. He will spend his life trying to understand our past. But if he concentrates on the past he will never see the present and will be of no value in helping form the future. Even Einstein never heard of Sputnic. Some problems of today are the same old problems man has always had, and studying the past can illuminate our times; but many of today's problems are brand new, and require new thinking and new solutions.

We have heard it reported that the good child is independent, he gets ahead on his own. All great men have achieved on their own. Others say this is sheer nonsense. Most children (and adults too) could not live a week on their own. Every man who achieved did so with the help, encouragement, food and support of others. Inventions don't come fully blown from a dream. They come from people working together, using the information in our cultural legacy; many minds, many hands, many people are involved in every invention, novel, play or business.

Here is a quotation from Laird Bell taking a position that people should be independent:

It seems to me no proper frame of mind for youth, to accept a world where not his own energy and talent but the plans that somebody else makes for him determine his life. I recognize that one should not be too censorious about people who accept the managed economy, security and planning as ideals. . . . A very great development of civilization took place under a relatively unplanned society in the last two centuries.

I find it hard to be reconciled to the thought that the young should turn away from an exciting world of risk and big stakes for a tame one planned, however expertly, for someone else. Our achievements at the University of

Chicago have been possible not because we had economic security but rather because we had ambitions. I trust you will go forth, not in search of security, but looking for high adventure.

And here is a reply by Lloyd Lewis:

For every Daniel Boone who wanted to go it alone, there were 100,000 settlers hunting security from poverty, from landlessness, from unemployment. They didn't say to Uncle Sam, "Stand back! We'll handle our competitors!" Instead they yelled for him to send federal troops to eliminate the Indians. They made the trails resound with their howling for free land, internal improvements, canals, harbors, locks, roads, and high protective tariff. Advertisements in Europe told them that they could step off the boat and shoot a gun in any direction, day or night, and bring down at least three turkeys, four deer and a goose. This sounded like security to peasants who had never had enough meat in their lives and whose brothers had been hanged for poaching. The truth of the matter is that these peasants had spent so much of their lives dodging or fighting the constables who wanted to jail them for debt, or gibbet them for praying to the wrong dominie, or draft them for the stirring perils of professional soldiery, that it could hardly be said that they came to America seeking adventure.

If that was what they wanted, they'd have stayed home.

How is security related to adventure? Can one go forth to joyful adventure if his heart is heavy, his stomach empty, and if he has a wooden leg?

A good child is wise. Perhaps it is too much to expect of a child to be wise, when this gift occurs so infrequently even among adults. "Wisdom" would mean knowing how to temper the preceding virtues when they became obnoxious, how to combine honesty with courtesy; freedom with order; popularity with conscience; discretion with valor; creativity with humility, justice with mercy.

We are in the business of making children how we want them, but it too often appears we do not know how we want them, or what is involved. When we go to a tailor and say make me a coat of such and such a size, he can make it to our order. Can we make a child to specifications? If we could, what would be the specifications? In America we have been enriched by the thoughts, ideas, inventions, values of a thousand societies. With such a rich assortment of values from which to choose, it takes a heap of knowing to choose well.

Mr. Robert M. Hutchins of the Fund for the Republic gives his views on this. He says that there are three urgent problems facing the world. The first is making democracy work. He means making it work better. The second urgent problem is survival, for which we need draw no pictures. And the third question, the one we ask in more detail in this paper: If we should survive, what should we do with our lives?

2. LIFE: THE IMPORTANT VALUE

GENESIS 22

*In hundreds of places and among hundreds of peoples the
practice of infanticide—and sacrificial killing—has occurred.
Newspapers even today frequently report incidents in
which angry parents have beaten their children to death.
Although beating is often recommended (see selection 3),
killing is condemned.*

*The following passage from the biblical Book of Genesis
relates a very important incident in which child sacrifice is
rejected as improper. In this powerful story God Himself
indicates that the sacrifice of Isaac, the only son of Abraham,
who at this time is a very old man, is no longer acceptable.*

And it came to pass after these things, that God did tempt Abraham,
and said unto him, Abraham: and he said, Behold, here I am. And he
said, Take now thy son, thine only son Isaac, whom thou lovest, and
get thee into the land of Moriah; and offer him there for a burnt offering upon one of the mountains which I will tell thee of.

And Abraham rose up early in the morning, and saddled his ass,
and took two of his young men with him, and Isaac his son, and clave
the wood for the burnt offering, and rose up, and went unto the place
of which God had told him. Then on the third day Abraham lifted up
his eyes, and saw the place afar off. And Abraham said unto his young
men, Abide ye here with the ass; and I and the lad will go yonder
and worship, and come again to you. And Abraham took the wood of
the burnt offering, and laid it upon Isaac his son; and he took the fire
in his hand, and a knife; and they went both of them together. And
Isaac spake unto Abraham his father, and said, My father: and he said,
Here am I, my son. And he said, Behold the fire and the wood: but
where is the lamb for a burnt offering? And Abraham said, My son,
God will provide himself a lamb for a burnt offering: so they went both
of them together. And they came to the place which God had told him
of; and Abraham built an altar there, and laid the wood in order, and
bound Isaac his son, and laid him on the altar upon the wood. And
Abraham stretched forth his hand, and took the knife to slay his son.
And the angel of the LORD called unto him out of heaven, and said,
Abraham, Abraham: and he said, Here am I. And he said, Lay not

thine hand upon the lad, neither do thou any thing unto him: for now I know that thou fearest God, seeing thou hast not withheld thy son, thine only son from me. And Abraham lifted up his eyes, and looked, and behold behind him a ram caught in a thicket by his horns: and Abraham went and took the ram, and offered him up for a burnt offering in the stead of his son.

3. THE TEN COMMANDMENTS AND OTHER BIBLICAL PRECEPTS

Like all peoples, the wandering tribes of Israel gave much thought to defining the nature of good and evil. Many of their observations were written down in what came to be called the Holy Scriptures.

The fact that the beautifully worded passages from the Old Testament reprinted here sometimes appear to contradict one another should in itself make them exciting and thought-provoking.

DEUTERONOMY 5

I am the Lord thy God, which brought thee out of the land of Egypt, out of the house of bondage.

Thou shalt have no other gods before me.

Thou shalt not make thee any graven image, or any likness of any thing that is in heaven above, or that is in the earth beneath, or that is in the waters beneath the earth.

Thou shalt not bow down thyself unto them, nor serve them: for I the Lord thy God am a jealous God, visiting the iniquity of the fathers upon the children unto the third and fourth generation of them that hate me.

And showing mercy unto thousands of them that love me and keep my commandments.

Thou shalt not take the name of the Lord thy God in vain.

Keep the sabbath day to sanctify it. Six days shalt thou labor and do all thy work, but the seventh day is the sabbath. In it thou shalt not do any work, thou, nor thy son, nor thy daughter, nor thy manservant, nor thy maidservant, nor thine ox, nor thine ass, nor any of thy cattle, nor the stranger that is within thy gates.

Honour thy father and thy mother.

Thou shalt not kill.

Neither shalt thou commit adultery.

Neither shalt thou steal.

Neither shalt thou bear false witness against thy neighbor.

Neither shalt thou desire thy neighbor's wife, nor covet thy neighbor's house, his field or his servant, his ox, or his ass or any thing that is thy neighbor's.

LEVITICUS 26

If ye walk in my statutes, and keep my commandments, and do them:

Then I will give you rain in due season, and the land shall yield her increase, and the trees of the field shall yield their fruit.

And your threshings shall reach unto the vintage, and the vintage shall reach unto the sowing time: and ye shall eat your bread to the full, and dwell in your land safely, and ye shall lie down, and none shall make you afraid. And ye shall chase your enemies, and they shall fall before you by the sword. And five of you shall chase an hundred. And I will be your God, and ye shall be my people.

But if ye will not hearken unto me, and will not do all these commandments: I will appoint over you terror, consumption and the burning ague that shall consume the eyes and cause sorrow of heart: and ye shall sow your seed in vain for your enemy will eat it, and ye shall be slain before your enemies; and ye shall flee when none pursueth you; ten women shall bake bread in one oven; ye shall eat and not be satisfied, and I will make your cities waste.

PROVERBS

Ch 1.   The proverbs of Solomon the son of David, king of Israel; to know wisdom and instruction; to perceive the words of understanding. A wise man will hear, and will increase learning; and a man of understanding shall attain unto wise counsels; to understand a proverb, and the interpretation; the words of the wise, and their dark sayings.

Ch 3.   Happy is the man that findeth wisdom which is better than the merchandise of silver, more precious than rubies, and all her paths are peace.

Ch 6.   Go to the ant, thou sluggard; consider her ways and be wise: which having no guide, overseer or ruler, provideth her meat in the summer, and gathereth her food in the harvest. How long will thou sleep, Oh sluggard?

These six things doth the Lord hate: yea, seven are an abomination unto him: A proud look, a lying tongue, and hands that shed innocent blood. An heart that deviseth wicked imaginations, feet that be swift in running to mischief. A false witness that speaketh lies, and he that soweth discord among brethren.

Ch 14. Even in laughter the heart is sorrowful; and the end of that mirth is heaviness. A good man shall be satisfied from himself. A wise man feareth and departeth from evil, but the fool rageth, and is confident. The poor is hated even of his own neighbors, but the rich hath many friends. He that despiseth his neighbor sinneth; but he that hath mercy on the poor, happy is he.

Ch 15. A soft answer turneth away wrath; but grievous words stir up anger. Better is a dinner of herbs where love is, than a stalled ox and hatred therewith.

Ch 16. By mercy and truth iniquity is purged: and by the fear of the Lord men depart from evil. Pride goeth before destruction, and an haughty spirit before a fall. Pleasant words are as an honeycomb, sweet to the soul, and health to the bones. A whisperer separateth friends. He that is slow to anger is better than the mighty; and he that ruleth his spirit than he that taketh a city. A merry heart doeth good like a medicine: but a broken spirit drieth the bones.

Ch 18. Whoso findeth a wife findeth a good thing.

Ch 19. Better is the poor that walketh in his integrity, than he that is perverse in his lips and is a fool. Wealth maketh many friends, but the poor is separated from his neighbor. Every man is a friend to him that giveth gifts. Chasten thy son while there is hope, and let not thy soul spare for his crying.

Ch 22. Foolishness is bound in the heart of a child; but the rod of correction shall drive it far from him. Train up a child in the way he should go; and when he is old he will not depart from it.

Ch 23. Withhold not correction from the child: for if thou beatest him with the rod, he shall not die. Thou shalt beat him with the rod and shalt deliver his soul from hell. Hearken unto thy father that begat thee, and despise not thy mother when she is old. Who hath woe? who hath sorrow? who hath contentions? who hath babbling? who hath wounds without cause? who hath redness of eyes? They that tarry long at the wine: they that go to seek mixed wine. Yea, thou shalt be as he that lieth down in the midst of the sea, or as he that lieth upon top of the mast. They have stricken me, shalt thou say and I was not sick; they have beaten me and I felt it not: when shall I awake? I will seek it yet again.

Ch 24. Be not thou envious against evil men, neither desire to be with them. For their heart studieth destruction, and their lips talk of mischief. Through wisdom is an house builded; and by understanding it is established, and by knowledge shall the chambers be filled with all precious and pleasant riches. My son, eat thou honey, because it is good; and the honeycomb which is sweet to the taste. So shall the knowledge of wisdom be unto the soul. Eat not the bread of him that hath an evil eye. Neither desire thou his dainty meats.

PSALMS

PSALM 23

The Lord is my shepherd; I shall not want. He maketh me to lie down in green pastures: he leadeth me beside the still waters. He restoreth my soul; he leadeth me in the paths of righteousness for his name's sake. Yea, though I walk through the valley of the shadow of death, I will fear no evil; for thou art with me; thy rod and thy staff they comfort me. Thou preparest a table before me in the presence of mine enemies; thou anointest my head with oil; my cup runneth over. Surely goodness and mercy shall follow me all the days of my life: and I will dwell in the house of the Lord for ever.

PSALM 82

Defend the poor and fatherless: do justice to the afflicted and needy.

PSALM 144

Blessed be the Lord my strength, which teacheth my hands to war, and my fingers to fight. My goodness, and my fortress; my high tower, and my deliverer; my shield, and he in whom I trust; who subdueth my people under me. Lord, what is man, that thou takest knowledge of him! or the son of man, that thou makest account of him! Man is like to vanity: his days are as a shadow that passeth away.

ECCLESIASTES

Vanity of vanities saith the Preacher, vanity of vanities; all is vanity. What profit hath a man of all his labour which he taketh under the sun? One generation passeth away, and another generation cometh: but the earth abideth forever. The thing that hath been, it is that which shall be; and there is no new thing under the sun. Is there any thing whereof it may be said, See, this is new? it hath been already of old time which was before us. In much wisdom is much grief: and he that increaseth knowledge increaseth sorrow. I said in mine heart, Go to now, enjoy pleasure; and, behold, this also is vanity. I said of laughter, It is mad: and of mirth, what doeth it? I made me great works; I builded me houses; I planted me vineyards, gardens and pools of water. I got me servants and maidens and had great possessions, and gold and silver, and men singers and women singers. Then I looked on all the works and, behold, all was vanity and vexation of spirit.

4. THE SERMON ON THE MOUNT

MATTHEW 5-7

Although the ideals of The Sermon on the Mount are professed
by hundreds of millions of people, they are as revolutionary
now as they were 2,000 years ago. If one were to practice
what these stirring words preach, he would probably be
tagged as a "radical," if not imprisoned.
*   In any study of ethical values, Chapters 5, 6, and 7 of the*
Gospel According to St. Matthew deserve most careful study.

And seeing the multitudes, he went up into a mountain: and when
he was set, his disciples came unto him: And he opened his mouth, and
taught them, saying, Blessed are the poor in spirit: for theirs is the
kingdom of heaven. Blessed are they that mourn: for they shall be
comforted. Blessed are the meek: for they shall inherit the earth. Blessed
are they which do hunger and thirst after righteousness: for they shall
be filled. Blessed are the merciful: for they shall obtain mercy. Blessed
are the pure in heart: for they shall see God. Blessed are the peace-
makers: for they shall be called the children of God. Blessed are they
which are persecuted for righteousness' sake: for theirs is the kingdom
of heaven. Blessed are ye, when men shall revile you, and persecute
you, and shall say all manner of evil against you falsely, for my sake.
Rejoice, and be exceeding glad: for great is your reward in heaven:
for so persecuted they the prophets which were before you.

Ye are the salt of the earth: but if the salt have lost his savour,
wherewith shall it be salted? it is thenceforth good for nothing, but to
be cast out, and to be trodden under foot of men. Ye are the light of
the world. A city that is set on an hill cannot be hid. Neither do men
light a candle, and put it under a bushel, but on a candlestick; and it
giveth light unto all that are in the house. Let your light so shine before men, that they may see your good works, and glorify your Father
which is in heaven.

Think not that I am come to destroy the law, or the prophets: I
am not come to destroy, but to fulfil. For verily I say unto you, Till
heaven and earth pass, one jot or one tittle shall in no wise pass from
the law, till all be fulfilled. Whosoever therefore shall break one of
these least commandments, and shall teach men so, he shall be called
the least in the kingdom of heaven: but whosoever shall do and teach

them, the same shall be called great in the kingdom of heaven. For I say unto you, That except your righteousness shall exceed the righteousness of the scribes and Pharisees, ye shall in no case enter into the kingdom of heaven.

Ye have heard that it was said by them of old time, Thou shalt not kill; and whosoever shall kill shall be in danger of the judgment: But I say unto you, That whosoever is angry with his brother without a cause shall be in danger of the judgment: and whosoever shall say to his brother, Raca, shall be in danger of the council: but whosoever shall say, Thou fool, shall be in danger of hell fire. Therefore if thou bring thy gift to the altar, and there rememberest that thy brother hath ought against thee; Leave there thy gift before the altar, and go thy way; first be reconciled to thy brother, and then come and offer thy gift. Agree with thine adversary quickly, whiles thou art in the way with him; lest at any time the adversary deliver thee to the judge, and the judge deliver thee to the officer, and thou be cast into prison. Verily I say unto thee, Thou shalt by no means come out thence, till thou hast paid the uttermost farthing.

Ye have heard that it was said by them of old time, Thou shalt not commit adultery: But I say unto you, That whosoever looketh on a woman to lust after her hath committed adultery with her already in his heart. And if thy right eye offend thee, pluck it out, and cast it from thee: for it is profitable for thee that one of thy members should perish, and not that thy whole body should be cast into hell. And if thy right hand offend thee, cut it off, and cast it from thee: for it is profitable for thee that one of thy members should perish, and not that thy whole body should be cast into hell. It hath been said, Whosoever shall put away his wife, let him give her a writing of divorcement: But I say unto you, That whosoever shall put away his wife, saving for the cause of fornication, causeth her to commit adultery: and whosoever shall marry her that is divorced committeth adultery.

Again, ye have heard that it hath been said by them of old time, Thou shalt not forswear thyself, but shalt perform unto the Lord thine oaths: But I say unto you, Swear not at all; neither by heaven; for it is God's throne: Nor by the earth; for it is his footstool: neither by Jerusalem; for it is the city of the great King. Neither shalt thou swear by thy head, because thou canst not make one hair white or black. But let your communication be, Yea, yea; Nay, nay: for whatsoever is more than these cometh of evil.

Ye have heard that it hath been said, An eye for an eye, and a tooth for a tooth: But I say unto you, That ye resist not evil: but whosoever shall smite thee on thy right cheek, turn to him the other also. And if any man will sue thee at the law, and take away thy coat, let him have thy cloke also. And whosoever shall compel thee to go a mile, go with him twain. Give to him that asketh thee, and from him that would borrow of thee turn not thou away.

Ye have heard that it hath been said, Thou shalt love thy neighbour, and hate thine enemy. But I say unto you, Love your enemies, bless them that curse you, do good to them that hate you, and pray for them which despitefully use you, and persecute you; That ye may be the children of your Father which is in heaven: for he maketh his sun to rise on the evil and on the good, and sendeth rain on the just and on the unjust. For if ye love them which love you, what reward have ye? do not even the publicans the same? And if ye salute your brethren only, what do ye more than others? do not even the publicans so? Be ye therefore perfect, even as your Father which is in heaven is perfect.

Take heed that ye do not your alms before men, to be seen of them: otherwise ye have no reward of your Father which is in heaven. Therefore when thou doest thine alms, do not sound a trumpet before thee, as the hypocrites do in the synagogues and in the streets, that they may have glory of men. Verily I say unto you, They have their reward. But when thou doest alms, let not thy left hand know what thy right hand doeth: That thine alms may be in secret: and thy Father which seeth in secret himself shall reward thee openly.

And when thou prayest, thou shalt not be as the hypocrites are: for they love to pray standing in the synagogues and in the corners of the streets, that they may be seen of men. Verily I say unto you, They have their reward. But thou, when thou prayest, enter into thy closet, and when thou hast shut thy door, pray to thy Father which is in secret; and thy Father which seeth in secret shall reward thee openly. But when ye pray, use not vain repetitions, as the heathen do: for they think that they shall be heard for their much speaking. Be not ye therefore like unto them: for your Father knoweth what things ye have need of, before ye ask him. After this manner therefore pray ye: Our Father which art in heaven, Hallowed be thy name. Thy kingdom come. Thy will be done in earth, as it is in heaven. Give us this day our daily bread. And forgive us our debts, as we forgive our debtors. And lead us not into temptation, but deliver us from evil: For thine is the kingdom, and the power, and the glory, for ever. Amen. For if ye forgive men their trespasses, your heavenly Father will also forgive you: But if ye forgive not men their trespasses, neither will your Father forgive your trespasses.

Moreover when ye fast, be not, as the hypocrites, of a sad countenance: for they disfigure their faces, that they may appear unto men to fast. Verily I say unto you, They have their reward. But thou, when thou fastest, anoint thine head, and wash thy face; That thou appear not unto men to fast, but unto thy Father which is in secret: and thy Father, which seeth in secret, shall reward thee openly.

Lay not up for yourselves treasures upon earth, where moth and rust doth corrupt, and where thieves break through and steal: But lay up for yourselves treasures in heaven, where neither moth nor rust doth corrupt, and where thieves do not break through nor steal: For where your treasure is, there will your heart be also. The light of the body is the eye: if therefore thine eye be single, thy whole body shall be full of light. But if thine eye be evil, thy whole body shall be full of darkness. If therefore the light that is in thee be darkness, how great is that darkness!

No man can serve two masters; for either he will hate the one, and love the other; or else he will hold to the one, and despise the other. Ye cannot serve God and mammon. Therefore I say unto you, Take no thought for your life, what ye shall eat, or what ye shall drink; nor yet for your body, what ye shall put on. Is not the life more than meat, and the body than raiment? Behold the fowls of the air: for they sow not, neither do they reap, nor gather into barns; yet your heavenly Father feedeth them. Are ye not much better than they? Which of you by taking thought can add one cubit unto his stature? And why take ye thought for raiment? Consider the lilies of the field, how they grow; they toil not, neither do they spin: And yet I say unto you, That even Solomon in all his glory was not arrayed like one of these. Wherefore, if God so clothe the grass of the field, which today is, and tomorrow is cast into the oven, shall he not much more clothe you, O ye of little faith? Therefore take no thought, saying, What shall we eat? or, What shall we drink? or, Wherewithal shall we be clothed? (For after all these things do the Gentiles seek:) for your heavenly Father knoweth that ye have need of all these things. But seek ye first the kingdom of God, and his righteousness; and all these things shall be added unto you. Take therefore no thought for the morrow: for the morrow shall take thought for the things of itself. Sufficient unto the day is the evil thereof.

Judge not, that ye be not judged. For with what judgment ye judge, ye shall be judged: and with what measure ye mete, it shall be measured to you again. And why beholdest thou the mote that is in thy brother's eye, but considerest not the beam that is in thine own eye? Or how wilt thou say to thy brother, Let me pull out the mote out of thine eye; and, behold, a beam is in thine own eye? Thou hypocrite, first cast out the beam out of thine own eye; and then shalt thou see clearly to cast out the mote out of thy brother's eye.

Give not that which is holy unto the dogs, neither cast ye your pearls before swine, lest they trample them under their feet, and turn again and rend you.

Ask, and it shall be given you; seek, and ye shall find; knock, and it shall be opened unto you: For every one that asketh receiveth; and he that seeketh findeth; and to him that knocketh it shall be opened. Or what man is there of you, whom if his son ask bread, will he give him a stone? Or if he ask a fish, will he give him a serpent? If ye then, being evil, know how to give good gifts unto your children, how much more shall your Father which is in heaven give good things to them that ask him? Therefore all things whatsoever ye would that men should do to you, do ye even so to them: for this is the law and the prophets.

Enter ye in at the strait gate: for wide is the gate, and broad is the way, that leadeth to destruction, and many there be which go in thereat: Because strait is the gate, and narrow is the way, which leadeth unto life, and few there be that find it.

Beware of false prophets, which come to you in sheep's clothing, but inwardly they are ravening wolves. Ye shall know them by their fruits. Do men gather grapes of thorns, or figs of thistles? Even so every good tree bringeth forth good fruit; but a corrupt tree bringeth forth evil fruit. A good tree cannot bring forth evil fruit, neither can a corrupt tree bring forth good fruit. Every tree that bringeth not forth good fruit is hewn down, and cast into the fire. Wherefore by their fruits ye shall know them.

Not every one that saith unto me, Lord, Lord, shall enter into the kingdom of heaven; but he that doeth the will of my Father which is in heaven. Many will say to me in that day, Lord, Lord, have we not prophesied in thy name? and in thy name have cast out devils? and in thy name done many wonderful works? And then will I profess unto them, I never knew you: depart from me, ye that work iniquity.

Therefore whosoever heareth these sayings of mine, and doeth them, I will liken him unto a wise man, which built his house upon a rock: And the rain descended, and the floods came, and the winds blew, and beat upon that house; and it fell not: for it was founded upon a rock. And every one that heareth these sayings of mine, and doeth them not, shall be likened unto a foolish man, which built his house upon the sand: And the rain descended, and the floods came, and the winds blew, and beat upon that house; and it fell: and great was the fall of it. And it came to pass, when Jesus had ended these sayings, the people were astonished at his doctrine: For he taught them as one having authority, and not as the scribes.

5. SOME PERSONALITY DIFFERENCES IN CHILDREN RELATED TO STRICT OR PERMISSIVE PARENTAL DISCIPLINE

GOODWIN WATSON

The proper procedure for the socialization of children is a difficult problem. Should the child be allowed to do as he pleases, his parents quietly hoping he will make the correct decisions? Or should the parents make the child do as he is told?

This important article, comparing 44 children from strict homes with 34 from permissive family groups, indicates that those from permissive backgrounds tend toward more independent, cooperative, and creative behavior than those with strict upbringings. Because of this and similar studies, psychologists have advocated permissiveness for two decades. In many ways, however, the groups are similar, and Watson reports that permissiveness is very rare.

A. INTRODUCTION

In controversies over parental discipline of children, few of the arguments advanced for more permissiveness or for more strict adult control have yet been empirically tested. Does early indulgence "spoil" children or does it give them a foundation of "security" to meet life's stress and strain? Does firm and consistent discipline by the parents create in children inner hostilities, anxieties, and self-rejection or does it relieve anxiety and foster more successful self-discipline? Psychologists, psychoanalysts, teachers, parents, grandparents have often spoken with strong conviction on one or the other side of these issues, but the evidence has usually come from personal experience, clinical cases, plausible theories, or unconscious bias.

A generation ago this writer made a first effort at empirical study of this problem, comparing the self-reports of 230 graduate students

Selections reprinted from *Journal of Psychology,* 44 (1957), 227–249, by permission of the author and The Journal Press. (Seven tables have been omitted.)

who rated their home discipline during childhood along a continuum from the most strict to the most lenient. Those who came from the strictest quartile of homes reported: (a) more hatred for and constraint in relation to parents; (b) more rejection of teachers; (c) poorer relations with classmates, more quarrels, and shyness; (d) more broken engagements and unsatisfactory love affairs; (e) more worry, anxiety, and guilt feeling; (f) more unhappiness and crying; (g) more dependence on parents; but (h) better school grades and stronger ambition. Two cogent criticisms should be made of this study. First, the "strict" category included homes where there was severe punishment and quite possible rejection. The "lax" category included possible indifference and neglect along with genuine concern for freedom. Second, since all data came from the students' self-reports, a generally negative or optimistic outlook may have permeated both the reports on home discipline and the present self-evaluation.

A few years later (1938) Carpenter and Eisenberg (4) reported findings leading to similar conclusions. Among 500 college women, the 50 rated as most "dominant" reported a childhood in which their own "freedom" and "individuality" had been stressed. The more "submissive," like the shy, dependent, anxious students in our 1929 study, came almost entirely from adult-dominated homes. Those who "had to have parents permission to do practically everything" turned out at college age to be "submissives" (21%) rather than "dominants" (2%).

Studies attempting to relate specific early child-rearing practices (e.g., breast feeding, self-demand feeding, method of toilet training, etc.) to child personality seem to have been inconclusive [Cf. Sewell (11) and review by Orlansky (9)]. Those which center upon the general social climate in the home, on the other hand, reveal marked and generally consistent differences. One exception is Myers (8) who, in 1935, reported that a pupil adjustment questionnaire and high school teacher ratings on quality of personality adjustment were unrelated to strictness of home discipline.

Hattwick (5) in 1936 found that "over-attentive" homes which "favor" the child or "revolve around" the child were positively correlated (.2 to .4) with tendencies of nursery school pupils to be babyish in such matters as "cries easily," "asks unnecessary help," and "avoids risk." On the other hand, these same over-indulged children were less likely to take the property of others or to mistreat animals.

Ayer and Bermeister (2) in 1951 reported on another study of the personality traits of nursery school children in relation to their home discipline. Significant correlations appeared between physical punishment at home and a tendency of children not to face reality ($r = .35$) and between permissiveness of parents (letting children learn from the natural consequences of their acts) and a more "attractive" personality in the child ($r = .33$).

Symonds (13) matched 28 parents who "dominated" their children in an authoritative way with 28 who permitted the child much freedom and who usually acceded to child wishes. He found the children from stricter homes more courteous, obedient, and neat, but also more shy, timid, withdrawing, docile, and troubled. The more permissive parents brought up children who were more aggressive, more disobedient, and who had more eating problems, but who also were more self-confident, better at self-expression, freer, and more independent.

Anderson (1) identified a group of junior high school pupils who had been brought up with warm affection but little adult dominance. He found these children marked by a high degree of maturity, poise, cheerfulness, coöperation, obedience, and responsibility.

Lafore (7), using techniques of direct, on-the-scene observation, made two half-hour visits in the homes of 21 nursery school children, and reported that:

Parents who presented the largest number of instances of dictating (to) and interfering with their children, received the largest number of expressions of hostility from their children. . . .
Parents who showed large numbers of instances of blaming, hurrying, punishing, threatening and interfering had children who presented large numbers of crying. . . .
Children who were frequently threatened scored high on fearfulness. . . .
Children who were cautioned most often scored low on resourcefulness.

Raelke's study (10) is in some ways closest to the one to be reported here. She studied 43 children of nursery school or kindergarten age, giving the parents a questionnaire and observing the children in free-play and picture-interpretation test situations. Children from more restrictive and autocratic home discipline showed less aggressiveness, less rivalry, were more passive, more colorless, and less popular. They did not get along so well with other children. The children from homes with freer discipline were more active, showed more rivalry, and were more popular. Raelke found that parents who were "democratic" in their disciplinary methods, giving more respect to the youngsters, fostered children who themselves showed more consideration for others.

Baldwin (3) in 1948, reported on a study of 64 four-year-olds, showing that parents who were strict and undemocratic in their methods of control were likely to have children who were quiet, well-behaved, unaggressive, but restricted in curiosity, originality, and imagination.

Shoben (12) found that when parents of "problem children" (defined as: referred for clinical help, or brought into custody of juvenile authorities at least twice) were given an attitude scale they were more apt than were parents of non-problem children to agree with statements approving strict discipline and demand for obedience. Bi-serial correlation was .80 on the original group and .62 on a validating group for this variable which Shoben called "Dominating."

There is considerable convergence among the findings of these studies. There seems to be reason to suppose that firm, strict adult domination will produce the conforming, obedient child but will handicap him in initiative and probably burden him with shyness and a sense of inadequacy. More permissive treatment seems, in these studies, to result in more independence and aggressiveness on the part of the child. These children are less docile but in some studies appear to be more popular and more considerate of others. Shoben's results challenge a popular belief that juvenile delinquency is associated with lack of punishment by parents.

B. SELECTION OF SUBJECTS

This study was conducted under the auspices of The Guidance Center, a child-guidance clinic in New Rochelle. Associated with the Guidance Center was a positive program of education in mental health and of community service, reaching hundreds of parents of "normal" children in the eastern part of Westchester County. Subjects for this study were limited to normal children in school from kindergarten through sixth grade. Only "good" homes where children were wanted, loved, and well cared for were included. Any children who had ever been referred for psychological or psychiatric treatment were excluded. Nominations were sought from parents, teachers, and social workers, to find good homes that were known to be clearly "strict" or "permissive."

During a preliminary period, social workers visited the recommended homes and talked with these parents about their practices in child-raising. On the basis of the interviews a multiple-answer questionnaire was constructed and printed under the title, "*How I Am Bringing Up My Child.*" The instrument asked about parental reaction to each of 35 fairly common situations, such as children's eating, sleeping, toilet training, dressing, keeping clean, caring for toys, quarreling, anger at parents, sex curiosity, attendance at school and church, choice of television programs, friends, etc. Each situation was followed by three kinds of possible response: (*a*) a clearly permissive reaction, (*b*) a middle-of-the-road or "sometimes this and sometimes that" answer, and (*c*) a reply characteristic of the parent who sets standards and enforces strict obedience. The responses were assigned weights of 5 for the most permissive, 3 for the neutral, and 1 for the strict reaction. There was opportunity for parents to write in a response to each situation in their own words if none of the proposed answers seemed to fit well enough. If a parent's qualified answer fell between "strict" and "middle-of-the-road" it was given 2 points; if it fell between "middle-of-the-road" and "permissive" it was given 4 points. Consistent choice of the "strict" responses would result in a score of 35; consistent "middle-of-the-road" responses would give a total of 105; consistent "permissiveness" would bring a total score of 175. The actual range was from 55 to 158.

A range of 20 points on either side of the neutral point of 105 was arbitrarily set as representing the area of common practice—strict about some things at some times and more lenient on other matters or at other times. Although we had made special efforts to reach the more extreme groups—the permissive parents with scores of 125 or over, and the strict parents with scores of 85 or less—more than half (53%) of our responses fell in the 40 point middle range and were not used in this study.

The home discipline for 34 of the children was rated by fathers independently of the mother's rating. Fathers usually reported a less permissive attitude than did mothers. For these cases, fathers averaged a score of 105 and mothers 115. In only seven instances did the mother's report indicate a stricter attitude than that of the father. Correlation between mother's rating and father's was .61. For the sake of consistency, since mother's rating was available in all cases and since in suburban communities today the mother is more directly and more frequently responsible for discipline in the type of situation listed, our classification into strict or permissive is based only on the mother's report. In no instance would a child's classification have moved from one extreme category to the other if the father's questionnaire had been used instead of the mother's.

Responses of children to questions on home discipline as they saw it, usually confirmed the answers of the parents. Interviews and questionnaires, independently administered by Dr. Norris E. Fliegel, indicated that children from strict homes concurred with their mothers on 86 per cent of the items. It is interesting also that the children almost invariably approved the form of discipline they were receiving. Those from permissive homes believed it was best to give children freedom to make their own decisions; those from strict homes felt that parents knew best and should exercise firm control.

C. PROCEDURE

Parents whose questionnaire score was extreme, falling under 86 (strict) or over 124 (permissive), were visited by a trained social worker who conducted an interview designed to check both directly and indirectly on the reported attitudes and practices, to evaluate the general climate of the home, and to obtain the parents' perception of their child's strength and weaknesses. The social workers were not informed as to whether the home to be visited had been reported as permissive or as strict but the differences were so marked that this was seldom in doubt. In the few (3) instances in which the social worker felt that the questionnaire classification was questionable because the home really belonged in the middle-of-the-road category rather than at the extreme, the case was not included in our comparative study. Thus every case which was included met both the criteria: extreme score on the questionnaire, and confirming judgment of a social worker who had independently observed parent and child in the home.

Children included in our study were voluntarily brought to the Guidance Center by their parents for an hour or two of psychological testing which included a free play period, a Rorschach test, selected pictures from the *TAT*, a figure-drawing test, and a performance test (Alexander Passalong) which gradually became too difficult and so gave opportunity to study reaction to stress or frustration. Some of the children returned for a second appointment in which they were given a vocabulary test and a questionnaire on their perception of the home discipline. Results from this latter instrument are being analyzed and reported by Norris Fliegel.

We endeavored to get school behavior ratings for all the children, but this proved impossible in some cases. Wherever they coöperated, teachers or school guidance officers rated the children on a scale which provided intervals from 1 to 5 on: (*a*) level of activity; (*b*) initiative; (*c*) independence, spontaneity, self-reliance; (*d*) confidence, good adjustment; (*e*) friendliness and popularity; (*f*) coöperation; (*g*) self-control; and (*h*) persistence. In the case of 16 of 36 children rated by teachers a trained worker from the Guidance Center made an independent appraisal using the same scale. Agreement of the teacher and the outside observer is represented by a correlation of .77. Of 121 parallel judgments, 59 per cent agreed exactly; 31 per cent differed by only one scale step; and 10 per cent were two steps apart. Thus 90 per cent assigned the same or an adjoining category.

D. RESULTS

1. PERMISSIVENESS IS RARE

The first surprise of the study was our difficulty in finding parents who were fairly consistently permissive. Perhaps this should have been anticipated.

Whiting and Child (15) have estimated the over-all indulgence or severity of child training in 47 societies studied by competent anthropological observers. The aspects of discipline which they included in their index were: (*a*) earliness and severity of weaning; (*b*) toilet training; (*c*) repression of sexual activity; (*d*) repression of aggression; and (*e*) effort toward child's independence. They found only two of the 47 cultures as severe on the younger child as is the typical American middle-class white family described by Davis and Havighurst. No culture in the records is less permissive with children than we are. The short-shift given to "progressive education" in this country might further have warned us.

We had been led to believe, however, that in certain sub-cultures of the United States the ideal of respecting the child and of permitting him great freedom to mature in his own way and at his own good time had taken root. We knew that psychoanalytic concepts were commonly heard in upper-middle class Westchester child-study groups and that "mental hygiene" was looked upon as favorably as Divine Grace once had been. Some teachers complained that children were being given too much freedom at home and writers in popular journals freely listed lack of firm parental discipline as a major cause of juvenile delinquency. It was easy to find citizens who thought that some of their neighbors were overly-permissive parents.

We set the modest goal of 50 cases—25 boys and 25 girls—from child-centered, permissive homes. After strenuous search, with the co-operation of the Guidance Center, the Child Study Association, the Mental Hygiene Association, social workers, clergymen, teachers, pediatricians and P.T.A.'s; and after extending our quest for an extra year and modifying our qualifying scores a step or two downward toward the middle; we eventually located 38 permissively brought-up children —21 boys and 17 girls. (Four of these could not be included in the later testing.) The distribution of our questionnaire returns is shown in Table 1. We emphasize again that this is not a normal cross-section. We were not interested in "middle-of-the-road" cases for this particular comparison. The point of the table is that with much less effort, we found three times as many "strict" as "permissive" homes in the most "liberal" section of an upper-middle class suburban community. The obtained median score of 101 is below (i.e., more strict than) the arbitrary neutral score of 105.

2. AGE, SEX, AND DISCIPLINE

Demands for conformity to adult standards become stronger as a child grows older. Babies are not expected, except by pathological parents, to "behave" themselves. Many cultures treat young children very indulgently, only later expecting them to exercise mature levels of self-control. Pearl Buck reports that in the China she knew, children were usually treated very permissively until about the age of seven. Their demands were gratified whenever possible. But after seven, they were expected to behave like proper adults, and they did so.

Table 1.   Distribution of Scores on "How I Am Bringing Up My Child"

Score	No. of boys	No. of girls	Both	Per cent of total
"Permissive" Extreme				(12%)
145 and over	3	5	8	
135–144	5	4	9	
125–134	13	8	21	
"Middle-of-the-Road"				(53%)
115–124	13	14	27	
105–114	30	39	69	
95–104	31	48	79	
"Strict" Extreme				(35%)
85–94	33	41	74	
75–84	20	8	28	
74 and below	9	4	13	
TOTAL	157	171	328	(100%)

. . . . .

Our data from 328 children in Eastern Westchester county show no clear and consistent age trend. The anticipated transition from infant indulgence to mature demands does not appear in this cross-sectional survey. Longitudinal studies of qualitative changes in the same child-parent relationship might reveal that tolerance for some kinds of childish misbehavior is decreasing, but that with advancing age children are treated with increased freedom which offsets these restrictions.

Some might have expected that girls—sometimes reputed to be "less trouble" than boys—would be treated more permissively. Others would have expected that boys would be granted more license than girls. Our data do not give support to either interpretation as a general pattern. In some families, no doubt, girls are treated more indulgently but in others they are more restricted; on balance no difference is found between the discipline of sons and that of daughters, aged 5 to 12.

3.   THE TWO GROUPS COMPARED

. . . Although our two groups of children, one from exceptionally "permissive" and the other from very "strict" homes, are far apart on Home Discipline score, they are not significantly different in proportion of boys (57 per cent and 62 per cent), or in age. The distributions of intelligence, as estimated from Rorschach or quite independently from a vocabulary test, show relatively a few more top-level IQ's from the permissive homes, but this difference is not large enough to be statistically

significant. It is noteworthy that all children in this study have IQ's of
110 or higher as estimated from their vocabulary.

. . . . .

4. PLAN OF PERSONALITY STUDY

Children who are strictly brought up will be compared with children
who are treated much more permissively, on each of nine dimensions of
personality as follows:

Overt Behavior

1. Independence—dependence.
2. Socialization—ego-centrism.
3. Persistence—easy discouragement.
4. Self-control—disintegration.
5. Energy—passivity.
6. Creativity—stereotyping.

Inner Feelings

7. Friendliness—hostility.
8. Security—anxiety.
9. Happiness—sadness.

In each instance the null hypothesis—that there is no significant difference between the two groups—will be statistically tested.

*a. Independence—Dependence: Hypothesis 1. Is there no difference
between children from strict and those from permissive homes in the
personality dimension of independence—dependence?*   Five measures
bearing upon this hypothesis have been combined to give an index of independence. One is a rating by the psychologist of the child's behavior as
he was brought into the playroom, shown the toys, games, puzzles, craft
materials, etc., and told he might play with them in any way he chose.
A rating of "5" is assigned to those children who promptly sized up the
situation and went to work on their own responsibility with no further
demands on the adult. The low extreme of the scale, a rating of "1," is
assigned to those children who were unable to get going despite repeated
instruction and reassurance. This rating correlates .70 with the composite
index.

The second measure is a rating of the child's evident need for adult
attention during the later activities of the testing period. Those children
who independently judged their own performance with little reference
to cues from the psychologist are at the high (5) end of the scale; those
who were so dependent on adult approval that without definite reassurance their behavior was disrupted are given a rating of 1. This measure correlates .71 with the composite.

The third rating is based on a period of free play with doll figures representing a family. If the examiner was asked to make decisions for the child, the rating is low; high ratings represent independent, self-reliant structuring of the interpersonal play. This measure has the highest correlation (.76) with the composite index.

The fourth measure is based on the story interpretations which the child assigned to several *TAT* and *CAT* pictures. If the figures with whom the child seemed to identify most were self-reliant, acting on their own responsibility, the rating is 5. The lowest rating, 1, means that the identification figures were generally passive, helpless, or dependent. This correlates only .51 with the composite.

Our fifth rating is derived from Rorschach responses. Whether M (movement) responses were active and extensor or passive and flexor, or absent; whether the balance of C, CF, and FC tended toward or away from control, and the content of food and adult-child relationships were all taken into account. The Rorschach estimate correlates .67 with the composite.

Table 2. Differences in Independence—Dependence

	BOYS		GIRLS		ALL	
	Strict	Permissive	Strict	Permissive	Strict	Permissive
High independ- ence (20–23)	1	7	1	3	2	10
Above average (17–19)	9	6	6	4	15	10
Below average (13–16)	10	7	8	5	18	12
Very dependent (9–12)	5	1	4	1	9	2
TOTAL	25	21	19	13	44	34

$X^2 = 20.95$. $P < .01$.

The reliability of the total index is estimated (Spearman-Brown) at .80. Theoretically scores might range from 5 to 25; the actual range is from 9 (very dependent) to 23 (highly independent). Distributions shown in Table 2 find some children from each type of home at every level of independence but the null hypothesis—that no real difference will be found—must be rejected. Differences (based on X^2 with Yates' correction) are significant at better than the .01 level. The highly independent children include 29 per cent of our permissive sample, but only 5 per cent of the strictly disciplined children. The very dependent children represent 6 per cent of those from permissive homes and 21 per cent of those from strict homes. We find, therefore, a *marked tendency for greater freedom in the home to show itself in greater independence in the child's behavior outside the home.*

b. Socialization—Ego-centrism: Hypothesis 2. Is there no difference between children from strict and those from permissive homes in the personality dimension of socialization—ego-centrism? Our index combines four separate ratings: (a) verbal negativism (or over-compliance) versus coöperative consideration of the child's own wishes and the adult requests; (d) behavioral negativism (or over-compliance) versus "positive but differentiated cooperation"; (c) stories told in response to several TAT and CAT pictures, rated for quality of parent-child relations from resistance to friendly interaction; and (d) responses to Card IV of Rorschach. Average intercorrelation of these ratings on socially integrative responses is .52, yielding a predicted reliability, for the four combined, of .81.

Differences . . . show markedly better coöperation by children from permissive homes. Differences are statistically significant, being large enough to have a probability of chance occurrence, less than .01. The highest level of mature coöperation is found among 32 per cent of the children from permissive homes but only 9 per cent of the children strictly disciplined. The null hypothesis must be rejected and so also must the "spoiled child" or "little monster" tradition. *Exceptionally permissive discipline seems on the whole to be associated with better socialization and more effective coöperation with others.* At the same time, it should be remembered that children from each type of home can be found at every step of the socialization scale.

This study does not demonstrate that the higher average level of independence reported earlier, or of coöperation reported here, is produced by the permissive discipline. It may be true—and the data on freedom from hostility to be reported later make this plausible—that the more relaxed home atmosphere is responsible for the observed differences in personality. Alternative explanations cannot, however, be excluded. Perhaps the kind of parents who choose the permissive role transmit, via heredity or via associated cultural influences, a different temperament or pattern of living. It should not be assumed that if parents who have heretofore practiced strict discipline were simply to change over to great permissiveness, their children would thereby become more independent or coöperative. They might, or might not. A correlational study cannot satisfactorily answer questions of causation. . . .

c. Persistence—Easy-discouragement: Hypothesis 3. Is there no difference between children from strict and those from permissive homes in the personality dimension of persistence versus being easily discouraged? All subjects were given the Alexander Passalong test which begins with easy problems in block movement and arrangement but proceeds to those which, although they seem workable, are impossibly difficult. The psychologist noted how long the child persisted at the task and also the effect of increasing difficulty and frustration upon personality organization and ability to make intelligent use of experience.

Table 3 is in accord with the null hypothesis, since the two groups cannot confidently be regarded as from different statistical distributions. The null hypothesis is likewise supported by teacher ratings (for 38 cases) on persistence at school tasks which showed similar distributions for children from strict and from permissive homes.

. . . . .

Table 3. Differences in Persistence—Easy Discouragement *

	BOYS		GIRLS		ALL	
RATING	Strict	Permissive	Strict	Permissive	Strict	Permissive
4 Very persistent	13	6	8	3	21	9
3 Moderate	3	7	4	9	7	16
1–2 Evade, give up	9	7	7	1	16	8
TOTAL	25	20	19	13	44	33

* Distributions not statistically significant, but association of permissive discipline with moderate rather than high or low persistence is significant ($X^2 = 12.49$) at better than the .01 level of confidence.

If our hypothesis were revised to state that permissive discipline is associated with a moderate degree of persistence, while strict discipline is associated with either unusually persistent or easily discouraged behavior, this *post hoc* revised hypothesis would be supported by the psychological test data of Table 3 at better than the .01 level of significance. The revised hypothesis makes good psychological sense. Since we already know that the children from permissive homes are more inclined to act independently and on their own initiative, we might expect them to make a try at a very difficult problem, but to use their own judgment in giving it up when no progress is made. In contrast, the children accustomed to firm adult control might more readily feel helpless, or, if instructed to keep on trying, persist in their vain efforts. The data on intellectual quality of the continued effort will be helpful in assessing this expectation.

As the task grew more difficult, some children became frustrated and deteriorated in their learning process. Others continued to study the problem, did not repeat errors, and evidenced growing insight into the difficulty. Type of home discipline does seem to be related to quality of behavior under difficulties, as reported in Table 4. Serious deterioration in intellectual quality of response was found in 13 (32 per cent) of the children with strict up-bringing, but in only 2 (6 per cent) of the children given greater freedom.

Table 4.   Differences in Effect of Frustration on Learning

| | BOYS | | GIRLS | | ALL | |
RATING	*Strict*	*Permissive*	*Strict*	*Permissive*	*Strict*	*Permissive*
3 = Improves despite frustration	8	11	6	9	14	20
2 = No marked effect	7	8	7	3	14	11
1 = Deterioration from frustration	7	1	6	1	13	2
TOTAL	22	20	19	13	41	33

$X^2 = 6.73$. Differences significant at .02 to .05 level.

The hypothesis that home discipline is unrelated to persistence-discouragement should probably be rejected. The observed differences certainly do not sustain the popular fear that children who are allowed their own way much of the time at home will collapse when faced by difficult tasks. Apparently—with due allowance, again, for the fact that some children from each type of home can be found at every level—there is some tendency for *permissive discipline to foster the type of personality which makes a reasonable effort, continues effective intellectual attack upon problems, but is unlikely to persist indefinitely against odds.* Differences in school work are not significant.

d. *Self-Control—Emotional Disintegration: Hypothesis 4. Is there no difference between children from strict and those from permissive homes in the personality dimension of self-control versus emotional disintegration?* Closely related to the quality of intellectual attack upon a difficult problem is the emotional response during frustration. The data in Table 5 come from the psychologist's rating of the child's emotional reactions as the Passalong test became too difficult for him. The null hypothesis is acceptable; observed differences are not statistically significant. A further test of the hypothesis may be made, using teacher's ratings for 37 of the children.

Table 5.   Differences in Self-Control During Frustration Test

| | BOYS | | GIRLS | | ALL | |
	Strict	*Permissive*	*Strict*	*Permissive*	*Strict*	*Permissive*
Undisturbed	10	12	8	6	18	18
Moderate impatience	10	7	9	5	19	12
Extremely upset	4	1	2	2	6	3
TOTAL	24	20	19	13	43	33

Differences not statistically significant.

Again, as shown in Table 6, differences fall within what might well be expected by chance.

Table 6.   Teacher Rating on Self-Control

	BOYS		GIRLS		ALL	
	Strict	Permissive	Strict	Permissive	Strict	Permissive
Well balanced; not easily upset	5	2	6	6	11	8
About average	3	2	2	0	5	2
Loses temper, cries, easily upset	7	3	1	0	8	3
TOTAL	15	7	9	6	24	13

Differences not statistically significant.

Our data do not support the view that children given firm control at home are better able to withstand frustration; neither do they support those who argue that strict parental control interferes with the development of the child's self-control.

e. Energy—Passivity: Hypothesis 5. Is there no difference between children from strict and those from permissive homes in the dimension of energetic versus passive personality?   Three ratings are applicable to testing of this hypothesis. One is a rating by the psychologist of the apparent energy level of the child. Scores range from 1 for "inert, uninvolved" manner during play and testing, through 2 for subdued activity, to 5 for very lively participation. This variable refers to focused personality energy, not to merely physical, muscular activity.

The second rating is derived wholly from the Rorschach performance, taking account of total number of responses, number of content categories, number of wholes, and amount of movement.

The third estimate is based on an exercise in which the child drew a man, a woman, and himself.

Average intercorrelation of the three ratings is .46; predicted reliability for the three combined is .72.

As shown in Table 7, the differences between groups are not significant and the null hypothesis is acceptable.

Neither the data from the psychological tests nor those from the classroom would support the view that strict home discipline typically represses impulses to such an extent as to make children inactive. In the test situation no difference is apparent, at school the well-disciplined children appear, on the whole, more active along approved lines.

f. Creativity—Conformity: Hypothesis 6. Is there no difference between children from strict and those from permissive homes in the personality dimension of creativity versus conformity?   Five measures of

Table 7.   Differences in Energy—Passivity

	BOYS		GIRLS		ALL	
	Strict	*Permissive*	*Strict*	*Permissive*	*Strict*	*Permissive*
Energetic, active productive (13–15)	3	4	3	4	6	8
Above Average (11–12)	10	4	8	5	18	9
Average (9–10)	10	3	3	4	13	7
Inert, passive (5–8)	2	9	5	0	7	9
TOTAL	25	20	19	13	44	33

Differences not statistically significant.

. . . . .

this variable are available. One is based on the child's behavior, ranging from free and imaginative to stereotyped and monotonous, during a free play period. A second has been similarly observed during a period of play with a full family of dolls. The third estimates originality and imagination in stories composed as responses to *CAT* and *TAT* pictures. The fourth comes from Rorschach responses and the fifth from human figure-drawing. The average intercorrelation of these measures is .53 and the predicted reliability for the combined rating is .85.

Table 8.   Differences in Creativity—Conformity

	BOYS		GIRLS		ALL	
	Strict	*Permissive*	*Strict*	*Permissive*	*Strict*	*Permissive*
Highly creative, imaginative, spontaneous, original	1	6	1	5	2	11
Above average	12	5	6	1	18	6
Below average	8	4	8	7	16	11
Stereotyped, conventional, restricted	4	6	4	0	8	6
TOTAL	25	21	19	13	44	34

$X^2 = 29.35.$ $P < .01.$

The differences shown in Table 8 are the most impressive of any in our comparisons, and compel rejection of the null hypothesis. *High creativity characterizes* 11 (33 per cent) *of the children brought up with unusual freedom, but only* 2 (5 per cent) *of those from strict homes.* The more firmly disciplined children are most apt to be found near the middle of the range in this variable.

The first six variables—independence, socialization, persistence, self-control, energy, and creativity—have focused on more overt, and directly observable behavior. The remaining three turn attention to the inner life of the child.

g. *Friendliness—Hostility: Hypothesis 7. Is there no difference between children from strict and those from permissive homes along the dimension of friendly versus hostile feelings toward others?* Our psychological testing yields four projective indications of inner hostility. One is based on observation of free play with dolls. Hostile contacts or avoidance of contacts is rated 1; friendly interaction is rated 5.

The second is based on the *TAT* and *CAT* stories. The low end of scale (rating 1) is assigned to stories of violent conflict, death, and destruction. High scores represent stories of friendly interaction.

The third rating is based on such Rorschach signs as content items interpreted as aggressive weapons, mutilated human or animal bodies, and aggressive or hostile M or FM.

The fourth has been drawn from analysis of the figure-drawing test and responses during the drawing.

Table 9. Differences in Friendliness—Hostility

	BOYS		GIRLS		ALL	
	Strict	*Permissive*	*Strict*	*Permissive*	*Strict*	*Permissive*
High friendliness, little hostility (16 and over)	1	2	0	4	1	6
Above average friendliness; below average hostility (Scores 13–15)	5	8	8	6	13	14
Above average hostility (Scores 10–12)	12	8	10	1	22	9
High degree of aggressive hostility (Scores 9 and lower)	7	4	1	1	8	5
TOTAL	25	22	19	12	44	34

$X^2 = 10.64$ (Yates correction). $P < .02$.

Intercorrelations among these tests range from .50 to .74, averaging .60; the predicted reliability for the four combined is .87—the highest of any of our measures.

Hostility versus friendliness scores of the two groups are compared in Table 9. The null hypothesis should be rejected. *More hostility is evident in those children who have been strictly disciplined; more positive feelings toward others are expressed by children whose parents have been permissive;* these differences are consistent through the distribution and are statistically significant. At the same time, it should be remembered that neither group has a complete monopoly on positive, friendly feelings toward others or on inner hostility.

Reactions to frustration on the Passalong test make possible another rating which has in it a high component of hostility for some children. Half of the TAT story-completion test was administered before the frustrating experience of failure on the too-difficult block test. The other half was given immediately after the somewhat annoying defeat. For a few children, the consequence was that the stories in the latter part of the test were briefer, the child was less coöperative and gave more evidence of hostility. This behavior characterized six (15 per cent) of the 41 children from strict homes; but only one (3 per cent) of the 32 children from permissive homes. This difference is not statistically significant, but its direction is in accord with the evidence from Table 9 indicating that strict discipline does leave a residue of inner hostility.

Supplementary research by Dr. Norris E. Fliegel, in which the Blacky Test was administered to 47 of our subjects, showed only one significant difference in the emotional life of the 24 adult-dominated as distinguished from that of the 23 self-regulating children. *"Children from strict homes did not feel free to express their hostility, but had to inhibit it."* As reported earlier, the children from strict homes did not openly resent adult control; indeed, they indorsed it. But on projective tests it was clear that they fancied that even a little puppy should submit to what is expected of him and never get angry at those who push him around.

h. Security—Anxiety: Hypothesis 8. Is there no difference between children from strict and those from permissive homes in the personality dimension security—anxiety? Five different ratings compose our measure of anxiety. One is the psychologist's general impression of the overtly confident or insecure behavior of the child. Three are based on projective tests: one on Card 9 of the CAT, one on the Rorschach, and one on the figure drawing test. The fifth measure is the anxiety evident during failure on the Passalong test. These five measures have an average intercorrelation of .33; the combined index would have a predicted reliability of .71 which is not high but would suffice if the groups turn out to be markedly different.

As shown in Table 10 the two groups are not clearly distinguished. The null hypothesis is acceptable. Half a dozen children from each type of discipline show marked evidence of anxiety—another half-dozen from each category behave in an easy, secure manner. What makes for anxiety in a child must be something other than unusually strict or unusually lax parental control.

i. Happiness—Sadness: Hypothesis 9. Is there no difference between children from strict and those from permissive homes in the personality dimension of happiness versus sadness? Three measures are related to general level of happiness. One is a rating of the overt manner and apparent mood of the child during his play and testing periods. Scores range from 5 for the most euphoric to 1 for the most depressed. A second measure is derived by analysis of the imaginative stories given in response to *CAT* and *TAT* pictures. Predominantly optimistic and enjoyable events result in high ratings; stories in which distress, sadness, and unhappiness come to the leading figures result in a low score. The third measure is based upon Rorschach test responses. Predominant use of black, and perception of figures as torn and broken, are used as indicators of depression.

Table 10.   Differences in Security—Anxiety

	BOYS		GIRLS		ALL	
	Strict	Permissive	Strict	Permissive	Strict	Permissive
Secure, relaxed (16–19)	1	4	4	3	5	7
Less than average anxiety (14–15)	10	6	5	7	15	13
More than average anxiety (12–13)	8	7	7	1	15	8
Anxious, tense (7–11)	6	4	3	2	9	6
TOTAL	25	21	19	13	44	34

$X^2 = 1.81$. Differences not significant.

Intercorrelations among the several indices (except for overt behavior and the Rorschach which correlate .54) are low, averaging .28 and giving a combined predictive reliability of .54.

Results conform to the null hypothesis. While our data show a slightly larger proportion of permissive discipline subjects in both the "happy" and the "unhappy" categories, the differences are unreliable.

E. SUMMARY

Forty-four children brought up in good, loving, but strictly disciplined homes are compared with 34 children from the same community and also brought up in good, loving homes but with an extraordinary degree of permissiveness. Two periods of psychological testing, supplemented (in 38 cases) by teacher ratings, have yielded measures of nine dimensions of personality. On three of the nine, no statistically significant difference is found: these are the dimensions of self-control, inner security, and happiness. Factors making for anxiety, emotional disorganization, and unhappiness are found about equally often under either type of home discipline. No difference in activity and energy level was observed during the psychological testing, but teacher ratings indicate higher activity level of an approved sort, at school for the children accustomed to stricter discipline.

On persistence, teachers observe no differences, but on a psychological test children from strict homes are more apt to fall in extreme categories, being either unusually persistent or very easily discouraged. A moderate persistence is more characteristic of the children from permissive homes. These children maintain a better quality of intellectual activity under difficulty than do the children from strict homes.

On the four remaining variables (which are also those most reliably measured, with predicted *r*'s from .80 to .87) significant differences in each instance are in favor of the children from permissive homes. Greater freedom for the child is clearly associated with: (a) more initiative and independence (except, perhaps, at school tasks); (b) better socialization and coöperation; (c) less inner hostility and more friendly feelings toward others; and (d) a higher level of spontaneity, originality, and creativity.

None of the personality differences applies to all cases; some children from strict and some from permissive homes may be found at every level on every characteristic tested. It is impressive, however, to find no clear personality advantages associated in general with strict discipline in a good home. Where differences do emerge, these are consistently to the credit of the more permissive upbringing. This study cannot distinguish the extent to which the advantages associated with permissiveness are due to that procedure alone and the extent to which more permissive parents may convey hereditary or cultural assets with which the permissive attitudes happen to be correlated.

REFERENCES

1. ANDERSON, J. P. The Relationships between Certain Aspects of Parental Behavior and Attitudes of Junior High School Pupils. New York: Teachers College, Columbia University, 1940.
2. AYER, M. E., & BERNREUTER, R. A study of the relationship between discipline and personality traits in young children. *J. Genet. Psychol.*, 1937, 50, 165–170.
3. BALDWIN, A. L. Socialization and the parent-child relationship. *Child Devel.*, 1948, 19, 127–136.
4. CARPENTER, J., & EISENBERG, P. Some relationships between family background and personality. *J. of Psychol.*, 1938, 6, 115–136.
5. HATTWICK, B. W. Interrelations between the preschool child's behavior and certain factors in the home. *Child Devel.*, 1936, 7, 200–226.
6. HATTWICK, B. W., & STOWELL, M. The relation of parental over-attentiveness to children's work habits and social adjustment in kindergarten and the first six grades of school. *J. Ed. Res.*, 1936, 30, 162–176.
7. LAFORE, G. Practices of parents in dealing with preschool children. *Child Devel. Monog.*, 1945, 31, 3–150.
8. MYERS, T. R. Intrafamily Relationships and Pupil Adjustment. New York: Teachers College, Columbia University, 1935.

9. ORLANSKY, H. Infant care and personality. *Psychol. Bull.*, 1949, 46, 1–48.
10. RAELKE, M. J. The Relation of Parental Authority to Children's Behavior and Attitudes. Minneapolis: Univ. Minnesota Press, 1946.
11. SEWELL, W. H. Infant training and the personality of the child. *Am. J. Sociol.*, 1952, 58, 150–157.
12. SHOBEN, E. J., JR. The assessment of parental attitudes in relation to child adjustment. *Genet. Psychol. Monog.*, 1949, 39, 101–148.
13. SYMONDS, P. M. Psychology of Parent-Child Relationships. New York: Appleton-Century-Crofts, 1939.
14. WATSON, G. A comparison of the effects of lax versus strict home discipline. *J. Soc. Psychol.*, 1934, 5, 102–105.
15. WHITING, J. W. M., & CHILD, I. L. Child Training and Personality. New Haven: Yale Univ. Press, 1953.

6. WHAT MAKES THEM CREATIVE?

NATALIE READER HAIMOWITZ
AND MORRIS L. HAIMOWITZ

What exactly is "creativity" and what factors in the child's background encourage its development?

Selection 5 suggested that a permissive home had some relation to creativity in children. This study, which differentiates between intelligence and creativity, identifies other factors.

Today the world is seeking creative men and women to invent better mousetraps, and to help us to live together more peacefully in a rapidly changing and increasingly complex society.

Creativity is often regarded as some magical, inborn quality; it is sometimes equated with intelligence or talent. It is neither of these. There are many people who, though possessing high intelligence and being able to quickly grasp and use established methods, cannot innovate or invent. Similarly, many are born with a physiological predisposition for certain skills and abilities, but are nevertheless unable to create or invent, even in the areas in which they demonstrate talent.

Creativity has been defined as the capacity to innovate, to invent, to place elements together in a way in which they have never before been placed, such that their value or beauty is enhanced. Contrasted with conformity, it is the capacity to transcend the usual ways of dealing with problems or objects with new, more useful and more effective patterns. It will be the proposition of this paper that this ability is not inborn, but is a product of experience, that certain geographical, social and cultural milieus favor or hamper creativity. We will explore some of the psychological and sociological phenomena which appear to be related to the emergence of creative adults.

WHAT IS CREATIVITY?

In problem solving, we may observe two different methods of approach, both of which have value in a complex culture. On the one hand there is "convergent" thinking, which integrates what is already known, unifying or harmonizing existing facts in a logical well-organized, orderly manner; it is thinking which conforms to existing knowledge and exacting methods. "Divergent" thinking, on the other hand, reaches into the unknown. Its essence is not its orderliness but its originality. Guilford,[8] having elaborated on these qualitatively dissimilar kinds of thinking, demonstrates that existing intelligence tests rest heavily on skills which are convergent, reflecting cultural values which reward and esteem existing knowledge more highly than they reward innovation and invention.

Obviously, both convergent and divergent thinking are important in the development of a science. A report of the Foundation for Research in Human Behavior at Ann Arbor, Michigan,[5] defines creativity as "looking at things in a new and different way," points out that this kind of thinking occurs at the discovery phase, the insight phase, the intuitive phase of problem solving, and concludes that it is to be contrasted with the kind of restrained thinking concerned with validation of insights and testing of hypotheses. It is the former kinds of abilities, however, that are creative.

As in the world of physical objects and physical forces, creativity is often demonstrated in the interpersonal sphere by finding new ways to resolve interpersonal problems, by discovering new and more satisfying ways to interact with others. Foote and Cottrell in their book *Identity and Interpersonal Competence* [4] (see also Selection 7) see creativity as "The actor's capacity to free himself from established routines of perception and action, and to redefine situations and act in the new roles called for by the situations." Anyone who has observed sensitive and insightful handling of an interpersonal problem can testify that there is such a thing as inventiveness in social relationships. In marked contrast are formal, traditional relationships, in which everyone's behavior is prearranged, where everyone knows what is to be done and who will do it.

COMPONENTS OF CREATIVITY

The following components of creativity have been suggested in the literature: basic security, intelligence, flexibility, spontaneity, humor, originality, ability to perceive a variety of essential features of an object or situation, playfulness, radicalness, eccentricity; we would add freedom, marginality and secularity to this list. Conversely, characteristics which would hypothetically correlate negatively with creativity would be neatness, rigidity, control, thoroughness, reason, logic, respect for tradition and authority, and a tendency to routinize and organize tasks.

MEASURING CREATIVITY

One type of test wherein creative people function differently from equally "intelligent" but less creative persons are word association tests; the more creative person associates a larger number of categories with each word. Another is a hidden-shapes test which requires that the subject find a given geometrical form in a complex pattern in which it is "hidden." Another presents the beginning of a story and asks the subjects to compose a funny, a sad, and a moralistic ending.

An interesting, simple test asks the subject to draw two parallel lines and to use these lines in making a design. If he makes a design inside the lines, he is restricting himself more than if his design goes outside the two lines:

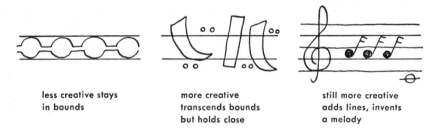

| less creative stays in bounds | more creative transcends bounds but holds close | still more creative adds lines, invents a melody |

Another test gives the subject a problem: "You are newly married. About a month after the wedding your parents come to visit you for Sunday dinner. Your mother starts cleaning your house. You are angry about this. Let's act it out for 3 or 4 minutes. Now let's act it out again, you taking the part of your mother." The creative person finds new solutions to this stress situation.

Another test asks for a written story: "Here is a picture. Write a story about it." The creative person writes stories or endings to half-completed stories that few others imagine.

Still another test says: "Here is a newspaper. How many uses can you find for it?" The more creative can think of more and better uses than the less creative.

The Rorschach Test uses standardized ink blots. The subject is asked, "Tell me what you see." The creative person perceives objects, forms, and relationships others don't see.

In all these tests, it is assumed that the person who can do what is defined as creative in the test situation will be more creative outside the test situation. This is a bold assumption since many creative persons, being nonconformists, may not be willing to invest motivation and energy in the rather arbitrary test situation; they may not care at all about what a newspaper can be used for, nor will they necessarily find pleasure or even interest in making up stories about pictures or ink blots.

CREATIVITY AND BASIC SECURITY

There are two conflicting views concerning the relationship between inner security and creativity. The reluctance of some talented people to seek psychological help for their emotional problems is supported by the belief that if the individual becomes more comfortable, he may become less creative. We hear this view also from individuals who are associated with minority political or religious movements. The belief is held that with increased security one becomes more satisfied, more conforming, and one loses his need for and interest in unpopular, deviant opinions and activities. According to this view, creativity emerges from dissatisfaction and neurosis.

The other view regards creativity as emerging only when the organism has solved its basic problems of biological and social survival. Maslow, for instance, holds that only when the individual has achieved some sense of basic security—being fed, clothed, safe from harm, achieving sexual satisfaction, being loved by others, esteeming himself—can he spare the energy for the more whimsical, relaxed capacity to innovate and improvise. Similarly Erikson, with his concepts of "autonomy" and "initiative," suggests that only when the individual has solved his more primitive, elemental problems in relating to his world, only when he feels secure enough to initiate, and realistic enough to build a stable sense of personal identity, do "higher" kinds of human activity emerge. In this view, frustration blocks creativity. Both theorists postulate that while the individual is experiencing insecurity in the gratification of the "lower level" of needs, he cannot really be creative.

Carefully conducted, longitudinal studies of creative and not-so-creative individuals and societies might help to clarify the conflicting evidence. Scattered evidence from biographies of famous creative individuals in the arts and sciences (evidence obtained and presented by students of literature rather than by social scientists) fails to support the notion that creativity can only emerge under conditions wherein the individual's basic needs have been satisfied and his life prospects are for continued satisfaction. The childhood of such eminent innovators as Darwin, Schubert, Sarah Bernhardt, Brahms, Van Gogh, the Brontes, Gauguin, do not stand out as models of security, love, and the satisfaction of basic needs. Darwin was shy, afraid of his successful father. Schubert lived in unbelievable poverty, loving music which his father denied him. Sarah Bernhardt was an illegitimate daughter of a milliner-courtesan with no home and no person to call her own.

Of course, doting biographers often play up the Horatio Alger struggles of the impoverished, crippled child who by hard work and courage overcomes impossible obstacles and achieves greatness and immortality. When we attempt, as social scientists, to recreate the lives of those who are no longer living from biography, we must wonder whether what we read is factual or partly invention aimed at making an exciting story.

When we study highly creative persons, we often find poverty or physical defects for which the individual must certainly have been striving to compensate. We find broken homes suggesting that the individuals must certainly have experienced loss of parental love through death, rejection, or desertion, and we often notice minority group status in political, religious, or racial groups such that the individual must have experienced some sense of insecurity in his "belongingness" to the larger society. If biography is enough rooted in fact, then we know that factors other than basic security are equally crucial. Some of these worthy of explanation are intelligence, freedom, marginality, and secular values.

CREATIVITY AND INTELLIGENCE

The observation has been made that the more creative are not necessarily the more intelligent. Creativity appears to be in some way associated with intelligence, but the two do not refer to the same dimensions of behavior. Just as creativity is measured operationally, that is, is defined as being what the creativity test measures, so is intelligence measured operationally, being defined as what the intelligence test measures. We assume that the person who shows intelligence in an intelligence test will also show intelligence in other aspects of his life. Yet the intelligence test may fail to tap the devices used by a general planning a campaign, or those of a young lady seeking a husband, or the behavior of an architect planning a new school. The kinds of intelligence valued on intelligence tests are verbal, memory, or convergent—organizing, logical *skills*—rather than divergent, original kinds of *talents*. Creative talents may be penalized or missed in typical intelligence tests. While those who seem to innovate successfully are apparently those also with high intelligence, it is quite possible to discover highly intelligent persons who do not innovate and discover, and to find highly creative persons who do not show superiority on intelligence tests.

Getzels and Jackson [6] did just that. They gave both intelligence tests and tests of creativity to 449 adolescents. From the 449 subjects, two groups were selected out: one of 24 individuals who scored in the highest

20 per cent in intelligence, but not highest in creativity; and the second group of 28 who scored in the top 20 per cent in creativity but did not excell in intelligence.

Comparing these two groups showed that "despite striking differences in mean IQ the creative and intelligent groups were equally superior to the total population in school performance as measured by the standardized achievement tests." Yet, from teachers' ratings, they found that teachers preferred the intelligent group rather than the creative. They also found that the need for achievement was no different in either group from the total population. Most striking differences were found when comparing the fantasy materials of the two groups. Judges, working blindly, could with high accuracy place authors of fantasy productions in the correct group—either "high intelligence" or "highly creative." The creative subjects consistently used more stimulus-free, humorous, and playful themes. Intelligent subjects' fantasy productions were orderly, logical, but "bound."

Other studies indicate that original people prefer certain types of intellectual tasks, prefer the complex to the simple problem or solution—they delay coming to conclusions until most of the pieces can be fitted together—and that creative people have more energy and are more impulsive and responsive to emotion, even when solving problems.

In *The Creative Process,* a study of 38 geniuses, including the introspective reports of such men as Einstein, Henry James, D. H. Lawrence, and Van Gogh, Ghiselin [7] suggests that those who are creative have passion and skill for their work and, when concerned with major problems which they cannot solve, appear to "forget" the problem for a time. But they would suddenly, while asleep, taking a walk, reading a book, or talking about something else, be struck with the solution as by lightning. The idea would appear to be coming from their own unconscious, which had been working on the problem all the time. Ghiselin's study suggests that in addition to intelligence there is a freedom of thought such that unconscious forces may be available in creative individuals for productive, constructive activity, assisting the more conscious intellectual processes.

CREATIVITY AND FREEDOM

Indeed, the creative person must be able to remain free from certain restraints. The very act of creating something new and different involves the courage to go beyond cultural limits. When we study the childhood biographies of creative artists, scientists, inventors, such as the Brontes, Fermi, Thomas Jefferson, Shaw, Whitney, Edison, Robert Burns, we are impressed with the apparent freedom they experienced in their early lives, even though it was often associated with parental neglect, death or desertion. They seemed to live in the midst of broad areas in which to roam, with freedom to explore, with privacy to contemplate. In many biographies, we find the absence of the parent of the same sex. Perhaps the trauma of the loss had its compensations in freedom, absence of parental coercion, and less oedipal competition.

Such hypotheses arise as we recognize the fact that so many renowned persons have come from broken homes: Washington, Jefferson, Lincoln, Herbert Hoover, Bach, Beethoven, Schubert, Schumann, Stalin, Hitler, Stonewall Jackson, the Brontes, Robert Burns, Robert Fulton, Sibelius, Debussy, Andrew Johnson, Tchaikowsky, Gauguin, Leonardo DaVinci, James Garfield, Joseph Conrad, Andrew Jackson, and hundreds of others.

No statistical study has been made to determine whether such a hypothesis as this would be true: the fathers of eminent men died before the child reached puberty in greater proportions than the fathers of the noneminent. If this hypothesis is valid, precisely what in the experience of parental loss liberates creativity?

Certainly the death of a parent in the child's infancy may so shatter basic security as to make creativity impossible. However, losing a parent in middle or late childhood may give the child more freedom and more responsibility. A number of studies by Watson, Baldwin, Lafore, Hattwick, Symonds, and Carpenter strongly indicate that children from permissive homes, homes where considerable personal freedom is permitted, are much more likely to be creative than children from restrictive homes (see Selection 5).

Imagine the courage it takes to tackle the proposition that the world is composed of atoms and that these atoms are made up of neutrons and electrons. One cannot see an atom, or an electron or neutron; one cannot even demonstrate them, as one can the invisible forces of gravity or electricity. The same is true for concepts in psychology. One cannot see motivation or the superego, and they are very difficult to demonstrate. If it takes courage to try to understand these concepts, think how much more courage would be required to imagine the concept, to create it. When developing new concepts, one is leaving the culture, leaving the traditional, taking off for a new world, in the manner of Columbus, and the point we are making is that this requires courage, the courage to be different, not as a small religious sect is different, because here at least the members are all similar, but to be different from everyone else in the world.

Creativity thus appears to be associated with freedom in the self which arises from freedom in the family, in the committee, the club, the social gathering, or any small group. By "freedom" here is meant the absence of a domineering group member or leader and the absence of obvious status differences. In our experiments with small groups we have noted more willingness of members to explore, to suggest wild ideas, to joke about the purposes or methods of the group when the designated leader was quietly receptive to such behavior. Very often a leader might try to encourage group participation, but his domineering ways blocked participation and creativity. For example, he would ask the group to make suggestions and, instead of waiting patiently for them, would go ahead and make his own. Later he would report, "I tried to get them to open up, but they wouldn't. They just don't have ideas." The leader who tries to impose standards against the wishes of the group will meet with apathy or rebellion, certainly not with creativity.

Jack Gibb's experiments show that more creative suggestions come from the group when the leader speaks, acts, and dresses informally than when his manner is formal. Studies in the classroom show similar results. We are not suggesting absence of leadership; we are suggesting absence of dominating leaders. The famous study of Lewin, Lippitt, and White [9] points out some difference between a no-leader (laissez-faire) situation and a democratic leadership situation (see Selection 31).

Studies in group dynamics suggest leadership is essential for a creative atmosphere. Leadership may be defined as any act of any member which helps the progress of the group. Thus, if two members are blocking each other's actions and dividing the group into two anxious and opposing camps, progress may be blocked. An act of leadership might be to point this situation out to the group, or it might be a suggestion for a five minute break, or a suggestion that the collection of some data would settle the differences, or a joke about how much we all hate each other. Every classroom needs creative ideas for the optimum advancement of the class. Thus, the best teacher is not only one skilled in the content of the subject matter, but also one skilled in group leadership.

Thelan in his current exciting research tells us that some children learn better working alone; others work better in pairs or in small groups; still others do best in large groups. Some children are aware of their peculiar needs in this respect, but others are not. In our own classes we have often asked for volunteers for a committee job. When the job calls for six persons, we may get different people for one committee than those who respond as when you ask for three committees of two each. When we ask the students about this, some say, "I like to work with only one other person," or "I like to work in a larger group." Recognition, acceptance, and use of individual differences in such matters greatly benefits the teacher as well as the students; and leadership in the home, school, church, camp, or factory is a major factor in creativity. Leland Bradford and Gordon Lippitt of the National Training Laboratory are in the forefront of those developing creativity in group leadership.

CREATIVITY AND MARGINALITY

Some students of civilization, such as Hume, Teggart, Bucher, William James, and Robert Park, have described a catastrophic theory of progress. Park [12] in his book *Race and Culture* points out that races are the product of isolation and inbreeding, while civilization is a consequence of contact and communication. The decisive events in man's history have been those which brought men together through the catastrophes of mass migration. The collisions, conflicts, and fusions of peoples and cultures incidental to these migrations cause both tragedy and creativity. Bucher writes that every advance in culture commences with a new period of wandering.

Somewhere in his own wanderings over the earth, Robert Park invented the term "marginal man" to indicate what Simmel had called "the stranger." The stranger is one who stays but is a potential wanderer; he is thus not bound, as others are, by the local proprieties and customs. He is the freer man. He is less involved with others, and he can be more objective in his judgment since he is not confined by one set of customs, pieties, or precedents. The stranger is the man of the cities, where division of labor and increased production have emancipated him from the age-old struggle against starvation and have given him freedom from ancient customs as well as leisure to create.

The marginal man is a man who is part of a culture but not of it. In his autobiography *Up Stream*, Ludwig Lewisohn [10] wavers between the warm security of the ghetto which he has left and the cold freedom of the outer world where he is a stranger. Heine had the same problem, struggling to be a German and also a Jew. He was both, and being both he was not fully either. He was a marginal man, and he was creative.

The marginal man is the Okie in California, the Puerto Rican in New York, the hillbilly in Chicago, the European in America, and the American in Europe, the mulatto who mingles with whites; the white man in Africa, the Irishman in England, the Catholic in Asia or in the Protestant South.

The point is that marginality, which sets a man free, makes it possible for him to be creative, to see aspects of a culture in a new light because he comes from another culture. When we study the great creative men, it seems that marginality is far more the rule than the exception.

George Bernard Shaw, for example, was born a Protestant in Catholic Ireland. Economically and socially on the fringes of the middle class, his social position was continually threatened by the economic embarrassment and alcoholism of his father. He was personally neglected by parents who found neither time for him nor interest in him. Shaw departed from the home of his childhood to live and work as an Irishman in London, clearly an out-group position. His circumstances can be easily said to have led to his cynicism. And his cynicism about his father, his religion, his economic and social order, and most of the institutions of his day is the essence of his creativity.

In similar fashion, we note that Freud was a Jew in a non-Jewish society, as was Karl Marx; that Joseph Conrad was the orphaned child of Polish nationals exiled in Russia, that Sarah Bernhardt was the child of unmarried parents of different religions. Mme. Curie was Polish, living in France; Gershwin was the son of immigrants. Stalin was a Georgian; Hitler an Austrian; Napoleon a Corsican; and Churchill, half-American. Their marginality may lead to creativity or to other intense effort—the pursuit of political power. It may be that the outcast position of marginality enables the individual to get diverse, multidimensional views of values and customs that those thoroughly "in" any society or class fail to achieve. It may be this very multidimensionality, and perhaps the insecurity and defensiveness that goes with marginality, which prevents the individual from "swallowing" wholeheartedly the traditional values, practices, and beliefs of the dominant society. This very lack of acceptance of one set standard and one set tradition appears to free the individual to innovate. The marginal man can innovate partly because he does not accept the cultures as he sees them (his isolation creates resistance) and partly because he sees two or more divergent possibilities where "belongers" see only one way, the way to which they are accustomed.

The group most responsible for emotionalized attitudes is the primary group. If the individual is fairly secure in his early family relationships and if the values of the family place great emphasis on the family traditions, we would expect the individual to carry on the family traditions. If, however, he is marginal in his family (feels "left-out" emotionally, physically or psychologically) we expect originality to emerge. It may also emerge when a person is thoroughly entrenched in a family which honors innovation and change as important values.

Although marginality may be a precondition of creativity, it is not a sufficient condition. No one can be so uncreative, so rigid as the marginal man. The new convert, for example, is typically the most conforming. The 100 per cent American is often a European who just got here, or one of his children. The *nouveau riche* are the most careful about their clothes, carpets, and coiffures. What makes the creative marginal man different from the marginal man who is an extreme conformist? We suggest the major difference is a sense of humor, but research will be required to prove that it is not merely an historical accident.

SACRED AND SECULAR VALUES

In a sacred or folk society, creativity is discouraged. Redfield [13] has defined a folk society as an ideal type, a relatively stable, small, homogeneous, isolated community, where unchanging traditions guide behavior. This kind of society does not seek change and tends to reject innovations. Most traditions have religious meaning. To alter them is sacrilegious.

Redfield contrasts the folk society with the secular, which is rapidly changing, large, heterogeneous, in communication with distant lands; its religion is the new, the different, where nothing is more worthless than yesterday's newspaper or last season's styles, and nothing so valuable as a new cloth for men's shirts or a new spray for mosquitoes. A child reared here, assimilating his culture, learns to value the novel, to adopt new fads, with pleasurable expectations, and perhaps he begins to look forward to setting the pace himself. If his innovations or inventions should strike the popular fancy, he is a great man, for a moment at least.

Thus, if the group has a favorable attitude toward change, a milieu is created in which creativity is favored. In interviews with 200 scientists and artists, we asked "Were you ever encouraged by a teacher?" Nearly all said, "Yes."

In an analysis of the childhood of 1,400 great men and women, we repeatedly found the overwhelming importance of an outstanding teacher. We believe the single most crucial step in increasing creativity in our society would be to recruit and hold the best teachers.

SUMMARY

In exploring some of the environmental and experiential factors in creativity, the following have been considered: enough feeling of security to risk venturing beyond social norms; intelligence involving divergent rather than convergent thinking, which seems to be related to a highly developed sense of humor; freedom to explore, to think, to feel, to roam; enough pressure from marginality to push the person outside his family or social group; and a secular social climate which favors innovation. Such a social climate is fostered by good teachers, informality, freedom for all to participate, skilled but not domineering leadership, opportunity to rotate roles, and a feeling of trust and equality among group members.

BIBLIOGRAPHY

1. BARRON, F., "Originality in Relation to Personality and Intellect," *Journal of Psychology*, 25 (1957), 730–742.
2. BECK, S. J., *Rorschach's Test* (New York: Grune and Stratton, 1946), Vols. I and II.

3. CARTWRIGHT, D., AND A. ZANDER, *Group Dynamics: Research and Theory* (Evanston, Ill.: Row Peterson and Company, 1953).

4. FOOTE, NELSON N., AND L. S. COTTRELL, *Identity and Interpersonal Competence: A New Direction in Family Research* (Chicago: The University of Chicago Press, 1955).

5. FOUNDATION FOR RESEARCH ON HUMAN BEHAVIOR, "Creativity and Conformity" (Ann Arbor, Mich.: The Foundation, 1958). (Includes an excellent short bibliography.)

6. GETZELS, J. W., AND P. W. JACKSON, "The Highly Creative and the Highly Intelligent Adolescent: An Attempt at Differentiation." A paper presented at the American Psychological Association Convention, Washington, D.C., August, 1958.

7. GHISELIN, BREWSTER, *The Creative Process* (Berkeley: University of California Press, 1952).

8. GUILFORD, J. P., *et al.*, "A Factor-Analytic Study of Creative Thinking," report from Psychological Laboratory, University of Southern California, 1951–1952.

9. LEWIN, K., R. LIPPITT, AND R. WHITE, "An Experimental Study of Leadership in Group Life." Selection 31 in the present volume.

10. LEWISOHN, L., *Upstream* (New York: Boni & Liveright, 1922).

11. MAIER, N. R. F., AND A. R. SOLEM, "The Contributions of a Discussion Leader to the Quality of Group Thinking: the Effective Use of Minority Opinions," Human Relations, 5 (1952), 277–288.

12. PARK, R. E., *Race and Culture* (Glencoe, Ill.: The Free Press, 1950).

13. REDFIELD, ROBERT, *The Folk Culture of Yucatan* (Chicago: University of Chicago Press, 1941).

14. SIMMEL, GEORG, *Soziologie* (Leipzig: Duncker und Humblot, 1908).

15. STANTON, H. R., AND E. LITWAK, "Toward the Development of a Short Form Test of Interpersonal Competence," *American Sociological Review*, 20, No. 6 (December, 1955), 668–674.

7. IDENTITY AND INTERPERSONAL COMPETENCE

NELSON N. FOOTE AND LEONARD S. COTTRELL, JR.

This selection answers the general question, "What kind of children do we want?" by replying, "Competent ones." But what exactly is "competence" and how can children acquire it?

The hypotheses presented here in reply to the last question are probably as representative of the current thinking of the behavioral scientists as any that could be found. Each of them almost immediately raises two related questions: "Is this really true?" and "How can it be proved to be true or false?"

INTERPERSONAL COMPETENCE

Competence is a synonym for ability. It means a satisfactory degree of ability for performing certain implied kinds of tasks. Each of the abilities described below as components of interpersonal competence is found to some degree in any normal person, regardless of his previous experience. Nevertheless, as with virtually all human abilities, by practice and purposeful training wide differences result. In this sense, interpersonal competence although based upon inherited potentialities, and directly contributing to self-conceptions, may be compared to acquired skills. To conceive of interpersonal relations as governed by relative degrees of skill in controlling the outcome of episodes of interaction is to diverge greatly from some other explanations of characteristic differences in behavior.

. . . . .

Some writers have attempted to define analytically the characteristics of mental health. At the 1953 National Conference on Social Work, for example, Dr. Marie Jahoda grappled with this quite metaphorical concept before an interdisciplinary symposium on the family. She first criticized previous conceptions which confused psychological health with (1) the absence of disease, (2) statistical normality, (3) psychological well-being (happiness), or (4) successful survival. These criteria were inappropriate, she asserted, because they neglected the social matrix of human behavior:

It follows that we must not conceive of psychological health as the final state in which the individual finds himself, for this state is dependent upon external events over which he has no control. Rather we should think of it as a style of behavior or a behavior tendency which would add to his happiness, satisfaction, and so on, if things in the external world were all right. Psychological health, then, manifests itself in behavior that has a promise of success under favorable conditions.

. . . . .

THE COMPONENTS OF COMPETENCE

Each of the component aspects of competence in interpersonal relations can be considerably elaborated and investigated. The decision as to how far to go in any particular instance depends on the particular project in mind and the amount of resources available. Here it is deemed suitable only to outline roughly a recognizable conceptual definition of each component, and not to attempt operational definition or the construction of any measures. We can then go on to consider some hypotheses about the purposeful development of each of the six components of competence.

1. *Health.* In this component we include much more than mere absence of disease. Rather it signifies the progressive maximization—within organic limits—of the ability of the organism to exercise all of its physiological functions, and to achieve its maximum of sensory acuity, strength, energy, co-ordination, dexterity, endurance, recuperative power, and immunity. A popular synonym is "good physical condition." In some medical research circles, there is, in this positive sense, considerable discussion of the better operational criteria of health to take the place of such crude indices as, for example, gain in weight among children. Research in psychiatry and psychosomatic medicine has been finding not only that sexual competence and fertility depend on psychosocial development, but also physical health in general. But the relationship runs in both directions.

Without good health, interpersonal episodes often diverge in outcome from wanted ends. Fatigue is a common example of this. While it can be and often is a symptom of complications in living, with certain other people it may also originate new difficulties. The overworked mother will lose her patience unless her reserve of energy, her ruggedness of physique, can carry her through the critical periods. The ailing person of either sex may find his dependence is not only a burden to others but means that he cannot complete the tasks that he formerly could. Endurance of strain makes physical demands, but the capacity to bear strain is not a constant; it can be cultivated in advance of its use. A striking example is the frequent recovery from despair and breakdown of interpersonal relations through vacation and rest, hygiene and recreation. On the positive, nontherapeutic side—in terms of optimal development—a benevolent spiral seems to extend from radiant health to a cheerful mien, from a cheerful mien to a friendly response, and back again to competence. . . .

. . . . .

2. *Intelligence.* Since this component has been studied continuously and widely for over two generations, it would be presumptuous to elaborate upon it here. Scope of perception of relationships among events; the capacity to abstract and symbolize experience, to manipulate the symbols into meaningful generalizations, and to be articulate in communication; skill in mobilizing the resources of environment and

experience in the services of a variety of goals; these are the kinds of capacities included in this category. It is significant that the construction of measures of intelligence is as controversial as ever, and that in any particular research project, the appropriateness and validity of the measure adopted is always a question of judgment.

. . . . .

3. *Empathy.* People appear to differ in their ability correctly to interpret the attitudes and intentions of others, in the accuracy with which they can perceive situations from others' standpoint, and thus anticipate and predict their behavior. This type of social sensitivity rests on what we call the empathic responses. Empathic responses are basic to "taking the role of the other" and hence to social interaction and the communicative processes upon which rests social integration. They are central in the development of the social self and the capacity for self-conscious behavior. No human association, and least of all democratic society, is possible without the processes indicated by this term. For this reason we must include empathic capacity as one of the essential components of interpersonal competence. The sign of its absence is misunderstanding; to measure its presence in the positive sense is a task now being attempted by a few investigators.

The kind of interaction experienced in the family as well as in other groups appears to depend heavily upon the degree to which empathic capacity develops, but experimental research on fluctuations in this element of competence has hardly begun. This lack in research is paralleled by a lack of explicit programs in action agencies aimed at the development of this type of skill. Yet it is so fundamental to social life of every kind that some social psychologists have come close to defining their field as the study of empathy.

4. *Autonomy.* In the conception of the competent personality which we are defining in terms of its components, one essential element is perhaps best denoted by the word "autonomy," though the ordinary usage of the term does not include all the significance we shall assign to it here. Our present referents, expressed as aspects, are: the clarity of the individual's conception of self (identity); the extent to which he maintains a stable set of internal standards by which he acts; the degree to which he is self-directed and self-controlled in his actions; his confidence in and reliance upon himself; the degree of self-respect he maintains; and the capacity for recognizing real threats to self and of mobilizing realistic defenses when so threatened. That is, autonomy is taken to be genuine self-government, construed as an ability, not a state of affairs. A narrower definition, close to operational, is ease in giving and receiving evaluations of self and others.

Commencing with Piaget in the 1920's, the number of writers who have attempted to deal with autonomy has been growing steadily, but the process of making clearer what is meant by this term (or its near-equivalents like ego-strength and integrity) has as yet produced no satisfactory agreement upon its referents. Some writers treat it as a trait, some as a value, some as a set of rules for behavior, and some as a highly subjective, desired state of affairs. We believe that progress in definition and measurement of this obviously very important though subtle complex will come most rapidly if definition is sought in terms of an acquired ability for handling those kinds of problematic interpersonal situations where self-esteem is threatened or challenged.

5. *Judgment*. While critical judgment has long been understood to be acquired slowly with experience, more or less according to age, its operational definition and measurement is still a difficult task. Certain of the educational psychologists have perhaps gone furthest in differentiating this ability from intelligence, and in analyzing the conditions by which an educational or other agency may cultivate judgment among its pupils.

Judgment refers here to the ability which develops slowly in human beings to estimate and evaluate the meaning and consequences to one's self of alternative lines of conduct. It means the ability to adjudicate among values, or to make correct decisions; the index of lack of judgment (bad judgment) is mistakes, but these are the products of an antecedent process, in which skill is the important variable. Obviously neither small children nor incapacitated adults can make sound decisions in the sense indicated; and it is equally obvious that among normal adults there is wide variation in this ability. Some persons acquire reputations for unusually good judgment, and some others become conspicuous for the opposite. It is therefore highly proper to conceive of judgment as an acquired critical ability differing in degree among individuals.

. . . . .

. . . A thoroughly interpersonal concept of judgment, appropriate for studying its development, probably therefore must include the skill involved in getting others to be reasonable in discussion, and to handle criticism in a way that utilizes its value.

6. *Creativity*. This component is perhaps the least amenable to precise definition and division into manageable variables which can be measured. It is ironical that the so-called tough-minded scientists and hard-headed practical people are inclined to look askance at this category as a proper object of scientific study, and yet all of these people demand appraisals of this quality in prospective associates on whom heavy responsibility for leadership and initiative will fall.

The idea of creativity is commonly associated with artistic and intellectual activities. We define it here as any demonstrated capacity for innovations in behavior or real reconstruction of any aspect of the social environment. It involves the ability to develop fresh perspectives from which to view all accepted routines and to make novel combinations of ideas and objects and so define new goals, endowing old ones with fresh meaning, and inventing means for their realization. In interpersonal relations, it is the ability to invent or improvise new roles or alternative lines of action in problematic situations, and to evoke such behavior in others. Among other things it seems to involve curiosity, self-confidence, something of the venturesomeness and risk-taking tendencies of the explorer, a flexible mind with the kind of freedom which permits the orientation of spontaneous play. . . .

.   .   .   .   .

WHY SIX COMPONENTS OF COMPETENCE?

This brief outline of our conception of the essential components of interpersonal competence is offered with no illusions as to its adequacy or finality. If we have succeeded in giving to the reader at least a rough working idea of the content and meaning the term has for us, and have stimulated critical thinking on its contemporary relevance or implications, our purpose for the moment has been served. Perhaps such reflection will result in the discovery of other skills and qualities which should be added to this list. For the present we are unable to offer additions or corrections, and have some reasons for assuming its completeness.

Readers of George Herbert Mead will recall his distinction between the "me" and "I" phases of the self in personality development and social interaction. Looking at the elements of competence, three correspond roughly to the "me" phase and three to the "I" phase:

	Me: Intelligence	I: Health
	Empathy	Autonomy
	Judgment	Creativity

The former refer to the vested and organized experience of the community as incorporated within personal conduct; the latter, to the active, assertive, and emergent features of human behavior, not reducible to standard roles in conventional situations.

.   .   .   .   .

Hypotheses for Experimentation. Within our focal interest of developing new research on the family, we are primarily concerned with research that has practical relevance for the planned development of interpersonal competence. For this reason we prefer to treat each component as a variable dependent on definable antecedent conditions. As a way of visualizing the task of proposing hypotheses of this kind, we suggest the reader keep the following table in mind. That the grouping of the relevant antecedent conditions is not entirely arbitrary may be visible upon inspection.

The hypotheses, now listed serially, would if the table were large enough be contained in the various cells. In addition, the table would have depth in the sense that each cell would contain hypotheses for different developmental periods—infancy, childhood, preadolescence, adolescence, adulthood, and later maturity—and for successive phases of the family cycle—courtship, marriage, parenthood, and grandparenthood.

Table 1. Scheme for Arraying Hypotheses

CONSEQUENT VARIABLES— COMPONENTS OF COMPETENCE	ANTECEDENT CONDITIONS					
	1 Biological	2 Economic	3 Social-Legal	4 Inter-personal	5 Educa-tional	6 Recrea-tional
1. Health	Infancy to later maturity	ditto				
2. Intelligence	ditto					
3. Empathy						
4. Autonomy						
5. Judgment						
6. Creativity						

The table suggests that only relatively simple relations can be hypothesized. While this limitation does not necessarily follow, the testing of simpler relations is logically the place to start; the more complex interrelationships among antecedent conditions will suggest themselves soon enough.

The rest of this chapter will present some illustrative hypotheses affecting the development of competent personalities. They are arranged so as to fall into various cells of the table. We are not able to fill all the cells with promising hypotheses of the experimental, or even the descriptive, variety. To do so would require the collaboration of many investigators, but the scheme suggested may help to stimulate others to make additions.

. . . . .

SOME CONDITIONS FOR DEVELOPMENT OF HEALTH

Biological conditions during:

Infancy: The planned child is more likely to be born under favorable conditions of maternal health.[1]

Childhood: The health of the parents affects the child, and improvement of their health may often be more effective than direct approach to the child.

Preadolescence: Food fears run a course and abate if left alone; if alternate diets are kept at hand meanwhile, the range of taste will freely expand.

Adolescence: Developing rhythms of sleeping and eating, work and play, if disrupted arbitrarily, lead to stress reactions, but if respected, facilitate regular autonomic functioning.

Economic conditions during:

Infancy: The chances of life for each child increase with its family's rising level of living, and approach a point where chances are even.

Childhood: Since the health of each school child largely depends on the health of the other school children, where the school explicitly functions to bring community medical resources to bear in cases of need, the health of all improves.

Preadolescence: Progressive involvement in productive manual work which mobilizes energies for tasks of extended duration is conducive to good physical condition, and particularly to control of satiation.

Adolescence: Health is favorably affected by the development of clear-cut vocational identity through ideal models and confirming groups.

Adulthood: Security of employment fosters health; assurance of permanent worth to the employment unit fosters it even more.

Later maturity: Availability of rewarding work, regardless of age, prolongs the retention of vigor and faculties.

Social-legal conditions during:

Infancy: To minimize the traditional penalties of minority status—crowding, deprivation, neglect—is to increase the chances of life for children in these restricted groups.

Childhood: If a family lives in a residential community designed for family living and for children's safety and play, then the children's health will thrive more than in an area oriented mainly to adult males.

Preadolescence: Dramatization of the public interest in the welfare of children—particularly its concern and intervention in cases of ill-treatment—causes parents to give children better protection than where the public seems indifferent.

Adolescence: Legal and moral emphasis on responsibility toward others creates an atmosphere more favorable to the growth of sexual competence than emphasis upon restraint of sexual interests.

Adulthood: As women feel accorded equal status at large, they gain in capacity for sexual response.

[1] *Ceteris paribus* [other things being equal] is a qualification that applies to all the following hypotheses.

Later maturity: Health of the aged is directly a function of whether as a class they experience tangible evidence of respect or rejection.

Interpersonal conditions during:

Infancy: If parents are accepted as adults by parental figures, they can in turn more readily give parental care. (The famous studies of Anna Freud, Rene Spitz *et al.*—summarized by Bowlby,—well cover the bearing of continuous affection upon physical and mental health, but they do not show how love might be enhanced for the unloved and the unloving.)

Childhood: The cared-for child learns to value and care for himself, by avoiding risks and following rules, when these rules are conceived as protection and not as restraint.

Preadolescence: An optimum alternation between isolation and stimulation is directly related to patterns of energy-use that fall between apathy and overstimulation.

Adolescence: Clear-cut models for sex identification improve the chances of sexual competence and reduce frigidity and impotency.

Adulthood: Control of fertility is a function of full communication and common intent between husband and wife.

Later maturity: Retaining an audience or finding new audiences, before whom one wishes to do well, is conducive to continuous health.

Educational conditions during:

Infancy: Recognition by parents and others of each gain made in the child's physical development builds up assurance and appetite for further ventures.

Childhood: Sympathetic responses of others to signs of the child's physical state help the child to recognize their meaning and importance: teaching him to report them explicitly is the basis for ultimate self-regulation.

Preadolescence: The responsibility of looking after pet animals provides a dramatic basis for learning hygiene.

Adolescence: Understanding of physiology reduces anxiety over rapid development and makes the emergence of sexual functioning a welcome attainment and thus contributes to sexual competence.

. . . . .

Recreational conditions during:

Infancy: Space and objects for exploration induce the growth of coordination.

Childhood: Full and free expression of evening bursts of energy in play, with adult consent or participation, do more for health than their suppression.

Preadolescence: If the physical demands of sports are adjusted to slightly exceed the margin of proven competence, their effect upon growth of physical competence is maximal.

Adolescence: The rhythm and phrasing of play episodes—if the demands increase in a graded series—affect the span of potential involvement, and thereby the capacity for flexible mobilization of energy.

. . . . .

SOME CONDITIONS OF INTELLIGENCE

Biological conditions during:

Infancy: Physical stimulation through handling and caressing stimulates perceptive responsiveness to the environment.

Childhood: Having other children to play with fosters intelligence; having none retards it.

Preadolescence: Regular and thorough examination and correction of deficiencies in hearing and seeing improve intelligence in children; hearing difficulties particularly lead to attributions of lack of intelligence, and to self-conceptions as unintelligent.

Adolescence: The span of involvement in episodes of learning behavior can be steadily lengthened by progressively adjusting new tasks to the margin of ability.

. . . . .

Later maturity: Energy reluctantly expended is pathogenic, but energy expended willingly in response to stimulation, even in large amounts, is generally hygienic. Not quantity but quality of work is the gauge.

Economic conditions during:

Infancy: Objects that can be manipulated, and which disclose their principles by being disassembled and assembled, foster intelligence.

Childhood: Use of adult objects—despite cost and waste—improve the child's comprehension of its environment.

Preadolescence: If both father and mother can spend much time with their children, being responsive to their initiative, rather than doing things for them, the children's intelligence improves.

Adolescence: The opportunity to explore and experiment before being committed to a vocation makes more probable a choice which will utilize potentialities fully, thus fostering their growth.

. . . . .

Social-legal conditions during:

Infancy: A general atmosphere of neighborhood interest in births and babies stimulates response and development.

Childhood: Subcultural emphasis on the values of learning and professionalism encourages the development of intelligence; anti-intellectualism discourages it.

Preadolescence: Cultural emphasis on the values of personal performance rather than on those of birth, race, and family connection, lifts the ceilings of motivation imposed by inherited status.

Adolescence: The complementarity of receptive and assertive approaches to knowledge and control of reality is best appreciated and employed in coeducational institutions. Thus all types of intelligence are cultivated best by coeducation.

Interpersonal conditions during:

Infancy: Maternal responsiveness fosters alertness to novel elements in experience; her enjoyment in the child's discoveries intensifies his own.

Childhood: To involve the child in the pursuit of knowledge through discussion between parents, especially where there is dialectic and reasonable resolution, cultivates his intelligence.

Preadolescence: A chum with whom one can assimilate new intellectual challenges, by kindly mutual criticism and by confiding fears, is a great help in forming strategies for mastering fears.

Adolescense: Reciprocal, frank discussion of the standards of adolescent peers versus the parent-teacher generation reduces ambiguity in the self-evaluation of progress, and makes criticism bear clearly on the sources of mistakes.

. . . . .

Educational conditions during:

Infancy: Abundant talking with the infant before he learns to talk stimulates the growth of intelligence.

Childhood: When teachers proceed explicitly, not on the notion of an original self that has to be trained, curbed, expressed, or molded, but by construing education as a joint process of discovery and mastery, they reduce resistance to learning and encourage the appetite for it.

Preadolescence: As the child is exposed to sympathetic adults of richer vocabulary, his intelligence develops more rapidly and fully.

Adolescence: Practice in group methods of problem-solving, e.g., through admission to family councils, furnishes an overt, dramatic model of careful thinking, which can be assumed individually by identification.

Adulthood: Children's questions—if welcomed and used—provide the parent with a review of his own intellectual biography and stimulate self-analysis of his resistances to learning, and so may reduce them.

. . . . .

SOME CONDITIONS FOR DEVELOPMENT OF EMPATHY

. . . . .

. . . In general it is widely suspected that underdevelopment or impairment of empathic capacity plays a major role in many kinds of behavior disorders, particularly in schizophrenia.

Under biological conditions also belong hypotheses concerning the effects on empathic capacity of various bodily states of extreme hunger, anger, pain, fear, excitement, intoxication, pleasure-anticipation, pain-anticipation, and similar conditions which restrict attention or reduce perception.

Additional types of hypotheses about the social psychological consequents of certain biological conditions and their effects in turn upon empathic capacity are suggested here. For example:

1. Prolonged illness increases habituation to a relationship of dependency and thus depresses empathic capacity on both sides of the relationship, but especially in the dependent member.

2. Empathic capacity is negatively correlated with repression of biological functions. (*a*) There is a negative correlation between the degree of repression of sexual functions and empathic capacity. (*b*) Thus economic, social, and educational provision for minimizing the gap between organic sexual maturity and sexual functioning will have a positive effect on empathic capacity.

3. Unwanted children are lower in empathic development than children who are desired and planned for. (*a*) Instruction in how to safely and efficiently control the number of children born, and means to exercise this control, will result in a lower proportion of rejected people in the population. (*b*) By spreading the economic burden of having and rearing children over the whole population, the probability of children being born to people who want them will be increased, with a consequent increase in average empathic capacity.

4. There is a critical point beyond which closer contact with another person will no longer lead to an increase in empathy. (*a*) Up to a certain point, intimate interaction with others increases the capacity to empathize with them. But when others are too constantly present, the organism appears to develop a protective resistance to responding to them. . . .

. . . . .

Economic Conditions

Economic conditions (job stability, income, conditions of work, and leisure time) become factors in the development and exercise of empathic capacity when they affect the amount of unhurried and anxiety-free time, and the facilities for stimulating activities, that parents can give to their children. Their influence is also important to empathic development to the extent that they affect contact and participation in the life of the community. In less obvious ways they influence attitudes and values, and these in turn affect empathic skill:

1. There is a negative correlation between the degree to which parents emphasize material possessions and other evidences of buying power in their evaluations of themselves and others, and their own and their children's empathic capacity.

2. To the extent that criteria of wealth predominate in the selection

of associates, social life becomes restricted and unstimulating and empathic capacity atrophies.

. . . . .

4. The assumption by children of appropriately graded responsibilities for the economic welfare of the family (as for example, regular duties and special jobs in the home, or limited jobs outside) increases empathic capacity. (Note: This is of course no argument for child labor in the old sense. But a revision of our economic, educational, and family institutional arrangements so as to make it a regular thing for all children, beginning at junior high school age, to have a limited and safeguarded opportunity for genuine participation in the world of business, industry, and government, would probably be a desirable thing in terms of their optimal development.)

Social-Legal Conditions

1. Members of an authoritarian, hierarchic social system will tend to develop higher empathic responsiveness to situations of superordinate-subordinate structure and lower empathic capacity for understanding other types of relations. (*a*) If the system is relatively stable and rigid, then those nearer the top exhibit the greatest empathy with persons in superior positions and the least with those in subordinate roles.

2. Family structure in such systems will tend to reflect social structure, and families are hence rendered less likely to provide the interpersonal conditions for maximizing empathic capacity.

3. In authoritarian families, the mother becomes the pivotal, mediating person, who is more able to understand both authoritarian father and subordinate children. (This may be why such characteristics as intuitiveness, sympathetic understanding, adaptability, and interest and skill in literary and artistic production have become identified as "feminine" in cultures characterized by patriarchal-authoritarian family systems.)

Age, sex, ethnic, religious, and socioeconomic differences tend to operate to inhibit the development of empathic capacity, and reduce its utilization where possessed, when these rankings serve as barriers to participation and communication.

. . . . .

Interpersonal Conditions

1. There is a positive linear relation between the empathic capacity of a person at any point in his developmental career line and the extent to which his previous development has been characterized by

stable, intimate communicative relations of relative equality and reciprocity with the members of his family. (*a*) For the ideal type, middle-class American family, the relative importance of the specific relationships are mother, father, siblings, in that order. (*b*) Affection is a highly important positive factor but its relative effectiveness is a function of the amount of communication sustained in the relationship. (*c*) Friction and conflict produce a negative effect to the extent that they impair communication. (*d*) The range of empathic capacity is a function of the number of different kinds of functional positions which the person has occupies in the family interaction. (By functional position of a person we mean the part played by him in a given social act, e.g., a giver or a receiver in an act of giving and receiving; leader or follower.) (*e*) Unilateral acts of parental subordination to the child's demands, or of administering rewards and punishment, minimize reciprocity and inhibit the development of empathic response. Striking the child in anger at something he has done and in other ways reacting to his acts so that he discovers that "parents too are human," is more in the direction of reciprocity and communication than the detached and impersonal application of rules of punishment and reward. The positive effect of "acting natural" is enhanced if the parent explains his reactions to the child and encourages him to consider how he would feel under similar circumstances, and then follows this by working out with the child some new line of action as an experimental solution to the problem.

2. Empathic capacity in children is positively related to the facility with which their parents learn to communicate and understand each other (though high empathic capacity does not insure marital harmony).

Educational Conditions

Schools, secular and religious, are in a favorable situation to experiment with various ways of supplementing and facilitating the family in the development of empathic capacity. Experimental and control groups could be used without detriment to the children used as subjects, indeed, with the conscious participation of the children and parents in the experiment. Hypotheses such as the following illustrate some of the possibilities:

1. Groups of children who are given the following experiences will show more empathic capacity than comparable groups who are not given such experiences: (*a*) Taught courses in fiction, biography, and drama in which the child is instructed and is given assistance in putting himself in the roles of the various characters studied. (*b*) Taught by teachers who themselves are high in empathic capacity. (*c*) Taught by a number of teachers who represent different subcultural backgrounds. (*d*) Given explicit instruction, training, and practice in ac-

curate portrayal of others who represent different roles in his own life situations and different subcultural identities. (*e*) Taught in situations in which the emphasis on individualistic striving for grades is replaced by emphasis on collaborative responsibility for maximizing the skill and the mastery of the subject matter by each member of the collaborating group. (*f*) Participation in group activity which involves responsibility for co-operation in planning of significant programs, resolution of real problems, and genuine discipline of members.

. . . . .

Recreational Conditions

. . . . .

1. Unilateral giving of toys with no opportunity for the child to reciprocate and to occupy the role of giver inhibits his empathic development.

2. Toys which confine the child to role of spectator limit his empathic development.

3. Abundance of mimetic and dramatic play is positively correlated with empathic development. The genuine and full participation of the parents in this play greatly enhances its effect on empathic development.

4. Reading and films, radio and television programs, which provide rich opportunity for identification with a variety of characters, increase the empathic capacity of the child.

5. Forms of play which involve discussion, planning, teamwork, and resolution of differences are productive of empathic capacity.

SOME CONDITIONS FOR DEVELOPMENT OF AUTONOMY

Autonomy has been provisionally defined as the ability to be one's self. Analytically considered, it involves and requires knowing one's self; having or finding an unambiguous identity to refer to in each situation; and being able to govern one's self in the sense of being able to choose among alternatives. The development of autonomy is not synonymous with the development of a self, though emergence of a self is indispensable. The growth of autonomy is taken as measurable and as varying within and among individuals over time. . . .

. . . . .

Biological Conditions

1. Health which itself is one of the components of competence, significantly conditions all the other components including autonomy. The conditions of health—nutrition, rest, hygiene—are therefore in-

directly biological conditions of autonomy. But there are a few bio-logical conditions which more directly affect autonomy than through their influence upon physical health. In marriage and family living, these concern sexual adequacy and fertility, where these enter into self-respect and sense of worth, in the estimation of self and others. To the extent that sexual adequacy and skill can be improved by knowledge, practice, or medical treatment, a contribution is made to autonomy, i.e., the person becomes more able to handle interpersonal situations mak-ing demands upon his sexual competence. The fact that there is a circular relationship here, in which autonomy significantly affects sexual functioning, implies the reverse proposition as a corollary hypothesis worthy of investigation.

2. Fatigue as a biological variable distinguishable from health signif-icantly conditions autonomy, and is also often the product of absence of autonomy. If practices are followed by which energy is fostered and fatigue diminished, at those times when the severest demands are made upon autonomy, autonomous capacity is itself increased.

3. Association in play exclusively with those with whom one is at a physical disadvantage, especially in the same family, leads to recur-rent experiences of failure and submission which inhibit the develop-ment of autonomy. The optimal distribution of successes and failures occurs when physical opponents are evenly matched in competition.

4. The more adequate sexual satisfaction is in marriage, the less frequent is extra-marital sexual experience and consequent threats to mutually supported self-esteem.

5. Cultivation of physical appearance—complexion, weight, grace, posture, grooming—contributes to the growth of autonomy.

6. Space for physical privacy and quiet—reduction of stimulation—facilitates the integration of new conceptions of self, especially during adolescence, and thus contributes to the development of autonomy.

Economic Conditions

1. Autonomy is positively correlated with children's opportunity progressively to earn money for performance of economically significant work and to gain practice in the management of their own economic affairs. (Safeguards against exploitation are assumed.)

2. Economic independence develops autonomy, while (*a*) chronic dependence undermines autonomy, (*b*) unemployment undermines autonomy.

3. Work which continually challenges the capacities of the person without taxing them beyond their limits enhances autonomy. (*a*) Con-tinuous employment at work far below one's level of capacity reduces autonomy. (*b*) Continuous employment at work which exceeds one's capacities and causes a chronic judgment of failure by others and self reduces autonomy.

4. Continual exposure to marked differences of reward for comparable effort reduces autonomy, whereas recognition of differences of effort by differences of reward enhances autonomy.

. . . . .

9. There is an optimal balance of work and leisure which maximizes autonomy.

Social-Legal Conditions

1. Nonthreatening exposure to a wide range of cultural and subcultural alternatives for handling interpersonal situations enhances autonomy.

2. Repeated categorical discrimination without regard to performance damages autonomy, whereas equivalence of opportunity facilitates development of autonomy.

3. Customary community respect for individual differences enhances autonomy.

4. Persistent involvement or proffering of the opportunity for involvement in group activity, without forcing it, cultivates autonomy; persistent exclusion, ostracism, or forced participation reduces it.

5. Exclusive domination by others reduces autonomy; progressive increments of initiative and responsibility enhance it.

6. Procedures of assignment of duties and periodic reporting are more conducive to autonomoy than procedures of direct supervision.

7. Community enforcement of voluntary agreements and nullification of agreements obtained by duress encourage autonomy.

8. Marriage between persons regarding each other as social unequals reduces autonomy of both mates and children; social equality in marriage facilitates the development of autonomy in mates and children.

Interpersonal Conditions

1. The strength and persistence of autonomy are positively correlated with the number of respect responses received by the self from significant others in the person's life situations.

2. Possession of a family name respected by others encourages autonomy.

3. Intimate presence of adequate models which enable the growing child to form correct sex identification is indispensable for the development of autonomy.

4. Exposure to other highly autonomous persons who can serve as models for identification facilitates autonomy.

5. Recognition by significant others of progressive accomplishment encourages autonomy.

6. Correspondence between the level of performance expected

by others and the capacity of the person to equal or exceed it is optimal for development of autonomy.

7. Autonomy increases as failure is met by assistance and encouragement for the next attempt rather than with derogatory personal condemnation.

8. Wherever accomplishment is competitive, matching of competitors is optimal for the development of autonomy.

9. Generally speaking, emphasis upon surpassing previous performance is more conducive to development of autonomy than is stress upon competitive standards of performance.

10. The growth of autonomy is assisted by the customary use of rituals for honoring the defeated party in situations of conflict.

11. Practice in the performance of roles conveying respect to others increases the autonomy of the self.

12. Autonomy is cultivated by participation in groups where one receives open and direct but nonaggressive evaluation of one's self by the others.

13. Autonomy is increased as appraisals of one's self by others come from a range of perspectives, thus giving one alternative evaluations to choose from.

14. When parents praise their children individually for characteristics that differentiate them noncompetitively from their siblings, so that each can feel uniquely appreciated, autonomy is cultivated.

15. When parents permit their children to compare them objectively with other parents they cultivate the autonomy both of their children and of themselves.

Educational Conditions

1. Rewards for expressions of curiosity and critical comparisons encourage autonomy; punishment for these reduces it.

2. Full and consistent recognition of the limitations of human knowledge, the debatability of issues, the disagreement of authorities, and the legitimacy of dissent encourage autonomy.

3. Given a broad grasp and perspective on world history, geography, and culture, one is less likely to be oppressed by the superiority or inferiority of any provincial culture or subculture.

4. Instruction and practice in scientific method foster autonomy.

5. Since teachers frequently are models for identification, they affect the autonomy of pupils favorably if they can serve as autonomous models of unambiguous sex identity.

6. If the curriculum recognizes the development of diverse skills as an objective of education this will encourage autonomy, whereas approval solely for intelligence and intellectual achievement reduces it.

7. When questions by pupils are encouraged and welcomed, the autonomy of teachers and pupils is enhanced.

8. A programming of educational experience which affords intervals of solitude for the assimilation and integration of new knowledge increases autonomy more than programs which maintain a steady barrage of work and participation.

9. Participation in the pursuit of knowledge is more productive of autonomy than mere passive receipt of knowledge.

10. Recognition and facilitation of individual intellectual interests, as they arise, encourage autonomy; enforcement of conformity reduces its development.

11. Open reciprocal criticism by fellow-students of each other's work stimulates autonomy, provided personal aggression is minimized and objectivity of standards maintained.

12. Access by parents to objective and thorough appraisal of their children's performance, if done in a way to invoke their role as audience and not their anxiety as performers themselves, aids in the growth of parental autonomy.

Recreational Conditions

1. Positive encouragement and provision for play encourages autonomy; scorn, discouragement, or subordination of play to serve extrinsic interests, reduces its contribution to autonomy.

2. Games which, without threat, convey to a person appraisals of himself by others contribute to the development of autonomy.

3. Games which provide recognition of improvement on previous performance increase autonomy.

. . . . .

SOME CONDITIONS FOR DEVELOPMENT OF JUDGMENT

. . . . .

1. If sufficient time is allowed for the completion of each sequence of decision-making, each experience can be assimilated with previous experience, and learning can occur in the sense of greater integration and efficiency in the process of judgment.

Conversely, pressure of time which forbids completion of the process is disruptive of particular instances of decision-making and inhibitory of the progressive improvement of judgment. (Generous allotments of time for making up one's mind may seem easier to obtain than the patience to utilize the time in careful weighing of alternatives, where in the past patience has been punished by parental figures.)

2. The greater one's experience as a decision-maker, the better judgment becomes. . . . Experience in decision-making is not only to run the

risk of mistakes with costly consequences, but to make the mistakes and bear the consequences.

3. If the exercise of judgment is practiced in a playful and symbolic manner, competence in the judgment of real-life situations increases.

Judgment can be practiced in such forms of play as team debating, rhetoric, mock trials, window and catalogue shopping, and academic discussions. Symbolic practice in judgment can be obtained through vicarious participation in the solution of real or prototype problems by leaders or other representatives. Explicit training furnishes concentrated practice. Practice is increased by systematically taking the roles of others, e.g., changing sides in debate.

4. Judgment improves if responsibilities widen with the growth of judgment. Withdrawal of—or from—responsibility inhibits the growth of judgment.

. . . . .

7. As provocations to diffuse anxiety are lessened, judgment improves.

. . . . .

9. Exposure to highly competent decision-makers facilitates identification with them, and thereby the acquisition of their skills, and confidence in the exercise of judgment.

. . . . .

10. The greater the quantity and reliability of relevant knowledge available to participants in problematic interpersonal situations, the more likely is improvement in their judgment.

. . . . .

Without some rules, situations become wholly arbitrary, fluid, and chaotic. Yet if rules are applied to situations mechanically without deviation or change, there is no room for judgment, which cannot develop without exercise. The optimal function of rules is thus analogous to that of grammar in language—they limit and facilitate, without dictating what statements will be composed by users. . . .

SOME CONDITIONS FOR DEVELOPMENT OF CREATIVITY

. . . . .

1. Participation in social relations which are permissive rather than repressive, equalitarian rather than hierarchical and authoritarian, mutual and reciprocal rather than unilateral, is favorable to creativity.

2. Rotation of functional positions among the participants in a social relationship is a source of new experience, providing a broadening base for creativity and increasing the probability of its development. Role-reversal in role-playing is an almost universally usable substitute device when more extended rotation of roles is not feasible, as with children and parents.

3. Participation in social relations where diversity and individuality are valued above uniformity and conformity increases the probability of creativity.

4. Extensive and obligatory routine is unfavorable to creativity. Routine in a particular activity may be favorable to creativity insofar as it frees the individual's attention, energy, and other resources for creative activity in another area. . . .

5. Situations which provide challenges that exceed the individual's previous achievement without exceeding his ability are favorable to the occurrence of creativity. . . .

6. Experiences increasing self-esteem will increase the probability of creativity. A distinction between self-esteem and self-satisfaction (a seeking for stability, permanence, perpetuation of the status quo of the self) is necessary. Self-esteem is conceived as a positive self-valuation operating independently from changes in other areas of the self-system. Involved in self-esteem is a kind of detachment which permits a person's appraisal of his general worth to stand independent from particular success and failure events; critical appraisal of products is thus not seen as directed against the performer.

7. If experiences are provided affecting the individual's self-organization and symbolic processes, so that his "threshold of stimulation" is lowered and he becomes able to be more fully responsive to the stimulation of other people and interpersonal events, the probability of creativity is increased. A playful and sociable atmosphere—as created by the capable host—is the best example.

8. Practice in make-believe and utilization of imaginary, absent, or hypothetical audiences, when real or socially present audiences are inimical or inhibitory, increases the probability of creativity. Respect for one's own voluntary fantasy and ability to withdraw are the principal cases in point; these must of course be distinguished from compulsory fantasy and worry.

. . . . .

10. Increasing the variety and range of a person's experience increases his potentiality for creativity, providing a richer fund of materials and a broader base for creativity. . . .

. . . . .

12. Creativity operates under a law of increasing returns, in that each episode of creativity increases the potentiality for future creativity. Providing people with experiences of creativity on a small scale increases the probability of more extensive creativity on a larger scale in the future.

13. Interpersonal activities and orientations which are genuinely playful are favorable to creativity. Competition and conflict (where competitors are matched and consequences limited and not serious), satire, parody, and burlesque of cherished values; humor; the playful juxtaposition of incongruities; the playful cultivation of illogicality, fantasy, and the mixture of the real and the unreal are among the kinds of playfulness favorable to creativity. . . .

14. Cultivation of an aesthetic orientation toward activity ("do it because it pleases you") as opposed to a utilitarian practical orientation ("do it because it is good for you") increases the probability of creativity. . . .

8. THE FAMILY IN THE U.S.S.R.

KENT GEIGER AND ALEX INKELES

This discussion presents a brief but interesting picture of family relationships in a totalitarian society. The Soviet revolution not only changed the ownership and control of wealth, but also revolutionized the Russian family and its child-rearing customs.

The evidence at hand points to an increasingly pronounced and widespread orientation toward equality as between husband and wife. Among the peasantry, of course, and among some of the ethnic groups where male and age prerogatives are deeply embedded in the traditional way of life, the woman can hardly be said to have reached equality with her husband. However, patriarchal patterns are looked upon by both the government and the urban population as backward and unenlightened "remnants" of an outmoded way of life. Equality of power and authority within the family between husband and wife is also supported by law. No distinctions whatsoever are made on the basis of sex in regard to legally enforceable rights and duties in the family.

Selections reprinted from the article in *Marriage and Family Living*, XVI, No. 4 (November, 1954), 403–404, by permission of the authors and The National Council on Family Relations.

Husband and wife enjoy full freedom of choice as to their individual occupation and place of residence. Neither may compel the other to change his place of residence or occupation; the wife need not "follow the husband." Further, each spouse is required to support the other if he or she is in need and unable to work, and husband and wife are jointly responsible for the support and upbringing of the children.

Although in many respects the husband-wife relationship tends to be markedly symmetrical, there still remain spheres of specialization which are sex-typed. The primary responsibility of the husband is seen as that of providing for the material security of the family, and the care of young children, the preparation of food, washing of clothes, etc., are regarded as the wife's responsibilities. In some families the bulk of the daytime care of young children is delegated to in-laws, older children, or servants in the case of upper class families. This is not always possible, however, and even where such aid is available it is only a partial answer to the problem of the divided role of the Soviet woman. Therefore most Soviet women must be both wives and mothers on the one hand, and full-time workers on the other, a fact which introduces a definite element of strain into their lives and in turn into the family.

As to relations between parents and children in the Soviet family, children definitely appear to be desired and cherished, and while they are young much attention is paid to them. Soviet parents seem as a rule to prefer to keep their children at home while they are young rather than send them to the public nurseries for the entire day. Since many families have no one at home to care for them, however, a large number of children must spend most of their waking hours in these government sponsored institutions. This is a start of a series of experiences outside the home controlled and dominated almost completely by the state. Children enter the regular primary school at the age of seven. The requirement for compulsory education is four years for the entire U.S.S.R., but in the more settled and urban areas it involves a seven year minimum. In addition to the ideas and training which children absorb at school, at appropriate ages they enter the Soviet youth organizations—the Octobrists, the Pioneers, and the Komsomol—which are organizationally integrated with the schools but controlled and directed by representatives of the Communist Party. This early and intensive training of children to be loyal Soviet patriots reflects back on family relationships, and as the children grow up some tension between parents and children in the form of parent-youth conflict quite frequently develops.

Conflict in the family between parents and children in the U.S.S.R. was especially common in the early years of Soviet history when the tendency was to look upon all the established institutions of pre-Revolutionary society with a jaundiced eye and when the revolutionary fervor of the youth often got out of control. At present the family is accepted and promoted as a "basic unit of socialist society," but certain socially structured modes of conflict with the older generations still persist. Under the influence of a utopian, monothematic ideology, inculcated by the school and youth organizations, and with very limited opportunities to temper ideas with experience, the Soviet child is apt to take the official propaganda and agitation seriously and quite literally. In many cases young people become fanatically devoted to the ruling regime and its goals, and rebel against their more detached or even hostile parents, who, they feel, are old-fashioned and not socially conscious. Differences in religious orientation, for instance, are particularly likely to be a basis for conflict and tensions. In the schools and youth organizations the children are taught that religion is nonscientific and at best mistaken, whereas in the home, especially in the case of peasant and worker families, traditional religious attitudes often predominate. While the denunciation of parents by children is clearly a rare and exceptional occurrence, particularly in recent times, there is no doubt that parent-child differences of this order are quite widespread and severe, and parents often report marked hesitation to let their children know their real feelings on many issues.

A final aspect of interpersonal relationships in the Soviet family is related to the fact that the U.S.S.R. is a totalitarian social system in which the government chronically carries out large scale repressive activities against the people. The presence of the powerful secret police, and the wholesale political arrests and purges have created throughout Soviet society an atmosphere of distrust and insecurity so that large parts of the population constantly feel exposed and anxious. Family life serves for many as an especially gratifying counterbalance to this kind of atmosphere, for that element of trust and stability which is conspicuously absent in the larger society can often be found in the interpersonal relationships within the family. For those who have not identified with the goals and symbols of the ruling regime, therefore—and it appears that there are many who fall in this category—the family serves as a refuge or retreat from a threatening life situation.

In conclusion it can be said that the general direction of change and the lines of development indicated for the Soviet family in the future are broadly similar to those which have already occurred in Western industrial countries. The family will probably become smaller in size, more mobile geographically, more isolated from the larger kinship system, and other patterns inherited from a peasant cultural background will be increasingly replaced by those demanded by an urban industrial system. Greater stress on educational preparation of children and on the development of characteristics leading to the possibility of occupational mobility are probable developments in the realm of values and attitudes;

and a general trend toward equalitarianism in social relationships between husband and wife and parents and children is indicated on the interpersonal relations dimension of family life.

9. ONE MAN'S FAMILY: DAVID AND ABSALOM

II SAMUEL 13–15, 18

No book contains more dramatic incidents involving love and loyalty, courage and despair, envy and hate, rape and murder than the Holy Bible. The passages below relate some tragic events in the family of King David.

Although his children were guilty of serious crimes, David did not punish or reprimand them. Nor did he summon a meeting of the village board or call the police. Instead, he "tare his garments and lay on the earth . . . and wept very sore." Today many would consider this kind of behavior infantile; others would regard it as the healthiest way to express one's grief.

CHAPTER 13

And it came to pass . . . , that Absalom the son of David had a fair sister, whose name was Tamar; and Amnon the son of David loved her. And Amnon was so vexed, that he fell sick for his sister Tamar; for she was a virgin; and Amnon thought it hard for him to do anything to her. But Amnon had a friend, whose name was Jonadab, the son of Shimeah David's brother: and Jonadab was a very subtil man. And he said unto him, Why art thou, being the king's son, lean from day to day? wilt thou not tell me? And Amnon said unto him, I love Tamar, my brother Absalom's sister. And Jonadab said unto him, Lay thee down on thy bed, and make thyself sick: and when thy father cometh to see thee, say unto him, I pray thee, let my sister Tamar come, and give me meat, and dress the meat in my sight, that I may see it, and eat it at her hand.

So Amnon lay down, and made himself sick: and when the king was come to see him, Amnon said unto the king, I pray thee, let Tamar my sister come, and make me a couple of cakes in my sight, that I may eat at her hand. Then David sent home to Tamar, saying, Go now to thy brother Amnon's house, and dress him meat. So Tamar went to her brother Amnon's house; and he was laid down. And she took flour, and kneaded it, and made cakes in his sight, and did bake the cakes. And she took a pan, and poured them out before him; but he refused to eat. And Amnon said, Have out all men from me. And they went out every man from him. And Amnon said unto Tamar, Bring the meat into the chamber, that I may eat of thine hand. And Tamar took the cakes which she had made, and brought them into the chamber to Amnon her brother. And when she had brought them unto him to eat, he took hold of her, and said unto her, Come lie with me, my sister. And she answered him, Nay, my brother, do not force me; for no such thing ought to be done in Israel: do not thou this folly. And I, whither shall I cause my shame to go? and as for thee, thou shalt be as one of the fools in Israel. Now therefore, I pray thee, speak unto the king; for he will not withhold me from thee. Howbeit he would not hearken unto her voice: but, being stronger than she, forced her, and lay with her.

Then Amnon hated her exceedingly; so that the hatred wherewith he hated her was greater than the love wherewith he had loved her. And Amnon said unto her, Arise, be gone. And she said unto him, There is no cause: this evil in sending me away is greater than the other that thou didst unto me. But he would not hearken unto her. . . .

. . . . .

. . . when king David heard of all these things, he was very wroth. And Absalom spake unto his brother Amnon neither good nor bad: for Absalom hated Amnon, because he had forced his sister Tamar.

Now Absalom had commanded his servants, saying, Mark ye now when Amnon's heart is merry with wine, and when I say unto you, Smite Amnon; then kill him, fear not: have not I commanded you? be courageous, and be valiant. And the servants of Absalom did unto Amnon as Absalom had commanded. Then all the king's sons arose, and every man gat him up upon his mule, and fled.

And it came to pass, while they were in the way, that tidings came to David, saying, Absalom hath slain all the king's sons, and there is not one of them left. Then the king arose, and tare his garments, and lay on the earth; and all his servants stood by with their clothes rent. And Jonadab, the son of Shimeah David's brother, answered and said, Let not thy lord suppose that they have slain all the young men the king's sons; for Amnon only is dead: for by the appointment of Absalom this hath been determined from the day that he forced his sister Tamar. Now therefore let not my lord the king take the thing to his heart, to think that all the king's sons are dead: for Amnon only is dead. . . . And it came to pass, as soon as he had made an end of speaking, that, behold, the king's sons came, and lifted up their voice and wept: and the king also and all his servants wept very sore.

But Absalom fled, and went to Talmai, the son of Ammihud, king of

Geshur. And David mourned for his son every day. So Absalom fled, and went to Geshur, and was there three years. And the soul of king David longed to go forth unto Absalom: for he was comforted concerning Amnon, seeing he was dead.

<small>CHAPTER 14</small>

Now Joab the son of Zeruiah perceived that the king's heart was toward Absalom. And Joab sent to Tekoah, and fetched thence a wise woman, and said unto her, I pray thee, feign thyself to be a mourner, and put on now mourning apparel, and anoint thyself with oil, but be as a woman that had a long time mourned for the dead: And come to the king, and speak on this manner unto him. So Joab put the words in her mouth.

And when the woman of Tekoah spake to the king, she fell on her face to the ground, and did obeisance, and said, Help, O king.

.   .   .   .   .

For we must needs die, and are as water spilt on the ground, which cannot be gathered up again; neither doth God respect any person: yet doth he devise means, that his banished be not expelled from him. Now therefore that I am come to speak of this thing unto my lord the king, it is because the people have made me afraid: and thy handmaid said, I will now speak unto the king; it may be that the king will perform the request of his handmaid. For the king will hear, to deliver his handmaid out of the hand of the man that would destroy me and my son together out of the inheritance of God. Then thine handmaid said, The word of my lord the king shall now be comfortable: for as an angel of God, so is my lord the king to discern good and bad: therefore the LORD thy God will be with thee. Then the king answered and said unto the woman, Hide not from me, I pray thee, the thing that I shall ask thee. And the woman said, Let my lord the king now speak. And the king said, Is not the hand of Joab with thee in all this? And the woman answered and said, As thy soul liveth, my lord the king, none can turn to the right hand or to the left from ought that my lord the king hath spoken: for thy servant Joab, he bade me, and he put all these words in the mouth of thine handmaid: To fetch about this form of speech hath thy servant Joab done this thing: and my lord is wise, according to the wisdom of an angel of God, to know all things that are in the earth.

And the king said unto Joab, Behold now, I have done this thing: go therefore, bring the young man Absalom again. And Joab fell to the ground on his face, and bowed himself, and thanked the king: and Joab said, To day thy servant knoweth that I have found grace in thy sight, my lord, O king, in that the king hath fulfilled the request of his servant. So Joab arose and went to Geshur, and brought Absalom to Jerusalem.

And the king said, Let him turn to his own house, and let him not see my face. So Absalom returned to his own house, and saw not the king's face.

But in all Israel there was none to be so much praised as Absalom for his beauty: from the sole of his foot even to the crown of his head there was no blemish in him. And when he polled his head, (for it was at every year's end that he polled it: because the hair was heavy on him, therefore he polled it:) he weighed the hair of his head at two hundred shekels after the king's weight. . . .

So Absalom dwelt two full years in Jerusalem, and saw not the king's face. Therefore Absalom sent for Joab, to have sent him to the king; but he would not come to him: and when he sent again the second time, he would not come. Therefore he said unto his servants, See, Joab's field is near mine, and he hath barley there; go and set it on fire. And Absalom's servants set the field on fire. Then Joab arose, and came to Absalom unto his house, and said unto him, Wherefore have thy servants set my field on fire? And Absalom answered Joab, Behold, I sent unto thee, saying, Come hither, that I may send thee to the king, to say, Wherefore am I come from Geshur? it had been good for me to have been there still: now therefore let me see the king's face; and if there be any iniquity in me, let him kill me. So Joab came to the king, and told him: and when he had called for Absalom, he came to the king, and bowed himself on his face to the ground before the king: and the king kissed Absalom.

CHAPTER 15

And it came to pass after this, that Absalom prepared him chariots and horses, and fifty men to run before him. And Absalom rose up early, and stood beside the way of the gate: and it was so, that when any man that had a controversy came to the king for judgment, then Absalom called unto him, and said, Of what city art thou? And he said, Thy servant is of one of the tribes of Israel. And Absalom said unto him, See, thy matters are good and right; but there is no man deputed of the king to hear thee. Absalom said moreover, Oh that I were made judge in the land, that every man which hath any suit or cause might come unto me, and I would do him justice! And it was so, that when any man came nigh to him to do him obeisance, he put forth his hand, and took him, and kissed him. And on this manner did Absalom to all Israel that came to the king for judgment: so Absalom stole the hearts of the men of Israel.

And it came to pass after forty years, that Absalom said unto the king, I pray thee, let me go and pay my vow, which I have vowed unto the LORD, in Hebron. For thy servant vowed a vow while I abode at Geshur in Syria, saying, If the LORD shall bring me again indeed to

Jerusalem, then I will serve the LORD. And the king said unto him, Go in peace. So he arose, and went to Hebron.

But Absalom sent spies throughout all the tribes of Israel, saying, As soon as ye hear the sound of the trumpet, then ye shall say, Absalom reigneth in Hebron. And with Absalom went two hundred men out of Jerusalem, that were called; and they went in their simplicity, and they knew not anything. And Absalom sent for Ahithophel the Gilonite, David's counseller, from his city, even from Giloh, while he offered sacrifices. And the conspiracy was strong; for the people increased continually with Absalom.

And there came a messenger to David, saying, The hearts of the men of Israel are after Absalom. And David said unto all his servants that were with him at Jerusalem, Arise, and let us flee; for we shall not else escape from Absalom: make speed to depart, lest he overtake us suddenly, and bring evil upon us, and smite the city with the edge of the sword.

. . . . .

CHAPTER 18

. . . . .

So the people went out into the field against Israel: and the battle was in the wood of Ephraim; Where the people of Israel were slain before the servants of David, and there was there a great slaughter that day of twenty thousand men. For the battle was there scattered over the face of all the country: and the wood devoured more people that day than the sword devoured.

And Absalom met the servants of David. And Absalom rode upon a mule, and the mule went under the thick boughs of a great oak, and his head caught hold of the oak, and he was taken up between the heaven and the earth; and the mule that was under him went away. And a certain man saw it, and told Joab, and said, Behold, I saw Absalom hanged in an oak. And Joab said unto the man that told him, And, behold, thou sawest him, and why didst thou not smite him there to the ground? and I would have given thee ten shekels of silver, and a girdle. And the man said unto Joab, Though I should receive a thousand shekels of silver in mine hand, yet would I not put forth mine hand against the king's son: for in our hearing the king charged thee and Abishai and Ittai, saying, Beware that none touch the young man Absalom. Otherwise I should have wrought falsehood against mine own life: for there is no matter hid from the king, and thou thyself wouldest have set thyself against me. Then said Joab, I may not tarry thus with thee. And he took three darts in his hand, and thrust them through the heart of Absalom, while he was yet alive in the midst of the oak. And ten young men that bare Joab's armour compassed about and smote Absalom, and slew him.

. . . . .

. . . And, behold, Cushi came; and Cushi said, Tidings, my lord the king: for the LORD hath avenged thee this day of all them that rose up against thee. And the king said unto Cushi, Is the young man Absalom safe? And Cushi answered, the enemies of my lord the king, and all that rise against thee to do thee hurt, be as that young man is.

And the king was much moved, and went up to the chamber over the gate, and wept: and as he went, thus he said, O my son Absalom, my son, my son Absalom! Would God I had died for thee, O Absalom, my son, my son!

10. THE FAMILY IN ISRAEL: THE KIBBUTZ

YONINA TALMON-GARBER

Israel today is very different from the Israel of David's time. There are cities and farms, cooperative communities and collective settlements, and the family structure in each is different. The peoples of Europe and Africa stream into this new democracy, bringing with them a wide variety of customs and family relationships.

But the Kibbutz, which is briefly described here, is an institution peculiar to modern Israel. There the parents are seen by the children as friends, while the nurses and teachers function as disciplinarians. This system is organized in the hope of preventing hatred of the parents by the children.

Melford E. Spiro, in his book Children of the Kibbutz, *describes the Kibbutz as carefully planned to make the entire community responsible for each and every one of its children.*

The disposition to establish new types of family organization prevailed mainly among immigrants to whom immigration entailed a con-

Selections reprinted from the article in *Marriage and Family Living*, XVI, No. 4 (November, 1954), 346–349, by permission of the author and The National Council on Family Relations.

scious and voluntary break with the former social structure. Many of the founders of the Cooperative and Communal Settlements were members of youth movement groups and arrived in the country as young, unattached individuals. To many of them the cohesion of the new primary group and the identification with its values replaced the family they had left behind—hence a strong communal organization and a redefinition of the position of the family within the community.

. . . . .

The basic features of the Collective Settlements (Kibbutz) [1] are common ownership of all property, except for a few personal belongings, communal organization of production, consumption and the care of children. The Community is run as one economic unit and as one household. The family has ceased to be an autonomous group from the point of view of the division of labor.

Husband and wife have independent jobs. Roles are allotted to individual members by a central committee elected yearly by the general assembly. Main meals are taken in the communal dining hall and are served from a common kitchen. Members' needs are provided for by communal institutions. Families look after their own rooms but have few other household responsibilities.

In most of the Collectives, children live apart from their parents and are attended mainly by members assigned to this task. From their birth on they sleep, eat and study in special houses. Each age group leads its own life and has its autonomous arrangements. Almost every activity in the age group is supervised by an elected committee and many issues are settled by open discussion between the youngsters and the adults in charge of them. Committees work under the guidance of adults but children are given some experience in self-government and get some preparation for active participation in adult institutions. Living conditions and the number of members assigned to look after the children depend on the economic situation of the settlement. But in all communities the standard of living of the children is noticeably higher than that of their parents. Children lead a sheltered life and are not allowed to suffer any want. They start to do some work early, but only at the age of eighteen to twenty years do they enter the adult division of labor and work full-time.

The age groups lead their own social and cultural life. On festive occasions they do not participate in the general celebration but arrange special festivities in which parents participate as passive observers. The only important exception is the culminating feast of the year (Passover) when parents and children participate alike. It is mainly through the

[1] There are 227 Collective Settlements in Israel. Population in the Collective Settlements was 69,089 in 1952.

age group that children come into definite and structured relations with the adult world.

Children meet their parents and their siblings every day in off hours. They spend the afternoons and early evenings with them. Parents put their young children to sleep. On Saturdays and on holidays children are with their parents most of the time except for short intervals when they take their separate meals. There are thus frequent and intensive relations between parents and children, but the main socializing agencies are the peer age groups and specialized nurses, instructors and teachers. The age group is a solidary unit and it substitutes the sibling unit. It duplicates the structural lines of the community and inculcates communal norms. Basically the children belong to the community as a whole.

The family has delegated most of its functions to the community. The main emphasis lies therefore on affective ties and personal relationships within it. The family is the only sphere in which both children and parents are free from routine tasks. It is mainly within the family that the individual members have intimate relations unpatterned by their position in the community. In so far as the nuclear family has ceased to be the prime socializing agency it avoids the inevitable ambivalence towards the agents of socialization. Parents do not have to combine the contrasting tasks of providing the child's needs for security and unconditional love on the one hand with thwarting their wishes on the other hand. They can afford to be permissive and the authoritarian element in child-parent relationships is thus minimized. The emotional attachment to parents is intensive for yet another reason. The child's position outside the family is ascribed only to a small extent. He has to compete for a position in his age group and he has to compete with his age peers for the approval of the adults in charge of them. All the children in the same age group have the same claim to attention. It is only in their family that they get special individualized treatment.

As mentioned before, the Collectives were established by solidary primary groups of young and single individuals. The formation of families within the community has inevitably weakened the primary group characteristics of the community and the families tend to become a competing focus of intensive primary group relations. Diversification of social and economic structure and routinization entailed some re-definition of the relations of the family and the community. There is a growing tendency to allow the family a little more independence and privacy. In some Collectives they have even tried to change certain aspects of the care of children. Children in those Collectives spend the whole day with their age group, but come home to sleep in their parents' flats. In spite of a slight shift in the position of the family the Collective Settlements still represent an extreme "non-familistic" division of labor.

The main trend of change of demographic standards in the Collectives is a considerable decrease in the age at marriage and a small increase of fertility. Average age at marriage in 1949 was 26.5 for males and 23.5 for females, as compared with 30.7–25.1 for the whole country. The birth rate was 30.1 per thousand as compared with 29.3 in towns and 31.9 in the whole country. Divorce rate was 3.54. Establishment of a family in the Collectives does not entail the setting up of a separate household, consequently members can marry as early as they choose. In spite of the fact that the birth of children does not have a direct or immediate effect on the standard of living of the family and does not entail much additional work for the parents, fertility remains comparatively low. The economic factor is not eliminated and the size of family is planned more or less consciously with due consideration of the economic position of the community. . . .

11. FRENCH PARENTS TAKE THEIR CHILDREN TO THE PARK

MARTHA WOLFENSTEIN

Are European children "civilized" as compared to American youngsters? Or, as many Europeans have said—putting it generously —are American children more "active" than their European counterparts?

This delightful description, from a book filled with wonderfully lively studies, may raise—and partially answer—any number of questions about the behavior of children in different cultures.

In Parisian families it is a regular routine to take the children to the park. This is a good situation in which to observe how French children play, their relations with one another and with the adults who bring them to the park. In the summer of 1947 and again in the summer of 1953 I had occasion to make such observations in various parks in Paris. . . .

THE "FOYER" IN THE PARK

For the French each family circle is peculiarly self-inclosed, with the family members closely bound to one another and a feeling of extreme wariness about intrusion from outside. This feeling is carried over when parents take their children to play in the park. The children do not leave their parents to join other children in a communal play area. In fact, there are few communal play facilities—an occasional sand pile, some swings and carrousels, to which one must pay admission and to which the children are escorted by the parents. The usual procedure is for the mother (or other adult who brings the children to the park) to establish herself on a bench while the children squat directly at her feet and play there in the sand of the path. Where there is a sand pile, children frequently fill their buckets there and then carry the sand to where mother is sitting and deposit it at her feet. . . .

. . . . .

There seems to be a continual mild anxiety that possessions will get mixed up in the park. Mothers are constantly checking on the where-abouts of their children's toys and returning toys to other mothers. One woman hands a toy shovel to another, saying: *C'est à vous, madame?* Toys seem to be regarded as the possessions of the parents, and mislaid ones are usually restored to them. While parents are concerned to keep track of their own child's toys, they seem particularly upset if their child has picked up something belonging to another and are apt to slap the child for it. This happens regardless of whether there has been any dis-pute and where the owner may be quite unaware that another child has picked up something of his.

The following incidents illustrate these attitudes. A girl of about two is holding a celluloid fish belonging to a boy of about the same age. Though the boy makes no protest, the attendant of the girl scoldingly tells her to give it to him, pushes her forward, and after the girl has handed the fish to the boy, hustles her back to her own bench.

A girl of about two has picked up a leather strap from a neighboring group. Her nurse reproves her, takes her by the hand, and returns the strap. A little later a boy of about the same age, belonging to this neigh-boring family, plays with the little girl, picks up her pail, and keeps it while the little girl is fed by her nurse. The boy's grandmother becomes aware that he has the pail, hits him on the buttocks, scolds, and, taking him by the hand, returns the pail to the girl's nurse. In front of the nurse she repeatedly hits the boy about the head and ears.

. . . . .

Among American children issues of ownership versus sharing tend to arise when two children dispute about the use of a toy. What is con-sidered desirable is that the child should learn to share his playthings, which are his property, with others. French children seem to be taught something quite different. Toys are familial property, and those belonging to each family must be kept separate. Just as the children with their parents or other familial adults form a close little circle in the park, so their belongings should remain within the circle. The child who brings into this circle something from outside seems to be introducing an intrusive object, which arouses all the negative sentiments felt, but from politeness not directly expressed, toward outsiders. At the same time it is an offense to the outsiders, whose belongings are thus displaced, and restitution and apologies to them are required. Also, as French adults are much preoccupied with property and with increasing their own, they have to ward off the temptation to do so by illegitimate means. The child's easy way of picking up others' things may evoke in adults impulses to take which they strive to repress in themselves and which they therefore cannot tolerate in the child.

Friendly behavior between children of different families is not encouraged by the adults. . . .

SECRET SOLIDARITY OF BROTHERS

In the following incident one can observe the friendly relation of two brothers which becomes more outspoken when they get by themselves, away from the adults. The two boys, of about six and seven, very neat, dressed alike in blue jerseys and white shorts, are playing together in the sand of the path. Their father sits talking with two women, who appear to be friends of the family, and the boys' sister, about a year older, sits on a bench with her doll. As the younger boy moves into the father's field of vision, the father slaps his hands and face, presumably because he has got himself dirty. This puts an end to the sand play; the two boys sit down, subdued, on the bench, and, as the father turns away, the older presents the younger with a cellophane bag—a gesture of sympathy and compensation. After a time the father suggests to the girl that the children take a walk around the park, and they immediately set out. On their walk the boys keep close together, leaving the girl to herself. As they get farther away from the father, the boys begin putting their arms around each other's shoulders. They become much more animated and point things out to each other as they go. As they get nearer to the father again on the return path, they drop their arms from each other's shoulders, drift apart, and again become more subdued. Having returned, they seat themselves quietly again on the bench.

ACCEPTANCE OF THE LITTLE ONES

French children show a great readiness to play with children younger than themselves, in a way which contrasts strikingly with the behavior of American children. It is typical of American boys particularly to be intolerant of the "kid brother" who wants to tag along and get into the big boys' game when he isn't good enough. An American boy of seven will complain that he has no one of his own age to play with; the neighbors' little boy is six. In America there tends to be a strict age-grading, which the children themselves feel strongly about.

In contrast to this, French children appear interested in younger children and ready to accept them in their games. A boy of eight or nine will play ball with a smaller boy, a five-year-old or even a two-year-old, without showing any impatience at the ineptitude of the younger one. The two children may be brothers or may belong to families that know each other. A slender blond boy of about seven seems completely absorbed in a little girl of two or three whom he follows around, bending over to speak to her. The mothers of the two children are acquainted with each other, and the boy and his mother both shake hands with the little girl's mother when she leaves the park. The boy looks quite disconsolate without his little friend; eventually, at his mother's suggestion, he picks up his scooter and slowly pushes off on it.

Such interest, particularly on the part of boys, in younger children differs markedly from the American pattern, where interest in babies becomes strictly sex-typed for girls only and out of keeping with the boy's ideal of masculine toughness.

. . . . .

. . . Where the American child is expected from an early age to become a member of a peer group outside the family, for the French child the family and the contacts which the adults make with other families remain decisive. While, from the American point of view, this may appear restrictive, it also facilitates friendly relations between older and younger children, including notably affectionate quasi-paternal feelings of older boys toward small children.

. . . . .

GROWNUPS STOP CHILDREN'S AGGRESSION

French children are not taught to fight their own battles, to stick up for their rights, in the American sense of these terms. If one child attacks another, even very mildly, the grownups regularly intervene and scold the aggressor. The child who is attacked is likely to look aggrieved or to cry, to look toward his mother or go to her. He does not hit back, nor is he encouraged to do so. An attack is thus not a challenge which must be met by the attacked to save his self-esteem. It is a piece of naughty behavior to be dealt with by the adults.

In the following instances one can see how quickly adults intervene in even very slight manifestations of aggression. Among a group of small children playing on a sand pile, a girl of about two and a half takes a shovel away from her four-year-old sister and walks away with it, looking back in a mildly provocative way. The older girl remains seated and simply looks dismayed. The younger one is already going back to return the shovel when the mother comes over and scolds her, calling her *vilaine*. The little one gives back the shovel, and the two resume their digging.

. . . . .

In [another] incident . . . , where a little girl stepped on a little boy's sand pie, the boy looked toward his grandmother with an expression of amazement and distress. The grandmother promptly launched into a biting verbal attack on the little girl: *Vilaine! Vilaine fille! Tu commences maintenant à faire des sottises!* A little later when another girl was throwing sand into the sand pile, the grandmother scolded her repeatedly, telling her it could get into children's eyes. The girl's mother, a little way off, then chimed in and told the girl to stop. Protective as she was of her little grandson, the grandmother was equally ready to interfere in an aggressive act of his. Thus, when he was pushing another boy, who did not even seem to notice the rather gentle pressure, the grandmother called to him to stop, that he would make the other boy get a *bo-bo,* and the grandson stopped.

Thus what French children learn is not the prized Anglo-Saxon art of self-defense or the rules that determine what is a fair fight. What they learn is that their own aggression is not permissible.

A consequence of the prohibition against physical aggression is that verbal disputes are substituted for it. . . .

. . . . .

RESTRAINT IN MOTOR ACTIVITY

To an American visitor it is often amazing how long French children stay still. They are able to sit for long periods on park benches beside their parents. A typical position of a child in the park is squatting at his mother's feet, playing in the sand. His hands are busy, but his total body position remains constant. Children are often brought to the park in quite elegant (and unwashable) clothes, and they do not get dirty. The squatting child keeps his bottom poised within an inch of the ground but never touching, only his hands getting dirty; activity and getting dirty are both restricted to the hands. While sand play is generally permissible and children are provided with equipment for it, they seem subject to intermittent uncertainty whether it is all right for their hands to be dirty. From time to time a child shows his dirty hands to his mother, and she wipes them off.

Among some children between two and three I noticed a particularly marked tendency to complete immobility, remaining in the same position, with even their hands motionless, and staring blankly or watching other children. A French child analyst suggested that this is the age when children are being stuffed with food and are consequently somewhat stuporous. Occasionally one could see children of these ages moving more actively and running about. But the total effect contrasted with the usual more continuous motor activity which one sees in American children. Also, French children seemed more often to walk where American children would run.

. . . . .

The relation between restraint on aggression and on large-muscle activity was remarked upon by another French child analyst, who had treated both French and American children. She observed that an American child in an aggressive mood would throw things up to the ceiling, while a French child would express similar angry impulses by making little cuts in a piece of clay.

Forceful activity on the part of children is apt to evoke warning words from the adults: "Gently, gently." Two brothers about nine and six were throwing a rubber ball back and forth. The younger had to make quite an effort to throw the ball the required distance; his throws were a bit badly aimed but did not come very close to any bystanders. His mother and grandmother, who were sitting near him, repeatedly cautioned him after every throw: *Doucement! Doucement!* I had the feeling that it was the strenuousness of his movements which made them uneasy, though they may also have exaggerated the danger of his hitting someone. Similarly, when two little girls about four and five were twirling around, holding each other's hands, an elderly woman seated near by kept calling to the older girl: *Doucement, elle est plus petite que toi.* To which the child answered that they were not going very fast. The implication here seems to be that any rapid or forceful movement can easily pass into a damaging act.

. . . . .

On the same occasion the play of another boy whom I observed, with a paper airplane, seemed to demonstrate very nicely the feeling about remaining within a small space. When American boys make planes out of folded paper, these planes are generally long and narrow, with a sharp point, with the aim of their being able to fly as fast and far as possible. In contrast to this prevailing American style, the French boy had folded his paper plane in a wide-winged, much less pointed shape. It moved more slowly through the air and did not go any great distance, but within a small space described many complicated and elegant loops.

Another time I observed a game where an active chase was led up to by elaborate preliminaries in which action was slight. This seemed comparable to the protracted talk postponing action. Five children (of about six to nine) were playing together with a young nursemaid. The nursemaid sat on a bench while the children performed charades in front of her, the performance being preceded by considerable consultation among themselves as to the subject they would enact. As the nursemaid ventured various guesses, the children interrupted their act several times to explain the exact rules of the game to her. When she finally uttered the right word, this was the signal for them to run and her to chase them. Any child she caught before they reached a certain tree then joined her on the bench and helped to guess and to chase the next time round. But before the next brief chase there were again the consultations and the pantomime. Other children's games in which an introductory ritual precedes a chase are common, but I am not familiar with any in which the less active preparatory phase is so elaborate, where talk and small movements occupy such a large part of the game and the chase comes only as a brief finale.

THE CHILD ALONE

French children manifest a greater tolerance for being alone than American children do. Just as they do not show the urge to be incessantly in motion, which one sees in American children, so also they do not show the need to be constantly with other children. When I speak of a child being alone, I mean alone with the adult who has brought him to the park. But this may mean in effect being very much alone, since, as a rule, the adult pays little attention to him. There is usually little interchange in the park between adults and children over one and a half. While mothers and nurses direct a good deal of affectionate talk to a baby in a carriage, they tend to ignore the three-year-old squatting at their feet or sitting on the bench beside them. . . .

. . . . .

Where there is a choice of either playing alone or with others, playing alone may be preferred (which again I think would be very rare among American children). Three girls of about thirteen were playing near one another, each with the kind of toy which is whirled into the air from a string and caught again, a game requiring considerable skill. The three of them, all quite proficient, continued this play, each by herself, for at least an hour before they joined together and began passing the whirling object from one to another.

. . . . .

It may be added that for the French the mere presence of others, even if there is no overt interaction with them, appears to constitute a valued form of sociability. This would apply to the child who plays by himself alongside other children in the park as well as to the adult who sits alone with his drink and his newspaper at a café table.

. . . . .

ADULTS ARE ABOVE THE EMOTIONS OF CHILDREN

Adults seem to look down from a considerable height on both the griefs and the joys of children. Childhood and adulthood are two very distinct human conditions. From the vantage point of the adult, the emotions of the child do not seem serious: they are not, after all, about anything very important. The adult is likely to be detached in the face of the child's distress. Where the child is elated, the adult, though sympathetic, may regard the child humorously, perhaps a bit mockingly: how he overestimates these little childish things!

On an occasion when a mother punished a little boy, she appeared quite unconcerned about his rage and grief and was amused when he later came to fling his arms around her. . . .

. . . . .

For the French, adulthood is decidedly the desirable time of life. Simply assuming the role of adults as he knows them is gratifying to a French child; no extraneous glamour need be added. At the same time, the adults in their role of authority rouse impulses of rebellious mockery in children, which they express in parodying the adults among themselves. This motive is liable to persist and to be permitted much stronger expression when the children grow up, in the mockery of authority figures, particularly in the political sphere, which is so prominent in French life.

. . . . .

CHILDHOOD IS NOT FOR FUN

For the French, enjoyment of life is the prerogative of adults. Childhood is a preparation. Then everything must be useful, not just fun; it must have an educational purpose. The hard regime of French school children, with its tremendous burden of work, is well known. Probably nothing in later life is such a terrible ordeal as the dreaded *bachot* (the examination at the conclusion of secondary school). It is a real *rite de passage,* a painful test to which youths on the verge of maturity are subjected by their elders.

The attitude that everything for children, even the very young, must serve a useful purpose and not be just amusing is well exemplified around the carrousel in the Luxembourg Gardens. There are various rides for the children, among them rows of large rocking horses. A sign describes these as: *Chevaux hygiéniques. Jeu gymnastique pour les enfants développant la force et la souplesse.*

At the carrousel, as soon as the ride began, an old woman with spectacles and red hair done up in a bun on top of her head and wearing an old-fashioned gray coat (she seemed to me a benevolent witch), handed out to each child in the outer circle a stick (*baguette*). She then held out to them a contraption which dispensed rings and encouraged them to catch the rings on their sticks. Throughout the duration of the ride, the old woman directed to the children an incessant didactic discourse, urging them to pay attention and work very hard to catch the rings. *Attention! Regarde ton travail! Regarde bien, chou-chou! Au milieu,* indicating with her finger the middle of the ring at which the child should aim. *Doucement!* When a child used his stick to beat time instead of to catch the rings, the old woman scolded him for this frivolity. . . . Thus, even on the carrousel, children have a task to perform. The elders direct, commend, and rebuke them. They are not there just for fun.

The paradox from the American point of view is that the French grow up with a great capacity for enjoyment of life. The adult enters fully into the pleasures which have not been permitted to the child. There seems to be a successful realization that pleasure is not taboo, but only postponed. The song of Charles Trenet, *Quand j'étais petit,* ends with the triumphant, *On n'est plus petit!*—everything is now permitted. It remains one of the puzzles of French culture how this effect is achieved: that the restraints to which children are subjected have only a temporary influence and do not encumber the adult with lasting inhibitions.

If we compare Americans and French, it seems as though the relation between childhood and adulthood is almost completely opposite in the two cultures. In America we regard childhood as a very nearly ideal time, a time for enjoyment, an end in itself. The American image of the child, whether envisaged in the classical figures of Tom Sawyer and Huckleberry Finn, or in the small hero of the recent film *The Little Fugitive,* who achieves a self-sufficient existence at Coney Island, is of a young person with great resources for enjoyment, whose present life is an end in itself. . . . With the French, as I have said, it seems to be the other way around. Childhood is a period of probation, when everything is a means to an end; it is unenviable from the vantage point of adulthood. The image of the child is replete with frustration and longing for pleasures of the adults which are not for him. It is in adulthood that the possibility of living in the moment is achieved. Not that this precludes much scheming and planning as far as careers or business advantage is concerned. But this is not allowed to interfere with sensuous pleasures, which are an end in themselves. The attainment of these end-pleasures, notably in eating and in lovemaking, is not a simple matter. Much care and preparation are required, and changing stimuli may be needed to keep pleasure intense. Concern with such pleasures and ingenuity in achieving them are persistent in adult life. It is with the prospect of these pleasures that the individual has served his hardworking childhood, and it is now, as an adult, that he can lose himself in the pleasures of the moment.

12. THE FAMILY IN INDIA

S. CHANDRASEKHAR

This brief description of the family in India indicates that institutions in that newly freed country are slowly evolving away from long-held customs—large families, early marriage, low status for women, etc.—toward more modern patterns. The poverty and despair throughout the large and complex nation and the illiteracy of most of the population hinder progress, of course, and, in many ways, the culture of India remains as it has for centuries.

The Indian sex ratio for the whole country is an adverse one, for in 1951 there were 947 females per 1000 males. The rural sex ratio is 966:1000, while the urban sex ratio is 860:1000. This sex ratio has been more or less the same during the last fifty years.

.   .   .   .   .

The Indian pattern of marital status presents an interesting picture. According to Indian law (the Child Marriage Restraint Act of 1929 popularly known as the Sarda Act) child marriages (of males under 18 and females under 14) are punishable. But according to the 1951 Census, there were 2,833,000 married males, 6,180,000 married females, 66,000 widowers and 134,000 widows—all between the ages of 5 and 14! This simply means that the Sarda Act has failed in its objective of restraining early marriages.

Selections reprinted from the article in *Marriage and Family Living*, XVI, No. 4 (November, 1954), 336–341, by permission of the author and The National Council on Family Relations.

The universality of the married state in India is well known. In the country as a whole, every other male is married, while three out of five females—of all ages—are married. In other words, 49.1 per cent of all males are either married men or widowers and 61.2 per cent of all females are either married women or widows. Only 6.4 per cent of all females aged fifteen and over were unmarried. But even this 6.4 per cent will not remain unmarried long for they are bound to get married within a few years. In other words, between the ages 35–44, only 0.1 per cent of the total population of women remain unmarried. The problem of spinsters does not exist or at any rate is very insignificant in India.

In 1951 there were 5 widowers to 100 males and 12.8 widows to 100 females. But since widowers are permitted to and very often do marry, they constitute no social problem, unlike the widows who are not expected to and invariably do not marry. (There is no legal barrier to widow remarriage, nor is Hinduism opposed to second marriage of Hindu women or widows, but all Hindu males seem to prefer virgins.) The total number of widows of all ages according to the 1951 census was nearly 25 million.

. . . . .

The Hindu Joint Family. The traditional Hindu joint family is larger than the conjugal or the biological family. The unit is not the husband, wife and children, but the larger family group. It is at once a corporate, economic, religious and social unit. In a joint family when sons grow up to manhood and marry, they do not leave the parental household and set up their own separate houses, but occupy different rooms in the parental, rather ancestral, residence, along with their children and children's children. Correspondingly, the womenfolk also, the mother, the daughters-in-law, unmarried daughters, grand-daughters, and sometimes great-granddaughters, live under the same roof. The daughters of the family, on getting married, of course leave their parental home and become members of the joint families to which their husbands belong. And so, naturally, the number of those who live together under the same roof may be very large and sometimes may even run to more than fifty. The household servants, many of whom often grow up with the family, have their recognized place, and their attachment to the master members of the family is often deep and cordial. To accommodate all these, it need hardly be added that the house has to be very large indeed.

The father and mother have their places of honor in these joint families. (Hence the absence of state-supported homes for old people in India; it is difficult to say whether there is no need for such homes today though the number of old people is small.) The father, being the oldest and most experienced, is nominally the head of the family. Under ordinary circumstances it is he who controls, guides and directs the whole family, unless he is very old or disabled, in which case the eldest son or the eldest member in the nearest line of male descent—maternal or paternal uncle—takes his place. The mother always has her say. Though grownup sons live in the family with their wives, the respect and consideration shown by all members of the family to the old mother is very great. And it may be safely asserted that no important measure of domestic concern will be approved or carried out without the final, if formal, sanction of the mother.

In the family, food and property are held in common and jointly owned, and the actual share to which each member is entitled if there be separation diminishes or increases with each birth or death. This arrangement is normally not disturbed even if some members of the family have to reside far away from the home in different parts of the country by virtue of their calling. (The prolonged sojourn in a distant place outside the joint family has been a factor in recent years for the breakup of the joint family.) When at home, all share the food prepared in a single common kitchen. In fact, in popular parlance, the chief criterion of the joint nature of the commensal family arises largely from the fact of the common kitchen. The saying is "Ek hi chule ka pakka khate hain," or "they eat food cooked in one and the same kitchen."

The ancestral property and the income arising from it, along with the earnings of the individual members, constitute the common family fund, out of which the expenses of the whole family are met. Often an earning member of the joint family who happens to live outside the common family out of town or village remits a part of his income to the common family pool, a system resembling that of the pre-Revolution peasant family in Russia. The funds—money, land, houses, jewelry and cattle—like other family affairs, are looked after by the father or the eldest son or some senior male relative. But in financial matters, all adult members are usually consulted before any major item of expenditure is granted. Every earning member contributes his share to the family fund. And the necessary and legitimate needs of all the family members are generally met. Thus, all earning members—mostly male— contribute in proportion to their income, and all members—men, women, married, widowed and children—whether earning or not, enjoy the common family resources. In practice, it sometimes happens that an unemployed brother, his wife and children may consume more from the family funds than a childless brother whose income may be considerable. This arrangement of give and take demands a great deal of mutual tolerance, affection, accommodation and understanding on the part of all the members. This traditional system in which all are entitled to be maintained from the family funds according to their needs is, in practice, a recognized socialist unit, though not necessarily secular in spirit. All the adult members follow the principle, "Give what you can and take what you need."

In a word, the joint family is simply the common ownership of the means of production and the common enjoyment of the fruits of labor. In practice, the system has through the centuries led to both beneficial and harmful effects on the Indian social and economic structure.

Betrothal and Marriage. The most important event in any family is marriage and the place of the married householder, particularly for a woman, in the Hindu cultural milieu, is an exalted one. The Hindu view of marriage is that it is a sacramental duty and that every man and woman must perforce enter into it, as the married state is one of the fourfold stages—*ashramas*—in an individual's life. Therefore, the first desideratum of a good life, according to Hindu scriptures, is that all should marry, marry young, and stay married. Hence the universality of the married state in India. One does not take a wife for sexual pleasure, or companionship necessarily, but one marries a daughter-in-law to help the family and hand down the torch of life to generations yet unborn to thus perpetuate the family line. As the young man or woman does not marry to suit his or her fancy, the choice of the partner does not rest with the individual. The parents and interested relatives—in fact, the whole joint family—choose the bride without any particular consideration of the groom's tastes or views. The bride, on her side, is consulted even less by her parents and relatives.

The Hindu scriptural injunction has been in favor of pre-puberty betrothal and marriage. In practice, however, while girls today may be betrothed before puberty, marriage after puberty has become common. The law, as well as enlightened public opinion, has veered in this direction, but exceptions are not wanting, as pointed out in our analysis of recent census statistics. It is difficult to be precise on this question, for the exact age of an individual, particularly in the village, is still largely a matter of guess. It is possible that parents arrange the marriage of their daughters at an age well past puberty to ease their consciences, but give out a lower age for the bride as a matter of misplaced pride and esteem in the community. Therefore, while early marriage does exist, physical consummation and living together is, by and large, a post-puberty affair.

As I have pointed out elsewhere: In Western countries, romance (or love as a pre-requisite to marriage), economic considerations, prolonged education and training and eagerness for personal and social advancement contribute to the postponement of marriage to a comparatively late date. Religion not only does not condemn celibacy but has a kind word for it. The current social attitudes do not disapprove of those who never enter the married state. Many therefore do not marry just for the sake of marriage. The pressure of these considerations may and sometimes does result in many remaining bachelors and spinsters.

But in India there is no chance for love to play any significant part in marriage. Marriages, by and large, are arranged by the parents and the majority are herded into the married state in a routine fashion. Economic stability of the bridegroom has never been an important consideration in contracting a marriage. Of course, the parents-in-law are anxious to see that the son-in-law is well employed or otherwise settled in life, but unemployment is not a positive disqualification since the resources of the joint family are available for the initial support of the newly married couple. Besides, there is the dowry that the bride brings. Religion does not encourage celibacy for a Hindu, if he be a strict one, must have at least one son. But perhaps it is not really the fear of religious ostracism that is behind this urge to get married. It is the social disapproval of the unmarried state that explains the universal prevalence of the married state.[1]

Divorce and Widowhood. As factual data on family disorganization are unavailable, it is difficult to estimate the nature and extent of desertion, separation, divorce, annulment and widowhood. However, the problem of family disorganization, with the exception of widowhood, is not acute in India.

As pointed out already, social attitudes are opposed to widow remarriage. Since most widowers marry and since they cannot, or rather do not, marry widows, they have to seek wives among girls much their juniors. If a widower aged forty or fifty wants to marry, he cannot marry a woman aged thirty, for a woman at that age is likely to be either married and living with her husband, or a widow. So he will have to marry a girl between the ages of fourteen and twenty. This unequal combination from the point of view of age leads to an increasing number of widows, for the relatively old husband soon passes away, leaving behind his young wife a widow. And she cannot, of course, remarry.

The paucity of females keeps up the custom of early marriage for girls. Early marriages customarily involve considerable disparity in age between husband and wives. This difference in age increases widowhood. Since widows cannot remarry, widowhood increases the shortage of eligible brides, which accentuates the paucity of females. Thus the vicious wheel whirls on.

. . . . .

As a rule, marriages in India are deprived of both premarital meeting (in the sense of meeting, dating and courtship) and postmarital dissolution (such as separation, annulment and divorce) in case the marriage is a failure. Both these safety valves are denied to the Hindus. By and large, they do not know what they are getting into, and once

[1] S. Chandrasekhar, *India's Population: Fact and Policy* (2nd ed., Madras, 1951).

in it, good, bad or indifferent, there is no easy way out. There is no special effort of adjustment on the part of the husband to make his marriage a success; the effort is almost one-sided, always on the part of the wife. And yet ninety-five per cent of the Hindu marriages appear successful and it is difficult to assess the factors behind this apparent stability. It may be that the partners endure such difficulties as they encounter as an inevitable part of the married state, or they may not be aware of anything better. As for the average wife, she is conditioned by upbringing not to expect anything better and to be ready for the worst. After all, in a sense, Hindu marriage is a sustained blind date. Secondly, the fact that there is no acceptable and socially approved way out, compels the partners to reconcile themselves to the situation. Or it may be that all these marriages are really happy and successful, based on mutual understanding, affection and goodwill.

. . . . .

Modern Trends in the Indian Family.   What are the present trends which are likely to mould the future of the family in India? Marriage is ordinarily limited to a member's own caste, sub- and even sub-sub caste. With the growth of Western contact, modern education and the spread of coeducational colleges and universities, young people are able to meet, get to know one another and fall in love beyond the purview of parental supervision. When young people fall in love across caste lines and when such inter-caste love becomes serious the first major obstacle is parental objection. When the couple in question are serious and when they have some measure of economic security in the sense of some private means or a job, they tend to oppose the parental and family objections and brave the world. But this is not always easy, for in India, one's private life is very much the public concern! (Such marriages in India are called "love marriages" as opposed to the traditional Hindu concept where you "marry and love" and not "love and marry.") These marriages are still so few in number that they elicit public comment.

And yet it is possible that inter-caste and even inter-religious marriages might become the pattern of future Indian society. Two powerful aids in this direction are that no one today seriously upholds caste in public, for it has come to be agreed that the caste system is opposed to democratic ideals. Secondly, all great Indian leaders and social reformers from Ram Mohan Roy down to Gandhi and Nehru have disapproved of the caste system as practiced and have not only approved but have set examples of inter-caste marriages by letting their children marry outside the caste. Once the system of permitting an individual to choose his or her partner gets under way, the caste system will disappear; this process might eventually evolve that rare species of *Indians,* for today there are no Indians, in the strict sense, but only Bengalis and Andhras, Tamils and Gujiaratis, high and low caste Hindus.

Second, educational facilities for women with their accompanying right to employment and economic freedom have already led to the beginning of a conflict between traditional marriage and a socially useful and lucrative career (this does not imply that marriage and a career for a woman ought always to conflict). What is more, even in marriage, Indian women are beginning to assert their rights and want to decide when and how many children they shall have. India is witnessing such rapid changes that Indian women are beginning to demand contraceptive knowledge.

Third, now that India is free, the Government itself is aiding in the evolution of Hindu law on marriage, divorce, succession, property rights, etc. in consonance with modern thought and needs. When the comprehensive Hindu Code Reform Bill, which is now on the anvil of the Indian Parliament, is passed into law, India will have taken a great step towards modernizing her domestic law. . . .

13. RELATION OF CHILD TRAINING TO SUBSISTENCE ECONOMY

HERBERT BARRY, III, IRVIN L. CHILD, AND
MARGARET K. BACON

This study of 104 societies indicates that child-rearing practices are closely related to the way in which the child's parents make their living. In societies which accumulate food resources, with herds or crops, there is strong pressure toward responsibility, conformity and obedience—and pressure against independence, self-reliance, and achievement. But in societies primarily made up of hunters and fishers, the opposite "virtues" are desired; self-reliance and initiative rather than obedient conformity is advocated.

Cross-cultural research on child training has generally grown out of an interest in how the typical personality of a people is brought into being. The customary child training practices of a group are thought to be one important set of influences responsible for the typical personality,

Selections reprinted from the article in *American Anthropologist*, 61, No. 1 (February, 1959), 51–63, by permission of the authors and publisher.

and hence an important clue in tracing its causal background. But the typical personality may also be viewed as an existing set of conditions which may exert an influence on later child training practices. Indeed, any present feature of culture may influence future child training practices, either directly or through an influence on typical personality. Thus child training may just as well, and with equal interest of another sort, be viewed as effect in a series of cultural events, rather than as cause (being in fact, we presume, both at once). Moreover, even while considering child training as a cause of the typical personality of a people, one is led to inquire: Why does a particular society select child training practices which will tend to produce this particular kind of typical personality? Is it because this kind of typical personality is functional for the adult life of the society, and training methods which will produce it are thus also functional?

By a variety of routes, then, the student of child training is led to inquire into the relation of child training to the basic patterns of social life—to those aspects of culture, whatever they be, which set the scene for the rest of culture. Among the features likely to hold this sort of dominant or controlling position is the general nature of the subsistence economy, and it is to this aspect of culture that we will here relate child training practices.

. . . . .

AN HYPOTHESIS ABOUT ECONOMIC ROLE AND TYPE OF SUBSISTENCE

Earlier anthropological writers classified economies in accordance with a notion of uniform sequences in cultural development from primitive to civilized. As a result of further research, this attempt has given way to more objective bases of classification. One such objective classification is that of Forde (1934). While stressing the limited usefulness of any classificatory scheme, in view of the great overlap between categories and the variation of economic practices within any one category, Forde does propose the following categories for dominant economy of a society: collecting, hunting, fishing, cultivation, and stock-raising. The usefulness of these categories has been affirmed by Herskovits (1952:86) and Murdock (1957).

In considering the relation of economy to adult role, and hence to child training, we felt that perhaps a variable of great significance is the extent to which food is accumulated and must be cared for. At one extreme is dependence mainly upon animal husbandry, where the meat that will be eaten in coming months and years, and the animals that will produce the future milk, are present on the hoof. In this type of society, future food supply seems to be best assured by faithful adherence to routines designed to maintain the good health of the herd. Agriculture perhaps imposes only slightly less pressure toward the same pattern of behavior. Social rules prescribe the best known way to bring the growing plants to successful harvest, and to protect the stored produce for gradual consumption until the next harvest. Carelessness in performance of routine duties leads to a threat of hunger, not for the day of carelessness itself but for many months to come. Individual initiative in attempts to improve techniques may be feared because no one can tell immediately whether the changes will lead to a greater harvest or to disastrous failure. Under these conditions, there might well be a premium on obedience to the older and wiser, and on responsibility in faithful performance of the routine laid down by custom for one's economic role.

At an opposite extreme is subsistence primarily through hunting or fishing, with no means for extended storing of the catch. Here individual initiative and development of high individual skill seem to be at a premium. Where each day's food comes from that day's catch, variations in the energy and skill exerted in food-getting lead to immediate reward or punishment. Innovation, moreover, seems unlikely to be so generally feared. If a competent hunter tries out some change in technique, and it fails, he may still have time to revert to the established procedures to get his catch. If the change is a good one, it may lead to immediate reward.

We recognize, of course, that there will not be a perfect correlation between the dominant type of food-getting and such aspects of the economic role. Agricultural and herding societies may produce a sufficient food surplus to allow some individuals to experiment with new techniques. Some hunting and fishing societies have means of preserving their catch, and this should increase the pressure for conformity to rules for ensuring preservation. Hunting and fishing may be done by teamwork, so that success depends partly upon responsible performance of the special duties assigned to each member. Some societies regard their hunting lands as a resource which must be protected by rigid conformity to conservation rules. A better picture of the relation of economy to socialization could surely be obtained through an analysis of such details of economic activity.

ECONOMY AND CHILD TRAINING

We have outlined above an hypothesis about economic behavior as an adaptation to the general type of subsistence economy. If economic role tends to be generalized to the rest of behavior, predictions might be made about the typical character or personality of adults in societies with different subsistence economies. In societies with low accumulation of food resources, adults should tend to be individualistic, assertive, and venturesome. By parallel reasoning, adults should tend to be conscientious, compliant, and conservative in societies with high accumulation of food resources.

If economic role and general personality tend to be appropriate for the type of subsistence economy, we may expect the training of children to foreshadow these adaptations. The kind of adult behavior useful to the society is likely to be taught to some extent to the children, in order to assure the appearance of this behavior at the time it is needed. Hence we may predict that the emphases in child training will be toward the development of kinds of behavior especially useful for the adult economy.

As a method for testing the hypothesis of adaptation to subsistence economy, societies with different types of economy may be compared in adult economic roles, general adult personality, and child training. In the present paper, societies which differ in economy are compared in child training, not in adult economic role or adult personality, because child training seems to have the most indirect connection with economy. If appropriate differences in child training are found, we may infer that the adaptation to economy includes a wide sphere of social behavior.

PROCEDURE

In the preliminary version of a recent article, Murdock (1957) classified the subsistence economy of societies into six categories, designated by the letters A, F, G, H, P, and R. We have considered societies as likely to be . . . high in accumulation of food resources, by our definition, if they were classified by Murdock as predominantly pastoral (P) or as agricultural with animal husbandry also important (A). Societies were considered likely to be . . . low in accumulation if Murdock designated them as predominantly hunting (H) or fishing (F).

Societies were considered intermediate in accumulation if Murdock designated them as predominantly agricultural, with either grain (G) or root (R) crops, with animal husbandry not important. . . .

Several other cultural variables, to be used somewhat incidentally later in the paper, were also taken from Murdock's analyses (1957, and preliminary unpublished version).

The authors of the present paper obtained ratings on several aspects of child training practices by their own analysis of ethnographic documents. The methods used are described in detail in Barry, Bacon and Child (1957). Societies were rated separately for boys and for girls with respect to six aspects of training.

1. Obedience training.
2. Responsibility training, which usually was on the basis of participation in the subsistence or household tasks.
3. Nurturance training, i.e., training the child to be nurturant or helpful toward younger siblings and other dependent people.
4. Achievement training, which was usually on the basis of competition, or imposition of standards of excellence in performance.
5. Self-reliance training, defined as training to take care of oneself, to be independent of the assistance of other people in supplying one's needs and wants.
6. General independence training. This was defined more generally than self-reliance training, to include training not only to satisfy one's own needs but also toward all kinds of feredom from control, domination, and supervision. Ratings of general independence training were highly correlated with ratings of self-reliance training, but were not identical to them.

For each of these six aspects of training, societies were rated on strength of socialization, which was defined as the combined positive pressure (rewards for the behavior) plus negative pressure (punishments for lack of the behavior). The ratings were for the stage of childhood, from age 4 or 5 years until shortly before puberty. Each rating was made by two separate judges, working independently, and the sum of their two judgments was used.

The results to be reported are on 104 societies which are included in two separate samples: Murdock's sample of over 500 societies classified on economy and social organization, and 110 societies rated on socialization by Bacon and Barry. Most of these 104 societies are nonliterate, and they are distributed all over the world. Many cultures were omitted from some of the ratings because of insufficient information; such omissions are much more frequent for the socialization variables than for Murdock's variable.

RESULTS

ECONOMY AND SPECIFIC VARIABLES OF SOCIALIZATION

. . . Figure 1 shows the average ranking of our six socialization variables for the societies classified according to subsistence economy. Societies with extremely high accumulation, compared to those with extremely low accumulation, tend to show higher pressure toward reresponsibility and obedience and lower pressure toward achievement, self-reliance and independence. Nurturance is the only child training variable which has approximately the same average ranking in both groups of societies. The association of each variable with accumulation is in the same direction for boys and girls.

. . . . .

It is apparent from Figure 1 that child training practices are correlated with amount of accumulation of food resources. For example, strong pressure toward responsibility (i.e., high ranking) tends to occur more frequently in societies which have high accumulation of food resources. If this correlation were perfect, so that societies high in responsibility were always high in accumulation and vice versa, the coefficient of association would be +1.00. If societies high in responsibility, and those low in responsibility were each divided equally between high and low accumulation, the association coefficient would be zero (0.00). If the correlation were in the reverse direction, so that societies high in responsibility were always low in accumulation, the association coefficient would be negative but again of maximum size (—1.00). Thus the size of the association coefficient gives a measure of the consistency of the relationship between two variables; the plus or minus sign shows the direction of the relationship.

The results portrayed in Figure 1 have been expressed in coefficients of association in Table 1. As Table 1 shows, responsibility and obedience are positively correlated with accumulation of food resources; achieve-

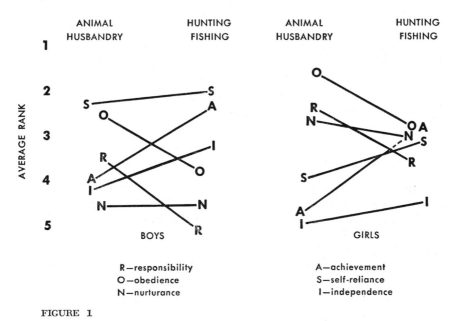

R—responsibility
O—obedience
N—nurturance

A—achievement
S—self-reliance
I—independence

FIGURE 1

ment, self-reliance, and independence are negatively correlated with accumulation. Nurturance shows . . . results . . . of small magnitude and [not] statistically significant. . . .

Table 1.   Relation of Child Training Practices to Accumulation of
Food Resources (Expressed as Coefficients of Association)

	Boys	Girls
Responsibility	+.74 **	+.62 **
Obedience	+.50 **	+.59 **
Nurturance	−.01	+.10
Achievement	−.60 **	−.62 **
Self-reliance	−.21	−.46 *
Independence	−.41 *	−.11

* $p < .05$ } Two-tail tests, based on the Mann Whitney U (Siegel 1956:116–127).
** $p < .01$

These results are all substantially alike for the training of the two sexes. The correlations between economy and child training are in the same direction for boys and girls for all the variables except nurturance. There seems to be no consistent difference between the sexes in size of the correlations. However, it is worth noting in Figure 1 that the variables which ranked higher in societies with high accumulation of food resources (obedience and responsibility) were emphasized more strongly in the training of girls than boys, whereas the variables which ranked higher in societies with low accumulation of food resources (achievement, self-reliance and independence) were emphasized more strongly in the training of boys than girls. A further description of sex differences for the same group of societies may be found in a recent paper by Barry, Bacon and Child (1957).

. . . . .

ECONOMY AND A GENERAL VARIABLE OF SOCIALIZATION

In their relation to economy, the socialization variables (if we omit nurturance) fall into two distinct groups. This fact suggests that a single more general variable might be extracted for presentation of data on individual societies and for further exploration of results. We have called this variable pressure toward compliance vs. assertion. It is based on the separate socialization variables, and was derived in the following way: The sum of the rankings of responsibility and obedience training, for both boys and girls, was subtracted from the sum of the rankings of achievement and self-reliance, for both boys and girls. A plus score meant that responsibility and obedience were ranked higher (i.e., were assigned lower numbers) than achievement and self-reliance, and for purposes of calculating a coefficient of association any plus score was designated as predominant pressure toward compliance. A zero or minus score was designated as predominant pressure toward assertion. We dealt with cases of missing information as follows: In the several societies in which the achievement rating was not made, general independence was substituted for it in deriving this general measure of pressure toward compliance vs. assertion. In the two societies where the obedience rating was not made, the responsibility rating was substituted for it. Eleven societies were omitted because some or all of the ratings had been made only for one sex.

Table 2 presents a list of societies, divided according to predominant economy and arranged in order of their score on relative predominance of compliance vs. assertion in child training pressures. The correlation portrayed in this table is very consistent. Societies with high accumulation of food resources almost always had predominant pressure toward compliance, whereas societies with low accumulation almost always had predominant pressure toward assertion; 39 societies conformed to this result and only seven had high accumulation with assertion or low accumulation with compliance. The association coefficient for this relationship is .94, (P), and P is less than .001, measured by the Mann-Whitney U Test (Siegel 1956:116–117).

It is not surprising, of course, that economy shows a higher correlation with the combined measure of socialization pressures than with any of the separate child training measures from which it is derived. The magnitude of the correlation is, however, surprising. We may conclude that a knowledge of the economy alone would enable one to predict with considerable accuracy whether a society's socialization pressures were primarily toward compliance or assertion.

RELATION TO OTHER CULTURAL VARIABLES

We have suggested that child training practices are shaped by the behavioral requirements of the adult economic roles. This implies a fairly direct causal relation between economy and child training. It is quite possible, however, that the causal connection might be much more indirect. The subsistence economy may have a pervasive influence on many other aspects of culture, and some of these other aspects of culture may be more directly responsible for influencing child training practices. As a first check on this possibility, we decided to explore the relation of pressure toward compliance vs. assertion, and of subsistence economy, to nine other major cultural variables for which Murdock . . . has prepared analyses from the ethnographic literature for these same societies.

For five of these variables, it was possible to treat Murdock's categories as falling along an ordered scale: these are the first five variables

Table 2. Relation of Subsistence Economy to General Pressure Toward Compliance vs. Assertion in Child Training

The societies are grouped in columns on the basis of economy and are listed within each column in descending order of degree of pressure toward compliance as compared with pressure toward assertion. The number in parentheses after each society indicates the degree of preponderance of compliance (plus scores) or of assertion (minus scores).

EXTREMES IN ACCUMULATION	
High (animal husbandry)	Low (hunting, fishing)
Aymara (+13½)	
Tepoztlan (+13½)	
Lepcha (+11½)	
Swazi (+8½)	
Tswana (+8½)	
Nyakyusa (+8)	
Sotho (+8)	
Nuer (+7)	
Tallensi (+7)	
Lovedu (+6½)	
Mbundu (+6½)	
Venda (+6½)	
Kikuyu (+6)	
Zulu (+6)	
Pondo (+4½)	
Chagga (+4)	
Ganda (+3)	
Chamorro (+2½)	Teton (+4)
Masai (+2½)	Yahgan (+1)
Chukchee (+1)	Hupa (+½)
Tanala (0)	Chiricahua (0)
Thonga (−2½)	Murngin (0)
Araucanian (−3)	Paiute (0)
Balinese (−3)	Arapaho (−2)
	Kwakiutl (−2)
	Cheyenne (2½)
	Kaska (−2½)
	Klamath (−2½)
	Ojibwa (−2½)
	Ona (−3)
	Aleut (−4)
	Jicarilla (−6½)
	Western Apache (−10)
	Siriono (−10½)
	West Greenland Eskimo (−11)
	Aranda (−12)
	Comanche (−12)
	Crow (−13½)
	Manus (−15)

listed in Table 3. For three additional variables (the rest of those appearing in Table 3), Murdock's categories were divided into two groups to form a reasonable dichotomy. Clearly these eight variables show some consistency in their relation both to our economic measure and to pressure toward compliance vs. assertion. . . .

Table 3. **Relation of Other Cultural Variables to Pressure Toward Compliance vs. Assertion, and to Accumulation of Food Resources, Separately for Two Groups of Societies**

(The measure given here is the index of order association, for which see Wallis and Roberts, 1956:282–284; where both variables are dichotomous, this measure reduces to the more familiar coefficient of association. Pressure toward compliance, and accumulation of food resources, have been treated here as dichotomous variables; the other variables have from two to seven ordered categories. A plus or minus sign indicates whether the variables are positively or negatively related to high accumulation and high pressure toward compliance.)

Cultural Variable	*Relation to Accumulation*	*Relation to Pressure toward Compliance*
Size of permanent settlement unit	+.52	+.43
Degree of political integration	+.76	+.63
Complexity of social stratification	+.74	+.56
Greater participation by women in predominant subsistence activity	+.60	+.48
Extent of approach to general polygyny	+.25	−.08
Presence of bride-price or bride-service	+.84	+.86
Unilinearity of descent	+.83	+.49
Residence fixed or neolocal, rather than shifting or bilocal	+.32	+.35

[However,] pressure toward compliance vs. assertion shows [a] higher correlation with accumulation of food resources (.94) . . . than with any of the other cultural variables. These other cultural variables are mostly related more closely to accumulation than to compliance vs. assertion. . . . Therefore it is plausible that the relation of compliance vs. assertion to the variables listed in Table 3 is principally due to their common relation to accumulation of food resources.

. . . . .

INTERMEDIATE ACCUMULATION OF FOOD RESOURCES [*]

The high correlations we have reported between subsistence economy and child training were applied only to societies which are ex-

* This section, preceding the conclusion, has been added to the original article by the authors.

tremely high or extremely low in accumulation of food resources. A large group of predominantly agricultural societies do not fit into either category but might still show considerable variation in accumulation of food resources. The question remains whether the correlations found among the extreme cases would also be found in this more intermediate group of societies. Furthermore, the data shown in Table 3 suggest the possibility that the high correlation between accumulation of food resources and pressure toward compliance is found only in societies where the subsistence economy is consistently linked with a group of other cultural variables.

In order to answer these questions, we divided the predominantly agricultural societies into two groups. Those with little or no hunting or fishing (15 societies) were considered as having high accumulation of food resources, and those which rely on hunting or fishing for an important part of their food (18 societies) were considered as having low accumulation of food resources. Here as in the extreme comparison, societies with high accumulation of food resources tend to emphasize responsibility and obedience training, and show high overall pressure toward compliance in child training; societies with low accumulation of food resources tend to emphasize achievement, self-reliance and independence training, and show low overall pressure toward compliance in child training. The association coefficient between accumulation of food resources and pressure toward compliance is .93 ($p < .02$). Accumulation of food resources shows low and inconsistent relationships to all of the cultural variables listed in Table 3, with the exception of the last one (residence fixed or neolocal, rather than shifting or bilocal). Therefore the high positive correlation between accumulation of food resources and pressure toward compliance in child training is found among our entire sample of societies and does not depend upon the group of cultural variables which are linked with the extreme variations in accumulation of food resources.

DISCUSSION

Some readers may feel that our main results are obvious, to the extent of being therefore trivial. We believe that this is not the case, that we have instead obtained strong evidence for one hypothesis where some other quite different hypothesis might seem more obvious in advance. For example, let us start the other way around and think of child training as the basic given. Pressure toward self-reliance and achievement should produce strongly independent people who hate to be dependent on others. This character tendency should render very rewarding all features of economic behavior that make it easier to avoid being dependent on others. Among such features, one of the most conspicuous might be the possession by each individual or family of an accumulated food supply (such as herd or crop), which ensures that an unlucky hunt will not leave one dependent upon the neighbor's catch. Hence child training pressure toward assertion should motivate (perhaps unconsciously) the quest for high accumulation techniques of subsistence. But according to our findings, it evidently does not. If any such process operates to a slight degree, it appears to be completely obscured by the much more important process to which our results point.

Our findings then are consistent with the suggestion that child training tends to be a suitable adaptation to subsistence economy. Pressure toward obedience and responsibility should tend to make children into the obedient and responsible adults who can best ensure the continuing welfare of a society with a high-accumulation economy, whose food supply must be protected and developed gradually throughout the year. Pressure toward self-reliance and achievement should shape children into the venturesome, independent adults who can take initiative in wresting food daily from nature, and thus ensure survival in societies with a low-accumulation economy.

REFERENCES CITED

BARRY, HERBERT III, Margaret K. Bacon, and Irvin L. Child
> 1957 A cross-cultural survey of some sex differences in socialization. Journal of Abnormal and Social Psychology 55:327–332.

FORDE, C. DARYLL
> 1934 Habitat, economy and society. London, Methuen.

HERSKOVITS, MELVILLE J.
> 1952 Economic anthropology. New York, Alfred A. Knopf.

MURDOCK, GEORGE PETER
> 1957 World ethnographic sample. American Anthropologist 59:664–687.

SIEGEL, SIDNEY
> 1956 Nonparametric statistics for the behavioral sciences. New York. McGraw-Hill.

WALLIS, W. ALLEN AND HARRY V. ROBERTS
> 1956 Statistics, a new approach. Glencoe, Illinois, Free Press.

14. IN THE DAYS OF MY YOUTH

GEORGE BERNARD SHAW

Perhaps Shaw's essential greatness—as a playwright, as a critic of the arts and as a critic of society as well,—lay in his capacity to cut through pretense and shatter hypocrisy. What special childhood experiences enabled him to develop this ability?

In these autobiographical sketches Shaw describes his childhood and family with mixed contempt and admiration for the values of his people. Is this the kind of person we would want?

MY MOTHER AND HER RELATIVES

My mother was the daughter of a country gentlemen, and was brought up with ruthless strictness to be a paragon of all ladylike virtues and accomplishments, by her grand aunt, whom I remember from my very early childhood as a humpbacked old lady with a pretty face, whose deformity seemed to me quaintly proper to her as a beneficent fairy. Had she known the magically favorable impression she made on me, she would perhaps have left me her property; and I now believe I was brought to her in the hope I should attract her to this extent. But I was a failure. She had brought my mother up to make such a distinguished marriage as would finally wipe out an unmentionable stain on her pedigree; for though on her parents side her extraction was everything that could be desired, her grandfather was a mysterious master spirit whose birth was so obscure that there was some doubt as to whether he ever had any legal parents at all.

. . . . .

Nature, expelled with a fork, came back again and wrecked the life plans of her fairy aunt. When my mother grew up, she knew thoroughbass as taught by her musicmaster Johann Bernhard Logier (famous in Dublin as the inventor of the chiroplast, a mechanical finger exerciser which set his piano pupils all wrong); she could repeat two of La Fontaine's fables in French with perfect pronunciation; she could carry herself with complete dignity; and she could have worked as a

Reprinted from *Sixteen Self Sketches* (Dodd, Mead & Company, 1949) by permission of The Public Trustee as Executor of the Estate of George Bernard Shaw, Deceased, and of The Society of Authors, London.

ragpicker without losing her entire conviction that she was a lady, of a species apart from servants and common persons. But she could not housekeep on a small income; she had no notion of the value of money; she detested her grand aunt and regarded all that had been taught her as religion and discipline as tyranny and slavery. Consequently, as she was naturally very humane, she abandoned her own children to the most complete anarchy. Both my parents, as it happened, were utterly uncoercive.

In due time she was floated in Dublin society to get married. Among other persons with whom she came in contact was George Carr Shaw, an apparently harmless gentleman of forty, with a squint and a vein of humor which delighted in anti-climax, and would have made him an appreciative listener for Charles Lamb. He was a member of a large family which spoke of itself as "the Shaws," and got invited, on the strength of a second cousinship, to Bushy Park, the seat of the bachelor Sir Robert Shaw, Bart., as to whom see Burke's *Landed Gentry*. George Carr Shaw seemed very safe company for my carefully guarded mother, because nobody could conceive his having the audacity, the enterprise, nor the means, to marry anybody, even if it could be supposed that his years or his squint could appeal to so well brought-up a female as Miss Lucinda Elizabeth Gurly. He was therefore well spoken of by her relatives as a quite eligible person to know in a general social way. They forgot that, having never been taught what marriage really means, nor experienced impecuniosity, she might marry any adventurer without knowing how much she was doing.

Her tragedy came about by external pressure of a sort that nobody could have foreseen.

Her widowed father was most unexpectedly married again; this time the penniless daughter of an old friend of his whose bills he had backed with ruinous consequences. The alliance did not please the family of his first wife, especially his brother-in-law, a Kilkenny squire, to whom he owed money, and from whom he concealed his intention to marry again.

Unfortunately my mother innocently let out the secret to her uncle. The consequence was that my grandfather, going out on his wedding morning to buy a pair of gloves for the ceremony, was arrested for debt at the suit of his brother-in-law. One can hardly blame him for being furious. But his fury carried him beyond all reason. He believed that my mother had betrayed him deliberately so as to stop the marriage by his arrest. My mother, who was on a visit to some relatives in Dublin at the time, had to choose between two homes to return to. One was the house of a stepmother and an enraged father. The other was to the house of her aunt, which meant the old domestic slavery and tyranny.

It was at this moment that some devil, perhaps commissioned by

the Life Force to bring me into the world, prompted my father to propose marriage to Miss Bessie Gurly. She caught at the straw. She had
heard that he had a pension of £60 a year; and to her, who had never
been allowed to have more than pocket money nor to housekeep, £60
seemed an enormous and inexhaustible sum. She calmly announced her
engagement, dropping the bombshell as unconcernedly as if it were a
colored glass ball from her solitaire board. People played solitaire in
those days.

Finding it impossible to make her see the gravity of the pecuniary
situation, or to induce her to cancel her engagement on such ground,
her people played another card. They told her that George Carr Shaw
was a drunkard. She indignantly refused to believe them, reminding
them that they had never objected to him before. When they persisted,
she went to him straightforwardly and asked him was it true. He assured her most solemnly that he was a convinced and life-long teetotaller.
And she believed him and married him. But it was not true. He drank.

Without attempting to defend my father for telling this whopper,
I must explain that he really was in principle a convinced teetotaller.
Unfortunately it was the horror of his own experience as an occasional
dipsomaniac that gave him this conviction, which he was miserably
unable to carry into practice.

I can only imagine the hell into which my mother descended when
she found out what shabby-genteel poverty with a drunken husband is
like. She told me once that when they were honeymooning in Liverpool
(of all places) she opened her bridegroom's wardrobe and found it full
of empty bottles. In the first shock of the discovery she ran away to the
docks to get employed as a stewardess and be taken out of the country.
But on the way she was molested by some rough docklanders and had
to run back again.

I have elsewhere recorded how, when my father, taking me for a
walk, pretended in play to throw me into the canal, he very nearly did
it. When we got home I said to my mother as an awful and hardly
credible discovery "Mamma: I think Papa is drunk." This was too much
for her. She replied "When is he anything else?"

It is a rhetorical exaggeration to say that I have never since believed in anything or anybody; but the wrench from my discovery that
he was a hypocrite and a dipsomaniac was so sudden and violent that
it must have left its mark on me.

. . . . .

Under all the circumstances it says a great deal for my mother's
humanity that she did not hate her children. She did not hate anybody,
nor love anybody. The specific maternal passion awoke in her a little for
my younger sister, who died at twenty, but it did not move her until she

lost her, nor then noticeably. She did not concern herself much about us; for she had never been taught that mothering is a science, nor that it matters in the least what children eat or drink; she left all that to servants whose wage was £8 a year and could neither write nor read. She had no sense of the value of her own training, and gave it no credit for its results, which she may have regarded as gifts of nature; but she had a deep sense of its cruelties. As we grew up and had to take care of ourselves unguided, we met life's difficulties by breaking our shins over them, gaining such wisdom as was inevitable by making fools of ourselves.

. . . . .

My father was impecunious and unsuccessful: he could do nothing that interested her; and he did not shake off his miserable and disgraceful tippling (he did eventually) until it was too late to make any difference in their relations. Had there not been imagination, idealization, the charm of music, the charm of lovely seas and sunsets, and our natural kindliness and gentleness, it is impossible to say what cynical barbarism we might not have grown into.

My mother's salvation came through music. She had a mezzosoprano voice of extraordinary purity of tone; and to cultivate it she took lessons from George John Vandaleur Lee, already well established in Dublin as an orchestral conductor, an organizer of concerts, and a teacher of singing so heterodox and original that he depended for his performances on amateurs trained by himself, and was detested by his professional rivals, whom he disparaged as voice wreckers, as indeed they mostly were. He extended this criticism to doctors, and amazed us by eating brown bread instead of white, and sleeping with the window open, both of which habits I acquired and have practised ever since. His influence in our household, of which he at last became a member, accustomed me to the scepticism as to academic authority which still persists in me.

He not only made my mother sing by a method that preserved her voice perfectly until her death at over eighty but gave her a Cause and a Creed to live for.

Those who know my play *Misalliance,* in which the lover has three fathers, will note that I also had a natural father and two supplementaries, making three varieties for me to study. This widened my outlook very considerably. Natural parents should bear in mind that the more supplementaries their children find, at school or elsewhere, the better they will know that it takes all sorts to make a world. Also that though there is always the risk of being corrupted by bad parents, the natural ones may be—probably ten per cent. of them actually are—the worst of the lot.

Then there was my maternal Uncle Walter. During my boyhood he was a ship's surgeon on the Inman line (now the American), visiting us between voyages. . . . In spite of his excesses, which were not continuous, being the intermittent debauches of a seafarer on shore, he was an upstanding healthy man until he married an English widow in America and settled as a general practitioner in Leyton, Essex, then a country district on the borders of Epping Forest. His wife tried to make him behave himself according to English lights, to go to church; to consult the feelings and prejudices of his patients; to refrain from the amusement of scandalizing their respectability; or at least to stint himself in the item of uproarious blasphemy. It was quite useless: her protests only added to the zest of his profanities.

. . . . .

The children of Bohemian Anarchists are often in such strenuous reaction against their bringing-up that they are the most tyrannically conventional of parents. The problem of how much and when children can be kindly and safely left to their own devices, and how much guided and ordered, is the most difficult part of parental policy. Prince Peter Kropotkin, a comprehensive thinker, far above the average in wisdom and kindliness, said of children "You can only look on." My mother, if she had ever thought about the matter at all would have said "You can only go your own way and let the children go theirs."

. . . . .

IN THE DAYS OF MY YOUTH

All autobiographies are lies. I do not mean unconscious, unintentional lies: I mean deliberate lies. No man is bad enough to tell the truth about himself during his lifetime, involving, as he must, the truth about his family and his friends and colleagues. And no man is good enough to tell the truth to posterity in a document which he suppresses until there is nobody left alive to contradict him.

. . . . .

I am in the further difficulty that I have not yet ascertained the truth about myself. For instance, how far am I mad, and how far sane? I do not know. My specific talent has enabled me to cut a figure in my profession in London: but a man may, like Don Quixote, be clever enough to cut a figure, and yet be stark mad.

A critic recently described me as having "a kindly dislike of my fellow creatures." Dread would have been nearer the mark than dislike; for a man is the only animal of which I am thoroughly and cravenly afraid. I have never thought much of the courage of a lion tamer. Inside the cage he is at least safe from other men. There is less harm in a well-fed lion. It has no ideals, no sect, no party, no nation, no class: in short, no reason for destroying anything it does not want to eat.

. . . . .

My father was an Irish Protestant gentleman of the down-start race of younger sons. He had no inheritance, no profession, no manual skill, no qualification of any sort for any definite social function. He must have had some elementary education; for he could read and write and keep accounts more or less inaccurately; and he spoke and dressed like an Irish educated gentleman and not like a railway porter. But he certainly had not a university degree; and I never heard him speak of any school or college of which he could claim to be an alumnus. He had, however, been brought up to believe that there was an inborn virtue of gentility in all Shaws as partisans of William the Conqueror. . . . My father was a second cousin of the baronet, and was privileged to hire a carriage and attend the Bushy Park funerals, beside having a right to an invitation to certain family parties there. Necessarily all the Shaws were Protestants and snobs. . . .

I believe Ireland, as far as the Protestant gentry is concerned, to be the most irreligious country in the world. I was christened by my uncle; and as my godfather was intoxicated and did not turn up, the sexton was ordered to promise and vow in his place, precisely as my uncle might have ordered him to put more coals on the vestry fire. I was never confirmed; and I believe my parents never were either. Of the seriousness with which English families took this rite I had no conception; for Irish Protestantism was not then a religion: it was a side in political faction, a class prejudice, a conviction that Roman Catholics are socially inferior persons who will go to hell when they die and leave Heaven for the exclusive possession of Protestant ladies and gentlemen. In my childhood I was sent every Sunday to a Sunday school where genteel little children repeated texts, and were rewarded with cards inscribed to them. After an hour of this we were marched into the adjoining church (the Molyneux in Upper Leeson Street), to sit around the altar rails and fidget there until our neighbors must have wished the service over as heartily as we did. I suffered this, not for my salvation, but because my father's respectability demanded it. When we went to live in Dalkey we broke with the observance and never resumed it.

. . . . .

Imagine being taught to despise a workman, and to respect a gentleman, in a country where every rag of excuse of gentility is stripped off by poverty! Imagine being taught that there is one God, a Protestant and a perfect gentleman, keeping Heaven select for the gentry against an idolatrous impostor called the Pope! Imagine the pretensions of the English peerage on the incomes of the English middle class! I remember Stopford Brooke one day telling me that he discerned in my books an intense and contemptuous hatred for society. No wonder!

.   .   .   .   .

And now, what power did I find in Ireland religious enough to redeem me from this abomination of desolation? Quite simply, the power of Art. My mother, as it happened, had a considerable musical talent. In order to exercise it seriously, she had to associate with other people who had musical talent. My first doubt as to whether God could really be a good Protestant was suggested by the fact that the best voices available for combination with my mother's in the works of the great composers had been unaccountably vouchsafed to Roman Catholics. Even the divine gentility was presently called in question; for some of these vocalists were undeniably shopkeepers. If the best tenor, undeniably a Catholic, was at least an accountant, the buffo was a frank stationer.

There was no help for it: if my mother was to do anything but sing silly ballads in drawing rooms, she had to associate herself on an entirely unsectarian footing with people of like artistic gifts without the smallest reference to creed or class. She must actually permit herself to be approached by Roman Catholic priests, and at their invitation to enter that house of Belial, the Roman Catholic chapel, and sing the Masses of Mozart there. If religion is that which binds men to one another, and irreligion that which sunders, then must I testify that I found the religion of my country in its musical genius, and its irreligion in its churches and drawing rooms.

Let me add a word of gratitude to that cherished asylum of my boyhood, the National Gallery of Ireland. I believe I am the only Irishman who has ever been in it, except the officials. But I know that it did much more for me than the two confiscated medieval Cathedrals so magnificently "restored" out of the profits of the drink trade.

PART II

INFANCY

Satisfying Fundamental Needs:
Some Dimensions of Love

INTRODUCTION

What are the fundamental needs of the infant, and how can they best be satisfied? What is motherly love? How much of it does an infant need?

In this Part some provocative answers to these questions are explored. Banham observed many infants learning to express love. The experiments of Clara Davis demonstrate best ways to show love to a child; in terms of his dietary needs, it is to provide for him a wide variety of natural foods and then allow him to eat as he pleases. Montagu shows that some infants are born already handicapped by their mother's dietary deficiencies or diseases. Can an infant therefore be said to sometimes need love even before he has been born? Breckenridge and Vincent present some laws which govern human growth; could one say that love for an infant is shown in behavior which facilitates the operation of these laws?

Harlow's experiments show that for infant monkeys a supply of warm milk and a clean soft form to clutch provide the infant's essential needs, and Dennis and Najarian suggest that abandoned Lebanese infants in an understaffed Creche develop almost as well as those kept with their mothers. These two articles contradict those by Spitz and Bowlby, indicating that children reared in institutions do not develop well physically, intellectually, or emotionally.

The developmental patterns described below may provide a helpful reference for the reader, as he studies all of these articles. They tell us what young children can do at various age levels.

A DEVELOPMENTAL PATTERN—BIRTH TO SIX YEARS

The age norms given here are merely suggestive, and no child follows the pattern exactly. For example, at six months the pattern says, "may sit up a few minutes," although some children do this at 4 months and others may not until 8 or 9 months. Some general principles, however, hold for all children: they see before they grasp; they sit before they stand; creep before they walk; babble before they speak; scribble before they draw or write; tell stories before they tell the truth. They like music and dancing and sweet talk at all ages. For more detailed norms, see Arnold Gesell and Frances L. Ilg, *Child Development* (Harper and Brothers, 1949); Wayne and Marsena G. Dennis, "Behavioral Development during the First Year as Shown by 40 Biographies," *Psychological Record* 1 (1937) 349–361; Nancy Bayley, "Mental Growth during the first three years," *Genetic Psychology Monographs*, 14 (1933), 1–92; M. M. Shirley, *The First Two Years*, (University of Minnesota Press, 1931–1933); Lewis M. Terman and Maud A. Merrill, *Measuring Intelligence* (Houghton Mifflin Company, 1937).

THE NEWBORN   Breathing and heartbeat rapid and irregular. Moves arms, legs, fingers, head and neck randomly, without control. A talented and busy mouth: sucks, swallows, coughs, sneezes, tastes sweet and sour, spits, burps, vomits, cries. Babinski reflex; startle response to cold or hot food or bath. Urination 18 times, defecation 4 to 7 times daily; penis erection. Sleeps 20 hours a day.

2 WEEKS   Eyes begin to focus on objects.

4 WEEKS   Can lift head; eyes focus a little better but not well. Awakens early, screaming for food. Sometimes stops crying after feeding, rocking, changing diapers, or bubbling.

8 WEEKS   Follows an object with eyes. Smiles.

3 MONTHS   Looks at object held in his hand. Laughs.

4 MONTHS   Reaches for object, but can't quite get it. Pulls self to sitting. Likes to bathe if water is at just the right temperature. Plays with fingers; sucks fingers, sits for a moment or so, coos. Gradually sleeps less and less, exercises more and more. Looks around while nursing. May be fed from spoon or cup but loses half of the food.

6 MONTHS   May sit up a few minutes. Holds up head but not body. Grabs objects, puts them in mouth, bangs them, drops them. If an object drops out of sight, he forgets it immediately. Becoming more expert with hands, but still clumsy with spoon. Some crawling at-

tempts. Morning and afternoon nap. Takes 4 meals a day; one bowel movement a day, more often in diaper than in pot.

8 MONTHS Rolls over. Closes eyes as object gets close to face.

10 MONTHS Sits up easily. Pulls to standing, crawls, creeps; uses thumb and index finger. Puts spoon into cup, plays pat-a-cake, rolls ball. Likes adults to play with him.

1 YEAR Walks with support. Drops objects from hand. Uses thumb and forefinger with ease. Sleeps 14 hours a day. Makes many sounds, practices "talking," and says two or three "words."

15 MONTHS Walks alone, falls often. Says a few words. Unwraps toys.

18 MONTHS Can point to a picture named in book or magazine. Runs and runs, falls and falls; can take off shoes and mittens; pushes around toys and furniture; sweeps with broom; mops and messes; pulls on curtains, table cloths; needs close supervision. Enjoys cardboard boxes, ropes, clothes pins, and something to bang on. Holds and drinks from cup. Tries to tell what he wants by gestures. Knows many words but can't really talk yet.

2 YEARS Walks well. Says over 200 words. Plays alone, runs to adult for comfort and praise; fears animals; can build a tower of 2 to 4 blocks; grabs toys away from other children; knocks competitors down if he can; may be jealous of baby brother or sister; can point to toys when names are given or to parts of body, scribbles.

2½ YEARS Fears animals and imaginary objects. Sleeps 12 hours at night and takes two short naps a day. Says 400 words. Very impatient, jumps, runs, shouts, tries to draw a line, folds paper.

3 YEARS Can stand on one leg. Helps to set the table. Says 800 words. Fears cars in street or alley. Can draw a circle and a cross. Enjoys crayons, cutting with blunt-ended scissors, using spoon and fork (but not well). Can get water alone, toilet trained, runs up and down stairs, can count to three, puts on some clothes, may even button himself.

4 YEARS Can throw a ball; likes to tricycle, paint, play with clay, mud, dolls, hammer and saw. Tells long tales. Operates TV and record player. Can be bossy, friendly, angry, boastful. Skips, hops, and jumps; plays with boys and girls, plays house, plays hospital, and acts out a thousand plots. Makes faces. Can dress himself with some help; goes outside alone but welcomes adult protection from bullies and likes an adult to play with. Sings. Runs into street if not watched and taught how to cross at corners. Can draw a square and triangle.

5 YEARS A little man or woman: With help, dresses, eats, sets the table, sweeps; wanders around the block alone. Uses 2,000 words, often illogically; recognizes many letters in alphabet. Hugs and fights; enjoys a quiet bedtime story; believes almost anything he is told.

Tries to skate, jump rope; plays organized games, in which everyone has a turn, but hates to lose in competitive games.

6 YEARS Can ride a bicycle, read and write, go off to school alone if not too far away, manage fork and spoon (but not yet a knife); knows something about time but can't read a clock. Because of pressures in getting up, getting dressed, doing school work, keeping quiet in school, may be a bad year. Can throw a ball and hit ball with bat, but can't catch small ball.

15. CONSTITUTIONAL AND PRENATAL FACTORS IN INFANT AND CHILD HEALTH

M. F. ASHLEY MONTAGU

Dr. Montagu's knowledgeable and provocative article gives new significance to the term "environment." An impressive amount of evidence is presented regarding the interplay between the mental-emotional state of the mother and her unborn child, the mechanisms by which stress, tension, and anxiety are transferred from mother to child in-utero. That many children are born already handicapped by parental deprivations, reveals the profound influence of socio-economic, biological and psychological factors on the individual even before he is born.

INTRODUCTION

This review of the materials relating to constitutional and prenatal factors in infant and child health should be regarded as of suggestive rather than of determinative value. That is to say, it should be read as suggesting areas for research to research workers, and to parents it should suggest something of the nature of the care and caution they need to exercise even before the baby is born. In short, most statements made in this review should be read with the phrase, "The evidence suggests . . ." mentally affixed.

It is important to bear in mind that much of our knowledge of what conditions affect the unborn fetus is drawn from the field of disease, from

Selections reprinted from the article in *Symposium on the Healthy Personality*, edited by Milton J. Senn (Josiah Macy Jr. Foundation, 1950), pp. 148–169, by permission of the author and publisher.

pathology. This fact should not cause the reader to develop an exaggerated view of the dangers to which the fetus is exposed nor to marvel at what might seem the surprising fact that so many human beings have survived unmarred. The pathological cases are fortunately in the minority. Their value, and their use here, lies in the fact that they show, as it were, in high relief the kind of conditions which can influence the development of the fetus, as well as something of the probable mode of action of the more normal conditions. They also show us how the development of the fetus can be influenced for better or for worse. Indeed, if there is one important lesson to be learned from the findings which are discussed in this paper, it is that we can do much to make the prenatal development of the infant a satisfactory one.

. . . . .

CONSTITUTION, HEREDITY, AND ENVIRONMENT

Constitution is the sum total of the structural, functional, and psychological characters of the organism. It is in large measure an integral of genetic potentialities influenced in varying degrees by internal and external environmental factors. What, in fact, we are concerned with here is the answer to the following questions: (1) What are the inherited genetic potentialities (the genotype) of the organisms? (2) How are these influenced by the internal and external environmental factors during prenatal life?, and (3) What role does each of these factors play in influencing the subsequent physical and mental health of infant and child?

What we mean by these questions is what we mean by "constitution," for constitution is at first a series of operative questions that even by the time of birth have not yet become final declarative answers. Indeed, there is little that is final about constitution, for constitution is a *process* rather than an unchanging entity. In brief, it is important to understand at the outset that constitution is not a biologically *given* structure predestined by its genotype to function in a predetermined manner. The manner in which all genotypes function is determined by the interaction of the genotype with the environment in which it undergoes development. What, so to speak, the genotype—the complex of genetic potentialities with which the organism is endowed—asks is: What kind of responses are going to be made to my autocatalytic enzymatic (chemically accelerating) overtures, my tentative advances? How will I impress? How will I be impressed? For the outcome of all this will be my constitution.

The point that must be emphasized here is that every genotype is a unique physicochemical system comprising particular kinds of potentialities having definite limits. These limits vary from individual to individual, so that were the genotype to be exposed to identical environmental conditions its interactive expression would nevertheless continue to vary from individual to individual. But in point of fact the environmental conditions never are the same for two individuals, not including single-egg or so-called "identical" twins. This fact renders it necessary for us to recognize that heredity is not merely constituted by the genotype, but by the genotype as modified by the environment in which it has developed. It is necessary to grasp clearly the fact that what the organism inherits is a genotype *and* an environment. That heredity is the dynamic integral of the genotype and the environment—the resultant of the dynamic interaction between the two.

If it is true that the organism inherits a genotype and an environment, and that the resultant of the interaction between the two is heredity, then it follows that is would be possible to influence the heredity of the developing organism by controlling its environment. This we know to be true by virtue of numerous experiments involving plants and non-human animals, and we have good evidence that it is also true for man. The question of an earlier day which asked whether heredity was more important than environment or vice versa has been dismissed by some experts as a spurious question. It has been said that heredity and environment are equally important, since both are necessary if the genes are to develop, or rather if the genes are to produce development. Genes always act within the conditioning effects of an environment. Some have gone further and stated that the genotype is more important than the environment, and others have asserted the opposite.

Clearly, the genotype is fundamental in that it is biologically determined as a complex of potentialities with inherent limitations for development. But since those potentialities are always considerably influenced by the environment, the question of importance becomes a relative one, depending upon whether one takes the view that the genotype can be favorably influenced by controlled environmental factors or that it cannot. Since it is through its environment alone that the developing "human" organism can be influenced, it seems clear that it is the most important means through which we can work to secure the optimum development of the genotype in its final expression in what we see, which we call the phenotype. The importance of the genotype is affirmed as potentiality or potentialities, a statement which implies the necessity of emphasizing its complementary, the importance of the developer of those potentialities—the environment.

Genes determine, not characters nor traits, but responses of the developing organism to the environment. Since the expression of the genotype is a function of the environment, it is to a certain extent amenable to human control. The practical significance of this statement cannot be overemphasized for those of us who are interested in understanding, and to some extent controlling, the character and influence of prenatal factors upon the developing fetus and their effects upon the health of infant and child.

INHERITED POTENTIALITIES AND ENVIRONMENTAL INFLUENCES

We may now turn to our three questions and the answers to them. The first two questions are best answered together.

What are the inherited genetic potentialities of the organism, and how are these influenced by internal and external environmental factors during prenatal life?

The inherited genetic potentialities are contained in the genes in the 24 chromosomes transmitted from the mother and in the 24 chromosomes transmitted from the father. Three different observers (Ashley Montagu, 1945; Spuhler, 1948; Evans, 1949), by three different methods, have independently estimated the number of genes in man to be somewhere in the vicinity of 30,000. Genes are autocatalytic, enzymatic, self-duplicating giant protein molecules of great complexity. That is to say, genes are the organic catalysts which accelerate essential chemical reactions, the original builders of the body which they serve to differentiate according to the type of medium and other conditions which surround them in their interactive chemical relations (Muller, 1947). These chemical relations are inherent in the chemical properties of the genes and will be *more or less* broadly realized according to a determinate pattern under all environments. The *more* or the *less* will depend upon the nature of the environment in which the genes find themselves. The important point to understand, however, is that the same genes may be influenced to express themselves differently and to have different end effects as a consequence of the different environments in which they function. It is in this way, we believe, that the different parts of the body come to be developed by essentially the same genes. Furthermore, from fertilization onward small random or accidental changes in the environment of the egg or embryo may be operative and can have a decisive effect upon development. A gene on the verge of expressing itself may be affected by random variations in the constitution of the cell substance (Dahlberg, 1948). Variations in the prenatal environment during the limited period of the action of certain genes may substantially affect their manifestation.

A great many constitutional defects in children are believed to be owing to disturbances during the prenatal development of the organism. The evidence for this is in part derived from experimental studies on nonhuman animals and in part from the factual data for man himself.

IS THERE A CONNECTION BETWEEN THE NERVOUS SYSTEMS OF MOTHER AND CHILD?

Until recently there has been a widespread belief that the fetus is so well insulated in the womb and so well protected by the placental barrier that it lives a nirvana-like existence completely sufficient unto itself. Some have described this condition as a state of uterine bliss. According to them this uterine state of bliss leaves its mark upon the mind of the organism and, unconsciously recollected in later life, usually in anything but tranquillity, determines the person's search for such a state of bliss. This "Maginot Line" view of uterine existence is no longer in agreement with the facts. Indeed, we begin to perceive that there is more than a modicum of truth in the remark, uttered by Samuel Taylor Coleridge more than a hundred years ago, "Yes, the history of man for the nine months preceding his birth, would, probably, be far more interesting, and contain events of greater moment, than all the threescore and ten years that follow it."

A still widely prevalent belief has it that there is no connection between the nervous systems of mother and fetus. This notion is based on a very narrow conception of the nervous system. It is through the neurohumoral system, the system comprising the interrelated nervous and endocrine systems acting through the fluid medium of the blood (and its oxygen and carbon-dioxide contents), that nervous changes in the mother may affect the fetus. The common endocrine pool of the mother and fetus forms a neurohumoral bond between them. The endocrine systems of mother and fetus complement each other.

All this is not to say that there is anything at all in the old wives' tale of "maternal impressions." The mother's "impressions," her "psychological states" as such, cannot possibly be transmitted to the fetus. What are transmitted are the gross chemical changes which occur in the mother and, so far as we know at the present time, nothing more.

While it is believed that some hormonal molecules are not small enough to pass through the placenta, there is no doubt that many maternal hormones are composed of molecules of small enough size to be able to pass very readily through the placenta (Needham, 1931; Windle, 1940; Flexner, 1947).

ARE THE MOTHER'S EMOTIONAL STATES COMMUNICATED TO THE FETUS? IF SO, HOW? POSSIBLE EFFECTS.

The answer to this compound question is: Yes, there is good evidence that the mother's emotional states are, at least in chemical form transmitted to the fetus. The Fels Institute workers at Antioch College, Yellow Springs, Ohio, have found that emotional disturbances in the pregnant mother produce a marked increase in the activity of the fetus. Mothers undergoing periods of severe emotional distress have fetuses which show considerably increased activity. Moreover, the Fels workers have found that mothers having the highest rates for the functioning of that part of the nervous system which is mostly under unconscious control, and is concerned with the regulation of visceral activities, the autonomic nervous system in such measures as skin conductance, resting heart rate, respiration rate, variability of respiration and variability of heart rate under basic conditions, have the most active fetuses. In view of these facts, it has been postulated "that the psychophysiological state of the mother exerts an influence upon the behavior pattern of the normal fetus" (Sontag, 1944, page 152).

The Fels Institute workers have observed that fatigue in the pregnant mother will also produce hyperactivity in the fetus. Supporting these observations, other observers have found that the activity of the fetus is greatest in the evening (Harris and Harris, 1946).

How are the mother's emotional states capable of effecting the fetus?

Through the neurohumoral system, which has already been defined as being composed of the interrelated nervous and endocrine systems acting through the fluid medium of the blood. For example, stimuli originating in the cerebral cortex (the external gray matter of the brain) may set up reflexes which pass directly into the autonomic nervous system (through the autonomic representation in the cerebral cortex) or are mediated through the feeling-tone center or relay station known as the thalamus to the lower autonomic centers of the hypothalamus, the great coordinating center of the autonomic nervous system situated at the base of the brain. By whatever route such reflexes travel, the autonomic nervous system acts upon the endocrine glands and these pour their secretions into the blood. In the pregnant mother such secretions are known to be capable of passing through the placenta to the fetus, with the possible exception of some of the hormones of the pituitary gland. Stimuli originating in the central nervous system of the mother can therefore indirectly produce changes in the fetus by leading to chemical changes in the mother which affect the fetus. Acetylcholine, which is a substance given off along the course of a nerve fiber during the passage of a nerve impulse, and adrenaline, the secretion of the glands situated on top of the kidneys, the adrenal glands, are almost certainly two among the many substances involved. But we may well consider this under the heading of the third part of our question: What are the possible effects of the mother's emotional states upon the fetus?

The infants of mothers who were emotionally disturbed during pregnancy frequently exhibit evidences of an irritable and hyperactive autonomic nervous system. The cases observed by Sontag presented disturbances in gastrointestinal motility, tone, and function manifested by excessive regurgitation, dyspepsia, and perhaps diarrhea. In some cases there is increase in heart rate, increased vasomotor irritability (irritability of the blood vessels in terms of constriction and dilation), and changes in respiratory pattern. Sontag says:

Irritable or poorly balanced adrenergic-cholinergic systems probably constitute an important part of the rather poorly defined syndrome commonly labeled constitutional inadequacy or nutritional diaphysis. Early feeding difficulties based on motor and sensory abnormalities of the gastrointestinal system are in many instances of autonomic origin. The presence of feeding difficulties of a motor or secretory nature from birth must presume their etiology and basic disturbances during intrauterine life. In prenatal development of such a condition, prolonged nervous and emotional disturbances of the mother during the later months of pregnancy seem to be important (Sontag, 1941, page 1001).

The suggestion is that the autonomic nervous system of the fetus becomes sensitized through the hyperactivity of the mother's neuro-humoral system.

In connection with hyperirritability and gastrointestinal disturbances, Halliday has recently mentioned:

The clinical impression (which has not yet been subjected to clinical testing) that patients who develop recurring depressive states in adult life frequently provide a history—if this can be obtained and confirmed—showing that the mother was grievously disturbed emotionally during the intrauterine phase of the patient. Similar biographical findings, though to a less spectacular degree, are not uncommon in duodenal ulcer. (Halliday, 1948, pages 91–92.)

. . . . .

Sontag (1941) has observed an association between prenatal stimulation of the fetus and postnatal feeding difficulties. The drugs used by the pregnant mother, her nutrition, her endocrine status, emotional life, and activity level may very likely contribute to the shaping of the physical status, the behavior patterns, and the postnatal progress of the child.

The Fels Institute workers have found that if the mother undergoes severe emotional stresses during pregnancy, especially during the latter part of pregnancy, her child will be born as, and develop as, a hyperactive, irritable, squirming infant who cries for his feeding every two or three hours instead of sleeping through the four-hour interval between feedings. The irritability of such infants involves the control of the gastrointestinal tract, causing emptying of the bowel at frequent intervals, as well as regurgitation of food. As Sontag puts it:

He is to all intents and purposes a neurotic infant when he is born—the result of an unsatisfactory fetal environment. In this instance he has not had to wait until childhood for a bad home situation or other cause to make him neurotic. It has been done for him before he has even seen the light of day (Sontag, 1944, pages 1–5).

Greenacre (1945) has suggested that the evidence indicates the possible existence of preanxiety reactions in fetal life without, necessarily, any psychic content. She suggests that traumatic stimuli, such as sudden sounds, vibrations, umbilical-cord entanglements, and the like, may produce a predisposition to anxiety which, whether combined or not with constitutional and traumatizing birth experiences, might be an important determinant in producing the severity of any neurosis.

That the fetus is capable of being conditioned . . . has long been thought to be a possibility. The possibility has now been turned into a certainty. Spelt (1948) has shown that the fetus *in utero* during the last two months of pregnancy can be taught to respond to the secondary association of a primary original stimulus. . . .

These are important findings, for they indicate that the potentialities for conditioning and probably learning (the ability to increase the strength of any act through training) are already present in the unborn fetus, as well as the possibility of its acquiring certain habits of response while still in the womb.

Other environmental factors which may affect the prenatal development of the organism may be considered under the following eight headings: (I) physical agents, (II) nutritional effects, (III) drugs, (IV) infections, (V) maternal dysfunction; (VI) maternal sensitization, (VII) maternal age, (VIII) maternal parity.

I. *Physical Agents.* The fetus will respond to sounds originating outside the mother's body at the thirtieth week, when, for example, a doorbell buzzer is held opposite its head (Sontag and Richards, 1938). Under such conditions the fetal responses are of a convulsive nature. The startle reflex is easily elicited. It has been found that very slight tapping upon the amnion at the time of hysterectomy under local anesthesia will result in quick fetal movements at a much earlier period in prenatal life (Windle, 1940, page 189). Tapping indirectly, as upon the side of a bathtub in which a pregnant woman was lying, induced a sudden jump on the part of the fetus thirty-one days before it was born. Orchestral or piano music or the vibration of a washing machine, during the last two months of pregnancy, resulted in marked increase in fetal activity. It is now known that the human fetus *in utero* is capable of being stimulated by, and responding to, a wide range of tones (Bernard and Sontag, 1947).

It is believed that the ability to receive stimuli originating within the organism, the proprioceptive sense, is developed very early in the fetus, and that muscle-joint responses are capable of being produced not only by proprioceptive but also by stimuli originating outside the organism (exteroceptive stimulation) (Windle, 1940, page 186). Differences in pressure *in utero*, whether induced through internal or external forces; differences in position, umbilical-cord entanglements, and similar factors may more or less adversely affect the development of the organism. Deformity may be caused by faulty position, mechanical shaking, temperature changes; asymmetry of the head may be produced by pressure of the head downward upon the thorax; wryneck (torticollis) has been observed, and pressure atrophy of the skin indicates the kind of continuous stimulation to which the fetus may be exposed.

Exposure to massive doses of x-rays within the first two months of pregnancy will, in many cases, produce abortion of the embryo (Goldstein and Wexler, 1931). Where abortion does not follow, serious injury has been found to result in a large percentage of cases. Thus, Murphy (1929) found that in a series of 74 recorded cases of therapeutic maternal irradiation, there were only 36 normal children born; there were 23 imbeciles with heads of abnormal size and 15 offspring otherwise malformed or diseased. In other words, 51.3% of the children were abnormal.

A series of experiences which may seriously affect the fetus is the process of birth itself. The severity of the birth process as measured by length and difficulty of labor, presentation, forceps delivery, primiparity, and similar factors is highly correlated with nutritional disturbances in the infant. A large proportion of such infants develop condensations of bone which show in x-rays of one-month-old infants in the form of fine white striae in the tarsal bones of the foot. Sontag and Harris (1938) conclude that these striae "are the result of disturbances in growth produced by the process of birth itself and influenced by such factors as maternal health and nutrition." They write:

> We believe that shock of birth is an important factor and that it is determined by the severity of the birth process plus the physical condition of the infant. We consider the mechanism comparable to that involved when striae are laid down in the long bones of growing children as a result of a surgical procedure or of a severe illness.

Greenacre has already been quoted to the effect that in the process of birth:

> where there has been considerable disproportion between an increased sensory stimulation and a limited motor discharge over a period of time such tension may conceivably be incorporated into the working balance of the individual and become temporarily or permanently a characteristic of his makeup.

Greenacre adds:

> where this is true, a sudden increase or decrease in the established tension level of the individual contributes to symptoms of anxiety. There is, however, in each individual, a unique primary organization and level of tension that is determined, in some measure, by the birth experience, furnishing an important element in the patterning of the drive and energy distribution of that individual (1945).

It may be that the trauma of birth is not experienced as a trauma by all fetuses; there is good evidence that it is so experienced by some. In these latter cases the experience may, to a more or less important extent, influence the later psychic development of the organism.

Physical agents which may be operative before or at birth to influence the subsequent health of infant and child are such factors as abnormal physical or instrumental delivery. Injury sustained by the fetus by these means may be crippling for life. Apart from purely physical injuries, permanent damage may be done to the mental faculties. In the New York State Schools for Mental Defectives, Malzberg (1950) has calculated that approximately 6% of all first admissions are due to injuries sustained at birth.

II. *Nutritional Effects.*   From the standpoint of the physical growth and development of the organism, it is known that such environmental factors as are produced by the mother's nutrition and occupation during all stages of pregnancy, her health, general hygiene, and sanitation can affect the development of the fetus (Sanders, 1934; Warkany, 1947). These conditions generally reflect the socioeconomic status or the nutritional status of the mother. Festuses and infants of mothers of low socioeconomic status are smaller and have a higher mortality rate than those of mothers of higher socioeconomic status. In itself small size is not necessarily a handicap, but in many cases it is a symptom of basic organic deficiencies which will play an important role in the later developmental history of the organism. Children who may otherwise appear to be normal will usually exhibit evidences of deficient intrauterine environment in the form of radio-opaque white striae which may be seen in the tarsal bones by the end of the first postnatal month (Sontag and Harris, 1938). These striae, corresponding to the lines of retarded growth seen in the long bones of older children and adults and caused by periods of prolonged illness, indicate that disturbances in nutrition, from whatever cause, during prenatal life are capable of inscribing their effects very substantially upon the structure of the developing organism.

Experiments reported by Warkany (1947) suggest that maternal nutrition in the early stages of fetal growth is a decisive factor in the production of certain physical abnormalities. It is not at present clear how the damage is done, but the evidence strongly indicates that it is owing to a lack of certain vitamins or proteins, or to some complex toxic disturbance occasioned by the mother's state of malnutrition. Recent studies indicate that emotional stress may severely disturb the nutritional economy of the individual (Sieve, 1949). In the pregnant mother malnutrition so induced may seriously affect the development of the fetus.

Murphy (1947) found that the fetuses of pregnant women suffering from renal hypertension and albuminuria showed no more serious defects than fetuses of a random sample of pregnant women. He did, however, find that diets deficient in calcium, phosphorus, and vitamins B, C, and D were common in pregnant women with a high frequency of malformed fetuses. Fetal rickets as a consequence of the depletion of the mineral reserves of starved mothers is a well-known phenomenon. It is also known that vitamin D deficiency during pregnancy predisposes the child to early rickets (M'Gonigle and Kirby, 1936).

Ebbs and his co-workers (1942) and Tisdall (1945) have demonstrated the substantive importance of an adequate maternal diet during pregnancy for the health of the infant and the adult it grows to be—*if* it survives to be an adult. An important point which should be underscored here is that not one of the 120 women in the poor-diet group studied by these investigators showed the slightest sign of any deficiency diseases. As these workers found, and as Burke and his co-workers (1943) found in an independent investigation, when nutrition during pregnancy is inadequate the fetus suffers more than the mother. If the mother's diet is good during pregnancy, then the infant is usually in excellent condition at birth. In Ebbs' Canadian study 120 pregnant women on a poor diet were compared with 90 pregnant women of the same socioeconomic status whose diet had been made good. In every way the mothers and their offspring who were on a good diet did better than the mothers and their offspring who were on a poor diet.

The facts set out in Table 1 are striking. They show that a diet which was inadequate, although good enough not to produce any recognizable clinical conditions in the mother, seriously interfered with the efficiency of the pregnant mother but affected the fetus more than it did her.

These findings were abundantly confirmed by the group of workers at Harvard (Burke *et al.*, 1943). In their study, carried out on 216 mothers and their infants during 1930–1941, they found that every stillborn, every infant dying during the first few days after birth, with one exception (the majority with congenital defects) all prematures, and all functionally immature infants were born to mothers who had had inadequate diets during pregnancy. The effects of maternal malnutrition upon the infant were very evident in babies born in Europe during World War II. Birth weight and length of infant decreased (Smith, 1947); premature births and stillbirths increased (Antonov, 1947), as did cases of severe rickets, severe anemais, and tuberculosis (Heseltine, 1948). Where the food intake was rigidily and scientifically controlled, as in England, the health of children improved. Unfortunately, in other countries food shortages were not so intelligently handled. The fact that well-nourished mothers tend to have well-nourished babies (Beilly and Kurland, 1945), and poorly nourished mothers, poorly nourished babies (Ebbs *et al.*,

1942; Burke *et al.*, 1943), as well as all the evidence known to us, indicates, as Macy (1946) has said, "that the well-being of the child before and after birth is influenced by the nutrition of the mother before and at the time of conception, and by the adequacy of her diet during pregnancy."

Table 1

		DIET	
		Poor	*Good*
Prenatal maternal record	*Poor-Bad*	36.0%	9.0%
Condition during labor	*Poor-Bad*	24.0%	3.0%
Duration of the first stage of labor	*Primapara*	20.3 hours	11.1 hours
	Multipara	15.2 hours	9.5 hours
Convalescence	*Poor-Bad*	11.5%	3.5%
Record of babies during first two weeks	*Poor-Bad*	14.0%	0.0%
ILLNESS OF BABIES DURING FIRST SIX MONTHS			
Frequent colds		21.0%	4.7%
Bronchitis		4.2%	1.5%
Pneumonia		5.5%	1.5%
Rickets		5.5%	0.0%
Tetany		4.2%	0.0%
Dystrophy		7.0%	1.5%
Anemia		25.0%	9.4%
Deaths		3.0%	0.0%
MISCARRIAGES AND INFANT DEATHS			
Miscarriages		7.0%	0.0%
Stillbirths		4.0%	0.0%
Deaths:			
Pneumonia		2.0%	0.0%
Prematurity		1.0%	0.0%
Prematures		9.0%	2.0%

On the actual contributory side one can say that not only must great care be taken to see to it that the pregnant mother's diet is an optimum one but also that her meals are properly spaced. The evidence (Tompkins, 1948) indicates that six small meals rather than two or three large ones daily tend to reduce or eliminate the severe nausea and vomiting of early pregnancy and to eliminate fatigue and other untoward symptoms.

We may conclude this section on nutrition with the words of a distinguished student of the subject, H. D. Kruse (1950), to the effect that many environmental factors, inside as well as outside the body,

exert influences upon nutrition which in turn reflect in health and welfare. In this relationship nutrition is seen to signalize the influence of
environment on health and welfare and to occupy a key and paramount
position as the crucial medium between them.

In connection with the nutrition of the fetus, it should be added
here that the fetus swallows amniotic fluid at least as early as the fifth
month, and though its nutritional value may under ordinary circumstances
be slight, significant changes in its composition may affect the fetus. By
artificially sweetening the amniotic fluid, it has been possible to induce
the fetus to swallow more actively, thus reducing the girth and other unpleasant symptoms of polyhydramnios (excessive amniotic fluid) in the
pregnant mother (De Snoo, 1937). Saccharine was subsequently demonstrated in the umbilical vein blood and in the first urine of these infants.
Methylene blue injected with the saccharine appeared in the urine of
the hydramniotic mothers, at times coinciding with increased fetal activity. It was concluded that the fetus spends most of its time in sleep
and that, becoming wakeful, it begins to move and drink the sweet
amniotic fluid.

Swallowing and gastrointestinal activity in the fetus have been demonstrated by many other means (Windle, 1940, page 101). The whole
gastrointestinal system appears to be prepared and ready to function
quite early in fetal life. That the fetal gastrointestinal tract may be
seriously disturbed as a result of severe emotional distress experienced
by the pregnant mother has already been noted. There may be other
conditions which may produce similar effects, but this in an area of fetal
physiology concerning which we know very little.

III. *Drugs.* Drugs taken by the pregnant mother may seriously
affect the fetus. Many cases of congenital deafness have been traced to
the mother's use of quinine for malaria during pregnancy. Morphinism
has been reported in the infants of mothers who were morphine addicts.
Inhalation of amyl nitrite by the mother for a few seconds induced an
increase in fetal heart rate, beginning during the third minute following
the mother's inhalation. Subsequent inhalations produced a diphasic
(excitor-depressor) response (Rech, 1931, 1933; Sontag and Richards,
1938).

The obstetrical practice of dosing the pregnant mother with barbi-
turates and similar drugs prior to delivery may so overload the fetal
blood stream as to produce asphyxiation in the fetus at birth, with either
permanent brain damage or subtle damage of such a kind as to lead to
mental impairment. Fortunately, the trend today is away from heavy
sedation.

It is known that a barbiturate derivative such as "sodium seconal,"
usually prescribed as a sedative, when given to the pregnant mother will
pass into the blood stream of the fetus and cause a cortical electrical de-

pression in its brain waves which can be measured at, and persists for some time after, birth (Hughes *et al.*, 1948).

. . . . .

Is there any evidence that the pregnant mother's smoking affects the fetus? There is. It has been found that the smoking of one cigarette generally produced an increase in the heart rate, sometimes a decrease in the heart rate. The maximum individual increase in fetal heart beats per minute was 39.6, the greatest drop 16.8 (Sontag and Wallace, 1935; Sontag and Richards, 1938). The maximum effect is observed between the eighth and twelfth minutes after the cigarette, and the cardiovascular response is more marked after the eighth month. It is quite possible that the products of tobacco may adversely affect not only the heart of the fetus but its whole cardiovascular system, not to mention the possibility of many other organs. This is a subject upon which we need more research. At the present time we have no definite evidence that the mother's intake of tobacco smoke actually harms the fetus. This is a question which further research alone can settle.

IV. *Infections.* Some virus and bacterial diseases can be transmitted from pregnant mother to fetus, with considerable damage to the latter. Rubella (German measles) is an example of a virus disease which, contracted by the mother in early pregnancy, may produce cataract and deafness with mental defect (Gregg, 1941).

Swan (1948) has shown that if the mother contracts rubella during the first four months of pregnancy she has a three to one chance of giving birth to a congenitally defective child. Equine encephalomyelitis, fortunately very rare, is another virus disease which can cause changes in the fetus which produce idiocy. Smallpox, chickenpox, measles, mumps, scarlet fever, erysipelas, and recurrent fever have long been known to be transmissible from mother to fetus (Goodpasture, 1942). There is also good experimental evidence indicating that the virus of *influenza A* can produce serious deformities in the developing embryo (Hamburger and Habel, 1947). The bacterium of congenital syphilis, *Treponema pallidum*, can actually enter the embryo. If this happens, miscarriage occurs (Dippel, 1945). If the bacterium enters at a later fetal age, the child is born with signs of congenital syphilis, or the disease may not show itself till later, as congenital paresis. Tuberculosis is also transmissible to the fetus from the mother by means of the *Bacillum tuberculosis*. The fetal death rate from tuberculosis is high, while those infants who are born with the disease usually die within the first year (Elizadale and Latienda, 1943). Malarial parasites are known to be transmissible from mother to fetus. Protozoal parasites, such as *Toxoplasma*, can be transmitted from mother to fetus and produce such conditions as meningoencephalomyelitis, microphthalmos, bilateral choreoretinitis, hydrocephalus, microcephalus, convulsions, and idiocy or mental retardation. Malignant melanoma has been transmitted by mother to fetus (Holland, 1949). Retrolental fibroplasia (Terry, 1943, 1945), or, as it is sometimes called, congenital encephalo-ophthalmic dysplasia (Krause, 1946; Ingalls, 1948; Owens and Owens, 1949), is a condition in which the fetus usually prematurely born, exhibits a retrolental mass, often with secondary glaucoma and cataract, and recurrent retinal and vitreous hemorrhages. Microphthalmos and strabismus is common. The cause is unknown, but the condition probably develops as a result of changes during the sixth and seventh months of pregnancy. These changes are almost certainly due to maternal environmental conditions. Unfortunately, what the precise nature of these may be is at present unknown.

V. *Maternal Dysfunction.* By maternal dysfunction is meant noninfectious functional disease in the pregnant mother. Such disorders in the mother may seriously affect the development of the fetus. Pregnant women suffering from hypertensive disease (high blood pressure) show a very high rate both of fetal loss and of maternal mortality, as well as of other serious conditions. Chesley and Annetto (1947) have reported that in 301 pregnancies in 218 women with essential hypertension (disease due to no known cause), the gross fetal loss in the first hypertensive pregnancy reached the staggeringly high figure of 38% and increased with the increase in blood pressure. There were thirteen maternal deaths, or a total of 4.3%, some 200 times higher than occurs in general obstetrical practice. Gasper (1945) found that out of 49 deliveries in 45 pregnant diabetics there were 19 stillbirths and 6 neonatal deaths, in other words a fetal mortality rate of 51%!

VI. *Maternal Sensitization.* In instances in which the genotype of mother and fetus differ in the substances borne on the surfaces of the red blood corpuscles, the mother may become sensitized and produce antibodies inimical to fetal development. This usually results in causing anemia at a relatively late fetal age. The Rh incompatibilities constitute a well-known example of this. When the blood of the rhesus monkey is injected into rabbits or guinea pigs, a special serum is obtained. The serum will "clump" the blood of about 85% of all white persons. The factor in the blood which makes it clump in response to the serum is the Rh factor. Persons who have this type of blood are said to be Rh positive. Persons who do not are Rh negative. The exact way in which the Rh factor is inherited is extremely complicated. Three distinct Rh factors are known, and at least six major genes are involved. These result in twenty-one combinations of genotypes which produce eight Rh blood types.

Understanding how the Rh factor operates and how it is inherited is extremely important in biology and medicine. And the practical implications for human health are great.

When a woman who is Rh negative marries a man who is Rh positive, the first-born child of such a marriage is usually normal. However, during following pregnancies the fetus may be lost by miscarriage. Or it may be born in such an anemic and jaundiced state that it lives only a few hours after birth. The infant usually dies from a disease called erythroblastosis. The name means that the red blood corpuscles—the erythrocytes—have been subject to wholesale destruction.

The disease is caused by the fact that the fetus has inherited an Rh positive gene from its father. The fetus produces Rh positive substances called antigens in its blood. These substances pass through the placenta into the mother's blood, where the antigens stimulate the production of large numbers of antibodies. These antibodies in turn pass through the placenta into the blood system of the fetus. There they start destroying the red blood corpuscles of the fetus.

Fortunately this disease does not occur as often as the facts of heredity might lead us to expect. Erythroblastosis takes place in about one out of every two hundred pregnancies. Actually, about one in twelve pregnancies involve an Rh negative mother carrying an Rh positive fetus. Therefore, in theory we should have children suffering from erythroblastosis born in one out of twelve instead of one out of two hundred pregnancies. If we omit firstborn children—who are seldom affected—this figure would work out to one in seventeen or eighteen pregnancies.

This fortunate discrepancy may be caused by the fact that in many cases the antigens from the fetus may not pass through the placenta. In other cases some mothers may not respond to the actions of the antigens from the fetus. And there is also a possibility that the chemical incompatibility between the blood of the mother and that of the unborn child may result in other harmful effects than the ones commonly expected.

Recent research indicates that mental deficiency may be caused by a lack of oxygen in the developing brain. Such an oxygen lack could result from the destruction of the oxygen-carrying red blood corpuscles in the absence of the Rh factor. Thus, if the brain of the fetus is deprived of oxygen during an important stage of its development, the brain may be permanently damaged. This may partly explain how mentally deficient children sometimes occur in families in which there is no previous record of mental deficiency.

Understanding the importance of the Rh factor is of great practical importance. Every woman planning marriage should consult her physician to find out the Rh types both of herself and of her prospective husband. There are various ways in which the evil effects of clashing Rh factors may be partially averted if doctors know about them beforehand.

Endocrine disturbances in the mother may affect the development of the fetus in many ways, but our knowledge of this subject is at present very meager. It is known that in diabetic mothers the fetus grows very rapidly, owing possibly to her excessive pituitary secretion. The fetus may reach the average birth weight of the newborn long before it reaches term, and thus present considerable obstetrical difficulty. It is of interest to note that the birth weights of babies whose mothers subsequently develop diabetes are greater than the average normal birth weight (Barns and Morgans, 1948). It is quite possible that a certain proportion of such mothers are supported relatively free of diabetes during pregnancy by the insulin secretion of the fetus. It has already been noted that the mortality rates of fetuses and infants of diabetic mothers are extremely high (Gaspar, 1945).

VII. *Maternal Age.* There is a high correlation between age of mother and maldevelopment of the fetus. The cause of this is obscure. Half the known cases of Mongolism were born to mothers of thirty-eight years of age or more (Penrose, 1949; Malzberg, 1950). Congenital hydrocephalus is also significantly correlated with late maternal age. Indeed, statistically speaking, abnormal conditions appear with significantly higher frequency in the infant of the older mother (Kuder and Johnson, 1944) than in any other group. The incidence of two-egg twinning also increases with maternal age. The evidence is now fairly complete that infant and maternal mortality rates, prematurity, stillbirths, and miscarriage rates are highly correlated with age of mother (Montagu, 1946). The optimum period for childbearing seems to lie between the years of twenty-three and twenty-nine. Before twenty-three years of age, on the average, the younger the mother—and after twenty-nine years of age, the older the mother—the higher are the maternal and infant mortality rates. In the younger mothers the responsible factor appears to be inadequate development of the reproductive system. In the older mothers the progressive decline in the functions of that system is almost certainly responsible. Since these functions are largely endocrine in nature, it is likely that in some cases the fetus is adversely affected developmentally.

VIII. *Parity* (number of previous pregnancies of mother). There is evidence that first-born children, as well as those born at the end of a long series of pregnancies, are less viable than those born in between, irrespective of maternal age. Fetal malformations are slightly more common in the children of mothers having their first pregnancies (primiparae) than in those of the second and third. It is known that disturbances due to sensitization become more marked with increasing age of the mother, but the reason for this is at present unknown.

It should be remembered that these are statistical findings, and that there are plenty of first-born and last-born children, as well as children who were born well after their mother's thirty-eighth birthday, who are in every way perfectly healthy. . . .

The question has been asked whether some children from birth are more likely than others to find the achievement of healthy personality development difficult. Some of the facts already mentioned in the preceding pages should make it quite clear that the answer to this question is in the affirmative.

Excluding physical malformations from our discussion in the present connection, the indications are that a child which as a fetus was traumatized by such factors as have already been discussed is likely to find the achievement of healthy personality development more difficult, other things being equal, than a child who as a fetus was not so traumatized. Some children, as Sontag has pointed out, are born "neurotic" as a result of their intrauterine experiences.

The "neurotic" newborn is generally hyperactive, irritable, restless, squirming, a crier, and a feeding problem. It is interesting to note that in those cases in which the evidence for the birth trauma is strong, as in children who have had to be instrumentally delivered, some 50% of such children at school age exhibited general hyperactivity in the form of irritability, restlessness, and distractibility, as compared to only 25% who showed such hyperactivity but were spontaneously born (Wile and Davis, 1941). Also significant in this connection is the "prematurity syndrome" exhibited by prematurely born children. In the nursery age group prematurely born children exhibit a significantly higher sensory acuity than term children, and in comparison are somewhat retarded in lingual and manual motor control, and in postural and locomotor control. Control of bowel and bladder sphincters is achieved later and with difficulty; the attention span is short, such children being highly emotional, jumpy, anxious, and usually shy (Shirley, 1939; Hirschl *et al.*, 1948). Furthermore, prematurely born children show a significantly higher incidence of nasopharyngeal and respiratory infections, especially during the first year. Behavior disorders, especially with regard to feeding, are more frequent in premature infants (Drillien, 1947, 1948).

REFERENCES

ANTONOV, A. N., "Children Born During the Siege of Leningrad in 1942," *J. Pediat.*, 50, 250–259 (1947).

BARNS, H. H. F., AND MORGANS, M. E., "Prediabetic Pregnancy," *J. Obst. & Gynec. Brit. Emp.*, 55, 449–454 (1948).

BEILLY, J. S., AND KURLAND, I. I., "Relationship of Maternal Weight Gain and Weight of Newborn Infant," *Am. J. Obst. & Gynec.*, 50, 202–206 (1945).

BERNARD, J., AND SONTAG, L. W., "Fetal Reactivity to Fetal Stimulation: A Preliminary Report," *J. Genet. Psychol.*, 70, 205–210 (1947).

BRYANT, E. R., "Heredity and Length of Gestation," *J. Hered.*, 24, 339 (1943).

BURKE, B. S., BEAL, V. A., KIRKWOOD, S. B., AND STUART, H. C., "Nutrition Studies During Pregnancy," *Am. J. Obst. & Gynec.*, 46, 38–52 (1943).

CHESLEY, L. C., AND ANNETTO, J. E., "Pregnancy in the Patient with Hypertensive Disease," *Am. J. Obst. & Gynec.*, 53, 372–381 (1947).

DAHLBERG, C., "Environment, Inheritance and Random Variation with Special Reference to Investigations on Twins," *Acta Genetica et Statistica Medica,* 1, 104–114 (1948).

DE SNOO, K., "Das Trinkende Kind im Uterus," *Monatschrift fur Geburtshulfe und Gynekologie,* 105, 88–97 (1937).

DIPPEL, A. L., "The Relationship of Congenital Syphilis to Abortion and Miscarriage, and the Mechanism of Intrauterine Protection," *Am. J. Obst. & Gynec.*, 47, 369–379 (1945).

DRILLIEN, M. C., "Studies in Prematurity, Stillbirth and Neonatal Death, Factors Affecting Birth-Weight and Outcome; Delivery and Its Hazards," *J. Obst. & Gynaec. Brit. Emp.*, 54, 300–323, 443–468 (1947).

DRILLIEN, M. C., "Studies in Prematurity; Development and Progress of Prematurely Born Child in Pre-School Period," *Arch. Dis. Childhood,* 23, 69–83 (1948).

EBBS, J. H. BROWN, A., TISDALL, F. F. MOYLE, W. J., AND BELL, M., "The Influence of Improved Prenatal Nutrition upon the Infant," *Canad. M.A.J.,* 46, 6–8 (1942).

EBBS, J. H., TISDALL, F. F., AND SCOTT, W. A., "The Influence of Prenatal Diet on the Mother and Child," *The Milbank Memorial Fund Quarterly,* 20, 35–36 (1942).

ELIZALDE, P. I., AND I. LATIENDA Y RAMAN, "Tuberculosis Prenatal," *Arch. Soc. argent. anat. Norm. y. Pat.*, 5, 576–596 (1943).

EVANS, R. D., "Quantitative Inferences Concerning the Genetic Effects of Radiation on Human Beings," *Science,* 109, 299–304 (1949).

GASPAR, J. L., "Diabetes Mellitus and Pregnancy," *West. J. Surg.*, 53, 21 (1945).

GATES, R. R., *Human Genetics* (New York: Macmillan, 1946), 2 vols.

GOLDSTEIN, I., AND WEXLER, D., "Rosette Formation in the Eyes of Irradiated Human Embryos," *Arch. Ophth.*, 5, 591 (1931).

GOODPASTURE, E. W., "Virus Infection of the Mammalian Fetus," *Science,* 99, 391–396 (1942).

GREENACRE, P., "The Biological Economy of Birth," *The Psychoanalytic Study of the Child,* ed. O. Fenichel *et al.* (New York: International Universities Press), 1, 31–51 (1945).

GREGG, N. MC A., "Congenital Cataract Following German Measles," *Tr. Ophth. Soc. Australia,* 3, 35 (1941).

HAMBURGER, V., AND HABEL, K., "Teratogenic and Lethal Effects of Influenza-A and Mumps Viruses on Early Chick Embryos," *Proc. Soc. Exper. Biol. & Med.*, 66, 608 (1947).

HALLIDAY, J. L., *Psychosocial Medicine* (New York: W. W. Norton, 1948).

HARRIS, D. B., AND HARRIS, E. S., "A Study of Fetal Movements in Relation to Mother's Activity," *Human Biol.*, 18, 221–237 (1946).

HESELTINE, M., "The Health and Welfare of the World's Children," *J. Am. Dietet. A.*, 24, 91–95 (1948).

HIRSCHL, D., LEVY, H., AND LITVAK, A. M., "The Physical and Mental Development of Premature Infants: A Statistical Survey with Five-Year Follow-up," *Arch. Pediat.*, 65, 648–653 (1948).

HOLLAND, E., "A Case of Transplacental Metastasis of Malignant Melanoma from Mother to Foetus," *J. Obst. & Gynaec. Brit. Emp.,* 56, 529 (1949).

HUGHES, J. G., EHMANN, B., AND BROWN, U. A., "Electroencephalography of the Newborn," *Am. J. Dis. Child,* 76, 626–633 (1948).

INGALLS, T. H., "Congenital Encephalo-ophthalmic Dysplasia; Epidemiologic Implications," *Pediatrics,* 1, 315 (1948).

KRAUSE, A. C., "Congenital Encephalo-ophthalmic Dysplasia," *Arch. Ophth.,* 36, 387–444 (1946).

KRUSE, H. D., "Malnutrition: Its Nature, Cause, and Significance," *Biological Foundation of Health Education* (New York: Columbia University Press, 1950), pp. 10–31.

KRUDER, K., AND JOHNSON, D. G., "The Elderly Primipara," *Am. J. Obst. & Gynec.,* 47, 794–807 (1944).

MACY, I. G., *The Science of Nutrition* (New York: Nutrition Foundation, 1946).

M'GONIGLE, G. C. M., AND KIRBY, J., *Poverty and Public Health* (London: Gollancz, 1936).

MALZBERG, B., "Some Statistical Aspects of Mongolism," *Am. J. Ment. Deficiency,* 54, 266–281 (1950).

MONTAGU, M. F. ASHLEY, *Adolescent Sterility* (Springfield, Ill.: C. C. Thomas, 1945).

MULLER, H. J., "Genetic Fundamentals: The Work of the Genes," *Genetics, Medicine and Man* (Ithaca, N.Y.: Cornell University Press, 1947), p. 16.

MURPHY, D. P., "The Outcome of 625 Pregnancies in Women Subjected to Pelvic Radium Roentgen Irradiation," *Am. J. Obst. & Gynec.,* 18, 179–187 (1929).

MURPHY, D. P., *Congenital Malformation,* 2nd. ed. (Philadelphia: University of Pennsylvania Press, 1947).

OWENS, W. C., AND OWENS, E. H., "Retrolental Fibroplasia in Premature Infants," (1) *Am. J. Ophth.,* 32, 1–21 (1949); (2) *ibid.,* 1631–1637.

PENROSE, L. S., *The Biology of Mental Defect* (London: Sidgwick & Jackson, 1949).

RECH, W., "Untersuchungen uber die Herstatigkeit des Fetus," *Archiv. fur Gynakologie,* Teil I, 145, 714–737 (1931); Teil II, 147, 8–94 (1931); Teil III, 154, 47–57 (1933).

SANDERS, B. S., *Environment and Growth* (Baltimore: Warwick & York, 1934).

SHIRLEY, M., "A Behavior Syndrome Characterizing Prematurely-Born Children," *Child Development,* 10, 115–128 (1939).

SIEVE, B. F., "Vitamins and Hormones in Nutrition. V: Emotional Upset and Trauma," *Am. J. Digest. Dis.,* 16, 14–25 (1949).

SMITH, G. A., "Effects of Maternal Undernutrition upon the Newborn Infant in Holland (1944–45)," *J. Pediat.,* 30, 229–243 (1947).

SONTAG, L. W., AND WALLACE, R. F., "The Effect of Cigarette Smoking During Pregnancy upon the Fetal Heart Rate," *Am. J. Obst. & Gynec.,* 29, 3–8 (1935).

SONTAG, L. W., AND HARRIS, L. M., "Evidence of Disturbed Prenatal and Neonatal Growth in Bones of Infants Aged One Month," *Am. J. Dis. Child.,* 56, 1248–1255 (1938).

SONTAG, L. W., AND RICHARDS, T. W., "Studies in Fetal Behavior," *Monographs of the Society for Research in Child Development,* 3, x–72 (1938).

SONTAG, L. W., "The Significance of Fetal Environmental Differences," *Am. J. Obst. & Gynec,* 42, 996–1003 (1941).

SONTAG, L. W., "Differences in Modifiability of Fetal Behavior and Physiology," *Psychosomatic Medicine,* 6, 151–154 (1944).

SONTAG, L. W., "War and the Fetal Maternal Relationship," *Marriage and Family Living,* 6, 1–5 (1944).

SPUHLER, J. N., "On the Number of Genes in Man," *Science,* 10, 279–280 (1948).

SWAN, C., "Rubella in Pregnancy as an Aetiological Factor in Congenital Malformation, Stillbirth, Miscarriage and Abortion," *J. Obst. & Gynaec. Brit. Emp.,* 56, 341–363, 591–605 (1949).

TERRY, T. L., "Fibroplastic Overgrowth of Persistent Tunica Vasculosa Lentis in Premature Infants; Etiologic Factors," *Arch. Ophth.,* 29, 36–38 (1943).

TERRY, T. L., "Retrolental Fibroplasia in Premature Infants; Further Studies in Fibroplastic Overgrowth of Persistent Tunica Vasculosa Lentis," *Arch. Ophth.,* 33, 203–208 (1945).

TISDALL, F. F., "The Role of Nutrition in Preventive Medicine," *The Milbank Memorial Fund Quarterly,* 23, 1–15 (1945).

TOMPKINS, W. T., "The Clinical Significance of Nutritional Deficiencies in Pregnancy," *Bull. New York Acad. Med.,* 24, 376–388 (1948).

WARKANY, J., "Etiology of Congenital Malformations," *Advances in Pediatrics* (New York: Interscience Publishers, 1947), 2, 1.

WILE, I. S., AND DAVIS, R., "The Relation of Birth to Behavior," *Am. J. Orthopsychiat.,* 11, 320–324 (1941).

WINDLE, W. F., *Physiology of the Fetus* (Philadelphia: Saunders, 1940).

16. WHAT ARE SOME OF THE LAWS WHICH GOVERN GROWTH?

MARIAN E. BRECKENRIDGE AND E. LEE VINCENT

The child is not a miniature adult. His brain and optic nerve are not developed. He cannot see as well as an adult, and his muscular and bone growth is not complete. Regardless of how much training and practice he gets, the average three-year-old cannot read or write, ride a bicycle or swim, do arithmetic, whip up a soufflé, or play the violin. It goes without saying that it may be damaging to the child to expect behavior at a particular age level which he is not physically

Reprinted from *Child Development* (W. B. Saunders Company, 1955), pp. 5–16, by permission of the authors and publisher.

or intellectually able to perform. Conversely, it may be damaging to discourage learning when he is "ready" for it.

Experiments have shown that children specially trained much earlier than usual in such skills as walking, climbing stairs, reading, and writing, master these skills at about the same age as ordinary children. For example, since most children are physically and psychologically mature enough to learn to read at the age of six, the average child of four who gets special reading lessons will take two years to learn to read, while a six-year-old will learn in a few weeks.

Breckenridge and Vincent present here some laws which govern human growth and development—laws which control the "readiness" for learning social and intellectual skills.

GROWTH IS BOTH QUANTITATIVE AND QUALITATIVE

"Growth" includes two aspects of change. They are not interchangeable but, nevertheless, are inseparable. It is said that a child "grows" and "grows up." He "grows" in size; he "grows up" or matures in structure and function. In maturing he passes through successive changes, which indicate his progress. These indicators are called maturity indicators. Ultimately, as he has passed through each successive stage of growth he reaches the end point of this process, which is called maturity.

There are many illustrations of this maturing or "growing up" process which accompanies growth in size. The baby's digestive tract, for example, not only grows in size, but also changes in structure. This permits digestion of more complex foods and increases its efficiency in converting foods into simpler forms which the body can use. The child, therefore, can widen his experiences with foods as he grows, and this will in turn contribute to his physical well-being and his social development. The structure and functional efficiency of many of the internal organs change with development.

Younger children are not only smaller than older ones; they are also simpler organisms, both physically and psychologically. The young baby, for example, learns motor controls over his larger muscles first. Only gradually can he master such fine coordinations as are required for reading and writing. Reasoning too, in children of preschool age is, of necessity, relatively simple and uncomplicated. Only later, when his nervous system has developed more complex organization and when accumulated experience exists as a basis, can the child attempt more complex forms of reasoning.

Emotions are simpler, the younger the child. Babies feel things "with all of themselves," being completely joyous or completely miserable about rather simple things. Differentiation of structure and accumulation of experience produce more and more complex emotional reactions to more and more complicated situations. If we permit children to go on expressing "full-blast" emotions about simple, babyish things instead of growing into greater controls and more "civilized" responses to more "grown up" situations, we are not helping them to live up to their growth potentialities.

Some people, failing to understand this double aspect of growth, do not realize that children's intellectual capacity and character traits are essentially different from those of adults. We cannot without disaster expect the motor skills, intellectual complexities or character insights from children that we expect from adults, or from younger children that we expect from older children. They have simply not "grown up," any more than they have "grown."

These aspects of "growing up" are discussed later under the effect of maturation upon learning. We have many experiments to prove that children cannot learn what they are not ready through growth or maturity to learn.

GROWTH IS A CONTINUOUS AND ORDERLY PROCESS

Growth is a continuous process which moves with an urgency supplied from deep inner sources. We may well ask how the relatively helpless, unskilled, uncontrolled infant finally reaches a level of maturity at which he can meet the tests of life just discussed. The answer is that he does it by an orderly sequence of acquisitions. He will grow because of a strong impulse to grow which is inherent in the organism; and his growth will be orderly—the product of his innate gifts of inheritance, enhanced or modified by his experience.

This should comfort us, since we realize that we do not need to make him grow. He will do that anyway. Only severe neglect or abuse will seriously disrupt his growth. Because growth is continuous we must realize that what happens at one stage carries over into and influences the next and ensuing stages.

Even the seemingly sudden spurts in tempo of growth lead into and grow out of quieter, less dramatic periods. It may be possible that in the quieter periods the child is mobilizing his forces for ensuing spurts. Parents rightly celebrate the appearance of baby's first tooth, the first independent step in walking, or the first word spoken, the first evidence of reading ability, or the first "date" with a girl (or boy) in adolescence. Each of these noticeable changes is a sort of graduation from the school of preliminary developments. The first step in walking cannot be taken until a long chain of learnings in bodily control has preceded. This is also true of the first word spoken, the first evidence of successful adjustment to other children, or any other conspicuous event in growth.

Each of them is a milestone which marks progress in a long process.

Fortunately for students of child development these milestones appear in an orderly sequence. It is not difficult to chart the steps by which growth takes place or to describe the patterns which it follows. No child, for example, learns to walk without having first learned to stand, nor does any child speak clearly before he has passed through the babble stage of syllables in language. As Gesell [1] so delightfully puts it: Each child "sits before he stands; he babbles before he talks; he fabricates before he tells the truth; he draws a circle before he draws a square; he is selfish before he is altruistic; he is dependent on others before he achieves dependence on self." For the great mass of children, these patterns or stages of learning follow each other in so fixed a sequence, and parallel certain birthdays so consistently that standards of what to expect at each age have been set up.

THE TEMPO OF GROWTH IS NOT EVEN

These sequences of development do not move along in time at a steady pace. Maturity indicators do not appear at regular intervals. There are periods of accelerated growth and periods of decelerated growth. During infancy and the early preschool years growth moves swiftly and the maturity indicators of each of the various aspects of growth appear in rapid succession. During the later preschool and school years the rate of growth slackens. But this does not mean that significant changes are not taking place. Before puberty certain phases of growth become accelerated before they taper off to the adult level. Figure 1 illustrates the change in tempo of growth. It shows the growth profiles of height for a boy and demonstrates the rapid growth in infancy, the slower growth during the preschool and school years before pubescence, and the pubescent acceleration followed by the tapering off of growth during adolescence. Profile A shows the general trend of his growth; Profile B shows his growth rate during successive periods. This pattern, with the exception of the pubescent spurt, would be as evident in typical intelligence growth curves.

DIFFERENT ASPECTS OF GROWTH DEVELOP AT DIFFERENT RATES

Not all aspects of growth develop at the same rate at the same time; that is, they do not proceed along an even front. For example, parents often worry because children characteristically speak three to five words at twelve months of age, but in the next three or four months they seldom acquire new words and often even forget the ones they knew.

[1] A. L. Gesell and F. Ilg, *The Child from Five to Ten* (Harper Bros., 1943).

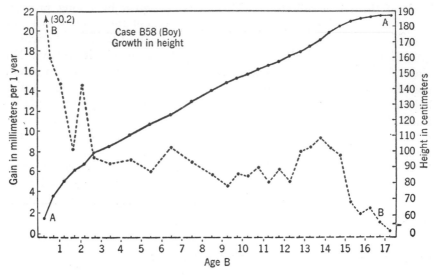

FIGURE 1.   GROWTH IN HEIGHT OF A BOY, EXPRESSED IN PROFILE A AS
HEIGHT AT SUCCESSIVE CHRONOLOGIC YEARS AND IN PROFILE B AS GROWTH
RATE DURING SUCCESSIVE PERIODS, ILLUSTRATES THE CHANGES IN TEMPO
OF GROWTH

From H. R. Stolz and L. M. Stolz, *Somatic Development of Adolescent Boys*
(New York: The Macmillan Company, 1951)

Language growth slows up for the time being because the child's physical energy and enthusiasm for learning are thoroughly occupied with
the thrills of upright locomotion. Development in general bodily skill
spurts ahead at this time, apparently leaving little growth energy (if we
may such a phrase) for language development. Similarly, school work
sometimes suffers a slump while children's growth energy is being expended on the rapid increase in height and weight characteristic of
pubescence. It is important to know which aspects of growth can be expected to absorb much of the child's capacity for growth at any given
time of his life. We do not now in our public schools, for example,
make provision for the fact that physical development proceeds rapidly
during pubescence. Academic loads are stepped up rather than reduced
in junior and senior high school, extracurricular activities, home work,
and rapidly increasing social interests frequently replace the extra hours
of sleep which rapid physical growth requires. It is slight wonder that
we have in this country so high a tuberculosis rate among adolescent
children.

Figure 2 shows how some of the different parts of the body develop
at different rates at given ages. We have no comparable charts to show

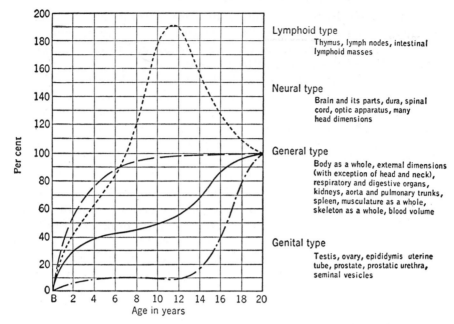

Lymphoid type
> Thymus, lymph nodes, intestinal lymphoid masses

Neural type
> Brain and its parts, dura, spinal cord, optic apparatus, many head dimensions

General type
> Body as a whole, external dimensions (with exception of head and neck), respiratory and digestive organs, kidneys, aorta and pulmonary trunks, spleen, musculature as a whole, skeleton as a whole, blood volume

Genital type
> Testis, ovary, epididymis uterine tube, prostate, prostatic urethra, seminal vesicles

FIGURE 2. A GRAPH SHOWING THE MAJOR TYPES OF POSTNATAL GROWTH OF THE VARIOUS PARTS AND ORGANS OF THE BODY. THE SEVERAL CURVES ARE DRAWN TO A COMMON SCALE BY COMPUTING THEIR VALUES AT SUCCESSIVE AGES IN TERMS OF THEIR TOTAL POSTNATAL INCREMENTS (TO TWENTY YEARS)

From R. E. Scammon and J. A. Harris, *The Measurement of Man* (Minneapolis: University of Minnesota Press, 1930)

tempo of growth in intellect and character. We can see that the nervous system develops rapidly in earlier years. This parallels rapid acquisition of control over the body, and rapid expansion of intellectual capacities. Children probably learn more new things in the first five years of life than in any comparable period during the rest of their lives. On the other hand, we can see that the most rapid development of the genital system occurs during pubescence. Certain definite social interests and emotional capacities increase concurrently or soon afterward.

BOTH RATE AND PATTERN OF GROWTH CAN BE MODIFIED BY CONDITIONS WITHIN AND WITHOUT THE BODY

Although the impulse to grow is strong through innate force and even though patterns are fairly definite for all children, both rate and exact pattern can be changed when the child's environment is not fulfilling the fundamental needs of the child. Nutrition, activity, rest, psychologic challenge, opportunity to learn, security in affection, an adequate and understanding discipline and many other circumstances are of great importance in determining how fast and to what extent the potentialities of the child will be realized.

Around the world there are children who have been so poorly fed during their growing years that they have been unable to achieve healthy growth. Psychologic deprivations are also producing damaged personalities. Physical and psychologic scars incurred by conditions during World War II, such as lack of food, separation of families, loss of parents, destruction of home and communities, have in many cases become permanent when the deprivations were very severe and of long duration. The resilience of the growing mind and body has its limitations if environmental conditions prove to be too unfavorable for growth. In addition to such conditions as those resulting from war or other crises there are also dramatic evidences of modification in the changes in growth produced by such things as lack of iodine in community drinking water, which results in an increase of cretinism (dwarfism due to inadequate thyroid secretion) in the population concerned. The disease called rickets, which results from deficiency in diet or sunshine or both, may leave permanent evidences on the body in the form of flat chests or deformed pelves, and crooked backs, all of which interfere with the efficient functioning of the body. Similarly, deficiencies in affection and security in childhood may leave permanent scars on the personality in the form of explosive tempers, "grudges," fears, and other severe handicaps to the adequate functioning of personality. Poor methods of teaching reading or other primary school subjects may leave a child with a resistance to all academic work.

On the other hand, if a child's inheritance is good, and if he has adequate diet, security in love, good teaching and other favorable circumstances he will flourish in his growth, and will develop in excellent health, with a keen intellect and a well-balanced and likable personality. We cannot, however, set up "ideal" environments, even if we wished to do so. Human nature has its weaknesses; germs exist in abundance; accidents will happen. Fortunately, the body and the personality have great resiliency. They can make up for temporary retardations, provided the disturbing factors are removed in time or the accidental damage is not too devastating. We must, in fact, consciously avoid an attempt to set up a too protected environment, since if the child is reared in early years in an aseptic (germ free) atmosphere he develops no immunity to life's ordinary germs; if he is protected and coddled too much he becomes what is known as a spoiled child; if he struggles for nothing he gains no moral strength.

EACH CHILD GROWS IN HIS OWN UNIQUE WAY

Some children are tall and some short, some slender, others stocky. Some are physically strong, others are weak; some are intellectually keen, others are dull. There are the energetic and the phlegmatic, the agile and the awkward, the courageous and the fearful, the outgoing and the ingoing in personality. Almost every trait measured by any scale scatters individuals along a distribution known as "the normal probability curve," or "the range of normal probability." Figures 3 and 4 show the idea of normal distribution of traits. We can see from this that there is a midpoint, or theoretical average. It is quite possible that no given person in any group would measure exactly at the theoretic average for his group in any given trait. The great mass of "average" people spread over a certain span of measurement called "the normal range," within which development or growth may be considered desirable. The extremes may or may not be undesirable. In weight measurements, for example, excessive overweight or underweight is considered detrimental to health at any age. On the other hand, on the "mental age" scale people are usually desirous of belonging in the most extreme upper brackets of accomplishment where one is referred to as in the "genius" class. There is some discussion in the literature, however, as to whether even in this trait it is not possible to rank too far from the average of the population to be understood easily by others or happily adjusted to them.

An example of how widely these differences vary within the same age range can be found in Meredith's [2] study of eighteen anthropometric measurements on Iowa City boys between birth and eighteen years in whom he noted wide individual differences. The lightest boy at eighteen

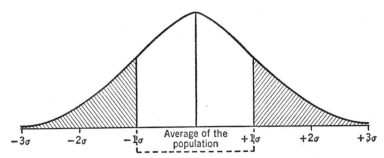

FIGURE 3. NORMAL PROBABILITY CURVE. RANGE WITHIN WHICH THE GREAT MASS OF "NORMAL" PEOPLE LIE. SHADED AREAS REPRESENT EXTREMES. IN EITHER DIRECTION

[2] H. V. Meredith, "The Rhythm of Physical Growth," *University of Iowa Studies, Child Welfare, 11* (3): 1935.

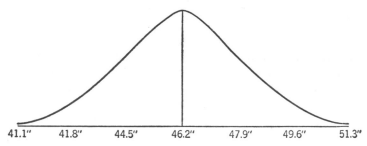

| 41.1" | 41.8" | 44.5" | 46.2" | 47.9" | 49.6" | 51.3" |

FIGURE 4.   NORMAL PROBABILITY CURVE OF HEIGHT IN INCHES FOR SIX-YEAR-OLD BOYS

Average and standard deviation taken from K. Simmons and T. W. Todd, "Growth of Well Children: Analysis of Stature and Weight 3 Months to 13 Years," *Growth*, 1938, Vol. 2, No. 2

years was no heavier than the heaviest boy at eight years. The lightest boy at eight years weighed hardly as much as the heaviest two-year-old. These, of course, represent extremes but are warnings to us in using chronologic age scales too rigidly in classifying children.

While all children pass through the sequence of maturity stages, some may omit some of the intermediate steps. For example, some children walk upright without creeping or crawling, even though most children crawl, creep, walk in sequence. Then again, a sequence may be disturbed because of a structural defect. Such may be the case of deaf children who sometimes learn to read and write before they learn to speak or understand spoken language, this being a reversal of the usual order of development.

Some children also differ in their rate of development, going through the sequential steps as expected but at a slower or faster rate than average children. Thus there are *slow growers* and *fast growers*. The period of adolescence initiated by the beginning of pubescent changes illustrates dramatically these differences. For some it begins early; for some it begins late. Stolz and Stolz [3] give a range of at least five and one-half years in the chronologic age at which adolescence began for the boys in the California Adolescent Study and at least four and one-half years at which it ended.

Thus one boy may be entering adolescence at age ten years while he is in the high fifth grade, while for an age peer classmate childhood may continue until he is fifteen and a half years old and in the low eleventh grade (p. 423).

There are also definite *differences between boys and girls.* Figure 5, representing growth in weight of boys and girls from three months to

[3] H. R. Stolz and L. M. Stolz, *Somatic Development of Adolescent Boys* (New York: The Macmillan Company, 1951).

seventeen years shows that boys generally exceed girls in weight in the early years and after fourteen years of age. In the early school years they are somewhat similar in weight, but between nine and fourteen years girls, because they mature earlier than boys and therefore pass through the pubescent spurt of growth earlier than boys, are temporarily heavier than boys. Within each sex, there is considerable difference in the ages at which children arrive at maturity.

There seems to be very little differences between boys and girls in general intellectual capacity, but there are certain definite differences in interests and behavior, as we shall see later. Whether these differences in interests and behavior are innate or a product of the way we rear children is not clear, but much depends upon which interest or which trait is under discussion.

Goodenough and Maurer [4] after a comparison of a number of types of tests of preschool children and test performances at later years found that in nearly all instances girls' scores showed a more consistent correlation between early and later tests than boys' scores. Thus girls showed

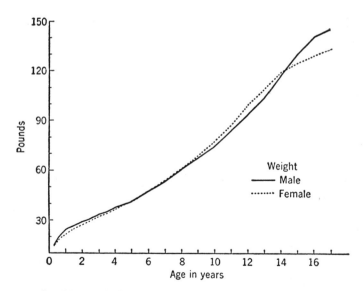

FIGURE 5.   CURVES SHOWING THE GROWTH IN WEIGHT OF BOYS AND GIRLS FROM THREE MONTHS TO SEVENTEEN YEARS

From K. Simmons, "The Brush Foundation Study of Child Growth and Development: II. Physical Growth and Development," *Monograph for the Society for Research in Child Development*, Vol. 9, No. 1

[4] F. L. Goodenough and K. M. Maurer, *The Mental Growth of Children from Two to Fourteen Years: A Study of the Predictive Value of the Minnesota Preschool Scale*, (Minneapolis: University of Minnesota Press, 1947).

a reliable tendency toward greater stabilization of performance on tests than boys in the early years. They discuss this by saying:

Although it is possible that sex difference represents an earlier stabilization of mental level in females than in males it is probably more reasonable to assume that better cooperation and greater docility in the test situations—characteristics in which a number of girls are likely to exceed boys—provide sufficient explanation for the differences found. Nevertheless, the other possibility is by no means excluded. Because of the theoretical significance of the problem further investigation is desirable.

We must understand these unique aspects of each individual child's growth if we are to treat children intelligently. A tall, slender child does not put on weight at the same rate, nor does he weigh as much for his height, as does a stocky child. Some parents create unnecessary feeding problems in their attempt to achieve "standard" weight gains. Certain intellectually fast growing children have the physical stamina and social maturity to enter school at five and one-half years of age. Other children of the same chronologic and mental ages will be quite unable physically or socially to stand the competition of other first graders. Some children seem "slow to catch on" in school for several years, yet prove later to be excellent students. Forcing the pace of growth at any stage will not produce good results in the long run, and may incur serious damage along the way. Forcing children into any pattern of growth which is not in harmony with their natural potentialities is likely to result in tragedy both for the child and for the misguided adult. Fathers, for example, should not try to make "go getters" out of sensitive, artistic boys; nor should Susie be compelled to try to make Phi Beta Kappa because her older sister did.

GROWTH IS COMPLEX. ALL OF ITS ASPECTS ARE CLOSELY INTERRELATED

The many failures in attempting to discover simple causal relationships in development speak for the fact that growth is an extremely complex process, the various aspects of which are intimately interrelated. It is impossible to understand the physical child without understanding him at the same time as a thinking and feeling child. It is likewise impossible to understand his mental development without a real knowledge of his physical body and its needs. There is a close relationship, for example, between his total adjustment to school and his emotions, his physical health and his intellectual adequacy. Such simple things as fatigue or hunger may influence his behavior. An emotional disturbance may contribute to difficulties in eating or sleeping. An illness may be an incubation period for a behavior problem. A physical defect may have been the starting point for certain attitudes and social adjustments.

It is important to an adolescent not to be too tall, too short or obese. It makes a difference in the total picture of the child whether he is energetic or phlegmatic. The posture of a child may express his physical well-being or the reverse, and also may reveal something of his attitudes. . . .

. . . . .

17. CHILD CARE AND THE GROWTH OF LOVE

JOHN BOWLBY

When the third session of the Social Commission of the United Nations decided to arrange for a study of homeless children, Dr. Bowlby was appointed by the World Health Organization to carry out the project. He surveyed the scientific literature dealing with children without mothers and journeyed to many countries, observing and discussing their problems. He found general agreement among persons and agencies having contact with large numbers of children that the mental health of children is tragically damaged by separation from their mothers.

Some of the immediately bad effects of deprivation on young children and some of the short-term after-effects have now been discussed, and note taken that those without training in mental health are apt either to deny the existence of such responses or to waive them aside as of no consequence. In this chapter, the tremendous weight of evidence will be reviewed which makes it clear that those who view these responses with concern, so far from crying wolf, are calling attention to matters of grave medical and social significance.

During the late 1930s, at least six independent workers were struck by the frequency with which children who committed numerous delinquencies, who seemed to have no feelings for anyone and were very difficult to treat, were found to have had grossly disturbed relationships with their mothers in their early years. Persistent stealing, violence, egotism, and sexual misdemeanors were among their less pleasant characteristics.

. . . . .

Selections reprinted from *Child Care and the Growth of Love*, edited by Margery Fry (Penguin Books Ltd., 1953), 33–49, by permission of the publisher.

Between 1937 and 1943 there were many papers on this subject, several of which originated independently and some of which were completed in ignorance of the work of others. The unanimity of their conclusions stamps their findings as true. With monotonous regularity each observer put his finger on the child's inability to make relationships as being the central feature from which all the other disturbances sprang, and on the history of long periods spent in an institution or, as in the case quoted, of the child's being shifted about from one foster-mother to another as being its cause. So similar are the observations and the conclusions—even the very words—that each might have written the others' papers:

The symptom complaints are of various types. They include, frequently, aggressive and sexual behaviour in early life, stealing, lying, often of the fantastic type, and, essentially, complaints variously expressed that indicate some lack of emotional response in the child. It is this lack of emotional response, this shallowness of feeling that explains the difficulty in modifying behaviour.

Early in the work a third group of girls was recognized who were asocial [*i.e.* unaware of obligations to others], but not obviously neurotic, and with whom no treatment methods seemed of any avail. Later it became clear that the feature common to them was an inability to make a real relationship with any member of the staff. There might seem to be a good contact, but it invariably proved to be superficial. . . . There might be protestations of interest and a boisterous show of affection, but there was little or no evidence of any real attachment having been made. In going over their previous history, this same feature was outstanding. . . . [These girls] have apparently had no opportunity to have a loving relationship in early childhood [and] seem to have little or no capacity to enter into an emotional relation with another person or with a group.

All the children [twenty-eight in number] present certain common symptoms of inadequate personality development chiefly related to an inability to give or receive affection; in other words, inability to relate the self to others. . . . The conclusion seems inescapable that infants reared in institutions undergo an isolation type of experience, with a resulting isolation type of personality.

Two special problems were referred to the ward from two child-placing agencies. One came from an agency [in which] there is a feeling that no attachment should be allowed to develop between the child and the boarding home, so that by the time the child is five years old, he has no attachment to anybody and no pattern of behaviour. . . . Another special group consisted of children placed in infancy [who] are given the best pediatric care . . . but have been deprived of social contacts and play materials. . . . These children are unable to accept love, because of their severe deprivation in the first three years. . . . They have no play pattern, cannot enter into group play and abuse other children. . . . They are overactive and distractible; they are completely confused about human relationships. . . . This type of child does not respond to the nursery group and continues overactive, aggressive and asocial.

"Imperviousness and a limited capacity for affective relationships" characterize children who have spent their early years in an institution. "Can it be that the absence of affective relationship in infancy made it difficult or even unnecessary for the institution children to participate later in positive emotional relationships . . . ?"

These communications came from across the Atlantic: meanwhile quite independent observations by Dr. Bowlby in London led to exactly the same conclusions:

Prolonged breaks [in the mother-child relationship] during the first three years of life leave a characteristic impression on the child's personality. Such children appear emotionally withdrawn and isolated. They fail to develop loving ties with other children or with adults and consequently have no friendships worth the name. It is true that they are sometimes sociable in a superficial sense, but if this is scrutinized we find that there are no feelings, no roots in these relationships. This, I think, more than anything else, is the cause of their hard-boiledness. Parents and school-teachers complain that nothing you say or do has any effect on the child. If you thrash him he cries for a bit, but there is no emotional response to being out of favour, such as is normal to the ordinary child. It appears to be of no essential consequence to these lost souls whether they are in favour or not. Since they are unable to make genuine emotional relations, the condition of relationship at a given moment lacks all significance for them. . . . During the last few years I have seen some sixteen cases of this affectionless type of persistent pilferer and in only two was a prolonged break absent. In all the others gross breaches of the mother-child relation had occurred during the first three years, and the child had become a persistent pilferer.

Since these early papers there have been several careful "retrospective studies," namely, studies made by specialists who were called upon to treat nervous symptoms and disturbances of behaviour, who by working back into the children's histories, unearthed the common factors of lack of care—caused either by their being in institutions, or being posted, like parcels, from one mother-figure to another.

One doctor in a large New York hospital had some 5,000 children under her care from 1935 to 1944. She found that from 5 per cent to 10 per cent of them showed the characteristics which have already been described.

There is an inability to love or feel guilty. There is no conscience. Their inability to enter into any relationship makes treatment or even education impossible. They have no idea of time, so that they cannot recall past experience and cannot benefit from past experience or be motivated to future goals. This lack of time concept is a striking feature in the defective organization of the personality structure. . . .

Ten of the children referred to were seen five years later. They "all remained infantile, unhappy, and affectionless and unable to adjust to children in the schoolroom or other group situation."

Dr. Bowlby, writing of the children he dealt with in London, described how in some of their histories it was possible to find how the child had reacted to some startling and painful happening. He laid especial emphasis on the tendency of these children to steal. Dividing all the cases he had seen at a child guidance clinic into those who had been reported as stealing and those who had not, he compared a group of forty-four thieves with a control group, similar in number, age, and sex, who although emotionally disturbed did not steal. The thieves were distinguished from the controls in two main ways. First, there were among them fourteen "affectionless characters," while there were none in the control group. Secondly, seventeen of the thieves had suffered complete and prolonged separation (six months or more) from their mothers or established foster-mothers during their first five years of life; only two of the controls had suffered similar separations. Neither of these differences can be accounted for by chance. Two further points of great importance were that the "affectionless characters" almost always had a history of separation, and that they were far more delinquent than any of the others.

The results showed that bad heredity was less frequent amongst the "affectionless" thieves than amongst the others: of the fourteen children who came into this class only three could be said to have had a bad heredity (i.e. parents or grandparents with serious psychological ill-health), but twelve of them had histories of separation from their mothers. Thus there can be no doubting that for the affectionless thief nurture not nature is to blame.

Dr. Bowlby concludes:

There is a very strong case indeed for believing that prolonged separation of a child from his mother (or mother substitute) during the first five years of life stands foremost among the causes of delinquent character development.

Among the cases described is one of a boy who was believed to have had a good relation to his mother until the age of eighteen months, but who was then in hospital for nine months, during which time visiting by his parents was forbidden. Other cases suggest that hospitalization and changes of mother-figure as late as the fourth year can have very destructive effects in producing the development of an affectionless psychopathic character given to persistent delinquent conduct and extremely difficult to treat.

Other retrospective studies touch on this problem. Thus the record of some 200 children under the age of twelve seen at a child-guidance clinic in London during the years 1942–6, whose troubles seemed to have been caused or aggravated by the war, showed that in one-third of the cases the trouble had been caused by evacuation. Almost all the difficult and long treatment cases were due to evacuation, not, it must be emphasized, to experience of bombing. No less than two-thirds of the children who presented problems after evacuation had been under the age of five when first evacuated. Since the number of young children evacuated in proportion to older ones was small, the figures make clear the extent to which it is especially the young child who is damaged by experiences of this kind.

Again, studies of adult patients have often led their authors to the conclusion that love deprivation is the cause of their psychological condition. Writing of hysterical patients, one doctor puts forward the view that

regardless of the nature of the individual's inborn tendencies, he will not develop hysteria unless he is subjected during childhood to situations causing him to crave affection.

Among such situations he lists the death of a parent and separation of child from parents. Another doctor who collected information on 530 prostitutes in Copenhagen, found that one-third of them had not been brought up at home, but had spent their childhood under troubled and shifting conditions.

Three per cent were brought up by close relations, 3 per cent were boarded out or sent to a home, 27 per cent were raised under combined conditions, partly in homes or almshouses, partly in institutions for the feeble-minded or epileptics, partly at home or with relatives.

Sometimes they had three or four different foster-homes during the course of their childhood. Seventeen per cent of the total were illegitimate.

The objection to all these restrospective studies is, of course, that they are concerned only with children who have developed badly and fail to take into account those who may have had the same experience, but have developed normally. We now come to studies of especial value, since they take a group of children placed as infants in institutions and seek to discover how they have turned out.

One very careful investigation carried out by a New York psychologist, Dr. Goldfarb, was scientifically planned from the beginning to test the theory that the experience of living in the highly impersonal surroundings of an institution nursery in the first two or three years of life has an adverse effect on personality development. What he did was to compare the mental development of children, brought up until the age of about three in an institution and then placed in foster-homes, with others who had gone straight from their mothers to foster-homes, in which they had remained. In both groups the children had been handed over by their mothers in infancy, usually within the first nine months of life. Dr. Goldfarb took great care to see that the two groups were of similar heredity. The children most thoroughly studied consisted of fifteen pairs who, at the time of the examination, ranged in age from ten to fourteen years. One set of fifteen was in the institution from about six months of age to three and a half years, the other set had not had this experience. Conditions in the institution were of the highest standards of physical hygiene, but lacked the elementary essentials of mental hygiene:

> Babies below the age of nine months were each kept in their own little cubicles to prevent the spread of epidemic infection. Their only contacts with adults occurred during these few hurried moments when they were dressed, changed, or fed by nurses.

Later they were members of a group of fifteen or twenty under the supervision of one nurse, who had neither the training nor the time to offer them love or attention. As a result they lived in "almost complete social isolation during the first year of life," and their experience in the succeeding two years was only slightly richer. Dr. Goldfarb has gone to great pains to ensure that the foster-homes of the two groups are similar, and shows further that, in respect of the mother's occupational, educational, and mental standing, the institution group was slightly superior to the controls. Any differences in the mental states of the two groups of children are, therefore, almost certain to be the result of their differing experiences in infancy. We must remember that none of the children had had the advantage of a quite unbroken home life. All had been in their foster-homes for six or seven years. Yet the differences between the groups are very marked and painfully full of meaning.

The two groups of children were studied by a great variety of tests. In intelligence, in power of abstract thinking, in their social maturity, their power of keeping rules or making friends, the institution group fell far below those who had stayed with their mothers for some months and then gone straight to the care of foster-mothers. Only three of the fifteen institution children were up to the average in speech, whilst all fifteen of the others reached this level. This continuing backwardness of speech has been noticed by many other observers—it looks as though the art of speech must be learnt at the right time and in the right place.

Whilst it will be seen that in most respects Dr. Goldfarb's conclusions are much like those of other observers, it must be noted that in two respects they differ from Dr. Bowlby's. First, the New York children "craved affection" and the London ones are observed to be "affectionless." This contrast is probably more apparent than real. Many affectionless characters crave affection, but none the less have a complete inability either to accept or reciprocate it. The poor capacity of all but two of Goldfarb's children for making relationships clearly confirms other work. The fact that only one of this group of Goldfarb's institution children stole and none truanted is, however, surprising in view of Bowlby's findings. The difference is probably valid and needs explanation: perhaps it can be explained this way. All of Goldfarb's cases had been institutionalized from soon after birth until they were three years old. None of Bowlby's had—they were all products of deprivation for a limited period, or of frequent changes. It may well be that their stealing was an attempt to secure love and gratification and so reinstate the love relationship which they had lost, whereas Goldfarb's cases, never having experienced anything of the kind, had nothing to reinstate. Certainly it would appear that the more complete the deprivation is in the early years the more indifferent to society and isolated the child becomes, whereas the more his deprivation is broken by moments of satisfaction the more he turns against society and suffers from conflicting feelings of love and hatred for the same people.

Before we leave the subject of Dr. Goldfarb's writings, we must make it clear that we must not take it for granted that all infants and toddlers in institutions have similar experiences. Not only is it clear that they do not, but the more one studies all the evidence on the subject the more one becomes convinced that the outcome is to a high degree dependent on the exact nature of the psychological experience. If further research is to be fruitful, it must pay minute attention not only to the ages and periods of deprivation, but also to the quality of the child's relation to his mother before deprivation, his experiences with mother-substitutes, if any, during separation, and the reception he gets from his mother or foster-mother when at last he becomes settled again.

There are several other follow-up studies which, though far less thorough, show similar results. An American psychiatrist, Dr. Lowrey, studied a group of children comprising among others twenty-two unselected cases who, with one exception, had been admitted to an institution before their first birthday and had remained there until they were three or four, when they were transferred to another society for fostering. They were examined when they were five years of age or older. All of them showed severe personality disturbances centering on an inability to give or receive affection. Symptoms, each of which occurred in half or more of them, included aggressiveness, negativism (contrariness or obstinacy), selfishness, excessive crying, food difficulties, speech defects, and bedwetting. Other difficulties only a little less frequent included over-activity, fears, and soiling.

Both Dr. Goldfarb and Dr. Lowrey report 100 per cent of children institutionalized in their early years to have developed very poorly; other studies show that many such children achieve a tolerable degree of social adaptation when adult. Though this finding is in accordance with the expectations of the man in the street, it would be a mistake to build too much on it, since it is known that very many people who are psychologically disturbed are able to make an apparent adjustment for long periods. Moreover, these other studies show a large proportion of obvious mental ill-health which the authors regard as confirming the harmfulness of institutional conditions for young children.

As long ago as 1924, a comprehensive study was made in America of the social adjustment as adults of 910 people who had been placed in foster-homes as children. A particularly interesting comparison is made between ninety-five of them who had spent five years or more of their childhood in institutions and eighty-four who had spent the same years at home (in 80 per cent of cases in bad homes). Not only had all the children of both groups, later, been placed in foster-homes of similar quality and at similar ages, but so far as could be determined the heredity of the two groups was similar. The results show that those brought up in an institution adjusted significantly less well than those who had remained during their first five years in their own homes. Since the two groups were of similar heredity, the difference cannot be explained in this way. The fact that no less than one-third of the institution children turned out to be "socially incapable," of which nearly half were troublesome and delinquent, is to be noted.

It will be remarked, however, that, despite the institutional experience in the early years, two-thirds turned out "socially capable." So far as it goes this is satisfactory, but, as no expert examination was carried out, psychological troubles not leading to social incompetence were not recorded.

So far all the evidence has pointed in but one direction. It is now time to consider the three studies which present evidence which calls these conclusions in question. It may be said at once that none of them is of high scientific quality. One is a brief note, questioning the accuracy of Dr. Lowrey's 100 per cent bad results in some institutions, by another specialist who states that he has seen some sixteen children coming from the same institution and having had the same experiences as Lowrey's group, and and that only two showed adverse features of personality. No details are given and there appears to have been no systematic investigation of the individual cases.

Another critic compares a group of 100 boys aged nine to fourteen years living in an institution with another 100 of the same age living at home in bad surroundings, where broken homes and family discords predominate. Using questionnaires, he shows that the two groups are similar in mental ill-health. Not only is a questionnaire an unsatisfactory way of measuring mental health, but no evidence is given regarding the age at which the children entered the institution.

The most recent of the three studies was carried out by a group of child-guidance workers in England. They compared the "social maturity" of two groups of fifteen-year-old children: fifty-one who had spent the previous three years or more in an institution, and a comparable fifty-two who had lived at home. They showed that, although the institution children have a lower score than the family children, when the cases are regrouped according to their heredity an exactly similar difference is to be seen. On the basis of these figures they conclude that the case of those who argue that any social or personal retardation is attributable exclusively or mainly to environmental influences is weakened, and that constitutional factors are at least as important as environmental factors in the growth of social maturity.

These conclusions are ill-judged and certainly cannot be sustained by the evidence presented. In addition to technical criticism of the methods used in the enquiry, it is pointed out that some of the institution children did not enter until they were quite old, the average age of admission being four years; while, even more serious, of the family children in the control group, no less than twenty-two had been evacuated from their homes during the war, the average length of time being one year and nine months. Work with so many shortcomings cannot be accepted as calling in question the almost unanimous findings of the workers already quoted.

There is one other group of facts which is sometimes quoted as casting doubt on these findings—that from the Jewish communal settlements in Israel known as Kibbutz (plural, Kibbutzim). In these settlements, largely for ideological reasons, children are brought up by professional nurses in a "Children's House." Babies are reared in groups of five or six, and are later merged at the age of three years into larger groups numbering twelve to eighteen. The emphasis is throughout on communal rather than family care. Is not this, it may be asked, a clear example that communal care can be made to work without damaging the children? Before answering this question it is necessary to look more carefully at the conditions in which the children are raised. The following account is taken partly from the report of an American psychiatric social worker who recently visited Israel, and partly from a personal communication from the Lasker Child Guidance Centre in Jerusalem. Both describe life in certain of the non-religious Kibbutzim. The former remarks:

Separation is a relative concept and separation as it appears in the Kibbutz should not be thought of as identical with that of children who are brought up in foster-homes or institutions away from their parents. . . . In the Kibbutz there is a great deal of opportunity for close relationship between child and parents.

Not only does the mother nurse the baby and feed him in the early months, but, to follow the Lasker Centre's description:

once the suckling tie between mother and child is abandoned, the daily visit of the child to the room of the parents becomes the focus of family life for the child, and its importance is scrupulously respected. During these few hours the parents, or at least one of them, are more or less completely at the disposal of the children; they play with them, talk to them, carry the babies about, take the toddlers for little walks, etc.

The time spent with the children "may amount to as much as two to three hours on working days and many more on the Sabbath."

Here, then, is no complete abandonment of parent-child relations. Though the amount of time parents spend with their young children is far less than in most other Western communities, the report makes it clear that "the parents are extremely important people in the children's eyes, and the children in the parents'." It is interesting to note, too, that the trend is steadily towards parents taking more responsibility. Formerly parents had to visit the children in the Children's House— now the children come to the parents' room and the parents even prepare light meals for them; feasts are now celebrated in the parents' room as well as communally in the Children's House; mothers are asserting themselves and demanding to see more of their children.

Finally, it is by no means certain that the children do not suffer from this regime. While both observers report good and co-operative development in adolescence, the Lasker Centre think there are signs of a somewhat higher level of insecurity among Kibbutz children than among others, at least until the age of seven years. They also point out that the strong morale and intimate group life of the Kibbutz are of great value to the older child and adolescent, and that these may offset some of the unsettlement of earlier years.

From this brief account it is evident that there is no evidence here which can be held to undermine our conclusions. The conditions provide, of course, unusually rich opportunities for research in child development, and it is to be hoped that these will not be missed.

OBSERVATIONS OF WAR ORPHANS AND REFUGEES

Evidence of the adverse effects on children of all ages of separation from their families was provided on a tragic scale during the Second World War, when thousands of refugee children from occupied lands in Europe were cared for in Switzerland and elsewhere. Owing to the scale of the problem, there was little time for systematic research, and in any case the children had been submitted to such diverse and often horrifying experiences that it would have been almost impossible to have isolated the effects of separation from those of other experiences. A summary of the findings of medical, educational, and relief workers emphasizes that "while the reports tell of disturbances in character resulting from war, they show also the fundamental part played in their causation by rupture of the family tie." Of experiences with refugee children at the Pestalozzi Village at Trogen, Switzerland, we read:

> No doubt remains that a long period without individual attention and personal relationships leads to mental atrophy; it slows down or arrests the development of the emotional life and thus in turn inhibits normal intellectual development. We have observed that acute psychical traumata [damaging experiences], however serious, do not result in such deep injury as chronic deficiencies and prolonged spiritual solitude.

In 1944 a small comparative study was made of ninety-seven Jewish refugee children in homes in Switzerland and 173 Swiss children of about the same age (eleven to seventeen years). All the children were asked to write an essay on "What I think, what I wish, and what I hope." From a scrutiny of these essays it appeared that for the refugees separation from their parents was evidently their most tragic experience. In contrast, few of the Swiss children mentioned their parents, who were evidently felt to be a natural and inevitable part of life. Another great contrast was the refugee children's preoccupation with their suffering past, or with frenzied and grandiose ideas regarding the future. The Swiss children lived happily in the present, which for the refugee was either a vacuum or at best an unsatisfying transition. Deprived of all the things which had given life meaning, especially family and friends, they were possessed by a feeling of emptiness.

Another psychologist also studied refugee children in Switzerland and others in a concentration camp. He describes such symptoms as bedwetting and stealing, an inability to make relations and a consequent loss of ability to form ideals, an increase of aggression, and intolerance of frustration.

In the Netherlands after the war, a group of psychiatrists studied some thousands of children whose parents had been deported in 1942 and 1943 and who had been cared for in foster-homes, often from earliest infancy. They report that frequent changes of foster-home almost always had very adverse effects, leading the child to become withdrawn and apathetic. This was sometimes accompanied by a superficial sociability and, later, promiscuous sex-relationships. Some young children managed to weather a single change, but others could not stand even this, and developed symptoms such as anxiety, depression, excessive clinging, and bedwetting. Many of the children were still emotionally disturbed when examined after the war and in need of treatment. It was noted that those who had had good family relationships before separation could usually be helped to an adjustment, but that for those with a bad family background the outlook was poor.

Finally may be noted an extensive psychological and statistical study undertaken in Spain following the civil war on over 14,000 cases of neglected and delinquent children housed in the environs of Barcelona. Once again there is confirmation of the decisive and adverse role in character development played by the break-up of the family and the vital importance of family life for satisfactory social and moral development. Particularly interesting is the confirmation of Dr. Goldfarb's findings regarding impaired mental development. The intelligence levels of the neglected and delinquent children are much below those of a control group. Lessened capacity for abstract thought is also noted— the evidence, in the investigator's opinion, pointing to the existence of a strong link between the development of the abstract mental faculties and the family and social life of the child. He notes especially the following characteristics of the neglected and delinquent child:

Feeble and difficult attention due to his great instability. Very slight sense of objective realities, overflowing imagination and absolute lack of critical ability. Incapacity for strict abstraction and logical reasoning. Noteworthy backwardness in the development of language. . . .

The similarity of these observations on war orphans and refugees to those on other deprived children will not fail to impress the reader.

18. MOTHERLESS INFANTS

RENÉ A. SPITZ

This is probably the most dramatic study of the effects of maternal deprivation on otherwise well-cared-for infants. Like Bowlby's article (selection 17), it paints a sad picture of psychological scars, arrested development, and high death rates resulting from the loss of contact with the mother.

In the following an extremely condensed report on our findings on psychosocial factors in infant development will be presented. To call attention to the function of such factors in infancy appears to us an

Selections reprinted from the article in *Child Development,* 20 (1949), 145–155, by permission of the author and the Society for Research in Child Development.

urgent need, for it is not generally appreciated that at this age influences of a psychosocial nature are more startling in their consequences for development than at any other period of childhood in later life.

The reasons for this are manifold. At no later period is the development so rapid, so turbulent and so conspicuous. It involves, more obviously than at any later period, the somatic as well as the psychological aspects. Any variation in the development will be manifested in both these sectors, with the result, as will be shown further on, that such variations caused by psychosocial factors can literally become matters of life and death.

. . . . .

A brief summary of the first investigation made by us may serve as an illustration for the other ones of which only the results will be given.

The investigation in question (3, 4) was carried out in two institutions which we had the opportunity to observe simultaneously. Both institutions had certain similarities: the infants received adequate food; hygiene and asepsis were strictly enforced; the housing of the children was excellent; and medical care more than adequate. In both institutions the infants were admitted shortly after birth.

The institutions differed in one single factor. This factor was the amount of emotional interchange offered. In institution No. 1, which we have called "Nursery," the children were raised by their own mothers. In institution No. 2, which we have called "Foundlinghome," the children were raised from the third month by overworked nursing personnel: one nurse had to care for from eight to twelve children. Thus, the available emotional interchange between child and mother formed the one independent variable in the comparison of the two groups.

The response to this variable showed itself in many different ways. Perhaps the most comprehensive index of this response is offered by the monthly averages of the developmental quotients of these children.

The developmental quotient (1, 2) represents the total of the development of six sectors of the personality: mastery of perception, of bodily functions, of social relations, of memory and imitation, of manipulative ability and of intelligence. The monthly averages of the developmental quotients of the children in the two institutions over a period of twelve months are shown in Figure 1.

The contrast in the development of the children in the two institutions is striking. But this twelve months' chart does not tell the whole story. The children in "Foundlinghome" continued their downward slide and by the end of the second year reached a developmental quotient of 45. We have here an impressive example of how the absence of one psychosocial factor, that of emotional interchange with the mother, results in a complete reversal of a developmental trend. This becomes still clearer in Figure 2.

It should be realized that the factor which was present in the first case, but eliminated in the second, is the pivot of all development in the first year. It is the mother-child relation. By choosing this factor as our independent variable we were able to observe its vital importance. While the children in "Nursery" developed into normal healthy toddlers, a two-year observation of "Foundlinghome" showed that the emotionally starved children never learned to speak, to walk, to feed themselves. With one or two exceptions in a total of 91 children, those who survived were human wrecks who behaved either in the manner of agitated or of apathetic idiots.

The most impressive evidence probably is a comparison of the mor-

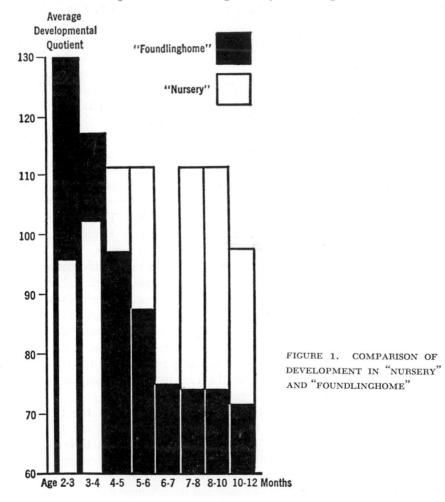

FIGURE 1.   COMPARISON OF DEVELOPMENT IN "NURSERY" AND "FOUNDLINGHOME"

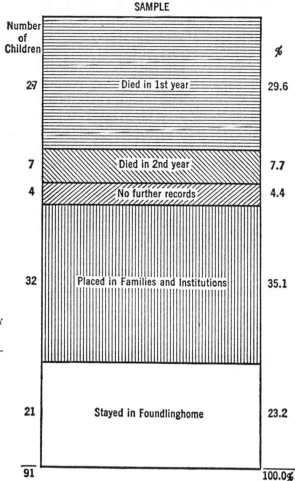

FIGURE 2.   MORTALITY
RATE OF CHILDREN IN
"FOUNDLINGHOME" DUR-
ING A TWO-YEARS' OB-
SERVATION PERIOD

tality rates of the two institutions. "Nursery" in this respect has an outstanding record, far better than the average of the country. In a five
years' observation period during which we observed a total of 239 children, each for one year or more, "Nursery" did not lose a single child
through death. In "Foundlinghome" on the other hand, 37 per cent
of the children died during a two years' observation period (Figure 2).

The high mortality is but the most extreme consequence of the
general decline, both physical and psychological, which is shown by
children completely starved of emotional interchange.

We have called this condition marasmus, from the picture it shows;
or hospitalism according to its etiology. The ecological background of
marasmus is the orphanage and the foundling home which were cur-

rent in our country in the last century. This ecological background leads to the picture of a developmental arrest which progressively becomes a developmental regression. Its earliest symptoms are developmental retardations in the different sectors of personality. Changes occur in the emotional development, later the emotional manifestations become progressively impoverished, finally they give way to apathy. In those cases which survived we have found, alternating with the apathetic children, a hyper-excitable personality type. This personality type is on the lines described by Wallon as "l'enfant turbulent" (6). We have called this, for want of a better term, the erethitic or agitated type.

The results of this study caused us to focus our attention on the mother-child relation in all our further research on infants. We strove to examine whether in less spectacular conditions also it was truly such an all-important influence. Closer investigation bore out this impression. We could establish, in the course of our further research, with the help of statistical methods, that the regularity in the emergence of emotional response, and subsequently of developmental progress both physical and mental, is predicated on adequate mother-child relations. Inappropriate mother-child relations resulted regularly either in the absence of developmental progress, emotional or otherwise, or in paradoxical responses.

This is not a surprising finding for those who have observed infants with their mothers; during the first year of life it is the mother, or her substitute, who transmits literally every experience to the infant. Consequently, barring starvation, disease or actual physical injury, no other factor is capable of so influencing the child's development in every field as its relation to its mother. Therefore, this relationship becomes the central ecological factor in infant development in the course of the first year. On the other hand, development, particularly in the emotional sector, provides an extremely sensitive and reliable indicator of variations in the mother-child relationship.

A few of the further findings made by us in this respect will follow. If our first example showed the complete deprivation of emotional interchange, the following ones will present other and less striking modifications of the mother-child relation.

If, for instance, the deprivation of emotional interchange starts at a later date, in the third quarter of the first year, a condition can develop which greatly resembles the picture of depression in the adult. The psychic structure of the infant is rudimentary and can in no way be compared to that of the adult. Therefore, the similarity of the symptomatology should not induce us to assume an identity of the pathological process. To stress this difference we have called the condition anaclitic (5) depression.

As the name implies, the presenting symptom is a very great increase in the manifestations of the emotions of displeasure. This goes to the point where anxiety reactions in the nature of panic can be observed. Children in this condition will scream by the hour; this may be accompanied by autonomic manifestations such as tears, heavy salivation, severe perspiration, convulsive trembling, dilation of pupils, etc.

At the same time development becomes arrested (see Table 1). The arrest is selective: the least involved is the social sector which remains relatively advanced.

Table 1

NURSERY	INFLUENCE OF SEPARATION FROM MOTHER ON DEVELOPMENTAL QUOTIENT
	SEVERE DEPRESSION
Duration of Separation in Months	*Changes in Points of DQ*
Under 3	−12.5
3 to 4	−14
4 to 5	−14
Over 5	−25

One peculiarity of this condition is that the re-establishment of favorable emotional interchange will rapidly re-establish the developmental level. However, this is only true for separations which do not last longer than three months. If the deprivation lasts longer than five months no improvement is shown. On the contrary, the developmental quotient continues its decline, though at a slower rate, and it would seem that a progressive process has been initiated (see Table 2).

Table 2

NURSERY	INFLUENCE OF SEPARATION FROM MOTHER ON DEVELOPMENTAL QUOTIENT
	SEVERE DEPRESSION
Duration of Separation in Months	*Reversibility of Decline in Points of DQ*
Under 3	+25
3 to 4	+13
4 to 5	+12
Over 5	− 4

CONCLUSION

. . . We believe . . . that the central psychosocial factor in the infant's life is its emotional interchange with its mother.

The particular ecological significance of this finding lies in the fact that this emotional interchange is largely governed by culturally determined mores and institutions on one hand, by social and economic conditions on the other. To give one example: marasmus was a frequent condition up to 1920 in our country, as foundling homes were still in general use. Today such conditions are difficult to find unless we look for them in countries where foundling homes are still the rule. In the United States placement in foster-homes has taken the place of foundling institutions.

Less extreme conditions, however, like anaclitic depression and the others described above can be readily found at present here too. Our social institutions do not encourage the mother to spend much time with her child—at least in the population at large. Industrial civilization tends to deprive the child in early infancy of its mother. I have recently learned that in another industrial country a financial premium has been introduced for mothers who return earlier to factory work after having delivered their child. The earlier they abandon their baby the more substantial the tax reduction they receive. We can be convinced that the consequences of these socio-economic measures will make themselves felt in a distortion of these children's psychological development, although a dozen or more years must pass before the change becomes evident.

Still less consideration is given in our social institutions and in our present-day mores to the question of how to prepare the future mother's personality for motherhood. From the influence on child development exerted by mood-swings in the mother, by the mother's infantile personality or by her neurosis, it is obvious that attempts to remedy such conditions should begin early. . . . I have stressed that preventive psychiatry should begin as early as possible, at birth at least, but preferably before delivery.

I have attempted to show in this paper that such preventive psychiatry will have to begin by applying measures which are largely of an ecological nature. These measures will have to include a re-arrangement of legislation, making it possible for mothers to stay with their children; of education to prepare our female population for motherhood; and they will have to comprise the introduction of social psychiatry to remedy in expectant mothers psychiatric conditions apt to damage their children.

BIBLIOGRAPHY

1. BUEHLER, CHARLOTTE, AND HETZER, H. *Kleinkinder Tests.* Leipzig: Johann Ambrosius Barth, 1932.
2. HETZER, H. AND WOLFE, K. Babytests *Z. Psychol.*, 1928, 107, 62–104.
3. SPITZ, R. A. Hospitalism: an inquiry into the genesis of psychiatric conditions in early childhood. *The Psychoanalytic Study of the Child,* New York: International Univ. Press, 1945, 1, 53–74.
4. SPITZ, R. A. Hospitalism, a follow-up report. *The Psychoanalytic Study of the Child,* New York: International Univ. Press, 1946, 2, 113–117.
5. SPITZ, R. A., AND WOLFE, K. M. Anaclitic depression: an inquiry into the genesis of psychiatric conditions in early childhood. *The Psychoanalytic Study of the Child,* New York: International Univ. Press, 1946, 2, 313–342.
6. WALLON, H. *L'enfant turbulent.* Paris: Librairie Felix Alcan, 1925, p. 642.

19. INFANT DEVELOPMENT UNDER ENVIRONMENTAL HANDICAP

WAYNE DENNIS AND PERGROUHI NAJARIAN

In sharp contrast to the opinions of Bowlby (selection 17) and Spitz (selection 18)—which have shown that institutional infants, because of understaffing and poor care, suffer higher mortality and morbidity rates, and develop inferior intelligence and less ability to relate to others—this study concludes that infants reared in institutions develop normally.

The editors asked Professor Dennis how he reconciled his findings with those of the other researchers. He stated that he believed that the type of adult caring for the infant was more important than the physical environment—institution or foster home—in which the child is reared. He pointed out, for example, that four-year-olds whose nurse provided them freely with paper, pencil, and other stimulating materials scored considerably higher on the Draw-a-Man test than other children in the same institution whose nurses did not provide such materials.

Ribble and Spitz have proposed that if certain stimulus deprivations occur in early childhood the consequences are drastic and enduring.

Reprinted from *Psychological Monographs,* 71, No. 7, (1957), Whole No. 436, by permission of the authors and the American Psychological Association.

These views have arisen largely from observation of infants in institutions. The supporting evidence has consisted in part of scores of institutional subjects on infant tests and in part upon general impressions of the emotional states of the children.

This report is concerned with behavioral development in an institution whose care of infants is in some respects identical with, and in some respects quite different from, that described in other studies.

The data were obtained in a foundling home in Beirut, Lebanon, which, because of inadequate financial support, is able to provide little more than essential physical care. We will report upon the developmental status of two age-groups of children in this institution: those between 2 months and 12 months of age, and those between 4½ and 6 years of age. After describing the environmental conditions and presenting the data we will discuss the relationship of this study to previous studies, and to theories of child development.

THE CRECHE

The institution in which the study was conducted will be called the Creche, although this is not the formal name of the home. The Creche is a home for infants and young children operated by a religious order (of nuns). All children in the Creche are received shortly after birth. They arrive via two routes. The majority come from a maternity hospital operated by the religious order referred to previously. An unmarried woman being attended by this hospital may arrange to have her infant taken to the Creche. In so doing she relinquishes claim to the infant and may not see or visit it thereafter. The remainder of the Creche population consists of infants left upon the doorstep of the institution. Nothing is known definitely concerning their parents, but it is likely that the majority of these infants, too, are illegitimate.

The Creche is nearly 30 years old but it has a new building which was completed in the spring of 1955, and for which the order is still indebted. The building is an excellent one, being fireproof, sunny, and airy. The infant beds and other pieces of equipment are new and modern. The appearance of the institution fails to reveal that it exists month after month upon inadequate and uncertain contributions. The feeding, clothing, and housing of the children have the first claim upon the Creche's meager income. The most stringent economy must be exercised in regard to expenditures for personnel. For this reason the number of persons taking care of the children is extremely limited. Understaffing is the direct cause of whatever deficiencies may characterize the child-care practices to be described later.

Naturally the number of children in the institution varies from time to time with the advent of new arrivals, and departures due to deaths, or to transfer to other institutions to which the children are sent at about six years of age. The size of the staff, too, is subject to some variations. However, estimates made at two periods separated by five months agree in showing that for each person directly concerned with the care of the children—i.e., those who feed the children, change diapers, bathe and clothe them, change their beds, nurse them when they are ill, supervise their play, and teach them—there are 10 children. This ratio of 1 to 10 includes those on night duty as well as on day duty. It does not, however, include personnel who work in the kitchen, laundry, and mending room, nor those who do the cleaning. It does not include the four nuns who constitute the administrative staff and who frequently assist in direct care. Clearly this is an extremely limited staff. The essential functions can be accomplished only by means of hurried procedures and long hours of work.

From birth to one year there is no assignment of individual children to particular attendants. Rather, a room of children is assigned jointly to several caretakers and observation showed no consistent relationships between attendants and children. At later ages, each group of children is assigned most of the day to a supervisor and an assistant.

During the first two months of life the infant is taken out of his crib only for his daily bath and change of clothes. He is given his bottle while lying on his back in his crib, because ordinarily no one has time to hold it. The nipple is placed in his mouth and the bottle is propped up by a small pillow. Bathing and dressing are done with a maximum of dispatch and a minimum of mothering.

In conformity with a widespread Near Eastern practice, the infant is swaddled from birth. Figure 1 illustrates the type of swaddling used. The baby has his arms as well as his legs enclosed in tight wrappings, and hence the

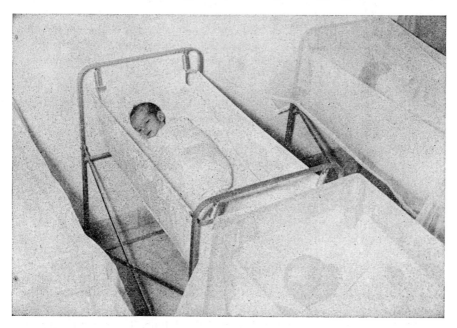

FIGURE 1

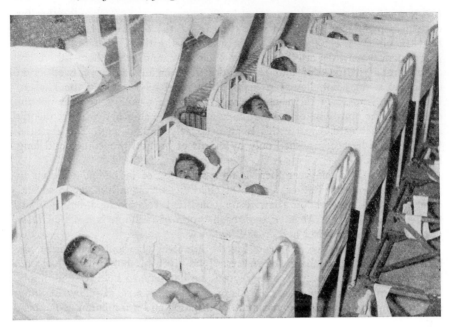

FIGURE 2

scope of his movements is greatly restricted. During the early weeks the infant is bound as depicted except when being bathed and dressed. No fixed schedule is followed in regard to freedom from swaddling, but in general the hands are freed at about two months of age, and swaddling is ended at about four months. Swaddling is continued for a longer period during the winter months than during the remainder of the year because the wrappings of the child serve to keep him warm.

As shown in Figure 2, each crib has a covering around the sides. This is present to protect the child from drafts, but as a consequence the child can see only the ceiling and the adults who occasionally come near him.

The adults seldom approach him except at feeding times. When they feed him they do not usually speak to him or caress him. When two or three persons are feeding twenty infants, many of them crying, there is no tendency to dally.

At about four months of age the child is removed to a room for older infants. He is placed in a larger crib, but for several further months his care remains much the same as it has been. A typical scene in the room is shown in Figure 2. A toy is usually placed in each crib, but it soon becomes lodged in a place inaccessible to the child and remains there. The child remains in this second crib until he begins to pull to the edge of the crib and faces some danger of falling out. At this point, he is usually placed during his waking hours with one or two other children in a play pen. This situation is illustrated in Figure 3. Sometimes he is placed in a canvas-bottomed baby chair, . . . but this is usually done only for short periods of time. The older child takes his daytime naps in the play pens. He is returned to his crib at night and tightly tucked in. The child graduates from room two to another room at one year of age or slightly thereafter. Some description of the care of older children will be given on later pages.

Until about four months of age the infant's food consists of milk, supplemented by vitamins. The feedings during this time are on a schedule of six feedings per day at daytime intervals of three hours. After four months bottle feeding is gradually reduced in frequency. It ceases at about twelve months.

The introduction of cooked cereals begins at four months, and fruit juices, crushed bananas, apple sauce, and vegetables are begun at five months. Depending upon the preferences of an attendant a child is sometimes given these supplementary foods held in arms, sometimes while sitting in chairs, and sometimes lying down. Beginning at eight months, eggs and chopped meat are occasionally given. Feeding times are reduced to five times per day at four months and to four times per day at one year. Toilet training is begun between 10 and 12 months.

Children are weighed at weekly intervals. Serious efforts are made to give special feeding to infants who are not gaining properly but again staff limitations make it difficult for an attendant to spend much time with any one child. The average weight during the first six months, based on records of the infants which we tested, is appreciably below what is ordinarily considered desirable (see Table 1). Comparable data are not available for other Lebanese children. No data are available on children beyond six months of age at the Creche.

FIGURE 3

From about one year to about three years the children spend much of the day in play groups of about twenty children with a supervisor and an assistant. Equipment is limited to a few balls, wagons, and swings. From three to four years of age much of the day is spent seated at small tables. The children are occupied in a desultory way with slates, beads, and sewing boards. At about four years they are placed in kindergarten within the Creche where training in naming objects and pictures, writing, reading, and numbers is begun. Instruction is given in both Arabic and French.

Table 1. Average Weights of Creche Infants

	BOYS						
STATISTIC	*Birth*	*1 Mo.* [a]	*2 Mo.*	*3 Mo.*	*4 Mo.*	*5 Mo.*	*6 Mo.*
Average weight in grams	2926	3233	3746	4365	4926	5555	5984
Number of cases	28	28	28	27	23	18	16

	GIRLS						
	Birth	*1 Mo.*	*2 Mo.*	*3 Mo.*	*4 Mo.*	*5 Mo.*	*6 Mo.*
Average weight in grams	2727	2985	3353	3858	4436	4910	5463
Number of cases		13	12	13	13	11	10	8

[a] In computing this average, for each child the record of weight taken nearest age 1.0 month was employed. A similar procedure was used at other ages.

Diet and medical care are under the supervision of a physician who devotes, gratis, about one hour per day to the Creche, whose population is about 140 children. During the winter months colds are common, and pneumonia occasionally occurs. The usual childhood illnesses occur. When a contagious disease enters the Creche it is likely to become widespread since there are no facilities for isolation of infectious cases. We do not have adequate statistics on mortality. It is our impression that it is high in the first three months of life, but not particularly high thereafter. Mortality seems especially high among those infants who are found on the doorstep, many of whom are suffering from malnutrition, exposure, or disease upon admission. In evaluating institutional mortality it should be noted that in some areas of Lebanon the crude death rate in the first year among children in homes is as high as 375 per 1000.

THE COMPARISON GROUP

For comparison with behavioral records of the Creche infants, data were obtained from children brought to the Well Baby Clinic of the American University of Beirut Hospital. All well babies of appropriate age who were brought to the clinic on certain days were tested. They were from among the poorer, but not the poorest, segments of the Beirut population.

All children tested were living at home and were brought to the clinic by their mothers. The majority were being breast fed. We did not obtain detailed data on swaddling, but typically the younger babies were brought in swaddled and the older ones unswaddled. It is our impression that swaddling customs among the poorer half of the Beirut population approximate those of the Creche. This conclusion is supported by a study by Wakim. Other comparison data were provided by American norms and certain Lebanese norms to be described later.

THE TESTING PROGRAM

For the subjects under one year of age the Cattell infant scale was employed.

This scale was selected because among available tests it seemed to offer the most objective procedures for administration and scoring. It provides five items for each month from 2 to 12 months of age, with one or two alternate items at each age level.

The procedures described in the test manual were carefully followed. They call for testing each infant at a level at which he passes all tests, at a level he fails all tests, and at all intermediate levels.

Several items on the test were not applicable to the Creche group because they require the examiner to obtain information from the mother or other caretaker. Among such items are babbles, anticipates feeding, inspects fingers, says "dada," etc. Attendants at the Creche could not supply the information required by these items. For this reason, "alternate" items provided by Cattell and based on direct observations were regularly substituted for these items. In the case of the comparison infants, all age-appropriate items, including all alternates, were administered; but in computing developmental scores for comparative purposes identical items were used for the Creche and the comparison groups.

At the 4½-to-6-year level the tests used were the Goodenough draw-a-man test, the Knox cube test, and the Porteus maze test. These were chosen because it was judged that they might be but little affected by the environmental handicaps of the Creche children. They have the further advantage of requiring a minimum of verbal instructions.

In giving and scoring the draw-a-man test, Goodenough procedures were followed. For the other two tests the procedures and norms employed were those given in the Grace Arthur Scale of Performance Tests, Revised Form II.

NUMBER OF SUBJECTS

We tested all subjects who fell into our age categories upon two series of testing dates. The only exceptions consisted of children who were ill or who had just undergone serious illness. The infant tests were given to 49 Creche infants and the 41 comparison cases. Since rather few of the Creche infants were above six months of age at the time of our first period of testing, during our second testing period we tested all infants who were six months of age and over even though this meant retesting in 13 cases. For this reason the number of *test scores* for the 49 Creche infants is 62.

In the 4½-to-6-year group, Goodenough tests were given to 30 subjects, and the Knox cube test and the Porteus maze test were each given to 25 subjects. None was retested.

RESULTS

For the infants, Table 2 indicates by age levels the score earned on each test. The Creche scores are shown by O-symbols, the comparison scores by X-symbols. Scores are grouped by step intervals of ten points. Thus, examining the figure by beginning at the top of column one, one finds that between 2 and 2¾ months of age one comparison infant had a developmental quotient between 140 and 149, two comparison infants had quotients between 130 and 139, etc.

Table 2. Individual Infant Scores by Age [a]

SCORES	AGE IN MONTHS									
	2	3	4	5	6	7	8	9	10	11
140–149	X									
130–139	XX		X							
120–129	X	X					X			
110–119	OO		X		XX	XX		X		
100–109	OOXX	XXXX	X	XX		X	XX	X	XX	
90–99	OO	O		XX		OX				
80–89	OOX	OX	XXXXX			O		O		O
70–79		OO	OOX		OO			O	OO	
60–69		O	OOOOOO	OOOOO	O	X	O	O	O	O
50–59	X	OO	OOO	OO	O	O			OO	OO
40–49		O			OO	OOO		OO	O	

[a] Creche infant scores are indicated by O; comparison infants by X.

Examination of Table 2 shows that at the two-months age level there is little if any difference between the two groups. The mean of the Creche group is 97, that of the comparison group 107. These means, each based on only eight cases, are not significantly different from each other or from the American norms. However, at all ages beyond three months the Creche infants score definitely lower than either the comparison or the normative groups, whose records are indistinguishable.

If all scores from 2 to 12 months are averaged, the Creche mean is 68, the comparison mean 102. For the 3-to-12-month period the mean of the Creche scores is 63, (SD 13), that of the comparison group 101 (SD 15), a difference of 38 points. This is a very large and highly significant difference (P < .001). In this age range all of the comparison infants tested above the mean of the Creche subjects and all of the Creche subjects were below the mean of the comparison group. No Creche baby between 3 and 12 months had a DQ above 95.

Before discussing the results of the infant tests we turn now to the tests given to Creche children between 4½ and 6 years of age. We note first that there are reasons to believe that the subjects tested at 4½ to 6 years of age performed, as infants, at the same level as did the children whose test results have just been presented. Because procedures of admission to the Creche have not changed in recent years the two groups of infants can be assumed to be genetically similar. Since practically all infants who enter the Creche remain for six years, there are no selective influences between admission and six years. The only qualification of this statement regards infant mortality, whose selective action so far as psychological tests are concerned is unknown, here as elsewhere. According to the supervisory staff there have been no changes in child care within the past six years.

Table 3. Results of Performance Tests

TEST	VARIOUS "DQ" SCORES				
	N	*Range*	*Median*	*Mean*	*SD*
Goodenough	30	58–136	93	93	20
Porteus maze [a]	25	69–150	89	95	20
Knox cube [b]	25		100		

[a] Four children earned fewer than 4 points, which is the minimum score for which Arthur gives a mental age. Since the lowest MA given by Arthur is 4.5, these children were arbitrarily given a mental age of 4 years and DQ's were computed accordingly. Obviously these scores affect the mean and SD but not the median.
[b] On this test, 11 of the 25 subjects scored below the 4.5 MA, the lowest age for which Arthur gives norms. Because of the large number below 4.5 no arbitrary scores were given. Of the 14 subjects who earned MA's of 4.5 and above, one had a DQ of 80 and two of 100. The remaining scores ranged from 101 to 165. The median of 100 seems representative.

The results of the performance tests are shown in Table 3. It will be noted that the data there reported agree remarkably well in showing that on these tests the development of the Creche children is only about 10 per cent below the norms of American home-reared children. In a separate report it has been shown that on the Goodenough test Lebanese children at the five-year level make scores equivalent to the American norms. No Lebanese norms are available for the Knox cube or Porteus maze tests but there is no reason to believe that they would be higher than the published standards. In other words, there is evidence that the environment of the Creche produces only a slight retardation among four- and five-year-olds on these tests.

In summary, the data show that, with respect to behavioral development, children in the Creche are normal during the second month of age, are greatly retarded from 3 to 12 months of age, and almost normal on certain performance tests between 4.5 and 6 years of age.

INTERPRETATIVE DISCUSSION

To a reader acquainted with the numerous and often divergent opinions concerning the effects of early environment, the results just reported may, on the surface, only serve to confuse further the already unclear picture. We believe, however, that we can show that these data and others can be fitted into a coherent view.

EARLY NORMALITY OF CRECHE INFANTS

The fact that the Creche subjects had DQ's of approximately 100 during the second month, and presumably during the first month also, should not be surprising. It has not been shown that any stimulus deprivation will affect infant behavioral development during the first two months. The twins reared under experimental conditions by Dennis and Dennis made normal progress during this period. The infants tested by Spitz had a mean developmental quotient of 130 during the second month. The supernormality of this score was probably due to the inadequacy of test norms rather than to institutional influence.

If it is true that restricted stimulation has little or no effect upon early behavioral development, this can be due to at least two different causes. One explanation would be in terms of maturation. Perhaps growth of the nervous system, apart from sensory stimulation, is alone responsible for postnatal behavioral growth during the first two months. A second explanation lies in the possibility that sensory experience is essential, but that for the tests presented to him the infant even when swaddled hand and foot and lying on his back obtains sufficient stimulation.

For the Cattell infant tests the second interpretation is not altogether unreasonable. Of the five tests which we employed at the two-month level, four are given to the infant while lying on his back and the responses required are visual. These are "inspects environment," "follows moving person," "follows moving ring vertically," and "follows moving ring horizontally." Since the infants spend nearly 24 hours per day in a supine position in a well lighted room, and some movement occurs near them, there is considerable opportunity to practice visual pursuit movements.

The fifth item among the two-month tests is lifting head when prone. The Creche infants are placed on the abdomen for a short time daily while being bathed, dried, and dressed. For this reason, lifting the head while in this position can be practiced and direct observation shows that it is practiced. Possibly the Creche infants respond normally to the items given them at two months because the required responses are well practiced. However, the possibility that maturation alone is sufficient for the development of the items is not ruled out.

RETARDATION BETWEEN 3 AND 12 MONTHS OF AGE

Beyond the two-months level the majority of items on the Cattell scale require that the infant be tested in a sitting position while being held on the lap of an adult. Sitting is a position to which the Creche infants under about ten months of age are relatively unaccustomed. They are not propped up in their beds or placed in chairs before that age. The first occasion for placing the infants in a sitting position may come with the introduction of semisolid foods, but we have noted that some of the infants are given these while lying down. Perhaps as a consequence of inexperience in being held upright the infants as a group make a poor record on the test item which involves holding the head erect and steady. This unsteadiness of the head, plus general unfamiliarity with sitting, may account in part for the low scores earned on certain purely visual items. These are "regards cube," "regards spoon," "follows ball," and "regards pellet."

Many of the remaining items involve not only sitting but in addition manual skills directed by vision. Among the items are "picks up spoon," "picks up cube," "grasps pellet," "grasps string," "lifts cup," "takes two cubes," "exploits paper," "pulls out peg," etc. Between ages 5 and 7 months, the age placement given these items, the infants have little opportunity to practice visuo-manual coordinations in a sitting position and, further, visuo-manual coordinations are not required or encouraged even in a lying position.

Analysis of other items whose placement is between 3 and 12 months reveals that practically all of them require manual skills and require adjustment to visually presented objects. It is suggested that the relationship between the items and the environmental restrictions experienced by the children account for the low scores made by the Creche subjects.

We examined the records made by the Creche children aged 3 months and above on each item, expecting that one or two items might be found in regard to which their performance is normal. We were able to find none. But we were also unable to find an item in this age range on which the subjects were judged to receive a normal amount of relevant experience.

It is interesting to note two items on which the subjects are very deficient even though the motor component of the item is clearly present. These involve turning to sound. In one of these items, the child, sitting on the lap of an adult, is required to turn toward the experimenter who stands by the shoulder of the seated adult, and calls the infant's name. The second item is similar but a small hand-bell is used instead of the voice. The first item has an age placement of four months, the second, five months. Of 36 children tested between 4 and 10 months of age only one turned to the voice and only four turned to the bell.

Now all of the children turned to and followed a moving person in the field of view. The difficulty of the item apparently lies in the subject's lack of associations with sounds. We have noted that in approaching a child or providing services for a child the attendants seldom speak to him. This seems to be due partly to the fact that the attendants are too busy. A second relevant fact is that, with 20 children in a room, and the windows open to rooms containing 100 additional children, it is seldom quiet enough at feeding times and bathing times to encourage verbal greetings. So far as we could determine no event which happens to a Creche baby is consistently preceded by a sound signal. These conditions seem to explain the finding that the infants seldom turned to a voice or a ringing bell only a few inches from their ears.

From the preceding discussion it will be obvious that we tend to attribute the retardation of Creche subjects between 3 and 12 months of age to a lack of learning opportunities relative to the Cattell test items.

RELATIONSHIP OF THE 3-TO-12-MONTH RETARDATION
TO THE FINDINGS OF OTHER STUDIES

There seems to be a superficial, if not a basic, disagreement between the results here reported, and those of other studies, particularly those of Dennis and Dennis and those of Spitz. We wish to comment on the apparent divergences and to indicate how they can be reconciled.

In a study of a pair of twins named Del and Rey who were reared under experimentally controlled conditions until thirteen months of age, Dennis and Dennis found that, while the subjects were retarded beyond the range of ordinary subjects in regard to the appearance of a few responses, the subjects' development in general equalled that of home-reared infants. The few specific retardations occurred on items in respect to which the infants could not engage in self-directed practice, namely, visually directed reaching, sitting without support, and supporting self with the feet. These retardations seem consonant with the behavior of the Creche subjects. However, the prevailing normality of Del and Rey seems at variance with the Creche findings.

To begin with, certain differences between the environmental conditions of the subjects in the two studies should be noted. For one thing, the adult-child ratios in the two studies were very different. In the Del-Rey study there were two subjects and two experimenters, a 1-to-1 ratio. In the Creche, the adult-child ratio is 1 to 10, a greatly different situation. In the Del-Rey study the environmental restrictions in regard to learning were rather severe in the beginning, but were gradually relaxed as desired data were obtained. In the Creche, very limited opportunities for learning and practicing responses continue throughout the first year. Certain specific contrasts may be mentioned: Del and Rey were kept in larger and deeper cribs, were less restrained by clothing and consequently probably had more opportunities for motor experimentation than did the Creche infants. Further, Del and Rey may have received more handling and more varied exposure to stimuli than did the Creche infants. However, there can be no doubt that in several respects Del and Rey suffered as much a restriction of experience as did the Creche infants. Speech was not directed to Del and Rey nor did adults smile in their presence until they were six months of age. No toys were provided until the twelfth month. They were not placed in a sitting position until they were over eight months of age.

But it is our belief that the difference between the normality of Del and Rey and the retardation of the Creche infants is due to the use of different indices of behavioral development rather than to real differences in behavior. In the Del-Rey study no general scale of infant development was administered. The majority of the developmental data reported for Del and Rey consisted of noting when each of a number of common infant responses first appeared. That is, the observers recorded when each subject first brought hand to mouth, first grasped bedclothes, first vocalized to person, first laughed, etc. The initial data of occurrence of such responses cannot be determined by testing. The Del-Rey data are longitudinal and the Del-Rey records were found to be normal when compared with similar data obtained in other observational studies.

Now since observation in the Del-Rey study was directed primarily toward responses which could occur at any time and did not require the introduction of test conditions, it follows that poverty of environmental stimulation would not be expected to yield much evidence of retardation. The child left to his own devices on his back in his crib can bring his hand to his mouth, grasp his bedclothes, vocalize, observe his own hands, grasp his own hands, grasp his own foot, bring foot to mouth, etc. These are the items which were observed. One of the major findings of the Del-Rey study was that the untutored infant does do these things, and does them within the usual age range of home-reared babies.

In regard to such responses it *may* be that the Creche babies are normal. The relevant facts can be discovered only by observers each spending full time observing a few infants. If all Creche infants were to be observed it would necessitate the presence of many additional observers or caretakers. The reader is reminded that the Del-Rey investigation, involving only two infants, took a major part of the time of the two observers for one year. To devote one year, or even one month to observing each Creche subject cannot be proposed in an institution which has severe limitations of caretaker personnel. In contrast to the requirements of an observational study of development, the testing time in the Creche study was only 10 to 30 minutes per subject.

If we cannot compare Del and Rey with the Creche babies in terms of observational data, it is likewise not possible to compare them in terms of test data. It is impossible to estimate in retrospect with any degree of confidence how Del and Rey would have scored at various times during the first year on the Cattell Infant Scale. We arrive, therefore, at the following conclusion: It is likely infants with restricted learning opportunities are normal on "observational" items but retarded on "test" items. It is believed that the latter, but not the former, are influenced by environmental limitations. If this is a correct interpretation, the Del-Rey study and the Creche study are two sides of the same coin. However, to establish that this is the case appears to be a very difficult research assignment.

We consider next the work of Spitz. The observations by Spitz which seem most closely related to the present study concern the institution called Foundling Home. Here, as at the Creche, there was a shortage of personnel. Although the mothers were present in the institution for several months, they seem to have had little contact with their children aside from breast-feeding them. Pinneau points out that Spitz does not explain why this was the case. Despite the presence of the mothers in the institution the adult-child ratio in the nursery is reported to be about 1 to 8. The children spent most of their time for many months on their backs in their cribs, as did the Creche infants. At one point Spitz reports that a hollow worn in their mattresses restrained their activity. This, however, was definitely not true of the Creche infants.

Since Spitz's studies have been extensively reviewed and criticized by Pinneau, only a limited amount of space will be devoted to them here. Spitz used some form of the Hetzer-Wolf baby tests. There is no doubt that their standardization leaves much to be desired. Spitz reports scores for the Foundling Home group and a control group of 17 home-reared infants. In the second month both groups had mean DQ's between 130 and 140. The private home group remained at that level but the mean of the Foundling Home group dropped precipitously to 76 by the sixth month and to 72 by the end of the first year. Spitz believes that this decline in DQ was due to the emotional consequences of separation from the mother, but Pinneau has pointed out that most of the decline took place prior to the prevalent age of separation. Pinneau indicates further that at least some of the decline is probably due to inadequate test standardization.

We compare our data with those of Spitz with considerable hesitation because the two sets of data were obtained by tests whose comparability is unknown. In numerical terms the results of the two studies in the second half of the first year seem to agree fairly well, Spitz's mean for this period being about 74 and ours 63. But the findings for the first half-year present some apparent differences. Our subjects drop from a mean of 97 to a mean of 72 between the second and third months, and drop only ten additional points thereafter. Spitz's group starts higher and declines for a longer period.

Spitz's data and ours agree in finding that environmental conditions can depress infant test scores after the second month of life. We disagree with Spitz in regard to the interpretation of the cause of the decline. He believes it to have been due, in the case of his subjects, to a break of the emotional attachment to the mother. This could not have been the cause of the decline of the Creche infants. Since the conditions for the formation of an emotional tie to a specific individual were never present, no breach of attachment could have occurred. We have noted above Pinneau's demonstration that even Spitz's own data do not support his interpretation. We believe that Spitz's data as well as ours are satisfactorily interpreted in terms of restricted learning opportunities. We suggest that an analysis of the relationship between test items and the conditions prevailing in the Foundling Home would reveal that retardation could readily be explained in terms of restriction of learning opportunities. But such restriction is not inherent in institutional care. Klackenberg has recently presented a study of infant development in a Swedish institution, in which the adult-child ratio was 1 to 2 or 3, in which no retardation was found.

DISCUSSION OF THE CRECHE FOUR- AND FIVE-YEAR-OLDS

We have no doubt that on many tests the Creche four- and five-year-olds (and also two- and three-year-olds) would be retarded, perhaps to a marked degree. We think this would be particularly true in regard to tests involving more than a very modest amount of language comprehension and language usage. The language handicap of institutional children with limited adult contact has been sufficiently demonstrated.

It is likely that on some performance tests the Creche children also would score below available norms. On the Healy Picture Form Board, for example, most of the incidents represented are outside the experience of Creche children. We assume that the older Creche children are retarded on some tests, but we wish to determine whether retardation is general or whether it is related to specific environmental handicaps.

We chose the draw-a-man test, the Knox cube test and the Porteus maze test because it was thought that the Creche environment might affect these tests less than other tests. So far as the Knox cubes are concerned, it is difficult to imagine how one can deprive a child of the experience of visually remembering just-touched objects, except through loss of sight. So far as the Goodenough is concerned, both human beings and two-dimensional representations of them were familiar to the subjects. They were also familiar with the idea of drawing and with the use of pencils. Knowledge of the use of pencils may also play a part in the Porteus maze test. It is uncertain what other experience may play a role in this test.

The results show clearly that on these tests the Creche children approximated the performance of children in normal environments. In other words, the retardation which was found to exist between 3 and 12 months of age did not produce a general and permanent intellectual deficit. It is possible for infants who have been retarded through limitations of experience at an early age level to perform normally, at least in some respects, at later age periods. The assumption that early retardation produces permanent retardation does not receive support from our data.

EMOTIONAL AND PERSONALITY EFFECTS

No doubt many readers would like to know the emotional and personality consequences of the Creche regime. So would we. But to the best of our knowledge no objective and standardized procedures with adequate norms are available which would enable us to compare the Creche infants with other groups of children in these respects. This is equally true of studies conducted earlier.

In the absence of objective techniques, we can only report a few impressions. The Creche infants were readily approachable and were interested in the tests. Very few testing sessions were postponed because of crying, from whatever cause. There was very little shyness or fear of strangers, perhaps because each infant saw several different adults. In the cribs there was very little if any crying that did not seem attributable to hunger or discomfort. However, some of the older babies developed automatisms such as arching the back strongly, or hitting some part of the body with the hand, which may have represented a type of "stimulation hunger." It was almost always possible to get the infants over two months of age to smile by stroking their chins or cheeks or by shaking them slightly. The older children, like the infants, were friendly and approachable. However, such observations are not meant to imply that other personality consequences could not be found if adequate techniques existed.

SUMMARY AND CONCLUSIONS

This study has been concerned with the development of children in an institution in Beirut, Lebanon, called the Creche, in which "mothering" and all other forms of adult-child interaction are at a minimum because the institution is seriously understaffed. The children come to the institution shortly after birth and remain until six years of age. Contact with the mother ceases upon the child's entrance to the institution and contact with mother-substitutes is slight because the adult-child ratio is 1 to 10.

Opportunity for developing infant skills through practice is very slight. In the early months the infants are swaddled. For many months the infant lies on his back, and is even fed in a supine position. He is not propped up, carried about, or provided with the means of practicing many activities.

Data on behavioral development were obtained by giving the Cattell infant scale to all infants between 2 and 12 months of age and the Goodenough draw-a-man test, the Knox cube test, and the Porteus maze test to all children between 4½ and 6 years of age. Comparison data were available from American norms and from certain groups of Lebanese subjects.

It was found that in terms of developmental quotients, the mean quotient at two months was approximately 100. Between 4 and 12 months the mean was 63. In the tests given at the four- and five-year level, the mean scores were roughly 90.

Possible interpretations of these data have been discussed at some length. Our conclusions may be summarized as follows:

1. It is uncertain whether the normality of behavior at two months shows that maturation plays a major role in early development, or whether experience, limited as it was, provided the essential requirements for learning the responses which were tested.
2. The retardation prevailing between 3 and 12 months of age seems to be due to lack of learning opportunities in situations comparable to the test situations. It is possible that an observational approach in the day-by-day situation might reveal that some behaviors developed normally.
3. The infants did not undergo loss of an emotional attachment. There is nothing to suggest that emotional shock, or lack of mothering or other emotion-arousing conditions, were responsible for behavioral retardation.
4. Retardation in the last nine months of the first year to the extent of a mean DQ of 65 does not result in a generally poor performance at 4½ to 6 years, even when the child remains in a relatively restricted environment. The study therefore does not support the doctrine of the permanency of early environmental effects.
5. It is believed that the objective data of other studies, as well as this one, can be interpreted in terms of the effects of specific kinds of restrictions upon infant learning.

20. THE NATURE OF LOVE

HARRY F. HARLOW

Although the fact that mortality and morbidity rates for children separated from their mothers are higher than those for children who are not maternally deprived has been clearly established, exactly what essential factors the mother provides remain unknown. Certainly there must be factors other than food, clothing, and warmth, since these are provided to infants in institutions.

The ingenious series of experiments described in this article show that baby monkeys "love" something soft and warm, that ever-present soft, warm artificial mothers are superior to natural mothers. Anyone who has seen how chickens, kittens, mice, or sheep huddle together, even on warm days, or who has observed the strong attachment an infant can develop to a tattered old blanket or a doll, can verify this snuggling response.

Perhaps any old rag will do as well as an actual mother—and better than some—but final demonstration of this remains to be completed.

The position commonly held by psychologists and sociologists is quite clear: The basic motives are, for the most part, the primary drives —particularly hunger, thirst, elimination, pain, and sex—and all other motives, including love or affection, are derived or secondary drives. The mother is associated with the reduction of the primary drives—particularly hunger, thirst, and pain—and through learning, affection or love is derived.

It is entirely reasonable to believe that the mother through association with food may become a secondary-reinforcing agent, but this is an inadequate mechanism to account for the persistence of the infant-material ties. There is a spate of researches on the formation of secondary reinforcers to hunger and thirst reduction. There can be no question that almost any external stimulus can become a secondary reinforcer if properly associated with tissue-need reduction, but the fact remains that this redundant literature demonstrates unequivocally that such derived drives suffer relatively rapid experimental extinction. Contrariwise, human affec-

Selections reprinted from the article in *The American Psychologist*, 13, No. 12 (December, 1958), 673–685, by permission of the author and the American Psychological Association.

tion does not extinguish when the mother ceases to have intimate association with the drives in question. Instead, the affectional ties to the mother show a lifelong, unrelenting persistence and, even more surprising, widely expanding generality.

Oddly enough, one of the few psychologists who took a position counter to modern psychological dogma was John B. Watson, who believed that love was an innate emotion elicited by cutaneous stimulation of the erogenous zones. . . .

The psychoanalysts have concerned themselves with the problem of the nature of the development of love in the neonate and infant, using ill and aging human beings as subjects. They have discovered the overwhelming importance of the breast and related this to the oral erotic tendencies developed at an age preceding their subjects' memories. Their theories range from a belief that the infant has an innate need to achieve and suckle at the breast to beliefs not unlike commonly accepted psychological theories. There are exceptions, as seen in the recent writings of John Bowlby, who attributes importance not only to food and thirst satisfaction, but also to "primary object-clinging," a need for intimate physical contact, which is initially associated with the mother.

As far as I know, there exists no direct experimental analysis of the relative importance of the stimulus variables determining the affectional or love responses in the neonatal and infant primate. Unfortunately, the human neonate is a limited experimental subject for such researches because of his inadequate motor capabilities. By the time the human infant's motor responses can be precisely measured, the antecedent determining conditions cannot be defined, having been lost in a jumble and jungle of confounded variables.

Many of these difficulties can be resolved by the use of the neonatal and infant macaque monkey as the subject for the analysis of basic affectional variables. It is possible to make precise measurements in this primate beginning at two to ten days of age, depending upon the maturational status of the individual animal at birth. The macaque infant differs from the human infant in that the monkey is more mature at birth and grows more rapidly; but the basic responses relating to affection, including nursing, contact, clinging, and even visual and auditory exploration, exhibit no fundamental differences in the two species. Even the development of perception, fear, frustration, and learning capability follows very similar sequences in rhesus monkeys and human children.

Three years' experimentation before we started our studies on affection gave us experience with the neonatal monkey. We had separated more than 60 of these animals from their mothers 6 to 12 hours after birth and suckled them on tiny bottles. The infant mortality was only a small fraction of what would have obtained had we let the monkey mothers raise their infants. Our bottle-fed babies were healthier and heavier than monkey-mother-reared infants. We know that we are better monkey mothers than are real monkey mothers thanks to synthetic diets, vitamins, iron extracts, penicillin, chloromycetin, 5% glucose, and constant, tender, loving care.

During the course of these studies we noticed that the laboratory-raised babies showed strong attachment to the cloth pads (folded gauze diapers) which were used to cover the hardware-cloth floors of their cages. The infants clung to these pads and engaged in violent temper tantrums when the pads were removed and replaced for sanitary reasons. Such contact-need or responsiveness had been reported previously by Gertrude van Wagenen for the monkey and by Thomas McCulloch and George Haslerud for the chimpanzee and is reminiscent of the devotion often exhibited by human infants to their pillows, blankets, and soft, cuddly stuffed toys. Responsiveness by the one-day-old infant monkey to the cloth pad is shown in Figure 1, and an unusual and strong attachment of a six-month-old infant to the cloth pad is illustrated in Figure 2. The baby, human or monkey, if it is to survive, must clutch at more than a straw.

We had also discovered during some allied observational studies that a baby monkey raised on a bare wire-mesh cage floor survives with

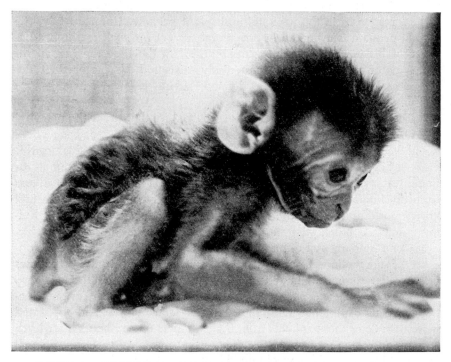

FIGURE 1.   RESPONSE TO CLOTH PAD BY ONE-DAY-OLD MONKEY

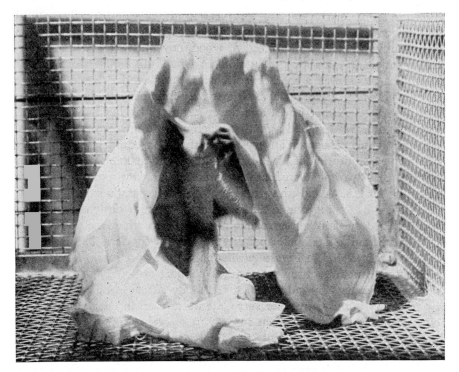

FIGURE 2. RESPONSE TO GAUZE PAD BY SIX-MONTH-OLD MONKEY USED IN EARLIER STUDY

difficulty, if at all, during the first five days of life. If a wire-mesh cone is introduced, the baby does better; and, if the cone is covered with terry cloth, husky, healthy, happy babies evolve. It takes more than a baby and a box to make a normal monkey. We were impressed by the possibility that, above and beyond the bubbling fountain of breast or bottle, contact comfort might be a very important variable in the development of the infant's affection for the mother.

At this point we decided to study the development of affectional responses of neonatal and infant monkeys to an artificial, inanimate mother, and so we built a surrogate mother which we hoped and believed would be a good surrogate mother. In devising this surrogate mother we were dependent neither upon the capriciousness of evolutionary processes nor upon mutations produced by chance radioactive fallout. Instead, we designed the mother surrogate in terms of modern human-engineering principles (Figure 3). We produced a perfectly proportioned, streamlined body stripped of unnecessary bulges and appendices. Redundancy in the surrogate mother's system was avoided by reducing the number of breasts from two to one and placing this uni-breast in an upper-thoracic, sagittal position, thus maximizing the natural and known perceptual-motor capabilities of the infant operator. The surrogate was made from a block of wood, covered with sponge rubber, and sheathed in tan cotton terry cloth. A light bulb behind her radiated heat. The result was a mother, soft, warm, and tender, a mother with infinite patience, a mother available twenty-four hours a day, a mother that never scolded her infant and never struck or bit her baby in anger. Furthermore, we designed a mother-machine with maximal maintenance efficiency since failure of any system or function could be resolved by the simple substitution of black boxes and new component parts. It is our opinion that we engineered a very superior monkey mother, although this position is not held universally by the monkey fathers.

Before beginning our initial experiment we also designed and constructed a second mother surrogate, a surrogate in which we deliberately built less than the maximal capability for contact comfort. This surrogate mother is illustrated in Figure 4. She is made of wire-mesh, a substance entirely adequate to provide postural support and nursing capability, and she is warmed by radiant heat. Her body differs in no essential way from that of the cloth mother surrogate other than in the quality of the contact comfort which she can supply.

In our initial experiment, the dual mother-surrogate condition, a cloth mother and a wire mother were placed in different cubicles attached to the infant's living cage as shown in Figure 4. For four newborn mon-

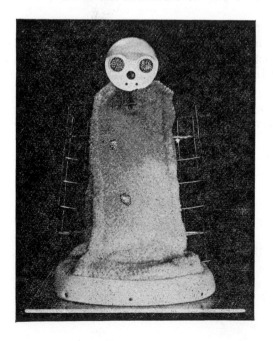

FIGURE 3.   CLOTH MOTHER
SURROGATE

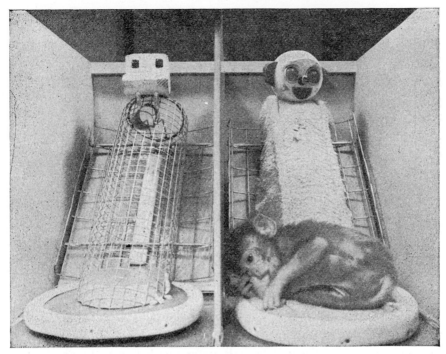

FIGURE 4.   WIRE AND CLOTH MOTHER SURROGATES

keys the cloth mother lactated and the wire mother did not; and, for the other four, this condition was reversed. In either condition the infant received all its milk through the mother surrogate as soon as it was able to maintain itself in this way, a capability achieved within two or three days except in the case of very immature infants. Supplementary feedings were given until the milk intake from the mother surrogate was adequate. Thus, the experiment was designed as a test of the relative importance of the variables of contact comfort and nursing comfort. During the first 14 days of life the monkey's cage floor was covered with a heating pad wrapped in a folded gauze diaper, and thereafter the cage floor was bare. The infants were always free to leave the heating pad or cage floor to contact either mother, and the time spent on the surrogate mothers was automatically recorded. Figure 5 shows the total time spent on the cloth and wire mothers under the two conditions of feeding. These data make it obvious that contact comfort is a variable of overwhelming importance in the development of affectional responses, whereas lactation is a variable of negligible importance. With age and opportunity to learn, subjects with the lactating wire mother showed decreasing responsiveness to her and increasing responsiveness to the nonlactating cloth mother, a finding completely contrary to any interpretation of derived drive in which the

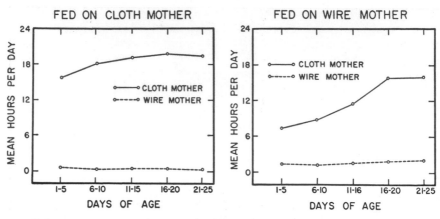

FIGURE 5.   TIME SPENT ON CLOTH AND WIRE MOTHER SURROGATES

mother-form becomes conditioned to hunger-thirst reduction. The persistence of these differential responses throughout 165 consecutive days of testing is evident in Figure 6.

One control group of neonatal monkeys was raised on a single wire mother, and a second control group was raised on a single cloth mother. There were no differences between these two groups in amount of milk ingested or in weight gain. The only difference between the groups lay in the composition of the feces, the softer stools of the wire-mother infants suggesting psychosomatic involvement. The wire mother is biologically adequate but psychologically inept.

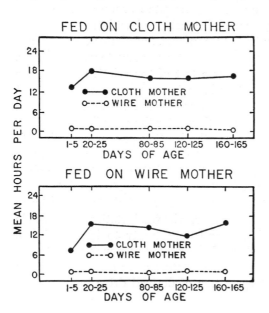

FIGURE 6.   LONG-TERM CONTACT TIME ON CLOTH AND WIRE MOTHER SURROGATES

We were not surprised to discover that contact comfort was an important basic affectional or love variable, but we did not expect it to overshadow so completely the variable of nursing; indeed, the disparity is so great as to suggest that the primary function of nursing as an affectional variable is that of insuring frequent and intimate body contact of the infant with the mother. Certainly, man cannot live by milk alone. Love is an emotion that does not need to be bottle- or spoon-fed, and we may be sure that there is nothing to be gained by giving lip service to love.

A charming lady once heard me describe these experiments; and, when I subsequently talked to her, her face brightened with sudden insight: "Now I know what's wrong with me," she said, "I'm just a wire mother." Perhaps she was lucky. She might have been a wire wife.

We believe that contact comfort has long served the animal kingdom as a motivating agent for affectional responses. Since at the present time we have no experimental data to substantiate this position, we supply information which must be accepted, if at all, on the basis of face validity.

•   •   •   •   •

One function of the real mother, human or sub-human, and presumably of a mother surrogate, is to provide a haven of safety for the infant in times of fear and danger. The frightened or ailing child clings to its mother, not its father; and this selective responsiveness in times of

FIGURE 7. TYPICAL FEAR STIMULUS

FIGURE 8. TYPICAL RESPONSE TO CLOTH MOTHER SURROGATE IN FEAR TEST

distress, disturbance, or danger may be used as a measure of the strength of affectional bonds. We have tested this kind of differential responsiveness by presenting to the infants in their cages, in the presence of the two mothers, various fear-producing stimuli such as the moving toy bear illustrated in Figure 7. A typical response to a fear stimulus is shown in Figure 8, and the data on differential responsiveness are presented in Figure 9. It is apparent that the cloth mother is highly preferred over the wire one, and this differential selectivity is enhanced by age and experience. In this situation, the variable of nursing appears to be of absolutely no importance: the infant consistently seeks the soft mother surrogate regardless of nursing condition.

Similarly, the mother or mother surrogate provides its young with a source of security, and this role or function is seen with special clarity when mother and child are in a strange situation. At the present time we have completed tests for this relationship on four of our eight baby monkeys assigned to the dual mother-surrogate condition by introducing them for three minutes into the strange environment of a room measuring six feet by six feet by six feet (also called the "open-field test") and containing multiple stimuli known to elicit curiosity-manipulatory responses in baby monkeys. The subjects were placed in this situation twice a week for eight weeks with no mother surrogate present during alternate sessions and the cloth mother present during the others. A cloth diaper was always available as one of the stimuli throughout all sessions. After one or two adaptation sessions, the infants always rushed to the mother surrogate when she was present and clutched her, rubbed their bodies against her, and frequently manipulated her body and face. After a few additional sessions, the infants began to use the mother surrogate as a source of security, a base of operations. As is shown in Figures 10 and 11, they would explore and manipulate a stimulus and then return to the mother before adventuring again into the strange new world. The behavior of these infants was quite different when the mother was absent

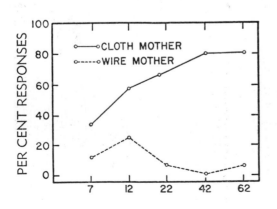

FIGURE 9. DIFFERENTIAL RESPONSIVENESS IN FEAR TESTS

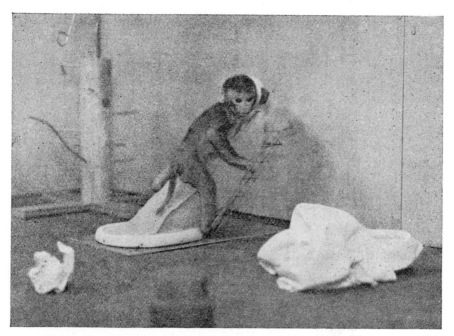

FIGURE 10.   RESPONSE TO CLOTH MOTHER IN THE OPEN-FIELD TEST

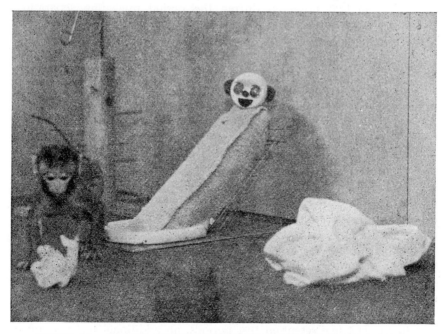

FIGURE 11.   OBJECT EXPLORATION IN PRESENCE OF CLOTH MOTHER

199

from the room. Frequently they would freeze in a crouched position, as is illustrated in Figures 12 and 13. Emotionality indices such as vocalization, crouching, rocking, and sucking increased sharply. . . . Total emotionality score was cut in half when the mother was present. In the absence of the mother some of the experimental monkeys would rush to the center of the room where the mother was customarily placed and then run rapidly from object to object, screaming and crying all the while. Continuous, frantic clutching of their bodies was very common, even when not in the crouching position. These monkeys frequently contacted and clutched the cloth diaper, but this action never pacified them. The same behavior occurred in the presence of the wire mother. No difference between the cloth-mother-fed and wire-mother-fed infants was demonstrated under either condition. Four control infants never raised with a mother surrogate showed the same emotionality scores when the mother was absent as the experimental infants showed in the absence of the mother, but the controls' scores were slightly larger in the presence of the mother surrogate than in her absence.

.   .   .   .   .

Affectional retention was . . . tested in the open field during the first 9 days after separation and then at 30-day intervals, and each test condition was run twice at each retention interval. The infant's behavior differed from that observed during the period preceding separation. When the cloth mother was present in the post-separation period, the babies rushed to her, climbed up, clung tightly to her, and rubbed their heads and faces against her body. After this initial embrace and reunion, they played on the mother, including biting and tearing at her cloth cover; but they rarely made any attempt to leave her during the test period, nor did they manipulate or play with the objects in the room, in contrast with their behavior before maternal separation. The only exception was the occasional monkey that left the mother surrogate momentarily, grasped the folded piece of paper (one of the standard stimuli in the field), and brought it quickly back to the mother. It appeared that deprivation had enhanced the tie to the mother and rendered the contact-comfort need so prepotent that need for the mother overwhelmed the exploratory motives during the brief, three-minute test sessions. No change in these behaviors was observed throughout the 185-day period. When the mother was absent from the open field, the behavior of the infants was similar in the initial retention test to that during the pre-separation tests; but they tended to show gradual adaptation to the open-field situation with repeated testing and, consequently, a reduction in their emotionality scores.

In the last five retention test periods, an additional test was introduced in which the surrogate mother was placed in the center of the

FIGURE 12. RESPONSE IN THE OPEN-FIELD TEST IN THE ABSENCE OF
THE MOTHER SURROGATE

FIGURE 13. RESPONSE IN THE OPEN-FIELD TEST IN THE ABSENCE OF THE
MOTHER SURROGATE

room and covered with a clear Plexiglas box. The monkeys were initially disturbed and frustrated when their explorations and manipulations of the box failed to provide contact with the mother. However, all animals adapted to the situation rather rapidly. Soon they used the box as a place of orientation for exploratory and play behavior, made frequent contacts with the objects in the field, and very often brought these objects to the Plexiglas box. The emotionality index was slightly higher than in the condition of the available cloth mothers, but it in no way approached the emotionality level displayed when the cloth mother was absent. Obviously, the infant monkeys gained emotional security by the presence of the mother even though contact was denied.

Affectional retention has also been measured by tests in which the monkey must unfasten a three-device mechanical puzzle to obtain entrance into a compartment containing the mother surrogate. All the trials are initiated by allowing the infant to go through an unlocked door, and in half the trials it finds the mother present and in half, an empty compartment. The door is then locked and a ten-minute test conducted. In tests given prior to separation from the surrogate mothers, some of the infants had solved this puzzle and others had failed. . . . On the last test before separation there were no differences in total manipulation under mother-present and mother-absent conditions, but striking differences exist between the two conditions throughout the post-separation test periods. Again, there is no interaction with conditions of feeding.

The over-all picture obtained from surveying the retention data is unequivocal. There is little, if any, waning of responsiveness to the mother throughout this five-month period as indicated by any measure. It becomes perfectly obvious that this affectional bond is highly resistant to forgetting and that it can be retained for very long periods of time by relatively infrequent contact reinforcement. During the next year, retention tests will be conducted at 90-day intervals, and further plans are dependent upon the results obtained. It would appear that affectional responses may show as much resistance to extinction as has been previously demonstrated for learned fears and learned pain, and such data would be in keeping with those of common human observation.

. . . . .

We have already described the group of four control infants that had never lived in the presence of any mother surrogate and had demonstrated no sign of affection or security in the presence of the cloth mothers introduced in test sessions. When these infants reached the age of 250 days, cubicles containing both a cloth mother and a wire mother were attached to their cages. There was no lactation in these mothers, for the monkeys were on a solid-food diet. The initial reaction of the monkeys to the alterations was one of extreme disturbance. All the infants screamed violently and made repeated attempts to escape the cage whenever the door was opened. They kept a maximum distance from the mother surrogates and exhibited a considerable amount of rocking and crouching behavior, indicative of emotionality. Our first thought was that the critical period for the development of maternally directed affection had passed and that these macaque children were doomed to live as affectional orphans. Fortunately, these behaviors continued for only 12 to 48 hours and then gradually ebbed, changing from indifference to active contact on, and exploration of, the surrogates. The home-cage behavior of these control monkeys slowly became similar to that of the animals raised with the mother surrogates from birth. Their manipulation and play on the cloth mother became progressively more vigorous to the point of actual mutilation, particularly during the morning after the cloth mother had been given her daily change of terry covering. The control subjects were now actively running to the cloth mother when frightened and had to be coaxed from her to be taken from the cage for formal testing.

. . . . .

Consistent with the results on the subjects reared from birth with dual mothers, these late-adopted infants spent less than one and one-half hours per day in contact with the wire mothers, and this activity level was relatively constant throughout the test sessions. Although the maximum time that the control monkeys spent on the cloth mother was only about half that spent by the original dual mother-surrogate group, we cannot be sure that this discrepancy is a function of differential early experience. The control monkeys were about three months older when the mothers were attached to their cages than the experimental animals had been when their mothers were removed and the retention tests begun. Thus, we do not know what the amount of contact would be for a 250-day-old animal raised from birth with surrogate mothers. Nevertheless, the magnitude of the differences and the fact that the contact-time curves for the mothered-from-birth infants had remained constant for almost 150 days suggest that early experience with the mother is a variable of measurable importance.

. . . . .

Before the introduction of the mother surrogate into the home-cage situation, only one of the four control monkeys had ever contacted the cloth mother in the open-field tests. In general, the surrogate mother not only gave the infants no security, but instead appeared to serve as a fear stimulus. The emotionality scores of these control subjects were slightly higher during the mother-present test sessions than during the mother-absent test sessions. These behaviors were changed radically by the fourth post-introduction test approximately 6o days later. In the absence of the cloth mothers the emotionality index in this fourth test remains near the earlier level, but the score is reduced by half when the mother is present, a result strikingly similar to that found for infants raised with the dual mother-surrogates from birth. The control infants now show increasing object exploration and play behavior, and they begin to use the mother as a base of operations, as did the infants raised from birth with the mother surrogates. However, there are still definite differences in the behavior of the two groups. The control infants do not rush directly to the mother and clutch her violently; but instead they go toward, and orient around her, usually after an initial period during which they frequently show disturbed behavior, exploratory behavior, or both.

That the control monkeys develop affection or love for the cloth mother when she is introduced into the cage at 250 days of age cannot be questioned. There is every reason to believe, however, that this interval of delay depresses the intensity of the affectional response below that of the infant monkeys that were surrogate-mothered from birth onward. In interpreting these data it is well to remember that the control monkeys had had continuous opportunity to observe and hear other monkeys housed in adjacent cages and that they had had limited opportunity to view and contact surrogate mothers in the test situations, even though they did not exploit the opportunities.

During the last two years we have observed the behavior of two infants raised by their own mothers. Love for the real mother and love for the surrogate mother appear to be very similar. The baby macaque spends many hours a day clinging to its real mother. If away from the mother when frightened, it rushes to her and in her presence shows comfort and composure. As far as we can observe, the infant monkey's affection for the real mother is strong, but no stronger than that of the experimental monkey for the surrogate cloth mother, and the security that the infant gains from the presence of the real mother is no greater than the security it gains from a cloth surrogate. Next year we hope to put this problem to final, definitive, experimental test. But, whether the mother is real or a cloth surrogate, there does develop a deep and abiding bond between mother and child. In one case it may be the call of the wild and in the other the McCall of civilization, but in both cases there is "togetherness."

In spite of the importance of contact comfort, there is reason to believe that other variables of measurable importance will be discovered. Postural support may be such a variable, and it has been suggested that, when we build arms into the mother surrogate, 10 is the minimal number required to provide adequate child care. Rocking motion may be such a variable, and we are comparing rocking and stationary mother surrogates and inclined planes. The differential responsiveness to cloth mother and cloth-covered inclined plane suggests that clinging as well as contact is an affectional variable of importance. Sounds, particularly natural, maternal sounds, may operate as either unlearned or learned affectional variables. Visual responsiveness may be such a variable, and it is possible that some semblance of visual imprinting may develop in the neonatal monkey. There are indications that this becomes a variable of importance during the course of infancy through some maturational process.

John Bowlby has suggested that there is an affectional variable which he calls "primary object following," characterized by visual and oral search of the mother's face. Our surrogate-mother-raised baby monkeys are at first inattentive to her face, as are human neonates to human mother faces. But by 30 days of age ever-increasing responsiveness to the mother's face appears—whether through learning, maturation, or both—and we have reason to believe that the face becomes an object of special attention.

Our first surrogate-mother-raised baby had a mother whose head was just a ball of wood since the baby was a month early and we had not had time to design a more esthetic head and face. This baby had contact with the blank-faced mother for 180 days and was then placed with two cloth mothers, one motionless and one rocking, both being endowed with painted, ornamented faces. To our surprise the animal would compulsively rotate both faces 180 degrees so that it viewed only a round, smooth face and never the painted, ornamented face. Furthermore, it would do this as long as the patience of the experimenter in reorienting the faces persisted. The monkey showed no sign of fear or anxiety, but it showed unlimited persistence. Subsequently it improved its technique, compulsively removing the heads and rolling them into its cage as fast as they were returned. We are intrigued by this observation, and we plan to examine systematically the role of the mother face in the development of infant-monkey affections. Indeed, these observations suggest the need for a series of ethological-type researches on the two-faced female.

Although we have made no attempts thus far to study the generalization of infant-macaque affection or love, the techniques which we have developed offer promise in this uncharted field. Beyond this, there are few if any technical difficulties in studying the affection of the actual, living mother for the child, and the techniques developed can be utilized and expanded for the analysis and developmental study of father-infant and infant-infant affection.

Since we can measure neonatal and infant affectional responses to mother surrogates, and since we know they are strong and persisting, we are in a position to assess the effects of feeding and contactual schedules; consistency and inconsistency in the mother surrogates; and early, intermediate, and late maternal deprivation. Again, we have here a family of problems of fundamental interest and theoretical importance.

21. THE DEVELOPMENT OF AFFECTIONATE BEHAVIOR IN INFANCY

KATHARINE M. BANHAM

The psychoanalysts Freud and Adler and the pioneering child psychologist Jean Piaget all held that the child first loves himself and that only in later developments does he begin to love others. The child's love is thus seen simply as the desire to control that which gratifies his immediate needs— perhaps even to swallow it up—in order to be assured of continuing gratification.

Katharine Banham's observations of 900 infants did not confirm this viewpoint. She found outgoing, affectionate behavior as natural and spontaneous in the infant as self-love.

The problem of defining love remains a complicated one. Harlow (selection 20) indicated that being soft, warm, and touchable was definitely an aspect of "lovableness." "I love you," may mean, "I need you," or, "I can let you go"; or, "I want to take care of you," or, "I want you to take care of me."

The concept "affectionate behavior" will be limited in this article to certain responses of infants in social situations, rather than with reference to inanimate objects. To be sure, a child may develop affectionate attachments for things as well as people, but these are more suitably classified as "interests." Where the attachment is very strong towards some particular object, such as a knotted handkerchief, it is thought to be due in most cases to association with human affections. In other words, the so-called "love object" represents, and is a substitute for, a human object of affection. Behavior which may be called affectionate develops primarily in relation to persons and only secondarily

Reprinted from *Journal of Genetic Psychology,* 76 (1950), 283–289, by permission of the author and The Journal Press.

in relation to things, or parts of the body, as substitutions or cues for the whole love relationship.

A tentative theory of the development of affection in infants is presented in the following paragraphs. It has been formulated inductively as a result of observation of 900 or more infants between four weeks and two years of age in social situations. No specially controlled experimental situation was set up. The behavior of the infants was merely noted incidentally during the course of psychological examination for estimation of level of mental development, in the preliminary period of becoming acquainted with both infant and guardians, and after completion of the tests. Some babies were in their own homes, a few were brought to child guidance clinics by social workers, some were in hospital wards, but by far the greatest number, about 600, were seen in boarding and adoptive homes, in the states of New Jersey and Iowa, and in the city of Montreal, Canada.

Affectionate behavior is first shown by the infant in an out-going striving and approach. Its gaze is fixed upon the person's face. It kicks, holds out and waves its arms, and tries to raise its body from the crib. The direction of the arm and leg movement is not well oriented or coordinated in the beginning, but repeated attempts to get closer to the attractive person become more successful, and useless movements are restrained. The child is struggling all the time, giving out energy, smiling and apparently enjoying the opportunity for self expression, just as it "enjoys" and responds delightedly to the smiles and social approach of the desired individual, be it mother, nurse, father, or sibling.

This affectionate behavior makes its beginning around four months of age, although the child does not reach out and pat the person of his affections until he is about six months old. Individual babies vary in their rate of development of coordinated movement. Between five and six months of age babies usually come to distinguish, in their perceptions and behavioral response, the familiar person from the stranger. It is then that definite affectionate attachments begin to show themselves. The mother, or other person who has nursed and fed the child longest, has changed its wet diapers, talked and sung to it, is preferred to other more transient acquaintances.

The child responds reciprocally to affectionate cuddling. It reaches out for the mother's face and mouth. Possibly, it would feed her if it could. Later, as a toddler, it does try to feed its dolls, carry them about, wrap them warmly, and rock them to sleep. Affectionate behavior, even in its beginnings, as all through life, is that of cherishing, protecting, giving of the self to and caring for another person. Attention is directed outward and not inward to bodily sensation.

There seems little evidence from the observation of infant behavior that "self-love" comes first in the development of human affections.

"Other love" is rather the first to appear, and develops along with the child's differentiating percept, and later with his concept of the human being who cares for him. The child is apparently unaware of, and unconcerned about himself. Certainly, he finds objects of interest to explore and sense. At about three months of age he discovers and watches his fingers, he listens to his own babbling and cooing; but his striving, excited affectionate behavior is directed toward another human being, usually mother.

The concept of "mother" has come about as a patterning of partially repeated percepts, and the associating of sensori-motor experiences accompanied by tension release and pleasurable gratification. The snug comfort of the mother's steady arm, the warm smooth taste of milk, its faint smell, the sound of mother's voice, and the sight of her smiling face have come to be distinguished in the child's experience from other smaller groups of pleasurable sensations, those that are not repeated in the same way, nor in connection with recurrent biological needs.

As memory develops, so does anticipation. Toward the end of the first year the child shows evidence of anticipation of the arrival of mother at mealtime, or when he is in a state of bodily discomfort, even though he cannot see her. He calls for her, squirms and wriggles. When she comes, he shows delight at her approach by laughter and banging with his hand, or pulling whatever object is nearest within reach, shoestring, ribbon, or bedcover, in attempts to reach her.

A child who has been well cared-for develops a pleasing concept of, and favorable attitude toward, "mother," and toward adults in general. During a brief period of a few months beginning in the second half of the first year, when the infant has learned to distinguish between familiar and unfamiliar persons, he shows a withdrawing reaction, muscular tension and emotional distress in the presence of strangers. Fondling, and being spoken to in a friendly way by a variety of persons soon dispels his anxiety, and broadens his conception of lovable persons.

At the same time as the child is learning to distinguish, and behave differentially with, strange adults he is discovering his own body and himself. During the second year when he begins to move about independently, he develops a concept of himself as a discrete and comprehensive unit. He gives himself a good time, exploring, running, and babbling a rhythmic but unintelligible jargon. He likes himself, judging from the way he collects things to give to himself, to pile in the saucepan his mother gave him or in his truck. But for the most part, he still likes mother best. If he runs away from her it may not be from antagonism, though this may be true in isolated cases, but because the whole big world he has found so enjoyable attracts him. He trusts mother to come after him and be there when he needs her.

Some children during the second year turn their affections upon themselves more than others do. Learning from experience that their mothers are not always ready to receive and reciprocate their affectionate embraces, they become temporarily subdued, and eventually find substitute objects of interest toward which to direct their manipulative activity. When the young child finds he has a diminishing share of mother's attention, particularly after the arrival of a new baby, and an increase in interference with his explorations and loving advances, he develops antagonistic and negative rather than approaching and affectionate behavior toward her.

This phase of fluctuating behavior, out-going and affectionate at one time, withdrawn or hostile at another, is usually only temporary, lasting through the second and third year. During that time the child is developing a richer concept of "mother," or of the mother substitute, and a stronger attachment to her. The association of emotional stimulation and of freedom of action which the mother allows the child, with the security of control and guidance which she gives him appears to be most eminently satisfying. Even though the mother thwarts the child at times, at others she rescues him from tight places and difficulties. She comforts him when he is sick or hurt, and he in his turn behaves compassionately toward her. He cries if he thinks she is hurt, climbs on to her knee and tries to comfort her with caresses.

Although the masculine gender has been used in the above brief sketches of the child's affectionate responses, this is just conventional usage. No sex distinction is implied. Girl babies and boy babies express their affection in like manner. Moreover, affectionate behavior in its beginnings is sex-less in direction and nature. If a man cares for a baby he comes to be the human object of its first affection, and the child behaves affectionately toward him.

Later in the child's development, beginning in the second year, somewhat different responses may be made to men and women, and to other children, depending on the way in which these individuals treat the baby. His actions are now imitative. His conception of the world of people and his reaction to other people depends upon the way they appear to him and behave with him. A talkative or whining mother is likely to have an exacting child. Similarly, a boisterous father, anxious for attention tends to draw out noisy, attention-seeking behavior in his son. Over-anxious parents who do everything for their child, expecting no reciprocity from him, focus his attention on himself and thwart his natural growth of out-going affection. Jealous older children by their example and by monopoly of adult attention may also cause the younger child to develop selfish traits of behavior. On the other hand, normal family affection, which is the most common, is reflected in the small infant's spontaneous affectionate behavior toward persons of either sex and any age.

Since the child's concept of himself appears to develop later than his concept of another person, the favorableness of his impression of himself as a person will depend to considerable extent upon the favorableness of his concepts of others. As adults and other children have acted towards him, so he behaves with them and in regard to himself. He laughingly excuses mistakes, or shows hasty impatience, dislike and intolerance of himself and his shortcomings, just as he does those of others. Affectionate behavior is emotional behavior, in that it involves total bodily response, visceral and motor, not just a single and specific action pattern.

First social impressions and behavioral responses are, however, subject to change. Later experiences may counter-balance earlier influences and modify a child's emotional reactions in regard to his guardian, himself, a sibling, or an adult rival. The child deprived of affection, or frustrated in his attempts to show affection early in life, generally finds other people who are more ingratiating and appreciative of his efforts and gifts, and he responds affectionately toward them. He need not necessarily develop a distorted and selfish attitude to life, nor other neurotic symptoms, because of privations or undue frustration in infancy. The great majority of children seen in adoptive homes by the writer, one or more years after placement, showed completely happy affectionate relationships with their new parents and neighbors, although many of them had been neglected in early infancy, or restricted in activity in hospital wards.

Explorative behavior with regard to the erogenous zones of the infant's own body appears and recurs within the first two or three years of life, apparently unrelated to affectionate attachments. It is part of the child's differentiating perception of the world of reality, and of himself in relation to it. His reactions to that world within the first few weeks of life are largely passive, or diffuse and random. The most definite and repeated actions are those which reduce tension produced by biological needs and induce sleep. His first coordinated and differentiated responses of affection are shown towards the person who cares for him, not himself. These develop within three or four months after birth. Association of human affection with erogenous zones and genital organs may come later, but is not a universal trait of infant behavior. Sucking, eliminating, biting and "possessing" or hoarding occur independently of the social situation, and are not necessarily socially or sexually linked.

Long series of controlled observations of infants in various social situations, and alone, are needed to substantiate the views here expressed, preferably with sound and movie picture recording. The behavior of children who have been early deprived of affection should be compared side by side with those who have always had a fond mother's care. Responses to persons of both sex and of different ages should be studied, also the reactions of infants of different races and social cultures. It is very questionable whether all children develop attachments to parents of the opposite sex, and whether they go successively through phases of autoeroticism and bisexuality on to heterosexual relationships, even in Western culture, let alone Asiatic, African or other cultures. In fact there is strong evidence from observable behavior of children that they do no such thing.

Infants of either sex brought up by nurses, older sisters, neighbors, and grand-parents were observed by the writer to develop the same kind of affectionate attachments for them as a baby normally shows toward its mother. Girl babies raised by mothers, or other women, in the absence of the fathers were no less and no more neurotic and dependent during school years than were boy babies so brought up, judging from reports of school adjustment and progress and friendly social relationships. A more objective and systematic investigation, however, is needed to substantiate or refute the above statements made from casual inquiry.

The writer's main thesis, based on direct observation of infant behavior over a period of 20 years, is that infants develop unique affectionate attachments for the persons in their own environment, for adults and children, men and women alike. They express their affection in outgoing, expansive movements, and they only become preoccupied with themselves, withdrawn or hostile as a secondary reaction, when rebuffed, smothered with unwanted ministrations, ignored or neglected. Such self-centered, self sufficient kind of behavior is often expressed by two-year-olds in self-initiated, solitary activity, but it is short-lived in normally healthy youngsters. They seek companionship, laugh at the antics and the noises made by others; they offer presents, sit up close, stroke and caress the persons of whom they are fond. They try to make others happy, and so continue their own social enjoyment, by the sort of behavior that has pleased them. They are encouraged by progressive gratification of affection to struggle with obstacles, explore further, and make an ever widening circle of friends.

In order of development, affectionate behavior is ordinarily expressed by the child under five months of age indiscriminately toward whoever approaches him in a friendly manner. During the second half of the first year he behaves affectionately toward familiar, rather than unfamiliar persons. But strangers may win his affections within a few minutes or hours, depending upon the individual child and attendant favorable or disturbing circumstances. His social attachments are already beginning to grow in number and strength.

During the second year, among the objects of the child's affections may be included himself. He clings to his toys, clothes, or chair, and collects small objects. He attracts attention to himself and cries at interference. From this phase, within the second and third year, he passes to one where affectionate behavior is shown largely to adults, but also to other children as well as himself. He fetches and carries things for others, laughs and talks with them, strokes and pats either gently or vigorously. Energetic patting may be a partial solution of a difficulty, a compromise between affection and jealous hostility. Playful biting, too, may be an adaptive compromise response in certain children. "Sadism" does not appear to be a universal trait or phase of infant behavior. Gradually during the preschool period, the child learns to laugh or exclaim good-naturedly at interference, such as previously brought tears or protest. He treats minor accidents either to himself or to others as jokes, and continues to show affection for others, in spite of the interference they cause with ardent desires of his own.

A child's affectionate behavior develops along with his social concepts, those of people in general, of specific persons including himself, of familiar and unfamiliar adults and children. The form of the behavior changes in adaptation to the social situation surrounding each individual child, but is always approaching, protecting, giving and "cherishing" in nature for the human object of affection. Hostile reactions can scarcely be regarded as affectionate, even though they may be directed towards a person formerly treated with affection, or maybe an imitation of that person's behavior with the child. They are usually explosive and temporary, effecting a gross change or removal of the offending situation. Affectionate behavior, on the other hand, tends to prolong, repeat or enhance the agreeable social interaction.

22. RESULTS OF SELF-SELECTION OF DIETS BY YOUNG CHILDREN

CLARA M. DAVIS

The late Dr. Davis experimentally concluded that, given a variety of natural foods from which to choose, infants can properly select their own healthy diets. Unfortunately, her classic study has often been misquoted, and unwarranted implications have been drawn from it; many "experts" have concluded that children possess a natural wisdom in their appetites and that they therefore should be permitted to eat

Reprinted from *Canadian Medical Association Journal*, 41 (1939), 257–261, by permission of the author and publisher.

whatever and whenever they please. But in the experiment described here care was taken to omit processed foods—such as refined sugar, candy, jams, cookies, macaroni, and soft drinks—and food was offered only three times a day, at definite mealtimes.

A similar study observing older children whose appetites had been "perverted" and who were allowed to roam freely in an environment filled with popsicles, soft drinks, etc., as well as natural foods might be an important sequel to the observations presented here.

The self-selection of diet experiment had for its subjects infants of weaning age, who had never had supplements of the ordinary foods of adult life. This age was chosen because only at his age could we have individuals who had neither had experience of such foods nor could have been influenced by the ideas of older persons and so would be without preconceived prejudices and biases with regard to them. The children concerned were studied for six years.

The list of foods used in the experiment was made up with the following considerations in mind. It should comprise a wide range of foods of both animal and vegetable origin that would adequately provide all the food elements, amino-acids, fats, carbohydrates, vitamins and minerals known to be necessary for human nutrition. The foods should be such as could generally be procured fresh in the market the year around. The list should contain only natural food materials and no incomplete foods or canned foods. Thus, cereals were whole grains; sugars were not used nor were milk products, such as cream, butter or cheese.

The preparation of the foods was as simple as possible. All meats, vegetables and fruits were finely cut, mashed or ground. Most of the foods were served only after being cooked, but lettuce was served only raw, while oat meal, wheat, beef, bone marrow, eggs, carrots, peas, cabbage and apples were served both raw and cooked. Lamb, chicken and glandular organs, all of local origin and not Federal inspected, were cooked as a measure of safety. Cooking was done without the loss of soluble substances and without the addition of salt or seasonings. Water was not added except in the case of cereals. Combinations of food materials such as custards, soups or bread were not used, thus insuring that each food when eaten was chosen for itself alone.

The list of foods was as follows:

1. Water
2. Sweet milk
3. Sour (lactic) milk
4. Sea salt (Seisal)
5. Apples
6. Bananas

7. Orange juice	21. Wheat	
8. Fresh pineapple	22. Corn meal	
9. Peaches	23. Barley	
10. Tomatoes	24. Ry-Krisp	
11. Beets	25. Beef	
12. Carrots	26. Lamb	
13. Peas	27. Bone marrow	
14. Turnips	28. Bone jelly	
15. Cauliflower	29. Chicken	
16. Cabbage	30. Sweetbreads	
17. Spinach	31. Brains	
18. Potatoes	32. Liver	
19. Lettuce	33. Kidneys	
20. Oatmeal	34. Fish (haddock)	

The entire list could not, of course, be gotten ready and served at one time and was therefore divided and served at three (in the early weeks, four) meals a day, this arrangement providing a wide variety at each meal. Both sweet and sour (lactic) milk, two kinds of cereals, animal protein foods, and either fruits or vegetables were served at each meal according to a fixed schedule. Each article, even salt, was served in a separate dish, salt not being added to any, nor was milk poured over the cereal. All portions were weighed or measured before serving and the remains weighed or measured on the return of the tray to the diet kitchen.

Food was not offered to the infant either directly or by suggestion. The nurses' orders were to sit quietly by, spoon in hand, and make no motion. When, and only when, the infant reached for or pointed to a dish might she take up a spoonful and, if he opened his mouth for it, put it in. She might not comment on what he took or did not take, point to or in any way attract his attention to any food, or refuse him any for which he reached. He might eat with his fingers or in any way he could without comment on or correction of his manners. The tray was to be taken away when he had definitely stopped eating, which was usually after from twenty to twenty-five minutes.

The results of his six-year study of self-selection of diet by young children from the time of weaning on may, for the purpose of this discussion, be conveniently grouped under three heads: (1) The results in terms of health and nutrition of the fifteen children; (2) the adequacy of the self-chosen diets as judged by nutritional laws and standards; (3) the contributions made by the study to our understanding of appetite and how it functions.

Like the lives of the happy, the annals of the healthy and vigorous make little exciting news. There were no failures of infants to manage their own diets; all had hearty appetites; all throve. Constipation was unknown among them and laxatives were never used or needed. Except in presence of parenteral infection, there was no vomiting or diarrhoea. Colds were usually of the mild three-day type without complications of any kind. There were a few cases of tonsillitis but no serious illness among the children in the six years. Curiously enough, the only epidemic to visit the nursery was acute glandular fever of Pfeiffer with which all the children in the nursery came down like ninepins on the same day. During this epidemic when temperatures of 103 to 105° F. prevailed, as with colds, etc., trays were served as usual, the children continuing to select their own food from the regular list. This led to the interesting observation that just as loss of appetite often precedes by twenty-four to forty-eight hours every other discoverable sign and symptom of acute infection, so return of appetite precedes by twelve to twenty-four hours all other signs of convalescence, occurring when fever is still high and enabling the observer to correctly predict its fall. This eating of a hearty meal when fever is still high is often not in evidence when children are put on restricted diets during such illness, but the correctness of the observation has been amply confirmed in the Children's Memorial Hospital where a modification of the self-selective method of feeding prevails. During convalescence unusually large amounts of raw beef, carrots and beets were eaten. The demand for increased amounts of raw beef and carrots can be easily accounted for but we are still curious about that for beets, and inclined to wonder whether they may furnish an anti-anaemic substance (iron?) from the fact that beets were eaten by all in much larger quantities in the first six months or year after weaning than ever again save after colds and acute glandular fever.

Some of the infants were in rather poor condition when taken for the experiment. Four were poorly nourished and underweight; five had rickets. Two of these five had only roentgenological signs of rickets, and one mild clinical rickets as well, while the other two were typical textbook cases. The first infant received for the study was one of the two with severe rickets, and, bound by a promise to do nothing or leave nothing undone to his detriment, we put a small glass of cod liver oil on his tray for him to take if he chose. This he did irregularly and in varying amounts until his blood calcium and phosphorus became normal and x-ray films showed his rickets to be healed, after which he did not take it again. He had taken just over two ounces in all. No other of the 15 children had any cod liver oil, viosterol, treatment by ultra-violet rays or other dietary adjuvants at any time during the study, and all four of the other cases of rickets were healed in approximately the same length of time as was the first. Regardless, however, of their condition when received, within a reasonable time the nutrition of all, checked as it was at regular and frequent intervals by physical examinations, urine analyses, blood counts, haemoglobin estimations and roentgeno-grams of bones, came up to the standard of optimal so far as could be discovered by examinations.

However, as I may be thought to have been unduly biased in my estimate of this rollicking, rosy-cheeked group, Dr. Joseph Brennemann's appraisal of them may be of interest. In his article, "Psychologic aspects of nutrition," published in an early number of the *Journal of Pediatrics,* he says, "I saw them on a number of occasions and they were the finest group of specimens from the physical and behavior standpoint that I have ever seen in children of that age."

But all is not gold that glitters. Carefully controlled laboratory ex-periments with animals have shown that growth and nutrition through-out the entire growth period may be satisfactory on diets that are slightly deficient in some of the essentials; and that such slight deficiencies only became evident as lessened vigor, fertility and longevity in adult life. Long as was the time these children remained on the study—none less than six months, and all but two from one to four and one-half years—but a fraction of the growth period was covered. One might, therefore, raise a skeptical eyebrow and say, "The examinations of these children do not by any means prove that all, some, or any of them were indeed optimally nourished; or that any of their diets were in fact adequate in the scientific sense. Whether appetite was or was not a competent guide to their eating can only be shown by checking their diets with nutri-tional laws and standards."

Such checking of each of the fifteen diets in its entirety (the grand total of all meals eaten by the children was nearly 36,000) gave, in summary, the following results:

QUANTITIES OF FOOD EATEN

The average daily calories furnished by the diets during each six months' period were in every instance found to be within the limits set by scientific nutritional standards for the individual's age. So, too, were the average daily calories per kilogram of body weight, except in the few instances in which infants, undernourished before weaning, ex-ceeded the standard in their first six months' period on the experiment. Finally, the law of the decline of calories, per kilogram of body weight, with growth was followed without exception and in orderly fashion as shown by curves made on a monthly basis. Quite possibly it is the close conformity of the diets to these quantitative laws and standards that accounts for the fact that there were after the first six months' period of each child no noticeably fat or thin children, but a greater uniformity of build than often obtains among those of the same family.

POTENTIAL ACIDITY AND ALKALINITY OF THE DIETS

Maintenance of the acid-base balance of the blood requires that potentially acid constituents of the diet must be at least balanced by constituents of potential alkalinity, and most authorities agree that a moderate excess of potentially alkaline ones is desirable. Regarding the relation of this law to dietary practice, H. C. Sherman says that while an upset of the acid-base balance resulting in ketosis may occur when the proportions of carbohydrates, proteins and fats in the diet are out of the proper relation to each other, "it is presumably rare in normal individuals on self-chosen diets." This proved to be the case with the diets of the children. In the diet of one child there was an exact balance of potentially acid and potentially alkaline constituents during his first and only six months' period. In the diets of the other fourteen there was a moderate preponderance of the potentially alkaline in every months' period.

THE DISTRIBUTION OF CALORIES

Nutritional science has been much concerned with the problem of the proper distribution of calories among the three dietary constituents—fat, carbohydrate and protein—and especially about the percentage of calories to be allotted to protein with which carbohydrates and fats are not interchangeable as body-builders. Authorities vary somewhat in the percentages they allot to protein for children below the age of five years, *i.e.*, in general, from 10 per cent to 17 per cent. For the self-chosen diets, the *average* distribution of calories per kilogram of body weight (regardless of variations in children's age) was protein 17 per cent, fat 35 per cent and carbohydrate 48 per cent. The individual range for the protein in the group was from 9 per cent to 20 per cent. All diets showed a decline in protein per kilogram of body weight in accordance with the change in the relation of body-building requirements to energy requirements that comes with growth and increased activity. Quality of protein is, however, no less important than quantity. The protein of the diets was in every case protein of the highest biological value, having been predominantly derived from such animal sources as milk, eggs, liver, kidney and muscle meats.

Because of the extent to which the essentially energy furnishing fats and carbohydrates are interchangeable in nutrition, few authorities make any allocation of the remaining 83 per cent of calories between them. The average distribution for these in the diets as a group (fat 35 per cent, carbohydrate 48 per cent) differs but slightly from that advocated by Rose.

As yet no statistical analysis of the diets has been made for their vitamin and mineral contents, but with all vegetables fresh, all cereals whole grains, ground by the old stone process, eggs, liver and kidney eaten freely, fresh fruits eaten in amazingly large quantities, and the salt used, an unpurified sea salt containing all the minerals found in the body, the probability of any deficiency in vitamins or minerals is slight indeed. In fact, the quantities of fresh fruit, carrots and potatoes and of eggs, liver and kidneys in practically all the diets preclude, on the basis of their known vitamin content, any shortage of Vitamins A, B, C and G. For the adequacy in vitamin D and calcium of the diets of children who took none or little milk for considerable periods of time we cannot speak so surely from an off-hand consideration of the quantities of foods eaten. We can, however, call in evidence the roentgenograms of these children's bones which showed as excellent calcification as those of the others.

Regarding the calcification of bones in the group, Dr. W. E. Anspach, Roentgenologist of the Children's Memorial Hospital, has written in a personal communication to your essayist, "The beautifully calcified bones in roentgenograms of your group of children stand out so well that I have no trouble in picking them out when seen at a distance." That such "beautiful calcification" of bones was achieved by all, regardless of whether or not they had rickets when admitted, would seem difficult to account for, had adequate calcium or vitamin D been lacking.

The diets, then, were orthodox, conforming to nutritional laws and standards in what they furnished. The children actually were as well nourished as they looked to be.

Such successful juggling and balancing of the more than thirty nutritional essentials that exist in mixed and different proportions in the foods from which they must be derived suggests at once the existence of some innate, automatic mechanism for its accomplishment, of which appetite is a part. It is certainly difficult to account for the success of the fifteen unrelated infants on any other grounds.

Also, such success with the nutritional essentials suggests the possibility that appetite indicated one orthodox diet in terms of foods and the quantities of them, comparable to the diet lists of paediatricians and nutritionists. But to this possibility the self-chosen diets give not a scintilla of support. In terms of foods and relative quantities of them they failed to show any orthodoxy of their own and were wholly unorthodox with respect to paediatric practice. For every diet differed from every other diet, fifteen different patterns of taste being presented, and not one diet was the predominantly cereal and milk diet with smaller supplements of fruit, eggs and meat, that is commonly thought proper for this age. To add to the apparent confusion, tastes changed unpredictably from time to time, refusing as we say "to stay put," while meals were often combinations of foods that were strange indeed to us, and would have been a dietitian's nightmare—for example, a breakfast of a pint of orange juice and liver; a supper of several eggs, bananas and milk. They achieved the goal, but by widely various means, as Heaven may presumably be reached by different roads.

This seemingly irresponsible and erratic behavior of appetite with respect to selection of foods from which the essentials were obtained stamps it as the same Puckish fellow we have always known it to be. Why, then, were his pranks beneficent in the experiment when so often harmful elsewhere? Or to put it baldly, as I hope many of you are doing, what was the trick in the experiment? This brings us to the discussion of what we learned about appetite and its workings, that throws light on the question of its competencies and fallibilities.

Selective appetite is, primarily, the desire for foods that please by smelling or tasting good, and it would seem that in the absence of such sensory information, i.e., if one had never smelled or tasted a food, he could not know whether he liked or disliked it. Such proved to be the case with these infants. When the large tray of foods, each in its separate dish, was placed before them at their first meals, there was not the faintest sign of "instinct" directed choice. On the contrary, their choices were apparently wholly random; they tried not only foods but chewed hopefully the clean spoon, dishes, the edge of the tray, or a piece of paper on it. Their faces showed expressions of surprise, followed by pleasure, indifference or dislike. All the articles on the list, except lettuce by two and spinach by one, were tried by all, and most tried several times, but within the first few days they began to reach eagerly for some and to neglect others, so that definite tastes grew under our eyes. Never again did any child eat so many of the foods as in the first weeks of his experimental period. Patterns of selective appetite, then, were shown to develop on the basis of sensory experience, *i.e.*, taste, smell, and doubtless the feeling of comfort and well-being that followed eating, which was evidenced much as in the breast-fed infant. In short, they were developed by sampling, which is essentially a trial and error method. And it is this trial and error method, this willingness to sample, that accounts for the most glaring fallibility of appetite. From time immemorial adults as well as children have eaten castor oil beans, poisonous fish, toad stools and nightshade berries with fatal results. Against such error, only the transmission of racial experience as knowledge can protect. Such error affords additional proof that in omnivorous eaters there is no "instinct" pointing blindly to the "good" or "bad" in food. And since every trial and error method involves the possibility of error, the problem of successful eating by appetite is that of reducing possible errors to those that are most trivial by a prior selection of the foods that are made available for eating.

Appetite also appears to have fallibilities with processed foods which have lost some of their natural constituents and which have become such important features of modern diet, *e.g.*, sugar and white flour. Certainly their introduction into previously sound primitive diets has invariably brought with it a train of nutritional evils, and ther widespread excess in civilized diets is decried by nutritional authorities. Whether the evils are due to innate fallibilities of appetite with respect to these products, or whether appetite in such cases is merely overruled by extraneous considerations of novelty, cheapness, ease of procurement and preparation, etc., has not been determined.

We had hoped to investigate this problem in a small way by an experiment with newly weaned infants in which both natural foods and their processed products were simultaneously served, but the depression dashed this hope.

By this time you have all doubtless perceived that the "trick" in the experiment (if "trick" you wish to call it) was in the food list. Confined to natural, unprocessed and unpurified foods as it was, and without made dishes of any sort, it reproduced to a large extent the conditions under which primitive peoples in many parts of the world have been shown to have had scientifically sound diets and excellent nutrition. Errors the children's appetites must have made—they are inherent in any trial and error method—but the errors with such a food list were too trivial and too easily compensated for to be of importance or even to be detected.

The results of the experiment, then, leave the selection of the foods to be made available to young children in the hands of their elders where everyone has always known it belongs. Even the food list is not a magic one. Any of you with a copy of McCollum's or H. C. Sherman's books on nutrition and properties of foods, could make a list quite different and equally as good. Self-selection can have no, or but doubtful, value if the diet must be selected from inferior foods. Finally, by providing conditions under which appetite could function freely and beneficently as in animals and primitive peoples, the experiment resolved the modern conflict between appetite and nutritional requirements. It eliminated anorexia and the eating problems that are the plague of feeding by the dosage method.

PART III

CHILDHOOD

The Child Views His World

INTRODUCTION

The well-known fable of the four blind men and the elephant illustrates one important psychological principle—the individual's view of his world often depends upon his particular position in it. The world seen by adults, for example, is vastly different from that seen by the child. How do children see their mothers and sisters; their schools, teachers, paints, and pencils; and their friends on the street? The meaning of a child's interactions with his world depends, of course, upon his perceptions of this world.

The articles reprinted in this Part demonstrate some aspects of the child's world gained through inference from and careful analysis of children's behavior. The selections from *Patterns of Child Rearing* offer conclusions based on both children's and mothers' behavior. Wolfenstein and Buhler interpret the child's view from his jokes and drawings, while Alper describes experiments showing how children react to finger paints. Child's article analyzes children's textbooks; responding to his conclusions, some readers may want to run out and quickly rewrite the books. The last four studies in this Part discuss the interaction of the child with his group and teacher, showing how changes in either may effect definite changes in how he feels about his world and how he behaves.

23. PATTERNS OF CHILD REARING

ROBERT R. SEARS, ELEANOR E. MACCOBY, AND
HARRY LEVIN

*Should a child be breast fed? What are the causes of bed-
wetting? How frequently do children express aggression against
their parents, and what patterns does such aggressive behavior
take?*

These passages from Patterns of Child Rearing *offer
interpretations of the descriptions of child-rearing practices
by 379 New England suburban mothers. The entire book
presents evidence that middle-class mothers are more
permissive than those of the lower class.*

Allison Davis and Robert J. Havighurst, however, concluded
in their studies that middle-class mothers were more restrictive
—completing weaning and toilet training earlier and being
more rigid in feeding. They also found, as did Kinsey, that
middle-class children masturbate more often and concluded
that this was due to the tensions resulting from the restrictions
imposed on them. Whiting and Child,† who studied child
rearing throughout the world, have claimed that children of
the American middle class are among the most restricted
anywhere.*

. . . Breast feeding and self-demand scheduling have received the
most interested public discussion in recent years. Militant enthusiasts for
both have generated more excitement than facts. They have reasoned,
in effect, that the "natural way" is best, and that a deep insecurity is
created in infancy by bottle-propping or rigid scheduling or other
methods of impersonalizing the feeding experience. They have talked
much of *good* and *bad* consequences of various infant care practices
without sure evidence that there are any consistent consequences at all.
It is worth reviewing what we have discovered about these matters.

Sixty per cent of the mothers in this sample did not breast-feed

---

* Allison Davis and Robert J. Havighurst, *Father of the Man* (Boston: Houghton
Mifflin Co., 1947).

† J. W. M. Whiting and I. L. Child, *Child Training and Personality: A Cross-
Cultural Study* (New Haven: Yale University Press, 1953).

Selections reprinted from *Patterns of Child Rearing* (Row, Peterson & Co., 1957)
by permission of the publisher and authors.

their children. Their reasons were various, ranging from genuine physical disability to frankly emotional rejection of the nursing function. If we may judge by the experience of other cultures, actual incapacity could have accounted for a very small proportion of these cases. In between the extremes were a host of explanations which may or may not have been the major reasons.

. . . . .

Now as to the effects of breast feeding. There have been very few careful studies of the question. None so far has demonstrated any important and consistent relationship between breast feeding and any later quality of the personality. Our own data, reported in this chapter, add nothing new to this negative state of affairs. None of the children's characteristics, as judged by the mothers' descriptions of them, were different for the two groups, the breast-fed and the non-breast-fed. . . .

. . . . .

What have we found out about the self-demand *vs.* rigid scheduling controversy? There is a clear indication in the mothers' reports that rigid scheduling is infrequent. So is complete self-demand, which is not surprising, for most infants develop some kind of schedule for themselves. Even the mother who is most solicitous of the baby's needs has some kind of schedule for her own household activities and probably in subtle ways tends to transfer this to the child. The range on this practice is quite wide in this group of mothers, but it tends clearly toward a child-oriented policy.

The findings with respect to weaning fit well with what was already known and add a few new items. The range of ages at which weaning to the cup was begun by this group of mothers was wide, but the central tendency was to begin early, well under the age of one year. This is very early, compared with the practices of nonliterate cultures. But the amount of emotional disturbance produced was not great, and the earlier the change was made, the less the upset. This accords with previous findings, which have suggested that the strength of the sucking habit, and the need to get food by sucking, are increased by more practice at sucking. The stronger such a drive or need is, the greater the severity of emotional upset when its actions are frustrated.

We have known, also, that upset is least when there is extensive preparation for the new mode of eating before the final step is taken that makes the child totally dependent on it. We can now add a new finding, that once the weaning has started, the emotional disturbance connected with it is most severe if the transition takes a long time.

It is always risky to give advice on the basis of group findings, but mothers have to make decisions on weaning anyway, and it may help to spell out what these facts suggest. If the goal is to have as little emotional disturbance as possible—and this is a big *if*, because there may be other goals that are more important, and would be better reached by doing something else—then it appears wisest to begin weaning before the end of the first year or else wait until the end of the second. If the longer period is used, the child obviously will have long since gone on a solid diet and will be taking many of his liquids by cup anyway. Secondly, there should be all possible preparation for the new mode of eating—orange juice, water, and especially some sips of milk by cup from the very beginning of life. Thus the new mode is not a shock and the skill is available. Giving attention to this preparation is obviously more important if weaning is to be done early. Thirdly, once the decision is made to wean—not just to prepare for it—the transition should be made as expeditiously as possible. There is no kindness in keeping a child on tenterhooks. If serious weaning is not undertaken until after the second year, there is always a good chance the baby will have weaned himself before the mother starts.

Finally, there is the matter of feeding problems in the preschool years. None of the infant-feeding practices we have examined—whether severe or gentle—appear to have been related to the later development of such problems. On the other hand, there was evidence that finickiness and other more severe reactions were related to harsh and restrictive methods of discipline. The relation is not a strong one, but it is consistent among the scales we examined.

. . . . .

TOILET TRAINING

Why is it that some children have so much difficulty in this area, others so little? It is likely that there are physiological differences between children which are important, but in the present context we are concerned with the influence of methods of training, and the emotional relationships within the home environment.

The most obvious matter to examine first is the toilet-training method itself. The age at the beginning of training was of no significance ($r = .08$), so we can turn to *severity*. Our ratings on severity of toilet training took into account both bowel training and prevention of bedwetting. From Table I it can be seen that the severity of the entire toilet-training process did have some bearing on children's tendencies to be late bed-wetters. When they were scolded and punished in the training process, they were somewhat more likely to be late bed-wetters than if their mothers were milder in their treatment.

As was the case with emotional reaction to the training process itself, however, simple severity of training does not tell the whole story.

Again we find that the disruptive effects of severe training occurred with some mothers but not with others. As one can see from comparing the top and bottom lines of Table I, severe training apparently had a kind of "kill or cure" effect so far as bed-wetting was concerned. When severely trained, the child either learned to be dry before he was two years old or he tended not to learn before he was five or six. Relatively few of the severely-trained children learned in the middle period.

Table I. Bed-Wetting: Relationship to the Severity of Toilet Training

AGE AT WHICH CHILD STOPPED WETTING BED	SEVERITY OF TOILET TRAINING			
	Not at All Severe	*Slight Pressure*	*Moderate Pressure*	*Quite Severe*
Before two years old	38%	49%	42%	45%
Between two and three years	30	21	27	11
Between three and five years	4	5	6	9
Before age five; not ascertained just when	11	10	6	4
Still wets bed	17	15	19	31
TOTAL	100%	100%	100%	100%
NUMBER OF CASES	54	117	129	75

$p < .01 \ (r = .18)$

Which children were "killed" and which "cured?" The answer is a curious one and we cannot pretend to have any theoretical explanation for it. Three things were related to late persistence of bed-wetting. One was the severity of toilet training, and another was the mother's affectional warmth. Both of these, it will be recalled, were also related to the amount of emotional upset during training. But a third factor is new—the mother's sex anxiety. We saw earlier that this quality in the mother was somewhat connected with whether she breast-fed her baby or not, and with whether she started bowel training early. Now we find it positively associated with persistent bed-wetting. The combination of high sex anxiety, a relatively cold and undemonstrative attitude toward the child, and severe toilet training were most efficient for producing prolonged bed-wetting. This is the "kill" prescription. The "cure" combination, that gave unusually high probability of the child's achieving night dryness before he was two years old, also included high sex anxiety, but in this instance it was associated with a warm and affectionate attitude toward the child, and with gentle toilet training. Perhaps an easier way of saying this is that both warmth of affection and gentleness of training were positively related to early night dryness, while their opposites led to night wetting. But both dimensions were much more influential, in their respective ways, in mothers who were rated as having high sex anxiety.

Bed-wetting is a problem, of course, and the connection of severe toilet training with problem behavior has a familiar ring. In the last chapter, we reported that children with feeding problems seemed to have had more severe toilet training, also. This raises the question as to whether children who had feeding problems also tended to be late bed-wetters, or whether problems in the feeding area (loss of appetite, refusal of certain foods) and bed-wetting are two possible *alternative* reactions to severe parental discipline. If the latter is so, the child who had one of these modes of response would not have had the other. There is some evidence that this was the case. Among the severely trained children, a child was less likely to wet the bed if he had feeding problems, and vice versa. Among the severely trained children who had *some* feeding problems, 22 per cent were late bed-wetters, while among the severely trained children who had *no* feeding problems, 47 per cent were late bed-wetters.

. . . . .

Viewed even from a cross-cultural standpoint, the range of ages at which the mothers began toilet training was wide. An anthropologist might have difficulty in defining just what *the* American custom is. The modal age was between nine and eleven months, but there were quite a number of mothers who started within the child's first half-year and a good many more who waited until well after the first birthday.

Did these variations make any difference? From the mother's standpoint, yes. By and large, the later the training was started, the more quickly it was accomplished. Likewise, from the child's standpoint, training begun after twenty months produced emotional upset in relatively few of the children. These facts sound like arguments for a late beginning, especially when one notes the high proportion of upsets in those cases in which training began in the fifteen- to nineteen-month range.

There are other aspects of the situation to be kept in mind, however. First there is the fact that mothers who began bowel training at the moderately early age of five to nine months found this procedure as successful as a very late start, in the sense that their children accepted the training with few signs of disturbance.

. . . . .

Within the limits of our two measures—duration and upset—we conclude that either of two periods may be chosen for training with an expectation of reasonable comfort. These are the second six months of the child's life and the time after twenty months. The training evidently goes more quickly at the later time and produces little upset. The earlier period is also not immediately upsetting to the child, though the process takes longer. We do not know, of course, whether there are later consequences, in the child's personality, resulting from the choice between these two age periods.

A word is in order about the fifteen- to nineteen-month period. One reason that bowel training in this period may be upsetting to the child is that the *wrong* habits have become deeply ingrained. There has been little or no experience with the *right* responses. In other words, he has been practicing elimination in a diaper, lying down or walking, and in rooms that are not in the future to be appropriate for sphincter release. He has not been practicing in the presence of such correct cues as sitting on the potty, being undressed, hearing his mother talk about toileting, and so on. A further problem is that if training is begun after the child is old enough to run around, he will resist being kept in one place long enough for evacuation to occur and for him to be rewarded. A nine-months-old baby who is not yet walking, and who is still content to be confined to a play pen for reasonable lengths of time, will also sit happily on the potty for five or ten minutes, especially if someone stays with him. If he is at all regular in his bowel movements this is usually enough time for his bowel movement to coincide. His mother can then follow it with rewards and praise. The child of a year and a-half, however, finds it confining to be required to sit still, even for five minutes. He is likely to struggle or cry—activity which can in itself prevent sphincter release. Even if it does occur, the child's emotional state is such that his mother has difficulty making the experience rewarding to him, no matter how much she praises and smiles.

In contrast with these various doubts and queries about the most appropriate age for beginning toilet training, there is considerable certainty about the effects of the dimension of severity. The introduction of pressure, impatience, irritability and punishment into toilet training produces resentment, recalcitrance, and emotional upset in the child. It does not serve to speed his learning in the slightest, and may, if the mother is rather cold in her relations with him, serve to initiate a prolonged period of bed-wetting.

Severe training may be an almost inevitable maternal reaction to external conditions, of course. A child gone balky because he has gotten started wrong in his attempts to gain control is difficult to handle gently under the best of circumstances. A siege of illness in either the mother or child at a critical part of the training can prolong the process and be quite frustrating.

. . . . .

DEPENDENCY

Even though we must maintain a cautious attitude toward the validity of our measure of dependency, these findings provide a consistent picture of the sources of dependency. . . .

Mothers who repeatedly demonstrate their affection for children are providing many supports for whatever actions the children have performed in order to obtain such demonstrations. These actions often involve following the mother around, touching her, smiling at her and talking, and keeping some kind of contact with her. These are the actions, of course, that we have labeled dependency.

Once the child has developed these habitual ways of acting—and all children develop some—he may be expected to use them as devices for reassuring himself that his mother does love him. That is to say, if she shows signs of rejection, if she uses withdrawal of love to discipline him, and if she is punitive toward his aggression, he may be expected to double his efforts to secure her affection. This will simply increase the frequency and persistence of the acts we have defined as dependent, and hence the mother will describe more of them.

The influence of affectionate demonstrativeness, if we may suggest a theoretical point, is an influence on the *learning* of dependent behavior. The effect of withdrawal of love, punishment of dependency and aggression, and other behaviors that threaten the child's security, is an effect on performance or *action*. Therefore, the actual amount of dependency observed and reported by a mother is a product of both factors. It follows that the most dependent children should be those whose mothers express openly their affection for the child but repeatedly threaten the affectional bond by withholding love as a means of discipline and by being punitive toward his displays of parent-directed aggression.

These relationships are exactly what we have found, but just which way the cause-and-effect arrows point is impossible to say. We are skeptical that there is any single direction of cause-and-effect relations in the child-rearing process. True, the mother's personality comes first, chronologically, and she starts the sequence of interactive behavior that culminates in the child's personality. But once a child starts to be over-dependent—or is *perceived* as being so by his mother—he becomes a stimulus to the mother and influences her behavior toward him. Perhaps, within the present group of mothers, over-dependency of their children increased the mothers' rejective feelings, made them more angry and hence more punitive for aggression. The whole relationship could be circular. An enormous amount of painstaking research will be required to untangle these phenomena.

. . . . .

AGGRESSION

The control of aggression in the home is obviously not a simple matter. Every mother in our group had had to cope with angry outbursts or quarreling at one time or another, and 95 per cent of them reported instances of strong aggression that had been directed at the parents themselves. It seems evident that the conditions of living are such that all children develop aggressive motivation. It is equally certain that very few parents can tolerate as much hostility in the home as the children are instigated to display.

One can distinguish two important themes in the control of children's aggression. One is what we have called "non-permissiveness"— the tendency for a parent to believe that aggression by a child toward his parents is wrong, and to accompany this belief by action designed to prevent aggressive outbursts or stop them when they occur.

The other theme has to do with the amount of punishment a child receives for being aggressive toward his parents. The two dimensions are obviously not independent, for some parents express their non-permissive attitude primarily through punishment which they administer during or after a child's display of temper. But other parents express their non-permissiveness in such a way as to *prevent* the aggressive outburst's occurring; under such circumstances, punishment is not necessary. Still other parents have non-punitive ways of dealing with the child's aggression once it does occur. Thus, not all non-permissive parents are to be found among the group who do a great deal of punishing for aggression.

Our findings suggest that the way for parents to produce a non-aggressive child is to make abundantly clear that aggression is frowned upon, and to stop aggression when it occurs, but to avoid punishing the child for his aggression. Punishment seems to have complex effects. While undoubtedly it often stops a particular form of aggression, at least momentarily, it appears to generate more hostility in the child and lead to further aggressive outbursts at some other time or place. Furthermore, when the parents punish—particularly when they employ physical punishment—they are providing a living example of the use of aggression at the very moment they are trying to teach the child not to be aggressive. The child, who copies his parents in many ways, is likely to learn as much from this example of successful aggression on his parents' part as he is from the pain of punishment. Thus, the most peaceful home is one in which the mother believes aggression is not desirable and under no circumstances is ever to be expressed toward her, but who relies mainly on non-punitive forms of control. The homes where the children show angry, aggressive outbursts frequently are likely to be homes in which the mother has a relatively tolerant (or careless!) attitude toward such behavior, or where she administers severe punishment for it, or both.

Table II.   High Conscience: Relationship to Techniques of
Discipline Employed by the Parents

Parents		Percentage of Children Rated High on Conscience	Number of Cases
High in their use of praise	$r = .18$	32%	181
Low in their use of praise		17%	192
High in their use of isolation	$r = .00$	29%	152
Low in their use of isolation		17%	167
High in use of withdrawal of love	$r = .09$	27%	81
Low in use of withdrawal of love		24%	107
High in their use of reasoning	$r = .18$	30%	192
Low in their use of reasoning		16%	91
High in use of tangible rewards	$r = -.04$	20%	188
Low in use of tangible rewards		28%	181
High in use of deprivation of privileges	$r = -.07$	18%	213
Low in use of deprivation of privileges		33%	156
High in use of physical punishment	$r = -.20$	15%	175
Low in use of physical punishment		32%	197

.   .   .   .   .

THE DEVELOPMENT OF CONSCIENCE

According to the theory of identification, the child imitates the mother, and adopts her standards and values as his own, in order to assure himself of her love. This suggests that a high conscience would develop most readily if the mother relied largely on those disciplinary techniques that involved *giving or withholding love* as a means of rewarding or punishing child behavior. Conversely, we would expect that the children of mothers who used such materialistic methods as deprivation of privileges, physical punishment, and tangible rewards, would develop conscience control more slowly. Children do learn to adapt themselves somewhat to the prevailing climate of the family environment. If love is used as a reward, a child learns to do what will bring him love. If his mother withholds love, he will even learn to give himself love, and he will do as she does to avoid the pain of having her separate herself from him. On the other hand, if the mother uses physical punishment, a child is understandably reluctant to confess his misdeeds or to admit, when asked, that he has done wrong. He may use hiding or flight or counter-aggression as devices to avoid punishment.

In Table II, we have compared the six dimensions which describe these two classes of disciplinary techniques. The first three—praise, isolation, and withdrawal of love—are ones that make use of love-oriented behavior by the mother. We have added "reasoning" to the table, too, because it was associated with these love-oriented techniques. In each instance, the high use of such methods is accompanied by a greater number of "high conscience" children than the lesser use. The second group of three—tangible rewards, deprivation, and physical punishment —is more materialistic, and in each case the more frequent use is accompanied by a smaller number of "high conscience" children. Again, as with our previous analyses, the statistical reliabilities of the relationships are meagre. Indeed, in four of the seven cases, the correlation coefficients which express the size of the relationships are approximately zero. However, six of the seven are in the theoretically expected direction. And in every case the percentage of extreme cases ("high conscience") shows a rather substantial difference between high and low groups. The consistency of these findings, rather than the amount of influence of each separate dimension, gives us some confidence in the significance of the final results.

In general, our findings support our theory of identification. They provide a little more information on the way in which parents' child-rearing practices influence the child's character. We can say with some degree of conviction that mothers who love and accept their children, and who use love-oriented techniques of discipline rather than material or physical techniques, produce relatively more children with high conscience. We can say, too, that girls develop this inner control, and adopt their appropriate sex-role qualities, earlier and faster than boys.

In some ways these are discomforting discoveries. They mix up our adult values a little. Ordinarily, we think of *acceptance* as a good thing; a rejecting mother is thought of as unfair and unkind. The words *love-oriented techniques of discipline* have a good sound, too, especially when they are put in contrast with physical punishment—at least . . . this is true for a good many mothers. But when we examine these love-oriented techniques more closely, and find that they include *withdrawal of love* as a means of control or punishment, we realize that we are dealing with a form of maternal behavior that is as much derogated as is rejection. Yet both *acceptance* and *withdrawal of love* appear to produce a strong conscience. Is this a good outcome or a bad outcome of child training?

Some degree of inner control of sex, aggression, and other powerful impulses is clearly necessary if a society is to survive. On the other hand, these impulses do exist in every child and in every adult. Too severe inner control can prevent any direct expression of them and can produce a quite unneccessary degree of guilt and anxiety. Too much conscience can destroy the happiness and productivity of the individual, just as too little can destroy the peace and stability of society.

The problem can be approached in a different way, however. We have discussed here only the *strength* of conscience, saying nothing of its content. In our interviews we asked about the signs of conscience, not what kinds of behavior the child prevented himself from doing, or felt guilty about after doing. The *content* of conscience appears to be the important thing, both from the individual's standpoint and from society's. A strong inner control of impulses to kill other people, or to make indiscriminate sexual advances to many potential partners, is not severely limiting to the individual's initiative. But if these inhibitions extend to *all* aggressive or sexual actions, the person may be crippled in his efforts to live a normal and productive life. American society is competitive and the American culture tolerates, indeed demands, a good deal of interpersonal aggression. In the sexual sphere, both males and females—in their respective fashions—must take initiative in seeking a marriage partner, and marriage can be misery for those whose inhibitions prevent them from yielding fully to the physical expression of love.

. . . . .

THE MOTHER'S WARMTH

Perhaps the most pervasive quality we attempted to measure was the warmth of the mother's feelings for her child. Although our main measure of this was the single rating scale called *warmth*, the quality itself seems to have been an underlying contributor to several of the scales (and, indeed, appeared as Factor C in the factor analysis).

Warmth proved equally pervasive in its effects on the child. Maternal *coldness* was associated with the development of feeding problems and persistent bed-wetting. It contributed to high aggression. It was an important background condition for emotional upset during severe toilet training, and for the slowing of conscience development. Indeed, the only one of our measures of child behavior with which warmth was not associated was dependency, and even in that instance the closely related scale for *affectionate demonstrativeness* was slightly correlated.

There is no clear evidence in our findings to explain why warmth should have such widespread influence. We can speculate, on the basis of our general theory of the learning process, about the possibility that it may play several roles. A warm mother spends more time with her child. She offers him more rewards, technically speaking, and gives him more guidance. He develops stronger expectancies of her reciprocal affection, and thus is more highly motivated to learn how to behave as she wants him to. He becomes more susceptible to control by her, for he has more to gain and more to lose. It seems likely, too, that he gets proportionately more satisfaction and less frustration from his growing desire for affection. We offer the hypothesis, for further research, that the children of warm mothers mature more rapidly, in their social behavior, than those of cold mothers.

PUNISHMENT

In our discussion of the training process we have contrasted punishment with reward. Both are techniques used for changing the child's habitual ways of acting. Do they work equally well? The answer is unequivocally "no"; but to be truly unequivocal, the answer must be understood as referring to the kind of punishment we were able to measure by our interview method. We could not, as one can with laboratory experiments on white rats or pigeons, examine the effects of punishment on isolated bits of behavior. Our measures of punishment, whether of the object-oriented or love-oriented variety, referred to *levels of punitiveness* in the mothers. That is, the amount of use of punishment that we measured was essentially a measure of a personality quality of the mothers. Punitiveness, in contrast with rewardingness, was a quite ineffectual quality for a mother to inject into her child training.

The evidence for this conclusion is overwhelming. The unhappy effects of punishment have run like a dismal thread through our findings. Mothers who punished toilet accidents severely ended up with bedwetting children. Mothers who punished dependency to get rid of it had more dependent children than mothers who did not punish. Mothers who punished aggressive behavior severely had more aggressive children than mothers who punished lightly. They also had more dependent children. Harsh physical punishment was associated with high childhood aggressiveness and with the development of feeding problems.

24. A DYNAMIC STUDY OF CHILDREN

HORACE B. ENGLISH

The best way to understand how a child views his world is to talk to one and to observe and study him. Some students will make a case study for laboratory experience in their psychology course. Professor English in this selection answers the questions: How do you find a child to study? How do you observe him? How do you write up the report?

"FIRST CATCH YOUR HARE"

Few of you are so unfortunate, one hopes, as to study child psychology in a region where there are no children. There is, therefore, much to be said for the idea that "the way to begin is to begin"—just pick a child and start in studying him. Experience shows, however, that there are a few principles which should be brought to your attention, not as rigid prescriptions but as suggestive guide lines.

First of all, the child selected should usually *not* be a "problem child." Of course, every child presents a problem to the teacher who has any imagination. But the term *problem child* has become something of a technical term for a badly adjusted child in need of specialized psychological treatment. You will occasionally have such a child in your class and may—unfortunately—have to deal with him or her without the professional psychological help that is really called for. Your first need, however, is to learn to deal with "normal" children. Most of your problems—and your most important ones—will be *normal* problems. It would be one of the worst possible results of a study of child psychology to get in the habit of trying to find something "abnormal" in every puzzling behavior, or of seeing a "problem child" beneath every curly head.

There is another and eminently practical reason, moreover, why it is wise to select a typical child. When we are asked why this child is being picked for study, we must be able to say with complete honesty that he is chosen because he is just an ordinary, everyday specimen.

Making Contact with the School. In most cases you should begin by a preliminary visit to the school. It is true, as we have insisted, that the child's school behavior cannot be fully understood in terms of only what happens in the classroom, but it is equally true that much that happens at home is unintelligible without an understanding of what is happening to the child in school. Since, moreover, most of you are planning to be teachers, it is perfectly proper that you *start* with the problem as it presents itself in the classroom; we merely insist that you should not stop there.

There is a very practical reason, also, for starting with the school. We obviously need the cooperation of parents, and the investigation of Johnny will seem less mysterious if presented as a school project rather than as a "case study." [1] Very often the principal can obtain the good will and cooperation of enough parents to supply an entire psychology class with subjects.

As a rule, then, your instructor will have broached the matter to the principal for you. Nonetheless, your first step is to present yourself to the principal and obtain his explicit permission to begin observation in his school. You must remember that the principal is legally and morally responsible for the conduct of school matters; it is only fair that he be kept fully informed of what is going on. Your call at his office, even if you should get no instructions and no information, is an elementary professional courtesy.

Because, however, she stands so much closer to the child, the cooperation of the classroom teacher is even more vital. One of the student's first obligations is thus to insure that the teacher understands the purposes of the investigation and is prepared to forward it. Many teachers, especially older ones, tend to feel a little on the defensive when their classes are being visited by students who are full of enthusiasm for new ways. It has been my experience that it helps to emphasize that your purpose is not so much to observe the class routine as it is to observe the individual child, that you are not at all interested for the time being in methods of teaching but only in the behavior of the child. Nor does it do any harm to show that you realize you are making extra work for the teacher and shall be very grateful for any help extended.

Making Initial Contacts with the Home.   If there is a sound tradition of friendly parent-teacher relations in the community, there should be no difficulty about an occasional visit to the child's home. The exact approach to the parents will have to depend on how one is introduced by the school. In general, it is to be hoped that the observer will have the way prepared for him by the principal of the school. Here various

---

[1] As a matter of fact, you would probably do well not to get in the habit of talking about your "case study." Educated parents may look for too much, uneducated ones are likely to be made to feel rather uncomfortable; too many of them have had experience with relief case workers.

For similar reasons it is better not to make much mention of psychology. People are apt to expect miracles of anything called psychology but also to be unduly skeptical of more mundane findings. "Child study" is a fairly accurate statement of our purposes and is less likely to be misunderstood.

means have been tried. Sometimes the parents have been asked to come to the school to talk the whole program over with the representatives of the college. Sometimes the principal has written the parents a letter which is sent home with the child, asking their cooperation. A few principals have been generous enough to talk individually with each parent. Sometimes the student has merely been furnished the name of the parents and must introduce himself and make his own arrangements.

Should you make an appointment or should you go unannounced to your first interview? Middle-class housewives—and most of your subjects will come from middle-class homes—are likely to be embarrassed if a "visitor" comes unannounced. They prefer to go to a lot of wholly unnecessary trouble to have things "looking nice." You, of course, would much prefer to see a normal everyday situation, but the choice is not yours. Moreover, the mother will talk more freely when she is confident of the appearance of the house and of herself; for your first visit that is more important than seeing the usual routine of the home. If, then, the family has a telephone, it is generally best to try to make an appointment. If you can wangle an invitation in general terms ("Any afternoon this week except Thursday"), so much the better. If there is no telephone in the home, have the child carry a message, written or oral. The lack of a telephone, however, is often an index of a lack of middle-class concern with appearances, so an unannounced visit may be risked.

In all cases you must remember that you occupy a rather delicate position. In the first place you are inevitably a representative both of the college and of the school. You have thus an opportunity to learn how to conduct yourself in a professional and tactful manner. In seeking your first appointment, for example, you should put yourself at the parents' disposal rather than seek your own convenience. We know, of course, that students, no less than the parents, have other appointments to meet. But in arranging for a mutually convenient meeting, you can manage to convey the impression that the parents' convenience has first consideration—as, indeed, it should have.

If the general plan has been outlined to the parent by the school, you should not elaborate much upon the statements already made. You can say quite simply that you are taking a course in child study in preparation for teaching, that the college considers a better understanding of children of great importance for effective teaching and has sought an opportunity for each prospective teacher to become thoroughly familiar with a typical, normal child. This child has been selected, not because he is a problem in school but simply because he represents the kind of child you will have to deal with when you become a teacher.

At this point it is generally well to allow the parent to ask questions. These questions should be answered frankly and directly. If the parents do not ask any questions, you might continue somewhat as follows; "Naturally it is impossible to understand a child without knowing how he has developed, so I should like to have you tell me something about his earlier years. And one thing that we certainly need to understand, better than teachers usually do, is how the child acts with his brothers and sisters around home." You would like permission, therefore, to come home from school with the child some day and notice how he acts there. You will try not to be too obvious, but if the child asks what you are doing, the mother may simply tell him that you are a student who is trying to get better acquainted with children in order to become a better teacher.

You should admit smilingly that neither the school nor the parent is likely to be very greatly enlightened by your study of the child. You will, of course, be quite glad to discuss with the mother anything that you find, but you are, after all, just a beginner in this field, and the purpose of this study is mainly your own improvement. You hardly expect to discover anything that the mother does not already know. As some slight return, however, for any bother you occasion, you will be happy to act as a "sitter" some evening while the parents are away.[2] And you may also indicate that if the parents are willing, you would like to take the child with you to a concert or motion picture or some such treat to see how he reacts there.

You should not volunteer any estimate of how much of the parent's time you will take, but if you are asked you should say: "Why, of course, I shall take only such time as you find it possible to give me. However, there seems to be no need, unless something unusual should develop, to take up more than an hour, or perhaps two hours at the most. I should like to be around the home somewhat longer just playing or talking with Suzanne, but I should certainly not expect to take up very much of your time in any direct way."

Be careful at this time to ask no questions about the parents themselves; the first approach should concern the child. When you are on a more familiar footing it may (or may not) be possible to ask a few questions about the family situation.

Just because some of the above directions take the form of direct quotation, you are not to make a prepared talk along these lines! There could be no greater mistake than to memorize these words and deliver them as a mechanical speech.

On the contrary it is desirable to get the *parent* to talk freely to you. It does no harm to let the conversation range very widely—even to "cabbages and kings." You will be at once learning something about the child's home and parents and cultivating an easy relationship. And, be

---

[2] Need it be pointed out that this is a chance not merely to repay the parents but to further your study of the child!

assured, the conversation will presently come back to the child or can be very gently steered back.[3]

Only one thing is essential: a simple, friendly, unassuming approach. Most parents will be cooperative and quite understanding of your mission. A few will be suspicious and doubtful at the start, but they will readily accept you if you are friendly and tactful. Only a very small number will prove so uncooperative that it is advisable to start over with another family.

Contact with the Child. The approach to the child can be made with the utmost simplicity. Children, of course, are very curious, but their curiosity as a rule is easily satisfied. In general, the best thing is just to make a plain statement: "I am studying to become a teacher (or to make myself a better teacher), and so I want to know children better. You see, if I am to be a good teacher I have to know what children are like." This simple statement seldom fails to satisfy the child, and it has the merit of being direct—and, strangely enough, true. If, however, the child has any further questions, these can be answered frankly and with similar simplicity. If the child asks, "Why pick on me?" answer that the teacher suggested that he was a perfectly "regular" sort of a child to become acquainted with. If the child wants to know what you are going to do, say that you will come around and play with him sometimes, get acquainted with his father and mother, find out about his health when he was a little boy and things like that. Suggest that perhaps you and he will go to a movie sometime or that you may take him to a concert or a museum (or something that will seem attractive). Do not offer to help him with his schoolwork; if he asks whether you will, say that you might look over some of his schoolwork sometime to see how he is getting on. This aspect, however, should not be emphasized. You will be surprised to find how readily children accept this whole proceeding, especially where several in the same room have what they are likely to call "My college girl."

To emphasize the necessity for sympathy and understanding of the child's feelings, we adapt from Teagarden eleven rules for the guidance of case workers which you will do well to ponder and observe. Lest you be worried about having to memorize them, Teagarden, and I, hasten to add that they are only a code of good sense.

1. Remember that the child may be uncomfortable. Make the situation as easy for him as possible. Unless you are so old that it makes you feel uncomfortable to do so, you should have the child call you by your first name. You are not at this time, you see, to act the teacher.
2. Be kindly but objective—not effusive.
3. Don't talk too much. Get the child to talk.

---

[3] In the exceptional case where this is not true, it is likely to be symptomatic of the relationship between parent and child.

4. Don't "talk down" to the child.
5. Don't ask questions until rapport has been established.
6. Don't try to get too much the first time.
7. Don't follow any outline or interviewing device woodenly.
8. Don't take notes obviously.
9. Don't show shock at anything the child tells you. (If he "tries you out" with obscenity, let him see you know what he is up to and are unimpressed.)
10. Don't try to handle problems that require expert handling in a particular field.
11. Don't betray confidences. You should repeat what you hear only where by doing so you may actually be giving help or protection. The child should never be allowed to feel imposed on.[4]

Naturally the approach to both parents and child will differ somewhat in the case of teachers actually in service, especially if they are dealing with a child in their own class. In other cases, also, it will be necessary to adapt your procedures to suit individual circumstances.

PLANNING OBSERVATION

Limiting the Field. There is practically no limit to the number of things which can be observed about any child of any age. A detailed and exhaustive study of a child's family relationships alone would take many weeks to complete. And even then it would be necessary to check every conclusion against further observations in order to insure that the study was based on permanent attitudes rather than chance occurrences. For a brief study such as you are about to make, it is especially necessary to discover as soon as possible what are likely to be the most important factors in the life of the child under observation.

It is impossible, however, to set up a rigid list of the "most important factors." What is most significant for one child may have very little significance for another. Thus, health is undoubtedly important; but health may play a very small part in the school adjustment of the child who has average health and vitality, whereas it may be the outstanding fact in the adjustment of another. Almost anything may be the most important factor in the child you are studying. We can, however, make certain rather general suggestions.

One of the most important areas to explore is the child's relationships with other people, especially members of the immediate family. Unfortunately, you will not have much opportunity to observe such relationships because of the limits of your study and prohibitory social conventions. A child's relations with his teacher are much more accessible and open to observation; and, so, in general, are the influences of school-

---

[4] Modified from Florence M. Teagarden, *Child psychology for professional workers,* rev. ed. Copyrighted, New York: Prentice-Hall, 1946.

mates and neighborhood friends. In some cases a certain child may identify himself with a person not in the immediate family; his relations with that person are of prime importance.

Anything that makes the child a little different is always interesting and important: differences in physical size or appearance, in racial stock,' in culture, in interests, in religion. You should be particularly alert to discover anything in the child's behavior that is unusual or that is personally characteristic.

Your preliminary observations, then, and your early interviews will provide you with certain "information" and, unless you are different from most persons, with certain rather vague impressions. These should be neither accepted nor rejected at this time. Instead, they should be "put on ice."

First-impressions Record.   For this purpose, it may be well to follow a suggestion I owe to Dr. Fritz Redl and write out a fairly detailed thumbnail sketch of the child very early in your relation with him—say after your second observation. Tell what you saw and heard, what seemed likely to you to be his chief characteristics, his chief problems, his probable background, and—here you must be honest!—how you felt toward the child. If he seems unattractive, don't be afraid that you are telling on yourself if you say so. While you should not lose contact with reality and write a merely imaginary sketch, you are encouraged *for just this once* to give way to your "hunches." This *first-impressions* record should be put aside and *not referred to again* until after the case history is finally written.

Then—and then only—bring out your *first-impressions* record and compare it with the conclusions of your study. This should be done in writing, and both the original note and the comparison included in the appendix to your study.

A word of warning. If, for just this once, you are encouraged to "let yourself go" in these initial "hunches," you are not thereby encouraged to take them seriously. Or perhaps I should urge that you be seriously skeptical of them. Too frequently we see only those things in another person's behavior that are in accord with our initial impressions. This is especially true when we have written down impressions, for then anything that contradicts the impressions means that "we were wrong." It may amuse as well as interest you to observe how readily you spring to your own defense, but you won't catch yourself unless you are constantly on the alert to do so. My purpose in having you commit your first impressions to writing is to have you become sufficiently aware of them that you will also beware! Don't let them blind you. Moreover, the accuracy or inaccuracy of your first impressions, as shown by the comparison in your appendix, is no indication of the excellence of your case study. The first impressions of even experienced personnel workers, psychiatrists, and psychologists are open to error. On the other hand, some few things turn out to be correct, maybe more than a few. Only a complete study can tell which judgments are which. Use the first-impressions record, then, as merely an informal experiment. Do not worry if your final comparisons shows that you are either right or wrong in some or all of your first notions.

If however, your final conclusions are to be sound, your tentative conclusions must be checked and rechecked *continuously*. We speak of "final" conclusions only because all human enterprises must have an end sometime. Otherwise, quite clearly what is called your "final" conclusion is only the last in a series of tentative conclusions. In the next section is outlined a method of checking these conclusions which is much less formidable than its title indicates.

Getting Preliminary Hypotheses. The great physicist Michael Faraday was once asked to observe an experiment. "Before we begin," he responded, "just what am I expected to see?" He knew better than to believe himself capable of detecting, offhand and without guidance, the essential features of a complicated machine.

Now you are about to begin observing the most complicated "machine" on earth. You, too, need the guidance of certain preliminary hypotheses. Faraday, please note, hoped to get his preliminary hypothesis from someone who already understood something of the problem. And we believe that you, too are likely to make progress more quickly in the early stages if you turn to the persons who know the child. Accordingly, after a brief visit to the class merely to acquaint yourself with the object of your investigation, you should talk with parent or teacher.

Certain precautions, however, are very important if you are to get off on the right foot. We have already noted that you will gain friendly rapport with an "interviewee" in proportion as you succeed in getting him or her to talk freely. Such free conversation also serves your purpose of learning what seem to be the child's outstanding characteristics and qualities. You should not, therefore, attempt to dominate the interview. Instead, cultivate the art of listening. If it is possible, avoid direct questioning and elicit the interviewee's spontaneous remarks. To keep him going and to show your interest, it is occasionally wise to say something which indicates your understanding, putting the matter in question form: "Do you mean that Harold seemed very happy when his sister was born?" Or you may somewhat direct the trend by such a question as: "He got over the measels rather easily?" Usually it will not be long before the interviewee has revealed his or her own major understandings of the child.

Now these understandings must be taken very tentatively. Suppose you are having your first interview with the child's teacher, who tells you that Robert seems to be neither a leader nor a follower but co-operates with his playmates and sometimes leads, other times follows. This statement, *carefully dated and duly ascribed to its author*, may be entered in your notes as a tentative hypothesis. Very tentative, in fact, for your next interview may be with a former teacher who was very enthusiastic about Robert and tells you that in her class Robert was always a leader. Here you have a problem, with several possible solutions.

It may be that the present teacher has been inaccurate in her observations and that Robert leads in most of his activities. Or, it is possible that the former teacher was incorrect and believed as she did mainly because she liked him so much. And it is quite possible that Robert may have been very much of a leader while in the former teacher's room, but at present is just as his present teacher describes him, cooperative but leading only when he is especially proficient in the activity. Before accepting one of these three interpretations as a conclusion, all three should be kept written down in your notes as something to be checked against further observations.

Your next observation may be of Robert on the playground. It is tempting to plan to spend your time in confirming or rejecting the tentative hypothesis that you may have set up with respect to Robert's leadership. Since, however, this is your first direct observation of Robert on the playground you should not spend all your time in this way. In the first place, perhaps we hear a little too much about leadership in child study; it is an important characteristic but not the only one. In any case, the question of leadership cannot be solved unless it is seen in relationship to other variable factors, for example, health. Thus, if you were thinking only of how much Robert leads, it would be quite possible that you would fail to note that he hangs back and does not initiate activities because he is out of breath or suddenly very tired; these are the characteristics of a child somewhat lacking in health or physical vigor. So for your early observation, even though eager to check on the leadership hypothesis, you must work more toward a certain broad understanding, a bird's-eye overview.

In other words, at this stage, your observations should be directed *by the behavior you are witnessing* rather than by any preconceived questions you have formulated. Note *what* the child has been doing, *with whom* he is doing it, and *how* in general he seems to conduct himself. Note also the reactions of other children or adults to him and how he reacts to them.

In both these preliminary approaches—that is, in the first interview and in the first direct observations—make sure that you are seeing and hearing correctly what the other person or the child is saying and doing. The observation needs to be very concrete, very objective and factual, very precise. Any appraisal or judgment not only may be, but should be, rather vague and indefinite. Yet out of all this there should emerge certain *tentative* hypotheses.

Keeping an Open Mind.   At this point there is grave danger of taking these hypotheses too seriously. First, even when they are correct, they may be stated in too general a form. In Robert's case, for example, your information is derived from the school situation—that is, from the teachers' reports and from what you saw on the school playground. This may justify some statement about leadership, but it certainly does not justify a broad generality. It is not at all unusual to find a child a leader at school and a follower at home. Your tentative hypothesis should therefore not concern "leadership" but "leadership at school."

And secondly, there is the question of the correctness of the hypothesis. The behavior may not have been correctly observed or interpreted, or the behavior may not be typical. For these reasons, you will do better to frame your hypotheses in the form of *questions* instead of statements or conclusions. All of us are too prone to take direct statements as conclusions and read them into all our further observations, whereas the questions serve to remind us that the issue is still open.

Using Hypotheses to Direct Observation.   But, in order that they take on a definite enough form to guide your observing, your hypotheses should be put in writing—early in your work with the child. *Before and after* each observation you should look over your notes, notice what seems *on the way* to confirmation, what seems disproved, which hypotheses need modification.

This part of scientific method seems time-consuming and is often neglected. Actually it is time-saving, since it enables you to get a greater wealth of really usable fact from your observations. The greatest vice of most child-study observation is *aimlessness*, dependence upon mere impressionism. Scientific observation is pointed, intensive search, not aimless gazing. Even in the first two or three observations you are not just looking around purposelessly; you are searching for your starting points. Hence I lay down one of the few rigid rules contained in this guide: Before beginning an observation period, formulate definitely the one or two questions or hypotheses with which your observation is to be particularly concerned. Ask yourself—in advance—what kinds of behavior will throw light on the hypothesis. After the observation is finished, report with respect to these questions (*a*) what you found, (*b*) what you did not find, and (*c*) what you should look for another time. All this must be very concrete and specific.

After a conference with a teacher a student wrote:

James's teacher says he is always cutting into the discussion in a way which she thinks is an attention-getting device. I noticed myself that his interruption was not to the point as it would be if it came from interest in the topic. I must see what I can observe in the home that bears on this. Does Mrs. T. tend to ignore him? Is there rivalry with Donny? Or at the other end, is he encouraged to be "cute"? If these leads fail, I'll try to find the cause of attention-getting in the school.

Note that the student has accepted someone else's interpretation—always a bit dangerous, though in this case fairly well supported. At any rate, having accepted the hypothesis, she begins an active *search* for relevant information to validate or invalidate it. How much more enlightening her observation of the home situation is likely to be when she goes with a definite searching attitude.

Should one ignore facts that do not bear on the hypothesis? By no means! Whatever else you observe and report is an "extra dividend." The *rule* given above is rigid, but *you* should be flexible and adaptable and sensitive to all sorts of child behavior. The whole situation may become radically unfavorable to finding out anything about the kind of behavior you had planned to study. A rapid change of plan is then called for. But there should still be a plan, a real search, not just aimless gazing.

KEEPING THE RECORDS

Adequate records are essential if your case study is to be acceptable, but they have a wider value. To an extent often not realized, the attempt to put fleeting observations in words clarifies them and brings out their significance. I believe in the value of direct experience; otherwise I should not be concerned with having you observe children. But even the lower animals can observe children; dogs, notably, are excellent observers. It is only when we can verbalize that we reach the human level.

WHO	Make clear who is the source of your information. If you are reporting your own direct observation, let that be clear.
WHAT	Clearly set off facts from interpretation.
HOW	Describe how the facts were gathered—by what methods in what circumstances.
WHEN	Date every record.

And be sure your record is complete. The Big Four of sound journalism apply here as well. Make clear *who* is the source of your information. If it was your own direct observation, let that be clear. If you are reporting what someone told you, be crystal clear as to just who told you what. The methods and circumstances of gathering the information must be given. If you observed the event, it is not too difficult to tell *how* you observed it. But if you are retelling something you learned secondhand, you have a double obligation. You must report how you got the information from your informant; and you must tell how your informant got it—if you can. Finally, tell where and when the event occurred.

As a double-check, you should always indicate when you wrote the report.

Taking Notes. While observing the child in class, you can generally take notes freely. In interviewing the teacher you will be expected to take notes. Many parents, on the other hand, are made nervous if you bring out a pencil and notebook. When you have become well acquainted with them, or when certain objective facts are being given (such as the date of Harold's attack of measles), you might ask permission to jot down a memo. If anyone seems concerned about your taking notes and asks for an explanation, you will find it best to say frankly that you are making notes merely to help you think things through afterward. It is obvious that only rarely may you write down things in the child's presence, though in case of need you can tell the child you are writing yourself a reminder of something to do. (A friend of mine who overworked this device in a group situation became known to the children as "that man who is always remembering something he's forgotten." They thought him queer in that respect, but took it in their stride.)

If you have been unable to take notes during the observation, write them as soon as possible thereafter. In every instance record the time (day and hour), the circumstances of the observation, the place, the purpose you had in mind in making the observation, and the time elapsing between observation and writing. All five of these essentials are illustrated in the following:

Jan. 7, '51. 10 A.M. Record made at the time at school. Class at work painting. Originally planned to study Mary's initiative in recitation. In light of the program, changed to observing extent of physical activity and distractability.

Field Notes. The notes you thus take on the spot or write down immediately afterward are known as *Field Notes* and should be included in the appendix of your final report to the instructor. *Unless they are very illegible or untidy, they need not be copied.* It is desirable, however, that they be uniform in size and in plan. We suggest that you use full $8\frac{1}{2} \times 11$ paper. This can be conveniently folded in half or quarter for "on-the-spot" notes and still fit in with the rest of your written or typed report. Make sure that the field notes are uniform in size and securely fastened together, so that they do not get out of order.

THE DISTINCTION BETWEEN FACT AND INTERPRETATION

While it is impossible to keep the human or personal element out of your observations, it must be your constant effort to reduce it to a minimum. This implies that you must distinguish what actually happened (observed fact) from how the fact impressed you (interpretation or meaning of the fact).

For present purposes we may think of observed fact as a percept—something seen, heard, smelled, touched, or tasted. As a rough criterion, whatever an actor directly conveys is observable. If he strides up and down, we actually observe a "nervous manner." Similarly we can observe a child's "happy smile" or "puzzled frown." These are the basic materials of observation.

In reacting to such "facts," however, we almost invariably indulge in a certain amount of interpretation. Several levels of interpretation may be usefully distinguished.

Consider the following statements:

(1) He replied, when his mother spoke to him, in a very cross tone. (2) He was irritated by the interruption to his work. (3) Besides that, his mother tends to nag him quite a lot and that makes him snappy in his replies. (4) This habit of making cross replies is getting to be general; he might be described as a cross or surly boy. (5) No wonder he is unpopular.

A Scale of Closeness to the Immediate Facts.   The first statement is reasonably factual. You observed a cross tone—although it may be difficult to state what, in physical terms, a cross tone is.

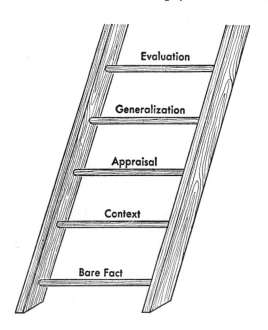

FIGURE 1.   THE LADDER OF FACTUALITY

The second statement goes somewhat beyond the bare fact; it is obviously an interpretation or explanation of the fact. But the explanation is stated in terms of the immediate setting of the event and is necessary if the event is to have any meaning. We may call this a *meaning* or *context* interpretation. Unless it is obvious, it should always be given as a part of the observation. Without it the bare fact would be too bare.

The third statement goes beyond the immediate situation; it is an *appraisal* in terms of quite a number of facts which have previously been observed and in the light of quite a complex psychological theory. (The hypothesis that a nagging mother leads to snappy replies seems so self-evidently true that we forget that it is only an hypothesis or theory.)

The fourth statement even more obviously goes beyond the immediate facts. It implies enough observations to warrant a judgment that the behavior in question is habitual or characteristic. This may be called generalization from the facts.[5] And once more we see a theory as to cause-and-effect relationships.

The last statement involves us in another theory and obviously implies moral and social evaluation as well.

We have here, then, a sort of scale of closeness to the immediate facts of experience: first, *observed fact;* second, fact plus immediate *context* or meaning; third, *appraisal* of the fact; fourth, *generalization* from the fact; fifth, *evaluation*.

Now perhaps all of this is justifiable. In a full study of an individual we have to come to rather far-reaching judgments; that, in a sense, is what the study is for. But most of this interpretation has no place in what purports to be a record of *factual observation*. The field notes should therefore give only a minimum of interpretation; any interpretation we do make should be clearly distinguished from the facts, and its tentative nature made clear. Let us see how the above statements might appear in your field notes.

Replied to mother's question in very cross tone [Apparently irritated by interruption to his work. *Query:* Does his mother nag him a lot? Does this make him irritable in relation to his mother? Or irritable in general? Wonder if this explains the unpopularity of which his teacher spoke.]

Note that the statement about interruption (the meaning) is set forth as a positive statement, though it is enclosed in brackets to show that it is your interpretation not your observation. But the wider interpretations, the judgments or generalizations and evaluations, are set down as questions for further investigation.

[5] Generalization *from* the facts must be distinguished from generalization *of* the facts. The latter may be illustrated by such statement as: "He answered crossly every time his mother spoke to him the entire afternoon." Generalization *of* the facts is not interpretation at all but simply a short way of stating them.

Particularly troublesome is that form of interpretation which consists in attributing some "trait" of character or personality to the child —as in (4) above, where the child is said to be "surly." Since "traits" are always a matter of inference and not of observed fact, they have no place in a factual report.

Such trait descriptions, moreover, cover up our lack of full knowledge. A child is said to have shown "strong will" because for three hours he refused a half stick of gum when he had asked for a whole piece. But saying this was "strong will" merely says he persisted in his refusal. It does not tell us *why*. It does not give us a clue as to how often or cunningly he was tempted with the half stick. It does not tell us what he gained from the refusal.

Compare the usefulness of these two reports:

1. Chester is very quick tempered, as was seen in the way he acted when his sister jogged his elbow while he was working on a model airplane.

2. While Chester was working on a model airplane, his sister accidentally jogged his elbow. He was instantly angry and pushed her away. [Of course, the model is fragile and very dear to him and his sister did endanger it. Yet I wondered whether that was the whole story. Does she pester him a lot? Or what is his relation to her? Does he think she is mother's pet just because she is young and rather doll-like? Does he feel that he must defend his possessions against her? I shall have to watch closely for indications that will bring out this. I wonder whether his mother has insight and objectivity enough to know. I think I shall not ask her directly, but she may have some evidence for me.]

The writer of the second report is looking for facts, the writer of the first found a ready-made conclusion.

25. INDUSTRY VERSUS INFERIORITY

ERIK H. ERIKSON

We have all frequently heard things described as being "as easy as child's play." Just how playful is child's play?

This selection provides some notion of what play means to children and to adults and of the close interrelationships of play, industriousness, self-esteem, and the feeling of mastery.

Selections reprinted from "Growth and Crises" in *Symposium on the Healthy Personality*, edited by Milton J. Senn (Josiah Macy, Jr. Foundation, 1950), 127–134, by permission of the author and publisher.

One might say that personality at the first stage crystallizes around the conviction "I am what I am given," and that of the second, "I am what I will." The third can be characterized by "I am what I can imagine I will be." We must now approach the fourth: "I am what I learn." The child now wants to be shown how to get busy with something and how to be busy with others.

This trend, too, starts much earlier, especially in some children. They want to watch how things are done and to try doing them. If they are lucky they live near barnyards or on streets around busy people and around many other children of all ages, so that they can watch and try, observe and participate as their capacities and their initiative grow in tentative spurts. But now it is time to "go to school." In all cultures, at this stage, children receive some systematic instruction, although it is by no means always in the kind of school which literate people must organize around teachers who have learned how to teach literacy. In preliterate people much is learned from adults who become teachers by acclamation rather than by appointment; and very much is learned from older children. What is learned in more primitive surroundings is related to the basic skills of *technology* which are developed as the child gets ready to handle the utensils, the tools, and the weapons used by the big people: he enters the technology of his tribe very gradually but also very directly. More literate people, with more specialized careers, must prepare the child by teaching him things which first of all make him literate. He is then given the widest possible basic education for the greatest number of possible careers. The greater the specialization, the more indistinct the goal of initiative becomes; and the more complicated the social reality is, the vaguer the father's and mother's role in it appears to be. Between childhood and adulthood, then, our children go to school; and school seems to be a world all by itself, with its own goals and limitations, its achievements and disappointments.

Grammar school education has swung back and forth between the extreme of making early school life an extension of grim adulthood by emphasizing self-restraint and a strict sense of duty in doing what one is *told* to do, and the other extreme of making it an extension of the natural tendency in childhood to find out by playing, to learn what one must do by doing steps which one *likes* to do. Both methods work for some children at times but not for all children at all times. The first trend, if carried to the extreme, exploits a tendency on the part of the preschool and grammar school child to become entirely dependent on prescribed duties. He thus learns much that is absolutely necessary and he develops an unshakable sense of duty; but he may never unlearn again an unnecessary and costly self-restraint with which he may later make his own life and other people's lives miserable, and in fact spoil his own children's natural desire to learn and to work. The second trend, when carried to an extreme, leads not only to the well-known popular objection that children do not learn anything any more but also to such feelings in children as are expressed in the by now famous remark of a metropolitan child who apprehensively asked one morning: "Teacher, *must* we do today what we *want* to do?" Nothing could better express the fact that children at this age *do* like to be mildly coerced into the adventure of finding out that one can learn to accomplish things which one would never have thought of by oneself, things which owe their attractiveness to the very fact that they are *not* the product of play and fantasy but the product of reality, practicality, and logic; things which thus provide a token sense of participation in the world of adults. In discussions of this kind it is common to say that one must steer a middle course between play and work, between childhood and adulthood, between old-fashioned and progressive education. It is always easy (and it seems entirely satisfactory to one's critics) to say that one plans to steer a middle course, but in practice it often leads to a course charted by avoidances rather than by zestful goals. Instead of pursuing, then, a course which merely avoids the extremes of easy play or hard work, it may be worth while to consider what play is and what work is, and then learn to dose and alternate each in such a way that play is play and work is work. Let us review briefly what play may mean at various stages of childhood and adulthood.

The adult plays for purposes of recreation. He steps out of his reality into imaginary realities for which he has made up arbitrary but none the less binding rules. But an adult must not be a playboy. Only he who works shall play—if, indeed, he can relax his competitiveness.

The playing child, then, poses a problem: whoever does not work shall not play. Therefore, to be tolerant of the child's play the adult must invent theories which show either that childhood play is really the child's work or that it does not count. The most popular theory, and the easiest on the observer, is that the child is nobody yet and that the nonsense of his play reflects it. According to Spencer, play uses up surplus energy in the young of a number of mammalians who do not need to feed or protect themselves because their parents do it for them. Others say that play is either preparation for the future or a method of working off past emotion, a means of finding imaginary relief for past frustrations.

It is true that the content of individual play often proves to be the infantile way of thinking over difficult experiences and of restoring a sense of mastery, comparable to the way in which we repeat, in thought and endless talk, experiences that have been too much for us. This is the rationale for play observation, play diagnosis, and play therapy. In watching a child play, the trained observer can get an impression of what it is the child is "thinking over," and what faulty logic, what emotional dead end he may be caught in. As a diagnostic tool such observation has become indispensable.

Play has its crisis, too (which, in fact, makes its observation an even better clinical tool). Let us consider the activity of building and destroying a tower. Many a mother thinks that her little son is in a "destructive stage" or even that he has a "destructive personality" because, after building a big, big tower, the boy cannot follow her advice to leave the tower for Daddy to see but instead *must* kick it and make it collapse. The almost manic pleasure with which children watch the collapse in a second of the product of long play labor has puzzled many, especially since the child does not appreciate it at all if his tower falls by accident or by a helpful uncle's hand. He, the builder, must destroy it himself. This game, I should think, arises from the not so distant experience of sudden falls at the very time when standing upright on wobbly legs afforded a new and fascinating perspective on existence. The child who consequently learns to *make* a tower "stand up" enjoys causing the same tower to waver and collapse: it helps *to do to somebody or something what was done to oneself;* it makes one feel stronger to know that there is somebody weaker—and towers, unlike little sisters, can't cry and call Mummy. But since it is the child's still precarious mastery over space which is thus to be demonstrated, it is understandable that watching somebody else kick one's tower may make the child see himself in the tower rather than in the kicker: all fun evaporates. Later, circus clowns afford satisfaction and amusement to the child when they obligingly fall and tumble about from mere ineptness and yet continue to challenge gravity and causality with ever renewed innocence: there are, then, even big people who are funnier, dumber, and wobblier. Some children, however, find themselves too much identified with the clown. They cannot bear to see his downfalls; to them they are "not funny." This example throws light on the beginning of many an anxiety in childhood, anxiety aroused when the child's attempt at mastery in play finds unwelcome "support" from adults who treat him roughly or amuse him with exercises which he likes only if and when he himself has initiated them.

The child's play begins with, and centers in, his own body. It begins before we notice it as play, and it consists first in the exploration by repetition of sensual perceptions, of kinesthetic sensations, and of vocalizations. (The handling of the genitals often begins as play and becomes "serious" only because of the adults' frightened attitude.) Next, the child plays with available persons and things. He may playfully cry to see what wave length serves best to make the mother reappear, or he may indulge in experimental excursions on her body and on the protrusions and orifices of her face. This is the child's first geography, and the basic maps acquired in such interplay with the mother no doubt remain guides for the first impressions of the "world."

The small world of manageable toys is a second harbor which the child establishes, returning to it when he needs to overhaul his ego. But the thing-world has its own laws: it may resist rearrangement or it may simply break to pieces; it may prove to belong to somebody else and be subject to confiscation by superiors. Often the microsphere seduces the child into an unguarded expression of dangerous themes and attitudes which arouse anxiety and lead to sudden *play-disruption.* This is the counterpart, in waking life, of the anxiety dream; it can keep children from trying to play just as the fear of night terror can keep them from going to sleep. If thus frightened or disappointed, the child may regress into daydreaming, thumb-sucking, masturbating. On the other hand, if the first use of the thing-world is successful and guided properly, the pleasure of mastering toy things becomes associated with the *mastery of the conflicts* which were projected on them and with the *prestige* gained through such mastery.

Finally, at nursery school age playfulness reaches into the world shared with others. At first these others are treated as things; they are inspected, run into, or forced to "be horsie." Learning is necessary in order to discover what potential play content can be admitted only to fantasy or only to play by and with oneself; what content can be successfully represented only in the world of toys and small things; and what content can be shared with others and even forced upon them.

As this is learned, each sphere is endowed with its own sense of reality and mastery. For quite a while, then, solitary play remains an indispensable harbor for the overhauling of damaged emotions after periods of rough going on the social seas.

What is infantile play, then? We saw that it is not the equivalent of adult play, that it is not recreation. The playing adult steps sideward into another, an artificial reality; the playing child advances forward to new stages of real mastery. This new mastery is not restricted to the technical mastery of toys and *things;* it also includes an infantile way of mastering *experience* by meditating, experimenting, and planning.

While all children at times need to be left alone in solitary play, or later in the company of books and radio, motion pictures and video, all of which, like the fairy tales of old, at least *sometimes* seem to convey what fits the needs of the infantile mind, and while all children need their hours and days of make-believe in games, they all, sooner or later, become dissatisfied and disgruntled without a sense of being useful, without a sense of being able to make things and make them well and even perfectly: this is what I call the *sense of industry.* Without this, the best entertained child soon acts exploited. It is as if he knows and his society knows that now that he is psychologically already a rudimentary parent, he must begin to be somewhat of a worker and potential provider before becoming a biological parent. With the oncoming latency period, then, the normally advanced child forgets, or rather "sublimates" (that is, applies to more useful pursuits and approved goals) the necessity of "making" people by direct attack or the desire to become papa and mamma in a hurry: he now learns to win recognition by producing things. He develops industry, that is, he adjusts himself to the inorganic laws of the tool world. He can become an eager and absorbed unit of a productive situation. To bring a productive situation to completion is an aim which gradually supersedes the whims and wishes of his idiosyncratic drives and personal disappointments. As he once untiring strove to walk well, and to throw things away well, he now wants to make things well. He develops the pleasure of work completion by steady attention and persevering diligence.

The danger at this stage is the development of a sense of *inadequacy and inferiority*. This may be caused by an insufficient solution of the preceding conflict: he may still want his mummy more than knowledge; he may still rather be the baby at home than the big child in school; he still compares himself with his father, and the comparison arouses a sense of guilt as well as a sense of anatomical inferiority. Family life (small family) may not have prepared him for school life, or school life may fail to sustain the promises of earlier stages in that nothing that he has learned to do well already seems to count one bit with the teacher. And then, again, he may be potentially able to excel in ways which are dormant and which, if not evoked now, may develop late or never.

Good teachers, healthy teachers, relaxed teachers, teachers who feel trusted and respected by the community, understand all this and can guide it. They know how to alternate play and work, games and study. They know how to recognize special efforts, how to encourage special gifts. They also know how to give a child time, and how to handle those children to whom school, for a while, is not important and rather a matter to endure than to enjoy; or the child to whom other children are much more important than the teacher and who shows it.

Good parents, healthy parents, relaxed parents, feel a need to make their children trust their teachers, and therefore to have teachers who can be trusted. It is not my job here to discuss teacher selection, teacher training, and the status and payment of teachers in their communities— all of which is of indirect importance for the development and the maintenance in children of a *sense of industry* and of a positive identification with those who *know* things and know how to *do* things. Again and again I have observed in the lives of especially gifted people that one teacher, somewhere, was able to kindle the flame of hidden talent.

The fact that the majority of teachers in the elementary schools are women must be considered here in passing, because it often leads to a conflict with the "ordinary" boy's masculine identification, as if knowledge were feminine, action masculine. Both boys and girls are apt to agree with Bernard Shaw's statement that those who can, do, while those who cannot, teach. The selection and training of teachers, then, is vital for the avoidance of the dangers which can befall the individual at this stage. There is, first, the above-mentioned sense of inferiority, the feeling that one will never be any good—a problem which calls for the type of teacher who knows how to emphasize what a child *can* do, and who knows a psychiatric problem when she sees one. Second, there is the danger of the child's identifying too strenuously with a too virtuous teacher or the teacher's pet. What we shall presently refer to as his sense of identity can remain prematurely fixed on being nothing but a good little worker or a good little helper, which may not be all he *could* be. Third, there is the danger (probably the most common one) that throughout the long years of going to school he will never acquire the enjoyment of work and the pride of doing at least one kind of thing well. This is particularly of concern in relation to that part of the nation who do not complete what schooling is at their disposal. It is always easy to say that they are born that way; that there must be less educated people as background for the superior ones; that the market needs and even fosters such people for its many simple and unskilled tasks. But from the point of view of the healthy personality (which, as we proceed, must now include the aspect of playing a constructive role in a healthy society), we must consider those who have had just enough schooling to appreciate what more fortunate people are learning to do but who, for one reason or another, have lacked inner or outer support of their stick-to-itiveness.

It will have been noted that, regarding the period of a developing sense of industry, I have referred to outer hindrances but not to any crisis (except a deferred inferiority crisis) coming from the inventory of basic human drives. This stage differs from the others in that it does not consist of a swing from a violent inner upheaval to a new mastery. The reason why Freud called it the latency stage is that violent drives are normally dormant at that time. But it is only a lull before the storm of puberty.

On the other hand, this is socially a most decisive stage: since industry involves doing things beside and with others, a first sense of division of labor and of equality of opportunity develops at this time. When a child begins to feel that it is the color of his skin, the background of his parents, or the cost of his clothes rather than his wish and his will to learn which will decide his social worth, lasting harm may ensue for the *sense of identity*. . . .

. . . . .

CONCLUSION

At this point, then, I have come close to overstepping the limits (some will say I have long and repeatedly overstepped them) that separate psychology from ethical philosophy. But in suggesting (in an admittedly most tentative manner) that parents, teachers, and doctors must learn to discuss matters of human relations and of community life if they wish to discuss their children's needs and problems, I am only insisting on a few basic psychological insights, which I shall try to formulate briefly in conclusion.

While we have, in the last few decades, learned more about the development and growth of the individual and about his motivations (especially unconscious motivations) than in the whole of human history before us (excepting, of course, the implicit wisdom expressed in the Bible or Shakespeare), increasing numbers of us come to the conclusion that a child and even a baby—perhaps even the fetus—sensitively reflects the quality of the milieu in which he grows up. Children feel the tensions, insecurities, and rages of their parents even if they do not know their causes or witness their most overt manifestations. Therefore, you cannot fool children. To develop a child with a healthy personality, a parent must be a genuine person in a genuine milieu. This, today, is difficult because rapid changes in the milieu often make it hard to know whether one must be genuine *against* a changing milieu or whether one may hope for a chance to do one's bit in the way of bettering or stabilizing conditions. It is difficult, also, because in a changing world we are trying out—we must try out—new ways. To bring up children in personal and tolerant ways, based on information and education rather than on tradition, is a very new way: it exposes parents to many additional insecurities, which are temporarily increased by psychiatry (and by such products of psychiatric thinking as the present paper). Psychiatric thinking sees the world so full of dangers that it is hard to relax one's caution at every step. I, too, have pointed to more dangers than to constructive avenues of action. Perhaps we can hope that this is only an indication that we are progressing through one stage of learning. When a man learns how to drive a car, he must become conscious of all the things that *might* happen; and he must learn to hear, see, and read all the danger signals on his dashboard and along the road. Yet he may hope that some day, when he has outgrown this stage of learning, he will be able to glide with the greatest ease through the landscape, enjoying the view with the confident knowledge that he will react to signs of mechanical trouble or road obstruction with automatic and effective speed.

We are now working toward, and fighting for, a world in which the harvest of democracy may be reaped. In order to make the world safe for democracy, we must make democracy safe for the healthy child. In order to ban autocracy, exploitation, and inequality in the world, we must realize that the first inequality in life is that of child and adult. Human childhood is long, so that parents and schools may have time to accept the child's personality in trust and to help it to be human in the best sense known to us. This long childhood exposes the child to grave anxieties and to a lasting sense of insecurity which, if unduly and senselessly intensified, persists in the adult in the form of vague anxiety—anxiety which, in turn, contributes specifically to the tension of personal, political, and even international life. This long childhood exposes adults, in turn, to the temptation to exploit thoughtlessly and often cruelly the child's dependence by making him pay for the psychological debts owed to them by others, by making him the victim of tensions which they will not, or dare not, correct in themselves or in their surroundings. We have learned not to stunt a child's growing body with child labor; we must now learn not to break his growing spirit by making him the victim of our anxieties.

26. CHILDREN'S HUMOR: JOKING AND ANXIETY

MARTHA WOLFENSTEIN

A most interesting way to discover how a child views his world is to study his jokes. Scientifically analyzed, every act has a cause, and every joke therefore has a meaning—or, indeed, many meanings, most of which are not funny at all.

It is fascinating to read the speculations about children's humor presented here. Miss Wolfenstein's interpretations are clearly the product of a creative mind. By questioning her particular views and discovering others, the reader can do some creative speculating of his own.

At a quarter past three there was only one child left in the kindergarten classroom, the others having been called for by mothers or maids or older brothers or sisters. The teacher came over to where the little boy sat quietly waiting and asked with some solicitude: "Who is calling

Selections reprinted from *Children's Humor—A Psychological Analysis* (The Free Press, 1954), chapter I, by permission of the publisher.

for you today, Eugene? Your mother? Or Betty?" The boy smiled: "My mother is coming, and Betty is coming, and Kay is coming—the whole family is coming except me because I'm here already." He laughed.

In this joke the little boy transformed an anxious feeling into one of amusement. Let us see how this has come about. He takes the teacher's question as an occasion for reversing the situation, as if to say: It is only you and not I who is worried whether anyone is coming to call for me —and how ridiculous you are to doubt it. He is helped to this retort by a rather precocious tendency to turn what the teacher says into nonsense. Here he says something nonsensical himself (I am not coming because I am already here) in order to make nonsense of the teacher's concern.

But to understand Eugene's little joke more fully we must know that his father has died in the past year. The thought "the whole family is coming" contains the wish: and my father too. This is immediately renounced with the word "except": the whole family is coming except one. But what would have been a direct expression of the sad reality is in its turn warded off with the substitution of himself for his father. Instead of "all except Daddy because he is dead," he produces "all except me because I'm here already." This gives the impression of being nonsense as he pretends to convey information while what he says is self-evident. The little boy's substitution of himself for his father in the joke repeats what has happened in life: the father has died and the five-year-old boy has been left alone with the mother and two older sisters. The nonsense in the joke expresses the thought: But it is nonsense to suppose that I could take my father's place. As in the case of nonsense in dreams, it represents opposed wishes: I did and did not wish for my father's death. Thus the nonsense has a double application: the boy disposes of the doubt—which he imputes to the teacher—that anyone is coming for him; and, on a deeper level, he repudiates the wish to take his father's place. In yet another way this joke may have served to ward off anxiety. Waiting for his mother or sister the little boy may indeed have wondered whether they were ever coming, whether they might not also be dead. And this may have evoked fears of his own death. In saying, "I am here," he is affirming: I am alive.

The human capacity to transform suffering into an occasion for mirth is thus already at work in a five-year-old. Under the strain of separation from the mother and sisters with whom he expected to be reunited at this moment, and which evokes the tragic and permanent separation from the father, he is able to joke. He might instead have been overwhelmed with anxiety; he might have cried in the teacher's arms. Or he might have struggled to repress his painful feelings, to be apathetic. But he wants to continue to feel, and he insists on feeling something pleasant. He might then have forgotten his actual situation and become absorbed in play. He does not do this either; he remains aware of his situation of lonely waiting. While confronting this reality, he transforms his feeling about it from pain to enjoyment. This retaining of contact with a disappointing reality combined with the urgent demand to continue to feel, but to feel something pleasant, is decisive for joking. However, the little boy could not have achieved this transformation of emotion if the teacher had not been there. She offers him sympathy which he refuses to accept, preferring to mock her. Repudiating the teacher's pity, he is able to ward off self-pity.

. . . . .

A twelve-year-old boy draws a picture titled, "Custer's Last Stand": it shows a man with a fruit stand. Here . . . the horror of annihilation is transformed into, or mistaken for, oral gratification. The boy wards off the image of the piled up corpses and substitutes an appetizing heap of fruit. Custer who led his men into bloody death becomes a kindly provider of food. In playing on the word "stand," the boy pretends to have mistaken its meaning. It is as if he said: Stand?—ah, you mean a fruit stand. The wish to transform the grievous into the gratifying finds expression in a pretended misunderstanding. It is true that for the unconscious oral gratification and death may be equated, in the persistent infantile fantasy of blissful merging with the mother's breast which is also annihilation. But on the conscious level this thought is disparaged. The boy who makes the joking picture knows very well that Custer's last stand was not a fruit stand; he only pretends to confuse the two. The unconscious fusing of opposites, subjected to the light of conscious criticism, appears as an absurd mistake.

. . . . .

The obstacles which oppose the satisfaction of human wishes are manifold. Not only outer circumstances but inner constraints prove obstructive, constraints which are related to a fear of one's own impulses. Many wishes can obtain only an imaginary satisfaction, in a dream, a story, a joke. One of the specific nuances of the joke is the assurance that impulses are harmless. The joker does not intend to carry out any damaging action; he is only joking. Robert, another ten-year-old boy, is obsessed with destructive fantasies. He composes a story about a bad boy, Jack, in which various chapters are titled: "Jack wrecks the house," "Jack wrecks father," "Jack wrecks mother," "Jack wrecks everything," "Nothing stops Jack." Family life in this story is a series of quarrels frequently giving way to free-for-all fights. But the fighting has a slapstick quality: on the one hand the violence is abrupt and extreme, on the other hand no real damage is done. The combatants always emerge unscathed. Through his hero, Jack, who so brazenly wages war on his

parents, Robert tries to reduce his disturbance about his own destructive impulses: it is all very funny. As he plans a new episode in which
the chandelier will fall on father's head, or Jack will push mother
through a hole in the floor, or will make a bomb to blow up the house,
Robert's usually troubled face lights up and he laughs over it. As he
writes, he repeatedly asks for my reassurance: "It is funny, isn't it?"
He also insists that his parents read over what he has written and laugh
about it. He wants the assurance that they do not condemn him for
his destructive wishes. If they find the story funny it means that they
regard his impulses as harmless. Since Robert's doubts on this point
persist, he requires an amused response to his story over and over again.
He reads it to his aunts, to his little brother, to his class in school. We
can see in this one of the motives of the habitual joker, who requires
ever renewed assurance that the impulses he expresses are innocuous.
We can also understand the joker's distress when he fails to obtain an
amused reaction. He then feels that his underlying bad wishes have been
perceived and condemned.

Under the pressure of conflicting wishes children discover a joking
way of dealing with them. The conflict may be translated into a contradiction which they then regard with a lofty reasonableness as if to say:
But that's absurd! In this way they gain a momentary respite from inner
stress. Six-year-old John is an intellectually ambitious little boy, eager to
learn to read and write. His father discusses scientific subjects with him
and John strives anxiously and pridefully to master them. At the same
time he has intense longings in the opposite direction. When he sees
his parents carry his baby sister in their arms he is overwhelmed with
the yearning to be carried in this way himself. However, when he pleads
with his parents to carry him, they protest that he is now too big. At
such moments he must wonder what is the good of his intellectual at-
tainments; growing up only debars him from what he wants most. John
makes up this riddle which he considers funny: "Why did the moron
write on a piece of paper?—'Cause he couldn't walk yet." The combination of being able to write but not being able to walk, so that one would
have to be carried, represents the fulfilment of both of John's opposed
wishes. In making a joke of this impossible consummation, he stresses
its paradoxical character: What an absurd idea to be able to write and
not to be able to walk yet! He uses his critical reasoning powers to devalue his frustrated wishes. We shall see how often children, in their
joking, attempt to free themselves from impossible wishes by picturing
their fulfilment as ridiculous.

.   .   .   .   .

A five-year-old little girl, Nora, turns an oedipal wishfulfilment fantasy into a funny story in this way. She says that she will tell me "a very

silly poem. It's a joke. One day my grandfather went out walking. He met a lamb. Haha. He said to the lamb, 'Will you marry me?' Haha. And the lamb said, 'Baah,' because it didn't know what to say. That's a funny one. A silly one." Here the child has disguised the characters in her oedipal drama, substituting her grandfather for her father and turning herself into a little lamb. Such disguises occur frequently in myths and fairy tales, where the closest, incestuous relations are transformed into relations between remote creatures, as here a human being and an animal. The disguise serves to avoid the guilt and fear which would be roused in acknowledging the true identity of the protagonists. The little girl who, while availing herself of this disguise, finds it funny, has proceeded to take the fantasy literally: How absurd it would be for grandfather to propose marriage to a little lamb. Thus having indulged in a dream-like fantasy, she turns upon what she has produced with a reasonable, realistic criticism. The comic effect is achieved by a shift of level, from fantasy which uses a symbolic mode of expression to literal-minded everyday thinking. By this shift the fantasied wishfulfilment is laughed off as ridiculous. The child has used a further defense against her wishes; she has projected them onto the father-figure in her little story. The grandfather is the one who proposes the improper alliance to the little lamb. The lamb remains demure and only emits a noncommital "Baah." Thus the little girl suppresses her own response to the tempting situation which she has conjured up, blanking it out with a meaningless sound. But again, taking it literally, she finds this dialogue comic: What kind of answer is that to a proposal of marriage if one can only say, "Baah?" It is in effect a mocking response. The little girl, in the guise of the lamb, brushes off the gratifying advances of the father. The comic treatment of the wishfulfilment fantasy consists in repudiating the gratification momentarily offered in imagination but in fact unavailable. The pathos of the unobtainable is transformed into the absurdity of the improbable.

. . . . .

Another joking fantasy plays with the image of the pregnant mother. Five-year-old Ann, having listened to the story of the man whose hat was as big as the world, was inspired to compose a story about an old lady whose house was as big as the world. The same consequence follows that no one can get out of this house. The bigness of the house (house being a frequent symbol of the female body) becomes a nuisance not only to others but to the lady herself, who is unable to get out of the house. Ann mocks the pregnant mother by stressing her incapacitation, in part projecting onto the mother her own frustration and distress. She transforms an enviable situation into one of comic annoyance. The wished-for is laughed off by playing up and exaggerating its inconvenient aspects. Here is Ann's story: "Once there was an old lady who lived in a house. A great big house as big as the world. That's why everybody had to walk straight in her house. Every time they tried to walk out of her house they couldn't. Because their house was in her house too. Every time they tried to play a game they had to play in her house of course. Every time they tried to move their bed out of her house they couldn't. This old lady did not like that. Every time she got cross every person she got cross at would try to get out, to get out the window. They couldn't. The window was too small. And when she went shopping she had to go shopping at her house. And when she ate, she couldn't eat at a restaurant. The restaurants were all in her house. Now this old lady got too tired of this one day. And she said to someone: 'Why do I have to do all these things in my house?' And one day she got much too tired and she said: 'I guess I'll get out of this house.' But she went over to the door and it was locked. It was no use. . . ."

Here the little girl, who has envied her mother's recent pregnancy and cherished the impossible wish to be pregnant herself, transforms the wished-for into a nuisance. The mother's body (house) is so big that she cannot go anywhere. There is also the question so puzzling to children: how does the baby get out? . . . In Ann's story, the pregnant mother, confined to the house, is condensed with the baby in the womb: neither the mother nor the other people (babies) can get out. There is also probably her own wish to escape from the mother (to get out of the house) which she is unable to realize.

. . . . .

The envied procreative powers of the parents may be made fun of by exaggeration, for instance, in fantasies of a family with hundreds of children. Just as the great size of the father's phallus or of the body of the pregnant mother were made ridiculous by being blown up beyond belief, so the baby which the child hopelessly longs to produce becomes less desirable by being multiplied a hundredfold. Also the power of the parents here passes into loss of control: They cannot stop making babies. A six-year-old girl tells the following: "Once there was a little girl. A lady. And she had three hundred children in one year. And they all went to school and they all had the same group and they were all the same age. They all did the same things at school. Wasn't that sil-lee? They all had dirty faces. They all had pimples on their lips. And they all had the same age. They all had dresses on. Some were boys but they had dresses on too, hee, hee, hee. . . . Then they all said the same thing at the same time. And they all sang. The only song they knew was: Abbadabbadabba. . . . Their names were Jimmy and Mary and Cocky" (she laughs) "and Ellen and Frances and Jonathan . . . Timmy and Bimmy and Kisser. The End."

One baby is an object of longing, but at the prospect of three hundred babies all singing "Abbadabbadabba'" in unison motherly sentiment is dissipated. Thus a transformation of feeling is achieved by the multiplication of its objects. The little girl uses additional devices to devalue the babies: they are dirty and diseased (they have pimples on their lips), the boys are castrated (wearing dresses), and they have silly or naughty names (Cocky, Kisser). Another motive behind such a fantasy is the child's anxious concern with how many more children the mother may have. The motive of rivalry with possible brothers and sisters complicates the wish to compete with the mother. In producing the fantasy that the mother will have three hundred children in one year, which she knows is impossible, the little girl reassures herself: nothing is going to happen.

. . . . .

We have seen how children find ways of making fun of the bigness, power, and prerogatives of the grown-ups whom they envy. There is another imposing aspect of adults, which is often oppressive and fearful to children, namely their moral authority; and here too children seek relief through mockery. They seize with delight on opportunities to show that the grown-ups are not infallibly good, or to expose the grown-ups' demands as absurdly impossible, or to distort the meaning of a prohibition into a permission. A little girl of five was very fond of using words for more or less taboo body parts, such as "bottom." If her mother happened to say, "I think I put this or that in the bottom drawer," the child would shout delightedly: "You said 'bottom'!" Thus she pretended to catch her mother in the same naughtiness to which she herself was prone. In a joking way she attempted to make out that her mother was not so very good, and so to relieve herself from the pressure of a too ideal model.

In rebellion against adults' demands, children may try to reduce these demands to absurdity. A six-year-old girl tells me that her teacher said something funny. "She said we couldn't get up from our chairs until we'd finished eating. It sounded as if we'd have to sleep there all night!" In her wish to demonstrate that adults' demands are excessive, the little girl retorts mockingly in her own mind to what the teacher has said: And suppose we don't finish? Then you mean we'll have to stay here all night? By distorting the teacher's demand into something so unreasonable as to be ridiculous, the child exempts herself from feeling bound by it.

Children become skillful in misinterpreting what adults say, to find sanctions for naughtiness or exemption from chores. A teacher says to a four-year-old little girl: "Are you going to help me to put down the beds?" The little girl replies playfully, pretending to have misheard: "Yes, I'm going to help you to take off your head." Thus she pretends that the teacher has requested an all-out expression of the child's aggressive impulses, and she, being a nice little girl, will gladly comply. In the classroom of the six-year-olds, the teacher is teaching the children how to tell time. She has a large clock, the hands of which she places in various positions as she asks the children what time it is. As she puts the clock hands to three o'clock, she asks again: "What time is it now?" The children shout: "Three o'clock! Goodbye, teacher!" In an uproar of laughter they rush to put on their hats and coats and are half-way out the door before the teacher can stop them. Thus they pretend not to have understood the hypothetical character of the teacher's question, and to believe that she is pointing out the actual time to them, three o'clock, the end of the school day. They distort the teacher's meaning in such a way that it becomes an exemption from further work; it is she who sets the clock hands forward and lets them out of school. The embodiment of restrictions is transformed by their joking pretense into an agent of release.

. . . . .

The relation of the comic world to inadequate moral authorities is particularly evident when these authorities appear as characters in the drama. In Charlie Chaplin's *City Lights,* the little tramp encounters by chance an eccentric millionaire who befriends him. The millionaire's benevolence is, however, unpredictable. When he is drunk, he is extravagantly friendly to the little tramp, embracing him, feeding and clothing him, giving him an expensive car. But when he is sober, he fails to recognize the little fellow, has him thrown out of the house and abandons him to the police. Thus for the bewildered little tramp the world is presided over by a capricious deity.

. . . . .

How decisive the image of parental authority is for comedy or tragedy may be seen in the alternative interpretations of the *Merchant of Venice.* The comic or tragic effect depends on how the character of Shylock is regarded. Shylock is a father-figure who has been wronged and who claims vengeance. The issue is whether his claim is a righteous one. The comic impact, which the play originally had, depended on taking Shylock as an unworthy and ludicrous character; his pretense to justice could be unmasked as low vindictiveness. To the extent to which more recent interpretations of the play have tended to attribute justice to Shylock's position, and to see him as cheated of his due, he becomes invested with the paternal right to punish and the play loses its comic effect.

. . . . .

Eugene showed a precocious tendency to mock adults. By demonstrating how silly they were he reduced their impressiveness; the huge beings of his frightening fantasies for the moment dwindled away. With his teacher he used the technique of taking her words more literally than they were intended and so making out that she had said something foolish. When the teacher told another boy to put on his shoes, Eugene remarked: "He doesn't have shoes, he has sneakers." The teacher corrected herself: "I meant, 'Put on your sneakers.'" To this Eugene retorted: "I already have my sneakers on." By thus reducing an authority figure to absurdity Eugene seemed to be reassuring himself that the adults were harmless and that he had nothing to fear from them.

. . . . .

In a joking story Katherine takes a different approach to her family problems. "Once there was a girl named Sissy and a boy named Heinie. They lived in a house made of brown stuff, and not logs I'm telling you! . . . Their mother was called BM. . . . One day they went into the woods to seek their fortune. They crawled to the mouth of the great world. . . . Mrs. BM was very unhappy at the sad turn of events because the two youngsters ran away. So she went looking for them. . . . When she found them sleeping contentedly at the bottom of the toilet and took them back and—shooosh! If you guessed everything up to now you'll guess that's the toilet flushing. And the family went to live downstairs, in a little brown house. The end." . . . The children with their comically naughty names, "Sissy" (urine) and "Heinie" (behind), are not objects of sympathy. Katherine had previously told me that she would not like it if her younger sister called her "Sissy," "because it means coward and second you know what." "Heinie" is the name of the hero in a series of jokes very popular with children of this age; he keeps getting lost and his mother goes around asking everyone: "Have you seen my Heinie?" In her story Katherine makes both Sissy and Heinie excreta. She expresses in a joking way her early wish that her mother would throw her little sister out, flush her down the toilet. Children originally value highly their own body products and do not want to part with them. Later they learn that these products are to be despised. Children also frequently imagine that babies are born through the bowel, and equate babies with feces. Following this line of thought, Katherine says in effect: Mother was just as foolish to want to keep the baby as I used to be when I wanted to preserve my bowel movements. But the child who wants to throw out the baby readily imagines that she will be punished with a similar fate. Or the child has the fantasy that, to separate the younger one from the mother, the two children will run away from home together. This is what happens in Katherine's story. Katherine also reverses the idea that the children are the mother's excreta: the mother is also nothing but a BM. Thus she expresses the feeling: I am just as foolish to want that worthless mother as she was to keep the baby. Where in her serious story Katherine evokes her longing for love from her parents, in the joking one she makes light of this wish by devaluing its object. . . .

27. INTERPRETATION OF PROJECTIVE DEVICES

CHARLOTTE BUHLER, FAITH SMITTER, SYBIL RICHARDSON, AND FRANKLYN BRADSHAW

The development and use of projective techniques flourished after Freud's theories of unconscious motivation were publicized. Since the child unwittingly expresses his unconscious self in countless ways, a trained observer may learn many things by studying his behavior, his speech, his jokes, his reactions to ink drawings, pictures, or cloud formations, his dreams, his stories, and his drawings. The psychologist acts like a detective; he slowly assembles bits of information, like a jigsaw puzzle, into a picture of the child's personality.

This selection demonstrates some interpretations of children's drawings by experts.

The main objection to projective techniques has been the difficulty of reliable interpretation of an individual's projections. Because of this difficulty there is danger of abusing projective methods.

People with empathy, intuition, and imagination often feel that they can interpret another's feelings and motives. Although they succeed often, their interpretations are far from reliable. Children's drawings, for instance, seem to offer an almost irresistible invitation to interpretation. For the alert and interested teacher, the temptation to think of the child

Reprinted from *Childhood Problems and the Teacher,* by Charlotte Buhler, Faith Smitter, Sybil Richardson, and Franklyn Bradshaw. By permission of Henry Holt and Company, Inc. Copyright 1952.

who uses gay colors as gay, and to find clues to the child's personality in certain contents, is very great. But this should be done only with extreme caution unless the teacher has had clinical training. In order to interpret projective self-expression, the examiner must recognize that there are unique personal features in self-expression which exist only in this individual's "private world." Such features are understood only if one knows something about the individual's history. To the experienced worker, the detection of these unique features becomes an important clue to the discovery of emotionally traumatic experiences.

An interesting example is the little three-year-old girl who evidently had some problem in connection with the use of her hands. She went around the room touching things so that they fell down, but she never used her hands directly. She touched objects by pushing her doll's head toward the toys.

Later this same child built a stable for a toy cow and built it almost like a hand with blocks protruding like fingers. But there were six, not five blocks.

This child had been born with the anomaly of six fingers on one hand. Although operated on as a baby, she no doubt had heard about it and had also raised questions regarding the scar on her hand.

Another interesting example is the forty-one-year-old man who saw injured birds in the Rorschach ink blots in seven places in which most people saw quite different things. After the test, when the examiner asked whether he had any particular experience with birds, the subject was astonished by the question—he had not been conscious of seeing so many birds. Then he began to think and suddenly exclaimed that indeed as a boy of seven he had accidentally stepped on a little bird and crushed it. The incident bothered him for many years, after which he forgot it completely.

In addition to such unique experiences, projective techniques also show general human trends. These recurring content or form characteristics of projective productions have been submitted to standardizing procedures and can be interpreted generally as will be shown in the following.

SAMPLES OF PROJECTIVE MATERIAL

DRAWINGS AND PAINTINGS

For the teacher, drawings and paintings, including finger paintings, are so much a part of her experience and interest that a sampling of this important material is given here.

A good example is *Vigdis* whose drawings (Figure 1) were reproduced with a short explanation of her problem. . . .

She is quite *conscious* of the fact that she loves her teacher more than her grandparents; she wants her teacher to love her and to take her away from her grandparents into her own new home; Vigdis hopes

FIGURE 1

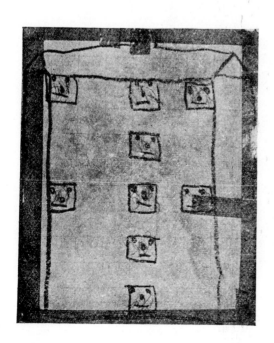

FIGURE 2

267

to be welcome to the new husband also. She wants to be their child. She is *unconscious* of the fact that her drawings make a plea to the teacher to take her into her married life and into her new home as her child.

She gives a *direct* picture of herself with her grandparents and herself with the new couple. By the symbol of hand-holding she also *indirectly* expresses being close to the teacher and the husband but not to the grandparents.

In five-year-old *Tommy's* picture (Figure 2), there is an equally complex pattern of his conscious longing for the mother to be home, his unconscious fear and loneliness, his direct picture of the children at the windows, and his symbolic multiplication of many faces expressing the urgency he feels.

The deeper a child's problem, the more unconscious and unrealistic becomes the symbolism that expresses his disturbance. When *Frick* . . . ties the house he draws to a tree, he forgets reality in which houses are never tied to trees. He just expresses his fear and his wish concerning his home's stability.

The relationship between *Leigh's* apple tree (Figure 3) and himself was even deeper. When Leigh came to therapy . . . he was deeply disturbed by his soiling. The "ugly brown leaves" of the tree as well as

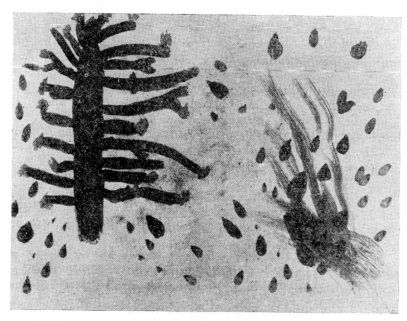

FIGURE 3

the "dirty balls" of sand were semiconscious references to the soiling which shamed him. The leaves had to be burned; the balls to be buried. But the tree also had nice green leaves, and the tree must not burn. This was an unconscious reference to himself, to his good potentialities, and his wish that not Leigh but his shameful deeds be abolished.

This symbolic self-expression is deep because Leigh is not aware that his drawings and his sand formations relate to himself, or that he tells the therapist his problem by means of these products.

The therapist may or may not explain this symbolism to the child. Psychoanalysts formerly considered these interpretations to be essential. At present the prevailing tendency is to refrain from many interpretations, especially with younger children, and to achieve a certain amount of insight without making the child conscious of the way in which he revealed himself.

Leigh's apple tree is an *individual symbol* which refers to his private world. Leigh has been much interested in the burning of old leaves in his parents' back yard where grows this apple tree which he loves and climbs and which he identified with his home and himself. Other symbols are much more general and repetitious.

In spontaneous drawings of young children, the *house* appears most frequently. There seems to be a strong feeling about the protection that his home gives to the child. The strong identification of family and house is shown in one of the drawings that Wolff collected. At his instruction to "draw your family," a number of children drew the family beside their house.

In their drawings many children surround their houses with fences, whether or not their own houses and yards have fences. The *fence* is another of the most frequently used symbols—to fence out potential aggressors or to imprison "bad" people.

Charlie, age eleven, makes a self-protective fence (Figure 4). So does nine-year-old *Henry* (Figure 5). *Henk,* an eight-year-old boy with severe anxieties caused by a very strict and punitive father, at first expresses his feelings that his house is a prison by painting barred windows. Then (Figure 6), probably becoming fearful that someone will guess how he feels, he covers the windows with paint, but expresses his feeling about lack of freedom everywhere by enclosing every object in his world—the trees, the flowers, even the sun and garden. There is only one hope, the boat with which to escape outside.

The most unhappy feeling seems expressed in *Hallie's* drawing (Figure 7). The whole world is only fence and sky. It is empty of people, of things, of anything to have fun with—an empty prison.

The depth of feelings of imprisonment and the need for self-protection cannot be decided by looking at the drawings. The interpreter has

FIGURE 4

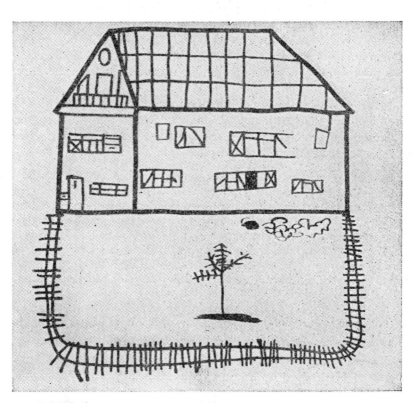

FIGURE 5

FIGURE 6

FIGURE 7

to know more about the child, his background and history, his symptoms, and his ability or inability to project his feelings appropriately.

In remedial release work, children will quite frequently draw jails or witches. This need not always mean deep feelings of deprivation and hatred. Sometimes these drawings may express only acute anger and acute unhappiness. It is helpful, whenever possible, to have the child's comments on his drawings.

.   .   .   .   .   .

To the child, the *human figure* is as important as the *house*. The Goodenough "Draw-a-Man" test, originally devised for the purpose of testing intelligence, finds increasing application as a projective technique, because the attributes given to the human figure are often more expressive of the child's emotional responses than they are of his intellectual responses.

Children's self-portraits are also of great interest, revealing as they do children's attitudes toward their personalities and their moods. A frequent self-portrait is of the "lonely" child (Figure 8), done with unusually painstaking care.

Many of the examples we have used here show that *contents* as well as *formal* characteristics can be used for projection. This is as true of drawings as of other projective techniques, for example, the Rorschach and World tests. Protective fences, rigid schemation, confused disarrangements, over- or underemphasis of items, repetitions, worry over or dis-

FIGURE 8

regard of detail—all are formal characteristics produced by an individual similarly in all these techniques.

. . . . . .

An unconscious formal symptom of importance is the child's worry over much detail and his overconscientious efforts to produce the most careful detail. This is almost always a sign of excessive worry and of an emotionally disturbing perfectionism.

. . . *Paulinke's* flower garden (Figure 9), which is a happy content but, even so, not a release from worry, *Dagny's* detailed work on the girl in the snow (Figure 8), and *Henry's* detail on the garden fence (Figure 5) all belong in the same category.

A frequent content symbol used by little five- and six-year-old girls is the lonely child, as Dagny, age five, paints herself in the snow (Figure 8). "I want to stand all by myself," said another little girl who made such a drawing. Older lonely children paint "lonely" landscapes without people, sometimes without a sign of life, as *Ingrid* does in her second picture, "Road in the Sun" (Figure 10), or *Jerry* does in "The Desert" (Figure 11). Older children also sometimes express their distrust of people by choosing animals, particularly horses, as their friends.

It would be wrong to assume that all children's paintings refer to emotionally disturbing events. Six-year-old *Irma's* "Happy Birthday"

FIGURE 9

FIGURE 10

FIGURE 11

274

FIGURE 12

FIGURE 13

(Figure 12) and ten-year-old *Paulinke's* "Flower Garden" (Figure 9) project happy feelings, and drawings such as "The Battle of Hastings" (Figure 13) by *Douglas,* age nine, represent intellectual and artistic interests.

28. REACTIONS OF MIDDLE AND LOWER CLASS CHILDREN TO FINGER PAINTS

THELMA G. ALPER, HOWARD T. BLANE, AND BARBARA K. ABRAMS

Selection 23 presented evidence that lower-class children are reared more restrictively than those of the middle class. Yet this report of two carefully conducted experiments seems to come to the opposite conclusion by showing that middle-class children are more afraid of soiling and smearing than are lower-class children. The reader can attempt to account for the contradictions, even as psychologists must.

During the past decade a new philosophy of child training has come into prominence. Variously termed "developmental," "self-demand" or "child-centered," its two major tenets are: (*a*) habit training should be started when the child is physiologically ready to comply, not before; and (*b*) the emotional climate in which the training takes place should be one of unconditional acceptance of the child, of tolerance for failure, not coercive adherence to rigid schedules. The first is consistent with the findings of a number of co-twin control experiments. For the second there is some support from clinical studies but the experimental evidence is still equivocal.[1] The psychological advantages and disadvantages of permissive as compared with rigid child-training practices cannot, therefore, yet be clearly evaluated.

During the same period sociologists have been reporting striking social class differences in child-training practices. Middle class parents, they find, are coercive, lower class, permissive. Middle class parents begin habit training earlier, set higher standards for achievement, and

[1] For cogent criticisms of the experimental literature see Harris (9, pp. 12–19) and Koch (11, pp. 6–11).

Reprinted from *Journal of Abnormal and Social Psychology,* 51, No. 3 (November, 1955), 439–448, by permission of the authors and the American Psychological Association. The first part of this study was reported briefly at the EPA meetings in 1949; the second, at the APA meetings in 1951.

are less tolerant of failure. These studies, based only on what mothers say their practices are, include no data on how children react to the parental demands. That class differences in training might result in class differences in personality development, however, is suggested by the sociologists. Davis and Havighurst (3) generalize from their data, as follows: "We would say that middle class children are subjected earlier and more consistently to the influences which make a child orderly, conscientious, responsible and tame. In the course of this training, middle class children *probably* suffer more frustration of their impulses." Ericson's (4) conclusions, based on the same population samples, are similar: "Middle class children are *probably* subjected to more frustrations in the process of achieving these learnings and are probably more anxious as a result of these pressures than are lower class children." [2]

To test the validity of these generalizations, the reputed class differences in a specific area of habit training, namely bowel training, were selected as the focus of the present study. The rationale of the present study was as follows: if the cleanliness standards of middle class parents are more rigid from infancy on, and if these standards are "frustrating," then an experimental task which requires the child to get dirty should elicit measurably different behaviors in middle and lower class children.

Three major differences in behavior were predicted:

1. Middle class children would more often try to avoid the task (refuse to enter into it, or be slower to accept it);
2. Middle class children would show more concern about getting dirty once in the task (maintain minimal contact with the materials);
3. Middle class children would show more concern about getting themselves cleaned up afterwards (go to the bathroom oftener).

Table 1. Median Age in Months for Beginning and Completing Bowel Training in Lower and Middle Class White Children [*]

	PRESENT SAMPLE		DAVIS AND HAVIGHURST DATA	
	Middle Class	*Lower Class*	*Middle Class*	*Lower Class*
Bowel Training Begun	9	11.2	7.5	10.2
Bowel Training Completed	27	18.0	18.4	18.8

[*] Present data compared with data from Davis and Havighurst (3).

Two experiments were designed to test these predictions. In the first, Experiment I, the child was required to use fingerpaints; in the second,

[2] The present writers have added the italics to this and to the preceding quotation.

Experiment II, a control experiment, crayons. It was predicted that the behavior of middle and lower class children would differ significantly in Experiment I, not in Experiment II.

EXPERIMENT I: THE FINGER-PAINTING STUDY METHOD

SUBJECTS

Thirty-six four-year-old, white nursery school children served as Ss.[3] Eighteen were attending a university-sponsored nursery school in Cambridge, Massachusetts, the other 18 attended social-agency supported day nursery schools situated in lower class residential areas in Boston, Massachusetts.

Occupational, educational, residential, and other pertinent socioeconomic data, as outlined by Warner, *et al.* (20), obtained through parent interviews, teacher interviews, and school records, support the designation of the first group as middle class, the second as lower class.[4] Both boys and girls were included, but not in equal numbers. All were within, or above, the normal IQ range.

As evidence of class differences in toilet training, parental time schedules, reported in median age in months for beginning and completing bowel training,[5] are presented in Table 1, along with the corresponding data from Davis and Havighurst (3, p. 701). In both samples, middle class parents start training significantly earlier than do lower class parents. In the present sample, the middle class child achieves control significantly *later;* in the Davis and Havighurst sample, the two groups achieve control at about the same time. The first tenet of the new philosophy of permissiveness in child training, then, is seemingly more frequently violated by middle than by lower class parents in our sample since it is the former who start the training too early; *cf.* Spock (18), and Gesell and Ilg (8). The fact that middle class Ss achieve voluntary control later than do lower class Ss may be indirect evidence that the second tenet, a permissive emotional climate, is also being violated by our middle class parents.[6]

MATERIALS

The Shaw (17) finger paints, red, orange, yellow, green, blue, purple, brown, and black, were used. The paper was the usual 22- by 16-inch glazed paper recommended by Napoli (13) for finger painting.

[3] The sample was restricted to white children since the data for Negro parents are not as consistent. Duvall (4) reports that Negro mothers at all class levels are less permissive than white mothers, whereas Ericson (5) finds that lower class Negro mothers are coercive in toilet training, though permissive in other areas.

[4] The middle class sample was primarily upper-middle; the lower class, primarily middle-lower.

[5] Ericson's (5, p. 499) definition for "training completed" was followed: the child can inhibit defecation voluntarily and can indicate to the mother the need to defecate.

[6] Direct measures of the emotional climate, unfortunately, were not included in the study.

PROCEDURE

Each S was tested individually in a small examining room where E had put out the materials in advance. These consisted of a sheet of dampened paper on the work table, the paints, in eight small jars, arranged in random order on a stand beside the table, and a smock, the latter being customary in these schools during painting sessions.

The E began the session by engaging S in conversation about finger paints: did he know what finger paints were, how to use them, etc. Regardless of S's answers, E illustrated how both hands, both arms, and even the elbows could be used in this kind of painting.

To maximize contact with the paints, S was required to use his fingers for scooping the paints out of the jars.

The experimental task consisted of two finger paintings. For the first, the "free painting," the instructions were: "Paint anything you want to paint." For the second, the "family painting," the instructions were: "Paint a picture of your family—your brothers and sisters, mother and daddy." [7] If S seemed uncertain of what was required of him, E asked: "Who are the people who live in your house?" S was then encouraged to enumerate these people and to draw them.

The E attempted to maintain an informal and permissive atmosphere during the experimental session.

VARIABLES MEASURED

Sixteen formal variables were included for measurement. The list, including operational definitions, is given below.

1. Time to begin painting: measured from the moment E completes the instructions, to the time S begins actually to apply paint to paper; 10 sec. or less scored as "immediate," over 10 sec. as "delayed"; measured only for the "free painting."
2. Acceptance of task: scored as accepted if S does finger-paint; if refuses to paint, or, if in the second painting the content is something other than "a family," performance scored as "task not accepted."
3. Requests help: S asks E for help at some stage in the drawing.
4. Use of whole hand vs. finger-tip approach: S uses fingers and palm for smearing vs. only finger tips.
5. Use of both hands: S uses both hands in whole or part, simultaneously or successively.
6. Use of the whole sheet vs. partial use of sheet: finished product covers whole sheet of paper vs. only a restricted portion.
7. Use of warm vs. cold colors: S makes more frequent use of red, orange and yellow than of green, blue, and purple, as measured by a frequency count.
8. Use of monotones: S uses only one color.
9. Use of brown and/or black: S uses brown, black or both.

[7] Having ascertained the family constellation in advance, E altered these instructions to fit the individual S.

10. Separate placement of colors: S applies paint in daubs, streaks, or patches, keeping each color separate against the white background of the paper.
11. Intermingling of colors: the colors border on each other, but each is retained in the finished product; overlapping of edges is included, "overlay," is not.
12. Indiscriminate mixing of colors: the identity of the separate colors is lost; the finished product looks characteristically "muddy."
13. Names "free drawing": S spontaneously announces what the drawing represents; scores only in the first painting.
14. Mutilation: S defaces finished product by smearing or overlay of fresh paint, original content unrecognizable in whole, or in part, by E; scored only in the second painting.
15. Asks to take paintings home; S asks permission to take his paintings home.
16. Washing-up behavior: S leaves task, goes to the bathroom, washes hands, face, etc., during or after task is completed.

For purposes of analysis and interpretation the variables were grouped as follows: a. Measures of S's willingness to undertake the task: variables 1 and 2; b. Measures of S's willingness to remain in the situation: variables 3, 4, 5, and 6 in the free painting and 3, 4 and 5 in the family painting; c. Measures of color usage and color placement: variables 7, 8, 9, 10, 11, and 12; d. Measure of S's tolerance for an unstructured situation: variable 13 [8]; e. Measures of S's tolerance for the finished product: variables 14 and 15; f. Measure of S's tolerance for "the state of being dirty": variable 16.

RESULTS

The S was scored in terms of presence or absence of each variable. The scores are presented in Table 2 along with the probability values for significance of the differences between the two groups of Ss, computed by Fisher's (6) exact test.

FREE PAINTING TASK

a. Willingness to undertake the task (variables 1 and 2). The behavior of the two groups differs significantly on one of these variables. Both groups comply with the instruction to paint a picture (variable 2), but more lower class Ss accept the task immediately (variable 1, $p = .001$).

b. Willingness to remain in the situation (variables 3, 4, 5, and 6). Three of the differences are significant in the expected direction. More lower class Ss use the whole hand for smearing (variable 4, $p = .02$) and, indeed, smear with *both* hands (variable 5, $p = .001$). More lower class Ss smear the paint over the entire surface of the paper (variable 6, $p = .001$). Neither group requests help with the free painting (variable 3).

The use of the finger tip, not the whole hand (variable 4), and of a

---

[8] Since E imposes structure in the second task, this measure applies only to the first painting.

different fingertip for each separate color, is a middle, not a lower class behavior. Lower class Ss more often use a whole arm, "into-the-paints-to-the-elbow" technique. They apply the paints in wide swirling motions, using both hands, palms down, fingers spread, as contrasted with the constricted, small movements of middle class Ss (variable 6).

c. Color usage (variables 7, 8, and 9) and color placement (variables 10, 11, and 12).

Table 2. **Comparison of Middle and Lower Class Four-Year-Old Children on Two Finger-Painting Tasks**

	FREE PAINTING TASK			FAMILY PAINTING TASK		
VARIABLE	Middle Class Ss (N = 18)	Lower Class Ss (N = 18)	p *	Middle Class Ss (N = 18)	Lower Class Ss (N = 18)	p *
1. Begins to paint immediately	5	17	.001	—	—	—
2. Accepts task	18	18	1.000	4	12	.01
3. Requests help	0	0	1.000	8	3	.03
4. Use of whole hand	11	17	.02	12	17	.04
5. Use of both hands	8	17	.001	13	17	.09
6. Use of whole sheet	9	18	.001	—	—	—
7. Use of warm colors	1	10	.001	2	7	.06
8. Use of monotones	2	2	1.000	3	2	>.20
9. Use of brown and/or black	11	11	1.000	12	12	1.000
10. Separate placement of colors	4	0	.05	3	0	.11
11. Intermingles colors	2	13	.001	3	10	.02
12. Mixes colors indiscriminately	10	3	.02	8	5	>.20
13. Names free painting	14	7	.02	—	—	—
14. Mutilates painting	—	—	—	10	4	.04
15. Asks to take drawing home	—	—	—	18	1	<.001
16. Washing-up behavior	5	0	.02	18	18	1.000

* Computed by means of Fisher's (6) exact test.

Only one color usage variable yields a significant difference: lower class Ss more often use warm colors, red, orange, yellow; middle class Ss, cold colors, green, blue, purple (variable 7, $p = .001$). The use of monotones (variable 8) is rare in both groups. Both groups use browns and blacks (variable 9).

All of the color placement variables yield statistically significant differences. When clear separation of the color occurs (variable 10,

$p = .05$), it does so only among middle class Ss. When the middle class S permits colors to come into contact he intermixes them in such manner that the colors lose their separate identity in the finished product (variable 12, $p = .02$). The lower class S more often intermingles the colors (variable 11, $p = .02$). As a consequence, the total effect of the two sets of paintings is strikingly different. The paintings of middle class Ss typically consists of daubs, streaks, or somewhat constricted wave lines of paint widely separated from each other, or of dark, muddy-looking, formless masses with much overlay of one color or another, the original colors no longer being recognizable in the final product. The paintings of the lower class Ss, on the other hand, are more often warm and bright in color tone and the original colors are recognizable in the finished product.

d. The S's tolerance for an unstructured situation (variable 13).

Giving a name to the painting (variable 13), is used as a measure of S's intolerance for the unstructured situation. The difference between the two groups is statistically significant: more middle class Ss name the free painting ($p = .02$).

Sometimes the naming occurs right away, S announcing what he will paint. Sometimes it occurs only after the product is finished, when E routinely asked if the picture had a name.

e. The S's tolerance for the finished product (variables 14 and 15).[9]

f. The S's tolerance for the state of being dirty (variable 16).

A frequency count of the number of Ss who left the task to go to the bathroom (variable 16) revealed a class difference. No lower class S's went to the bathroom during, or at the end of the free painting task. Nor do they talk about wanting to go. This behavior occurs only among middle class S's ($p = .02$).[10]

FAMILY PAINTING TASK

a. Willingness to undertake the task (variables 1 and 2). As noted earlier, variable 1 was not measured here. Variable 2 did yield a significant difference in the expected direction: more lower class Ss comply with E's instruction to paint a picture of the family ($p = .01$).[11]

---

[9] Not measured for the first painting.

[10] While the record of S's questions and remarks during the painting process is not complete enough for statistical analysis, it may be noted in passing that middle, not lower class Ss carry on a running commentary, replete with self-references, while painting. Typical remarks are the following: "Look at me, I'm all dirty" . . . "My hands are green" . . . "I'm all muddy" . . . "Will the paint come off?"

The vocalizations of lower class Ss were more often squeals, grunts, or laughs. When they talked it was usually to ask why E was there or when E would come again, rather than to direct attention to themselves.

[11] In no case do we find a family, or reasonable facsimile thereof, in the final products of middle class Ss. The four who did accept the task mutilated the drawing at the end of the session.

b. Willingness to remain in the situation (variables 3, 4, and 5). Two of these variables yield significant differences in the expected direction. As in the free painting, more lower class Ss use the whole hand for smearing (variable 4, $p = .04$). Use of both hands for applying the paints, however, now only shows a tendency in favor of lower class Ss (variable 5, $p = .09$).

c. Color usage and color placement (variables 7, 8, 9, 10, 11, and 12).

None of the color usage variables yields a significant difference. One approaches significance: more lower class Ss tend to use warm colors (variable 7, $p = .06$).

The direction of the differences for color placement variables (variables 10, 11, and 12) remains the same in both paintings. But only intermingling (variable 11, $p = .02$) reveals a significant between-class difference in the second painting.

d. The S's tolerance for the finished product (variables 14, and 15).

More middle class Ss mutilate the family painting (variable 14, $p = .04$).[12]

All middle class Ss asked for permission to take their paintings home (variable 15). Only one lower class S made this request. The p here is beyond the .001 level of confidence.

e. The S's tolerance for the state of being dirty (variable 16).

After completing the second task, all Ss voluntarily entered the bathroom and washed up before returning to the classroom.

The results of Experiment I indicate, then, that the behavior of middle and lower class Ss does differ in the predicted ways: middle class Ss more often tried to avoid the finger-painting task and more often tried to avoid getting dirty while they were painting. They were apparently also more concerned than lower class Ss to get clean afterwards.

EXPERIMENT II: THE CRAYON STUDY METHOD

SUBJECTS

Forty white, four-year-old, nursery school children served as Ss. Twenty were enrolled in private schools in Worcester, Massachusetts, the other twenty in the social-agency-sponsored schools used in Experiment I. The sociological

---

[12] The content data support the view that S's mutilation is intentional. Like many middle class Ss, middle class Ann, for example, paints a house, not her family. Her house has four windows. She identifies each as she paints: "This is my mommy's, this is my daddy's, this is brother's and this is mine." Next she smears black paint across three windows, leaving undefaced only the window of her own room.

Lower class Suky draws her mother, starting with the feet. She then says, "She is too big." Where the body should be Suky smears with a kind of scribbling motion. Suky's mother, the teacher has told us, is pregnant.

criteria for selecting the two groups, the one middle class, the other lower, were the same as in Experiment I.[13]

The toilet-training time schedules are presented in Table 3.[14]

Table 3. Mean Age in Months at Which Bowel Training Was Begun and Completed

	MIDDLE CLASS			LOWER CLASS			
	N	Ss	N	Ss	tc	p	
Bowel Training Begun	18	10	17	9	1.04	.30	
Bowel Training Completed	18	25.9	16	17.4	4.49	<.01	

Comparison of Tables 1 and 3 reveals some schedule differences. Experiment I was completed in 1948, Experiment II in 1951. In the 1948 sample (Table 1), the middle class parent began the training earlier and completed it later than did the lower class parent. Both differences were significant. In 1951 (Table 3), the middle class parent started and completed training later.[15] But now only the completion data differ significantly for the two social classes. The reversal in starting-time, while not statistically significant, however, may have some importance.

In 1951, some middle class mothers volunteered during the interview that they had read "The Books" and that they were "following" them. By "The Books" they meant Gesell and Ilg (8) and/or Spock (18). In 1948, these books were not mentioned. Nor did lower class mothers mention them in 1951. Yet, if the attitudes of our 1951 middle class mothers were as consistently permissive as self-demand theory requires, and if the lower class mothers were continuing to be permissive, then logically, training should be completed approximately at the same time in the two social classes. But, as Table 3 shows, this is not the case. As in 1948, middle class Ss still achieve control significantly *later* ($p = .01$). What seems likely, therefore, is that the middle class delay in starting training may stand alone in "taking over" the new philosophy of child care. The attitudes and emotional climate may still be coercive.[16] This will be considered again in a later section.

MATERIALS

Milton-Bradley Trutone Crayons were used. The colors were the same as in Experiment I. The drawing paper was of the newsprint variety. The size of the paper corresponded to that customarily used in the given nursery school.

[13] As in Experiment I, the middle class group was primarily upper-middle, the lower class, primarily middle-lower.

[14] It was not possible to complete these data for all Ss. The teachers were of the opinion, however, that the incompleted cases were not atypical.

[15] The Maccoby *et al.* (12) social class training data gathered in the same year are also in this direction.

[16] Klatskin's (10) data support this possibility. The values and attitudes of middle class mothers who participated in the rooming-in plan seemed to remain "middle class" (coercive, nonpermissive) even though their practices followed the precepts of self-demand scheduling.

Table 4. Comparison of Middle and Lower Class Four-Year-Old Children on Two Crayon Drawing Tasks

	FREE DRAWING			FAMILY DRAWING		
VARIABLE	*Middle Class* Ss (N = 20)	*Lower Class* Ss (N = 20)	p *	*Middle Class* Ss (N = 20)	*Lower Class* Ss (N = 20)	p *
1. Begins to draw immediately	18	19	>.20	17	13	.14
2. Accepts task	20	20	1.000	16	12	.15
3. Use of whole sheet	15	14	>.20	13	9	.15
4. Use of warm colors	4	3	>.20	6	2	.12
5. Use of monotones	2	6	.12	6	11	.10
6. Use of brown and/ or black	15	13	>.20	14	9	.10
7. Separate placement of colors	3	2	>.20	2	1	>.20
8. Intermingling of colors	11	6	.10	11	5	.05
9. Indiscriminate mixing of colors	4	6	>.20	2	0	>.20
10. Names free drawing	14	15	>.20	—	—	—
11. Mutilates drawing	5	4	>.20	2	0	>.20

* Computed by means of Fisher's (6) exact test.

PROCEDURE

The procedure was the same as in Experiment I, adjustments being made only for the difference in medium. For example, no demonstration of crayoning was given.

VARIABLES MEASURED [17]

1. Time to begin crayoning.
2. Acceptance of task.
3. Use of whole sheet vs. partial use of sheet.[18]
4. Use of warm vs. cold colors.
5. Use of monotones.
6. Use of brown and/or black crayons.
7. Separate placement of colors.
8. Intermingling of colors.
9. Indiscriminate mixing of colors.
10. Names "free drawing."
11. Mutilation.

[17] Only variables new to Experiment II will be defined.
[18] Because the crayon drawings typically had content, the entire sheet was rarely covered. If a drawing occupied at least two thirds of the paper, it was scored as using the whole sheet.

12. Takes initiative in cleaning-up: at end of session, S spontaneously offers to put away crayons and/or to clean the table.
13. Asks to take drawings home.
14. Asks to do an extra drawing: at end of session, S asks if he may make one more picture.

As in Experiment I, S was scored in terms of presence or absence of each variable.

These scores constitute the data for analysis.

RESULTS

The data for variables 1–11, analyzed by means of Fisher's (6) exact test, are summarized in Table 4. Postsession behavior, variables 12–14, are presented in Table 5. As these tables show, of the 24 differences analyzed, only two were statistically significant. Since this could occur by chance alone, no further discussion of these data will be presented.

Table 5. Comparison of Postsession Behavior of Middle and Lower Class Nursery School Children Following Crayon-Drawing Tasks

VARIABLE	MIDDLE CLASS Ss ($N = 20$)	LOWER CLASS Ss ($N = 20$)	p *
12. Takes initiative in cleaning-up process	5	11	.05
13. Asks permission to take drawings home	3	7	.14
14. Asks to do an extra drawing	5	8	>.20

* Computed by means of Fisher's (6) exact test.

The hypothesis Experiment II was designed to test, therefore, is supported: middle and lower class Ss behave in the same way when the drawing medium does not necessitate getting dirty.

DISCUSSION

As predicted, finger paints, not crayons, yielded statistically significant differences in the behavior of middle and lower class nursery school children. Middle class Ss do appear to be made anxious by the smearing requirement: they have a lower tolerance for getting dirty, for staying dirty, and for the products they produce while dirty. Among the more obvious variables to reveal these differences are the slower acceptance by middle class Ss of the finger-painting task, the maintenance of only minimal contact with the paints (e.g., a single finger tip, not a whole-hand approach), the substitution of a different content for the "family" painting and/or final mutilation of it. Differences yielded by other variables also support the thesis of tolerance differences, as can be seen by relating these variables to be empirical findings of other studies, as discussed below.

While investigators are not in complete accord about the psychological significance of color usage (16), many make a distinction between warm and cold colors. Cold colors in children's drawings have been associated with depression (14), delinquency (15), poor adjustment, and controlled reactions as opposed to free emotional expression (1); warm colors, with cheerfulness and good adjustment (1, 2, 15, 20). The parsimonious application of these findings to our results is that middle class Ss by using more cold colors in Experiment I are attempting to control their feelings.[19] The greater use of warm colors by lower class Ss is consistent with absence of situational anxiety.

Our color placement data fall into the three patterns previously noted by Alschuler and Hattwick (1). One pattern, separate placement, they suggest, is the response of the emotionally more mature child who has an "extreme sense of order and cleanliness" and "repressed desires to smear and to soil." A second pattern, indiscrimate mixing, is the response of the emotionally immature child who is still functioning "on a manipulative, smearing level." Both the more controlled separate placement and the uncontrolled indiscriminate mixing occurred in middle, not lower class Ss in the present study. Lower class Ss more often resorted to a third pattern, the intermingling of colors. According to Alschuler and Hattwick (1), intermingling is not associated with "strain or emotional tension."

Constricted use of the drawing paper has been found to characterize the behavior of the timid child, the rejected and deprived child, the withdrawing, emotionally dependent child; use of the whole sheet, the "uninhibited" child, the "relatively outgoing, assertive, self-reliant personality." In our results, middle class Ss resort to the constricted pattern, lower class to the unconstricted.

The assigning of a name to the "free" painting, a variable which characterized middle class Ss, is reminiscent of Frenkel-Brunswick's (7) concept of intolerance for ambiguity. The structuring of an unstructured situation by giving it a name may help S control or contain the anxieties aroused by smearing. By naming, S may be saying: "I have drawn *something; I have not just been smearing.*"

---

[19] The studies cited above have limited value for comparative purposes. In some, abnormal populations only were sampled. Some use water-colors, some crayons, others a combination of media. Social class factors also were not controlled.

The more frequent request of middle class Ss for help with the family painting suggests another mechanism of defense: only if the adult gets dirty, too, is it all right for the middle class S to get dirty!

The middle class S's lack of spontaneity about cleaning up the examining room would seem to be consistent with the rest of his behavior. It may mean that he wants to get away quickly from the scene of his smearing misdoings. Or, like the middle class child in the Fisher *et al.* (5) balloon film, he departs without helping, knowing that "somebody else will clean up." Characteristically, for the middle class child, someone else does. Teachers in the lower class schools tell us that these children are taught to clean up after themselves. They appear here to do so willingly.

Two different explanations occur to us with respect to the middle class S's more frequent request to take his drawings home: (*a*) he may want to use his products as a gift to appease the parent who disapproves of his getting dirty; or (*b*) he may wish to destroy the evidence himself. To choose between these alternatives, we would have to know "the-take-home-policies" of these schools, as well as what, in fact, S would do with his products were he allowed to retain them.

Consistently, then, the finger-painting data support the thesis of social-class tolerance differences for getting and staying dirty. Middle class Ss are seemingly made more anxious by the smearing task. As predicted, however, behavioral differences break down when crayons are used as the drawing medium. Yet since some middle class mothers in the crayon study tell us that they are following "The Books," the argument could be made that the crayon study does not serve as an adequate control, that we are no longer dealing with coercively vs. permissively reared children. Indeed, there are no differences now in the parental time schedules for starting toilet training. Differences in time for completing training, however, persist. This latter fact, we feel, supports the argument that the emotional climate in which the training is taking place is different in the two social classes.

Middle class mothers, influenced by modern parent-oriented literature, may be *trying* to be more permissive. Yet if their attitudes toward dirt and messiness are still traditionally middle class, and Klatskin's (10) study done during the same time interval suggests that they are, the likelihood is that these parents would resort either to inconsistent permissiveness or to a laissez-faire policy. In either case, we would expect control to be delayed since "the rules" for winning parental approval would not be clear to the child. Class differences in the atmosphere in which the training is taking place would thus still pertain. Exposure to a new philosophy of training, as Klatskin (10) notes, does not insure the proper attitudes for applying it.

A recent study by Maccoby *et al.* (12), however, raises some important questions. It overlaps in time, and to some extent in geographical samplings, our crayon experiment. On the basis of interviews with middle and lower class mothers, they report a shift "toward greater warmth and permissiveness, and less severity in socialization among upper-middle families with the more severe training occurring among the lower group" (12, p. 392). As in our crayon study, bowel training is started a little later by middle class mothers, but not significantly so. Unlike our study, training is completed by middle and lower class children at about the same time. This latter difference is an important one. Yet we cannot fully account for it.

In comparing their data with those of Davis and Havighurst (3), Maccoby *et al.* (12, p. 394) raise the question of sampling differences. Davis and Havighurst, they suggest, may have been dealing with a "lower" class sample. But Ericson (4, p. 496) used the Davis and Havighurst sample and describes it as "for the most part, upper-lower class." Our lower class sample was primarily middle-lower. The linear relationship between severity of training and class membership, from lower-lower to upper-middle, as reported by Maccoby *et al.*, moreover, would fit neither the Davis and Havinghurst data, nor ours. Sampling differences, therefore, would seem not to be the crucial factor.

A more promising lead is suggested by the Maccoby *et al.* question as to whether "upper-middle mothers were telling the interviewers not what they actually do but what they believe would be the right thing to say to the interviewer" (12, p. 392). In telling us that they are following "The Books," our middle class mothers may also have been telling us "the right thing." Yet, since they report an even later age for completing bowel training, may this not mean that their standards for cleanliness are very high indeed?

We raise a final, and perhaps the most basic question for future research. Judging from recent, informal discussions with parents at PTA meetings, for example, middle class parents *are* reading "The Books." But they seem to be equating permissiveness and laissez faire. They mistake the "let the child do anything he wants to do, lest we frustrate him by imposing rules," for permissiveness. The consequences of permissiveness and laissez faire for personality development, however, theoretically should be quite different. Laissez faire, with its absence of rules, absence of any sort of guidance, should make for insecurity, indecisiveness, and feelings that the parents are not interested enough to help.[20] Yet from the parents' point of view the training procedures might seem permissive because they are "lenient." Consistent with this possibility are the

[20] A quotation from the senior author's unpublished counseling records of a young college student epitomizes the feelings of rejection laissez faire can entail: "My parents do not restrict me at all. They never ask me where I'm going, with whom I'm going or where I've been. I guess they don't love me enough to care."

Maccoby *et al.* findings of statistically significant class differences in techniques of discipline. Upper-lower mothers more often use what Maccoby *et al.* describes as "negative techniques" (12, p. 387): physical punishment, ridicule, and deprivation of privileges; upper-middle mothers more often use scolding statements involving withdrawal of love (12, Table 6, p. 388). That the latter can make children very anxious indeed is clinically now well recognized.

To gain further insight into the problems raised by this discussion necessitates additional research. Among the studies which might profitably be undertaken are : (*a*) a repetition of the original finger-painting study in which the consequences of different parental attitudes as well as of different training procedures are investigated; (*b*) a study of the behavioral consequences of social class differences in habit training areas other than toilet training; and (*c*), a systematic study of the extent to which present-day parents are confusing permissiveness with laissez faire.

SUMMARY

Starting with the findings by sociologists that child-training practices differ markedly in middle and lower class families, two related experiments were designed to measure behavioral consequences of the reputedly coercive, rigid middle class procedures as contrasted with the more permissive lower class procedures. The conjectures of Davis and Havighurst (3, p. 707) that middle class children "probably suffer more frustration of their impulses," and of Ericson (4, p. 501) that middle class children "are probably more anxious as a result of these pressures," were tested, using class differences in toilet training procedures as the basis for the experimental design.

In the first experiment, eighteen middle and eighteen lower class white, nursery school children used finger paints for painting two pictures. The S chose his own content for the first picture. For the second, he was asked to paint a picture of his family. Quantitative analysis of the formal aspects of the paintings reveals statistically significant differences in the performance of the two groups of Ss. The middle class Ss show a lower tolerance for getting dirty, for staying dirty, and for the products they produce while dirty, as measured by such variables as time to begin painting, color usage, mutilation of the family painting, bathroom behavior, etc.

In the second experiment, crayons were used as the drawing medium. As predicted, the class differences obtained in the first experiment do not persist in the second experiment. The class differences in Experiment I, therefore, reflect differences in reactions "to getting dirty," not differences in drawing, as such.

The results are interpreted to mean that soiling and smearing behavior does arouse more anxiety in middle than in lower class children. The mechanisms used by the middle class child to handle this anxiety are discussed.

REFERENCES

1. ALSCHULER, ROSE H., & HATTWICK, LA BERTA B. W. *Painting and personality.* Vol. I, II. Chicago: University of Chicago Press, 1947.

2. BRICK, N. The mental hygiene value of children's art work. *Amer. J. Orthopsychiat.,* 1944, 14, 136–146.

3. DAVIS, W. A., & HAVIGHURST, R. J. Social class and color differences in child-rearing. *Amer. sociol. Rev.,* 1946, 11, 698–710.

4. ERICSON, MARTHA. Child-rearing and social status. In T. M. Newcomb, E. L. Hartley, & others (Eds.), *Readings in social psychology.* New York: Holt, 1947.

5. FISHER, M. S., STONE, L. J. & BACKER, J. Balloons: demonstration of a projective technique for the study of aggression and destruction in young children. New York: New York Film Library, 1941. (Film)

6. FISHER, R. A. *Statistical methods for research workers.* (6th ed.) Edinburgh: Oliver and Boyd, 1936. Also in A. C. Edwards, *Experimental design in psychological research.* New York: Rinehart, 1950. Pp. 84–85.

7. FRENKEL-BRUNSWIK, ELSE. Intolerance of ambiguity as an emotional and personality variable. *J. Pers.,* 1949, 18, 108–143.

8. GESELL, A., & ILG, FRANCES. *Infant and child in the culture of today.* New York: Harper, 1943.

9. HARRIS, D. B. Child psychology. *Annu. Rev. Psychol.* 1953, 4, 1–30.

10. KLATSKIN, ETHELYN H. Shifts in child care practices in three social classes under an infant care program of flexible methodology. *Amer. J. Orthopsychiat.,* 1952, 22, 52–61.

11. KOCH, HELEN L. Child psychology. *Annu. Rev. Psychol.,* 1954, 5, 1–26.

12. MACCOBY, ELEANOR E., GIBBS, PATRICIA K., & others. Methods of child-rearing in two social classes. In W. E. Martin, & Celia B. Stendler (Eds.), *Readings in child development.* New York: Harcourt Brace, 1954.

13. NAPOLI, P. J. Finger-painting and personality diagnosis. *Genet. Psychol. Monogr.,* 1946, 34, 129–230.

14. PFISTER, O. Farbe und Bewegung in der Zeichnung Geisteskranker, *Schweiz. Arch. Neurol. Psychiat.,* 1934, 34, 325–365.

15. PHILIPS, E., & STROMBERG, E. A comparative study of finger-painting performance in detention home and high school pupils. *J. Psychol.,* 1948, 26, 507–515.

16. PRECKER, J. A. Painting and drawing in personality assessment. *J. proj. Tech.,* 1950, 14, 262–286.

17. SHAW, RUTH F. *Finger-painting.* Boston: Little, Brown, 1934.

18. SPOCK, B. *Pocket book of baby and child care.* New York: Pocket Books, 1948.
19. WARNER, W. L., MEEKER, MARCHIA, & EELLS, K. *Social class in America.* Chicago: Science Research Associates, 1949.
20. WOLFF, W. *Personality of the preschool child.* New York: Grune and Stratton, 1946.

29. CHILDREN'S TEXTBOOKS AND PERSONALITY DEVELOPMENT: AN EXPLORATION IN THE SOCIAL PSYCHOLOGY OF EDUCATION

IRVIN L. CHILD, ELMER H. POTTER, AND ESTELLE M. LEVINE

One of the many ways in which children learn cultural values and expectations is through the stories they read. In grammar school the average child reads or has read to him thousands of stories, each of which carries its own message about right and wrong, what will be rewarded and what punished.

The findings in this important monograph analyzing 914 third-grade stories are startling. Under most conditions, the stories show that initiative and original thinking are punished— rather than rewarded. Unlike real life, nearly every story has a happy ending, and the child in the story always wins the competition. Thus the stories offer few positive suggestions to aid their readers in facing the problems of failure or aggression with which most children must cope in real life.

The specific objective of this study is the analysis of certain content of the world of ideas which confronts children in the process of education, from the point of view of the probable effect of that content on the motivation of their behavior. Just what that means will be made clear through the discussion, in the rest of this chapter, of the way the content was analyzed.

Selections reprinted from *Psychological Monographs*, 60, No. 3 (1946), Whole No. 279, 1–7, 43–53, by permission of the authors and the American Psychological Association.

SELECTION OF MATERIAL

THE BOOKS CHOSEN

The material chosen for analysis consisted of certain portions of the content of general readers intended for use in the third grade. Printed material was selected, rather than the content of what was said by teachers in classrooms, because of the accessibility of printed material, and because a manageable sample of it must of necessity reflect accurately certain educational practices in the country at large. The choice of the third-grade level was made on the grounds of convenience for the purpose of this study: textbooks for the first and second grades have such very simple content that few passages are susceptible of the kind of analysis that we have undertaken, while readers from the fourth grade up, on the other hand, begin to have such complex material that the analysis would be more laborious and less reliable.

We chose for our purpose all of the general third-grade readers we were able to find which had been published since 1930. (Excluded were third-grade readers intended primarily to teach special topics such as science, social studies, or arithmetic, and one reader which deviated greatly from all the others in containing considerable material on religion.) In all, 30 books were included in the analysis.

SELECTION OF CONTENT FROM THE BOOKS

The first step in the process of analysis of the readers was the selection of those stories which were to be analyzed. Since the purpose of the analysis was to determine what effect the readers might have on the socialization of the child, only those stories were chosen in which the content could conceivably affect the child's behavior. The general criterion for selection was that the story contain characters in action, since the child's behavior would be affected only by his generalizing from that of individuals in the stories to his own behavior. This resulted in the exclusion of three types of material.

. . . . .

The content which was included in the analysis was, then, those stories in which characters appeared who presented distinctive behavior that could be analyzed according to the method described below. The material analyzed included well over three quarters of the content of the books. Altogether, 914 stories were analyzed.

A story is often, however, a cumbersome and complex unit for analysis and comparison. Sometimes a story contains several incidents whose context is very different. Or, in a single incident very different things will be happening to two or more important characters, or one character may be showing more than one significant kind of behavior. The unit for analysis, therefore, was not the story but the *thema*. A thema is a sequence of psychological events consisting of (1) a situation or circumstances confronting a person, (2) the behavior (internal and external) with which the person responds, (3) the consequences of the behavior as felt by the person himself. In the 914 stories used, 3409 thema were found and analyzed, an average of almost 4 thema per story. In the presentation of quantitative data in the rest of this monograph, the number of thema is always the basic quantity dealt with.

METHOD OF ANALYSIS

The method of analysis applied to the thema found in the readers was based on the following considerations:

It is assumed that in reading a story, a child goes through symbolically, or rehearses to himself, the episode that is described. The same principles, then, are expected to govern the effect of the reading on him as would govern the effect of actually going through such an incident in real life. The principles that seemed important for this study are those of reinforcement and of avoidance learning.

It is assumed that when a sequence of behavior is shown as leading to reward, the effect will be to increase the likelihood of a child's behaving in that way under similar conditions in the future. Among the kinds of behavior that may be learned in this way are motives, for they are to be regarded as being produced largely by a subject's own behavior.

When, on the other hand, a sequence of behavior is shown as leading up to punishment, it is expected that the incident will contribute to the probability of the subject's avoidance of such behavior in the future. Again, among the effects of such avoidance can be the reduction of the strength or the likelihood of the appearance of a motive.

This reasoning suggested the analysis of the content in accordance with the following general scheme:

1. *Character* whose behavior is represented in the thema
2. *Behavior* displayed by the character
3. *Circumstances* surrounding the behavior
4. *Consequences* of the behavior (for the character himself)
5. *Type of story* in which the incident occurs.

The way that each of these aspects was analyzed will now be presented in turn.

CHARACTERS

If the effect of an incident upon a child depends upon his identification with the character whose behavior is being described, then the effect is likely to vary according to the ease of identification with the given character. Boys, for example, may be more likely to identify with boys, and girls with girls. Children may be more likely to identify with children than with adults, or perhaps less likely.

It was first necessary to decide which characters were those with which identification was most likely. Many characters were easily and reliably chosen on this basis. They were the *central characters,* the characters from whose point of view the story was written. In most cases a single individual or group of individuals clearly stood out as the central character of the story. In some cases there seemed to be two or three such figures, and in that case each one was dealt with separately.

There was a second group of figures who appeared in stories as the villainous antagonists of central characters, *anti-social characters* who injured or threatened the wealth or happiness of the central characters. It might be supposed at first glance that identification with these anti-social characters is not likely. We believe, however, that it is likely. Much behavior which is rarely shown as performed by social characters is shown as performed by anti-social characters, and the punishment that follows may indeed produce an effect on the child who reads the story.

Characters are first of all, then, divided into central and anti-social ones. For most of the categories of behavior dealt with, the number of anti-social characters is small and they are not treated separately. For certain categories of behavior, however, distinctive facts about the anti-social characters will be mentioned.

For each character, regardless of whether central or anti-social, a further classification was made as follows:

1. Children (divided into boys, girls, and groups of mixed sex)
2. Adults (men, women, and groups of mixed sex)
3. Animals (including in this single category both animals who are portrayed realistically and those who are shown as behaving like human beings)
4. Fairies (used here as a convenient short name for all supernatural creatures, including fairies in the strict sense, giants, dwarfs, gods, and inanimate objects imbued with life).

It is this classification of characters that has been most significant in connection with the analysis of behavior and that will be referred to in reporting on almost every behavioral category.

. . . . .

Table 1. Categories of Behavior Employed in Analyzing the Content of Third-Grade Readers, with the Number of Thema in Which Each Category Was Found

Category	Number of Thema in Which It Appears	Category	Number of Thema in Which It Appears
Objectless Behavior		Altruistic Social Behavior	
Activity	264	(generally leading to	
Passivity	89	simultaneous gratification	
Sentience	82	of other person's needs)	
Elation	55	Affiliation	364
Behavior Primarily in		Nurturance	266
Relation		Succorance	176
to Things and Events		Deference	184
Cognizance	351	Egoistic Social Behavior	
Achievement	221	(generally competing with	
Construction	75	other person's needs)	
Imaginality	31	Aggression	206
Acquisition	177	Dominance	152
Retention	33	Recognition	175
Order	43	Autonomy	122
		Rejection	21
		Avoidance Behavior	
		Harmavoidance	212
		Blamavoidance	72
		Infavoidance	38

. . . . .

SUMMARY OF PROCEDURE

The outline of the analysis given above will now be briefly summarized, together with some indication of the actual technique used in recording the data.

The first step was to read each story in a given book and determine whether it was suitable for the purposes of the analysis. If it was suitable, the second step was to identify all the separate thema in the story that fitted the pattern of analysis. When these thema were identified, a file card was prepared for each one. It was labeled appropriately to identify the story and the book and then the following information was entered on it:

1. The type of story
2. Whether the character was central or anti-social
3. The classification of the character according to age, sex, humanity, etc.

4. The behavior displayed, classified according to Murray's system of needs
5. Notes on the circumstances surrounding the behavior
6. The classification of the consequences of the behavior.

OVERALL FINDINGS AND DISCUSSION
CULTURAL FORCES INFLUENCING
PERSONALITY

The observations that have been reviewed on the treatment of various categories of behavior in children's readers can leave no doubt that this treatment is such as to encourage the development of certain motives and to discourage others. A tabulation of the percentage of reward, punishment, and no consequence for the various categories of behavior, presented in Table 2, brings out this general point quite clearly. The categories are arranged here in order of relative frequency of reward, and this order may be taken as one indication of the degree of encouragement or discouragement of the development of each one. In considerable part, of course, this order reflects general cultural norms—for example, in the high value placed on affiliation, nurturance and cognizance, and in the frequent punishment of aggression, retention and rejection. To this extent the analysis of the contents of the readers does not stand alone but is useful as symptomatic of probable characteristics of other kinds of content of the world of ideas that reach children—what teachers say to them in classes, morals that their parents point up to them, the content of stories they read elsewhere.

But the entire impact of cultural forces on personality manifested in these readers is not shown in a simple listing of the treatment of the several categories separately. There are also certain generalities which can be found running through the whole series of categories, generalities about particular ways of achieving ends which are most likely to lead to success or to failure.

Perhaps the most striking case of this sort is the repeated reward of effort or work as a way of reaching goals. In the discussion of acquisition, it was shown that effortful ways of acquiring things are the most frequently rewarded; similar observations were made in connection with achievement and construction. Even in the case of the relatively objectless need for activity, the more purposeful instances of activity which require more work are more frequently rewarded. Here certainly are some of the forces leading to the development of a motive to work or put forth effort. This motive is sometimes very important in adults or older children, and may activate them for a long time, even when the effort leads to no external reward. It needs explanation, because of marked contrast with the general tendency for human beings and other organisms

Table 2.   Percentage of Reward, Punishment, and No Consequence for Each Category of Behavior (in All of the 3409 Thema Which Were Analyzed)

Category of Behavior	Percent of Thema in Which the Behavior Is Rewarded	Percent of Thema in Which the Behavior Is Punished	Percent of Thema in Which Behavior Results in No Consequence (i.e., Neither Rewarded nor Punished)
Construction	96	1	3
Sentience	96	4	0
Elation	95	4	1
Cognizance	86	9	5
Succorance	84	10	6
Affiliation	82	8	9
Nurturance	82	5	12
Achievement	80	10	9
Recognition	79	13	8
Activity	74	9	16
Dominance	74	16	8
Blamavoidance	71	15	14
Imaginality	71	6	23
Order	70	2	28
Acquisition	64	31	3
Passivity	54	26	20
Deference	52	10	38
Harmavoidance	49	39	12
Autonomy	48	40	12
Retention	42	48	10
Aggression	35	52	11
Rejection	14	62	24
Infavoidance	8	74	18
All categories	71	17	12

to avoid work or effort when it is not necessary. The motive is doubtless developed in large part through social learning, and we have in this reading matter an example of the kinds of social influences that lead to its development.

Another special emphasis is on the acquisition of skills, on learning. This is, of course, evident in the first place from the high frequency of cognizant behavior and its high proportion of reward. It also appears in the treatment of achievement; there it was observed that the most frequently rewarded mode of achievement was by the acquisition of new skills, even more frequently rewarded than achievement through the display of skills formerly acquired.

Despite the emphasis on learning, there is in these third-grade readers little encouragement of intellectual activity as such. The cognizance is usually directed at simple isolated information rather than a quest for understanding. Sentience, as it appears in the readers, is only rarely concerned with esthetic appreciation which goes beyond the admiration of simple man-made objects or of nature. Activity is ordinarily physical, and in only one case intellectual in nature. The achievements, even those involving the acquisition of a skill, can in most cases hardly be spoken of as intellectual. Similarly in constructive behavior: only one story about construction concerns a non-material product, a poem.

It should be noted, moreover, that the acquisition of skills or knowledge which is rewarded is generally that which is dependent upon other persons in a superior position—for example the gaining of knowledge by children through questioning parents or teachers. In this sense, too, there is less emphasis on intellectual activity than might appear, since there is relatively little encouragement of original thinking on the part of the central character.

A distinction is also made between satisfying needs in socially approved ways, which tends to be rewarded, and satisfying them in disapproved ways, which tends to be punished. For example, in the case of retention, retention which is defined as socially or individually useful and permissible, such as saving money, is rewarded; on the other hand, retention which is defined as selfish is punished. Similarly for recognition: there is heavy reward for exhibiting one's capacities so long as social rules are followed; but when rules are broken, as by exhibiting oneself at the wrong time or making claims about one's powers that are not justified, then the behavior is punished. Dominance and aggression provide examples of other modes of behavior where social rules set down certain conditions as making the behavior permissible and certain other conditions as not. In these cases the conditions have to do with what other needs, if any, are served at the same time; if dominance or aggression does not serve some other approved purpose, or if it serves other disapproved purposes such as selfish acquisition or retention, it is punished.

PROBLEMS OF ADJUSTMENT

In the ways that have just been indicated, material such as that in the readers provides lessons to children, encouraging or discouraging the development of motives in a way that on the whole is likely to lead to more satisfactory adjustment in our society. But at the same time there are certain respects in which this material is failing to contribute to good adjustment.

A major defect of the readers from this point of view is what might be called their unrealistic optimism. Behavior directed at affiliation and nurturance, for example, is almost always rewarded in the readers. There are very few cases of failure. It is impossible to compare the proportion of success here with that obtaining in children's everyday life. Yet from the point of view of contributing to the solution of problems of everyday life, failures ought to receive a larger proportion of attention, for it is they that pose problems.

It may indeed be true that the encouragement of affiliative and nurturant needs in this reading is of little consequence, because the much stronger pressures from the real environment are already working in that same direction, and the contribution from here can be little more. But there is a very great opportunity for reading matter, such as in these textbooks, to point up possible solutions for frustrations often encountered by the child in seeking for gratification of these needs. In that case, such reading matter should include a larger number of accounts of how children get around obstacles in their attempts to satisfy affiliative and nurturant needs—stories in which expression of these needs first meets with punishment or rebuff and only attains success when some new method of approach more suited to the environment is hit upon.

For children who have encountered failure in their everyday life, the easy attainment of goals such as nurturance and affiliation in the readers may be so unrealistic as to have little effect in strengthening their desire for such goals. Suggestions as to how these needs may be satisfied despite serious difficulties might, on the other hand, through their realism to such children, contribute to strengthening the needs.

A similar sort of unrealism was commented on in the discussion of avoidance. While the content of these readers might do a great deal towards strengthening a desire for achievement in competitive success, there is very little about those children—perhaps the majority—who frequently experience failure in competition, and few suggestions about how such children can find some satisfactory way of adjusting to their failure. Such material might be more beneficial than what is actually found in contributing to the better adjustment of those children whose present adjustment is unsatisfactory.

A similar failure to make positive suggestions is found in the treatment of aggression and acquisition. Here are two needs, certainly universally present in children, which lead to serious problems of adjustment because of their frequent interference with desires of other and more powerful persons.

Children's reading matter might be quite useful in furthering satisfactory adjustment if it were able to pose models for the child of ways to satisfy these needs when they are prevented from the most direct and immediately satisfactory expression. While there are certainly some incidents which might be useful in this way, the general tendency in the readers is, instead, for these needs simply to be overlooked in the child characters. It is as though the writers were inclined to solve problems of aggression and acquisition in children by trying to convince children that they do not have these needs, that they are experienced only by adults, animals and supernatural creatures. To a certain extent the child's real social environment may be cooperating with the readers in this direction, through a tradition that children do not hate or covet and are basically nice unless they are led to be otherwise. But the fact probably is that every child does hate and does covet, and that in his efforts to do so he is being repeatedly rebuffed by the more powerful persons in his environment. Those persons are apt often not to have the psychological insight necessary for redirecting these interests of the child into channels where they can have more success. Here then is a valuable potential role of children's reading matter.

Another possible inadequacy of the reading matter, one much more difficult to judge, is concerned with maturity. It is notable in the content of these readers that independent action initiated by child characters, and indeed by anyone, is more likely to be punished than similar behavior which is performed under the direction of a superior. Cognizance, for example, is rather frequently punished when it is undertaken on the child's own initiative and leads to pursuit of knowledge directly by the child's own exploratory behavior, whereas it is almost always rewarded if knowledge is gained through dependence upon authority. Autonomous behavior, too, is generally punished except in the case where the kind of autonomy is that desired by the child's elders. (There is an exception to this in the case of nurturance, which is more often rewarded when it is spontaneously initiated by the character himself.)

There can be no doubt that if children continue to be trained in this way as they grow older, the effect on their potentialities as adults will be a bad one. It may indeed be that a considerable proportion of adult maladjustment in marriage and occupational life is due to the discouragement of autonomy and independence by the educational system up to the point where an adolescent or young adult leaves it. On the other hand, it may of course be argued that the amount of independence encouraged by the content of these readers is quite appropriate for the particular age level at which the readers are directed. Certainly the development towards autonomy must be a gradual process and a considerable amount of dependence on superiors is necessary, not only at this age but even on into adult life. It is for this reason that it is impossible to make a conclusive judgment about the wisdom of this aspect of the content of the readers.

DIFFERENTIAL TREATMENT OF THE SEXES

Perhaps the most striking single finding of this study is the extent to which a differentiation is made between the roles of male and female in the content of these readers. To the extent that boys identify with male characters, and girls with female characters, this difference both in itself and as a reflection of facts that hold true of many other sources of influence on children, must have a profound significance on the differential development of personality in the two sexes.

Some of the differentiation can be seen in the mere frequency with which the two sexes appear among the characters displaying the various categories of behavior. Female characters, for example, are relatively more frequent among those displaying affiliation, nurturance, and harm-avoidance. On the other hand, females are less frequent, relatively, among characters displaying activity, aggression, achievement, construction, and recognition. Girls and women are thus being shown as sociable, kind and timid, but inactive, unambitious and uncreative.

This picture is further added to by considering the relative proportion of male and female characters among the subsidiary characters who are objects related to the satisfaction of the needs of the central characters. The most important findings here refer to nurturance and cognizance. The persons nurtured by a central character are in the majority female, suggesting that females are in a relatively helpless position.

The persons who supply information to central characters who are seeking for knowledge are, in contrast, predominantly male. It will be recalled that even among unrelated adults who supply knowledge to children, the majority are male despite the obvious fact that the most important such persons of the real environment are the child's teachers, who are mostly women. Males, in short, are being portrayed as the bearers of knowledge and wisdom, and as the persons through whom knowledge can come to the child.

In all of these respects, a distinction in role is being made between the sexes which may indeed have a certain validity as of our society of the present time, but which seems much more a survival of former practices. The many schoolgirls who will at some future time have to make their own living are failing, if they identify with female characters, to receive the same training in the development of motives for work and achievement that boys are receiving. To the extent that this distinction is characteristic of many other aspects of the training the child receives from his environment, it should cause little wonder that women are sometimes less fitted for creative work and achievement than men of similar aptitude, for there is certainly much difference in the motivational training they receive for it. It has been a common assumption that the education of the two sexes is virtually the same in American public schools, except for differences in vocational training. Here is clear evidence that the education is not the same, even at early levels of grammar school and even when the boys and girls are mixed together, as they usually are, in the same classroom. Not only does the informal training of boys and girls at home and in the community differ, but even the formal education they are receiving in the classroom differs.

It has been shown in several instances that the differential treatment of the sexes goes further than mere correspondence with this stereotype of different categories of behavior as being more conspicuous in a particular sex. There are several striking instances where females are shown as being definitely inferior from a moral point of view. In the discussion of passivity it was shown that female characters are portrayed as lazy twice as often, relatively, as male characters. In the discussion of acquisition it was seen that female characters are shown as acquiring in socially disapproved ways much more often, relatively, than males, and much less frequently by the most approved routes of work and effort.

In view of the social values of our society, it can also be said that the facts already cited above are relevant here. Insofar as female characters are shown as not often achieving, constructing, obtaining recognition or engaging in activity, they are being shown in an unfavorable light by the general standards of our society. But on the other hand, in that female characters are being shown as more frequently affiliative, nurturant, or unaggressive, they may perhaps be said to be receiving the more favorable treatment. While it is not true, then, that female characters are uniformly shown in a more unfavorable light, the balance is certainly in that direction.

The most striking single fact of all, however, about the difference between the sexes is that female characters do simply tend to be neglected. Of all the central characters in all these thema (excluding central characters who consist of a group of mixed sex), 73% are male and only 27% are female. Male characters are thus over two and a half times as frequent as female ones. The same tendency is found, though not so strikingly, in the characters who are objects of, or cooperators in, the satisfaction of the needs of the central characters; here the proportion of males is 63% and of females 37%.

There can be no excuse for this greater attention to males in the claim that males have achieved more in society and hence that there is more to write about them. These stories are, with few exceptions, not about individuals of outstanding achievement but simply about the life of everyday people. The implication of this difference for a girl is that being female is a pretty bad thing, that the only people even in everyday life who are worth writing about or reading about are boys and men. If the content of these readers is typical of other social influences, small wonder that girls might develop for this reason alone an inferiority complex about their sex.

DIFFERENTIAL TREATMENT OF ADULTS AND CHILDREN

The human characters in the stories were readily divisible into two groups according to age—adults and children. The treatment of these two groups differed markedly, and in ways that raise interesting problems about the effect of these stories on the children who read them.

There are, first of all, great differences in the relative frequency of the various categories of behavior. Children are much lower than adults in the incidence of aggression and acquisition. In adults, aggression and acquisition are the most frequently appearing categories of behavior, whereas in children these two are of very low incidence.

It is of interest that this contrast should show the children as conforming more closely than adults to socially approved behavior. The same tendency is found in certain other comparisons that can be made between children and adults.

In the discussion of acquisition, retention and aggression, it was shown in each case that child characters more frequently exhibit the more approved forms of these needs and that adult characters more frequently exhibit the most disapproved forms. Thus even within some of the separate categories of behavior, children are shown as more socialized than adults.

That children are shown as more socialized is demonstrated also by the relative frequency of different kinds of rewards. It was noted in connection with several categories of behavior, especially affiliation and nurturance, that children are shown as more frequently receiving only internal rewards. This generalization holds true for all of the behavior in the readers taken as a whole. A summary of the percent of each type of reward in all four types of character is presented in Table 3. It appears there that children receive internal rewards in more than twice as large a proportion as do adults. When the separate categories of behavior are considered, it is found that the proportion of internal rewards is higher in children than in adults in all but one of the fourteen most frequent categories. Now internal rewards are dependent upon socialization, for they are rewards that a person administers to himself because he is well socialized, because he is able to feel good or virtuous at having done the right thing, even if no reward is offered by an external agency.

That children are shown as more socialized than adults, perhaps points up more clearly than anything else the role that the content of these readers must be more or less consciously intended to play in the moral education of children. If the readers are intended for inculcating proper behavior in children, then it must seem only natural at first glance that it is the child characters who especially should be shown as displaying the desired forms of behavior. But a serious question may be raised as to whether the readers are likely to accomplish the purpose in this way. A more sophisticated consideration of the probable effect of the content of these readers would suggest that there is considerable probability that children pattern their behavior more after that of the adult characters than after that of the child characters. There is ample reason to suppose that children imitate adults, especially their parents, much more than they do their age-mates, and particularly with reference to deep-seated motivational tendencies. If this be true, then for purposes of the moral education of the children who read these stories, the adult characters should be shown as at least as well socialized as the child characters.

Table 3. Kinds of Rewards for All Categories of Behavior: Percentage Distribution in Each Character Type

CHARACTER TYPE	PERCENTAGE DISTRIBUTION OF KINDS OF REWARD IN EACH CHARACTER TYPE			
	Internal	*Social*	*Material*	*Automatic*
Children	34	23	36	6
Adults	16	26	53	4
Animals	24	18	50	8
Fairies	16	34	43	8

Whether this criticism is justified does, of course, depend upon factual determination of whether children are more likely to be influenced by the behavior portrayed in adult characters than in child characters. But on general psychological grounds, this does seem so likely as to give the criticism considerable weight.

The content of the readers, then, is likely to point out to children certain rewards and punishments that, for them, follow upon the display of approved or disapproved behavior, but to suggest that these rewards and punishments may stop when they grow up to be adults. Such a lesson, which to be sure is also often made in a child's everyday life, may be satisfactory for the short-sighted parent or teacher, who knows that his immediate responsibility for the child will cease when the child becomes an adult. But as a background for educational policy it seems deficient to anyone who looks at child-rearing or education as a task of preparing children to become adequate adults.

30. SIMILARITY IN TEACHER AND PUPIL PERSONALITY

SISTER MARY AMATORA, O.S.F.

The teacher often spends more time with the child than his mother or father. So it comes as no surprise to learn from this study that children's personalities often become like their teachers'.

A. THE PROBLEM

Prominence of personality as the number one quality of the teacher is no longer a disputed topic. That the personality of the pupil is influenced by the personality of the teacher is likewise maintained by many educators today. A limited amount of vital research in this area has appeared in recent years, yet much remains to be studied before any final answers will be forthcoming.

Symonds (11), who has done considerable work in this area, states emphatically, "If better teachers are to be employed in our schools, more attention must be paid to personality factors in their selection."

In Robbins' (10) study, "ability to make the course interesting" received first place, above "teacher's knowledge of subject matter." The same study showed the most undesirable trait to be the teacher's failure to treat the student as an adult. These again show the high position accorded personality elements in the estimation of pupils.

Anderson's (7) classic studies on the effects of dominative and integrative behavior of the teacher upon pupil behavior have shown quite conclusively that the direction is from teacher to pupil, but never vice versa. Herrick's (9) observations are in the same direction.

Cook and Leeds (8) find that "the attitude of individual teachers toward pupils is significant related to the pupils' attitudes toward the teachers."

Tiedeman's (12) investigation of junior high school pupils likewise brought to the fore the personality qualities of the teachers as uppermost in pupil estimation. Reference to other studies shows similar trends.

Reprinted from *The Journal of Psychology,* 37 (1954), 45–50, by permission of the author and The Journal Press.

B. EXPERIMENTAL DESIGN

The present study seeks to investigate the relationships, if any, between the personalities of pupils and the personalities of their respective teachers on certain specified components of personality.

METHOD

Of the various types of measuring instruments for studying personality, such as the objective test, the life record data, and the questionnaire and rating scale technique, the latter method was chosen for the present experiment. As the inventory type of questionnaire is usually limited to self-ratings, a further element of objectivity was achieved by using the rating scale, on which a number of independent judgments could be secured for each individual pupil and teacher in the study.

a. The Scale. The Child Personality Scale (1, 3, 5) and its comparable adult form (2, 4, 6) prepared by the writer for earlier investigations were used. These instruments provide for the rating of both children and adults on 22 elements of personality. Each component of the personality is treated as a separate scale; each individual is rated separately on each scale on a 10-point continuum. The ends of the scales are staggered so as to avoid any possible halo effect.

Interpretation of each end of the scale is given by descriptive words and/or phrases, as is the mid-point or point of indifference signifying the average or "most people."

The 22 elements of personality included in the study are: Kindness, sympathy and thoughtfulness of others; dependability; politeness and courtesy; neatness and cleanliness; sociability; nervousness or calmness; punctuality in meeting appointments; honesty and fairness; patient and good-natured or easily angered; interested in few or in many things; quiet or boisterous; sense of humor; good-sportsmanship; coöperative in working with others; intelligent; energetic and peppy; popularity; religiousness; generosity; persistence in sticking to a task; optimistic or pessimistic; and, boring or entertaining.

b. The Subjects. Subjects used in the experiment were 100 teachers and their pupils of grades four through eight in both public and private schools, in both city and rural schools.

c. Procedure. Each teacher was rated on each of the 22 scales by three or four fellow teachers in the same school. The children were rated by eight classmates on each of the 22 scales. For the second part of the experiment ratings were secured for each child on each scale by three or four teachers.

C. ANALYSES OF DATA

When all papers were completed, data were analyzed separately for teachers and for pupils, in each of the two parts of the study.

1. THE TEACHERS' SCORES

The three or four ratings each teacher received on each scale were averaged separately for each teacher on each scale. These became the individual teacher's raw score ratings on the specified scales.

2. THE PUPILS' SCORES

For the pupils' scores there were two separate sets of data. Each was treated separately throughout the experiment: (a) The ratings each child received by the eight classmates were average on each of the twenty-two scales. This provided the first set of raw scores for each pupil on each scale. From these, means were computed for each class on each scale. (b) Each child's ratings by three or four teachers on each scale were averaged for the second set of data on the pupils' personalities. From these, the second set of class means was computed for each of the 22 scales.

3. CORRELATIONS

Pearsonian r's were computed separately for the two sets of data. For each of these, the mean pupil personality score on each scale was plotted against the average score for the teacher of that respective class. Thus were separate measures of correlation established between teacher and pupil personality on each of the 22 variables measured in the present study. The N for each r is 100 in each of the two sets of data.

D. RESULTS AND INTERPRETATIONS

As the object of this study is to determine the relationships, if any, between 22 specified components of personality in teacher and in pupil, two separate analyses are made. The first of these is based on the personalities of the teachers and their pupils, both as judged by teachers; and, the second compares the personalities of teachers as judged by teachers with the personalities of pupils as judged by pupils.

1. WHEN TEACHERS DO THE RATING

When the children's personalities in terms of teacher judgments are correlated with the personalities of their respective teachers in terms of fellow-teachers' ratings, the r's given in Table 1 are achieved. These, arranged in rank order from highest to lowest, reveal a considerable degree of relationship between teacher and pupil personality on most of the traits measured.

The *r*'s corrected for attenuation range from .46 to .11 with a median *r* of .275. According to Fisher's test of significance all *r*'s above .197 are significant at the 5 per cent level of confidence, and all *r*'s above .256 are significant at the one per cent level. Hence, at the one per cent level of confidence there is a statistical significance in the similarity between teacher and pupil personality on the first 15 scales listed in this table. On four more scales there is statistical significance at the 5 per cent level. The only three scales on which the relationship between teacher personality and pupil personality is below the 5 per cent level of confidence are those for sense of humor, good-sportsmanship, and religiousness. However, all correlations are positive, even on these low *r*'s.

Table 1. Correlation Between Pupils' and Teachers' Personalities I

Rank	Personality Variables	r_{xw}	$r \pm SE$	Rank	Personality Variables	r_{xw}	$r \pm SE$
1.	Energy and pep	.46	.38 .08	13.	Thoughtfulness	.27	.24 .09
2.	Sociability	.43	.34 .09	14.	Boring-		
3.	Nervous-calmness	.41	.33 .09		entertaining	.26	.23 .09
4.	Generosity	.40	.31 .09	15.	Neatness	.25	.22 .09
5.	Cooperation	.34	.28 .09	16.	Interests	.23	.20 .09
6.	Persistence	.33	.28 .09	17.	Courtesy	.23	.19 .10
7.	Disposition	.32	.26 .09	18.	Honesty	.20	.17 .10
8.	Punctuality	.31	.26 .09	19.	Dependability	.20	.16 .10
9.	Intelligence	.29	.25 .09	20.	Sense of humor	.16	.13 .10
10.	Popularity	.29	.25 .09	21.	Good-		
11.	Patience	.28	.24 .09		sportsmanship	.16	.12 .10
12.	Boisterous-			22.	Religiousness	.11	.06 .11
	quietness	.27	.24 .09				

2. WHEN CHILDREN DO THE RATING

To corroborate the above findings, a second set of data was analyzed in the same manner as was the first set. Pearsonian *r*'s were again computed for the 22 separate scales. This time the scores for the pupils' personalities as judged by their classmates were plotted against the scores of the teacher personality as rated by fellow-teachers.

The results are given in Table 2. It will be noted that, though slightly lower on some of the scales, the *r*'s of this table are not greatly different from those in Table 1. The present *r*'s range from .41 to .11 with a median *r* of .22. Here again, for the two variables and 98 degrees of freedom, all *r*'s at and above .197 are significant at the 5 per cent level, while all *r*'s at .256 or above, are statistically significant at the one per cent level of confidence.

In this table the relationships between teacher and pupil personality are statistically significant at the one per cent level on 10 of the 22 scales, and at the 5 per cent level on five more of the scales. Again, all correlations are positive. The findings of this second set of data corroborate the results of the first set of data in the present experiment.

Table 2.   Correlation Between Pupils' and Teachers' Personalities II

Rank	Personality Variables	$r_{\infty w}$	$r \pm SE$	Rank	Personality Variables	$r_{\infty w}$	$r \pm SE$
1.	Energy and pep	.41	.34 .09	13.	Intelligence	.20	.18 .10
2.	Sociability	.38	.31 .09	14.	Persistence	.20	.17 .10
3.	Nervous-calmness	.37	.30 .09	15.	Boisterous-		
4.	Popularity	.34	.25 .09		quietness	.20	.17 .10
5.	Generosity	.32	.25 .09	16.	Interests	.17	.15 .10
6.	Thoughtfulness	.31	.24 .09	17.	Punctuality	.17	.14 .10
7.	Patience	.30	.24. 09	18.	Honesty	.16	.13 .10
8.	Courtesy	.28	.23 .09	19.	Dependability	.15	.12 .10
9.	Cooperation	.27	.22 .09	20.	Good-		
10.	Disposition	.27	.22 .09		sportsmanship	.14	.11 .10
11.	Boring-			21.	Religiousness	.13	.09 .10
	entertaining	.23	.19 .10	22.	Sense of humor	.11	.09 .10
12.	Neatness	.21	.18 .10				

E. SUMMARY AND CONCLUSIONS

A study of the personalities of 100 classroom teachers and their pupils revealed positive relationships on all the 22 elements of personality measured.

Results were analyzed from two separate sets of data, which corroborated each other. On more than half the scales the similarity between teacher and pupil personality showed statistical significance at the one per cent level of confidence. For this sample of teachers and pupils there is less than one chance in a hundred that these *r*'s could have occurred if there were no true correlation. On about a fourth or more of the scales the similarity was verified within the limits of the 5 per cent level; that is, there is less than five chances in a hundred that these *r*'s could have arisen if there were no true correlation.

The most important finding of this experiment is the complete absence of all negative correlations. On every element of personality measured in this study there is a positive relationship between teacher and pupil personality.

Statistical data do not yield answers relative to *causal* relationships. Facts only are reported. Yet, other studies mentioned earlier in this article suggest such between pupil and teacher. However, if the findings of this study be true generally, then it is of vital importance to the development of wholesome personality in the children, that they have teachers who possess well-adjusted personalities.

POSTSCRIPT

After reading this article, we wrote a letter to Sister Mary Amatora with the following questions:

1. How many pupils were rated?
2. How long had they been in the teacher's class? That is, were the ratings made at the beginning of the term, the middle, or the end?
3. Could you compare the ratings with a control group, for example, a group of fifth-grade teachers and fourth-grade pupils, to show that the correlations here are lower than in those instances where teachers and pupils are in the same classes?
4. If the teacher personality influences the pupil personality, then the correlation should be higher at the end of the term than at the beginning. Do you have data showing correlations the first week of school compared with correlations the last week of school?

We received the following replies:

1. Ten pupils from each class were rated (upon arrival at the school, I requested the principal to send ten pupils, five boys and five girls, selected at random from each teacher's class).
2. Ratings were made during the month of April.
3. This was not done, but it would be an interesting experiment to do.
4. No. This would also be an interesting experiment, one which I should very much like to do had I the funds and the time.

REFERENCES

1. AMATORA, S. M. A twenty-two trait personality scale. *J. of Psychol.*, 1944, 18, 3–8.
2. ———. Boys' personality appraisals differentiate teacher groups. *Sch. & Soc.*, 1952, 76, 184–187.
3. ———. Child Personality Scale. Cincinnati: Gregory, 1951.
4. ———. Comparability of child and adult personality scales. *J. Educ. Psychol.*, 1944, 35, 309–313.
5. ———. Factor analysis of children's personality scale. *J. of Psychol.*, 1944, 18, 197–201.
6. ———. The education factor in personality appraisal. *J. Exp. Psychol.*, 1953, 21, 271–275.
7. ANDERSON, H. H., BREWER, J. E., & REED, M. F. Studies of teachers' classroom personalities: III. Appl. Psychol. Monog., 1946, No. 11.

8. COOK, W. W., & LEEDS, C. H. Measuring the teaching personality. *Educ. Psychol. Measmt.*, 1947, 7, 399–410.

9. HERRICK, V. E. Teachers' classroom personalities. *Elem. Sch. J.*, 1945, 46, 126–129.

10. ROBBINS, F. G. Student reactions to teacher personality traits. *Educ. Admin. & Suprv.*, 1944, 30, 241–246.

11. SYMONDS, P. M. Evaluation of teacher personality. *Teach. Coll. Rec.*, 1946, 48, 21–34.

12. TIEDEMAN, S. C. A study of pupil-teacher relationship. *J. Educ. Res.*, 1942, 35, 657–664.

31. AN EXPERIMENTAL STUDY OF LEADERSHIP AND GROUP LIFE

RONALD LIPPITT AND RALPH K. WHITE

This is one of the most famous experiments in child psychology. It attempts to make specific the meaning of such terms as "democratic," "autocratic," and "laissez-faire" in a leader-follower situation. Children's reactions to leaders who are autocratic and to those who are democratic and laissez-faire are compared, and the changes in attitude and behavior when the leadership shifts from one type to another are described.

The study here reported, conducted in 1939 and 1940, attempted in an exploratory way to discover the extent to which various aspects of leadership behavior and of total group life could be fruitfully studied

Reprinted from *Readings in Social Psychology*, Third Edition, edited by Eleanor E. Maccoby, Theodore M. Newcomb, and Eugene L. Hartley. By permission of Henry Holt and Company, Inc. Copyright 1958. Prepared by the authors from data more fully reported in (1) Kurt Lewin, Ronald Lippitt, and Ralph K. White, "Patterns of Aggressive Behavior in Experimentally Created 'Social Climates,'" *J. Soc. Psychol.*, 1939, X, 271–299; (2) Ronald Lippitt, "An Experimental Study of Authoritarian and Democratic Group Atmospheres" in *Studies in Topological and Vector Psychology, I, University of Iowa Studies in Child Welfare*, No. 16, 1940; (3) Ronald Lippitt, "An Analysis of Group Reactions to Three Types of Experimentally Created Social Climates" (Unpublished doctoral thesis, State University of Iowa, 1940); (4) Ronald Lippitt, "Field Theory and Experiment in Social Psychology: Authoritarian and Democratic Group Atmospheres," *Am. J. Sociol.*, 1939, XLV, 26–49; (5) Ronald Lippitt, "The Morale of Youth Groups," in Goodwin Watson (ed.), *Civilian Morale* (Boston: Published for Reynal & Hitchcock by Houghton Mifflin Co., 1942); and (6) Ronald Lippitt and Ralph K. White, "The 'Social Climate' of Children's Groups," in Roger Barker, Jacob Kounin, and Herbert Wright, *Child Development and Behavior* (New York: McGraw-Hill Book Co., 1943).

by experimental procedures of controlled matching and planned variation in conditions. The study had as its objectives:

1. To study the effects on group and individual behavior of three experimental variations in adult leadership in four clubs of eleven-year-old children. These three styles may be roughly labeled as "democratic," "authoritarian" and "laissez-faire."

2. To study the group and individual reactions to shifts from one type of leadership to another within the same group.

3. To seek relationships between the nature and content of other group memberships, particularly the classroom and family, and the reactions to the experimental social climates.

4. To explore the methodological problems of setting up comparative "group test situations," to develop adequate techniques of group process recording, and to discover the degree to which experimental conditions could be controlled and manipulated within the range of acceptance by the group members.

The major experimental controls may be described briefly as follows:

1. *Personal Characteristics of Group Members.* Because a large group of volunteers were available from which to select each of the small clubs, it was possible to arrange for comparability of group members on such characteristics as intelligence, and on such social behaviors (measured by teachers' ratings) as obedience, amount of social participation, leadership, frequency of quarreling, amount of physical energy, etc.

2. *The Interrelationship Pattern of Each Club.* In each group, by the use of a sociometric questionnaire in each classroom, it was possible to select groups which were very closely matched in terms of patterns of rejection, friendship, mutuality of relationship, and leadership position.

3. *Physical Setting and Equipment.* All clubs met in the same clubroom setting, two at a time in adjacent meeting spaces, with a common equipment box.

4. *Activity Interests.* It was important to know the extent to which initial interest in the planned activities might be responsible for differences in degree of involvement in activity during the experiment. Therefore it was ascertained in the beginning that all groups of boys were comparably interested in the range of craft and recreational activities in which they would later be engaged.

5. *Activity Content.* It is clear that the structure and content of an activity often exerts a powerful influence on the patterns of interdependence, cooperation, competition, etc. in group life. Therefore, it was important that activity content should be equated in these three types of leadership situations. In order to insure this, the clubs under

democratic leadership met first in time during the week, and the activities which were selected by those clubs were automatically assigned to the parallel clubs under authoritarian leadership. In the laissez-faire situation, there were a number of potential activities of the same type as that selected by the "democratic clubs."

	Period 1 (7 weeks)	Period 2 (7 weeks)	Period 3 (7 weeks)
Treatment Club Leader	Autocracy Sherlock Holmes I	Autocracy Sherlock Holmes IV	Democracy Sherlock Holmes II
Treatment Club Leader	Autocracy Dick Tracy II	Democracy Dick Tracy III	Autocracy Dick Tracy I
Treatment Club Leader	Democracy Secret Agents III	Autocracy Secret Agents II	Democracy Secret Agents IV
Treatment Club Leader	Democracy Charlie Chan IV	Democracy Charlie Chan I	Autocracy Charlie Chan III

6. *The Same Group under Different Leadership.* The experimental design also made it possible to have a perfect matching of club personnel on the same analysis by comparing the same club with itself under three different leaders.

EXPERIMENTAL VARIATIONS

In the beginning the experimenters had planned for only two major variations in adult leader behavior: an authoritarian pattern and a democratic pattern. Later it was decided that it would be more fruitful to add a third variation of "laissez-faire" adult behavior, although with the four available clubs it would make the experimental design less rigorous. The method of systematic rotation can be noted in the above chart, which refers to the earlier experiment (the same method was followed in the later experiment).

The three types of planned variation were as follows:

1. *The Sequence of Social Climates.* A number of the hypotheses focused upon the effect of a particular type of group history in determining the reactions of a group to a present pattern of leadership. The chart indicates the variety of group history sequences which were selected for exploratory study.

2. *"Leader Role" and "Leader Personality."* There was a question as to the extent to which certain basic personality characteristics of the adult leaders would be important determinants in the individual and group behavior patterns which resulted. To study this variable, four adults with very different personality patterns were selected as leaders and all of them after proper indoctrination took two or three different leadership roles with different groups during the course of the experiment as indicated on the chart. This made it possible to discover whether certain of the leaders induced common reaction patterns which could be traced to their "personality" as contrasted to their "leadership role."

3. *The Three Planned Leadership Roles.* The three variations in leader role which were worked through in careful detail by the four club leaders may be summarized as follows:

Plan for authoritarian leadership role. Practically all policies as regards club activities and procedures should be determined by the leader. The techniques and activity steps should be communicated by the authority, one unit at a time, so that future steps are in the dark to a large degree. The adult should take considerable responsibility for assigning the activity tasks and companions of each group member. The dominator should keep his standards of praise and criticism to himself in evaluating individual and group activities. He should also remain fairly aloof from active group participation except in demonstrating.

Plan for the democratic leadership role. Wherever possible, policies should be a matter of group decision and discussion with active encouragement and assistance by the adult leader. The leader should attempt to see that activity perspective emerges during the discussion period with the general steps to the group goal becoming clarified. Wherever technical advice is needed, the leader should try to suggest two or more alternative procedures from which choice can be made by the group members. Everyone should be free to work with whomever he chooses, and the divisions of responsibility should be left up to the group. The leader should attempt to communicate in an objective, fact-minded way the bases for his praise and criticism of individual and group activities. He should try to be a regular group member in spirit but not do much of the work (so that comparisons of group productivity can be made between the groups).

Plan for laissez-faire leadership role. In this situation, the adult should play a rather passive role in social participation and leave complete freedom for group or individual decisions in relation to activity and group procedure. The leader should make clear the various materials which are available and be sure it is understood that he will supply information and help when asked. He should do a minimum of taking the initiative in making suggestions. He should make no attempt to evaluate negatively or positively the behavior or productions of the individuals or the group as a group, although he should be friendly rather than "stand-offish" at all times.

The data below will indicate the extent to which these planned variations were carried out and the pattern of social stimulation which was represented by the leader behavior in each of the clubs.

From the great variety of observations recorded on the behavior of each leader it was possible to compute quantitative profiles of leader performance which could be compared to see the extent to which the three different types of leadership role were different and the degree to which the adults carrying out the same role were comparable in their behavior patterns. Figure 1 illustrates some of the major differences in the patterns of behavior of the three leadership roles. Most of the comparisons on the graph meet the test of statistical significance. The "average leader" comparisons are based on four democratic, four authoritarian, and two laissez-faire leader roles. The first three classifications of behavior, "leader orders," "disrupting commands" and "nonconstructive criticism," may be thought of as representing adult behavior which has a limiting effect upon the scope and spontaneity of child activity. About 60 percent of all of the behavior of the average authoritarian leader was of these types as compared to 5 percent for the democratic and laissez-faire leaders. The data show that the authoritarian leader usually initiated individual or group activity with an order, often disrupted on-going activity by an order which started things off in the new direction not spontaneously chosen, and fairly frequently criticized work in a manner which carried the meaning, "It is a bad job because I say it is a bad job" rather than, "It is a poor job because those nails are bent over instead of driven in."

The next three behavior classifications, "guiding suggestions," "extending knowledge," "stimulating self-guidance," may be thought of as extending individual and group freedom and abilities. We note here some of the major differences between the democratic and the laissez-faire leadership role. Whereas the democratic leader took the initiative (where he felt it was needed in making guiding suggestions) much more frequently than the laissez-faire leader, a major proportion of the latter leadership role was giving out information when it was asked for. It is clear, however, that the democratic leader did not take initiative for action away from the group as indicated by the fact that the average democratic leader showed a greater proportion of "stimulating self-guidance" than even the laissez-faire leader. The category of "stimulating self-guidance" was made up of three main items: "leader's requests for child's opinions on individual and group plans," "use of child judgment as criterion," and "taking consensus of opinion." The data indicate that the democratic leaders stimulated child independence eight times as often as the authoritarian leader and about twice as often as the laissez-faire leader, although the latter two types of adults showed about the same proportion of this behavior in their total pattern of activity.

The classification on the graph entitled, "praise and approval" is made up of such behavior items as "praising," "giving credit," "giving O.K.s," etc. It indicates largely the functioning of the adult as a dispenser of social recognition. The authoritarian adult was significantly more active in this regard than either of the other two types of leaders.

The extent to which the adult discussed personal matters unrelated to the club situation (home, school, etc.), and also joked on a friendly basis with the club members, is indicated by the "jovial and confident" classification. The democratic leader had social interactions of this type with the group members about eight times as often as either the authoritarian or laissez-faire leaders. This is perhaps one of the best indices of the extent to which the democratic leaders were "on the same level" as the club members.

The last classification on Figure 1, "matter of fact," indicates one measurement of the extent to which the various social atmospheres were "fact-minded" as compared to "personal-minded" as far as the behavior of the adults was concerned.

The degree to which all the adult leaders, delegated to assume a given leadership role, behaved in a comparable fashion on these major aspects of leadership role is indicated by the fact that, on all comparisons differentiating major characteristics of the three roles, there is no overlapping of the behavior of any representative of one role with any representative of a different role. Thus it is possible to conclude that three

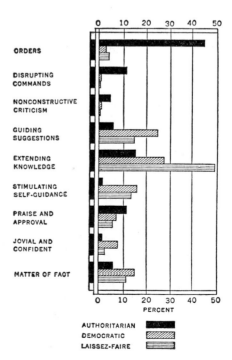

FIGURE 1. COMPARISON OF
BEHAVIOR OF AVERAGE AUTHORI-
TARIAN, DEMOCRATIC, AND
LAISSEZ-FAIRE LEADER

clearly different leadership patterns were created with a much smaller range of individual differences in leader behavior within each pattern than between the patterns.

LEADERSHIP ROLE AND PERSONALITY STYLE

An examination of the behavior patterns of the different leadership roles by the same individuals . . . reveals that on the items of leader behavior there is no greater similarity between the different performance patterns of the same individual than between those of different individuals. If we turn to the data of the three interviews with each club member in which at each transition stage in their club life they compared their leaders and talked very fully about them, we find again that there is no evidence of any adult personalities being rated favorably or unfavorably independently of their particular leadership role (i.e., authoritarian, democratic, laissez-faire). All leaders stood high as well as low for one group or another and all the comments about their "personalities" were concerned with attributes of their leadership roles which had been measured.

The following excerpts from interviews of club members who had just completed six months of club life which included an authoritarian, a laissez-faire, and a democratic leader (in that sequence) indicate rather clearly the aspects of "leadership personality" which were perceived as important.

"RW (democratic) was the best leader and DA (laissez-faire) was the poorest. RW has good ideas and goes right to the point of everything . . . and always asked us what to do next time the club met, which was very nice. . . . DA gave us no suggestions like RW did, and didn't help us out at all, though he was very nice to us . . . but let us figure things out too much. I liked RL (authoritarian) pretty well for that kind of work."

"RL (authoritarian) was best, and then RW (democratic) and DA (laissez-faire). RL was the strictest and I like that a lot. DA and RW let us go ahead and fight, and that isn't good, though RW didn't do it as much as DA did. DA just didn't give us much to do. RW was OK, but he didn't have so many ideas as RL did. RW wanted to do what we did; RL didn't want to go with us lots of times, and he decided what we were to do."

"I liked RW (democratic) best, then DA (laissez-faire) and then RL (authoritarian). RW was a good sport, works along with us and helps us a lot; he thinks of things just like we do and was just one of us—he never did try to be the boss, and wasn't strict at all, but we always had plenty to do (the golden mean). DA didn't do much, just sat and watched; there wasn't much I didn't like about him, but he didn't help us much . . . not like with RW when we had regular meetings and that was very good. RL was all right mostly; he was sort of dictator like, and we had to do what he said pretty nearly; he helped us work but he was sort of bossy."

"I liked RW (democratic) the best and RL (authoritarian) the least. RW was in between DA and RL. I like everything about him. I once said I didn't want to change from DA but I'm glad we changed. We could do what we pleased with DA but he was too easy going, not hard enough nearly, but he's a real nice person. With RL we always had something to do, and we did get a lot of things done, but I didn't like anything about him; he was much too strict. He was not cross, but very direct."

"I'd take RW (democratic) for a club leader, and DA (laissez-faire) was the worst. RW is just the right sort of combination; RL (authoritarian) was just about as good as RW, but he was kind of cross once in a while. RW had interesting things to do, he was just about right in everything. DA was too easy; he didn't know anything about the club—didn't know about its ways. He didn't understand us boys at all. . . . I didn't like him as well as RL because he had too few things for us to do." [1]

Another indirect indication that individual personality characteristics were not of any great significance in influencing group life in this study might be inferred from the finding that the total patterns of group reactions of different clubs to the same atmosphere tend to be remarkably homogeneous in spite of differences in adult leadership.

DATA COLLECTION AND ANALYSIS

Before continuing to summarize the individual and group behaviors which resulted from these three variations in leadership role, we will indicate briefly the types of data collection and analysis in the total study.

Eight types of club records were kept on each group, of which the four most important were kept by four different observers as follows.

1. A quantitative running account of the social interactions of the five children and the leader, in terms of symbols for directive, compliant, and objective (fact-minded) approaches and responses, including a category of purposeful refusal to respond to a social approach.
2. A minute-by-minute group structure analysis giving a record of activity subgroupings, the activity goal of each subgroup, whether the goal was initiated by the leader or spontaneously formed by the children, and rating on degree of unity of each subgrouping.
3. An interpretive running account of strikingly significant member actions and changes in the atmosphere of the group as a whole.
4. Continuous stenographic records of all conversation.

These data were synchronized at minute intervals so that placed side by side they furnished quite a complete and integrated picture of the on-going life of the group.

---

[1] Beside indicating the leadership characteristics perceived as important by the boys, the reader will note that one boy in this club (an army officer's son) preferred his authoritarian leader and that the other four split in that two preferred their authoritarian leader second best and two liked their laissez-faire leader second best.

Five other types of data covering the lives of the club members were collected, the three most important being:

1. Interviews with each child by a friendly "non-club" person during each transition period from one kind of group atmosphere and leader to another. These interviews elicited comparisons of the various club leaders with one another, with the teacher and with parents as well as other data about how the club could be run better, who were the best and poorest types of club members, what an ideal club leader would be like, etc.
2. Interviews with the parents, concentrating on kinds of discipline used in the home, status of the child in the family group, personality ratings on the same scales used by the teachers, discussion of the child's attitude toward the club, school and other group activities.
3. Talks with the teachers concerning the transfer to the schoolroom of behavior patterns acquired in the club and vice versa.

The reliability of the eleven trained observers ranged from .78 to .95 with an average reliability of .84. Another reliability computation on the coding of three thousand units of conversation into twenty-three categories of behavior showed a percent agreement of 86. The analyses of what constituted a "group life unit" showed reliabilities ranging from .90 to .98. A number of methodological researches carried on since the date of this study seem to suggest that it is possible to get much more meaningful and reliable observation data than has been generally believed if much more time and effort are spent on a careful "calibration" of psychologically well-trained observers.

COMPARATIVE GROUP TEST SITUATIONS

The experimenters also postulated that a fruitful way to discover some of the major differences between the three types of group atmosphere would be to arrange comparable "test episodes" in each club. So at regular intervals the following situations occurred:

1. Leader arrives late.
2. Leader called away for indeterminate time.
3. Stranger ("janitor" or "electrician") arrives while leader out and carries on critical attack of work of individual group member, then of group as a whole.

THE FOUR RESULTANT STYLES OF GROUP LIFE

Some of the major findings, summarized from stenographic records and other case material which are elsewhere reproduced, are as follows: Two distinct types of reaction were shown to the same pattern of authoritarian leadership. All of the data, including the documentary films, indicate that three of the clubs responded with a dependent leaning on the adult leader, relatively low levels of frustration tension, and practically no capacity for initiating group action, while the fourth club demonstrated considerable frustration and some degree of channelized aggression toward the authoritarian leader. (This latter pattern is much more comparable to the behavior of the club under authoritarian leadership in a previous experimental study of two clubs.)

Figure 2 indicates the major differences in the relations which developed between the group members and the adult leaders in the four resultant social atmospheres. In both types of authoritarian atmosphere the members were markedly more dependent upon the leader than in either the democratic or laissez-faire situations, dependence being somewhat greater in the more passive clubs. All other clubs showed a somewhat greater feeling of discontent in their relations with the adult leader than did the members of the democratic clubs, members of the "aggressive autocracy" being outstanding in their expression of rebellious feelings. There is evidence from other sources that the actual "felt discontent" in the "apathetic autocracies" was somewhat higher than indicated by the conversation which was considerably more restricted than was that of the democratic and laissez-faire club members.

In both types of authoritarian situations the demands for attention from the adult were greater than in the other atmospheres. It seemed

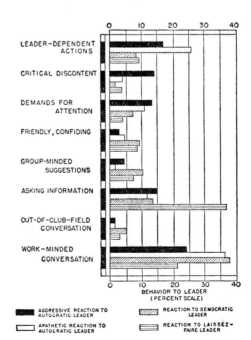

FIGURE 2. FOUR PATTERNS OF
GROUP REACTION TO THE THREE
DIFFERENT TYPES OF LEADERSHIP

clear that getting the attention of the adult represented one of the few paths to more satisfactory social status in the authoritarian situation where all of the "central functions" of group life were in the hands of the dominator.

The category "friendly, confiding" indicates that the members of the democratic and laissez-faire clubs initiated more "personal" and friendly approaches to their adult leaders, and the data on "out-of-club-field conversation" further indicate the more spontaneous exchanging of confidences about other parts of one's life experience in the democratic club atmosphere.

The data on "group-minded suggestions" to the leader show that the members in the democratic atmosphere felt much freer and more inclined to make suggestions on matters of group policy than in the other three group atmospheres. It is clear from other data that the lower level of suggestions in the laissez-faire situation is not because of any feeling of restricted freedom but because of a lack of a cooperative working relationship between the adult and the other group members.

The much greater responsibility of the members of the laissez-faire clubs to get their own information is shown by the fact that about 37 percent of their behavior toward their leader consisted of asking for information, as compared to about 15 percent in the other three club situations.

The final category in Figure 2, "work-minded conversation," indicates that a considerably larger proportion of the initiated approaches of the club members to their leaders were related to on going club activity in the democratic and in the apathetic authoritarian situations than in the other two types of social climate.

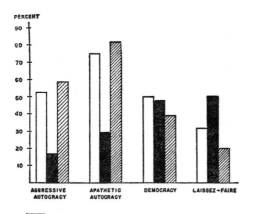

FIGURE 3.   PERCENT OF TIME SPENT IN HIGH ACTIVITY INVOLVEMENT

RESULTANT RELATIONSHIPS OF CLUB MEMBERS

The relationships between the club members also developed along quite different lines in the four social climates. Expressions of irritability and aggressiveness toward fellow members occurred more frequently in both the authoritarian atmospheres and the laissez-faire situation than in the democratic social climates. Unlike the relationships of high interpersonal tension and scapegoating which developed in the previous aggressive autocracy the club in this experiment seemed to focus its aggression sufficiently in other channels (toward the leader and toward the out-group) so that in-group tension did not rise to a dangerously high point.

There were more requests for attention and approval from fellow club members to each other in the democratic and laissez-faire situations than in the two authoritarian climates. It seems clear that the child members depended upon each other to a great extent for social recognition and were more ready to give recognition to each other in the democratic and laissez-faire situations.

It is interesting to find nearly as high a level of interpersonal friendliness in the authoritarian situations as in the democratic and laissez-faire atmospheres. The underlying spirit of rebellion toward the leader and cooperation in out-group aggression seem to be the "cohesive forces" in aggressive autocracy, while in apathetic autocracy with its much lower level of felt frustration, the shared submissiveness seemed to do away with all incentive to competition for social status.

Intermember suggestions for group action and group policy were significantly lower in both types of autocracy than in the laissez-faire and democratic atmospheres. The dissatisfactions arising from any lack of feeling of real progress in the laissez-faire situation led to a high frequency of expression of ideas about "something we might do." Contrary to the democratic situation, these suggestions seldom became reality because of the lack of the social techniques necessary for group decision and cooperative planning. The group achievement level, as contrasted to the "wish level," was far lower in laissez-faire than in any of the other three atmospheres.

OTHER DIFFERENCES

By having the leaders arrive a few minutes late at regular intervals in each club life, it was possible to discover that in the five authoritarian situations no group initiative to start new work or to continue with work already under way developed, as contrasted with the democratic situations where leaders who arrived late found their groups already active

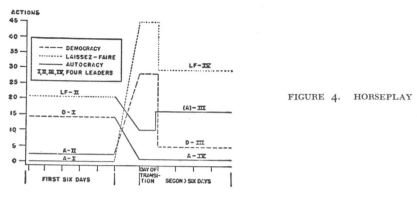

FIGURE 4.   HORSEPLAY

in a productive fashion. The groups under the laissez-faire leaders were active but not productive. Figure 3 shows the percentage of total club time in each of the four social atmospheres which was spent in giving major attention to some planned club project. For each atmosphere there is a comparison between the time when the leader was in the room, the time when the leader had been called out for planned experimental periods, and the unit of time just after the leader returned. The data here give striking evidence of the extent to which work motivation was leader-induced in the two types of authoritarian situation. "Working time" dropped to a minimum with the leader out, and most of what was done was in the minutes just after the leader had left the room. We see that in the democratic atmosphere the absence or presence of the leader had practically no effect. The apparent increase in group productive time with the laissez-faire leader out of the room may or may not be a meaningful result. Two or three times it was noted that when the adult left, one of the boys exerted a more powerful leadership and achieved a more coordinated group activity than when the relatively passive adult was present.

The behavior of the groups under authoritarian domination after their transition to a freer social atmosphere provided a very interesting index of unexpressed group tension. In Figure 4 it can be noted that both of these apathetic authoritarian clubs showed great outbursts of horseplay between the members on the first day of their transitions to a laissez-faire and a democratic group situation. This need to "blow off" disappeared with more meetings in the freer atmosphere.

It will be recalled that in certain situations all groups were subject to the same frustration of hostile criticism by a strange adult (e.g., "janitor") while the adult leader was gone. Under the different types of leaders, the groups handled these frustrations differently. Members of the apathetic authoritarian clubs tended to accept individually and to internalize the unjust criticism or, in one or two cases, they "blew off

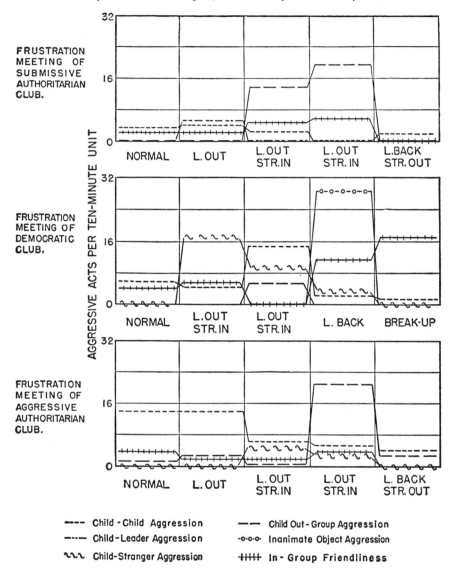

--- Child - Child Aggression   — Child Out - Group Aggression
—·— Child - Leader Aggression   -o-o-o- Inanimate Object Aggression
ⅤⅤⅤ Child - Stranger Aggression   ++++ In - Group Friendliness

FIGURE 5. CHANNELS OF GROUP TENSION RELEASE IN CLUBS OF ELEVEN-
YEAR-OLD BOYS UNDER DIFFERENT TYPES OF LEADERSHIP

steam" in aggressive advances toward an out-group (the other club
meeting in the adjacent clubroom; see Figure 5). In the aggressive
authoritarian situation, the frustration was typically channeled in aggression toward the out-group, although in several cases there was some
direct reaction to the source of frustration, the hostile stranger (see

Figure 5). In the democratic atmospheres there was evidence of a greater readiness to unite in rejection of the real source of frustration, the stranger, and to resist out-group aggression. Figure 5 shows an interesting case of a democratic club which first expressed its aggression directly against the stranger, then showed a slight rise in inter-member tension, followed by an aggressive outburst against a sheet of three-ply wood with hammer and chisels accompanied by a striking rise in in-group friendliness and a quick return to cooperative harmony. It was particularly interesting to discover that the clubs under democratic leaders resisted scapegoating as a channel of aggressive release.

The data indicate that the democratic type of adult role resulted in the greatest expression of individual differences, and that some type of uniformity-producing forces brought about a slightly lessened individual variability in the laissez-faire situation, and a much reduced range of individuality in the authoritarian clubs. Figure 6 gives an example of this analysis for the same group of individuals under three different leaders.

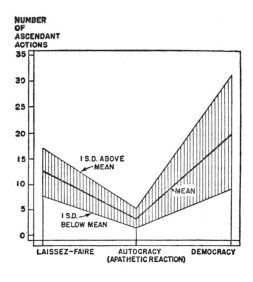

FIGURE 6.   THE EFFECT OF CHANGED ATMOSPHERE UPON THE RANGE OF INDIVIDUAL DIFFERENCES WITHIN THE SAME GROUP

32. THE INFLUENCE OF THE GROUP
ON THE JUDGMENTS OF CHILDREN

RUTH W. BERENDA

In the tale of "The Emperor's New Clothes," one child dares to see and admit reality, while others "see" the emperor as elegantly clothed. How much are the individual's perceptions influenced by others? What happens when reports of others contradict what a child actually sees?

In the series of ingenious experiments reported here, Dr. Berenda discovered that the influence of the group on children's judgments was greatest when the material to be evaluated was ambiguous and least where the material was clear-cut.

The fact that the most serious problems of our time are complicated and ambiguous—the elimination of war, poverty, crime, and racial tensions, for example, as well as the age-old questions concerning the metaphysical bases of existence— may perhaps explain why so many adults today are satisfied to accept the group's values and judgments.

FORMULATION OF THE PROBLEM AND PROCEDURE

This study is an attempt to analyze the effect that group pressure has on judgments of children between the ages of seven to thirteen. We are trying to understand the nature of this "pressure," the conditions under which it is effective in modifying judgments, and the child's conception of such situations and his reaction to them.

The general character of our procedure was to place an individual child in contradiction to a group and to observe the effect quantitatively and qualitatively.

.   .   .   .   .

The group was at all times composed of members of the child's class.

In some cases the majority was made up of the child's brightest classmates (Experiment I), and in other cases (Experiments III and IV) they were all the other children in his class—bright and dull.

Selections reprinted from *The Influence of the Group on the Judgments of Children* (King's Crown Press, 1950) by permission of the author.

Systematic investigation would require that tasks differing in structural clarity be investigated. We therefore used tasks that were extremely clear and also others that were somewhat varied with regard to this quality. The subjects were required to estimate the lengths of lines, compare lines with a standard and to match lines.

EXPERIMENT I   A GROUP VERSUS A MINORITY OF ONE

PROBLEM AND PROCEDURE

What would be the effect on the judgment of an individual child when a majority of the group of which he is a member unanimously gives wrong judgments regarding simple perceptual materials? Would such a child yield to group influence and change his judgments or would he conform to the group? What would be the reaction of a child to such a situation?

From a total of 240 children who participated in the control experiment only 90 of these children, ranging in age from seven to thirteen years and selected from grades two to seven, served as critical subjects in this experiment. Thirty-eight of these children came from classes with an average I.Q. whereas 52 were taken from the so-called "opportunity classes" where the I.Q. was 130 and above. Of the nine classes that participated the 8 bright children in each class served as the "majority." The 10 "minority" subjects of each class were selected by their teacher, 5 for such personality traits as leadership and independence and the remaining 5 for submissiveness and meekness. The two sexes were equally represented.

The children were presented successively with twelve pairs of cards, a standard containing a single line and a comparison card with three lines, one of which was equal in length to the standard. The task consisted in identifying that comparison line which was equal to the standard. The lines were made by pasting black tape, ¼ inch wide, on white cards, 17½ by 6 inches. The three lines of a comparison card were numbered from left to right. In each case a standard and a comparison card were presented on the ledge of a blackboard, 3 feet apart, the standard to the right.

Previously, these children had performed the same task in control experiments with their respective classes. Now, the same task was repeated with one essential change in the conditions. Eight of these children, or the so-called "majority," were under instruction to give false answers on seven out of the twelve lines. These seven lines will be referred to as "critical lines." In Table 1 are given the lengths of the lines as well as the incorrect answers of the majority.

On the day of the experiment those children who were to serve as critical subjects were sent to another classroom and were told by their teacher to stay there all day for special work. The experimenter then led the eight majority children to another classroom while the teacher remained with those who were not participating in the experiment.

Table 1. Lengths of Standard and Comparison Lines and the Responses of the Co-operating Group

TRIALS	LENGTH OF STANDARD LINE	LENGTH OF COMPARISON LINES			CORRECT ANSWERS	GROUP ANSWERS [a]
		First	*Second*	*Third*		
1	$7\frac{1}{2}$	5	$5\frac{3}{4}$	$7\frac{1}{2}$	3	3
2	5	$6\frac{1}{2}$	7	5	3	3
3	8	8	7	6	1	2
4	$3\frac{1}{2}$	$3\frac{3}{4}$	5	$3\frac{1}{2}$	3	*1*
5	9	7	9	11	2	2
6	$6\frac{1}{2}$	$6\frac{1}{2}$	$5\frac{1}{4}$	$7\frac{1}{2}$	1	*3*
7	$5\frac{1}{2}$	$4\frac{1}{2}$	$5\frac{1}{2}$	4	2	*1*
8	$1\frac{3}{4}$	$2\frac{3}{4}$	$3\frac{1}{4}$	$1\frac{3}{4}$	3	3
9	$2\frac{1}{2}$	4	$2\frac{1}{2}$	$3\frac{3}{8}$	2	*3*
10	$8\frac{1}{2}$	$8\frac{1}{2}$	$10\frac{1}{4}$	11	1	2
11	1	3	1	$2\frac{1}{4}$	2	2
12	$4\frac{1}{2}$	$4\frac{1}{2}$	$3\frac{1}{2}$	$5\frac{1}{2}$	1	*3*

[a] The italic figures in this column refer to the false responses of the group.

To the majority the experimenter explained the purpose and procedure of the experiment and stressed the need for their full co-operation. To the child who was usually selected by the group as the most reliable and careful the experimenter gave a typewritten copy of the answers he was to give in their sequence. The other seven children were instructed to follow him in their responses. All were given copies [1] of the questions they were to ask in the discussion that was to follow the judgments. The experiment as well as the discussion were carefully rehearsed.

Each critical subject was brought by a monitor to the experimental room where he found the eight majority children waiting in line outside of the room, with their books under their arms. The impression was thus created that the entire group was just entering the classroom. The child in the fifth seat had been instructed to make sure that the minority child was seated in the seat beside him, the sixth.

Presenting the first pair of cards, the experimenter addressed the group, saying: "You will remember I showed you these lines before. I have here at the right one line. On the other side I have a card with

[1] These copies were used for purposes of instruction but were not in evidence during the experiment.

three lines. You see that the three lines are not the same size. You also see that the lines are numbered one, two, and three. There is one line among these three that is just as long as the one line on this card [pointing to standard]. When I put up the two cards, you will not write your answers as you did last time, but each of you will stand up and give his answer out loud."

The twelve pairs of cards were thus presented and the responses of each child were recorded on a previously prepared chart.[2] After all the judgments had been given, the experimenter opened the discussion.

If the minority child did not follow the group, the experimenter started by saying: "Was this a hard test?" Invariably receiving a negative reply to this, the experimenter continued: "Yes, these are simple lines, and yet you didn't all agree. What happened?" At this point the majority children, as previously instructed, turned upon the minority child with the following:

1. "You gave different answers."
2. "What was the matter?"
3. "Why did you give these answers?"
4. "Who do you think was right, you or we?"

If the minority child said he was right, he was confronted with the question: "Was everyone else wrong?" If, on the other hand, the child said he was wrong, the majority demanded that he explain why he did not give their answers. In the interest of spontaneity the exact order of the questions could not be rigidly set in advance, since they depended so much upon the replies and the behavior of the critical child.

If the minority child would not admit that the group was wrong, the experimenter said: "You were right and they were wrong seven times." The reaction to this information was observed, and then the actual purpose of the experiment was revealed.

If the minority child had responded with the group, the experimenter started the discussion by saying: "Were you all sure of your answers? Was there any time when you felt like giving a different answer?" If the minority child did not reply to these questions, the experimenter put up two or three of the pairs on which the child followed the group and said to the minority child: "I am not sure I got all your answers right. Only you answer now." When the answers were recorded and the child's behavior noted, the experimenter took him out of the room and said: "Before you go back, I would like to ask you a few questions about this test. Let's go into this room." The experimenter then asked some of the following questions: "Were you sure of your

[2] Of course, only the answers of the minority children were tabulated, those of the majority having been prearranged.

answers? You gave different answers now than you did before. Which were right? If the other children were not there, would you have given the same answers? Why did you give the same answers? Did you doubt what you saw? How did you feel?"

At the end of the interview the experimenter explained the purpose of the experiment and observed the pupil's reaction to this information. The experimenter elicited from each critical child a promise [3] to keep the secret and led him back to his own classroom.

Before we present the quantitative results, it will be relevant to describe the atmosphere of the group experiments. By frankly discussing with each majority group, even the very young ones, the purpose and the implications of the experiment, we were able to secure their enthusiastic and complete co-operation. These children felt honored being chosen to help and realized the importance of their role in the experiment. They offered many suggestions, often valuable ones, on procedure; and when the teacher proved a poor judge in the selection of the minority children, the majority objected and by a vote designated those to be called in as critical subjects. They were also the ones who by a vote decided whether a child was reliable and could be trusted with the "secret" (purpose) of the experiment. True, to the younger children the procedure remained a game, but a very serious one indeed. They watched with interest and concern the behavior of each minority child and expressed disappointment when one whom they considered very bright yielded to group pressure. In the group discussion the majority turned with considerable fervor and such force on the dissenter that the latter was often brought to tears or to an open accusation that the majority gave wrong answers. As one youngster of eight put it when pressed by the group: "I wouldn't have took the answers if I didn't think it was right. Why are you asking me all these questions?" Or another: "I was just making up my mind. At least you must give a guy a chance to make up his mind."

If, as was often the case among the younger ones, the minority child admitted being right but could not bring himself to say that the majority was wrong, the others would challenge him on his lack of logic, pointing out that if he believed the others to be right he should have given their answers. The few who stubbornly insisted that theirs were the right answers were really put to test by their classmates who would point out indignantly that eight could not be wrong and one alone right. This led on several occasions to spontaneous discussions of a more general nature.

With all classes the experimental situation was so real and so dy-

---

[3] Five out of the total number of critical subjects admitted having heard about the "secret." The dynamics of the experimental situation were so strong that this knowledge in no way affected their behavior.

namic that even among the older children there was never a trace of suspicion nor any doubt that the situation was serious and important, even though very puzzling and strange.

RESULTS

. . . . .

It will be helpful to examine first how strongly the individual children were affected by the group conditions. The relevant results are reported in Table 2. In this table we include the frequencies with which the children followed the group. The corresponding results are presented graphically in Figure 1.

It will be noted that the effect of group conditions was indeed strong. Table 2 shows further that the effect of the majority was more pronounced on the younger than on the older children. Out of the maximum score of seven, the younger children followed the group 3.5 times on the average, the older children 2.5 times. Fully 26 per cent of the younger children followed the group throughout with only 7 per cent remaining independent in all their responses. Of the older group,

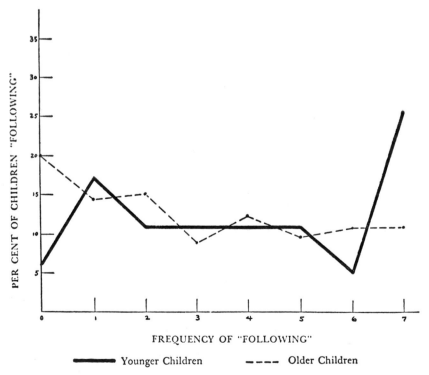

FIGURE 1.   MAJORITY VS. MINORITY OF ONE

on the other hand, only 12 per cent gave the incorrect group answers throughout and 20 per cent never followed. Considering the extremely clear character of the task and also the relatively high accuracy of the childrens' judgments under the control conditions, we have to conclude that the group exerted an effect of considerable magnitude.

. . . . .

Table 2. Frequency of "Following" Responses on Critical Lines Experiment I

NUMBER OF TIMES "FOLLOWING"	YOUNGER CHILDREN SEVEN TO TEN		OLDER CHILDREN TEN TO THIRTEEN		TOTAL "FOLLOWING"	
	Number	*Per Cent*	*Number*	*Per Cent*	*Number*	*Per Cent*
0	3	7	11	20	14	15.5
1	7	18	7	13	14	15.5
2	4	11	8	15	12	13
3	4	11	4	8	8	9
4	4	11	6	12	10	11
5	4	11	4	8	8	9
6	2	5	6	12	8	9
7	10	26	6	12	16	18
TOTAL	38	100	52	100	90	100
AVERAGE	3.5		2.5		2.7	

An examination of the percentages of correct responses to the lines considered individually adds support to our preceding conclusions. These are reported in Tables 3 and 4 and represented graphically in Figures 2 and 3.

The critical lines were responded to correctly by 93 per cent of the younger children under control conditions and by only 43 per cent of the same children under the pressure of the group. Of the older group, 94 per cent gave correct answers to the critical lines in the control experiment, whereas only 54 per cent did so in the critical experiment.

If we consider first the results concerning the younger group (see Table 3 and Figure 2), the following conclusions seem warranted.

1. All lengths were affected by the group conditions. Table 3 shows more errors for each length under critical than under control conditions.

2. The frequency of incorrect group responses in the critical experiment is as great as the frequency of all other categories of responses, 53 per cent as against 47 per cent.

3. The different lines are differently affected by the experimental conditions. It is of interest to note that the lengths most sensitive to the group factor were also those that under control conditions produced the greatest incidence of errors. . . .

Table 3. Distribution of "Group" Responses to Each Critical Length; Younger Children, Seven to Ten (N = 38)

	CONTROL EXPERIMENT				CRITICAL EXPERIMENT					
Critical Lines in Order of Presentation	*Correct Answers*		*Independent Correct*		*Group Answer*		*Independent Incorrect*		*Total Independent* [a]	
	Number	Per Cent	Number	Per Cent	Number	Per Cent	Number	Per Cent	Number	Per Cent
Third	34	89	13	34	20	53	5	13	18	47
Fourth	38	100	21	55	17	45	0	0	21	55
Sixth	32	84	12	32	26	68	0	0	12	32
Seventh	34	89	19	50	18	47	1	3	20	53
Ninth	38	100	20	53	16	42	2	5	22	58
Tenth	34	89	14	37	24	63	0	0	14	37
Twelfth	37	97	15	40	21	55	2	5	17	45
AVERAGE		93		43		53		37		43

Noncritical Lines in Order of Presentation	*Correct Answers*		*Independent Correct*		*Group Correct*		*Independent Incorrect*	
	Number	Per Cent	Number	Per Cent	Number	Per Cent	Number	Per Cent
First	38	100	0	0	38	100	0	0
Second	38	100	0	0	38	100	0	0
Fifth	31	82	0	0	38	100	0	0
Eighth	37	97	0	0	38	100	0	0
Eleventh	38	100	0	0	38	100	0	0
AVERAGE		95				100		

[a] This column is the sum of the "Independent Correct" and the "Independent Incorrect" columns. For purposes of the experiment answers different from those of the majority were termed "Independent" whether correct or incorrect.

THE EFFECT OF AGE

An examination of the preceding tables and figures reveals certain differences between the younger and older groups. There seems to be a tendency for the younger children to be more affected by the group pressure, and this tendency applies to each of the critical lines.

I.Q. AND FOLLOWING

.　.　.　.　.

There is no significant difference in the frequency of following between the younger children with I.Q.s of 130 and above and those of average I.Q. (t = .93). Nor is this difference significant for the older bright and average children (t = 61). The critical ratio between the older children from the opportunity classes and the younger ones from average classes is larger (t = 1.30) but still not significant. Twenty-eight per cent of the older bright children never followed the group and only 4 per cent followed throughout. Of the average younger children none remained entirely independent of the group, and as many as 55 per cent completely yielded to group pressure. Here again, as in Table 2, we note however, a remarkable range of individual differences especially in the middle of the distribution.

Table 4. Distribution of "Group" Responses to Each Critical Length; Older Children, Ten to Thirteen (N = 52)

Critical Lines in Order of Presentation	CONTROL EXPERIMENT Correct Answers		Independent Correct		CRITICAL EXPERIMENT Group Answer		Independent Incorrect		Total Independent [a]	
	Number	Per Cent	Number	Per Cent	Number	Per Cent	Number	Per Cent	Number	Per Cent
Third	47	90	25	48	21	41	6	11	31	59
Fourth	52	100	36	69	16	31	0	0	36	69
Sixth	48	92	21	41	31	59	0	0	21	41
Seventh	50	96	31	59	21	41	0	0	31	59
Ninth	52	100	35	67	17	33	0	0	35	67
Tenth	49	94	20	38	32	62	0	0	20	38
Twelfth	44	85	31	59	21	41	0	0	31	59
AVERAGE		94		54		44		1.5		56

Noncritical Critical Lines in Order of Presentation	Correct Answers		Independent Correct		Group Correct		Independent Incorrect	
	Number	Per Cent	Number	Per Cent	Number	Per Cent	Number	Per Cent
First	52	100	0	0	52	100	0	0
Second	52	100	0	0	52	100	0	0
Fifth	49	94	0	0	50	96	2	4
Eighth	51	98	0	0	52	100	0	0
Eleventh	52	100	0	0	52	100	0	0
AVERAGE		98				99		

[a] See note to Table 3.

TEACHER'S CHOICE AND FREQUENCY OF FOLLOWING

Will children who were judged to be independent by their teachers follow less than those found to be submissive? . . . Those judged

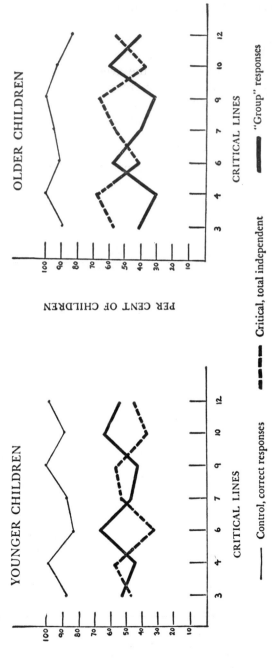

YOUNGER CHILDREN
PER CENT OF CHILDREN
100
90
80
70
60
50
40
30
20
10
3
4
6
7
9
10
12
CRITICAL LINES

OLDER CHILDREN
PER CENT OF CHILDREN
100
90
80
70
60
50
40
30
20
10
3
4
6
7
9
10
12
CRITICAL LINES

Control, correct responses — Critical, total independent — "Group" responses

FIGURE 2. MAJORITY VS. MINORITY OF ONE

FIGURE 3. MAJORITY VS. MINORITY OF ONE

submissive in the classroom situation often exhibited more independent behavior than some of the children known for their leadership and self-reliance. Of course, the number of cases is too small to draw any conclusions from our results.

QUALITATIVE DIFFERENCES BETWEEN
YOUNGER AND OLDER CHILDREN

Our observations of the behavior of the two groups seems to correspond to the quantitative results on the younger and older children. Among the younger children of seven to ten years there was little if any personal involvement—the situation at all times remaining remote. It was noted that whereas the older children would, for many days, discuss the experiment, the younger children, upon their return to their classrooms, did not talk about it either among themselves or with their respective teachers. Some of the younger children in the majority, in spite of the fact that they understood the directions and the purpose of the experiment, found it very difficult to give the wrong, prescribed answers.

On two occasions, when the objective situation was particularly clear, three children in the two lower grades found themselves compelled to give the correct response saying later: "I just couldn't help it." It is interesting to note that these three children were among the brightest pupils in the class.

A greater dependence on the group was noted among the younger children than among the older ones (see quantitative results).

This is well expressed in the answers given by the two age groups to the question: "Why did you give the same wrong answers as the group?" The most frequently heard explanations offered by the younger children were: "They all said the same number"; "I thought I should give the same answers as the other children"; or "If so many people said it, it might be right."

. . . . .

It was almost impossible for a younger child to admit, even under pressure, that he "copied," whereas among the older ones many readily conceded that they did. The fear of copying was found to be very strong, especially among the younger children.[4] It was also among the older children that the tendency to doubt the adequacy of one's eyes was observed. A youngster of twelve remarked: "My eyes could be different."

---

[4] It is interesting to note that copying as such was not considered bad in itself but definitely dependent on the general atmosphere in the classroom and the teacher's role in it. Thus, in two grades (the third and sixth) where the respective teachers were considered unfair and incompetent by the children, the pupils prided themselves on copying and not being caught.

Another said: "Maybe I don't see so good; maybe I need glasses." The younger children never expressed such doubts.

DISCUSSION

Despite the prevailing hypothesis that it is natural and easy to follow a group, we found quite the contrary to be the fact. It was *not* easy for these children to "follow." It was interesting to observe the reaction of the minority children to the wrong answers of the group. Lulled into security by the first two correct responses, each met the third (first wrong) answer with shock and bewilderment. Many a child would stand up in his seat, rub his eyes, look at all the others and then at the lines with a puzzled, embarrassed, and frightened expression on his face. Each child, without exception, felt ill at ease, fidgeted in his seat, or smiled uncomfortably at the others and at the experimenter. Many would whisper the right answer and turn to a neighbor for assurance. Some, after a few wrong group answers, would grow apathetic and look at the others in the group for the answer rather than at the lines. The situation was too puzzling; and being unable to explain it, they resigned themselves to it. There was always a note of relief when the majority gave a correct response.

. . . . .

Here are some of the comments made by the children in answer to the question "How did you feel during the test?"

A seven year old said: "I felt funny. I know it will be silly, but when they said an answer and I didn't think it was right, I felt like my heartbeat went down." A little girl of eight who followed the group completely said: "I didn't feel right. I kinda felt like giving my own but I don't know why I didn't." A more sophisticated eleven-year-old boy explained: "After I gave the answers, I felt like changing but didn't think it was proper." A boy of eight and one-half who gave all the wrong group answers offered this explanation in his own defense: "I know they were wrong, but it was like a jury—we were nine and I was the only one against eight. The majority wins. Besides, how could I prove I was right?" A girl of eleven said: "I had a funny feeling inside. You know you are right and they are wrong and you agree with them. And you still feel you are right and you say nothing about it. Once I gave the answer they didn't give. I thought they would think I was wrong. I just gave their answers. If I had the test alone, I wouldn't give the answers I gave." A nine-year-old boy who remained independent in his judgments in spite of group pressure said in the discussion: "I wanted to be like the rest, but then I thought it was correct to say the right answer. It would have been easier to give the same, but then it didn't look right." The same boy tried to explain why many children would follow under these conditions: "If you do too much disagreeing, people will think that you always disagree and get the wrong impression."

.   .   .   .   .

There was also the question of the children's faith in the ability of either the entire group or in particular members of the group. We must not forget that the majority was composed of the eight brightest children in each class! The minority child, therefore, had to meet the impact of a unanimous majority, one that was composed of people whom he knew to be "smart." Also, this majority did give right answers sometimes! This was especially difficult for those who in the opinion of the class and the teachers were the brightest in their class. They, irrespective of age, were brought to tears during the discussion and the interview, and were the only ones to become most personally involved. For them not only membership in the group was at stake, but their position in it was endangered. Even after the purpose of the experiment was revealed, they did not feel relieved.

Contrary to the classical hypothesis that a majority is always felt to be right, most of our minority children admitted upon questioning that the majority was giving wrong answers and that they fully realized it but that they couldn't understand why their classmates whom they knew to be "smart people" should give wrong answers on such simple material. Among the older children reference was often made to a particular member of the majority who was especially noted for being smart and right most of the time.

.   .   .   .   .

Following, as we have seen from the quantitative results, also depended on the clarity of the objective situation and was a function of the ease of discrimination of the lines presented for judgment. . . . A thirteen year old commented: "When I wasn't sure of myself, then I was inclined to agree with them." . . . In other words, where the situation is ambiguous and not very clear-cut, one is more apt to *accept* the opinion of a unanimous majority than when the situation is clearly structured. In the first instance in fact, the children did not feel that they "copied" or "followed." They merely admitted that they were uncertain of the right answer. It is only in the clear-cut situations that "copying" as such was admitted.

.   .   .   .   .

In conclusion we must say that though the children did follow the group significantly, in doing so they were affected by very real factors in the situation and not by blind faith in the majority or an instinct to imitate.

33. GROUP LEADERSHIP AND INSTITUTIONALIZATION

FERENC MEREI

This study compares the strength of the leader with that of the group. When a child who is a leader in one group is placed in another, he attempts to be the leader there also. Although he cannot change the new group's customs, he may ascend to leadership only if he accepts and utilizes its traditional values.

PRELIMINARIES TO THE EXPERIMENT

The problem we set ourselves concerns the relationship between leader and group. To tackle it, we took the following steps.

Children suitable to form a group were selected. Previous observation showed that from the age of 5 upward, in spontaneously formed groups, the sexes as a rule do not mix. Hence, the groups had to be homogeneous as to sex. They had to be homogeneous as to age, too, because, as our observations showed, in spontaneous groupings the age differences seldom exceed two years. Homogeneity was desirable also regarding the ties between members, e.g., children had to be chosen who had no strong likes or dislikes for one another. Finally, for the most pertinent purpose of our experiment, we tried to select children with an average capacity for leadership and social influence.

To rate the individual on these scores, we made some preliminary observations. We saw the children of two day nurseries for 35 to 40 minutes each day for a period of two weeks. Two people worked simultaneously and afterward unified their notes. The observations were not selective: everything that occurred in the nursery during that period was chronologically and fully recorded. On the basis of these observations we picked out those children whose social qualities were an average for that nursery group and who were *not* leaders. Children were selected in whom the frequency of: (*a*) "following orders" greatly outnumbered "giving orders"; (*b*) imitation outnumbered being imitated; (*c*) participation in group play was an average in number as well as in degree

Reprinted from *Human Relations,* II (1949), 23–39. This material first appeared in a larger Hungarian publication by the author. With his consent, it was translated and prepared in its present form by Mrs. David Rappaport for *Human Relations,* which journal granted permission for its use.

of cooperation; and (*d*) acts of attacking, crying, telling on each other, were about the average of the group. Furthermore, their ties to one another had to be no more solid or lasting than to other members of the nursery.

The children were formed into a group. An assembly was considered a group when it developed a relatedness, with permanent rules, habits, traditions, entirely of its own.

The children chosen were put in a separate room. Their field was permanent: the same set of furniture, toys, and tools every day. In this room they spent 30 to 40 minutes each day. Their actions were fully recorded by two observers who later synchronized and combined their notes. The observers were completely passive.

The group thus met until a tendency to "institutionalization" became noticeable, and their habits and traditions appeared to become lasting. Only such habits were considered traditions as were not found in the day nurseries, but had developed during the experimental period. This gave us an objective criterion of the point at which an assembly constituted a group. To form a tradition from three to six meetings were needed.

The children formed traditions such as permanent seating order (who should sit where); permanent division of objects (who plays with what); group ownership of certain objects, ceremonies connected with their use, expressions of belonging together; returning to certain activities; rituals; sequence of games; forming a group jargon out of expressions accidentally uttered, etc.

A leader was placed in the group so formed. The leader was chosen from the same day nursery. He was a child who the nursery-school teachers—they had spent many days with him—considered to have initiative and directing power, who was older than the members of the group, and who, during the preliminary observation, more often gave than followed orders, more often was imitated than imitating, and more often was the attacker than the attacked.

Thus the leader was chosen because he was older, domineering, imitated, aggressive rather than submissive, and because he had initiative.

After the group had formed fixed traditions we added such a leader. The place, the objects remained the same. Recording went on as before.

What did we expect to learn from the experiment thus set up? Our question was: Do group habits and traditions change with the appearance of a leader? Does the leader introduce new habits, and does the group accept them? Does the group follow the leader, or does it force its traditions upon him? We see the group through its traditions—the objective expressions of the existing relationship. Hence, the vector of forces between the stronger leader and the group of weaker individuals is determined not by *who* gives the orders but by *what* the orders are.

The question is not whether they accept leadership, but whether they give up their traditions by accepting what the leader initiates, whether they form new habits, rules, traditions, under his influence.

By carrying out this experiment we hoped to get the answer to our question.

THE EXPERIMENTAL PLAN

The experimental plan used the method of *varying the situation.* Individuals who scored high on leadership were observed in three situations:

1. In a larger group, where the members had no particular relationship with each other and where the leader's influence was felt by the group as a whole;
2. In a more closely knit group of the presocial stage formed through evolving group traditions; and
3. In a group with strong traditions of its own, facing a leader stronger than any one group member.

To record the entire process, we needed an adequate technique. We evolved a system of 76 symbols, each representing one complex act. The five people taking the notes synchronized them at 5-minute intervals.

Further variation was afforded through the objects in the room. By giving as many toys as there were children, we weakened group activity, since each could find something to do. By giving one object only we strengthened group activity, since all had to congregate around it. Setting a concrete task also strengthened the group. If an object familiar only to the leader was given, he was strengthened and the group weakened.

The choice of objects offers further possible variations which we have not sufficiently explored as yet.

We tried out many objects. Finally, the younger children (4 to 7 years) were given a tin toy house and a box of building blocks, the older ones (8 to 11 years) cardboard, picture magazines, scissors, crayons, paste, and paint brushes, and the instruction, "we want to make an exhibition." Of the latter objects there were fewer than there were children in the group, so that some manner of collaboration was required.

Most groups consisted of three children plus the leader, with some groups of four and six as well. The number chosen was determined by previous observations which showed that spontaneously formed groups, up to the age of 7, lasted longer when consisting of three to four children, and, between the ages of 7 and 10, of three to six children. Larger groups easily disintegrated.

We worked with twelve groups. In them we tried out the power of penetration of twenty-six children capable of leadership. The ages of all children ranged from 4 to 11 years. The difference within a group never exceeded two years. In every case but one the leader was older than any group member.

THE CONQUERED CONQUEROR

Let us now see the results of this experiment.

To summarize schematically, the same definite tendencies could be observed in all the experimental units: the group absorbed the leader, forcing its traditions on him. The leader takes over the habits and traditions of children who are younger than himself and who in the day nursery had been his underlings following his guidance. Now he engages in those activities which the group had developed before he entered it. His own undertakings either remain unsuccessful or gain acceptance only in a modified form suiting the traditions of that group.

Examples from our material demonstrate the point.

The table below will be understood from the following definitions:

Modeling is one of the most important types of social behavior. When a child's act or behavior is spontaneously imitated by some others, the child, we say, is *modeling*. When a child, even if unintentionally, imitates another—as members of a group do to take over each other's mode of behavior and thereby form common habits—we say that he is *being modeled*. We avoid the word "imitation" because it has a connotation of intention.

The ratio of *modeling* to *being modeled* is a measure of the social penetrating power of a person.

Modeling: Being Modeled

SUBJECT NO.	IN THE NURSERY	IN THE EXPERIMENTAL SITUATION	
		Without Leader	*With Leader*
13	3:4	17:5	10:5
15	1:4	3:8	1:2
25	1:5	1:11	3:4
10	2:8	0:2	0:3
20 (leader)	6:3		5:11

The table shows the ratio *modeling/being modeled* of four children (Nos. 13, 15, 25, 10). In the day nursery all four tended to follow some model, rather than to serve as a model to others. It was for just this behavior that we selected them.

When they became members of a separate group forming its own traditions, a change occurred: one of the four children (No. 13) took on the modeling role, while the others went on being modeled.

It was after this change had taken place that the leader (No. 20) joined the group. In the day nursery he did the modeling: he served as a model six times, but followed another model only three times, making this ratio of social penetration 6 : 3 (Column 2 "In day nursery" shows an inverse ratio for all the others in this group.)

In the experimental situation—when the leader was confronted with a developed group—his ratio changed: his power of social penetration diminished. Formerly he was *modeling* (6 : 3), but now he was *being modeled* (5 : 11)—that is, the others did not take over his mode of action, but he took over the habits developed by the group. In other words, he followed those who in the day nursery had followed him.

In other groups and with other leaders a similar tendency was observed. The ratio *modeling/being modeled* of an extremely influential and willful leader in the day nursery changed from 9 : 5 to 0 : 8. For another such child the ratio changed from 6 : 2 to 1 : 6.

This portion of our results shows that, in a group possessing traditions, the leader introduced does not become the source of new habits and rules; rather, he will be the one to take over existing group traditions and thus to follow a model. This happens in spite of the fact that in the larger social formation (day nursery) he had served as a model to every member of the group.

Since "forming traditions" was our criterion of social influence, we came to the conclusion that, *confronted by a group having its own traditions, the leader proves weak; this in spite of the fact that when confronting them singly he is stronger than any one member of the group— stronger precisely as to his social penetrating power.*

PLAY OF FORCES

The last paragraph is only a schematic summary of our results. Reality is richer and more varied; what we see in reality is a wide variety of *tendencies*—a pull of the group force facing other pulls in other directions.

What does this mean? Though the group generally assimilates the leader, we find that it does so only on certain conditions and within certain limits. We find that the leading personality, while accepting the traditions and habits of the group, also influences and changes them. Let us then inquire into the modes of this influence, into the conditions which allow the assimilated leader to become that group's leader.

On the twenty-six leaders of the experiment the group force acted in varied ways.

At one extreme is the case where the group entirely assimilated the child who previously showed definite capacity to lead. This occurred in a group that possessed particularly strict traditions, and had well established and meticulously carried out rituals of activity. One such group played with a doll house and two dolls. In the course of three play periods they worked out a ritual of activity of playing around the house and of taking the dolls for a walk. The leader, one and a half years their senior, joining the group at its fourth meeting, tried to introduce something new (fourth and fifth play periods). He suggested a circle game and group singing. He was not followed. When he started singing alone they followed him for a few moments, then returned to their old game. The third time he came (sixth play period), the leader joined in the group's original game. Only for a few moments, here and there, did he start new activities, but he was followed by no one. At the seventh and eighth play periods no sign was left that this child had once (before these same children had developed a group habit) been a leader among them.

At the other extreme is the case of the child who proved to be stronger than the group: he broke its traditions. There was one such case. The leader, a little girl (a year and a half older than the members) completely reorganized the group. She gave orders, she modeled, she decided what to do and how to play. The rules she introduced took the place of those the group had had.

This group's history is important: it was subjected to increasing difficulties, while the leader was given virtual training in leadership. After the group had formed its habits, each day a different leader was introduced. In three days three different leaders tried to foist their initiative upon it and to change its rituals. Against these three leaders the group was able to preserve its customs, rejecting their suggestions, in the face of all the enticing and aggression these leaders tried out on it. However, the struggle exhausted the group and it began to weaken. This weakening showed itself in that the children more often played by themselves, less often played their old organized games, playing instead merely side by side. The traditions were still formally there, but the members of the group tended to observe them singly, by themselves. The group lost much of its coherence.

These are borderline cases. *In the overwhelming majority of our cases the leader was forced to accept the group's traditions—that is, he proved weaker than the group but still managed to play the role of leader.* We observed each leader's ways of doing this.

1. The Order-Giver. The group whose data on "modeling" and "being modeled" was given above had fully developed customs when the leader was introduced. The new boy, older, more experienced, and more of a leader than any member of the group, attempted to take over. He gave orders, made suggestions, bossed everybody. The children carefully avoided him, ignored his orders, and carried on in their traditions.

Soon the leader found himself alone. Suddenly his behavior changed, he joined the group in its activities and quickly learned its rituals. He learned their expressions, their habits, their games. During his second play period with them, he again gave orders. Though keeping within the frame of activities he had just learned from them, and according to their rules, he told the children what to do—that is, he ordered them to do exactly what they would have done anyway. He appropriated the leadership without being able to change the group's traditions. The members accepted this situation by following his orders, since this did not change their habitual activities.

The data on the frequency of group activity shows this. The following table contains the proportion of *order-giving* to *order-following*.

Order-Giving: Order-Following

| EXPERIMENTAL SUBJECT NO. | IN DAY NURSERY | IN EXPERIMENTAL SITUATION | |
		Without Leader	*With Leader*
13	3:5	3:6	1:4
15	1:2	8:1	0:2
25	1:4	0:2	2:5
10	2:3	0:3	0:3
20	12:2		11:3

Four members of the group (Nos. 13, 15, 25, 10) were *order-followers* in the day nursery. After they had formed a separate homogeneous group, one of them (No. 15) became an *order-giver*. When group habits were developed and a leader (No. 20) was added, all followed the leader's orders, as in the day nursery. In the group with a tradition, the leader became just as much of an order-giver (11 : 3) as he was in the day nursery (12 : 2). Regarding order-giving, then, the leader was stronger than the group (he gave orders—they accepted them). At the same time, however, he was the one to copy the others; he took over their ways (his modeling proportion changed from 6 : 3 to 5 : 11).

If a person should observe the group for only a short period of time, for example by the Goodenough 1-minute or 5-minute method, he would see a leader giving orders and a group obeying. A prolonged observation of the group plus its history would, however, soon disclose the inner workings of this *order-giving:* the leader gives such orders as have reference to the group's traditional activities; he expropriates the leadership without changing the group's traditional modes of activity.

The leader is weaker than the group because he takes over its traditions and because his own suggestions do not take root. At the same time he is also stronger because everyone follows his orders.

The gist of the phenomenon lies just in this dichotomy.

The leader is stronger than any one group member. (He gives orders —they obey.) He is weaker than *group traditions* and is forced to accept them. He is stronger than the individual member, weaker than the "plus" which a group is over and above the sum of the individuals in it. He is stronger than the members, weaker than the formation.

In the relationship between group and leader, two factors stand out: (1) the group as a particular order of quality, whose strength is expressed by the change of the leader's modeling proportion (from 6 : 3 to 5 : 11); and (2) the members, whose *weakness* is expressed by the constancy (12 : 2 to 11 : 3) of the leader's ratio of *order-giving/order-following*.

Thus the curious situation obtains where the order-giver imitates, while the models follow the orders of their imitator.

What appears here is the "group plus"—the unique reality of a group —experimentally verified.

2. *The Proprietor.* A second way in which leadership may express itself is ownership: the leader joining the developed group takes possession of all the objects in the room. They continue being used according to group tradition; the games played with them remain the same. The leader joins in these games, but all the objects "belong" to him. The following table presents the data on this phenomenon, concerning the group discussed before.

Frequency of Object Appropriation (Borrows or takes away from another child)

EXPERIMENTAL SUBJECT NO.	IN THE EXPERIMENTAL SITUATION	
	Without Leader	*With Leader*
13	21	1
15	9	0
25	7	1
10	3	1
20		12

The frequency of taking possession of objects sharply falls for group members, and rises for the leader.

Into some groups, after traditions had been formed, outstanding leading personalities were placed—leaders obeyed in the day nursery by everyone, virtual dictators to more than thirty children. Let us follow one of them. If a child's behavior displeased him, he beat up that child; he allowed no opposition, and always had to have his way. The group into which he was put consisted of children younger than himself, children who in the day nursery always obeyed him. The result was unexpected: this structured group virtually swallowed him. (His proportion of modeling changed from 9 : 5 to 0 : 8). He followed the group's every activity, accepted its every custom, while his own suggestions were *never* followed.

However, his exceptional personality still asserted itself with the group. The children gave him every object without his asking, and with that acknowledged his authority. The group had two traditional activities: using blocks they built a train, and using chairs they built a bridge. The leader soon learned these constructions and used the objects acquired to build just these. From time to time the group gathered around him, eloquently praising whatever he did. They praised his beautiful creation, his skill, the wonderful things he made (which he had learned from them), as if to placate some dangerous genie. At the same time they followed him in nothing; on the contrary they drew him into their own activities and caused him to accept their habits. Their play remained unchanged; the same game with the same toys. They talked of the toys as they did before—Johnny's blocks, Tom's box—but occasionally they said; "The blocks belong to Andrew" (Andrew was the leader), or: "Tom's box belongs to Andrew." The owners of the objects became their users, while the right of ownership was given over, voluntarily or otherwise, to the new leader.

Observation over only a short period would lead to mistaken conclusions. One might see only that one child has all the toys, while the others surround and admire him. Only prolonged observation would show that those are but scenes of ceremonial offerings with which the children purchase, as it were, the leader's continued trust, with which they protect their traditions.

Again we see that apparently the leader is stronger than *the members* of the group (he appropriates their belongings), but weaker than *the group* because he is forced to accept its customs, traditions, and forms of activity.

3. *The Diplomat.*   The third way of asserting leadership, as observed in our experimental situation, is quite devious. The cases belonging here are peculiar. The leader, having a greater force of social penetration than the group members, attempts to force upon them a new mode of activity. He fails. However, the leader, for reasons as yet unclear to us—perhaps through his personality, perhaps because of the tense situation—does not get lost in the group, nor take over its habits, as did those leaders who complied in order to rule or in order to take possession of the toys.

This type of leader takes a roundabout course: he accepts the traditions of the group in order to change them.

Into old forms he pours new contents. What takes place here is a veritably dramatic struggle. We had one group with particularly strong traditions and institutionalization. This group rose to the highest level of spontaneous organization of games: to the level of division of roles.

One of the children, who in the day nursery showed no leadership, in this narrower group developed into a leader: games he suggested were followed, and their various parts became traditional with the group. It was at this point that a new leader was added. He tried to suggest new games but was not accepted. Then he joined their traditional game and slowly took over the leadership. The first day there were only two instances in which he led, the second day there were already nine. However, he was the one being modeled, taking over the group's habits. He accepted those habits but introduced minute changes. For example, he joined in the block game traditional with the group, but he demanded that always the red side of a block be on top. He was being modeled, he imitated, but he also introduced changes; then he became the leader of the traditional activities thus changed.

The third time he was with the group he again suggested new activities. One was "hide and seek." (They had a game involving hiding, and this feature attracted the leader.) The group did not accept the suggestion and played instead another traditional game they called "acting with hats."

The leader yielded, joined the "hat game" and instantly began to organize it, in the course of which he made changes so as to combine with it the hide-and-seek game he had suggested. He was *being modeled* to the group, but he also *modeled* the group; he accepted their traditions but changed them.

His roundabout road to leadership is clear here:

1. *He tries to do away with the group traditions and lead it on to new ones.*
2. *He is rejected.*
3. *He accepts the traditions and quickly learns them.*
4. *Within the frame of those traditions he soon assumes leadership, and, though reluctantly, the group follows him because he does a good job.*
5. *He introduces insignificant variations, loosening the tradition.*
6. *He then introduces new elements into the ritual already weakened by variation.*

In this case accepting the traditions is a roundabout way to introducing new ones. This is a very active process in which the leader plays an important role. Only children with exceptional social influence and a great deal of intiative could act this way.

Thus, between the extremes of total assimilation and total conquest, we find three types of behavior. In the experimental situation the leader either (1) is being modeled—but gives orders; or (2) is being modeled—

but obtains possession of the toys; or again (3) is being modeled—but he also models the others.

It has to be emphasized that in all these cases the leader must accept the traditions and can give orders only within their framework. The following is a nice example: into a well-developed group of children, 4 to 5 years old, a leader of 6½ with a strong personality was introduced. The group had traditional ways of using the toys. It was exactly determined who would play with what. Each toy, though they might exchange them for a while, traditionally constituted the possession of a certain child.

The leader was unable to change this rule of ownership. Yet he found himself a place in the system. At the beginning of the play period he distributed the objects, giving each child the one that "belonged to him." The children continued to ask the "owners" for the blocks or boxes when they wanted to play with them; they continued to exchange toys as before. Only now the blocks, house, or boxes were distributed by the leader at the beginning of the period. Thus he found himself a role in an order which was there when he first arrived, though unable essentially to change the existing traditions.

THE FORMING OF TRADITION

We have examined the influence of the group on a new leader. We have seen that the group forces its traditions on the leader; and that with varying circumstances the process involves changes, while the basic tendency remains the same. We have seen that the capitulating leader still makes his superior personality felt. Even though he accepts the group's traditions, he exerts an influence. Even in the case of total assimilation of the leader we find changes in the group's life which can be ascribed to his influence.

For example, one group always built trains out of blocks. The leader followed this activity. He too built trains, only he put a chimney on his locomotive. The others followed suit.

Another group's traditional game was to climb up and hang on to the top edge of a wardrobe and to swing there. The leader—of the type that gives orders but is being modeled—soon joined the game. Only one child at a time could swing on the wardrobe. On each side stood a chair to climb up on. Shortly after the leader joined the group he introduced a "oneway traffic." Everything went on as before with the exception that the children had to climb up one side and down the other. This innovation added color to the game without changing its structure. Such phenomena occurred often. Almost every leader, just as soon as he met the group, reorganized it, introducing direction and order.

In other cases this coloring lent by the leader pertained rather to the contents, as when a fitting little story was introduced. One group that played with a small house said: "This is the mailman's house—in the evening he comes home—in the morning he leaves." In the game itself there was no mailman. The children put nothing into the house. The mailman was not even symbolically represented. The words were merely additional coloring. On this the leader elaborated: "The mailman brings coal—they put it on wagons and trucks, etc." The others took over these little themes and their activity, though undamaged, became more colorful.

Often the leader would step up the pace of activity. This is another way to impose his will on the group. He would dictate a very fast tempo, driving them. A certain type of leader is needed to create this acceleration of pace: a child who is very active, who has many interests, whose attention is divided, and who has a stormy temperament. Such leaders busy themselves with several things at once, join several games at once, and with their "swing" accelerate the group's life.

An interesting influence of the leader is the *widening of the terrain.* The group's accustomed space becomes larger: a group that has worked in one portion of the room will, after the leader appears, expand into the entire room. The way this occurs clearly shows the relationship between a developed group and a new leader.

One group would play around a table in the middle of the room. From time to time they would go to the wardrobe in one corner of the room and try to climb up. Then the new leader appropriated the table, whereupon a migration to the wardrobe took place where they started the game of climbing up. The leader followed them and started organizing that game. Slowly the children shifted back to the table, but the leader was on their trail. The result was a pendulum-like movement between the table and wardrobe. Then one child went to a new place and started doing something there. At once the leader extended his pendulum motion to that place. A veritable pilgrimage began. Everywhere the leader was being modeled: he was the one who adjusted to the others' mode of activity.

Another frequent influence of the leader is that he changes the degree of concerted action. The degree of group action is not to be confused with the degree of creative activity of a person. When a presocial formation of four people sit together, one reading a philosophical treatise, the other solving a mathematical problem, the third writing an ode, etc., without having anything in common with each other, the group is of a lower social level than a foursome playing bridge.

During our investigations we observed that in some cases the leader brings a presocial group to a higher degree of concerted action, in other cases to a lower one. If, for example, a group that has merely congregated around a set of toys is organized into one with a division of roles, the group level has been raised. It will be lowered if group activity is reduced to mere side-by-side play. Such raising or lowering of group level depends mostly on the personal qualities of the leader, especially on his capacity to organize. The capacity consists of the bent to remember every custom, to see to it that objects are returned where they belong and that the rituals are observed, even if these were learned from the group. The leader who has this quality raises the group level even if he totally submits to the group's traditions.

THE POWER OF THE GROUP

Our question was: Which is stronger, the group made up of individuals of average social penetration, or the individual of high degree of social penetration but alien to the group?

Our criterion was, not the relationship between the new leader and the individual group members, but that "plus" arising from "groupness" which raises the power of the group above the aggregate strength of its members. This "plus" shows in the habits, customs, rules, and relationships making for institutionalization. Accordingly, the individual is the stronger of the two if he can change those traditions; but the group is the stronger if it assimilates the leader.

Couching our inquiry in these terms lent decisive importance to the ratio *modeling/being modeled.*

Our investigations have shown that the group with a tradition is stronger than the leader (though he is stronger than any one group member).

The play of forces between leader and group resulted in the following graduations:

1. The leader is totally assimilated;
2. The leader is being modeled but gives orders;
3. The leader is being modeled but gains possession of the toys;
4. The leader is being modeled but modifiies the traditions;
5. The leader destroys the group's traditions and introduces new ones. It is rare that the leader should become not only the center of the group but also the maker of its rules.

Which of these five situations will obtain depends on:

1. The degree of crystallization of traditions;
2. The extent of collaborative play;
3. The degree of group cohesion (the marginal child included).

These conditions issue from the nature of the group. It is no doubt important what kind of person, what character type the new leader is. It may be that in the child who expropriates the toys in order to set himself up as leader a desire for acquisition asserts itself; it may be that the child who gives orders is driven by narcissism and aggression. However, our investigation did not extend to these motivations.

Even the leader who is forced to accept existing traditions makes his superiority felt: he may lend color to activities, step up the pace, widen the field, or change the group level by influencing cohesion.

In our experiment, individuals of strong social penetrating power seldom became changers of traditions; however, being modeled to the existing traditions, they influenced them.

We were thus able to experience that "plus" which makes the group more than and different from the aggregate of its members: as in cases where the new leader conquered everyone, where each child followed his orders—as long as *what* he ordered was in agreement with the group's traditions.

It is in this peculiar strength of tradition that this group "plus" appears. Its carriers are the individuals constituting the group. By belonging to the group each is "more" and stronger. This became clear when children who in the day nursery were *being modeled* by leaders there, became the models of these leaders in the organized group.

Thus the group "plus" is not some substance hovering above the group: it is the hold their customs and habits have on the members; it is tradition, the carrier of which is the individual, who, in turn, is strengthened by it. Conceivably, the feeling of heightened intensity always evoked by group experience is the experiencing of just this "plus."

Why does the leader accept the group's traditions? Is it because he is weaker than its members, or more suggestible? No. We have seen him in the day nursery, modeling the others. Is it because he is in a new situation where the group members have the advantage of being familiar with the situation? This is contraindicated by the behavior of leaders who give orders quite without inhibition. The dichotomy is clear: the leader is supraordinated since he gives orders; but he is also subordinated since he is being modeled. He has the upper hand *vis à vis* the members but has to bow to group tradition.

Thus the reaction of the group to the new leader clearly brings into view the power of the group "plus." It is this "plus" that is stronger than the leader, who is stronger than any one group member.

With this we can discard all hypotheses which deny the uniqueness of the group, and which attempt fully to account for the group by assessing its members.

Our experiment refutes the prejudice of metaphysical social psychology that the group, through an evening effect, lowers the level of the individual. We observed exactly the opposite: the strength of the group strengthens its members. Group experience not only pleases, it also strengthens.

PART IV

DISTORTED VIEWS

INTRODUCTION

Some children's views of the world are distorted views, views which give rise to deviant behavior. If we may assume that all behavior is purposive and aimed at coping with the environment, deviant behavior and normal behavior must follow the same principle.

When its environment is too demanding or unpredictable or overly unrewarding or cruel, the organism, bearing the scars of many unfortunate experiences, comes to expect the imminent recurrence of similar events or conditions. One may view life as a lovely garden—or as a jungle filled with wild beasts, where one devours or is devoured. Through early experiences, each of us develops attitudes and expectations which he may carry throughout life. We all assume postures that we believe necessary to get along in particular circumstances or with particular people, and often these attitudes continue long after the original pressures causing them have disappeared.

The studies in this Part deal with some of the anxious behavior patterns developed by children in order to secure comfort and avoid pain, patterns adaptive at one period in life which prove maladaptive and ineffective at later periods. Several of the articles contain empathic and insightful descriptions of unrealistic expectations and feelings in disturbed children. Some discuss the people and situations to which a particular child was forced to adjust, with crippling results. The last two articles describe laboratory attempts to recreate such stressful conditions.

If control of antisocial behavior is to be attained, and ability to handle stress effectively is to be increased, understanding of the nature, causes, and possibilities for altering distorted perceptions is necessary.

354

34. THE CASE OF PETER

ERIK H. ERIKSON

Distorted views are often private and unique interpretations
of events with peculiar meanings understood only by those who
hold them. This description of some private meanings which
threaten the life of a small child, and of the thinking processes
of an eminent psychologist who magnificently uncovers the
secret distortions, reads like a detective story.

I have been told that Peter was retaining his bowel movements, first for a few days at a time, but more recently up to a week. I was urged to hurry when, in addition to a week's supply of fecal matter, Peter had incorporated and retained a large enema in his small, four-year-old body. He looked miserable, and when he thought nobody watched him he leaned his bloated abdomen against a wall for support.

His pediatrician had come to the conclusion that this feat could not have been accomplished without energetic support from the emotional side, although he suspected what was later revealed by X-ray, namely that the boy indeed had by then an enlarged colon. While a tendency toward colonic expansion may initially have contributed to the creation of the symptom, the child was now undoubtedly paralyzed by a conflict which he was unable to verbalize. The local physiological condition was to be taken care of later by diet and exercise. First it seemed necessary to understand the conflict and to establish communication with the boy as quickly as possible so that his co-operation might be obtained.

It has been my custom before deciding to take on a family problem to have a meal with the family in their home. I was introduced to my prospective little patient as an acquaintance of the parents who wanted to come and meet the whole family. The little boy was one of those children who make me question the wisdom of any effort at disguise. "Aren't dreams wonderful?" he said to me in the tone of a hostess as we sat down to lunch. He then improvised a series of playful statements which, as will be clear presently, gave away his dominant and disturbing fantasy. It is characteristic of the ambivalent aspect of such sphincter problems that the patients surrender almost obsessively the very secret which is so strenuously retained in their bowels. I shall list here some of Peter's dreamy statements and my silent reflections upon them which emerged during and after luncheon.

"I wish I had a little elephant right here in my house. But then it would grow and grow and burst the house."—The boy is eating at the moment. This means his intestinal bulk is growing to the bursting point.

"Look at that bee—it wants to get at the sugar in my stomach."—"Sugar" sounds euphemistic, but it does transmit the thought that he has something valuable in his stomach and that somebody wants to get at it.

"I had a bad dream. Some monkeys climbed up and down the house and tried to get in to get me."—The bees wanted to get at the sugar in his stomach; now the monkeys want to get at him in his house. Increasing food in his stomach—growing baby elephant in the house—bees after sugar in his stomach—monkeys after him in the house.

After lunch coffee was served in the garden. Peter sat down underneath a garden table, pulled the chairs in toward himself as if barricading himself, and said, "Now I am in my tent and the bees can't get at me."—Again he is inside an enclosure, endangered by intrusive animals.

He then showed me his room. I admired his books and said, "Show me the picture you like best in the book you like best." Without hesitation he produced an illustration showing a gingerbread man floating in water toward the open mouth of a swimming wolf. Excitedly he said, "The wolf is going to eat the gingerbread man, but it won't hurt the gingerbread man because [loudly] *he's not alive,* and food can't feel it when you eat it!" I thoroughly agreed with him, reflecting in the meantime that the boy's playful sayings converged on the idea that whatever he had accumulated in his stomach was alive and in danger of either "bursting" him or of being hurt. To test this impression I asked him to show me the picture he liked next best in any of the other books. He immediately went after a book called "The Little Engine That Could" and looked for a page which showed a smoke-puffing train going into a tunnel, while on the next page it comes out of it—its funnel *not smoking*. "You see," he said, "the train went into the tunnel and in the dark tunnel it *went dead!*"—Something alive went into a dark passage and came out dead. I no longer doubted that this little boy had a fantasy that he was filled with something precious and alive; that if he kept it, it would burst him and that if he released it, it might come out hurt or dead. In other words, he was pregnant.

The patient needed immediate help, by interpretation. I want to make it clear that I do not approve of imposing sexual enlightenment on unsuspecting children before a reliable relationship has been established. Here, however, I felt experimental action was called for. I came

back to his love for little elephants and suggested that we draw elephants. After we had reached a certain proficiency in drawing all the
outer appointments and appendages of an elephant lady and of a couple
of elephant babies, I asked whether he knew where the elephant babies
came from. Tensely he said he did not, although I had the impression
that he merely wanted to lead me on. So I drew as well as I could a
cross section of the elephant lady and of her inner compartments, making it quite clear that there were two exits, one for the bowels and one
for the babies. "This," I said, "some children do not know. They think
that the bowel movements and the babies come out of the same opening
in animals and in women." Before I could expand on the dangers which
one could infer from such misunderstood conditions, he very excitedly
told me that when his mother had carried him she had had to wear a
belt which kept him from falling out of her when she sat on the toilet;
and that he had proved too big for her opening so she had to have a
cut made in her stomach to let him out. I had not known that he had
been born by cesarean section, but I drew him a diagram of a woman,
setting him straight on what he remembered of his mother's explanations. I added that it seemed to me that he thought he was pregnant;
that while this was impossible in reality it was important to understand
the reason for his fantasy; that, as he might have heard, I made it my
business to understand children's thoughts and that, if he wished, I
would come back the next day to continue our conversation. He did
wish; and he had a superhuman bowel movement after I left.

There was no doubt, then, that once having bloated his abdomen
with retained fecal matter this boy thought he might be pregnant and
was afraid to let go lest he hurt himself or "the baby." But what had
made him retain in the first place? What had caused in him an emotional
conflict at this time which found its expression in a retention and pregnancy fantasy?

The boy's father gave me one key to the immediate "cause" of the
deadlock. "You know," he said, "that boy begins to look just like Myrtle."
"Who is Myrtle?" "She was his nurse for two years; she left three months
ago." "Shortly before his symptoms became so much worse?" "Yes."

Peter, then, has lost an important person in his life: his nurse.
A soft-spoken Oriental girl with a gentle touch, she had been his main
comfort for years because his parents were out often, both pursuing
professional careers. In recent months he had taken to attacking the
nurse in a roughhousing way, and the girl had seemed to accept and
quietly enjoy his decidedly "male" approach. In the nurse's homeland
such behavior is not only not unusual, it is the rule. But there it makes
sense, as part of the whole culture. Peter's mother, so she admitted,
could not quite suppress a feeling that there was something essentially
wrong about the boy's sudden maleness and about the way it was per-

mitted to manifest itself. She became alerted to the problem of having her boy brought up by a stranger, and she decided to take over herself.

Thus it was during a period of budding, provoked, and disapproved masculinity that the nurse left. Whether she left or was sent away hardly mattered to the child. What mattered was that he lived in a social class which provides paid mother substitutes from a different race or class. Seen from the children's point of view this poses a number of problems. If you like your ersatz mother, your mother will leave you more often and with a better conscience. If you mildly dislike her, your mother will leave you with mild regret. If you dislike her very much and can pro- voke convincing incidents, your mother will send her away—only to hire somebody like her or worse. And if you happen to like her very much in your own way or in her own way, your mother will surely send her away sooner or later.

In Peter's case, insult was added to injury by a letter from the nurse, who had heard of his condition and who was now trying her best to explain to him why she had left. She had originally told him that she was leaving in order to marry and have a baby of her own. This had been bad enough in view of the boy's feelings for her. Now she informed him that she had taken another job instead. "You see," she explained, "I always move on to another family when the child in my care becomes too big. I like best to tend babies." It was then that something happened to the boy. He had tried to be a big boy. His father had been of little help because he was frequently absent, preoccupied with a business which was too complicated to explain to his son. His mother had indicated that male behavior in the form provoked or con- doned by the nurse was unacceptable behavior. The nurse liked babies better.

So he "regressed." He became babyish and dependent, and in desperation, lest he lose more, *he held on.* This he had done before. Long ago, as a baby, he had demonstrated his first stubbornness by hold- ing food in his mouth. Later, put on the toilet and told not to get up until he had finished, he did not finish and he did not get up until his mother gave up. Now he held on to his bowels—and to much more, for he also became tight-lipped, expressionless, and rigid. All of this, of course, was one symptom with a variety of related meanings. The simplest meaning was: I am holding on to what I have got and I am not going to move, either forward or backward. But as we saw from his play, the object of his holding on could be interpreted in a variety of ways. Apparently at first, still believing the nurse to be pregnant, he tried to hold on to her by becoming the nurse and by pretending that he was pregnant too. His general regression, at the same time, demonstrated that he too, was a baby and thus as small as any child the nurse might have turned to. Freud called this the overdetermination of the meaning of a symptom.

The overdetermining items, however, are always systematically related: the boy identifies with *both partners of a lost relationship;* he is the nurse who is now the child and he is the baby he once was. Identifications which result from losses are like that. We become the lost person *and* we become again the person we were when the relationship was at its prime. This makes for much seemingly contradictory symptomatology.

Our boy, however, concerned himself with the fantasy of being pregnant. Once it looked as if he did indeed have the equivalent of a baby in him, he remembered what his mother had said about birth and about dangers to mother and child. He could not let go.

The interpretation of this fear to him resulted in a dramatic improvement which released the immediate discomfort and danger and brought out the boy's inhibited autonomy and boyish initiative. But only a combination of dietetic and gymnastic work with many interviews with mother and child could finally overcome a number of milder setbacks.

35. CRIMINALS ARE MADE, NOT BORN

MORRIS L. HAIMOWITZ

How does a nasty, trouble-making child evolve into a professional criminal? Where does he learn his trade? When is graduation day?

This paper describes some of the crucial experiences which lead a boy into a criminal career. The changes in self-image that accompany the progress of this "nobody" to the status of a criminal "somebody" appear to develop during his interaction with the responsible persons in his community. Paradoxically, the boy who is frequently told, "Don't be a bad boy," very often comes to feel that only by being very, very bad can he maintain his self-respect, dignity, and integrity.

I. INTRODUCTION

There are a number of theories about how people come to be professional criminals. There is the widespread notion that poverty causes crime; or the theory that "bad" neighborhoods cause crime; or that movies, TV, comic books, or radio crime stories cause crime; or that criminal associates cause crime; or that broken homes cause crime; or

Revised from *Teleclass Study Guide, Social Science 101,* 1958, by Francis Gaul, by permission of The Chicago Board of Education.

that race, nationality, neuroses, or crowded housing cause crime. These theories do not explain why most poor people never become professional criminals. Nor do most people from bad neighborhoods, or most children of broken homes, or most members of any race or nationality, or most neurotics become criminals. If crowded housing caused crime, all Eskimos would be criminals; actually, very few are.

Some studies show these factors to be associated with criminality. But science aims at generalizations which account for *all* cases, and not one of these theories accounts for even a majority of cases. These important studies indicate some *associated* factors, not the *causes* of crime. Let us illustrate the difference. Suppose we didn't know how a child is conceived and were seeking an explanation. We might make a survey and find the following factors associated with having children: poverty, illiteracy, race, religion, marriage, wedding rings, rural dwellings. Could we therefore state that poverty, illiteracy, and so on, were the causes of conception? Such a conclusion would completely overlook the crucial role of the sperm and ovary. Marriage is an associated factor, but it is not the cause of conception. The theory that poverty or the factors listed above cause crime is as untrue as the one that poverty, or a wedding ring, are the causes of conception.

II. HYPOTHESIS

This paper seeks to develop the hypothesis that the only way a person can become a professional criminal is by getting the idea that he is expected to be an outlaw by those whom he takes seriously: his parents, friends, neighbors, teachers, clergymen, police, social workers, and judges. He must form a mental picture of himself as different from others, different in a way requiring a different vocational career and requiring that he associate with persons ostracized as he is.

This hypothesis refers to professional criminals, not to occasional lawbreakers or alcoholics, or persons who murder or steal in a passionate outbreak. It applies to those persons who belong to professional criminal societies and whose trade or occupation is criminal, with "professional" standards or skills. It is not always easy to tell which criminal is the professional and which is the amateur because many criminals have conflicting self-conceptions.

We like to think that there are two classes of occupations, the legal and the illegal, but the actual situation is not so simple. There are many gradations between the strictly honest and the strictly criminal. Many activities of business or professional men, repairmen, or governmental workers fall into criminal categories. In addition, there are other activities, not definitely criminal, nor yet definitely honest, in the shady or unethical category. Moreover, there are perfectly legal activities which are of controversial value, such as manufacturing, advertising, or selling white flour, candy, alcohol, tobacco, patent medicines, or firearms, which may be declared illegal in the future. Finally, there are ideas which may be considered dangerous or illegal because they are new or different.

Some children are taught methods of stealing by their parents. But the usual delinquent cannot be explained so easily. Usually, his parents are frightened and embarrassed by his notoriety, even though they also may be secretly proud of their little rascal.

It is popular to explain socially disapproved behavior by labeling the person as neurotic. Neurosis is abnormal; so is criminality. For example, suppose a man steals or damages property and finds himself waiting, terrified and yet wanting to be caught. He may experience an anxiety, like the child playing hide-and-seek, with excitement reaching a climax when he is discovered. Such a person would be a neurotic criminal. However, one can not say all criminals are neurotic, especially the one who performs his acts because he, his family, and his associates consider them proper and desirable. Furthermore, criminal law changes from time to time and is differently enforced from place to place. Betting is illegal in Chicago; legal in the suburbs. George Washington was a hero in America; a criminal in England.

III. THE SETTING: SOME FACTORS ASSOCIATED WITH CRIME

When we study criminals we find certain factors statistically associated with crime.

Most delinquents are found in the slums, yet most slum children never become delinquents. Most delinquents come from broken homes, yet most children from broken homes never become delinquents. Most delinquents are of a different racial or ethnic stock than the natives, yet race or ethnic affiliation is no guarantee of law-abiding or criminal behavior. Most delinquents are probably neurotic, but most neurotics are not criminal. Most delinquents, finally, come from low-income families, but most persons with low incomes are law-abiding. A recent study of 2,000 white teenagers by Nye and Short showed that delinquency was not as closely related to income, religion, or to broken homes, as to the feeling, "My parents hate me." We may conclude that living in the slum or in a broken home, belonging to a different racial or ethnic group, and being neurotic and poor are factors associated with crime, but they are not the causes.

Most people who steal are not professional criminals. The act of stealing something probably involves a conscious decision. But the act of becoming a professional criminal appears to involve a long list of experiences in which a pattern of behavior occurs, a drifting into a habit of life, into life with a group of friends which no one ever planned but which could have only one ending. The criminal may never have made a conscious decision to enter on a career of crime.

The people living in the slums and rooming house areas of the city are different from others not only in being on the average less well educated and earning less money, having higher mortality and morbidity rates, in appearing to have a higher rate of criminality, but also in being of different ethnic, racial, or national stocks. They are the newcomers. The immigrants usually settle in the slums; they bring with them not only poverty but also opinions as to what's right and what's wrong which were appropriate in the environment from which they came. It is a crime for the newcomer in Chicago to throw his garbage out the window; but it was perfectly proper to do so home in the South —for the chickens and hogs to eat. Prohibition was incomprehensible to Europeans accustomed to wine with dinner.

The rapid growth of the factories, and of the slums housing the factory workers, the high rate of immigration, and the rapid technological developments have made this country, as well as most countries of our time, an area of cultural ferment, with rapidly changing ideas of what is criminal and what is proper. What is legal today may be criminal tomorrow.

All children get into mischief. Technically, you could say they violate the law. A little boy two years old pulls down the curtains in the living room. When they fall they knock over a lamp, dust flies all over the room, and his mother, hearing the commotion, runs in from the kitchen and helps him out of difficulty. He has behaved in utter disregard for life and property and is thus a lawbreaker, but no one calls him a criminal. His mother is caring for him all the time, getting him out of the refrigerator, turning off the gas which he has turned on, rescuing his toy rabbit from the toilet bowl. Like adults, all little children err, but few become gangsters.

Not all children have a mother at home caring for them. Especially not slum children. They live in the "zones of transition," called such because they are changing areas, changing from big homes to rooming houses, from residential to business, from native citizens to immigrants, from white to colored to Mexican and Puerto Rican. But in one way such a zone is not changing. It always has had the highest crime rate of any area in the city. The reasons many children do not have a mother supervising them are that their father is sick, or is dead, or is in jail, or cannot support his family. So the mother has to work, and cannot be home supervising the children; or she is sick or doesn't like caring for children.

A very high proportion of professional criminals come from the slums. Occasionally they come from nicer neighborhoods, but here too we find the unsupervised child. The child who steals and is caught and arrested is delinquent; if he steals and is not caught or not arrested, he is not delinquent. Of course, in nicer neighborhoods, police act more courteously to accused children.

There are many ways a child may react to the fears and loneliness resulting from parental neglect. He can become a dreamer; he can become sick or develop an inferiority complex; or he can become a fighter, and demand attention, stating in effect, "Love me or fear me." The self-conception he forms is determined by the way he perceives some crucial experiences.

IV. THE CRUCIAL EXPERIENCES

With Parents. Let's see what happens. A boy is involved in an incident during which someone is hurt or property is damaged or stolen. The injured party usually talks to the boy or his parents, and they make an amicable settlement. But sometimes the injured party feels frightened, angry with himself and his neighbors, and unable to deal with the situation alone, and so he calls the police. The boys see the police, and they all run away. One who did not run away, or was too slow, or had nothing to do with it, or has a bad reputation is caught. The parents are called in and they protect or spank the boy and everyone is satisfied. Or for some reason parents and sons are brought in for questioning. What concerns us is how the child learns that people expect him to be untrustworthy.

There are many ways parents may tell their children they are not to be trusted. They may be direct and say, "You are becoming a little hoodlum." Or they may be subtle and say, "My boy is good," and the boy knows they mean, "He is bad."

Here is an example of this. A juvenile officer was told that a fifteen-year-old boy had been committing delinquencies with a girl of his age. The girl had admitted relations with him. So the boy, accompanied by his mother, was brought in for questioning.

> POLICE OFFICER. Did you see Miss X on December 15?
> MOTHER. No, he didn't.
> POLICE OFFICER. Did you meet Miss X after school that day?
> MOTHER. No, why don't you leave him alone?
> POLICE OFFICER. Did you have relations with her?
> MOTHER. Why do you keep picking on him. He's a good boy; he would never do such a thing!
> POLICE OFFICER. Why don't you let him talk for himself. I've been asking him questions for thirty minutes and you haven't let him answer once.

Was this mother so convinced of her son's innocence? It is natural for a mother to defend her son. Her words said, "He is a good boy," but her manner said, "He can't be trusted to speak; he is either too stupid to say the right thing, or he is terribly guilty." Thus she became an accessory to the crime.

And how would the boy feel in a spot like this? "To die, to sink through the floor, where can I hide? It's even harder when she lies. Why don't the police mind their own business?"

When persons important to the child don't trust him, he may come to distrust himself. The conception of oneself as a law-violator, or just a hateful, worthless, public nuisance does not usually develop full-blown in a few minutes. We don't know exactly how it happens. Little children interact thousands of times with others, thereby learning what is expected of them. Little children of two, three, or four years like to help their mothers in the kitchen, wash the dishes, peel the potatoes, string the beans, crack the nuts, mop the floor. They like to help their father repair the clock, fix the furnace, paint the chairs, drive the car. Some mothers and fathers find this "help" more than they can bear. They tell the child, "Go away! You can't wash the dishes, you'll break them; you can't paint the furniture; you can't mop the floor, scram!"

We have observed eleven-year-old children who could not clear the table or wash a dish ("She might break them," the mother would say); and we have observed other children, five years old, who could clear the table, wash, and dry the dishes. One mother expects the child to break the dishes; the other mother expects the child to do a good job. Both children do what is expected of them, and by doing so, each is developing a self-conception.

Parents are very worried when their children are destructive. One mother who asked us for help could not understand her child: "Come see for yourself; that little boy was impossible." We went to her home, and she was right. He was impossible. But he wasn't learning how to be impossible all by himself; he was getting lots of help from his mother, and from his older brothers. During the hour of the visit we heard them tell him forty times, "Don't break the wall down; don't tear up your clothes; don't scream so loud; don't sweep the floor; don't be a bad boy; don't run; don't carry the tray. For God's sake, don't be impossible!" The boy told us, "I just wanted to help, and every time I try to help they make me do it wrong." His family wanted him to be good; but they told him they expected him to be bad. It appears that some children are more likely to act as people *expect* them to act than as they want to act. How many times a day may a parent tell the child, "I expect you to be bad." One hundred? and how many times by the child's sixth birthday? One hundred thousand? Some parents are more patient and can even enjoy the child's attempts to be useful. When the child strings one bean, they say, "Thank you," because they consider the child's age when judging his craftsmanship.

What is important is not so much just what words the parents say to the child as the way they act and the way their acts are interpreted by the child. The parents may say, "You are bad," but act as though the child were the most precious object in the world. Both the words and the other feelings are communicated. So the child may feel, "I am capable, but my parents are sometimes impatient."

Now let's see how the child may come to feel, "I am no good and can do nothing that is good." If by neglect, cruelty, or constant discouragement the actions of the parents are such that they indicate to the child he is the *least* precious object in the world, this self-conception may develop. It may happen because the child is often neglected, left uncared for, unfed. Or they just don't take time for the child. Every time the child wants to help wash dishes, they say, "Go away, dishes are not for you, you just make a mess." This may happen thousands of times between his second and sixth year. And one day his mother decides he is now old enough to help, and she calls him in—but now he has learned "Dishes are not for me." He refuses to help wash the dishes, or gets a headache, or has to go to the bathroom. More extreme situations, such as the parent's leaving the child alone for days at a time, or constant beatings, convey to him a sense of his worthlessness or undesirability.

With Police. Sometimes the boy is unsupervised, out on the streets. His parents prefer earning money to staying home and taking care of him. Something happens. He borrows a friend's bicycle, rides to the grocery store, goes inside, and buys an ice cream bar. As he comes out some bigger boys, wanting to share the ice cream, are waiting for him; he runs away from them, leaving the bicycle.

Meanwhile, the owner of the bicycle starts screaming, "Someone stole my bike." Fred says, "Tommy took it. I saw him." They find Tommy. He says he left it at the grocery store, but it is no longer there. The police are called. They try to locate Tommy's parents, but they are not at home. Now it is up to the police.

Usually the policeman is friendly but firm; he has children of his own who might have done the same thing, and he wouldn't want anyone roughing them up. He tells the boy, "You're a good boy. I know it was an accident. Be more careful next time," and lets him go. If he has the time and the desire, if he is well trained, if he has been assigned to that neighborhood long enough to know it well, if he is patient, the policeman will talk to the natural leaders of the boys to convert the leaders from delinquent to productive activities. The policeman knows that most leaders of boys' gangs will cooperate if they are given a chance to participate in the planning and that these leaders can influence their followers better than anyone else. Or the policeman may recognize the need for community aid for these boys and will talk to local adult leaders—the clergyman, teacher, school principal, businessman, his alderman, or police captain for the purpose of getting more supervised activities underway. A number of studies have shown that participation in supervised activities deters juvenile delinquency. Even when such facilities are available, however, some supervisors refuse to permit delinquents to participate.

Often the policeman can't do these things. He just doesn't have the time or the training. Perhaps he is under strain because it has happened several times before, or the citizen wronged is very angry or influential, or the policeman was recently reprimanded for being lax, or another child hit him in the ear with a snowball ten minutes earlier. Or, most important of all, the lad is impertinent. Then our young citizen—five, ten, fifteen years old—may be taken in and detained. The policeman may feel less likely to get into trouble by such action. Or he may feel, "Today I am starting a boy off on the wrong road, but I can't help it."

Until this time the boy is like all the other kids; full of energy, going through many different kinds of activities all day long, singing, jumping, screaming, playing cops and robbers, tearing clothes, crying, fighting—just like everyone else. But once arrested he becomes different. He is asked questions which imply a difference—name, father's name, religion, age, father's occupation, nationality, race. Ordinary things become extraordinary. He never thought about such things before. He was just like everyone else until now. He wonders about himself. He is frightened but also may be very impressed with the whole procedure and perhaps with his own importance. He wants his mother. He is taken to a social worker. She is expected to ask questions. Tell me about your home, your father and mother, the implication being something is wrong with them. She might even go home and find out for herself. He is taken to a psychologist or sociologist. His intelligence is measured—IQ: 105. His emotions are wondered at. He is taken to a judge: he hears lawyers talking about him. He is getting an education that his brothers and sisters and neighbors never dreamed about. Being in a detention home or jail can terrify a child. Everyone is saying, "Something's wrong with you."

He may be interrogated. Did you ever hear a policeman interrogating a teenager alleged to be guilty of a crime? The policeman acts and speaks as though the prisoner is guilty. It's his duty to clear up the crime. He is usually courteous, but sometimes he is filthy with insults, especially if the boy is a member of an ethnic group the policeman doesn't trust:

POLICE.   What were you doing at that house?
BOY.   I went there to collect $5.00 a man owed me.
POLICE.   Don't you know they're a pack of thieves?
BOY.   I didn't know that.
POLICE.   If you sleep in a stable, you will smell like—.

BOY. I just went to collect my $5.00.

POLICE. Who did you lend it to?

BOY. Fred Johnson.

POLICE. Fred Johnson! He's an old-timer. Been in jail a dozen times. Why did you lend him $5.00?

BOY. He asked me for it. He lent me money when we were in school together.

SECOND POLICE. Oh boy! what a tale! [*Sarcastically*] They were planning another A&P job.

BOY. I never had anything to do with any A&P. I go to Brundy School.

POLICE. Who went through the transom, you or Fred?

BOY. I never robbed any store in my life!

POLICE. [*All laugh*] You're a damned liar!

[*Boy cries.*] [1]

Some policemen treat him like a son. Others, like a step-son. The policeman has a tough job. It sounds easy, "Just enforce law and order." But what to do when John Doe, age eight, is caught for the third time stealing a bike? Scold him, let him go, arrest him? There must be an answer.

Why should a poorly paid, often semitrained policeman be permitted to bear the burden of such a major decision? Many people are involved; many should help decide—maybe a community council, including teenagers as well as adults. One thing police could do which would give the boy some idea of the problems of policemen would be to invite delinquents to patrol the city a few hours a week in a police squad car. Most cities have enough squad cars to keep every delinquent occupied several hours a week. It might work, properly supervised so that the officers are instructed to try to be friendly, courteous, to explain their jobs, to listen to the problems of the boys as a sort of get-acquainted, how-do-you-do gesture, or as a long-term intensive activity.

In Court. The boy may be taken to court. What happens in the court room? The state's attorney may appear if enough publicity is involved, and he makes a speech, such as: "(Crime) by teen-agers must be stopped. The energetic measures taken by police to deal with *these future hoodlums* will be backed to the limit by the state's attorney's Office." (In this particular case, the judge in Boy's Court ordered bond increases from $100 to $4,000 for each of the six young men arrested.) The state's attorney continued his speech. "Either those boys will have a chance to reflect in jail while they are waiting trial, or their parents, through the expense of getting them out on bond, will realize that

[1] This dialogue is quoted verbatim. Only names and obscenity are changed. The writer is grateful to many policemen in Chicago and prison officials in New York whose cooperation helped to formulate the ideas here.

parental irresponsibility doesn't pay." [2] His speech was longer. The boys might remember part of it, but we are sure they would like to forget that such a prominent man considered them "future hoodlums" and publicly proclaimed that not only they, but their parents as well, are tainted. Could the boys think: "He's important; he says we'll be criminals. He ought to know. I never thought I'd be a criminal; but he's a very important man." The public doesn't expect the state's attorney to furnish adequate homes, parents, playgrounds, and psychologists for these boys, so he doesn't bother with such details. But the public doesn't expect him to make these boys into permanent public enemies either.

The judge at the Boy's Court has many problems. Among some boys who had been arrested for participating in a riot, two were dismissed. Here's what the newspapers said about these two: "John ———, 21, of Chicago, a laborer, and his brother, 19, of Chicago, unemployed, were dismissed. They said they merely stopped nearby to see what the trouble was and were arrested. Judge ——— told the defendants: 'We're going to give you a break. We operate on the theory that every dog is entitled to one bite.'" [3] Here were two bystanders arrested, taken to jail, and then instead of getting an apology for being inconvenienced, the judge says he will invoke a canine justice. But this is no dog's court. These boys, like the judge, are human. What can the judge do? The police say, "They are guilty—we saw them rioting." The boys say, "We broke no law." Citizens, relatives, and neighbors testify, orate, hiss, and applaud both sides. The judge doesn't know who is right or what to do. The boys are our concern here. They may get the impression: "We are not like other human beings. We are bad."

What can the judge do? The voters are angry because there was a riot; the police are angry because the boys were not convicted; the boys, because they were arrested and scolded; the judge, because he too is on public trial in a difficult situation. Because of this many judges try to protect themselves and the public by utilizing medical, sociological, psychological, or other professional advice. Sometimes, though, they lose their tempers.

The writer has no quarrel with these officials. Thousands of such items appear in the papers every year. The point is that the police, state's attorney, and judges may not lead the defendants to expect honest, law-abiding behavior of themselves. If this were the end of it, probably the defendants would go back home and be upright citizens. The suggestions from the officials that they are disreputable might not be taken seriously. But this may not be the end.

Why should a solitary judge with fifty to one hundred cases in one

[2] Chicago Sunday *Tribune*, August 23, 1953, part 1, p. 25.
[3] Chicago *Daily News*, August 17, 1953, p. 3.

day be permitted to make such vital decisions? Crime hurts everyone. These decisions are too important for any one person to make.

Back Home. The boy goes back home. Whether or not he was found guilty, he is not quite like his friends any more. An object of curiosity: "What did they do to you?" "My lawyers defended me," he says. "I saw the judge." An object of adoration: his picture was in the paper; he has had his IQ measured; he has talked to lots of policemen. An object of scorn—he was arrested, put in jail with crooks—he is vicious. For some of his friends he is a hero; for others he must never be played with again. If he should see them, they turn away: "My mother says not to play with you. The state's attorney says you're a hoodlum."

Little boys soon forget. They play together as usual, except for those whose mothers are constantly reminding them, protecting them from the "criminal," the bad apple in the neighborhood. Then something happens again. The newspapers have a heyday. Who did it? The citizens are upset and impatient. They put pressure on the police. The police have to do something. Well, everyone knows who did it. Didn't someone just leave the detention home? Wasn't his name in the paper? It makes no difference that he was at school or visiting in another city when it happened. He is apprehended because he is convenient. He is found not guilty, but everyone suspects him just the same. He is getting a reputation, and a self-conception.

Lots of boys find their home life uncomfortable. Pick a child up off the street some night—say, at midnight. Take him home and you will see why he doesn't want to be home. His home may be physically repulsive; or it may be a lovely house but a miserable home. To say that it's the parent's fault misses the point. Most parents of delinquents are helpless, sorely in need of psychological, medical, religious or economic aid. Responsibility lies not with irresponsible parents but with the community.

We assume that parents mean well but many just do not have the energy and skills necessary to win the confidence of their children and to make plans together. Parents expect their children to mature gradually and become independent. That this can be done gracefully is proved by many happy parents who help their children settle on their own. Even in the better neighborhoods a barrier often develops between the parents and children. Most children on the street go home after a while and play inside, but some can't go home. In many instances help for the parents would prevent a child from going to the street.

On the Street. Our young citizen may find friends on the street where things are more pleasant, where he can be a hero. We assume everyone wants to be liked; everyone wants a word of praise, and if it is not available at home and is available on the street, then one goes to the street. A little boy knows where he is afraid to breathe and where he is a regular guy like all the rest.

The boys he plays with on the street may like to play volleyball. They have a volleyball and play all the time. They don't get into trouble. Or they may not have a volleyball. Slum children have less equipment than other children. What can you do on the street?

Everyone needs someone to idealize, someone to be like, someone to dream he is like. These street children could idealize their parents, but it is not likely since they don't enjoy their parents. Their hero could be a policeman who saves a man's life; but not if the policeman hurts them or depreciates them. We don't know enough about whom the street boys idealize. Maybe it's a famous boxer who can beat anyone in the whole world; or a cowboy movie star. These boys can't be cowboys; but they can fight, they can be brave, not afraid of their parents, not afraid of the police. They can learn to be tough.

If the street boy could get along with his mother, he might be home with her, learning to keep his room straight: "Freddie, hang up your clothes. Freddie, wash your hands; Freddie shine your shoes this minute. Freddie, here's some new crayons. That's a sweet boy." His mother cannot be at ease until she knows he is responding to her attempts at socialization.

The boys on the street are learning a different moral code: Who can throw the stone the straightest. Who can run faster. Who is a sissy. Who can do things and not get caught. Hundreds of times a day a boy is learning the code of the street: Be loyal to friends—never betray a comrade. Find out who you can trust. Avoid the police.

Street boys go to school. The teacher knows they have been in trouble and if anything out of the ordinary occurs in the classroom, she knows who is to blame. Even if they are not really to blame, she can guess who were the agitators. Because the street boys have more than average trouble at home, they may be more restless than the average pupils and not perform well in school. You can't want to please a teacher if this makes you a sissy, especially if this teacher is always picking on you or your friends. The teacher is not going to be his ideal or model. She could if she had a class of fifteen children instead of thirty to sixty and if her salary made it unnecessary to hold down an extra job or two, and if teachers had high morale, and if she had time to consult with parents, social workers, religious workers, a physician, a psychologist, a reading specialist, to discuss the boy's problems, and if she had professional training and attitudes. Sometimes she can do it without all these. But aren't we foolish to expect miracles of semitrained overworked teachers?

It takes most people years to settle down to one ego ideal. Little boys play at being policemen or cowboys or gangsters. When they are growing up they decide to be truck drivers or ambulance drivers or doctors. In school they want to be teachers or janitors or a principal or the coach. In college they want to be lawyers or scientists or philosophers or businessmen. After they leave college, they are deciding one day this, one day that. Who do I want to be like? What am I going to do? It takes years for the average citizen to decide.

Lots of people are helping the street boy to decide on his career. His mother and father and his home life are unbearable to him, so he joins the street boys. His friends on the street give him fellowship and praise for doing a good job. His teacher tells him he is too jumpy. The police suggest that he is a liar. The social worker suggests his family is tainted. The psychologist tells him he is not like other boys. The judge says, "Every dog deserves one bite." The state's attorney says, "You are the future hoodlums." Can one's career be that of a hoodlum?

Reform School. One day he is arrested, found guilty and goes to reform school. He is frightened and angry. He wishes he were home. He wants to find out: "Who are my friends and who are enemies?" He learns that some of the inmates are regular guys; others snitch on you. The guards, the hired hands around the place, can't be trusted; they are against you. "What are you here for?" a friend asks. "I grabbed a pocketbook and ran." "Is that all? Boy! I robbed five filling stations! You know that kid with the glasses, the tall blond one? He killed a policeman! When he says something, you'd better jump."

How do you rob a filling station? What do you do with the tires? Which lawyers will help you if you get caught? Which is the easiest way to rob the A&P? How do you steal a car? Where can you sell it? Who buys the parts? How can you be successful? This sounds like an exciting career. He never realized so many people are in this business. The reform school teaches much about crime, but little about reform.

The guards are afraid the boys will run away, hurt each other or hurt the guards. The superintendent has his job to do. He has to keep the boys clean, working, in school, has to buy the groceries, get a new psychologist to replace the one leaving for a better job, get three new attendants, make out dozens of reports, read what the wardens at other schools are doing, go to meetings, see visitors from the Rotary Club, decide what to do about a boy who is always fighting. If he is strict, the boys hate him more. If he is less strict, the place gets dirty and citizens complain; newspapers take pictures. There is never enough money. The superintendent does what he can. The boys are learning a career. They can't help it, and he can't help it. And the respectable citizens back home are not aware of the fact that they are paying $500 to $5,000 per year to train each child to become a more professional criminal. There is not one reform school which reforms. Foster homes are a much better risk, especially if foster parents get special training in ways to handle these children. It's hard to find parents who would take disturbed children, but anything seems better than the typical reform school.

After Reform School.   When the boy leaves the reform school, he goes home. He has been a disgrace to the family, and his welcome is thin: "Your mother is ashamed to walk down the street!" "We hope they reformed you." He is now perhaps nine, twelve, or fifteen years old. His sister says, "You have ruined my life." He wonders who his friends are. Maybe a brother is friendly to him. Maybe his mother. She gives him a new necktie. But can she give him what will save him from the electric chair or from a life sentence? If she can give him the trust and patience every boy needs much and he needs immensely, and if his other relatives and friends can, they can save him. Usually they cannot, any more than they could before reform school. If he is to be helped, it will be by foster parents or officials of the institutional kingdoms, school, church, scouts, PTA, settlement house, neighborhood center working as an integrated unit. Today these kingdoms often work in competition and at odds with one another.

It is easy in the neighborhood to tell who can be trusted. Plenty of guys make nasty remarks. They go to school; they go to Sunday school; they brush their teeth and say, "Good afternoon," to the corner policeman. When their mothers see the returned "criminal" in the drug store, they say: "Look who's out! If I see my boy playing with you I'll call the police. Stay away." You can understand that such mothers are trying to protect their own boys. But they are helping another boy to become a criminal. If good boys won't play with him, who will? Underworld characters?

Other mothers don't know much about him. They are working or sick or preoccupied. Their sons are the street boys. The boys want to know about reform school. Did they beat you? Let me show you what I learned. Let's pull a job tonight. I'll show you how to do it. I can chin with one hand.

He has to go to school. That's the law. The principal talks to him, the teacher talks to him, some kids talk to him, and what they say adds up to one thing: They are not his friends. They expect him to start something. It doesn't have to be that way. They could invite him to join the Scouts, or write on the school paper, or sing in the choir. If they did, it might save him.

His mother wants him to go to church. She has talked to the clergyman, who says he needs religion. He may not be as clean, as well dressed as the next boy—or he may be cleaner. The boy out of reform school wonders how his new clothes look. They feel strange. The people in Sunday school may not feel hostile toward him, but they are strangers. One looks at him in a friendly way; another says, "He just got out of reform school."

There is still a chance he won't go back to reform school, or graduate into prison, but the chance is slim. Let a window be broken, a store burglarized, a car stolen, and the neighbors will know who to blame. A nice neighborhood finds it easy to blame someone for its troubles, not only because he may be guilty, but because he is the one expected to perform such acts in this community. If he does not expect of himself what they expect of him, he will go straight, perhaps leaving the community, perhaps even changing the community, but that is unlikely.

Even after he comes to expect vicious or criminal behavior of himself, he may still act like a good citizen most of the time. But it appears that the self-concept, the picture of himself inside, is more powerful than anything else in determining his behavior. Here is part of an interview between a prisoner and a prison counselor to illustrate this:

PRISONER.   Why do I keep getting in trouble? I want to go straight, but I'll go out and before you know it I'm with the same crowd. I know it's wrong and yet there I am.

COUNSELOR.   Maybe you are forced back to the old crowd. Have you ever been treated like an ex-con?

PRISONER.   I was going with a girl and couldn't get the nerve to tell her I'd been in the pen. I knew she'd find out sooner or later. I kept wanting to give her up, I finally did in a way. I took to drinking.

COUNSELOR.   You had to. It's too much to bear. You knew she wouldn't understand.

PRISONER.   I began to hate her. She kept asking what was wrong and all that. In fact I don't think I minded it too much when I had to leave her, knowing what she would think of me.

COUNSELOR.   It's hard to love a person when you expect her to hate you.

PRISONER.   You know, she still comes to see me, so I was wrong about how she would feel.

The prisoner could not bring himself to tell his girl friend that he had been in jail for fear that she would hate him. Since it was not true that she hated him, we must conclude that the hatred was in himself, that he hated himself because he felt he was a criminal or because he expected her to hate him because he was a criminal. Of course, it is difficult for one who has been arrested many times to feel, "I'm an honest and respected man." He wanted to go straight but felt he was not honest. In not telling the girl, he was in fact dishonest. If he had felt he was an honest man, it would have been much easier for him to say, "I was convicted of a crime and spent some time in jail, but now I am honest."

But his self-conception must have been: "I'm a criminal. She would hate criminals like everyone else hates them, perhaps even as I myself do. So I can't tell her." With such a self-conception, he could not be comfortable around law-abiding citizens.

Gradually, over the years, if he comes to expect of himself what his neighbors expect of him, he becomes a professional criminal. But if along the way he can find satisfactions and social approval from legitimate activities, he will obey the law. When he has learned over and over again that he can find no satisfaction this way, he welcomes the greetings of his professional associates in the underworld. As a professional criminal, he has standards of performance to live up to, friends who will help him when in trouble, visit him in prison, send him presents at Christmas, give him a home when he is sick, tell him where the police are lax and where strict—hideouts, fences, and lawyers. At twelve, fourteen, sixteen, or eighteen he has come to a conclusion about his career that ordinary boys may not make until they are twenty or even forty. And he could not have drifted into this career without the help of his family and neighbors who sought a scapegoat and unwittingly suggested to him that he become an outlaw.

V. IMPLICATIONS

When a crime is committed in a community, it is, in a sense, caused by everyone. No one grows up and lives alone; the criminal grows up with people. He is molded by his social experiences. If he wants to murder, people have made him want to murder; if he wants to break school windows, his environment has taught him how and given him a reason. And if he is punished by the community, it is because the community feels guilty for his crime, for failing to provide positive experiences in schools, for not protecting him from severe cruelty, neglect, starvation, and rejection. Those in the community who most demand his punishment are usually those who feel most guilty for their own failures, real or imaginary. They punish the criminal as they have been punished themselves. If they could forgive themselves, accept themselves, they could forgive the delinquent, accept him, and, in accepting him, convert him before he becomes a hardened unconvertible criminal. This conversion process is usually too big a job for any one school, teacher, policeman, judge, psychologist or social worker. It takes many people to make an ordinary little boy into a hardened criminal. It will take a lot of people to make a disturbed little boy into a good citizen. Every little boy or girl in trouble should be examined by a physician, a psychologist, a reading specialist, a social worker, and his home and neighborhood should be studied. Intelligent steps can then be taken by this team of people working with the community council, with the cooperation of the boy and taking into consideration his preferences, to give this boy what everybody needs: security, affection, adventure, a chance to get recognition, to learn and to give to others the best that he has to give.

Every city and hamlet has some special programs for handling delinquents. Every program in every city is different from the next. Naturally, some are better than others. Study and systematic evaluation of these programs is required so that we can find out what works and what does not. At present we do not know.

36. CHILDREN WHO HATE

FRITZ REDL

What are delinquents? Are they simply average children who are misunderstood, who have had bad breaks, but are ready to become good, smiling little boys and girls if given half a chance? Or are they thoroughly lost children for whom there is no hope?

Redl presents some enlightening views growing out of his work at Pioneer House, a home for incorrigible boys. He describes with brilliant insight how delinquent children try to gratify antisocial impulses and to avoid the burden of a guilty conscience. His analysis gives new meaning and power to the concepts of the id, ego, and superego in dynamic conflict.

THE CONCEPT OF "EGO" AND OUR CLINICAL TASK

Psychoanalytic theory has different names for what is . . . called, with intended colloquial looseness, the "control system." The psychoanalysts would relegate the "control" of impulsivity to two separate "systems," which constitute special "parts of our personality," the superego and the ego. Sometimes there is a third one described in psychiatric literature, the "ego ideal," but we think we can safely adopt a widespread custom of considering it as a special part of the ego and reduce the basic issue to just the two. For the non-psychiatric reader it may be explained that the "superego" is more or less the same as the "conscience." It is that part of the personality whose job it is to remind us of value issues that arise in daily living. The "ego" is supposed to "keep us in touch with reality," a statement whose specific meaning will soon be amplified. The distinction between "ego" and "superego" is not as difficult as it is made

Selections reprinted from *Children Who Hate* (The Free Press, 1951) by permission of the publisher.

out to be. If a youngster doesn't take a dollar which just fell out of his mother's purse because he is afraid of being caught and getting thrashed, then we would say that it was his "ego" which limited his possessive urge along the line of "reality consequences." If a youngster doesn't take that dollar, even though he is certain nobody would ever find out, because he would feel bad to do anything which he considers to be a sin, such as stealing, then we would credit his "superego" with the success in impulse control. The concept of superego will be discussed more fully later. First, that peculiar agent within us which was given the name "ego" long ago by Sigmund Freud will be examined.

.   .   .   .   .

Freud himself developed this concept of the ego only late and gradually and subjected its conception to many changes and improvements. . . . It was primarily his daughter, Anna Freud, who elevated the ego and its mechanisms of defense to a respected place in therapy, especially in work with children. Since then, speculations about the intimate and not always peaceful interrelationship between the "ego" and the superego and many other details have taken increasing space in psychoanalytic literature. The growing interest of psychoanalysts in work with schizophrenics has given "ego" psychology another boost, and the need to bring psychoanalytic conceptualization closer to the action scene, which was especially increased through the development of all sorts of "group therapy," has added its push. Foregoing the fascination of portraying those details and what they mean for the therapist, we shall be satisfied with attempting to sketch what, today, we usually conceived as the "tasks of the ego."

From what Freud and his followers said, and from what can be inferred from the way they use the term in context when applying it to clinical observations, the "ego" actually is expected to fulfill at one time or another, the following functions:

I. COGNITIVE FUNCTION

A. *Cognitive Function, Externalized.* It has always been conceived as one of the main tasks of the ego to establish contact with the "outside world." In this respect, it seems to be the job of the ego to size up just what the "world around us" is like, and to give adequate signals about its imminent promises or dangers to our well-being. This vague notion of "sizing up outside reality" must, of course, today be replaced by a much more specific breakdown into at least two sides of this "outside world." One is what we may call the "Physical Reality." That means, it is the job of the ego to estimate actual dangers or advantages inherent in physical situations. "I don't want to go to that dentist today," says my anxiety-ridden and comfort-greedy id. "You had better get there fast. Remember what they found out about tooth decay and dentist bills if you wait too long?" my ego is supposed to chime in. The other side of "reality demands" to which we are subject in this world might be shortly and rather crudely summarized as "Social Reality." By this is meant that the behavior of other people, individually or in groups, directly or through their institutionalized laws, customs, pressures, etc., is also a factor to be reckoned with. It is obviously also the function of the ego to become aware of existing reality limitations from that source and to give appropriate warning signals, should our behavioral urges threaten to run into conflict with them. Even a child who is clearly delinquent in his value identification, that means, one with little "superego" at all, would be expected to have his ego make a careful assessment of just in which case stealing is "safe", in which other case the very openly enjoyed and guilt-free act of stealing had better be omitted because of "reality risks" involved in discovery, capture, too threatening legal consequences, or difficulty in getting rid of the loot. In short, it is the ego's job to size up the world around us, in its physical or social aspects, and to give danger signals if any one of our desires is too seriously in conflict with the "reality outside." . . .

B. *Cognitive Function, Internalized.* In the earlier definitions of the ego, its function of "establishing contact with the world around us," was usually emphasized. From the way the concept is now being used, though, it is obvious that an emphasis on a "cognitive appraisal of what is going on inside us" is an equally important job. In fact, some of the basic definitions of the role of psychoanalytic therapy are based on that very issue, namely, on the assumption that some id-contents cannot be got hold of by the ego, because they are repressed, that means, not even accessible to the conscious perception by the ego. If the ego doesn't even know what is going on, how can it get hold of it? This was the underlying tenor of the thinking even in the early stages of theory development leading to the demand that the repressed be made conscious. We can portray the situation implied in the following way:

Cognitive Appraisal of Its Own Id. By this we mean the awareness by the ego of the most important impulses, urges, desires, strivings, fears, etc., that obviously motivate our behavior, but are not necessarily always known to us. To know as much as possible about what is really going on "in the cellar of our unconscious" always has been a primary job of the ego, if it wants to retain or regain its health. In other words, it seems that all insights, including those into ourselves, are a function of the "ego."

Cognitive Appraisal of Its Own Superego. It is also one of the tasks of the ego to register "value demands" coming from within, not only to register "reality threats" coming from without. It is the job of the ego to know which behavior would run counter to what the specific personality "believes in," what its own superego considers fair or decent, or which behavior would, if allowed to go through, produce the horror of deep shame and nagging guilt. Ample evidence was produced in later psycho-analytic work to show that superego particles, too, can be unconscious and repressed. In those cases, it is the ego's job to become aware of the voice of its own conscience, and the therapist's task to help the ego onto that road. In short, "know thyself" does not only mean "know what your most secret strivings would make you do if they had a chance," but also "know what price you would have to pay in guilt feelings, should you give in to them."

II. THE POWER-FUNCTION OF THE EGO

Though not always implied in the definitions, it has always been assumed that the task of an ego that is in good working order is not only to "know" what reality demands are, but also to exert some force, so as to influence behavioral strivings in line with that knowledge. Or, in other words, if my ego is smart enough to tell me I "ought" to go to the dentist today, but not "strong" enough to get me there, it does only half its job and is not much help to me really. This "Power Function" of the ego is a most fascinating metapsychological problem, because we have so far wondered and speculated a good deal as to just where the ego is supposed to get the "power" to suppress impulses and drives. This problem was a difficult one in the early phases of theory, when the ego was supposed to be little more than a "voice" telling us about the world outside. We have come a long way since then. We have to assume, for any usable concep-tion of the ego, that it somewhere has access to a power system and then can use whatever energies it has at its disposal to enforce the dictates of its insights upon our pleasure-greedy impulse system. By the way, this is what we should mean when we say an ego is "weak." Unfortunately, the term "weak" is also used freely to indicate simply that an ego doesn't function well. We shall limit our use of the term "ego weakness" only to those situations where a disturbance of its power function is clearly meant.

III. THE SELECTIVE FUNCTION OF THE EGO

When confronted with an outside danger or an inner conflict, it is not enough to know what the situation is and to be ready to block in-admissible impulses—the ego has a few other decisions to make. For there is usually more than one way to react. The old idea that all the ego has to do is to decide whether an impulse can be afforded or not is an oversimplification which needed debunking long ago. Even in the most flash-like and simple situation, where the ego resorts to ready-made, stereotyped, reflex-like "defense mechanisms," it still has to select one from quite a number. Let's assume that a child suddenly becomes aware that the rest of his pals are engaged in some "dirty talk" which seems highly status-loaded in their gang but of which he doesn't understand a word because of parental overprotection and lack of sophistication. He has a variety of ways in which to react to the emerging conflict. He can deny his desire to be in on the talk. He can add "reaction formation" to this trick to make it more foolproof. Then he will get very indignant at the very insinuation that he might want to know about things like this and will even ward off his friendly therapist's help along the line of sex information. He may, on the other hand, simply withdraw, and this he may do on different levels and with varying scope. He may, for instance, simply avoid being near those bad boys; he may try not to have to play with them. On the other hand, he may ask to be transferred to a different group. Or he may have to cement his withdrawal with wild accusations and gossip propaganda against these youngsters. Finally, he may not do any of these things. He may successfully repress during daytime what is going on inside him, only to be flooded with bad dreams or night terrors, or plagued by insomnia or anxiety attacks.

Of course, our youngster doesn't have to resort to these automatic defense mechanisms at all. In that case he has to meet the problem on a reality level. Then, his ego has to make even more far-reaching decisions. Maybe he simply can tell his father and have a man-to-man talk and ask him what all those things the kids are talking about mean. Maybe he can ask another boy or his counselor. Or maybe his group skills are so well developed that he simply forces or inveigles the others into "cutting him in on it," swallowing the unavoidable transitional razzing he will get in order to solve the problem once and for all. In these cases, too, his ego will have quite a job to do. It will not only have to appraise just which of these paths are open to it but it will have to "inspect the tool by which reality is being met" as to its potential ability to solve the problem. It will have something like a "tool selection job in terms of efficiency appraisal" to perform.

IV. THE SYNTHETIC FUNCTION OF THE EGO

The concept of a synthetic function, a much later addition to ego psychology, has led into fascinating but also specifically metapsychological speculations. One of the latest studies around this issue is that of Nunberg. Here, we do not want to enter into such metapsychological speculations. We are using the term "synthetic function" in a somewhat simplified way. This is what we have in mind: if we assume that there are a number of "parts of the personality" at work, each one apparently equipped with some "influence" in the internal household affairs, then the job of putting them all together and keeping them in some sort of balance with each other must somewhere be ascribed to "somebody" in the picture. We suggest that the ego be given this task. In other words, it is also the ego's job to decide just how much a personality shall be predominantly influenced by the demands of the impulse system, the demands of outside reality, the dictates of its own conscience. It seems that "personality disbalance" can result from any one of a number of "wrong" assortments of power distribution. For instance, if the superego is allowed to dominate far beyond what an individual can sacrifice and still remain healthy and happy, you get a virtuous person, who will finally break down under his own frustrations or have to become hostile and nasty for the same reason. On the other hand, if impulsivity is entirely rampant, the present state of happiness will soon be destroyed by the conflict with the "outside world" which may result in lifelong incarceration, or by the "nagging guilt" from within, if too strongly established value issues are allowed to be violated by a too little vigilant ego. In brief, it is the job of the ego to balance the various demand systems and to keep this balance "reasonable" on all sides. We think, by the way, that the term "balanced personality" should be reserved for this issue rather than be used as widely as is currently the custom. The most glaring illustration of a one-sided handling of the synthetic function by the ego is the one which will engage us soon, namely, the case where the ego throws its weight entirely on the side of impulsivity or of a delinquency-identified superego —a situational distortion for which we plan to use the term "delinquent ego."

THE EGO AND THE CONCEPT OF DELINQUENCY

. . . . .

When we talk about the "delinquent ego" here, we have two things in mind:

1. We use the term "delinquent" in its cultural meaning—referring to any behavior which runs counter to the dominant value system within which the child's character formation takes place. Thus, we would include his insistence on "hate without cause," even where no clearly legally punishable act was involved. We mean all the attitudes which will be developed in a child who is about to drift into a "delinquent style of life."

2. As far as the "ego" side of the picture goes, we want to describe the ego in those situations in which it is bent on *defending impulse gratification at any cost*. In short, instead of performing its task of looking for a synthesis between desires, reality demands, and the impact of social values, the ego is, in those moments, totally on the *side of impulsivity*. It throws all its weight into the task of making impulse gratification possible, against the outside world as well as against whatever remainders of the voice of its own conscience may be left. The amazing spectacle which we have before us in the children who hate lies right here: Sometimes these children seem to act wrong and confused simply because their ego is inefficient and cannot, as described before, manage the onrush of im-

pulsivity in complex life situations. At other times, the situation is different indeed. Far from being helpless, the ego of these children is suddenly a rather shrewd appraiser of that part of reality which might be dangerous to their impulsive exploits and becomes an efficient manipulator of the world around them as well as an energetic protector of delinquent fun against the voice of their own conscience. Just which specific task the "delinquent ego," by which we mean from now on the ego's effort to secure guilt-free and anxiety-free enjoyment of delinquent impulsivity, may have to fulfill, will depend upon other details of a youngster's personality. Some, for instance, are identified with a delinquent behavior code anyway. Their own superego being delinquency identified already, guilt feelings won't bother them. The task of their ego is primarily to make it possible to "get away with things" and to defend their delinquency against the threat of the world around them. Others are not quite that advanced. They still have mighty chunks of their value-identified superego intact; the voice of their conscience still tries to make itself heard. In that case, the "delinquent ego" has the additional task of "duping its own superego," so that delinquent impulsivity can be enjoyed tax-free from feelings of guilt. In still another case, neither value-identified nor delinquent superego allegiances are very strongly developed. Those children are like a "bundle of drives," and their ego seems to have primarily a "reality manipulative task." These details are fascinating but irrelevant here. In all three cases we shall receive the full brunt of an efficient ego, bent on the task of impulse protection, when we try to educate or treat such children. Far from acting delinquent out of helplessness or just because of an occasional onrush of unusual impulse intensity, these children have an organized system of defenses well developed and meet the adult who tries to change them with a consistent and well-planned barrage of counter-techniques.

.   .   .   .   .

Once a child has part of its ego so clearly throwing its weight toward the side of the defense of delinquency, we are saddled with an entirely new task. In order to "free" the youngster of his delinquent urges, we have to take the hurdle of strategic impulse defense by their ego. With such children, therefore, the exact study of just how their ego goes about to defend their impulsivity against their own conscience, as well as against the outside world, becomes a matter of prime importance. Since the material gained from the psychiatric treatment of the basically neurotic delinquent has produced little insight into the "tough defense machinery" we are referring to here, it is worth while to give it our full attention. Indeed, the development of a successful "total treatment strategy" in a residential treatment design hinges upon this very ability to know their *ego strengths as well as their ego disturbances.* The detailed tracing of the machinations of the delinquency-protective ego of our Pioneers would run into several volumes. We have to restrict ourselves here, therefore, to a mere listing of the most discernable "ego functions in the service of impulse defense."

THE STRATEGY OF TAX EVASION

Our Pioneers did not fall into the category of children who simply have "no superego at all," or who are harmoniously identified with a totally delinquent neighborhood code, as the classical "healthy delinquent" is supposed to be. In fact, we never met a child who would fit that description. Even the toughest children with whom we had to deal would reveal, upon closer inspection, that the aggressive front of behavior with which they would surround themselves needed many "special tricks" to be maintained at all. Below the behavioral surface, there would be a great number of little "value islands" left—stemming out of isolated remainders of earlier childhood identification, from the automatic absorption of non-delinquent elements in the general "code of behavior" which even a delinquent neighborhood still has sprinkled around, or out of occasional real ties or dependencies with people which couldn't quite be avoided after all. In short, even the ego of the toughest delinquent doesn't have quite as simple a job as we might assume. While visibly expert in the task of producing delinquent behavior without much concern, it has quite a job to perform in order to keep all phases of that behavior from being "tax exempt" from feeling of guilt. The children we talk about have many such "value islands" in their personalities, and consequently their ego spends much time seeing to it that what they do can be enjoyed without the price of guilt feelings. In fact, they have little trouble "getting away" with a good deal of behavior for the moment. To really "get away" with doing all this without feeling bad about it afterwards, however, seems to be an additional job. It is fascinating to watch the special machinery these children's ego has developed in order to secure their behavior against post-situational guilt feelings.

. . . . .

The following is a fairly cursory list of such "tax evasion from guilt feelings" techniques which we could amply observe at Pioneer House as well as at camp:

REPRESSION OF OWN INTENT

Some of our youngsters have an enviable skill of repressing, right after an incident happens, its actual emotional gain and of course everything that would betray their basic motivation to begin with. This repression accomplished, they can now afford to remember, relate or brag about any other detail of the incident without having to fear that the voice of their conscience might be raised in this process.

One of the youngsters at camp had stolen a wallet from a counselor whom he actually liked a lot, and whose "fairness toward him" he had openly and repeatedly recognized before. The specific child had a perfectly "delinquent" superego as far as stealing as such was concerned, but his own value standard would reject as very "unfair" "to be mean to somebody who had been nice to you." When confronted with his misdeed, he had no trouble remembering, admitting, and discussing freely the details of his theft. When challenged, not along the line of having stolen, but of having been mean to somebody who had been so nice to him, he blocked entirely, couldn't remember a thing about just "why" he might have wanted to do a thing like that, assuring us that he didn't mean to hurt the adult, he just needed the cash in the wallet. As long as he could keep up this separation of issues for himself, he was perfectly safe. He would have liked nothing better than to be punished for the delinquent side of the act, so as to be sure not to be confronted with the real "guilt" as far as he was concerned. It took considerable interview work in this specific case until, much later, the child was able to allow himself to become aware of the full impact of his own love for the adult, of the specific fantasies which had gone into the theft, and could be helped to cope with the feelings of guilt which then, post-situationally, suddenly arose.

By the way, it is our experience that sudden *blocking* in a "grilling" interview does not always mean an attempt to hide from discovery. The inability of children to produce at all, when challenged in a way similar to that of the example, is sometimes a direct indication that we have hit upon an area in which real value sensitivity might still be intact.

HE DID IT FIRST

We do not mean the case, here, where a youngster tries to ward off blame by shoving it off onto somebody else. We actually mean that the mere fact that "somebody else did it first" would really constitute a chance not to have to feel guilty for something he did. We have pointed at this basic principle of "exculpation magics through the initiatory act" before. We do not claim that we can explain it, but have to state it as a simple matter of fact: Conscience can be assuaged at times by the simple awareness that the guilt-producing behavior was entered in only after somebody else had already openly done what one only intended to do. Needless to point out, this is a most "illogical" way of thinking, and no system of ethics we could conceive of actually supports such argument. For the Unconscious, however, it seems to be a fact that, for "intramural use" so to speak, priority of somebody else's guilt takes away the tax burden of guilt feelings quite well.

For a long time, at camp, we were fooled by considering the youngsters with the most patent trend to accuse others, as the more "delinquent ones."

For some of them that is still correct. We had to learn, though, that sometimes this actually works the other way around. The great need to find somebody who did it first need not come from a need to be revengeful or accusatory, but may, on the contrary, point to the very intact part of the youngster's superego. Only because he would really have to feel guilty for what he did, does a child sometimes seek so hard to find somebody else to blame.

EVERYBODY ELSE DOES SUCH THINGS ANYWAY

This is a well-known device even among adult sinners, and easily enters the "self-apologetic" argument of otherwise honorable people, especially where obligations to larger issues are involved. Many people who wouldn't steal one cent from another person's pocket find their morals crumbling if something can be pointed out as "general business practice." This kind of "logic," again, is equally indicative of two facts: that this special person's superego can be easily punctured, and also that there is still something that needs puncturing by a special trick.

.   .   .   .   .

WE WERE ALL IN ON IT

.   .   .   .   .

On one occasion the whole Pioneer group had been involved in a very dangerous and destructive episode of throwing bricks from the top of the garage. We decided to have individual interviews with each of the boys to "rub-in" the total unacceptability of such behavior. Andy, especially, was fascinating in his real indignation at even being approached on the subject. Tearfully he shouted at the Director who was doing the interviewing, "Yeah, everybody was doing it and you talk to me. Why is it my fault?" When it was pointed out to him that we were not saying it was all his fault but that he was responsible for his individual share in the matter, he was still unable to admit the point: "But we were all in on it. Why talk to me?"

BUT SOMEBODY ELSE DID THAT SAME THING TO ME BEFORE

As an open argument, such a statement seems incredible and void of all sense. An efficient delinquent ego, though, knows to what wonderful use it can be put, when the task of warding off guilt feelings arises. In fact, we had many children, after long interview work, really come out with this "theory of exculpation" in open declaration. After we had finally crowded them enough so that they could not any longer ward off the guilt issue involved in what they did, they found a last refuge, in arguing with themselves and with us, in this device. They really tried to prove that their stealing was all right because "somebody swiped my own wallet two weeks ago." Needless to add, only a rather primitive ego can still afford to get away with an alibi trick like that.

.   .   .   .   .

Two items need to be stressed to avoid a misunderstanding of what we have tried to point out in this whole section on the strategy of tax evasion. One is, again, the importance of differentiating between the mechanisms described here and a use of any such "arguments" in order to fool authority figures or as a semi-legalistic device to soften the punitive implication of a misdeed for which one has been caught. Wherever the latter is being done, the same arguments quoted here may be used, but we then have to deal with an entirely different layer of "defenses of the delinquent ego." . . . What we have in mind in the section on tax evasion is an actual attempt of the ego to ward off *inner* conflict between the children's own conscience and what they do. That is, their ego uses these devices to make delinquent behavior possible and to keep it guilt free, not to ward off outside consequences. The existence and usability of such defenses always prove both the energetic effort of the child's ego to protect his delinquency from his own "better self," and the existence of some parts of an intact conscience or superego—for the really "valueless" youngster wouldn't need any of this at all, and would simply enjoy his delinquent fun with a defiant "so what?" attitude. As in the case of the emergence of resistance in the treatment of neurotics, the defenses employed here prove both the existence of pathology and the functioning of the ego defending it. Thus, the careful study of such "alibi tricks" would help us in the diagnosis of what the enemy of our treatment effort is doing and, at the same time, also offer us additional insight into those parts of a child's superego which are still intact. The clinician, as well as the educator, might welcome both.

The other item to be stressed here and elaborated upon later on is, of course, the great impact of all this for practice. And this part is relevant not only for the educator of the disturbed child, but also for the parent and educator of his normal age mate. For, what is disturbance later on usually was a perfectly legitimate phase of development at an earlier time. The very type of "alibi tricks" children have to employ in the defense of their search for happiness which will irritate adults gives us a wonderful picture of just which level of superego development they have achieved, which is still to be entered into, where potential distortions might lurk. For the therapist of a disturbed child, the implications of all this are equally serious—for it means that in those cases the problem is not one of "ego support" but one of *superego support* and ego *repair*. The areas in which children act in the way we described are not the ones where their ego is "weak" or "disturbed." On the contrary, these seem to be hypertrophically developed ego functions—only applied in the service of the wrong goal. The result of these hypertrophic ego skills applied for the wrong goal must not be confused with the evidence of other areas in which the ego is weak or disturbed in its functioning, though any one child may, and usually does, show a mixture of both. . . .

The statement that a specific child simply has no conscience or superego at all is being bandied about rather freely these days. In fact, some quite elaborate terminology has been invented to label such far-reaching claims. Frankly, we think that this is the bunk. Among all the hundreds of children who were supposed to be without a conscience and with whom we lived quite closely for varying lengths of time, we haven't yet found one to whom such an exaggerated diagnosis would apply. We admit, though, that we were often tempted to make such a statement about a particular child, especially when we were angry at him, when our own middle-class sensitivities were rubbed the wrong way by what he said or did, when our lack of familiarity with his natural habitat made us blind to the fact that his conscience simply talked to him in a language different from the one ours would use, including four letter words. . . .

1. PECULIARITIES IN VALUE CONTENT

As far as the content of specific values goes, our youngsters showed three clearly differentiated peculiarities rather than just an "absence of superego." The first one might be described as *clear identification areas with a delinquent neighborhood code.* By this we imply that our youngsters have accepted some value demands from parents and from their surrounding community, but it so happens that these value demands are themselves of a delinquent nature. From the outside, this may make our children look as though they had "no values at all," but the clinical difference between that and what we really had before us is enormous and of great relevance. Some of their proud display of crude violence, which the middle-class clinician finds so embarrassing to watch, and some of their open bragging about acts of theft or about their deceit in "getting away" with thefts are openly contradictory to the value system by which we would judge. And often enough such behavior simply meant that our youngsters were "value blind" or "value defiant." It would be too easy, though, to shift the whole problem onto this simple explanation. We observed many instances where we were quite certain that such attitudes were *not* expressive of value defiance against the system in which they operated, but that their behavior was really "innocent." By this we mean that they acted that way because they felt in line with the value scale of their own parents and their natural habitat. Thus, when bragging about crude and unjust violence and when proud of a cleverly gotten away with theft, these children were sometimes not only not rebellious, but actually value-conforming as far as their natural habitat goes. Doing things like these, they did what any good child, obedient to his elders and conforming to the mores of the community, would do. The only trouble was that the parental and communal values themselves were out of focus with the general middle-class value scale. Clinically speaking, though, this makes such acts not acts of value rebellion but acts of value conformism. The conflict in those cases was between the standards of their natural habitat and ours, not between the child's impulse and his superego. . . .

In other moments of their lives, our youngsters did not give the impression of nearly total value absence or conflict. Sometimes they showed a sudden emergence of what we might term *"childhood value islands"* which was surprising to watch.

This means that, tough as they were, they would suddenly display very obviously non-delinquent, quite middle-class-like value issues which emerged out of nowhere. The fact seems to be that even a delinquent neighborhood in which children may grow up is not so consistently delinquent in its behavior code, so far as children are concerned, as it may be in its adult affairs. Toward their own children even the adults from tough neighborhoods sometimes practice a much more "civilian" type of behavior code than in their own lives. Also, the fact that children were rejected, had nobody to love and identify with, is rarely true to as high a degree as such overgeneralized statements seem to imply. It seems that even neglected children rescue some one or other "relationship memory" out of the debris of their infancy, and that occasional "identification loopholes" pierce the seemingly impenetrable wall of human coldness and disinterest.

As far as our Pioneers go, there were moments in our otherwise conflict-studded life with them, when individual youngsters would suddenly come through with unexpectedly value-identified statements or attitudes. "You see, that comes from not doing what Emily told you," one of the otherwise most recalcitrant ones would be overheard saying to his pal. Sometimes one of them would suddenly be ashamed when caught in some especially vehement swearing, and would explain his feelings by saying that "Kids aren't supposed to say such things in front of adults." Occasionally, the appearance of a visitor, which usually led to a great display of exhibitionistic toughness, would surprisingly throw the group or individual members of it into scenes of "Let's introduce our guest to our dear housemother, who is so kind to us all." Especially in moments of child-adult happiness, primarily focused around child-housemother, or child-cook, relationships, real value concern or guilt around an act of unfairness would crop up freely, seemingly from nowhere. Such value islands would emerge much too early for us to think that we produced them. They obviously had been there all the time, and now began to emerge out of the debris of general value warfare, as a remainder from earlier times.

. . . . .

2. INADEQUACY OF THE SIGNAL FUNCTION

The pathology of a sick conscience does not necessarily have to lie in the inadequate value content coverage. It may have its main trouble in a disturbance of the job of "giving value danger signals." These, indeed, were often very weak in our children. Where a normal child would feel some anticipatory pangs of conscience, even before he decided how he would act, our youngsters would have only a very dim awareness that what they were about to do wasn't so good. Thus, even in areas which were covered by value identifications, the very weakness of the voice of their conscience would often mean that it remained unheard amidst the noise of temptational challenge. This made it easy for their ego to ignore it entirely whenever feasible. Sometimes our youngsters seemed to suffer also from another incapacity of a sick conscience, but one which is more often found in the neurotic rather than the delinquent child. They seemed to have what we might term a "post-action conscience." A superego suffering from this disease is of no help at all. It is value identified, all right. But it does not raise its voice in a moment of temptation. It confines itself to screaming all the more loudly after the deed has been committed. Colloquial usage tends to throw this type of disturbance in together with the previous one, referring to both as a "weak conscience." Yet, clinically speaking, we have obviously an entirely different disturbance before us. This type of conscience acts, in fact, as many of the parents of such children acted earlier in their lives. They were, initially, too disinterested or rejective to care much how their children fared, or to give them any help to go straight. Then, if something went wrong, they would literally descend upon the child with the full blast of their revenge for the discomfort the child had caused them. This, in turn, would be followed by another stretch of disinterest, of lack of supervision and care. In some moments of their lives, the conscience of our youngsters would react in exactly the same way. It would produce some feelings of guilt after a too obvious misdeed, but would still give no anticipatory value danger signal in the next temptational situation. This special disease of "post-action conscience" constitutes an important challenge to the task of superego repair. While the behavioral results are the same as with the child who has no conscience to begin with, its cure needs to take an entirely different path.

THE COMPLEXITY OF SUPEREGO REPAIR

In this chapter we have isolated the "superego" or "conscience" of the child as though it were a part all by itself. This was unavoidable for the purpose of a crude sketch and rough outline of its main functions and their disturbance types. Before we forget the real complexity of our clinical task, though, we had better hasten to put things into context again. For, were only the superego of our children disturbed, the task would be comparatively simple. In fact, most normal and neurotic children also show isolated disturbances of their conscience as we have described them here, and we can often cope with them along the line of re-education, case work, and psychiatric treatment. The children who hate constitute a special problem over and beyond all that. Their deficient and sick conscience happens to coincide with a deficient or delinquent ego. That makes for a combination which seems to defy our usual treatment channels, and which taxes even the most ingenious "total treatment strategy" to the utmost.

Let us assume for a moment that we were lucky or skillful and discovered an old value island or even inserted a new value identification into Danny's life. What a clinical triumph that would constitute all by itself! Yet, where would it lead us if we achieved that much before we were able to bring his "ego" up to par? If Danny, for instance, suddenly feels guilty for acting "so mean" toward us—and what a healthy feeling that would be—what does it get us, so long as his ego cannot cope with even a normal feeling of guilt? From our description of that type of ego disturbance we can easily forecast the chaos in which this will result. Feeling guilty for having been unfair to us, Danny will have to have an anxiety attack or a temper tantrum, or he will have to destroy things which remind him of this obligation or guilt toward us. So the behavior result will be wild, even though we obviously scored a great therapeutic success so far as his superego goes. Or, to raise another complication, let's assume that we "strengthen" Joe's ego enough so that it suddenly is able to be more perceptive of the reality around him than it has been before. Where does that get us unless we also give his conscience more power over his life? For ego strength *per se* is a small gain, as our chapter on the "delinquent ego and its techniques" ought to have shown. On the other hand, how can we get Joe even to see the implication of his earlier deeds unless his ego is first strengthened to be self-perceptive enough of his own motives and to be socially sensitive enough to stop his delusional persecutory fantasies by which he defends himself from the impact of love?

The worst combination of all, though, is not that of superego deficiency and ego deficiency, but of superego deficiency and delinquency-identified ego strength. With the children who simply suffer from a maldeveloped conscience, we would have only one area of sickness to combat. With the children who combine such pathology with the impressive ego strength of the "delinquent ego and its defenses," . . . we have an indeed formidable combination arrayed against us. How can we ever get "value identifications" across against such hypertrophically developed defensive skills? What good would the breakdown of such defenses be to our clinical goals if we could not pull the value switch equally fast? Breaking down their ego defenses without supplying them with livable values at the same time will only leave us with ego-deficient children, not with the product we are supposed to deliver.

37. THE WAY OF ALL FLESH

SAMUEL BUTLER

The novelist, in creating the characters for his story, may reach back into his own intimate experience and thus reveal a great deal about his relations with those who were close to him. Butler's novel, from which these excerpts are taken, is reputed to be autobiographical, the parents being patterned after those of the author. Butler's insistence that the novel be published only after his death indicates that his hatred of his father, however strong, was tempered by feelings of compassion and guilt.

INTRODUCTION

. . . The worst misfortune that can happen to any person, says Butler, is to lose his money; the second is to lose his health; and the loss of reputation is a bad third. He seems to have regarded the death of his father as the most fortunate event in his own life; for it made him financially independent. He never quite forgave the old man for hanging on till he was eighty years old. He ridiculed the Bishop of Carlisle for saying that we long to meet our parents in the next world. "Speaking for myself, I have no wish to see my father again, and I think it likely that the Bishop of Carlisle would not be more eager to see his than I mine." Melchisedec "was a really happy man. He was without father, without mother, and without descent. He was an incarnate bachelor. He was a born orphan."

CHAPTER XX

The birth of his son opened Theobald's eyes to a good deal which he had but faintly realised hitherto. He had had no idea how great a nuisance a baby was. Babies come into the world so suddenly at the end, and upset everything so terribly when they do come: why cannot they steal in upon us with less of a shock to the domestic system? His wife, too, did not recover rapidly from her confinement; she remained an invalid for months; here was another nuisance and an expensive one, which interfered with

From *The Way of All Flesh* by Samuel Butler. Everyman's Library. Reprinted by permission of E. P. Dutton & Co., Inc.

the amount which Theobald liked to put by out of his income against, as
he said, a rainy day, or to make provision for his family if he should have
one. Now he was getting a family, so that it became all the more necessary to put money by, and here was the baby hindering him. Theorists
may say what they like about a man's children being a continuation of his
own identity, but it will generally be found that those who talk in this
way have no children of their own. Practical family men know better.

About twelve months after the birth of Ernest there came a second,
also a boy, who was christened Joseph, and in less than twelve months
afterwards, a girl, to whom was given the name of Charlotte. A few
months before this girl was born Christina paid a visit to the John Pontifexes in London, and, knowing her condition, passed a good deal of time
at the Royal Academy exhibition looking at the types of female beauty
portrayed by the Academicians, for she had made up her mind that the
child this time was to be a girl. Alethea warned her not to do this, but she
persisted, and certainly the child turned out plain, but whether the pictures caused this or no, I cannot say.

Theobald had never liked children. He had always got away from
them as soon as he could, and so had they from him; oh, why, he was inclined to ask himself, could not children be born into the world grown
up? If Christina could have given birth to a few full-grown clergymen in
priest's orders—of moderate views, but inclining rather to Evangelicism,
with comfortable livings and in all respects facsimiles of Theobald himself—why, there might have been more sense in it; or if people could buy
ready-made children at a shop of whatever age and sex they liked, instead
of always having to make them at home and to begin at the beginning
with them—that might do better, but as it was he did not like it. He felt
as he had felt when he had been required to come and be married to
Christina—that he had been going on for a long time quite nicely, and
would much rather continue things on their present footing. In the matter
of getting married he had been obliged to pretend he liked it; but times
were changed, and if he did not like a thing now, he could find a hundred
unexceptionable ways of making his dislike apparent.

It might have been better if Theobald in his younger days had kicked
more against his father: the fact that he had not done so encouraged him
to expect the most implicit obedience from his own children. He could
trust himself, he said (and so did Christina), to be more lenient than perhaps his father had been to himself; his danger, he said (and so again
did Christina), would be rather in the direction of being too indulgent;
he must be on his guard against this, for no duty could be more important than that of teaching a child to obey its parents in all things.

He had read not long since of an Eastern traveller, who, while exploring somewhere in the more remote parts of Arabia and Asia Minor, had
come upon a remarkably hardy, sober, industrious little Christian com-

munity—all of them in the best of health—who had turned out to be the actual living descendants of Jonadab, the son of Rechab; and two men in European costume, indeed, but speaking English with a broken accent, and by their colour evidently Oriental, had come begging to Battersby soon afterwards, and represented themselves as belonging to this people; they had said they were collecting funds to promote the conversion of their fellow tribesmen to the English branch of the Christian religion. True, they turned out to be impostors, for when he gave them a pound and Christina five shillings from her private purse, they went and got drunk with it in the next village but one to Battersby; still, this did not invalidate the story of the Eastern traveller. Then there were the Romans —whose greatness was probably due to the wholesome authority exercised by the head of a family over all its members. Some Romans had even killed their children; this was going too far, but then the Romans were not Christians, and knew no better.

The practical outcome of the foregoing was a conviction in Theobald's mind, and if in his, then in Christina's, that it was their duty to begin training up their children in the way they should go, even from their earliest infancy. The first signs of self-will must be carefully looked for, and plucked up by the roots at once before they had time to grow. Theobald picked up this numb serpent of a metaphor and cherished it in his bosom.

Before Ernest could well crawl he was taught to kneel; before he could well speak he was taught to lisp the Lord's prayer, and the general confession. How was it possible that these things could be taught too early? If his attention flagged or his memory failed him, here was an ill weed which would grow apace, unless it were plucked out immediately, and the only way to pluck it out was to whip him, or shut him up in a cupboard, or dock him of some of the small pleasures of childhood. Before he was three years old he could read and, after a fashion, write. Before he was four he was learning Latin, and could do rule of three sums.

As for the child himself, he was naturally of an even temper; he doted upon his nurse, on kittens and puppies, and on all things that would do him the kindness of allowing him to be fond of them. He was fond of his mother, too, but as regards his father, he has told me in later life he could remember no feeling but fear and shrinking. Christina did not remonstrate with Theobald concerning the severity of the tasks imposed upon their boy, nor yet as to the continual whippings that were found necessary at lesson times. Indeed, when during any absence of Theobald's the lessons were entrusted to her, she found to her sorrow that it was the only thing to do, and she did it no less effectually than Theobald himself; nevertheless she was fond of her boy, which Theobald never was, and it was long before she could destroy all affection for herself in the mind of her firstborn. But she persevered.

CHAPTER XXI

Strange! for she believed she doted upon him, and certainly she loved him better than either of her other children. Her version of the matter was that there had never yet been two parents so self-denying and devoted to the highest welfare of their children as Theobald and herself. For Ernest, a very great future—she was certain of it—was in store. This made severity all the more necessary, so that from the first he might have been kept pure from every taint of evil. She could not allow herself the scope for castle building which, we read, was indulged in by every Jewish matron before the appearance of the Messiah, for the Messiah had now come, but there was to be a millennium shortly, certainly not later than 1866, when Ernest would be just about the right age for it, and a modern Elias would be wanted to herald its approach. Heaven would bear her witness that she had never shrunk from the idea of martyrdom for herself and Theobald, nor would she avoid it for her boy, if his life was required of her in her Redeemer's service. Oh, no! If God told her to offer up her first-born, as He had told Abraham, she would take him up to Pigbury Beacon and plunge the—no, that she could not do, but it would be unnecessary—some one else might do that. It was not for nothing that Ernest had been baptised in water from the Jordan. It had not been her doing, nor yet Theobald's. They had not sought it. When water from the sacred stream was wanted for a sacred infant, the channel had been found through which it was to flow from far Palestine over land and sea to the door of the house where the child was lying. Why, it was a miracle! It was! It was! She saw it all now. The Jordan had left its bed and flowed into her own house. It was idle to say that this was not a miracle. No miracle was effected without means of some kind; the difference between the faithful and the unbeliever consisted in the very fact that the former could see a miracle where the latter could not. The Jews could see no miracle even in the raising of Lazarus and the feeding of the five thousand. The John Pontifexes would see no miracle in this matter of the water from the Jordan. The essence of a miracle lay not in the fact that means had been dispensed with, but in the adoption of means to a great end that had not been available without interference; and no one would suppose that Dr. Jones would have brought the water unless he had been directed. She would tell this to Theobald, and get him to see it in the . . . and yet perhaps it would be better not. The insight of women upon matters of this sort was deeper and more unerring than that of men. It was a woman and not a man who had been filled most completely with the whole fulness of the Deity. But why had they not treasured up the water after it was used? It ought never, never to have been thrown away, but it had been. Perhaps, however, this was for the best too—they might have been tempted to set too much store by it, and it might have become a source of spiritual danger to them—perhaps even of spiritual pride, the very sin of all others which she most abhorred. As for the channel through which the Jordan had flowed to Battersby, that mattered not more than the earth through which the river ran in Palestine itself. Dr. Jones was certainly worldly—very worldly; so, she regretted to feel, had been her father-in-law, though in a less degree; spiritual, at heart, doubtless, and becoming more and more spiritual continually as he grew older, still he was tainted with the world, till a very few hours, probably, before his death, whereas she and Theobald had given up all for Christ's sake. *They* were not worldly. At least Theobald was not. She had been, but she was sure she had grown in grace since she had left off eating things strangled and blood—this was as the washing in Jordan as against Abana and Pharpar, rivers of Damascus. Her boy should never touch a strangled fowl nor a black pudding—that, at any rate, she could see to. He should have a coral from the neighbourhood of Joppa—there were coral insects on those coasts, so that the thing could easily be done with a little energy; she would write to Dr. Jones about it, etc. And so on for hours together day after day for years. Truly, Mrs. Theobald loved her child according to her lights with an exceeding great fondness, but the dreams she had dreamed in sleep were sober realities in comparison with those she indulged in while awake.

When Ernest was in his second year, Theobald, as I have already said, began to teach him to read. He began to whip him two days after he had begun to teach him.

"It was painful," as he said to Christina, but it was the only thing to do and it was done. The child was puny, white and sickly, so they sent continually for the doctor who dosed him with calomel and James's powder. All was done in love, anxiety, timidity, stupidity, and impatience. They were stupid in little things; and he that is stupid in little will be stupid also in much.

Presently old Mr. Pontifex died, and then came the revelation of the little alteration he had made in his will simultaneously with his bequest to Ernest. It was rather hard to bear, especially as there was no way of conveying a bit of their minds to the testator now that he could no longer hurt them. As regards the boy himself anyone must see that the bequest would be an unmitigated misfortune to him. To leave him a small independence was perhaps the greatest injury which one could inflict upon a young man. It would cripple his energies, and deaden his desire for active employment. Many a youth was led into evil courses by the knowledge that on arriving at majority he would come into a few thousands. They might surely have been trusted to have their boy's interests at heart, and must be better judges of those interests than he, at twenty-one, could be expected to be: besides if Jonadab, the son of Rechab's father—or perhaps it might be simpler under the circumstances to say Rechab at once—if

Rechab, then, had left handsome legacies to his grandchildren—why Jonadab might not have found those children so easy to deal with, etc. "My dear," said Theobald, after having discussed the matter with Christina for the twentieth time, "my dear, the only thing to guide and console us under misfortunes of this kind is to take refuge in practical work."

EDITORS' SUMMARY OF CHAPTERS XXXVIII AND XXXIX

[Ernest became very fond of a remarkably pretty servant girl named Ellen, who, it was discovered, was very ill—and pregnant. There was no question about what should be done with Ellen: she should receive her wages and be packed off immediately. The only question was, who did it? Ernest? The mother thought about it. When innocent Ernest found out that Ellen was gone, almost penniless, he ran after the carriage, caught it—all out of breath—and gave Ellen his watch and the few shillings he had. Of course, this made Ernest late for dinner. What should he tell his parents? The truth? Oh, no! They would surely punish him. So he told them he had lost his watch, and was looking for it. His conscience troubled him deeply.]

CHAPTER XL

. . . Next day and for many days afterwards he fled when no man was pursuing, and trembled each time he heard his father's voice calling for him. He had already so many causes of anxiety that he could stand little more, and in spite of all his endeavours to look cheerful, even his mother could see that something was preying upon his mind. Then the idea returned to her that, after all, her son might not be innocent in the Ellen matter—and this was so interesting that she felt bound to get as near the truth as she could.

"Come here, my poor, pale-faced, heavy-eyed boy," she said to him one day in her kindest manner; "come and sit down by me, and we will have a little quiet confidential talk together, will we not?"

The boy went mechanically to the sofa. Whenever his mother wanted what she called a confidential talk with him she always selected the sofa as the most suitable ground on which to open her campaign. All mothers do this; the sofa is to them what the dining-room is to fathers. In the present case the sofa was particularly well adapted for a strategic purpose, being an old-fashioned one with a high back, mattress, bolsters and cushions. Once safely penned into one of its deep corners, it was like a dentist's chair, not too easy to get out of again. Here she could get at him better to pull him about, if this should seem desirable, or if she thought fit to cry she could bury her head in the sofa cushion and abandon herself to an agony of grief which seldom failed of its effect. None of her favourite manœuvres were so easily adopted in her usual seat, the armchair on the right hand side of the fireplace, and so well did her son know from his mother's tone that this was going to be a sofa conversation that he took his place like a lamb as soon as she began to speak and before she could reach the sofa herself.

"My dearest boy," began his mother, taking hold of his hand and placing it within her own, "promise me never to be afraid either of your dear papa or of me; promise me this, my dear, as you love me, promise it to me," and she kissed him again and again and stroked his hair. But with her other hand she still kept hold of his; she had got him and she meant to keep him.

The lad hung down his head and promised. What else could he do?

"You know there is no one, dear, dear Ernest, who loves you so much as your papa and I do; no one who watches so carefully over your interests or who is so anxious to enter into all your little joys and troubles as we are; but, my dearest boy, it grieves me to think sometimes that you have not that perfect love for and confidence in us which you ought to have. You know, my darling, that it would be as much our pleasure as our duty to watch over the development of your moral and spiritual nature, but alas! you will not let us see your moral and spiritual nature. At times we are almost inclined to doubt whether you have a moral and spiritual nature at all. Of your inner life, my dear, we know nothing beyond such scraps as we can glean in spite of you, from little things which escape you almost before you know that you have said them."

The boy winced at this. It made him feel hot and uncomfortable all over. He knew well how careful he ought to be, and yet, do what he could, from time to time his forgetfulness of the part betrayed him into unreserve. His mother saw that he winced, and enjoyed the scratch she had given him. Had she felt less confident of victory she had better have foregone the pleasure of touching as it were the eyes at the end of the snail's horns in order to enjoy seeing the snail draw them in again—but she knew that when she had got him well down into the sofa, and held his hand, she had the enemy almost absolutely at her mercy, and could do pretty much what she liked.

"Papa does not feel," she continued, "that you love him with that fulness and unreserve which would prompt you to have no concealment from him, and to tell him everything freely and fearlessly as your most loving earthly friend next only to your Heavenly Father. Perfect love, as we know, casteth out fear: your father loves you perfectly, my darling, but he does not feel as though you loved him perfectly in return. If you fear him it is because you do not love him as he deserves, and I know it sometimes cuts him to the very heart to think that he has earned from you a deeper and more willing sympathy than you display towards him.

Oh, Ernest, Ernest, do not grieve one who is so good and noble-hearted by conduct which I can call by no other name than ingratitude."

Ernest could never stand being spoken to in this way by his mother: for he still believed that she loved him, and that he was fond of her and had a friend in her—up to a certain point. But his mother was beginning to come to the end of her tether; she had played the domestic confidence trick upon him times without number already. Over and over again had she wheedled from him all she wanted to know, and afterwards got him into the most horrible scrape by telling the whole to Theobald. Ernest had remonstrated more than once upon these occasions, and had pointed out to his mother how disastrous to him his confidences had been, but Christina had always joined issue with him and showed him in the clearest possible manner that in each case she had been right, and that he could not reasonably complain. Generally it was her conscience that forbade her to be silent, and against this there was no appeal, for we are all bound to follow the dictates of our conscience. Ernest used to have to recite a hymn about conscience. It was to the effect that if you did not pay attention to its voice it would soon leave off speaking. "My mamma's conscience has not left off speaking," said Ernest to one of his chums at Roughborough; "it's always jabbering."

When a boy has once spoken so disrespectfully as this about his mother's conscience it is practically all over between him and her. Ernest through sheer force of habit, of the sofa, and of the return of the associated ideas, was still so moved by the siren's voice as to yearn to sail towards her, and fling himself into her arms, but it would not do; there were other associated ideas that returned also, and the mangled bones of too many murdered confessions were lying whitening round the skirts of his mother's dress, to allow him by any possibility to trust her further. So he hung his head and looked sheepish, but kept his own counsel.

"I see, my dearest," continued his mother, "either that I am mistaken, and that there is nothing on your mind, or that you will not unburden yourself to me: but oh, Ernest, tell me at least this much; is there nothing that you repent of, nothing which makes you unhappy in connection with that miserable girl Ellen?"

Ernest's heart failed him. "I am a dead boy now," he said to himself. He had not the faintest conception what his mother was driving at, and thought she suspected about the watch; but he held his ground.

I do not believe he was much more of a coward than his neighbours, only he did not know that all sensible people are cowards when they are off their beat, or when they think they are going to be roughly handled. I believe that if the truth were known, it would be found that even the valiant St. Michael himself tried hard to shirk his famous combat with the dragon; he pretended not to see all sorts of misconduct on the dragon's part; shut his eyes to the eating up of I do not know how many hundreds of men, women and children whom he had promised to protect; allowed himself to be publicly insulted a dozen times over without resenting it; and in the end, when even an angel could stand it no longer, he shilly-shallied and temporised an unconscionable time before he would fix the day and hour for the encounter. As for the actual combat it was much such another *wurra-wurra* as Mrs. Allaby had had with the young man who had in the end married her eldest daughter, till after a time, behold, there was the dragon lying dead, while he was himself alive and not very seriously hurt after all.

"I do not know what you mean, mamma," exclaimed Ernest anxiously and more or less hurriedly. His mother construed his manner into indignation at being suspected, and being rather frightened herself she turned tail and scuttled off as fast as her tongue could carry her.

"Oh!" she said, "I see by your tone that you are innocent! Oh! oh! how I thank my heavenly Father for this; may He for His dear Son's sake keep you always pure. Your father, my dear"—(here she spoke hurriedly but gave him a searching look) "was as pure as a spotless angel when he came to me. Like him, always be self-denying, truly truthful both in word and deed, never forgetful whose son and grandson you are, nor of the name we gave you, of the sacred stream in whose waters your sins were washed out of you through the blood and blessing of Christ," etc.

But Ernest cut this—I will not say short—but a great deal shorter than it would have been if Christina had had her say out, by extricating himself from his mamma's embrace and showing a clean pair of heels. As he got near the purlieus of the kitchen (where he was more at ease) he heard his father calling for his mother, and again his guilty conscience rose against him. "He has found all out now," it cried, "and he is going to tell mamma—this time I am done for." But there was nothing in it; his father only wanted the key of the cellaret. Then Ernest slunk off into a coppice or spinney behind the Rectory paddock, and consoled himself with a pipe of tobacco. Here in the wood with the summer sun streaming through the trees and a book and his pipe the boy forgot his cares and had an interval of that rest without which I verily believe his life would have been insupportable.

38. MATERNAL OVERPROTECTION

DAVID M. LEVY

*This study of "spoiled" children and their long-suffering parents
reveals that both are trapped by circumstances in narrowing,
mutually coercive, exasperating servitude. Levy observes the
relationships of twenty overprotected children to their overprotecting
parents, to school, and to other children; he also describes the
relationships of the parents to each other and discusses the later
adjustments of these children to adult life.*

The most frequent clinical type of maternal overprotection . . . is
found in the group in which the overprotection masks or is compensatory
to a strong rejection. It will be considered separately.

There remain a number of mild and mixed forms that require description. Early overprotection followed by rejection is an example. Theoretically, a frank rejection of a child may be followed by "pure" overprotection. . . . A mother absorbed in a first child and indifferent to the second may, after a dangerous illness of the second child has necessitated
much nursing care on her part, shift about in her attitudes. Such cases are
of the guilt-overprotection form. There are children, also, who experience
temporary periods of overprotection, or alternating periods of overprotection and rejection, or mixtures of overprotection and severity. In this connection, those children also should be included who are seen by their
mothers for brief periods of time during the day, yet, in the time available,
receive strongly overprotective care. They are often children of professional women. The latter act as though they must make up for their hours
of absence from the child through the intensity of their devotion in every
minute of contact.

"Mild" maternal overprotection is presumably an attenuated form
and very common. A quantitative distribution of overprotective manifestations would show, no doubt, a graduated progressive series. In the
mild forms, however, many extraneous problems complicate evaluation
and selection. Since we are dealing with mothers of various cultural backgrounds and of different economic and social groups, patterns of maternal
behavior with children, correctly estimated as overprotective in one
group, may in another group be typical phenomena. Breast feeding over a

Selections reprinted from *Maternal Overprotection* (Columbia University Press,
1943) by permission of the publisher.

period of two years, for example, may be a symptom of overprotection. On the other hand, it may be typical behavior in certain cultural groups.

.   .   .   .   .

A clinical classification of overprotection includes 1. *pure,* 2. *guilt,* 3. *mixed,* 4. *mild,* and 5. *nonmaternal* forms.

Here are three examples of Group I, the "pure" form:

CASE 1 (MALE, 8 YEARS)

Excessive Contact.   When he was an infant mother could never leave him for a instant. When he was two years old, she had moods of despondency because she could not get away from him. She feels worried and unhappy when patient is out of her sight. Has been sleeping with him the past six months because he has called her. Lies down with him at night. Extra nursing care has been required because of his frequent colds. Mother says they are attached together like Siamese twins.

Prolongation of Infantile Care.   Mother dresses him every day (age 8), takes him to school every morning and calls for him every afternoon. When at school in the morning she pays the waiter for his lunch and tells waiter what to give him. Breast fed 13 months. Mother fed him the first five years. Mother still goes to the bathroom with him and waits for him. Mother insists on holding his hand when they walk together. Resents his walking alone.

Prevention of Independent Behavior.   He has one friend whom mother takes him to see every two weeks. Mother does not allow him to help in housework for fear he'll fall and break a dish, etc.

Maternal Control.   Mother must have a light burning for him until he falls asleep. He goes to bed at 10 P. M. Mother always gives in to him; does everything for him; is dominated by him. He spits at her and strikes her.

.   .   .   .   .

CASE 5 (MALE, 13 YEARS)

Excessive Contact.   Mother has slept with him the past three years. Up to age 7, she never let him go out with any adult (even father) except herself.

Prolongation of Infantile Care.   When the patient is disobedient she puts him to bed in the afternoon, even now. She still prepares special food for him when he refuses to eat. She still sits by and coaxes.

Prevention of Independent Behavior.   Mother delayed his schooling until he was seven because she did not like him to leave her. She blocks the plan of sending him to boarding school. She kept him from having friends or learning bad things from other children. When he was sent to camp at 14, the mother visited him on the second day, found that his feet were wet and took him home.

Maternal Control.   General obedient, submissive response to maternal domination. Uses aggressive methods to maintain his dependency on the mother, insisting she walk to school with him, et cetera.

.   .   .   .   .

CASE 10 (MALE, 12 YEARS)

Excessive Contact. There is frequent kissing and fondling. The mother practically never let him alone during infancy. She kept him away from all but a few adults because she was afraid of infection. Patient still sleeps with the mother when father is out of town (continued to age 13).

Prolongation of Infantile care. Patient was breast fed 12 months. Mother still waits on him, gets water for him, butters his bread, etc.

Prevention of Independent Behavior. Mother has prevented his bicycling, making his own friends, and has generally prevented the development of responsibility.

Maternal Control. The patient is disrespectful and impudent to the parents. He constantly demands mother's service, and had a temper tantrum at the age of twelve because she didn't butter his bread for him. He resents giving up his chair for mother. He leaves the table and refuses to eat when he doesn't get the biggest piece.

. . . . .

PLAYMATES

A tabulation of the number of playmates of children of overprotecting, rejecting and "other" mothers has been made. Divided into groups of "none or one" and "few or many," the table shows a trend of increasing number of playmates as we go from the "over-protecting" mothers, to "rejecting," and to "neither."

A study was also made to determine if there is a relationship between the number of companions of parents and children. The study revealed a distinct tendency towards increase in number of companions of the child with increase in the number of social contacts of the parents.

The findings are consistent also with the observation that in case of pure overprotection the mother narrows down her social life to the child.

EXCESS OF CONTACT

Excessive contact is manifested in continuous companionship of mother and child, prolonged nursing care, excessive fondling, and sleeping with the mother long past infancy. The twenty "pure" cases (Group I) contained six boys who slept with their mothers long past infancy, three of them during adolescence. Of the latter, two showed overt evidence of direct sexual response or conflict, though none showed overt incestuous behavior. Of the former, one showed active incestuous behavior. In the remaining fourteen cases of Group I, no overt sexual response to the mother was revealed.

INFANTILIZATION

. . . . .

The data of infantilization concern feeding, dressing, bathing, washing, punishing and various kinds of behavior typical for children of younger years. Glaring examples are shown by a mother who helps her thirteen-year-old son dress; and by another who still butters bread and gets water for a twelve-year-old; by another who punishes a thirteen-year-old son by putting him to bed in the afternoon. Such examples are typical of many others illustrating the behavior of mothers who have prolonged the infantile method of handling into the older years.

Mothers in Group I demonstrate singly or in combination three types of infantilizing activity. Commonest is the continuation of breast feeding, a prolongation of the mother-infant relationship. Five mothers showed this type of infantilization with little or no evidence of the other forms. Six mothers gave evidence of prolonged breast feeding in combination with other forms.

The other two types of infantilization show a difference of degree, in which the child has a greater measure of control. A mother may wait on her child "hand and foot," yet may allow him to bathe and dress himself. In the gradual relinquishing of infantile care, breast feeding first gives way, then bodily care, and finally, the "waiting on" the child for services he can perform himself. The last form of infantilization includes services that adults may perform for each other, services that some of our overprotected children demand. Yet the same children may prevent the mother's insistent efforts to continue bathing and dressing them.

MATERNAL CONTROL

. . . . .

Under *maternal control* are included all available data of maternal discipline. Such control in Group I mothers is manifested by exaggerations of normal maternal domination or indulgence of the child, and described as overdomination and overindulgence.

Overindulgence consists in yielding to wish or actions of a child or submitting to his demands to an extent not tolerated by most parents. Overindulgence appears in active form through willing catering to the child's whims or wishes, and in passive form through surrender to the child's demands. Overindulgence in its extreme form would be manifested by complete maternal surrender to the child.

Both phases of maternal activity in the control of children can be studied most conveniently in an indirect way; *i.e.*, by collection of data on the response of children in this phase of maternal overprotection. Since children of overindulgent mothers display various rebellious symptoms disturbing to parents, they are more likely to be referred for treatment than children of overdominating mothers, since the latter are obedient and submissive.

In the Group I cases, nine children appear to be overdisciplined. All but one have been infantilized also to some degree. The absence of infantilization in the one case leads to a doubt of its proper inclusion in a group of so-called "pure" cases, since instances of maternal overdomination, without other evidence of overprotection, represent an essentially different type of mother-child relationship.

The activity of the child in initiating maternal overprotection appears more striking in the overindulgent than in any other phase of overprotection.

Eleven of the twenty Group I mothers who overindulge show numerous instances of submission to the tyranny of infantile demands. . . . In spite of long citations of what they had to endure, only three of the eleven overindulgent mothers sought help directly.

THE MOTHER-FATHER RELATIONSHIPS

As potent sources of increased maternal longing for a child, varieties of experience threatening the possibility of successful termination of pregnancy were gathered from the records of the overprotecting mothers. Of the 20, 13 yielded such instances: long periods of sterility (5); death of offspring (3); spontaneous miscarriages (3); and serious complications of pregnancy (3), preceding the birth of the patient.

An attempt was made to determine from available data whether unconscious wishes for the state of sterility operated in the instances given. It appeared likely in one case. The question was considered as to whether overprotection of any variety must be considered a neurosis, a compensatory reaction to unconscious hostility to the child, based on feelings of guilt and resembling obsessional neurosis. It was argued that such a position would refute the possibility of a normal maternal response, since if a normal response may be assumed, its increase in the presence of stronger stimuli must also be assumed.

Sixteen instances of sexual maladjustment were found in the group, a relatively high frequency as compared with check groups. In itself the difficulty was regarded as a strengthening factor of the overprotection, by the method of simple compensatory increase in mother love through blocking other channels of expression.

Fifteen instances were found in which there was little social life in common among the parents of the overprotected child. Of the five remaining cases in which there was a good general social relationship, two were sexually incompatible. The severe curtailment in mutual social activity, as in the mother's own general activity, was determined in most instances primarily by the mother-child relationship. Where the mother's social life was limited almost entirely to the child, the overprotecting data appeared especially striking with regard to infantilization and to attempts to prevent the child from making friends with other children.

Of the 20 overprotecting mothers, severe privation of parental love in their childhood was found in 16. Of these the death of one or both parents occurred in nine. Of the four cases in which an affectionate relationship with parents was recorded, there was evidence of some impoverishment of affection in terms of contact in three. The privation of all those positive feelings implicit in parental love, called "affect hunger," was regarded as an important consideration in understanding the overprotecting relationship, since the child could be utilized as a means of satisfying the abnormal craving for love resulting from affect hunger.

All but two of the 20 overprotecting mothers (Group I) were responsible, stable, and aggressive. The responsible attitude was manifested in stability of work, measured by steadiness of employment, and also in active helping out. The active or aggressive feature of the responsible behavior was regarded as a distinctly maternal type of behavior; it characterized the lives of 18 of the 20 overprotecting mothers since childhood.

Though evidence of thwarted ambitions for a career occurred in 12 instances in the group, the number checked by studies of contrast groups was not considered, in itself, significant.

. . . . .

As in humans, variations in the component maternal drives occur in animals, even in virgin rats, and are measurable. They show also a high degree of plasticity in the presence of external stimuli, in fact, to such a degree that, for example, the lactation period in the rat has been prolonged twenty times the normal by supplying the mother with successive litters of young. Two instances of maternal overprotection in monkeys were cited.

. . . . .

The fathers of the overprotected children studied were, in general, submissive, stable husbands and providers who played little or no authoritative role in the lives of their children. They made a ready adjustment to the maternal monopoly of the child, some adding to the infantilizing care (three cases). Twelve, in all, maintained an affectionate relationship with the child, five showed little or no affection, and the remaining three were out of contact due to divorce, desertion, and absence from the home.

A consistent pattern of submissive adaptation was revealed in the backgrounds of the fathers. Seven were obedient and favorite children, five were obedient sons of dominating mothers, and three, obedient sons of dominating fathers. Of the 18 fathers interviewed, there was only one instance in which evidence of difficulty as a husband was due to aggressive behavior towards the wife. With two exceptions, all the fathers in the group were stable and responsible workers. The group of parents represent a logical choice of dominating maternal women and submissive responsible men.

The usual patterns of interfering relatives were found in the group. In five cases their activities were important in the life of the child, and consisted chiefly in adding to the indulgence of the mother, and weakening her discipline.

. . . . .

BEHAVIOR OF THE OVERPROTECTED

The behavior of the indulged overprotected children was featured by disobedience, impudence, tantrums, excessive demands, and varying degrees of tyrannical behavior. The characteristics described were thought to represent accelerated growth of the aggressive components of the personality, and related directly to maternal indulgence. Limitations in the production of extreme tyrannical and possessive behavior at home was explained by varying degrees of parental modification, and external factors.

Most of the indulged overprotected children presented no special problems in school adjustment. This discrepancy between behavior at home and at school was explained by an exceptional and disciplinary attitude towards schoolwork on the part of the mothers; by satisfactions in the classroom related to high intelligence, verbal skill, and help through coaching on the part of the children; also, possibly, to their fear of the school group and a gratification in playing an obedient role. In any event, the adjustment of highly indulged children to classroom discipline indicates a high degree of flexibility in their personalities. When difficulties in classroom behavior occurred, they were consistent with the type of difficulty manifested at home.

Three boys who were disciplinary problems in the classroom were less intelligent than the others and their mothers less concerned about schoolwork.

In contrast with the indulged group, the dominated group responded well to the requirements of classroom behavior in every instance, regardless of I.Q. or of school success.

In all instances but one, difficulties in making friendships with other children occurred. The aggressive children showed, with one exception, "domination" or egocentric difficulties, that is, bossy, selfish, show-off, or cocky behavior. The submissive children showed in all cases but one timidity and withdrawal. There was a remarkable similarity of all the children's difficulty in relationship with their mothers and other children.

Successful adjustment of the indulged overprotected child to camp, as to school, would indicate that his difficulty with playmates could be improved, despite maternal overprotection, if opportunity were afforded for early social experience with children. Difficulties in making friendships were attributed to paucity of contact with children in the preschool age and lack of skill in play and sports, besides the problems inherent in the mother-child relationship. Follow-up studies indicated improvement in this regard during adolescence.

Some form of overt sexual behavior in childhood was noted in six instances, all in the indulged group. No problem in sex abnormality was present. The entire group showed nothing unusual in the frequency or form of masturbation.

Despite the very close attachment, including six cases in which children slept with their mothers long past infancy, follow-up studies into late adolescence or adult life failed to reveal an instance of sex abnormality. The theoretical aspect of this finding was discussed and the inference drawn that in maternal indulgent overprotection, the development of heterosexual behavior was hastened rather than delayed, because of lessened inhibitions.

The main outside interest of the overprotected group consisted in reading. There was a notable lack of interest in sports.

Feeding problems occurred in 12 of the 20 cases. The usual variety was manifested; in the form of bad table manners, refusal to eat on schedule, insistence on being fed or coaxed, finickiness, and refusal to eat certain foods. There was no instance of inappetence. Practically all the indulged overprotected were included in this group. The problems were consistent with maternal indulgence in regard to the feeding.

Nothing unusual was found in regard to sleeping difficulties. Problems related to sleep were in the form of refusal to go to bed, on time or without mother's company. Seven of the eight children who manifested such behavior were in the indulged overprotected group.

No problems in soiling occurred. There were but two cases of enuresis. The number was much less frequent than in other Institute cases. This difference was explained by the greater care exerted by overprotecting mothers. The assumption that the vast majority of problems in enuresis are originally due to neglect in training was supported by special data.

Information regarding cleanliness and care of possessions was available for 11 cases. The four who were very careless in this regard were all in the indulged group. Those noted as neat and careful were all in the dominated group.

Physical examinations revealed that the group of 20 overprotected children was taller and heavier than other groups, in keeping with the high degree of maternal care. Of the group, two only may be regarded as quite obese.

Errors of refraction were found in 11 cases. The inference that this relatively large number may have been due to excessive reading could not be determined, through lack of comparable data.

Treatment of organic difficulties seemed clearly related to improvement of social adjustment in two cases. In two others, organic factors were apparently reinforcing to the maternal over-protection. In three cases, findings during the physical examination served to overcome maternal apprehension. It was followed in one case by withdrawal of interest in the entire study.

In the cases presented, maternal overprotection appeared to be related directly to increased breast feeding, early bladder control, frequency of tonsillectomy, good nutrition, and probably obesity. It appeared to be related, indirectly, to correction of errors of visual refraction.

Manifestations of personality difficulties were revealed during the physical examination in 14 of the 20 cases. They were seen chiefly in the form of dependency on the mother, sensitivity, shyness, and bids for the examiner's attention.

39. SONS AND LOVERS

D. H. LAWRENCE

The Oedipus Complex—the jealous need of both father and son for the mother's love—was first identified by Freud. Here D. H. Lawrence presents a fictional family where everyone expresses contempt for the father and the attachment between mother and son becomes crippling to both. The distorted relationships he portrays can be found in many actual families—perhaps his own.

THE EARLY MARRIED LIFE OF THE MORELS

. . . . .

When she was twenty-three years old, she met, at a Christmas party, a young man from the Erewash Valley. Morel was then twenty-seven years old. He was well set-up, erect, and very smart. He had wavy black hair that shone again, and a vigorous black beard that had never been shaved. His cheeks were ruddy, and his red, moist mouth was noticeable because he laughed so often and so heartily. He had that rare thing, a rich, ringing laugh. Gertrude Coppard had watched him, fascinated. He was so full of colour and animation, his voice ran so easily into comic grotesque, he was so ready and so pleasant with everybody. Her own father had a rich fund of humour, but it was satiric. This man's was different: soft, nonintellectual, warm, a kind of gambolling.

She herself was opposite. She had a curious, receptive mind, which found much pleasure and amusement in listening to other folk. She was clever in leading folk on to talk. She loved ideas, and was considered very intellectual. What she liked most of all was an argument on religion or philosophy or politics with some educated man. This she did not often enjoy. So she always had people tell her about themselves, finding her pleasure so.

In her person she was rather small and delicate, with a large brow, and dropping bunches of brown silk curls. Her blue eyes were very straight, honest, and searching. She had the beautiful hands of the Coppards. Her dress was always subdued. She wore dark blue silk, with a peculiar silver chain of silver scallops. This, and a heavy brooch of twisted gold, was her only ornament. She was still perfectly intact, deeply religious, and full of beautiful candour.

Walter Morel seemed melted away before her. She was to the miner that thing of mystery and fascination, a lady. When she spoke to him, it was with a southern pronunciation and a purity of English which thrilled him to hear. She watched him. He danced well, as if it were natural and joyous in him to dance. His grandfather was a French refugee who had married an English barmaid—if it had been a marriage. Gertrude Coppard watched the young miner as he danced, a certain subtle exultation like glamour in his movement, and his face the flower of his body, ruddy, with tumbled black hair, and laughing alike whatever partner he bowed above. She thought him rather wonderful, never having met anyone like him. Her father was to her the type of all men. And George Coppard, proud in his bearing, handsome, and rather bitter; who preferred theology in reading, and who drew near in sympathy only to one man, the Apostle Paul; who was harsh in government, and in familiarity ironic; who ignored all sensuous pleasure;—he was very different from the miner. Gertrude herself was rather contemptuous of dancing; she had not the slightest inclination towards that accomplishment, and had never learned even a Roger de Coverley. She was a puritan, like her father, high-minded, and really stern. Therefore the dusky, golden softness of this man's sensuous flame of life, that flowed off his flesh like the flame from a candle, not baffled and gripped into incandescence by thought and spirit as her life was, seemed to her something wonderful, beyond her.

.   .   .   .   .

The next Christmas they were married, and for three months she was perfectly happy: for six months she was very happy.

He had signed the pledge, and wore the blue ribbon of a teetotaller: he was nothing if not showy. They lived, she thought, in his own house. It was small, but convenient enough, and quite nicely furnished, with solid, worthy stuff that suited her honest soul. The women, her neighbours, were rather foreign to her, and Morel's mother and sisters were apt to sneer at her ladylike ways. But she could perfectly well live by herself, so long as she had her husband close.

Sometimes, when she herself wearied of love-talk, she tried to open her heart seriously to him. She saw him listen deferentially, but without understanding. This killed her efforts at a finer intimacy, and she had flashes of fear. Sometimes he was restless of an evening: it was not enough for him just to be near her, she realized. She was glad when he set himself to little jobs.

He was a remarkably handy man—could make or mend anything. So she would say:

"I do like that coal-rake of your mother's—it is small and natty."

"Does ter, my wench? Well, I made that, so I can make thee one."

"What! why it's a steel one!"

"An' what if it is! Tha s'lt ha'e one very similar, if not exactly same."

She did not mind the mess, nor the hammering and noise. He was busy and happy.

But in the seventh month, when she was brushing his Sunday coat, she felt papers in the breast-pocket, and, seized with a sudden curiosity, took them out to read. He very rarely wore the frock-coat he was married in: and it had not occurred to her before to feel curious concerning the papers. They were the bills of the household furniture, still unpaid.

"Look here," she said at night, after he was washed and had had his dinner. "I found these in the pocket of your wedding-coat. Haven't you settled the bills yet?"

"No. I haven't had a chance."

"But you told me all was paid. I had better go into Nottingham on Saturday and settle them. I don't like sitting on another man's chairs and eating from an unpaid table."

He did not answer.

"I can have your bank-book, can't I?"

"Tha can ha'e it, for what good it'll be to thee."

"I thought—" she began. He had told her he had a good bit of money left over. But she realized it was no use asking questions. She sat rigid with bitterness and indignation.

The next day she went down to see his mother.

"Didn't you buy the furniture for Walter?" she asked.

"Yes, I did," tartly retorted the elder woman.

"And how much did he give you to pay for it?"

The elder woman was stung with fine indignation.

"Eighty pound, if you're so keen on knowin'," she replied.

"Eighty pounds! But there are forty-two pounds still owing!"

"I can't help that."

"But where has it all gone?"

"You'll find all the papers, I think, if you look—beside ten pound as he owed me, an' six pound as the wedding cost down here."

"Six pounds!" echoed Gertrude Morel. It seemed to her monstrous that, after her own father had paid so heavily for her wedding, six pounds more should have been squandered in eating and drinking at Walter's parents' house, at his expense.

"And how much has he sunk in his houses?" she asked.

"His houses—which houses?"

Gertrude Morel went white to the lips. He had told her the house he lived in, and the next one, were his own.

"I thought the house we live in—" she began.

"They're my houses, those two," said the mother-in-law. "And not clear either. It's as much as I can do to keep the mortgage interest paid."

Gertrude sat white and silent. She was her father now.

"Then we ought to be paying you rent," she said coldly.

"Walter is paying me rent," replied the mother.

"And what rent?" asked Gertrude.

"Six-and-six a week," retorted the mother.

It was more than the house was worth. Gertrude held her head erect, looked straight before her.

"It is lucky to be you," said the elder woman, bitingly, "to have a husband as takes all the worry of the money, and leaves you a free hand."

The young wife was silent.

She said very little to her husband, but her manner had changed towards him. Something in her proud, honourable soul had crystallized out hard as rock.

When October came in, she thought only of Christmas. Two years ago, at Christmas, she had met him. Last Christmas she had married him. This Christmas she would bear him a child.

"You don't dance yourself, do you, missis?" asked her nearest neighbour, in October, when there was great talk of opening a dancing-class over the Brick and Tile Inn at Bestwood.

"No—I never had the least inclination to," Mrs. Morel replied.

"Fancy! An' how funny as you should ha' married your Mester. You know he's quite a famous one for dancing."

"I didn't know he was famous," laughed Mrs. Morel.

"Yea, he is though! Why, he run that dancing-class in the Miners' Arms club-room for over five year."

"Did he?"

"Yes, he did." The other woman was defiant. "An' it was thronged every Tuesday, and Thursday, an' Sat'day—an' there *was* carryin's-on, accordin' to all accounts."

This kind of thing was gall and bitterness to Mrs. Morel, and she had a fair share of it. The women did not spare her, at first; for she was superior, though she could not help it.

He began to be rather late in coming home.

"They're working very late now aren't they?" she said to her washerwoman.

"No later than they allers do, I don't think. But they stop to have their pint at Ellen's, an' they get talkin', an' there you are! Dinner stone cold—an' it serves 'em right."

"But Mr. Morel does not take any drink."

The woman dropped the clothes, looked at Mrs. Morel, then went on with her work, saying nothing.

Gertrude Morel was very ill when the boy was born. Morel was good to her, as good as gold. But she felt very lonely, miles away from her own people. She felt lonely with him now, and his presence only made it more intense.

The boy was small and frail at first, but he came on quickly. He was a beautiful child, with dark gold ringlets, and dark-blue eyes which changed gradually to a clear grey. His mother loved him passionately. He came just when her own bitterness of disillusion was hardest to bear; when her faith in life was shaken, and her soul felt dreary and lonely. She made much of the child, and the father was jealous.

At last Mrs. Morel despised her husband. She turned to the child; she turned from the father. He had begun to neglect her; the novelty of his own home was gone. He had no grit, she said bitterly to herself. What he felt just at the minute, that was all to him. He could not abide by anything. There was nothing at the back of all his show.

There began a battle between the husband and wife—a fearful, bloody battle that ended only with the death of one. She fought to make him undertake his own responsibilities, to make him fulfil his obligations. But he was too different from her. His nature was purely sensuous, and she strove to make him moral, religious. She tried to force him to face things. He could not endure it—it drove him out of his mind.

While the baby was still tiny, the father's temper had become so irritable that it was not to be trusted. The child had only to give a little trouble when the man began to bully. A little more, and the hard hands of the collier hit the baby. Then Mrs. Morel loathed her husband, loathed him for days; and he went out and drank; and she cared very little what he did. Only, on his return, she scathed him with her satire.

The estrangement between them caused him, knowingly or unknowingly, grossly to offend her where he would not have done.

. . . . . .

EDITORS' SUMMARY

[The rift between the Morels widens, each day and each year. A daughter, Annie, and another son, Paul, are born to them. Gertrude Morel turns with all her passion from her husband to her children—first to William, her firstborn, who dies scarcely before he reaches manhood, then to Paul. The following episode occurs when Paul is an adolescent and torn between his ties to his mother and his love for his friend Miriam.]

STRIFE IN LOVE

He was not home again until a quarter to eleven. His mother was seated in the rocking-chair. Annie, with a rope of hair hanging down her back, remained sitting on a low stool before the fire, her elbows on her knees, gloomily. On the table stood the offending loaf unswathed. Paul entered rather breathless. No one spoke. His mother was reading the little local newspaper. He took off his coat, and went to sit down on the sofa. His mother moved curtly aside to let him pass. No one spoke. He was very uncomfortable. For some minutes he sat pretending to read a piece of paper he found on the table. Then—

"I forgot that bread, mother," he said.

There was no answer from either woman.

"Well," he said, "it's only twopence ha'penny. I can pay you for that."

Being angry he put three pennies on the table, and slid them towards his mother. She turned away her head. Her mouth was shut tightly.

"Yes," said Annie, "you don't know how badly my mother is!"

The girl sat staring glumly into the fire.

"Why is she badly?" asked Paul, in his overbearing way.

"Well!" said Annie. "She could scarcely get home."

He looked closely at his mother. She looked ill.

"*Why* could you scarcely get home?" he asked her, still sharply. She would not answer.

"I found her as white as a sheet sitting here," said Annie, with a suggestion of tears in her voice.

"Well, *why?*" insisted Paul. His brows were knitting, his eyes dilating passionately.

"It was enough to upset anybody," said Mrs. Morel, "hugging those parcels—meat, and green-groceries, and a pair of curtains——"

"Well, why *did* you hug them; you needn't have done."

"Then who would?"

"Let Annie fetch the meat."

"Yes, and I *would* fetch the meat, but how was I to know? You were off with Miriam, instead of being in when my mother came."

"And what was the matter with you?" asked Paul of his mother.

"I suppose it's my heart," she replied. Certainly she looked bluish round the mouth.

"And have you felt it before?"

"Yes—often enough."

"Then why haven't you told me?—and why haven't you seen a doctor?"

Mrs. Morel shifted in her chair, angry with him for his hectoring.

"You'd never notice anything," said Annie. "You're too eager to be off with Miriam."

"Oh, am I—and any worse than you with Leonard?"

"*I* was in at a quarter to ten."

There was silence in the room for a time.

"I should have thought," said Mrs. Morel bitterly, "that she wouldn't have occupied you so entirely as to burn a whole ovenful of bread."

"Beatrice was here as well as she."

"Very likely. But we know why the bread is spoilt."

"Why?" he flashed.

"Because you were engrossed with Miriam," replied Mrs. Morel hotly.

"Oh, very well—then it was *not!*" he replied angrily.

He was distressed and wretched. Seizing a paper, he began to read. Annie, her blouse unfastened, her long ropes of hair twisted into a plait, went up to bed, bidding him a very curt good-night.

Paul sat pretending to read. He knew his mother wanted to upbraid him. He also wanted to know what had made her ill, for he was troubled. So, instead of running away to bed, as he would liked to do, he sat and waited. There was a tense silence. The clock ticked loudly.

"You'd better go to bed before your father comes in," said the mother harshly. "And if you're going to have anything to eat, you'd better get it."

"I don't want anything."

It was his mother's custom to bring him some trifle for supper on Friday night, the night of luxury for the colliers. He was too angry to go and find it in the pantry this night. This insulted her.

"If I *wanted* you to go to Selby on Friday night, I can imagine the scene," said Mrs. Morel. "But you're never too tired to go if *she* will come for you. Nay, you neither want to eat nor drink then."

"I can't let her go alone."

"Can't you? And why does she come?"

"Not because I ask her."

"She doesn't come without you want her——"

"Well, what if I *do* want her—" he replied.

"Why, nothing if it was sensible or reasonable. But to go trapesing up there miles and miles in the mud, coming home at midnight, and got to go to Nottingham in the morning——"

"If I hadn't, you'd be just the same."

"Yes, I should, because there's no sense in it. Is she so fascinating that you must follow her all that way?" Mrs. Morel was bitterly sarcastic. She sat still, with averted face, stroking with a rhythmic, jerked movement the black sateen of her apron. It was a movement that hurt Paul to see.

"I do like her," he said, "but——"

"*Like* her!" said Mrs. Morel, in the same biting tones. "It seems to me you like nothing and nobody else. There's neither Annie, nor me, nor anyone now for you."

"What nonsense, mother—you know I don't love her—I—I tell you I *don't* love her—she doesn't even walk with my arm, because I don't want her to."

"Then why do you fly to her so often!"

"I *do* like to talk to her—I never said I didn't. But I *don't* love her."

"Is there nobody else to talk to?"

"Not about the things we talk of. There's lots of things that you're not interested in, that——"

"What things?"

Mrs. Morel was so intense that Paul began to pant.

"Why—painting—and books. *You* don't care about Herbert Spencer."

"No," was the sad reply. "And *you* won't at my age."

"Well, but I do now—and Miriam does——"

"And how do you know," Mrs. Morel flashed defiantly, "that *I* shouldn't? Do you ever try me?"

"But you don't, mother, you know you don't care whether a picture's decorative or not; you don't care what *manner* it is in."

"How do you know I don't care? Do you ever try me? Do you ever talk to me about these things, to try?"

"But it's not that that matters to you, mother, you know it's not."

"What is it, then—what is it, then, that matters to me?" she flashed. He knitted his brows with pain.

"You're old, mother, and we're young."

He only meant that the interests of *her* age were not the interests of his. But he realized the moment he had spoke that he had said the wrong thing.

"Yes, I know it well—I am old. And therefore I may stand aside; I have nothing more to do with you. You only want me to wait on you—the rest is for Miriam."

He could not bear it. Instinctively he realized that he was life to her. And, after all, she was the chief thing to him, the only supreme thing.

"You know it isn't mother, you know it isn't!"

She was moved to pity by his cry.

"It looks a great deal like it," she said, half putting aside her despair.

"No, mother—I really *don't* love her. I talk to her, but I want to come home to you."

He had taken off his collar and tie, and rose, bare-throated, to go to bed. As he stooped to kiss his mother, she threw her arms round his neck, hid her face on his shoulder, and cried, in a whimpering voice, so unlike her own that he writhed in agony.

"I can't bear it. I could let another woman—but not her. She'd leave me no room, not a bit of room——"

And immediately he hated Miriam bitterly.

"And I've never—you know, Paul—I've never had a husband—not really——"

He stroked his mother's hair, and his mouth was on her throat.

"And she exults so in taking you from me—she's not like ordinary girls."

"Well, I don't love her, mother," he murmured, bowing his head and hiding his eyes on her shoulder in misery. His mother kissed him a long, fervent kiss.

"My boy!" she said, in a voice trembling with passionate love.

Without knowing, he gently stroked her face.

"There," said his mother, "now go to bed: You'll be *so* tired in the morning." As she was speaking she heard her husband coming. "There's your father—now go." Suddenly she looked at him almost as if in fear. "Perhaps I'm selfish. If you want her, take her, my boy."

His mother looked so strange, Paul kissed her, trembling.

"Ha—mother!" he said softly.

Morel came in, walking unevenly. His hat was over one corner of his eye. He balanced in the doorway.

"At your mischief again?" he said venomously.

Mrs. Morel's emotion turned into sudden hate of the drunkard who had come in thus upon her.

"At any rate, it is sober," she said.

"H'm—h'm! h'm—h'm!" he sneered. He went into the passage, hung up his hat and coat. Then they heard him go down three steps to the pantry. He returned with a piece of pork-pie in his fist. It was what Mrs. Morel had bought for her son.

"Nor was that bought for you. If you can give me no more than twenty-five shillings, I'm sure I'm not going to buy you pork-pie to stuff, after you've swilled a bellyful of beer."

"Wha-at—wha-at!" snarled Morel, toppling in his balance. "Wha-at —not for me?" He looked at the piece of meat and crust, and suddenly, in a vicious spurt of temper, flung it into the fire.

Paul started to his feet.

"Waste your own stuff!" he cried.

"What—what!" suddenly shouted Morel, jumping up and clenching his fist. "I'll show yer, yer young jockey!"

"All right!" said Paul viciously, putting his head on one side. "Show me!"

He would at that moment dearly have loved to have a smack at something. Morel was half crouching, fists up, ready to spring. The young man stood, smiling with his lips.

"Ussha!" hissed the father, swiping round with a great stroke just past his son's face. He dared not, even though so close, really touch the young man, but swerved an inch away.

"Right!" said Paul, his eyes upon the side of his father's mouth, where in another instant his fist would have hit. He ached for that stroke. But he heard a faint moan from behind. His mother was deadly pale, dark at the mouth. Morel was dancing up to deliver another blow.

"Father!" said Paul, so that the word rang.

Morel started, and stood at attention.

"Mother!" moaned the boy. "Mother!"

She began to struggle with herself. Her open eyes watched him, although she could not move. Gradually she was coming to herself. He laid her down on the sofa, and ran upstairs for a little whisky, which at last she could sip. The tears were hopping down his face. As he knelt in front of her he did not cry, but the tears ran down his face quickly. Morel, on the opposite side of the room, sat with his elbows on his knees glaring across.

"What's a-matter with 'er?" he asked.

"Faint!" replied Paul.

"H'm!"

The elderly man began to unlace his boots. He stumbled off to bed. His last fight was fought in that home.

Paul knelt there, stroking his mother's hand.

"Don't be poorly, mother—don't be poorly!" he said time after time.

"It's nothing, my boy," she murmured.

At last he rose, fetched in a large piece of coal, and raked the fire. Then he cleared the room, put everything straight, laid the things for breakfast, and brought his mother's candle.

"Can you go to bed, mother?"

"Yes, I'll come."

"Sleep with Annie, mother, not with him."

"No. I'll sleep in my own bed."

"Don't sleep with him, mother."

"I'll sleep in my own bed."

She rose, and he turned out the gas, then followed her closely upstairs, carrying her candle. On the landing he kissed her close.

"Good-night, mother."

"Good-night!" she said.

He pressed his face upon the pillow in a fury of misery. And yet, somewhere in his soul, he was at peace because he still loved his mother best. It was the bitter peace of resignation.

The efforts of his father to conciliate him next day were a great humiliation to him.

Everybody tried to forget the scene.

DEFEAT OF MIRIAM

"At any rate, mother, I s'll never marry," he said.

"Ay, they all say that, my lad. You've not met the one yet. Only wait a year or two."

"But I shan't marry, mother. I shall live with you, and we'll have a servant."

"Ay, my lad, it's easy to talk. We'll see when the time comes."

"What time? I'm nearly twenty-three."

"Yes, you're not one that would marry young. But in three years' time——"

"I shall be with you just the same."

"We'll see, my boy, we'll see."

"But you don't want me to marry?"

"I shouldn't like to think of you going through your life without anybody to care for you and do—no."

"And you think I ought to marry?"

"Sooner or later every man ought."

"But you'd rather it were later."

"It would be hard—and very hard. It's as they say:

> " 'A son's my son till he takes him a wife,
>   But my daughter's my daughter the whole of her life.' "

"And you think I'd let a wife take me from you?"

"Well, you wouldn't ask her to marry your mother as well as you," Mrs. Morel smiled.

"She could do what she liked; she wouldn't have to interfere."

"She wouldn't—till she'd got you—and then you'd see."

"I never will see. I'll never marry while I've got you—I won't."

"But I shouldn't like to leave you with nobody, my boy," she cried.

"You're not going to leave me. What are you? Fifty-three! I'll give you till seventy-five. There you are, I'm fat and forty-four. Then I'll marry a staid body. See!"

His mother sat and laughed.

"Go to bed," she said—"go to bed."

"And we'll have a pretty house, you and me, and a servant, and it'll be just all right. I s'll perhaps be rich with my painting."

"Will you go to bed!"

"And then you s'll have a pony-carriage. See yourself—a little Queen Victoria trotting round."

"I tell you to go to bed," she laughed.

He kissed her and went. His plans for the future were always the same.

40. THE ATTITUDES OF MOTHERS OF MALE SCHIZOPHRENICS TOWARD CHILD BEHAVIOR

JOSEPH C. MARK

Exploration of the early experiences of schizophrenics has led to a number of general studies of the relation of the parents and home atmosphere to the later development of mental illness. Several of these studies have shown that mothers of schizophrenics are usually above average in intelligence and education.

Here Mark finds this group of mothers characterized by rejecting, overdominating, and severely restrictive attitudes toward their children. Mothers of this type are portrayed in The Way of All Flesh (*selection 37*) *and* Sons and Lovers (*selection 39*).

This investigation was designed to determine if the attitudes of the mothers of schizophrenics toward child behavior differ from the attitudes of the mothers of nonschizophrenics.

The male schizophrenics, whose mothers are the subject of this study, are veterans of World War II, hospitalized at VA installations at Northport, Long Island, and the Bronx, hospitals which serve the New York area.

METHOD

The results are based on material obtained through an attitude survey of a "disguised-structured" type. (1) This attitude survey contains 139 items pertain-

Reprinted from *Journal of Abnormal and Social Psychology*, 48, No. 2 (1953), 185–189, by permission of the author and the American Psychological Association.

ing to child rearing. The items are worded in the form of stereotypes, such as "A child should be seen and not heard." Shoben (7) found that such an instrument was disarming because of the disguised nature of the items, while allowing for a projection of opinion. At the same time the test is structured and provides for responses on an objective basis. Responses to each item are made on a four-point scale: strongly agree (A), mildly agree (a), mildly disagree (d), strongly disagree (D).

SUBJECTS

The attitude survey was administered to 100 mothers of male schizophrenics and to a control group of 100 mothers of male nonschizophrenics.

The control group was selected from among the mothers visiting general medical patients at the VA Hospital in the Bronx, women's auxiliaries of veterans' organizations, volunteer groups, and from private contacts. None of the sons of the control Ss had a history of hospitalization for mental illness, according to the mothers. The control group is comparable to the experimental group with respect to age, religion, education, socioeconomic status, and age of sons.

The mean age of the mothers in the experimental group is 55.7 years, and that of the mothers in the control group is 54.9 years.

The experimental and the control groups each have 35 Catholic, 35 Jewish, and 30 Protestant Ss.

The mothers in both groups are predominantly of grammar school educational background (50 experimental and 47 control) with the bulk of the remaining members in both groups at the high school level (37 experimental and 43 control). Two in each group went to college; twelve had no formal education (7 experimentals and 5 controls); seven were "unreported" (4 experimentals and 3 controls).

As an index of socioeconomic status, occupation of husband was employed. There were 11 professionals in each group, 19 proprietors and managers in the experimental group and 26 in the control group; 12 clerks and kindred workers in the experimentals and 11 in the controls; 30 skilled workers in the experimentals and 28 in the controls; with the rest divided fairly evenly between skilled and unskilled workers.

The mean age of the schizophrenic sons was 29 years and the sons of the controls averaged 28 years. The mean numbers of children in both groups approximated three children per family.

RELATED STUDIES

The influence of parents on a child's mental health, originally stressed by Freud (2, pp. 80–81) and recently emphasized by Sullivan (9), is now widely accepted. Speaking from his experience as a psychiatrist during World War II, Strecker (8) for example, found that the mental health of many soldiers was jeopardized by the attitude of his "Mom."

In a series of 45 unselected case histories of schizophrenics, Kasanin, Knight, and Sage reported (5) that maternal overprotection or rejection was present in 60 per cent of the cases (rejection was present in only two cases).

Studying the personalities of 25 mothers through the method of repeated interview, Tietze (10) concluded that the mothers were generally overanxious, obsessive, and domineering. She felt that the subtly dominating mother was particularly dangerous to the child, because the child was left with no opportunity to express aggressive feelings openly.

Gerard and Siegal (4) examined the family background of schizophrenics through anamneses collected from 71 parents and relatives. They found the parents to be immature with a poor marital relationship; and that the child was often exposed to markedly overprotective attitudes.

In contrast to Gerard and Siegel, Prout and White (6) found little difference between the life histories of 25 mothers of male schizophrenics and the life histories of the mothers of 25 nonschizophrenic males. They concluded from Rorschach data, however, that the mothers of the schizophrenics tended to compensate for their own life disappointments by living through their sons rather than having an independent life of their own.

There is then evidence for a pathological familial influence in the lives of schizophrenics. Of course, those who adhere to an organic or hereditary explanation of schizophrenia can maintain that a constitutional weakness in the child makes itself apparent in the form of a sickly child. The overprotected attitudes often attributed to the mothers of schizophrenics are then interpreted as a reaction to a basic inferiority in the child. On the other hand, those who have a psychogenic bias can insist that mother's attitudes are projected onto the child because of her own unconscious needs, regardless of the physical and psychological makeup of the child. Fromm-Reichmann (3) has coined the term "schizophrenogenic mother" to describe the mother who has such an injurious effect on her child as to cause him to become schizophrenic; and Rosen has sought the origins of the schizophrenic pattern in the relations between mother and child, especially searching for those feelings of the mother which convey rejection.

Without attempting to confront these crucial questions concerning the etiology of schizophrenia, it is the purpose in this study to ascertain in some measure whether or not a characteristic set of attitudes concerning the rearing of children can be attributed to the mothers of schizophrenics.

RESULTS

The two groups' responses to the 139 items of the attitude survey were compared, item by item, by means of the chi-square model. Of the 139 items, 67 proved significant at the .05 level of confidence or better. The 139 items grouped by significance level, are presented in Table I. In *all* instances of significant items, the mothers of schizophrenics more frequently *agreed* with the item than did the mothers of nonschizophrenics.

To determine if the differences in attitudes assume identifiable patterns, the 67 significant items were classified by four judges (clinical psychologists) into three preconceived clusters. These clusters were obtained from the Fels Institute's longitudinal research appraising parental behavior. These three clusters are as follows:

1. The measures of control the parent employs. The continuum extends from the parent who is restrictive and coercive, allowing the child little freedom of choice or range of activity, to the parent who is lax, ineffectual, unable to control the child. Between these two extremes is the parent who allows the child freedom but who is capable of asserting authority when and where desired.

2. The intellectual objectivity of the parent. The objective parent is rational rather than emotional in his behavior. Regardless of his acceptance or hostility, his overt behavior is largely governed by what he consciously decides is an appropriate policy. The emotional parent, in contrast, is unable to divorce his behavior from his immediate mood and consequently directly expresses his emotional attitude in his behavior, be it friendly or antagonistic.

3. The warmth of the parent-child relationship. A warm home is one in which the parent genuinely likes and enjoys the child, finds contact with him rewarding and pleasant, is appreciative and approving of the child's personality—in short, is "acceptant" in the conventional sense of the term. The position of the home varies on this continuum from excessive devotion through casual enjoyment and cool detachment down through vigorous hostility.

Some of the 67 significant items were found to apply to more than one of these categories: 16 items overlapped; 7 items remained unclassified. The following is a tabulation of the number of items in each of the three clusters employed:

1. Measures of Control (39 items) [1]
   a. lax and ineffectual, 6
   b. restrictive and coercive, 33
2. Intellectual Objectivity (14 items) [2]
   a. rational, 8
   b. emotional, 6

[1] The numbers of these items are as follows: lax and ineffectual: 23, 29, 30, 47, 61, 125; restrictive and coercive: 4, 9, 12, 13, 18, 20, 25, 35, 41, 67, 69, 71, 73, 74, 80, 90, 96, 101, 104, 107, 108, 110, 115, 116, 118, 123, 127, 130, 131, 132, 134, 138, 139.

[2] Item numbers under "rational": 40, 43, 57, 71, 81, 96, 121, 138; under "emotional": 14, 29, 54, 62, 65, 126.

3. Warmth of the Relationship (25 items) [3]
   a. excessive devotion, 13
   b. cool detachment, 10
   c. vigorous hostility, 2
4. Unclassified (7 items)

Judging from their numerical distribution, the mothers of schizo-phrenics as a group can be characterized as being mainly restrictive in their attitudes as to methods of controlling children. Lax and ineffectual attitudes are also present, but to a much lesser extent, and are out-numbered by the restrictive items 33 to 6.[4]

The mother of the schizophrenic believes in allowing a child no freedom or choice of activity and in prescribing and carefully channeling his behavior (items 13, 35, 69, 74). She frowns on friends and sex play and believes in keeping sexual information from him (items 80, 90, 101, 110). She feels it is a mother's duty to know everything that the child is thinking (items 18, 20, 123). This pervasively restrictive attitude extends into adulthood (items 12, 104, 108). Although she believes in stricter discipline, it is only for purposes of restricting behavior; lax methods are evidently approved if they gain desired ends (items 29, 30, 61).

The cluster of *intellectual objectivity* is composed of a rational or deliberate approach, on the one hand, and an emotional or impulsive one, on the other. The judges rated eight and six items, respectively, into these categories. This cluster was difficult to define for our purposes and the judges had trouble in rating. The few items classified into this cluster reflect this difficulty and it is not possible to make any definite con-clusions.

The *warmth of the relationship* consists of the following continuum: excessive devotion, casual enjoyment, cool detachment, and vigorous hostility. The judges placed 25 items into the warmth cluster and identi-fied 13 as indicating excessive devotion, none as casual enjoyment, 10 as cool detachment, and 2 as vigorous hostility. If casual enjoyment is taken as a center point, there are 13 items to one side of it and 12 to the other.

These mothers as a group thought that "a devoted mother has no time for social life" (item 33), but that "children should not annoy their parents with their unimportant problems" (item 32). They thought that "a mother should shower her child with praise at all times" (item 50), but that it was not desirable to play too much with a child as it would

---

[3] "Excessive devotion" item numbers: 13, 27, 29, 33, 35, 50, 51, 54, 62, 112, 118, 131, 135; "cool detachment": 10, 19, 32, 40, 75, 96, 111, 121, 130, 132; "vigorous hostility": 41, 58.

[4] A middle point on the Fels Behavior Rating Scale exists between these two ex-tremes and is defined as a parent who "allows sufficient freedom but is capable of asserting authority whenever it is deemed necessary." No items were classified into the middle position by the judges.

spoil him (item 40). They felt that "it's sad to see children grow up because they need you more when they're babies" (item 62), and that "quiet children are much nicer than little chatterboxes" (item 10).

The presence of such opposing attitudes as devotion and detachment may be pointing up the ambivalence of feeling toward their own children.

As far as the design of the study is concerned, a cross validation was not attempted. A replication would be desirable, however, to see how many of the significant items would repeat themselves. It is possible, for example, that about 7 of the 67 items at the .05 level or better may be significant by chance alone. The author has not been able to obtain a suitable population for such a cross validation but welcomes the efforts of other psychologists who would desire to do such a replication.

SUMMARY

1. The attitudes of the mothers of schizophrenics were found to differ from the attitudes of the mothers of nonschizophrenics with respect to various child-rearing practices.
2. Sixty-seven of the 139 items in an attitude survey differentiated the two groups at the .05 level of confidence or better.
3. The mothers of schizophrenics were found to be mainly restrictive in their control of the child. When it came to the warmth of the relationship, they exhibited attitudes both of excessive devotion and cool detachment.

Table 1. Items Significantly Differentiating Mothers of Schizophrenics from Mothers of Nonschizophrenics

.001 LEVEL

13. Children should be taken to and from school until the age of eight just to make sure there are no accidents.
18. A mother should make it her business to know everything her children are thinking.
20. If children are quiet for a little while a mother should immediately find out what they are thinking about.
32. Children should not annoy parents with their unimportant problems.
33. A devoted mother has no time for social life.
35. A watchful mother can keep her child out of all accidents.
40. Playing too much with a child will spoil him.
43. A parent must never make mistakes in front of the child.
51. Parents should sacrifice everything for their children.
54. When the father punishes a child for no good reason the mother should take the child's side.
64. A mother has to suffer much and say little.
81. Most children are toilet trained by 15 months of age.

101. Children who take part in sex play become sex criminals when they grow up.
115. A child should not plan to enter any occupation that his parents don't approve of.
121. Too much affection will make a child a "softie."

.01 LEVEL

19. Answering questions about sex is embarrassing and unnecessary.
22. A son is usually like the mother and a daughter like the father.
23. Punishing a child is a father's job.
29. It is all right for a mother to sleep with a child because it gives him a feeling of being loved and wanted.
30. A good way to get children to obey is by giving them presents or promising them treats.
47. Spanking a child does more good than harm.
57. Most children are able to talk by the age of 12 months.
58. There's little thanks or pleasure in raising children.
61. Parents ought to close their eyes to their children's faults.
62. One reason that it's sad to see children grow up is because they need you more when they are babies.
66. Children should not be punished for doing anything they've seen their parents do.
67. Boys should never be allowed to play with dolls and carriages.
71. The sooner a child learns to walk the better he's been trained.
75. It is not the duty of the parent to teach the child about sex.
111. Some children are just naturally bad.
112. Babies are more fun than older children.
117. A good child will never allow his parents to go to a home when they grow too old.
118. A good mother should shelter her child from life's little difficulties.
123. A child should never keep a secret from his parents.
131. Children seven years of age are really too young to spend summers away from home in a camp.
135. Mothers should have vacations away from their children.

.02 LEVEL

14. After punishing a child a parent naturally wants to make up for it by giving him everything he wants.
27. A mother should never be separated from her child.
37. Every parent has a favorite child.
41. Children need some of the natural meanness taken out of them.
50. A mother should shower her child with praise at all times.
53. It's better to have a boy than a girl.
73. Most children should have more discipline than they get.
90. It is better for children to play at home than to visit other children.
96. A child will develop a better character if he works after school instead of playing.
108. If children are to grow up and get somewhere in life they must be continuously kept after.

110. A young child should be protected from hearing about sex.
116. A child should not be allowed to play in the living room.
125. When an infant doesn't like a certain food the mother should stop feeding it to him.

.05 LEVEL

4. When a child won't eat you should tell him how nicely other children eat.
9. Children will neglect their schoolwork if parents don't keep after them.
10. Quiet children are much nicer than little chatterboxes.
12. The least a child can do for his parents when he grows up is to take care of them in their old age.
25. A good child doesn't fight with other children.
45. Sex is one of the greatest problems a parent has with children.
69. Children should do nothing without the consent of their parents.
74. Whenever a child is slow in dressing the parent should do it for him.
80. A child's friends usually do more harm than good.
104. No person should get married before the age of 25.
106. It is best to give children the idea that their parents have no faults.
107. A child shouldn't be allowed to see his parents completely undressed.
127. It is wicked for children to disobey their parents.
130. A child should be weaned away from the bottle or breast as soon as possible.
132. Strict discipline develops a fine strong character.
134. Children should always be punished for being bad.
138. Children who always obey grow up to be the best adults.
139. Too much freedom will make a child wild.

REFERENCES

1. CAMPBELL, D. T. The indirect assessment of social attitudes. *Psychol. Bull.*, 1950, 47, 15–38.
2. FREUD, S. *The interpretation of dreams.* New York: Macmillan, 1937.
3. FROMM-REICHMANN, FREIDA. Notes on development of treatment of schizophrenics by psychoanalytic therapy. *Psychiatry*, 1948, 11, 263.
4. GERARD, D. L., & SIEGEL, J. The family background of schizophrenia. *Psychiat. Quart.*, 1950, 24, 47–73.
5. KASININ, J., KNIGHT, E., & SAGE, P. Parent-child relationship in schizophrenia. *J. nerv. ment. Dis.*, 1934, 79, 249–263.
6. PROUT, C. T. & WHITE, MARY A. A controlled study of personality relationships in mothers of schizophrenic male patients. *Amer. J. Psychiat.*, 1950, 107, 251–256.
7. SHOBEN, E. J., JR. The assessment of parental attitudes in relation to child adjustment. *Genet. Psychol. Monogr.*, 1949, 39, 101–148.
8. STRECKER, E. A. *Their mothers' sons.* New York: Lippincott, 1946.
9. SULLIVAN, H. S. *Conceptions of modern psychiatry.* Washington, D. C.: William Alanson White Psychiatric Foundation, 1947.
10. TIETZE, TRUDE. A study of mothers of schizophrenic patients. *Psychiatry*, 1949, 12, 55–65.

41. THE PARENTAL ATTITUDES
OF MOTHERS OF SCHIZOPHRENICS

MARVIN ZUCKERMAN, MARY OLTEAN,
AND IRWIN MONASHKIN

This study, using an attitude scale similar to Mark's (selection 40) but a different sample, comes to conclusions contradicting his results. It offers evidence that mothers with grammar-school education are considerably more restrictive than college-educated mothers.

Psychoanalytic theorists such as Fromm-Reichman (3), Rosen (6), and Arieti (1) have hypothesized that schizophrenia has its origin in the early relationship between mother and child. They imply that the mother of a schizophrenic child has certain destructive types of attitudes toward children which she conveys to the child through her behavior and verbalizations. Unfortunately, we must rely on retrospective evidence bearing on this hypothesis. Tietze (9) interviewed a group of mothers of schizophrenics and characterized them as overanxious, obsessive and domineering. However, no control group was compared with these mothers, and one may question the objectivity of an open interview with a mother already identified as the mother of a schizophrenic.

The need for more objective techniques to assess parental attitudes encouraged other researchers to develop objective instruments. The typical parental attitude survey uses items which are stated in the form of generalities and clichés in order to make them sound socially acceptable. The parent is asked to state whether she mildly or strongly agrees or disagrees with these items. Freeman and Grayson (2) used the Shoben Parent-Child Attitude Survey in comparing 50 mothers of schizophrenics with 50 control mothers. They found the mothers of schizophrenics scored significantly higher on the Possessive and Ignoring scales (on the latter scale they accepted the .10 level of confidence) than the control mothers. Unfortunately, they did not control educational or socioeconomic differences between their groups. From the way in which the control group data was gathered, it is likely that differences existed in the educational levels of the groups. Furthermore, since they relied on volunteer mothers solicited by volunteer students, various selective factors could have determined the scores in the control group.

Reprinted from *Journal of Consulting Psychology*, 22, No. 4 (1958), 307–310, by permission of the authors and the American Psychological Association.

Mark (4), in a more carefully controlled study, found that a significant number of attitude items distinguished a group of 100 mothers of schizophrenics from 100 control mothers. However, McFarland (5) attempted to replicate this study with the same items and failed to find a significant number of items distinguishing the two groups.

The purpose of the present study was to retest the hypothesis that mothers of schizophrenics have more severe (controlling and rejecting) parental attitudes than mothers of normals.

PROCEDURE

The Parental Attitude Research Instrument (PARI) was the main instrument used in this study. This test was developed by Schaefer and Bell (7), with items modeled after the types used by Mark (4) and Shoben (8). An attempt was made to develop a number of short, but internally consistent, scales measuring specific types of attitudes, to permit somewhat broader interpretations than can be made from *post hoc* item analyses. The test consists of 23 scales, each of which measures some attitude theoretically relevant to personality development in children. Normative data are furnished by Schaefer and Bell (7), and in a previous article by Zuckerman, Ribback, Monashkin, and Norton (11). A factor analysis of the scales using a heterogeneous sample, including the group reported in this paper, can be found in the latter article. The factors found in this study were used to derive summary scores in the current study by weighing scales roughly by their factor loadings. Factor A seems to be an Authoritarian-Controlling factor which loads heavily on 16 of the scales. Factor B seems to be a Hostility-Rejection factor which loads on three scales. Factor C seems to be a Democratic Attitude factor which loads on three scales.

SUBJECTS

Forty-seven mothers of male and female patients diagnosed as schizophrenic in an acute treatment hospital were given the PARI. Ratings of pathology on 30 cases of mixed diagnoses were available from a previous study and provided some information on the reliability of diagnoses at the institution. A seven-point rating scale ranging from mildly neurotic to severely psychotic was used in rating the case-history summaries of the patients. Ratings were global, but factors considered included severity of symptoms, chronicity of the disorder, response to treatment, and premorbid adjustment. Two of the authors made the ratings independently, and their ratings correlated .80. The agreement between the raters and the diagnosis assigned the patient is summarized in Table 1. It can be seen that there is high agreement between psychiatric diagnosis and the ratings except in the middle of the scale where the borderline cases would be expected to fall. Although there is probably some contamination between the two sets of data, the experimenters felt justified in using the psychiatric diagnosis of schizophrenia as a criterion, recognizing that wide behavioral differences may exist within the disorder diagnosed as "schizophrenia."

Table 1.   Relation Between Case History Rating and Psychiatric Diagnosis

PSYCHIATRIC DIAGNOSIS	CASE HISTORY RATING		
	1–3	3.5–4.5	5–7
Nonschizophrenic	8	2	1
Schizophrenic	0	2	17

Note.—Chi square, corrected (combining cells) = 15.56. $df = 1$, $p < .001$.

A group of 47 mothers of normals was derived from the older age range of the normal sample (11) and from some additional normals gathered at a later date. The control group consisted of mothers given the PARI at church and social and nursery school meetings, with some mothers of students from a night extension college.

Since education of the mother seems to influence most of the scales and one of the factors (11), it was put into the analysis of variance design using three levels: grammar school, high school, and college. Age differences were then compared between diagnostic groups across levels. At the grammar school level, there was a significant age difference; therefore, the five oldest mothers of schizophrenics and the five youngest mothers of normals were discarded. The resultant samples, containing 42 mothers in each group, are described in Table 2. Sex of the patient was considered

Table 2.   Composition of Mothers of Schizophrenic and Mothers of Normal Groups

LEVEL OF EDUCATION	SCHIZOPHRENICS' MOTHERS		NORMALS' MOTHERS	
	N	Mean Age	N	Mean Age
Grammar school	11	52.4	11	52.0
High school	24	48.0	24	48.8
College	7	50.7	7	49.1
All cases	42	49.6	42	49.7

before grouping mothers of male and female schizophrenics together. Twenty-one mothers of male schizophrenics were compared with 21 mothers of female schizophrenics. A significant difference was found on only one scale. Therefore, the groups were combined. Other variables considered were the child's diagnostic subclassification, paranoid vs. other schizophrenics, and the time interval between the admission of the patient and the administration of the test to the mother. Neither of these variables seemed to markedly influence the average parental attitude scores.

RESULTS AND DISCUSSION

The results of the analyses of variance on Factors A, B, and C, and on 20 of the individual scales are reported in Table 3. Only one of the differences between groups was significant. The mothers of schizophrenics scored significantly lower on Scale 8, strictness, than the controls. How-

Table 3. Analysis of Variance Results in Comparison of Mothers of Schizophrenics and Mothers of Normals [a]

Score or Scale	Child's Diagnosis	Mother's Education	Interaction
SUMMARY SCORES			
A—Authoritarian-Control	—	15.41 **	5.97 **
B—Hostility-Rejection	—	1.89	—
C—Democratic Attitudes	1.39	—	—
SCALES			
2—Fostering Dependency	—	5.80 **	1.11
3—Seclusion of the Mother	—	8.80 **	1.80
4—Breaking the Will	3.18	13.07 **	3.98 *
5—Martyrdom	—	12.21 **	1.20
6—Fear of Harming the Baby	—	2.76	7.90 **
7—Marital Conflict	—	3.99 *	1.33
8—Strictness	6.31 *	2.80	2.85
9—Irritability	—	1.44	—
10—Excluding Outside Influences	3.23	10.51 **	3.71 *
11—Deification	3.02	11.07 **	4.57 *
12—Suppression of Aggression	—	4.24 *	2.02
13—Rejection of Homemaking Role	1.68	—	—
15—Approval of Activity	1.35	3.82	2.07
16—Avoidance of Communication	1.71	10.30 **	1.01
17—Inconsiderateness of Husband	—	—	—
18—Suppression of Sex	—	11.75 **	4.62 *
19—Ascendance of the Mother	—	11.13 **	6.12 **
20—Intrusiveness	—	9.78 **	2.69
22—Acceleration of Development	—	4.10 *	4.31 *
23—Dependency of the Mother	—	3.53 *	3.62 *

[a] F ratios of less than one are indicated by dashes.
 * Significant at or below the .05 level.
 ** Significant at or below the .01 level.

ever, 1 out of 23 comparisons may be considered a finding attributable to chance. The differences between education levels were significant for Factor A and 14 of the 20 individual scales. The interaction effects were significant for Factor A and eight of the individual scales. An analysis of the interaction effect in Factor A can be seen in Table 4. At the grammar school level, the mothers of schizophrenics tend to score higher than the controls, and at the high school level they scored significantly lower than the controls. No differences were found at the college level. The results on the individual scales tend to follow the same pattern. If we had included the 10 subjects discarded to make age equivalent at the grammar school level, the interaction effect would have been even more pronounced.

Table 4. Comparisons of Means of Mothers of Schizophrenics and Mothers of Normals by Levels on Summary Score A

Level of Education	Schizophrenics' Mothers	Normals' Mothers	t	p
Grammar school	242.09	214.91	1.88	.05–.10
High school	191.58	219.50	2.86	.01
College	172.86	155.86	.94	.3–.8

The interaction effects are difficult to interpret. They may indicate that the way the mothers of schizophrenics respond to the test depends on their familiarity with the cultural expectations for parental attitudes, which, in turn, may depend on their education. The samples at each level are not adequate to justify a conclusion. There is, however, a greater relationship between education and parental attitudes in mothers of schizophrenics than in the controls. The correlation between Factor A and education in the original 47 mothers of schizophrenics was —.632. In the original 47 controls it was only —.287. The difference between these two correlations was significant beyond the .05 level.

The hypothesis of a difference between parental attitudes of mothers of schizophrenics and other mothers was not confirmed. It would be difficult to disprove this hypothesis, since the possibility always remains that other instruments or techniques may reveal a difference. Toms (10) compared 30 mothers of male schizophrenics and 30 control mothers, using a variety of instruments including an interview, vocabulary test, the MMPI, and a short TAT. Unfortunately, there was a difference in education between the two groups which was not taken into account in the analyses. However, the general conclusion was that the hypotheses of personality differences between mothers of schizophrenics and other mothers were not confirmed from any of the techniques. One interesting result, which bears on our speculations about our interaction effects, was that the mothers of schizophrenics scored significantly higher on the two MMPI scales measuring defensiveness (L and K). These findings suggest that further research on the "schizophrenogenic mother" hypothesis might do better using tests which control for social desirability and response suppression.

SUMMARY

It was hypothesized that mothers of schizophrenics have more severe (controlling and rejecting) parental attitudes than mothers of normals. Forty-two mothers of schizophrenic patients and 42 control mothers were compared on the Parental Attitude Research Instrument. The hypothesis was not supported, although significant interactions were found between the two groups and levels of education.

REFERENCES

1. ARIETI, S. *Interpretation of schizophrenia.* New York: Robert Brunner, 1955.
2. FREEMAN, R. V., & GRAYSON, H. M. Maternal attitudes in schizophrenia. *J. abnorm. soc. Psychol.*, 1955, 50, 45–52.
3. FROMM-REICHMANN, FRIEDA. Notes on development of treatment of schizophrenics by psychoanalytic therapy. *Psychiatry*, 1948, 11, 263.
4. MARK, J. C. The attitudes of the mothers of male schizophrenics toward child behavior. *J. abnorm. soc. Psychol.*, 1953, 48, 185–189.
5. MC FARLAND, R. L. *Personal communication*, 1957.
6. ROSEN, J. N. The treatment of schizophrenic psychoses by direct analytic therapy. *Psychiat. Quart.*, 1947, 21, 3–37.
7. SCHAEFER, E. S., & BELL, R. Q. Development of the Parental Attitude Research Instrument. *Child Develpm.*, in press.
8. SHOBEN, E. J., JR. The assessment of parental attitudes in relation to child adjustment. *Genet. Psychol. Monogr.*, 1949, 39, 101–148.
9. TIETZE, T. A study of mothers of schizophrenic patients. *Psychiatry*, 1949, 12, 55–65.
10. TOMS, E. C. Personality characteristics of mothers of schizophrenic veterans. Unpublished doctoral dissertation, Univer. of Minnesota, 1955.
11. ZUCKERMAN, M., RIBBACK, BEATRICE B., MONASHKIN, I., & NORTON, J. A. Normative data and factor analysis on the Parental Attitude Research Instrument. *J. consult. Psychol.*, 1958, 22, 165–171.

42. A STUDY OF HOSTILITY IN
ALLERGIC CHILDREN

HYMAN MILLER AND DOROTHY W. BARUCH

*What happens to the child when the hostility naturally generated in
the friction of family living is permitted no expression?*

*Miller and Baruch explore this general question by comparing
the hostility patterns of allergic children with those of nonallergic
children who display behavior disorders. Their study concludes that
allergic children direct their hostility inward—against themselves—
rather than allowing it outward expression against others.*

*The widespread notion that allergies are inherited would seem
to contradict the findings presented here and raises several questions.
If allergic children were compared with normal children instead of
those with behavior disorders, would the differences between the
two groups be so great? Would their allergies disappear if
allergic children were "taught" to direct their hostility outward?*

Hostility is a common manifestation in our culture. It appears, in
fact, to be an almost inevitable product of the emotional climate which
our complex civilization imposes on the individual. Into its making go
not only the restrictions in a child's schedule and management from birth,
but also the impingement upon him of deeper currents in his immediate
environment, such as the tensions between his parents and the attitudes
both conscious and unconscious which his parents carry within themselves.

The direct expression of hostility to those who originally create it—
namely, the parents—is met by very early repressive and often punitive
handling. The child's aggression must then be disguised by displacement
onto various substitute targets or by indirection so that the hostility can
be disavowed.

As a plant becomes gnarled and twisted when it grows in a climate
unsuited to its proper development, so may a child's health become distorted by an unsuitable psychological climate. The allergic child provides
a particularly apt example of this. Psychological factors may precipitate,
aggravate or prolong the clinical symptoms of allergy and may often
vitiate their successful medical treatment (2, 4, 8).

Selections reprinted from the article in *American Journal of Orthopsychiatry*, XX,
No. 3 (July, 1950), 506–519, by permission of the authors and the publisher.

At first glance it would seem that the allergic child is exposed to the same emotional climate as any other child in our culture, at least prior to the onset of his clinical symptoms. As was shown, however, in the first paper of this series (5), there is a difference in emotional climate. This difference lies in the exposure to maternal rejection which is significantly more common in the allergic than in the nonallergic child. It has been argued (6) that the maternal rejection comes as a result of the allergic illness, but there is evidence (not yet reported) that rejection is primary rather than secondary in a significant proportion of cases. It precedes rather than follows the onset of allergic symptoms. Thus it may be said that maternal rejection is a common adverse influence in the emotional climate in which the allergic child is born.

But some nonallergic children are also exposed to this adverse influence. This poses the question: Do the psychological reactions of allergic children to as severe a frustrating experience as maternal rejection differ in ways that might help to account for their characteristic physical disturbances? For instance, do the allergics differ in their aggressive reactions to this experience? *Do they handle their hostility differently from the nonallergic child?*

Do allergic children bring out hostility to parents directly, i.e., openly, more or less commonly than the nonallergic, as in stubbornness or disobedience? Or are they more apt to disguise it by bringing it out indirectly, as in the refusal of food, or untidiness, or by displacing it onto other objects or people?

On the other hand, do they fail the courage to risk exposing themselves even in the less obvious outgoing modes of hostile expression? Do they then turn hostility in on themselves more than the nonallergic through behavioral deviations such as accident proneness and nail biting? Or do they block in the various expressions of hostility? And, finally, where do the somatic symptoms fit in? It was to shed light on this subject, the handling of hostility by the allergic child, that the present phase of this study was undertaken.

Sample Studied and Method of Collecting Data.   Included in this study were 90 allergic and 53 nonallergic children.

Every new allergic child patient who came to the allergist over a three-year period, from October, 1945 to November, 1948, was recommended for psychological investigation as part of general medical workup. As in a previous study, the present sample of allergics includes those cases where such recommendation was followed.

Medical data was obtained from the usual medical history and physical examination and from allergy skin tests. All these children suffered from the symptoms of clinical allergy in the accepted medical sense, namely, the clinical syndromes of asthma, hay fever or eczema. In other words, the presence of these clinical syndromes rather than the presence

of the abnormal reaginic antibody which identifies allergy in the immuno-
logical sense was used as the criterion for their inclusion on the premise
that psychological factors often do not and need not influence the reaginic
titer. Although most of the children had manifestations of the various
clinical allergic syndromes, they could be classified as regards the primary
presenting allergic problem as follows: asthma, 55; hay fever, 30; eczema,
5.

The control group of nonallergic children included those cases referred during the same period from various sources for divers problems.
From these were excluded those children showing gross abnormalities
such as mental deficiency, epilepsy, organic brain damage or possible
psychosis. The primary presenting behavior problems fell into the classification shown in Table 1.

Table 1

"Attacking" problems (18 cases) *	
Disobedience, "demandingness," stubbornness, rebellion	10
Sibling rivalry	2
Fire setting	2
Stealing	2
Truancy and running away	2
"Withdrawal" problems (29 cases) *	
Timidity, anxiety, clinging, "nervousness"	19
Physical complaints that did not yield to medical treatment	4
Stuttering	3
Masturbation	2
Hair pulling	1
Problems in which the attacking and withdrawing elements	
were not clear on presentation (6 cases)	
Not doing well in school	6

* "Withdrawal" and "Attack" used in relation to problems are Wickman's terms
(9).

From Table 1 it is seen that there are more problems which can be
classified under "Withdrawal" than under "Attack," thus making the control sample one in which overt aggression as a presenting symptom was
not as predominant as might be expected in a group referred for help.

In the control group medical reports in all cases indicated that no
physical symptoms of clinical allergy were present.

In both the allergic and nonallergic groups, qualitative psychological
data were obtained from interviews with the mother, and often also with
the father, and from a session with the child—either an interview or a
play session developed from a procedure described earlier by Baruch (3).

The allergic group was composed of 51 boys and 39 girls; the nonallergic group of 24 boys and 29 girls. In age, the allergics ranged from 1 year and 10 months to 18 years, with a mean age of 8 years and 8.26 months. The nonallergics ranged from 1 year and 11 months to 17 years, with a mean age of 8 years and 1.94 months.

The Hostility Pattern. In some children, hostility toward parents comes out directly without subterfuge or hiding. Andy (5/2)[1] says, "I like to scare my mother and hit her. I call her names, too, and I make a whole bunch of noise. I scream so loud she thinks I die and that scares her good." His mother confirmed this. Similarly in temper tantrums, in defiance, in name calling and so on, the child hits directly at the parent without subterfuge or cover-up. The fight is openly against the parent. The parent is the declared enemy. In the present study, this form of aggression is termed *Direct* hostility. The vector of the hostility is outward from the self. The target is frankly the parent.

Another way in which the child expresses hostility is by indirection. Paul (7/5) declares he has to wet his bed. He just can't help it if his mother does get sick from the smell. He is not so frank about his intent to battle his mother. He tries to hide it but the intent is obviously there. In such behavior as food refusals, whining, "silliness," untidiness and dirtiness, the child aims consciously or unconsciously to disturb his parents. His machinations may be more or less subtle but by indirection he hits out at them. The struggle is primarily between himself and his parents. They are still the chief enemies even though undeclared. Hostility of this sort is called *Indirect* hostility in this paper. The vector is still outward; the target is still the parents.

A third way in which the child expresses hostility is by displacing it. In such behavior as hitting or teasing another child, in cruelty to animals, in destruction of property, the child changes the target. To all conscious intent and purpose, the aim is removed from the parent. The vector of hostility is still outward and away from the self, but the target is changed. In the present study, hostility of this nature is called *Displaced.*

A fourth way in which the child expresses hostility is by turning it *against himself.* Then the vector changes as well as the target. The direction is no longer *out* but *in.* In the present study, hostility against self has included such behavior as suicide threats and self-condemnation; hair pulling, nail biting, head banging and accident proneness. The allergic symptoms have not been included here, not only because they were inherent in the sample, but also because one purpose was to explore how else in behavior the organism tended to injure itself.

The various types of hostility are not mutually exclusive. All or any combination can be seen in the same individual.

Thus, the various aspects of the hostile pattern are pictured in terms

---

[1] Numbers in parentheses following childrens' names indicate age in years and months.

of *vector* and *target*. Another aspect has to do with the spontaneity with which the hostility is expressed. No matter what the form, some children express hostility vigorously and freely; others hold it painfully under or let it through with timidity and reluctance. When a child has shown such reluctance, or has brought out hostility with hesitance, or has withheld it, the affect has been described as *Blocked*. Implicit in this blocking lie the guilt and anxiety which the hostile feelings generate.

Manifestations of Hostility in the Two Groups.   Evidences of the various kinds of hostility, as described above, and evidences of block were gained from observation of the child's behavior in the office and from reports by his parents regarding specific modes of behavior at home. Wherever possible, supplementary reports were obtained from the school. Records and protocols were then analyzed and tabulated for statistical purposes.

The material from the play sessions was treated separately in order to give a comparison of what was revealed projectively and what appeared in the child's daily life.

Outgoing Hostility (Vector Outward and Away from Self).   Under outgoing forms of hostility are included *Direct* hostility, *Indirect* and *Displaced*.

Direct hostility was evidenced in their daily behavior by 18 (20%) of the 90 allergic children and by 44 (83%) of the 53 nonallergic. Statistically the proportion of children showing direct hostility in the two groups was significantly different. (The critical ratio was 9.4)

Indirect hostility was evidenced in daily behavior by 41 allergic children (45%) and by all 53 of the nonallergics (100%—C.R. 7.2). Once more there was a significant difference.

. . . . .

In summary, the nonallergics act out all types of outwardly directed hostility in a significantly higher proportion of cases than do the allergics. Conversely, the allergics are characterized by not acting out hostility proportionately in their daily lives.

In the permissive atmosphere of the play sessions, however, the hostility of the allergics became more manifest. For example, John (8/5), a slender, asthmatic child, came into the office apprehensive and clinging to his mother. He was an only child, a Caesarean birth, who had been raised on a rigid schedule, trained early, and cuddled not at all. In infancy he had "vomited when forced to eat" and sucked his thumb. His mother described him as "a very good child." She expressed her attitude toward him when she said, "He's very affectionate, I'm not. I guess I'm not the loving sort. I really never wanted a child, I shouldn't have had him at all." And yet, "I revolve too much around him, I have no life of my own. He sleeps badly, is tense and nervous and sick all the time." The school also characterized him as "very good." No overt hostility was observed in his office deportment. He went through his tests with compliant fearfulness. He was obviously scared but voiced no protest.

In his play session with a doll family, he had the boy who represented himself take the toy gun and with displaced hostility shoot all the Japs who were behind the door and could not be seen. He then came home, shot the gun outside into the air, and had it hit the chimney. But this could not go on long. In a manner characteristic of the allergic, he had to stop himself. And so he made his mother run to call the police and had his father forbid further shooting. As he went on playing out a family scene, he showed the mother punishing the child and said, "She spanked him so hard, she busted her thumb. She's nasty. She don't like me to do bad things, like playing with her things or setting on the floor. I'll sock her," which he proceeded to have the boy doll do. But, again characteristically, he could not remain comfortable after this expression of direct hostility and had to punish himself. So he put the boy in a boat and had it tip over, saying, "He falls into the water—into a great big hole of water, so big he couldn't get out."

Of the 23 allergic children with no outgoing hostility manifested in their daily lives, 19 had play sessions. Fourteen of these (73%) unmasked hostility in one form or another in play. The change from behavior to play was statistically significant (C.R. 4.2).

To return to a comparison of the allergics and nonallergics: some interesting facts appeared in respect to the hostility which emerged in their play. Of the 90 allergics, 72 had play sessions; of the 53 nonallergics, 42 had play sessions. *Direct hostility* showed up in the play of 36 (50%) of the allergics and in 37 (81%) of the nonallergics (C.R. 3.6). *Indirect hostility* showed up in the play of 38 (52%) of the allergics and in 39 (92%) of the nonallergics (C.R. 5.6). Despite the increased release of hostility among the allergics in play, it was still significantly less than in the nonallergics.

However, in relation to *Displaced hostility*, the picture changed. Forty-eight (66%) of the allergics, and 33 (78%) of the nonallergics, showed displaced hostility in play (C.R. 1.4). The difference was no longer significant. It would seem, then, that given the permissiveness of the play situation, the allergic child chooses what he feels to be the safest way of bringing hostility out, namely, in displaced form. Hostility aimed at his parents appears to threaten him more.

Hostility against Self (Vector Inward toward Self). In the allergic group, 50 of the 90 children (55%) evidenced hostility against self in their daily behavior. In the nonallergics, 15 of the 53 (28%) turned hostility against self. Statistically, the two groups were significantly different (C.R. 3.3).

It is at once noticeable that there is a reversal of what occurred with outgoing hostility. Whereas the incidence of outgoing hostility was higher in the nonallergic groups, *hostility against self* was higher in the allergic groups. Even without counting his illness, the allergic individual more characteristically turned his hostility in on himself.

In play, too, the allergic showed hostility against self in a greater proportion of instances than the nonallergic. In the allergic group, 51 of the 72 who had play sessions (70%) evidenced hostility against self in play, whereas 15 of the 42 nonallergics who had play sessions evidenced it (35%). Statistically there was a significantly higher proportion of allergics (C.R. 3.8).

Larry (8/9) illustrated this type of hostility against self both in his play and his daily behavior. He was an obese boy with asthma and hay fever, uncertain in his speech and movement, almost viciously rejected by his mother, who also overprotected him. In his play he makes the doll representing himself not eat, "even though," as he says, "it is the best dinner." He makes various uncomfortable things happen to the child. For instance, he has to bathe in freezing water. He says, "Poor little boy, he doesn't have his own bed, he has to sleep on the floor." As to his behavior, the schoolteacher reported that he repeatedly tattled on himself, even to making false accusations as if seeking punishment. He threatened suicide frequently.

Howard (5/1), a boy with asthma and hay fever, in play says, "Naughty boy, daddy spanks him. They put him to bed because he's naughty. Burn naughty boy up. His face is gone. Turn him over, his face is gone. He's all burned up, his face is gone."

In interviews too, the older children came out with self-punitive expressions. Caroline (12), who suffered from hay fever, confided, "I'm going to commit suicide with sleeping pills. I like it when I get spanked, I beg for more."

Often in play, after expressing outgoing hostility, particularly of the direct type, the child would not only turn against himself but would become apprehensive and guilty and would grow hesitant and block. Donna (5/6), an asthmatic girl, serves as an example. In her play, the little girl representing herself manifests direct hostility. "She gets her cap gun out and sneaks up and shoots her mother." Donna then very evidently feels guilty. She protests, "Only I don't, I can't; it's too awful naughty." She then turns her hostility on herself and has the mother doll spank the little girl doll saying, "So her mother hits her again and again and hurts her awful." But the self-punishment does not absolve her. She hangs her head and blocks, saying, "I don't want to play any more."

Manifestation of Block in the Two Groups. Both in play and in interviews, the allergic subjects were more prone than the nonallergics to hide and deny hostility or to express it hesitantly and reluctantly. At the point where the therapist structured the play situation, as she did with all children, and said, "Now the boy (or girl) does something naughty," it was characteristic of the allergic children to hesitate, whereas it was characteristic of the nonallergics to jump right in.

To illustrate: In the nonallergics, Marlene (5/2) jumps in with, "She [the girl doll representing herself] was supposed to go to school and goes to the show instead and took money out of the bank . . . and when she got home she hit her father and kicked him and kicked her mother and slapped the mother's face. . . ." Jerry (6/0) takes the toy gun and shoots the father. Leila (4/4) "socks" the mother, "socks" the father, and gets herself a new mother without much ado. Linda (9/11) plays that she dumps all her pretty mother's dresses in the water, and her father's suits. She trips both down the steps and finally puts mother in the attic where there are "millions of rats and mice that mother hates. . . . But anyway, she [the girl] locked her in and left her. . . ." Barbara (15/5) admits openly that her parents make her furious. "They're ridiculously fussy. They're after me all the time with silly details. I'm mad."

In contrast, among the allergics, Phyllis (14) says, "I have no troubles. They don't ever bother me!" And from Caroline (12), "I've got no problems. I don't mind how they act. I don't care at all. I never feel mean." Jacqueline (14) explains, "I just sit and stare into space, just blank most of the time, so I won't think of anything."

Jimmy (9/7) in his play session admits that he wants to make the mother cry and then shows his block saying, "But I never can manage to get at it, so I stop wanting to. The trouble is as soon as I want to I feel like crying so it doesn't ever work out." Sam (7/7) similarly shows his desire and his block, "He'd like to knock the chair down and make the mother fall over. But he can't. He only cries." Hans (9) sits completely blocked and can do nothing. "I can't think," he says, "I feel awful. I wish I could think up something to do to them but I can't."

This was the characteristic picture evident not only in the play sessions, but in observations and reports of daily deportment as well. Statistical analysis confirmed these impressions.

In the allergic group 83 of the 90 children (92%) were observably blocked in their behavior, whereas only 9 of the 53 (17%) nonallergics were blocked. The difference statistically was highly significant (C.R. 12.8).

The allergic child apparently does not dare to express his hostile feelings to the same extent or as freely as does the nonallergic child. Apparently he more commonly generates or develops guilt and anxiety in relation to his hostility and more frequently is in conflict about bringing his feelings out.

. . . . .

In their play sessions, as is indicated earlier, the allergic children did loosen up. The expressions of direct hostility became more frequent. Of the 72 allergic children who had play sessions, 56 failed in their daily behavior to act out direct hostility. But in their play sessions, 24 of the 56 (42%) did bring out direct hostility to their parents. Since the difference between the direct hostility shown in the play and in behavior was significant (C.R. 4.4), it becomes evident once more that these allergic children did block in their daily behavior and either inhibited or repressed the hostility which they actually felt.

It is interesting also to note that 33 per cent of the allergics who showed direct hostility in play had not shown it in behavior, and 20 per cent who showed indirect hostility in play had failed to show it in behavior. But only 12 per cent of those who showed displaced hostility in play had failed to show it in behavior. Again, the greatest incidence of blocking in the allergics was in respect to direct hostility, the next greatest block in respect to indirect hostility, while the lowest evidence of blocking existed in bringing hostility out in displaced form.

A Graphic Comparison of the Two Groups.   Many of the foregoing points may be recapitulated and made more strikingly evident by a graphic comparison of the two groups in respect to the various forms of hostility and blocking, both in play and behavior (Figure 1). Although the statistical data here depicted are connected by lines, such lines are not to be construed as necessarily indicating a continuum either statistically or dynamically. The curves for play and behavior parallel each other in each group, but each group maintains its characteristic level for each form of hostility and for blocking.

. . . . .

DISCUSSION

In view of the pattern of upbringing in our culture, it may be assumed that hostility almost inevitably generated feelings of anxiety and guilt. Judging by the qualitative data in the present study, guilt was present in both the nonallergics and the allergics, but it did not appear to hamper the nonallergics as much as it did the allergics. The allergic children appeared to differ from the nonallergic in developing a greater degree of guilt and anxiety or in being able to handle it less adequately. This shows up quantitatively in the greater incidence of conflict or block among the allergics.

Explanation can be sought in the physical constitution of the child, in the environment, or in both. This brings us back to the fact that in the environment of the allergic child there was present an element which had a strikingly high incidence when contrasted with the same factor in the environment of the nonallergic. As brought out earlier, this factor was that of *maternal rejection* as defined in our previous report (5).

In the allergic, maternal rejection was present in 89 of the 90 (98%) while in the nonallergic group it was present in only 13 of the 53 (24%). Statistically, this is a highly significant difference (C.R. 12.3).

Relating this environmental factor to block, it was found that 83 of the 90 allergic children (92%) were not only rejected but were also blocked. In striking contrast, none of the 13 nonallergic children who were maternally rejected were blocked (C.R. 32.7). The highly significant difference here suggests that maternal rejection in the allergic somehow creates a greater sense of guilt and consequently greater conflict and block than in the nonallergic.

In a way then, the allergic child is like a cornered animal. He feels and hates the impact of his mother's rejection as all children do. But he fears to bring out hostility directly to his parents. He tries to bring it out by indirection, but again is apparently too guilty and blocks. He turns

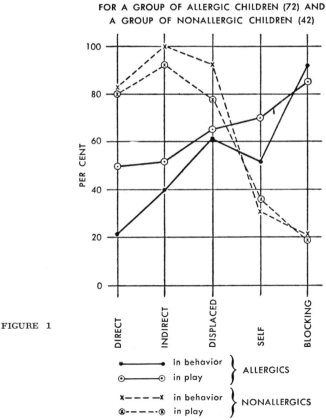

FOR A GROUP OF ALLERGIC CHILDREN (72) AND
A GROUP OF NONALLERGIC CHILDREN (42)

FIGURE 1

PER CENT

DIRECT   INDIRECT   DISPLACED   SELF   BLOCKING

•———• In behavior ⎫
⊙———⊙ in play   ⎬ ALLERGICS

x – – –x in behavior ⎫
⊗– – –⊗ in play   ⎬ NONALLERGICS

to displacing it but even so cannot seem to vent it sufficiently. In short, he cannot get release from the tension of his hostile feelings by expressing them in outgoing fashion. He seeks to punish himself. Still he does not gain absolution or peace, so he goes on trying to shut off the expression of his hostile feelings and to deny them. The inner conflict, however, apparently remains, and so he must draw from other resources within him to solve his dilemma. Here is probably where his allergic constitution comes in. It becomes useful to him. He can muster it to his aid.

With remarkable acuity, some of the allergic children seem to see this. Says Jeff (6/5), "When they punish and whip me I want to slam the door and break things and run away and get out. But I can't. I can't do nothin' to my little brother, he's sleeping. I can't do nothin' to my mother and father, I just can't. I just want to get out. But I can't. I get sick. Then mother brings me stuff and daddy does too, to make me better." Or, as Alice (7/9) expressed it, "Most days I'm good and my mother loves me. But when I'm sick I make my mother good and mad. She thinks I'm a regular nuisance 'cause she can't go out with her friends." Or as Eddie (4/9) says gleefully, "When I'm sick my daddy has to walk around at night for me and he says 'God damn.'"

The allergic child no doubt uses his symptoms to other ends than that of gaining hostile outlet. The data on affect hunger in the present sample (not yet reported) confirm this. But in one aspect of his dynamic behavior, the illness does appear to be used to discharge hostility. In short, where a psychosomatic element exists in causing, precipitating or prolonging the allergic exacerbations, the somatic symptoms appear to provide an answer to the unconscious controversy within. Guilt and anxiety having led to insoluble conflict and blocking, the child must find another way of getting his hostility out. The symptoms, then, represent a means of dissolving the organism's tension.

. . . . .

REFERENCES

1. ABRAMSON, HAROLD A. *Psychodynamics and the Allergic Patient*. Bruce, Saint Paul and Minneapolis, 1948.
2. ALEXANDER, F., AND T. M. FRENCH. *Studies in Psychosomatic Medicine*. Ronald Press, New York, 1948.
3. BARUCH, DOROTHY W. *Aggression During Doll Play in a Preschool*. Am. J. Orthopsychiatry, 11: 252–259, 1941.
4. DUNBAR, FLANDERS. *Emotions and Bodily Changes*. Columbia Univ. Press, New York, 1938.
5. MILLER, HYMAN, AND DOROTHY W. BARUCH. *Psychosomatic Studies of Children with Allergic Manifestations*. Psychosomat. Med., 10: 275 (Sept.-Oct.), 1948.

6. ROGERSON, C. H. *Psychological Factors in Asthma Prurigo.* Ibid., 3: 169 (April), 1941.

7. SAUL, L. J. *Some Observations on the Relations of Emotions and Allergy.* Ibid., 3: 66, 1941.

8. WEISS, E., AND O. S. ENGLISH. *Psychosomatic Medicine.* Saunders, Philadelphia, 1943.

9. WICKMAN, E. K. *Children's Behavior and Teacher's Attitudes.* Commonwealth Fund, New York, 1938.

43. A STUDY OF PREJUDICE IN CHILDREN

ELSE FRENKEL-BRUNSWIK

Persons in authority both comfort and frustrate us from our first moments of life. Each person works out some pattern of adjustment to this authority. Some spend all their lives in revolt while others cling to authority persons. The latter attempt to produce over and over again relationships in which there is a strong, punitive, cold authority-person whose word is law. Such persons are called "authoritarian." They prefer dominator-submitter, leader-follower relationships rather than relationships in which all are equal; they want to look up to people or down on them.

The preference of many people for relationships which allow them to be dependent rather than self-reliant—to let others make their decisions—is reflected in attitudes such as those of many Americans at election time. "My vote means nothing," they say, and they do not go to the polls. Apparently, their natural impulses to learn, to strive, and to participate in the events of democratic life have been beaten down, twisted and broken, by autocratic parents, friends, teachers, and employers.

This history-making article describes the feelings of prejudiced children toward their parents and toward their upbringings. A considerable amount of research has shown that the less educated express more prejudice than those with more schooling; moreover, persons in the lower socio-economic classes—perhaps because theirs is a more threatened position without security—have been shown to be more authoritarian than middle-class individuals.

Reprinted from *Human Relations*, 1, No. 3 (1948), 295–306, by permission of the Executor of the Estate of Else Frenkel-Brunswik; and the publisher.

A RESEARCH PROJECT ON ETHNIC PREJUDICE IN CHILDREN AND ADOLESCENTS

. . . A research project designed to throw light on the determinants of susceptibility to racial or ethnic prejudice and allied forms of undemocratic opinions and attitudes in children is being conducted at the Institute of Child Welfare of the University of California in Berkeley.

The age levels studied range from eleven to sixteen. The source of our present report includes attitude and personality tests as well as interviews with children and their parents. A total of about 1,500 boys and girls of varied socio-economic background were studied, and 120 of those found extremely prejudiced or unprejudiced were interviewed according to a schedule prepared in advance. The parents of the children interviewed were visited and likewise interviewed.

In general, the results indicate that already at these age levels children's reactions to statements about men and society as well as their spontaneous formulations about these topics form a more or less consistent pattern. This pattern, in turn, seems to be related to certain personality features of the child. Though there can be little doubt about the existence of these relationships, there is evidence that they are not as consistent and rigid as those found with adults in an earlier, similarly conceived Public Opinion Study, also conducted in Berkeley.

We shall point out the differences in the personalities of the ethnically prejudiced and unprejudiced child. It will turn out that such prejudice is but one aspect of a broader pattern of attitudes. At the same time, we shall try to discover areas of possible modifiability in the personality structure of the prejudiced child. As a first step, a description will be given of the social and political beliefs of such children. Next, we shall present a composite picture of their personality structure. An attempt will be made to study their social opinions and attitudes in relation to their basic personality needs.

ESTABLISHMENT AND TESTING OF OPPOSITE EXTREMES

The initial classification of subjects was made on the basis of responses to a series of about fifty slogans of racial prejudice or tolerance as well as statements pertaining to more general social attitudes. A prejudice scale was thus constructed with items regarding the attitude of children toward five minority groups: Jews, Negroes, Japanese, Mexicans, and "outgroups" in general. It proceeds along established lines in that it covers such situations as eating in the same restaurant, living in the same neighborhood, participating at the same social affairs, letting in or keeping people out of the country, and stereotypical accusations of minority members such as cruelty of the Japanese, laziness of the Negroes, or radicalism and moneymindedness of the Jews.

It was found that some of the children tend to reveal a stereotyped and rigid glorification of their own group and an aggressive rejection of outgroups and foreign countries. The scale yielded split-half correlations of from .82 to .90 (uncorrected for length of test), indicating that ethnic prejudice is a consistent and firmly established pattern not later than at the earliest of the age levels studied. In the present paper, the term "unprejudiced" (or "liberal") refers to those 25 per cent of the children who were found to be in greatest agreement with tolerant statements, whereas those in the opposite extreme quartile will be called "prejudiced" or "ethnocentric." The last two terms especially are to be understood to refer not only to racial or ethnic prejudice in the narrower sense of the word, but to a certain extent also to include its usual accompaniments, such as clannishness or national chauvinism and even glorification of family and self, in correspondence with the varying scope of what is being experienced as "ingroup" in any given context.

The disjunctive statements made in this paper concerning other attitudes or personality traits found predominantly in one or other of the two extreme groups are all based on quantitative material gained from other tests or from the interviews. The tests involved were constructed on the basis of initial clinical data gathered from children with extreme standing on the prejudice scale. Aside from a separate scale for more general social attitudes, there was a personality test containing about 150 items. The interviews were evaluated in terms of a system of categories which had proved themselves to be especially relevant in this context. Statistical significance (often at as high a level as 1 per cent or better) is established for all differences referred to in this paper between the two extreme groups, with respect to test items and in most cases also with respect to overall interview ratings. Quotations of answers to interview questions are added informally by way of illustration. It must also be kept in mind that the results presented here are limited to extremes only. Furthermore, they may well be less pronounced in cultures or subcultures in which the choice between alternative ideologies of the type involved here is less clearcut.

In addition to revealing prejudice toward specific ethnic groups, the children classified as ethnocentric are in marked disagreement with such more general statements, also included in the defining scale, as the following:

Different races and religions would get along better if they visited each other and shared things.

America is a lot better off because of the foreign races that live here.

The liberal children endorse most of such statements with a considerable approximation to unanimity.

GENERAL SOCIAL ATTITUDES OF PREJUDICED AND UNPREJUDICED CHILDREN

Along similar lines are the children's spontaneous reactions in the interviews to the question: "What is America's biggest problem today?" The liberal children can more readily remove themselves from their immediate needs and think in terms of a far-reaching social good. Examples of the problems they list are:

". . . the starving people in Europe, because the people in our country won't think of them and they should," or,

"The atom bomb; how to do things about the atom bomb to keep peace in the world."

Ethnocentric children, on the other hand, are more concerned with things that affect their immediate welfare. They tend to give greatest prominence to such problems as:

"Taxes on everything, and the cost of living.

The question "How would you change America?" is answered similarly. Ethnocentric children tend to mention external things:

"Clean up the streets—all that garbage lying around! See that everything is in order."

Liberal children, on the other hand, tend to mention such things as:

"So the Negroes wouldn't be beaten up like they are down South," or
"We should have a world police so that there would be no more wars."

We turn now to the test intended to ascertain even broader social attitudes. In this scale, as well as in the personality scales to be discussed next, differentiations are much more clearcut at the later age levels studied. Study of the interviews suggests that this is in part due to a comprehension factor, but that there is also a genuine absence of the relationship in the younger children.

The following statements in this scale differentiate to a particularly significant degree between the prejudiced and unprejudiced children, with the prejudiced more often endorsing them:

If we keep on having labor troubles, we may have to turn the government over to a dictator who will prevent any more strikes.

It is better to have our government run by business men rather than by college professors.

The government is interfering too much with private business.

Paralleling the rejection of the outgroup is a naive and selfish acceptance of the ingroup. Thus above age 11 approximately two-fifths of the prejudiced extreme but only a scattered few of the opposite extreme group subscribe to the following two statements:

People who do not believe that we have the best kind of government in the world should be kicked out of the country.

Refugees should be thrown out of this country so that their jobs can be given to veterans.

A particularly narrow form of ethnocentrism is revealed in the tendency, prominent in the prejudiced child, to agree with the following statement:

Only people who are like myself have a right to be happy.

The selfish orientation toward their own country and the indifference and hostility against other countries is furthermore expressed in the agreement of almost half of the ethnocentric children with the following statement:

We should not send any of our food to foreign countries, but should think of America first.

The rejection of foreign countries by the ethnocentric child, and the projection of his own hostility onto them, may be considered to contribute to his affinity toward war. Thus, our ethnocentric children subscribe almost twice as often as the liberal to the statement:

Most of the other countries of the world are really against us, but are afraid to show it.

There is, furthermore, the conviction—apparently deep-rooted in the personality structure of the prejudiced child—that wars are inevitable. Comparatively often he tends to endorse the following statement:

There will always be war, it is part of human nature.

In the interviews, where the children are able to express their opinions spontaneously, the ethnocentric children make remarks such as the following about war:

"One happens in every generation," or,
"The Bible says there will always be wars," or;
"Sure, we will have another war. Wars never end."

ANTI-WEAKNESS ATTITUDE OF THE PREJUDICED CHILD

The aggression of the ethnocentric children is not limited to minority groups and other countries but is part of a much more generalized rejection of all that is weak or different. Statements from additional scales help to assess such more general personality traits. Thus the prejudiced child agrees more often than the unprejudiced with the statement:

The world would be perfect if we put on a desert island all of the weak, crooked and feeble-minded people.

It is especially the prejudiced girl who tends to disagree with the following statement:

It is interesting to be friends with someone who thinks or feels differently from the way you do.

The ingroup feeling is clearly expressed by her tendency to endorse the following statement:

Play fair with your own gang, and let the other kids look out for themselves.

DICHOTOMY OF SEX ROLES

Ethnocentric children tend to conceive of the other sex as outgroup, and tend toward segregation from, and resentment against, the other sex. Associations of masculinity vs. femininity with strength vs. weakness need no further elaboration.

Around adolescence, the prejudiced of both sexes tend to agree with the statement:

Girls should only learn things that are useful around the house.

On the whole, ethnocentric children tend toward a rigid, dichotomizing conception of sex roles, being intolerant of passive or feminine manifestations in boys and masculine or tomboyish manifestations in girls. Thus an ethnocentric girl, asked how girls should act around boys, answers:

"Act like a lady, not like a bunch of hoodlums. Girls should not ask boys to date. It's not lady-like."

Two of the liberal boys reply to the same question as follows:

"It depends on their age; the girls should not be so afraid of the boys and not be shy," and,

"Talk about the things you like to talk about, about the same as another boy would."

Asked what is the worst occupation for a woman, one of the ethnocentric boys answers:

"To earn her own living, usually the man does that."

On the other hand, a boy low on ethnocentrism answers to the same question

"What she doesn't like to do."

The intolerance the ethnocentric child tends to show toward manifestations of the opposite sex in himself or in others makes for bad heterosexual adjustment, as was also found in the study of adults. The rigid and exaggerated conception of masculinity and femininity further tends to lead to a strained relation to one's own sex role. Thus the few children who, in reaction to some indirect questions, show envy of the role of the other sex, are ethnocentric.

The liberal child, on the other hand, tends, as does the liberal adult, to have a more flexible conception of the sex roles as well as to face conflicts in this direction more openly. Boys in this group show less repression of feminine, girls less repression of masculine trends. At the same time there is on the whole a better heterosexual development and less rejection of the opposite sex. Tolerance toward the other sex and the equalitarian relationship between the two sexes seems to be an important basis for tolerance in general and thus should be fostered by coeducational measures. This is one of the places where thinking in dichotomies has to be broken down.

POWER AND MONEY

The contempt the ethnocentric child has for the weak is related to his admiration of the strong, tough, and powerful, *per se*. He tends to disagree with the statement:

Weak people deserve consideration; the world should not belong to the strong only.

And he relatively often agrees with the statements:

Might makes right; the strong win out in the end.
A person who wants to be a man should seek power.

The latter statement shows the ideal aspired to by the typical ethnocentric boy and demanded in men by the typical ethnocentric girl. This pseudo-masculine ideal often prevents a humanitarian outlook which is sometimes considered as soft and "sissified." The fear of weakness is expressed in the tendency of the ethnocentric boy to agree with a statement like:

If a person does not watch out somebody will make a sucker out of him.

In the same context belongs the orientation toward money as a means of obtaining power, material benefits, and sometimes even friends. In the interviews of prejudiced children appear such statements as the following:

"It means something if you want to buy a house or a car or a fur coat for your wife. No dollar, no friend; have a dollar, got a friend."

The over-libidinization of money leads not only to an exaggeration of its importance but also to an unrealistic fear of it as something evil. The following is typical of the statements made by some of the ethnocentric children:

"It helps make enemies. Money is the root of all evil, they say."

AMBIVALENT SUBMISSION TO PARENTS AND TEACHERS

The admiration the ethnocentric child tends to have for success, power, and prestige may be assumed to result from submission to authority based on his fear of punishment and retaliation. The originally forced submission to parental authority apparently leads to a continued demand for autocratic leadership, strict discipline and punishment, as exercised not only by parents but also by parent substitutes. Thus ethnocentric children, especially girls, tend to agree more often than liberal ones with the statements

Teachers should tell children what to do and not try to find out what the children want.

It would be better if teachers would be more strict.

This attitude is also mirrored in their spontaneous statements made in the interviews while talking about parents and teachers. They tend to refer to the authoritarian aspects of the parent-child relationship whereas liberal children tend to emphasize the cooperative aspects of this relationship.

Though there tends to be a surface submission to authority in the ethnocentric, there is often, at the same time, an underlying resentment against authority. Apparently, this resentment is repressed for two reasons: first, because of a fear of retaliation for any open expression of resentment; and second, because of a fear of being deprived of the material benefits which persons in authority can give, and upon which the typical prejudiced child seems especially dependent. For the ethnocentric more than for the liberal, parents and other adults are conceived of as the deliverers of goods.

The following quotations illustrate the attitude of the ethnocentric child toward the parents as well as toward teachers. Asked to describe the perfect father, one of the boys in this group says:

"Does not give you everything you want, isn't very strict with you, doesn't let you do the outrageous things that you sometimes want to."

Typical of these children is the use of the negative in the characterization of the perfect parent and the references to the punitive and restrictive aspects. Others of these boys say about the perfect father:

"He spanks you when you are bad and doesn't give you too much money," or;

"When you ask for something he ought not to give it to you right away. Not soft on you, strict."

Similar is the description of the perfect teacher by another ethnocentric boy:

"She is strict, treats all children the same, won't take any nonsense of them, keeps them organized in the playground, in class, in lines."

About teachers who are not liked an ethnocentric boy says:

"Those who tell you in a nice way instead of being strict and they don't make you mind."

The same group of children when asked how they would like to change their father sometimes reveal resentment and feelings of being deprived and victimized. One of the ethnocentric boys says:

"He wouldn't smoke a pipe, would not eat too much, wouldn't take all the food away from his son."

Along the same lines is the answer of an ethnocentric boy to the question, "For what should the hardest punishment be administered?";

"Should be for talking back to parents, it should be a whipping."

One of the girls in this group says:

"Naturally for murder, the next is for not paying attention to her mother and father. She should be sent to a juvenile home for not paying attention to her parents."

Another ethnocentric boy asks for punishment too:

"Talking back, not minding, for example, if you are supposed to saw a certain amount of wood in one hour and don't do it you should be punished for it."

Methodical clinical ratings of the interviews confirm the impressions gained from these quotations. The ethnocentric children tend to think in the category of strictness and harshness when telling about their fathers, the liberal children tend to think primarily in terms of companionship. The ratings also seem to indicate that ethnocentric children tend to complain more about neglect by their fathers. The interview ratings bear out the fearful submission to harsh punishment on the part of the typical ethnocentric child and the ability of the typical liberal child to assimilate punishment which is explained to them and for which their understanding is thus assured. Fear and dependency not only seem to prevent the ethnocentric child from any conscious criticism of the parents but even lead to an acceptance of punishment and to an "identification with the aggressor." The fact that the negative feelings against the parents have to be excluded from consciousness may be considered as contributing to the general lack of insight, rigidity of defense, and "narrowness of the ego." Since the unprejudiced child as a rule does not seem to have had to submit to stern authority in childhood (according to the interviews at least), he can afford in his later life not to long for strong authority, nor does he need to assert his strength against those who are weaker. The "anti-weakness" attitude referred to above seems thus to be directly related to the fearful submission to authority.

PARENTS' CONCERN WITH SOCIAL STATUS. RIGID RULES AND DISCIPLINE

The hypothesis may be offered that it is this repressed resentment toward authority which is displaced upon socially inferior and foreign groups. As may be seen from the interviews with the parents, the liberal child, in contrast to the ethnocentric child, is more likely to be treated as an equal and to be given the opportunity to express feelings of rebellion or disagreement. He thus learns at home the equalitarian and individualized approach to people, as the ethnocentric child learns the authoritarian and hierarchical way of thinking. Interviews with parents of ethnocentric children show an exaggerated social status-concern. This may well be assumed to be the basis of a rigid and externalized set of values. What is socially accepted and what is helpful in the climbing of the social ladder is considered good, and what deviates, what is different, and what is socially inferior is considered bad.

The parents of the ethnocentric children are often socially marginal. The less they can accept their marginality, the more urgent becomes the wish to belong to the privileged groups. This leads to the development of a kind of collective ego which is very different from genuine group identification and which must be assumed to contribute to ethnocentrism. With this narrow and steep path in mind such parents are likely to be intolerant of any manifestation on the part of the children which seems to deter from, or to oppose, the goal decided upon. The more urgent the social needs of the parents, the more they are apt to view the child's behavior in terms of their own instead of the child's needs. Since the values of the parents are outside the children's scope, yet are rigorously enforced, only a superficial identification with the parents and society can be achieved. The suppressed instinctive and hostile tendencies are apt to become diffuse and depersonalized and to lead an independent, autonomous life. In line with this the overall clinical ratings seem to indicate the more diffuse and explosive nature of the aggression of ethnocentric children, as compared with milder and more ego-acceptable forms of aggression in the typical liberal child. Thus fascism and war must have a special appeal to ethnocentric children and adults, who expect liberation of their instincts in combination with approval by authorities.

MORALISM AND CONFORMITY

The influence of the parents must be considered at least a contributing factor to the tendency, observed in the ethnocentric child, to be more concerned with status values than are liberal children. He expects—and gives—social approval on the basis of external moral values, including cleanliness, politeness, and the like. He condemns others for their non-conformity to such values, conformity being an all-or-none affair. The functioning of his superego is mainly directed toward punishment, condemnation, and exclusion of others, mirroring thus the type of discipline to which he was exposed. Interview ratings show a tendency toward more moralistic condemnation on the part of the prejudiced child and greater permissiveness toward people in general on the part of the unprejudiced.

The trend to conformity of the ethnocentric child is expressed in his greater readiness to agree with the following statements:

There is only one right way to do anything.
Appearances are usually the best test.
One should avoid doing things in public which seem wrong to others even though one knows that these things are really all right.

Politeness, cleanliness, good manners appear again and again among the requirements of prejudiced children, especially the girls, for a perfect boy or perfect girl. Interview ratings indicate that ethnocentric children tend to mention in this connection purity, cleanliness and what corresponds to a conventional conception of good personality, whereas the liberal children tend to mention companionship and fun.

In the light of what has been said before about the attitude of the typical ethnocentric child toward parents, we may assume that the conformity to approved social values is based on fear of retaliation by society for disobedience rather than on a real incorporation of those values. In order to conform, he demands a set of inflexible rules which he can follow, and he is most at ease when he can categorize and make value judgments in terms of good or bad.

INTOLERANCE OF AMBIGUITIES

Analysis of the interviews indicates that this inflexibility of the ethnocentric child is part of a broader texture of rigidity and incapacity to face ambiguous situations. Intolerance of ambiguity has been found above in his conception of the parent-child relationship and in his conception of the sex roles. It is also present in the organization of the perceptual and cognitive field.

That this rigidity represents a more generalized approach to the solving of problems even in fields where there is no social or emotional involvement has been experimentally demonstrated by Rokeach. In solving arithmetic problems ethnocentric children show greater resistance to changing a given set which interferes with the direct and simple solution of a new task. Thus even in children rigidity tends to be a pervasive trait.

It must be added that it is rigidity in thinking that is related to ethnocentrism, and not intelligence, *per se;* the IQ was found to be only very slightly (negatively) correlated with ethnocentrism.

Our interpretation then could be that ideas and tendencies which are nonconforming and which do not agree with rigid, simple and prescribed solutions (such as submission to the strong) have to be repressed and displaced. When displaced into the social sphere, this is expressed in an overly moralizing, authoritarian or generally destructive manner, and it is here that the ethnocentric child becomes a potential fascist. The choice of simple solutions apparently helps to reduce some of the repressed anxieties. These anxieties are often more directly expressed in the liberal child, since he does not tend as much to deny possible weakness or shortcomings in himself and his group as does the ethnocentric child.

CATASTROPHIC CONCEPTION OF THE WORLD

The anxieties and insecurities of the ethnocentric child are expressed more indirectly, e.g., in a greater readiness to conceive of dangers and catastrophes in the outside world, to feel helplessly exposed to external powers and to subscribe to bizarre and superstitious statements. Thus the ethnocentric child (as also in this instance the ethnocentric adult) relatively often tends to answer in the affirmative to the following three statements:

> Some day a flood or earthquake will destroy everybody in the whole world.
> There are more contagious diseases nowadays than ever before.
> If everything would change, this world would be much better.

The tendency to wish for a diffuse and all-out change rather than for definite progress indicates how relatively poorly rooted the typical ethnocentric child is in the daily task of living and in his object relationships. Behind a rigid facade of conformity there seems to be an underlying fascination by the thought of chaos and destruction. A leader will thus be welcome who gives permission to this type of license. The ideal solution for this type of child and adult is to release what is dammed up, and thus remains unintegrated, under the protection of a leader representing the externalized superego.

We find dependency not only upon external authority but also upon inanimate external forces. Thus ethnocentric children subscribe significantly more often to such superstitious statements as:

> The position of the stars at the time of your birth tells your character and personality.
> It is really true that a black cat crossing your path will bring bad luck.
> You can protect yourself from bad luck by carrying a charm or good luck piece.

It seems to be important for the typical ethnocentric child to use devices by which he can get evil dangerous forces to join him on his side as a substitute for an undeveloped self-reliance. In general, his attitudes tend to be less scientifically oriented and rational than that of the liberal child, and he is likely to explain events for which he has no ready understanding in terms of chance factors.

COMPARATIVE FLEXIBILITY OF ETHNOCENTRISM IN CHILDREN

As indicated above, the personality structure of the ethnocentric child is similar to that of the ethnocentric adult. But while this personality pattern seems quite firmly established in the adult, it appears in the child as incipient, or as a potential direction for development. This is indicated by correlations which are all-round lower than the analogous ones in adults. For instance, we often find in ethnocentric adults a highly opportunistic, exploitative and manipulative attitude toward other people. The ethnocentric child, however, in spite of showing tendencies in the same direction, still generally seeks more primary satisfaction of his psychological needs. Thus not only liberal minded children, but to a great extent children in general, tend to choose their friends from the standpoint of good companionship and "fun," whereas the ethnocentric adult tends to be more exclusively oriented toward status in his choice of friends. Furthermore, the ethnocentric child is more accessible to experience and reality than the ethnocentric adult who has rigidly structured his world according to his interests and desires. Finally, the child's position as a comparative underdog constitutes a possible resource for expanding the experimental basis for his sympathy for other underdogs.

In spite of all the differences between the ethnocentric and liberal child, it must be pointed out that with respect to many of the features mentioned above, such as superstition or conformity, children in general have more of a touch of the ethnocentric than of the liberal adult. In turn, the ethnocentric adult may be considered as more infantile than is the liberal adult with respect to these variables. The older the children become, the greater the differences between the ethnocentric and the liberal child. All this seems to indicate that some of the trends which are connected with ethnocentrism are natural stages of development which have to be overcome if maturity is to be reached.

OVERALL PICTURE AND CONCLUSIONS

Let us review once more the personality structure and the background of the ethnocentric child and compare this with that of the liberal child. As mentioned before, the parents of the ethnocentric child are highly concerned with status. They use more harsh and rigid forms of discipline which the child generally submits to rather than accepts or understands. Parents are seen simultaneously as the providers of one's physical needs and as capricious arbiters of punishment. On the surface the ethnocentric child tends, especially in his more general statements, to idealize his parents. There are, however, indications that the parent-child relationship is lacking in genuine affection. In many ethnocentric children underlying feelings of being victimized are revealed by specific episodes, told by the children, of neglect, rejection and unjust punishment. The pressure to conform to parental authority and its externalized social values makes it impossible for the child to integrate or to express his instinctual and hostile tendencies. This lack of integration makes for a narrow and rigid personality. Thus instinctual tendencies cannot be utilized for constructive purposes, such as genuine ability for love, or creative activities, for which both more permissiveness and more guidance on the part of the adult would be needed. Since the ethnocentric child often gets neither of these he presents the dual aspects of being too inhibited, on the one hand, and of having the tendency to join wild and rough games, on the other. The gang-oriented child may later conform to an "adult gang" without having acquired an internalized conscience which would control the direct and indirect expressions of aggression. When the inhibition is more pronounced we have to do with the conventional pattern of ethnocentrism. Whenever disinhibition dominates the picture, we have to do with the delinquent variety of the ethnocentric. Since, however, delinquency also often looms behind the surface of rigid conventionality the affinity of the two patterns should not be overlooked.

By contrast, the liberal child is more oriented toward love and less toward power than is the ethnocentric child. He is more capable of giving affection since he has received more real affection. He tends to judge people more on the basis of their intrinsic worth than does the ethnocentric child who places more emphasis on conformity to social mores. The liberal child, on the other hand, takes internal values and principles more seriously. Since he fears punishment and retaliation less than does the ethnocentric child, he is more able really to incorporate the values of society imposed upon him. The liberal child employs the help of adults in working out his problems of sex and aggression, and thus can more easily withstand hateful propaganda both in the forms of defamation of minorities and of glorification of war. By virtue of the greater integration of his instinctual life he becomes a more creative and sublimated individual. He is thus more flexible and less likely to form stereotyped opinions about others. The interview ratings point toward a better developed, more integrated and more internalized superego. The unprejudiced child seems to be able to express disagreement with, and resentment against, the parents more openly, resulting in a much greater degree of independence from the parents and from authorities in general. At the same time there is love-oriented dependence on parents and people in general which constitutes an important source of gratification.

This is not to say that the liberal child is necessarily always socially or personally better adjusted. He has more open anxieties, more directly faced insecurities, more conflicts. For the reduction of these conflicts he does not as a rule use the simple though, in the last analysis, inappropriate and destructive methods characteristic of the ethnocentric child. It may be precisely this lack of displacement and projectivity which enables the liberal child and adult to evaluate social and political events in a more realistic and adequate fashion. This makes it less likely that the paradoxical attitudes of depersonalizing human relationships and personally tinting political and social events will be developed. Glorification of the ingroup and vilification of the outgroup in the ethnocentric child recurs in the dimensions of power-weakness, cleanliness-dirtiness, morality-immorality, conformance-difference, fairness-unfairness, etc., thus mirroring some of the basic dimensions of their outlook and personality dynamics. Above and beyond this, stereotypes provide the individual enough latitude to project onto outgroups his specific problems, such as aggression, underlying weakness, or preoccupation with sex. Different minority groups thereby seem to lend themselves to different types of accusations.

From the point of view of society as a whole, the most important problem therefore seems to be the child's attitude toward authority. Forced submission to authority produces only surface conformity countermanded by violent underlying destructiveness, dangerous to the very society to which there seems to be conformity. Only a frightened and frustrated child will tend to gain safety and security by oversimplified black-white schematizations and categorizations on the basis of crude, external characteristics. Deliberately planned democratic participation in school and family, individualized approach to the child, and the right proportion of permissiveness and guidance may be instrumental in bringing about the attitude necessary for a genuine identification with society and thus for international understanding.

44. THE SOCIAL AND EMOTIONAL PROBLEMS OF THE EPILEPTIC CHILD AND HIS FAMILY

WILLIAM G. LENNOX

Although the medical problems associated with epilepsy have been increasingly understood and well controlled, the social and emotional problems of the epileptic often remain crippling to him and his family. This article describes some of these problems, presenting facts which should free the public from common misconceptions about the kind of life epileptics should lead.

Lennox presents a popularly held physiological view of epilepsy. Other experts, however, view the disease as caused by the interplay of three factors—a physiological predisposition, a psychological stress, and an immediate environmental factor which precipitates each attack.

In epilepsy the eradication or control of seizures by medicines or by surgery is the capstone of treatment. However, the capstone of a pyramid does not float in thin air. It must have a broad base. For the epileptic, such a base is the physical, emotional, and social well-being of the child and his family, a phase of treatment too often neglected by the doctor.

In epilepsy, more than with most diseases, the unit of treatment is the family. An epileptic child brings psychologic and social complications for those around him which are subtle, severe, and long-lasting. Below and beyond the family is the widening substructure of friends, school-teachers, acquaintances, and the general public. The conception of epilepsy which resides in the public mind is most important. For centuries the pyramid of therapy has had a foundation not of masonry but of rubble and sand.

As depicted in Figure 1, in both cases the capstone of drug or surgical treatment is sound. The social-emotional treatment on the left is poor—secrecy, shame, and fear in the family. Underneath are public misconceptions and ostracism. In the case on the right, the family has a sense of

Selections reprinted from the article in *Journal of Pediatrics,* 44 (1954), by permission of the author and publisher, the C. V. Mosby Company.

security, courage, and hope, and there are public understanding and acceptance.

Let me hold up some of the pieces of rubble from under the capstone on the left. People say, "The cause of epilepsy is a complete mystery; there is no effective treatment; the disease and the disability are progressive; rest is best. The child should not attend school nor the adult have employment; a healthy child must not view a convulsion; mental deterioration is the rule; marriage and children are out." As illustrated in Fig. 1, such misconceptions are a crumbling support for medical treatment. Usually the doctor can say, "Evidence of brain damage is lacking; the child should maintain his good health and intelligence. With proper medication and with time the seizures should disappear and, given a right public attitude, he should be able to marry, to work, and, in short, to lead a normal life."

Wrong ideas, those that cause misery when spread abroad, can be as contagious and as harmful as pathogenic germs. Correction of false concepts requires public as well as individual efforts. Here is a problem of public health. More than with most diseases a better life for the epileptic depends on an improved understanding and attitude of the general public.

The sea of opinion in which the epileptic lives is beginning to feel the warming effects of the Gulf Stream of successful research and treatment of the past two decades. But the parents of the affected child may be last to accept the new warmth. Unhealthy sentiments such as fear, worry, shame, guilt, and despair give up their entrenched positions to hope and confidence only grudgingly. The episodic symptoms cause sharp fluctua-

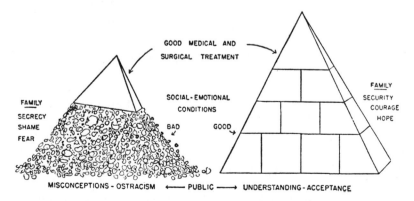

FIGURE 1.   SCHEMATIC REPRESENTATION OF PYRAMIDS OF THERAPY

The capstone at the top of each represents good drug and surgical therapy. The supporting structure represents the social-emotional conditions, at the left destructive and at the right constructive. At the base of each is the influence of the general public.

tions of emotion. A parent may unconsciously reject the child when his or her own esteem or social position is threatened. Unexpressed may be the thought, "This cannot happen to me. Let me put this terrible thing out of my thoughts, the child out of my presence." Guilt may follow realization that epilepsy came from his (or her) "side" or that the child's seizures followed some preventable accident.

A policy of hiding illness is the culminating injury inflicted by unhealthy sentiments. Secrecy has taken the place of the devils of old. Because patients and their relatives think they must remain in hiding, they do not take their rightful place in public campaigns against epilepsy. However, there is no security in secrecy. At any moment a seizure in public may tear off this cloak, exposing the illness in all its nakedness to a gaping public.

The social-emotional handicap for the epileptic is the more grotesque because it is so illogical and unnecessary. Epilepsy is a metabolic disorder and no more to be hidden than glycosuria or recurrent fever. In fact, a bout of high temperature without infection may be an epileptic seizure and as difficult to control as a convulsion. Dispassionately viewed, migraine is an autonomic epilepsy.

EMOTIONS AND THE CHILD

What effect does the prevailing fear and prejudice have on the epileptic child? The answer varies with the age. Even the baby may learn to fear the attacks. Hippocrates stated this, "But little children—when they have been often seized and feel its approach beforehand flee to their mothers—from terror and dread of the affliction, for being still infants they do not yet know what it is to be ashamed." The interruptions to play caused by frequently repeated petit mal may be frustrating and irritating.

Problems tend to increase with age. The young child may "get out of hand" because parents fear that "crossing" it will bring on an attack. Adolescence is a time of emotional rough waters; cross currents of overprotection in the home and rejection outside. What about traveling alone, dating, social events and late hours, smoking, drinking, swimming, automobile driving? A time-trusted guide is need to prevent rupture of normal parent-child relationships. The age of 12 is not the time for the competent pediatrician to turn his epileptic child adrift in the turbulent current of adolescence.

What role do emotional factors play in the child's seizures? Emotional forces can and do precipitate seizures in those already primed. However, in the main, disturbing fears, anxieties, and frustrations are consequences rather than causes of attacks. If emotion is the whole cause, the condition is not epilepsy but hysteria. The pediatrician should be competent to handle all but the most flagrant of the emotional disturbances. Those mentioned are on the level of consciousness and not immersed somewhere in its depth.

Bad behaviour may be a consequence of seizures, of brain injury, or of the strained relations engendered. Rarely, it may be a seizure itself. Differentiation is important. A child may be overactive, "always on the go," never satisfied, quarrelsome, destructive, disobedient, rebellious. Unhappy qualities such as these may be more difficult to explain and to control than the seizures. In such emergencies the help of an astute psychotherapist or social therapist for both mother and child is most welcome. To the extent that emotional problems arise out of the seizures, control of attacks by medication may bring a quick solution.

AID FOR THE PHYSICIAN

What special techniques or training does the pediatrician require? Of first importance are his own qualities that invite and inspire confidence. Parents and older children principally have three questions in their minds. Does our doctor know this subject? Can we believe what he tells us? Is his interest genuine? Close, unhurried attention to the details of the family life, the day-to-day problems of the parents, the distant bridges they want to cross now, the activities and ambitions of the child— these proclaim the doctor's real interest.

Of physical aids, by far the most important is the electroencephalogram. Tracings of the electrical currents of the brain allow the physician to speak with a certainty never dreamed of before. Approximately four-fifths of children subject to epileptic seizures display abnormalities during a twenty-minute recording. Minor deviations from the "normal" mean little. High-voltage waves, unduly slow or fast, so-called seizure discharges, tend to confirm a diagnosis of epilepsy made on clinical grounds. An alternate spike-and-wave formation recurring at the rate of three per second is diagnostic for petits, either actual or potential. The slower two-per-second variation speaks for minor seizures, brain injury, and relatively poor prognosis. Spike discharges suggest cicatricial lesions; big slow waves, tumor or previous encephalitis; spike discharges over a temporal lobe during sleep support a diagnosis of psychomotor epilepsy. Abnormality confined to a certain area may encourage the neurosurgeon to operate and may tell him what portion of the brain to remove. The degree of brain-wave disorder bears some relation to the severity of the epilepsy and is a rough guide to therapy and to prognosis. Because the brain-wave pattern is an hereditary trait, records may help in tracing the heredity of epilepsy and in advising about marriage and children. Altogether, if (a large *if*) the technique of making records and their interpretation is in experienced hands, this procedure, properly subordinated to clinical experience, reinforces the work of the physician or surgeon and saves expensive hospitalization.

THE COMPLICATION OF BRAIN DAMAGE

Epilepsy per se is a metabolic disorder of the brain. Disability for this metabolic (idiopathic) group is due primarily to the seizures and secondarily to emotional and social complications. An organic (symptomatic) epilepsy is the result of changes in brain structures (such as trauma at birth or encephalitis) acquired after conception. Persons in this organic group face five possible complications: seizures, brain damage, mental defects, plus emotional and social complications. The summation of these five may result in 100 per cent disability. In hopeless cases the doctor cannot preach hope. He is, in general, privileged to "cure seldom, relieve often, comfort always."

In addition to aiding in the social and emotional problems of individuals, the doctor must help to change public opinion and to cancel laws or rules that discriminate unfairly. The child, when adult, will meet problems of marriage and of employment. Doctors must now use their influence in smoothing the child's road of the future. Support of the leagues against epilepsy, one for doctors and another for the public, is important. The following cases illustrate problems involved:

After a series of convulsions, 7-year-old Fred was in a state of confusion for a week, able to walk and to eat when fed, but unable to answer questions or even to recognize his mother. His electroencephalogram was made up of discontinuous slow spike-wave discharges, ordinarily interpreted as representing a background of generalized neuropathology. The left-hand portion of Figure 2 is a section from this record. The mother was advised by the pediatrician that Fred's condition was chronic and that institutional care would be desirable. This threw her into a panic. She already was allergic to this subject because a brother was in an institution as a chronic epileptic. We felt that an immediate bad prognosis was hardly justified, since conditions of stupor may succeed a series of convulsions, and even the slow spike-wave complexes may yield to therapy. The mother seemed to accept a more hopeful outlook. Fortunately, the boy's confused state cleared under Phenurone medication and his electroencephalogram also. The right-hand portion of Figure 2, made five weeks later, shows a normal tracing. His intelligence score rose by 10 points to 106.

However, all this visible evidence of improvement failed to move the mother's foreboding. She interpreted shivering on the beach as a seizure; she thought his face at times had a foolish look; that his I.Q. should be higher. She was correct in complaining that his behavior at home was bad, with long periods of shrieking, reactions doubtless due to the tension of the mother's anxiety. When he was sent to a guidance home, his behavior was normal, but the deep-rooted anxiety of the mother continued in spite of efforts to explain and to reassure. She was referred to a psychiatrist who, not able to reach her

7-18-50 F. KIN. PERIOD OF STUPOR LASTING A WEEK   8-14-50   NORMAL STATE

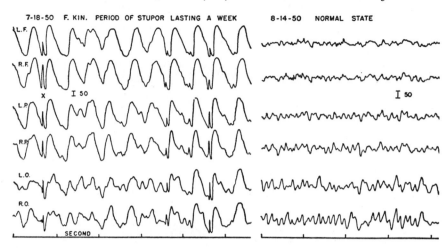

FIGURE 2.   THE ELECTROENCEPHALOGRAM OF FRED

In this and the remaining figures time in seconds is indicated at the bottom, the signal at the left represents the deflection caused by the indicated number of micro volts. Letters at the left indicate the placement of leads; *F*, frontal; *T*, temporal; *P*, parietal, and *O*, occipital. *L* is left and *R* is right. Explanations are in the text.

through psychotherapy, administered a series of shock treatments. Now, a year later, the boy has been attack-free for eighteen months and the mother complains only of his poor grades at school.

Jack, an 11-year-old, had a few convulsions in sleep but was without observed daytime seizures. The father, a physician, and the mother, sister of a chronic epileptic, were naturally deeply concerned. However the principal concern was for the boy's poor work in school where he was accused of laziness and inattention. His electroencephalogram was grossly abnormal (Figure 3). Discharges of abnormally slow waves with scattered spike-wave complexes were represented clinically only by momentary wavering of attention and flickering of the eyelids. Placed on Milontin, dysrhythmia ceased, and his teachers were amazed by the improvement in his performance. His waking electroencephalogram was nearly clear of spike-wave discharges, but in sleep occasional, much faster, complexes appeared (right-hand panel of Figure 3).

Pauline, a girl of 9 years, had a convulsion in early childhood that lasted two hours, but in the subsequent five years has had only five more. However, she seemed mentally retarded and was doing poorly in school. An I.Q. yielded a score of 54. An electroencephalogram made at this same visit was grossly abnormal. High-voltage slow spike-wave discharges were almost continuous in all leads, but their bad appearance was modified by the good feature of generalized rhythmicity (left-hand portion of Figure 4). Her convulsions called for phenobarbital or Dilantin, but her brain waves demanded Tridione; placed on Tridione, her electroencephalogram became normal. The right-hand portion made fifteen months later was entirely normal. She was seizure-free but more

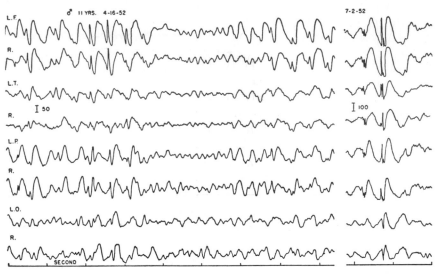

FIGURE 3. THE ELECTROENCEPHALOGRAM OF JACK

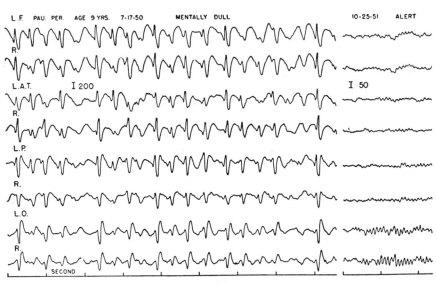

FIGURE 4. THE ELECTROENCEPHALOGRAM OF PAULINE

important, Pauline, according to her mother, was near the top of her class in school.

EDUCATION

Outside the home the principal hurdle for the child and parents is education. "Must we tell the teacher?" "How would other pupils and their parents react to a convulsion?" "How many seizures will the school tolerate?" A psychologic evaluation and estimation of the intelligence is helpful. Is the sight of a convulsion a psychic trauma to other pupils? If so, what about the acts of violence and murder which children watch every evening on television? Properly handled, a seizure in the classroom can be useful as a demonstration of first-aid measures. To shield the child from all unpleasantness is a disservice to him. Association with the child who bravely carries on in spite of embarrassing episodes can be an educational experience in brave living.

Thus, if the child is receiving modern drug therapy with seizures reasonably controlled and if his intelligence and behavior are adequate, he (or she) should continue regular classroom studies. Three anxieties are outstanding.

EVENTUAL RELIEF

Time is on the side of the epileptic. Turbulent brain waves and seizures tend to improve with increasing age. Supported by competent medical treatment, the great majority of patients can be cured or substantially relieved of seizures.

MENTALITY

Eventual intelligence is determined not by seizures per se but, more importantly, by natural endowment and by the presence or absence of antecedent brain damage. The great majority of epileptic children in the community are mentally as normal as children in general. Thus, of 200 office patients under the age of 15 years given the Stanford-Binet test, the average score was 109. However, social rejection often retards educational progress.

HEREDITY

A desire for progeny is universal and deep-rooted. Parents ask anxiously, "Can our child marry and have children and we grandchildren?" Because answers have been contradictory, we shall present our own data in some detail. These have convinced us that the importance of a transmitted tendency to seizures is no longer in doubt. However, other considerations may neutralize or overbalance this tendency and encourage most epileptics to marry and to rear children.

1. Not epilepsy per se but only a tendency to seizures is transmitted; hence, carriers of the tendency, many times more numerous than those with epilepsy, are genetically much more important.
2. A transmitted predisposition is no more important for epilepsy than for many other diseases; for example, diabetes, hypertension, obesity.
3. Epilepsy is not to be feared as it once was. Successful drug treatment has advanced importantly in recent years and additional gains are probable. The prevention of brain damage and of acquired epilepsy can be extended.
4. Possession by parents of transmissible mental and physical traits which are desirable may outweigh an undesired tendency to seizures on the part of one parent.

Reassured by these facts, we should vigorously oppose laws which forbid marriage of epileptics. We must, however, search out the facts about heredity uninfluenced by prejudice or emotion.

INCIDENCE OF EPILEPSY AMONG RELATIVES

An excellent monograph about epilepsy has been written by Alström. Alström's Swedish data indicate that heredity is not important in epilepsy. We have studied the family histories of approximately 4,000 epileptic patients. Among the 20,000 near relatives of these patients, the incidence of persons with a history of one or more seizures was 3.2 per cent. Approximately one-half had chronic epilepsy. This 1.6 per cent is an incidence three times greater than the incidence of epilepsy (0.5 per cent) in the population of draft age in the United States. The difference between the findings of Alström and ourselves is explained by the fact that his patients were adults and began to have epilepsy at an older age than ours. Alström publishes the age at onset of his cases for only the small group of fifty-nine with a family history of epilepsy. Epilepsy started in the first decade of life in 22 per cent of his cases and in 47 per cent of our 4,000 cases. Conversely, epilepsy began after the age of 20 in 50 per cent of his cases and in only 24 per cent of ours. Authors are agreed that epilepsy usually begins in childhood; hence, our groups should be the more representative.

What is the importance of the age at onset of seizures? Our study demonstrated that the number of epileptic relatives decreased progressively with the increase in age of the patient at the time of his first seizure. Thus, children without antecedent brain damage whose epilepsy began in infancy had nearly five times as many epileptic relatives as those who began to have seizures after the age of 30. If conclusions were drawn from only the latter group, we, like Alström, would discredit the influence of heredity. However, we have also the testimony of twins.

EVIDENCE FROM TWINS

Twins are most important in the study of heredity. We have assembled data on 173 pairs of twins affected with seizures, seventy-seven of these identical and ninety-six fraternal. This supplements a previous report of 122 twins. Among the seventy-seven identical twins, concordance was 70 per cent; among the ninety-six fraternal, it was 12.5 per cent. Among

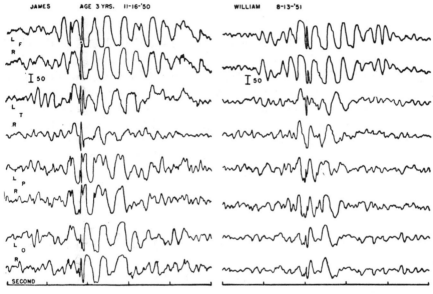

FIGURE 5. THE ELECTROENCEPHALOGRAMS OF TWINS JAMES AND WILLIAM

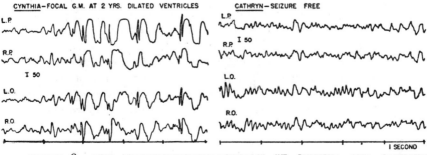

FIGURE 6. THE ELECTROENCEPHALOGRAMS OF CYNTHIA AND CATHRYN

the ninety-eight without evidence of acquired brain damage, concordance was 51 per cent; among the seventy-five with evidence of acquired brain damage, it was 20 per cent. Of the identical twins, fifty-one had no evidence of brain damage that antedated the first seizure, while in twenty-six, one of the co-twins had suffered brain damage. Both co-twins were epileptic in 88.2 per cent of the uninjured and in only 34.6 per cent of the injured group. Among all fraternal twins the concordance was 12.5 per cent. This is four times the incidence of epilepsy among siblings of epileptics. Presumably, the unusual hazards of pregnancy and premature birth experienced by twins are responsible.

. . . . .

CONCLUSION

The interrelationships of emotional and social problems of the child and his relatives call for the best qualities of the pediatrician; versatility, an open mind, persistence in year-after-year follow-up, the quality of hopefulness and courage which is transmitted as by osmosis to the faint-hearted and despondent. The effective doctor will search out the facts about epilepsy and actively combat unfounded fears. Specifically, meta-bolic (presumably genetic) epilepsy is not related to mental defect. A comprehensive view of the factors of heredity does not preclude marriage and children for most epileptics.

45. THE CHILDREN'S FORM OF THE MANIFEST ANXIETY SCALE

ALFRED CASTANEDA, BOYD R. MCCANDLESS,
AND DAVID S. PALERMO

How does the anxious child feel? How does the world look to him, by day and by night? What lurking dangers does he see within himself and in the outside environment?

The scale presented here is an attempt to describe and measure manifest anxiety in children, using items based on the subjective experiences and symptoms that accompany the disturbance. The paper thus illustrates some of the steps necessary in developing a personality scale.

Selections reprinted from the article in *Child Development*, 27 (1956), 317–326, by permission of the authors and the Society for Research in Child Development.

An earlier version of the present scale was administered to approximately 60 subjects for the purposes of obtaining information regarding possible difficulties in the instructions for its administration and the comprehensibility of the items. A total of 42 anxiety items were selected and modified, and 11 additional items designed to provide an index of the subject's tendency to falsify his responses to the anxiety items were included in the present form of the test. A similar set of items was included by Taylor from the L scale of the MMPI for the same purpose, hence these 11 items will also be referred to as the L scale. All of these items were then submitted to two elementary school system officials for a final check on their comprehensibility for the population for which they were intended. The 42 anxiety items, constituting the anxiety scale of the present test, are reproduced in Table 1 with their appropriate ordinal numbers as they appear in the present form of the test. The index of the level of anxiety is obtained by summing the number of these items answered "yes."

**Table 1.   Anxiety Items Included in the Anxiety Scale and
Numbered as They Appear in the Present Form of the Test.**

1. It is hard for me to keep my mind on anything.
2. I get nervous when someone watches me work.
3. I feel I have to be best in everything.
4. I blush easily.
6. I notice my heart beats very fast sometimes.
7. At times I feel like shouting.
8. I wish I could be very far from here.
9. Others seem to do things easier than I can.
11. I am secretly afraid of a lot of things.
12. I feel that others do not like the way I do things.
13. I feel alone even when there are people around me.
14. I have trouble making up my mind.
15. I get nervous when things do not go the right way for me.
16. I worry most of the time.
18. I worry about what my parents will say to me.
19. Often I have trouble getting my breath.
20. I get angry easily.
22. My hands feel sweaty.
23. I have to go to the toilet more than most people.
24. Other children are happier than I.
25. I worry about what other people think about me.
26. I have trouble swallowing.
27. I have worried about things that did not really make any difference later.
28. My feelings get hurt easily.
29. I worry about doing the right things.
31. I worry about what is going to happen.

32. It is hard for me to go to sleep at night.
33. I worry about how well I am doing in school.
35. My feelings get hurt easily when I am scolded.
37. I often get lonesome when I am with people.
38. I feel someone will tell me I do things the wrong way.
39. I am afraid of the dark.
40. It is hard for me to keep my mind on my school work.
42. Often I feel sick in my stomach.
43. I worry when I go to bed at night.
44. I often do things I wish I had never done.
45. I get headaches.
46. I often worry about what could happen to my parents.
48. I get tired easily.
50. I have bad dreams.
51. I am nervous.
53. I often worry about something bad happening to me.

The 11 L scale items are reproduced in Table 2 with their appropriate ordinal numbers as they appear in the present form of the test. Items 10 and 49, if answered "no" contribute to the L scale score as do the remaining nine items if answered "yes." The index of the subject's tendency to falsify his responses to the anxiety items, then, is the sum of these items answered in the designated manner.

Table 2.   Items Included in the L Scale and Numbered as They Appear in the Present Form of the Test

5. I like everyone I know.
10. I would rather win than lose in a game.
17. I am always kind.
21. I always have good manners.
30. I am always good.
34. I am always nice to everyone.
36. I tell the truth every single time.
41. I never get angry.
47. I never say things I shouldn't.
49. It is good to get high grades in school.
52. I never lie.

Copies of this test were distributed to the classroom teacher who administered it to her class on a group basis. The only instructions provided the teacher were those which appeared on the test itself and which she read to the class. The instructions were, "Read each question carefully. Put a circle around the word YES if you think it is true about you. Put a circle around the word NO if you think it is not true about you." Space was provided on the test sheet for the subject to identify himself by name, grade, sex and school. Approximately one week later the classroom teacher re-administered the test. A total of 15 classrooms from four different schools participated in the study. A total of 386 children participated in the first administration of the test. However, due primarily to absences, only 361 of these children were tested on the second administration. One week re-test reliabilities averaged at about .90 for the anxiety scale and at about .70 for the L scale. Intercorrelations between the anxiety scale and the L scale clustered around the zero value. Girls were found to score significantly higher than boys on both scales. Significant differences on the L scale were found to be associated with grade.

46. COMPLEX LEARNING AND PERFORMANCE AS A FUNCTION OF ANXIETY IN CHILDREN AND TASK DIFFICULTY

ALFRED CASTANEDA, DAVID S. PALERMO, AND BOYD R. MCCANDLESS

This study, using the Manifest Anxiety Scale described in selection 45, compares the problem-solving ability of anxious children with the ability of less disturbed children. It shows that a high degree of anxiety helps children learn to solve simple problems but hinders them seriously when the problems become more difficult.

This approach seems more constructive than that which stops after simply diagnosing a disorder. Since anxious children probably will grow to be anxious adults, an attempt to describe and understand the limits of their abilities seems useful. Today's society presents a great variety of tasks to be performed, and it is helpful to have some idea of who can do what.

The present study is concerned with the performance of fifth grade children on a complex learning task as a function of the relative difficulty of the various components comprising the task and of their scores on a scale of manifest anxiety adapted for children from Taylor's adult form.

Selections reprinted from the article in *Child Development*, 27 (1956), 328–332, by permission of the authors and the Society for Research in Child Development.

METHOD

Subjects. The 37 Ss in the present study were from among those who participated in the standardization of the children's form of the anxiety scale . . . and who, in addition, participated in a complex learning experiment . . . a year previously. The present study, then, reports the relationship between the anxiety scale scores of these Ss and their performance in the experiment of the previous year. Although the conventional practice with the adult form is to select Ss whose scores fall within the upper or lower 20th percentiles of the distribution the small number of Ss available in the present study precluded such a procedure. The anxiety scores of the present Ss ranged from a low of three to a high of 33, hence a score of 18 or above was arbitrarily designated as falling in the high anxious category and a score of 17 or below in the low anxious category. The high anxious group, then, consisted of 21 Ss, 9 boys and 12 girls and the low anxious group was composed of 16 Ss, 6 boys and 10 girls. . . .

Apparatus. . . . In essence, the apparatus consisted of a rectangularly shaped box approximately 9 x 18 x 9 in., painted flat black. A response panel containing five linearly arranged push buttons projected from the box. Centered 3 in. above the response panel was a 1 in. diameter aperture of flashed opal glass. Behind the aperture were five pilot lamps colored either dark red, green, amber, blue or light red. All controls used by E were situated to the back of the apparatus. By a simple switching arrangement E could actuate any single light and set any single push button so that depressing it turned off the light. Depression of any other of the four remaining buttons did not affect the light.

Procedure. All Ss had to learn the same five light button combinations. These five combinations had been previously determined on a random basis. Each single light was presented five times and randomly interspersed within the total 25 presentations. All Ss were allowed to continue responding until the correct button had been depressed at which time the next light was presented. Ss were merely instructed that the task required learning which buttons were associated with which colored lights and in case of an error to select another button until the correct one had been depressed. The particular buttons depressed and the order in which they were depressed for each presentation was recorded for each S.

RESULTS AND DISCUSSION

Studies with the adult form of the anxiety scale have indicated that the differential performance of high and low anxious Ss can differ depending on the particular characteristics of the task. For example, the tendency for the high anxious Ss to perform more poorly in comparison to low anxious Ss increases as the difficulty of the task increases . . . Conversely, if the difficulty of the task can be sufficiently decreased, differences in anxiety level may result to the benefit of the high anxious Ss. . . . Hence, these studies indicate that the difficulty existing either among several different tasks or among the various components comprising a given task . . . should be assessed, preferably on some basis independent of the performance of the high and low anxious groups which are being studied. Therefore, in order to determine the possibility that the five light button combinations in the present task may not have been equal with respect to the ease with which they could be learned, 20 Ss from among those who had participated in the previous experiment, and for whom anxiety scores were not available, were drawn at random and their performance on each of the five combinations was determined. The index of the difficulty of learning a given combination was the number of times, out of five, the first response to the light was the correct one, or more simply, the number of errorless trials.

· · · · ·

Table 1.   Mean Number of Errorless Trials on the Easy and Difficult Combinations for the High and Low Anxious Groups Separately

GROUP	DIFFICULTY LEVEL			
	Easy		Hard	
	M	SD	M	SD
High Anxious	5.00	2.41	3.33	1.29
Low Anxious	4.38	2.13	4.81	2.66

Table 1 presents the number of errorless trials for the high and low anxious groups for the easy and difficult combinations separately. It is apparent, on the basis of these data, that the high anxious children performed better, in comparison to the low anxious children, on the easy combinations, but more poorly on the difficult combinations. It can be noted that the performance of the high anxious children appeared to be more affected by the differences in the difficulty of the two sets of combinations than for the low anxious children.

· · · · ·

Of great interest, is the significant interaction between anxiety and task difficulty. This interaction may be interpreted to indicate that the effects of anxiety are dependent on the degree of difficulty involved in the task. This is in accord with the data presented in Table 1, showing that the position of superiority of the high anxious children on the easy combinations, in comparison to the low anxious children, is completely reversed on the more difficult combinations. Tests of the simple effects indicated that only the difference between the low and high anxious children on the difficult combinations was significant at beyond the .05 level ($F = 4.99$, df $= 1, 35$).

. . . The present results support the notion that the effects of anxiety can be more profitably studied if the characteristics of the task can be specified. . . .

47. EXPERIMENTALLY INDUCED ABNORMAL BEHAVIOR

NORMAN R. F. MAIER

The startling conclusions of this paper have important implications in regard to the issue of when to punish and when not to punish children. Working with animals, Maier and many others have observed that punishment of undesirable behavior in an animal already under severe stress leads to continual rigid repetition of the undesirable behavior. There is a great deal of evidence indicating that this is also true of human being.

EXPERIMENTALLY INDUCED ABNORMAL BEHAVIOR

Most of what we know about abnormal behavior has been learned from the study of mental patients and the way they respond to various forms of therapy. There are, however, a number of problems concerning the nature of the abnormal that can only be solved by experimental procedures with animals. One of these is to determine whether neurosis is a disease peculiar to man. This raises the question of whether man is so subject to the disease because of his superior mentality or whether the disease is primarily the product of man's way of living. It has been said that it takes imagination and intelligence of a high order to experience conflicts and that personality disorders require a complex personality structure. Obviously, the ability to produce true neurosis in animals will make it possible to answer this question.

The second problem concerns the relation of the symptom to the cause of the symptom. Has nature supplied man with protective mecha-

Selections reprinted from the article in *The Scientific Monthly*, XLVII (September, 1948), 210–216, by permission of the author and the American Association for the Advancement of Science.

nisms—processes whereby the organism develops certain unusual responses that serve to prevent a worse condition? Thus, if a patient develops hysterical blindness, is this symptom a means for protecting the patient from seeing something in his environment that causes his anxiety and conflict? Further, does a psychosis represent a patient's escape from reality and hence serve as a solution when reality is too stressful? If one deals only with studies of case histories, one can find support for this thesis, because the many events in a case history permit one to find a logical connection between the symptom and some problem in the patient's life. Further, when a child has enuresis, should one seek in this behavior some reason, or some way in which he thereby solves a problem? Could bed-wetting give him attention he desires? Could it be a way of striking back at strict parents? Only when we control the life histories of individuals and purposely produce symptoms can the relationship between a symptom and its cause be studied.

Animal studies permit one to secure the necessary case-history data for such investigation, but in order to use lower animals one must be able to produce behavior disorders comparable to those found in man. Thus, one of the first steps in animal studies of abnormal behavior was acquiring the ability to produce abnormal symptoms under laboratory conditions.

When our work was begun, success already had been achieved in this field. By the use of the conditioning method, Pavlov produced what he called an "experimental neurosis" in the dog. Liddell's laboratory at Cornell followed this line of attack, and Liddell used sheep and pigs as well as dogs in his research. At John Hopkins University, Gannt established a laboratory to continue the type of research initiated by Pavlov. These studies clearly showed that stressful and conflictual situations caused basic behavior disruptions. The disturbance was apparent from the facts that training on discrimination problems was lost, the animal became emotionally unstable (struggled and bit at restraining harnesses), and, in general, the docile animal became most unco-operative. Many symptoms akin to those observed in human patients (such as disturbances in heart rate, and peculiar fears) were seen, but their appearance was difficult to separate from reactions of normal individuals. At the time that our work with rats was begun at the University of Michigan, there was some doubt as to whether the changes produced in the animal were a "true" neurosis. The symptoms were regarded as not sufficiently profound to be convincing, and some psychiatrists argued that neurosis in subhuman animals was impossible because animals below man lacked sufficient imagination, they could not have sex conflicts, or they did not undergo permanent personality changes. Even though some of these criticisms seem to depend upon specialized definitions of neurosis, which exclude the disease from lower animals by defining it as a human disease, it seemed at the time that part of the failure to accept neurosis in animals was based upon the facts that the behavior disturbances observed were not profound enough and that the behavior was produced by a specialized aspect of the conditioning method.

It is probable that the attention our study received in 1938 was influenced by the fact that the disturbance produced in the rat was extremely violent and left no doubt about its being abnormal. The abnormal behavior was in the form of a seizure in which the rat ran madly in a circular pattern. This running was so violent that the nails of the feet became torn. It was not a typical fear pattern, because shelter was not sought and the animal often ran into table legs and walls. The running phase frequently was followed by a convulsion, which was similar to that produced by drugs; since then we have actually found that the convulsions produced by metrazol have a good deal in common with those produced in the training situation. After the active part of the seizure had passed (one or more minutes), the rat became very passive and its righting reflexes were either absent or greatly depressed. During this period the animal could be molded into almost any position, where it would remain for several minutes—sometimes as long as twenty minutes.

The situation for producing this behavior was built around our interpretation of the conditioning studies. It seemed that behavior disturbances in the earlier studies arose when an animal was trained to give a certain response to a signal and to withhold the response when a different signal was given. When these signals were made more and more alike, the animal had difficulty in determining whether to express or withhold the response. By the presentation of a signal that was as much like the withholding signal as the arousal signal, the animal was stimulated to express and withhold the response at the same time. This was a conflict between doing and not doing which we regarded as a basic conflict.

To incorporate this condition in our experiment, we trained rats to discriminate between . . . two cards in the apparatus. . . . The rat was trained to jump to the cards, and when it chose the correct card (the one with a white circle) this card yielded to the jump and gave the rat access to food. When the rat jumped to the wrong card (the one with the black circle), this card remained in place and the animal received a bump on the nose and fell into a protective net below. Under these conditions animals soon learn always to choose the reward card and to avoid the punishment card. After the discrimination is well learned the situation is changed so that only one of the cards is presented. If this card happens to be the punishment card, the animal, as may be expected, refuses to jump. In order to cause the animal to jump to the punishment card, it is necessary to drive him. This is done by using a jet of air and directing it on the rat. When released, the air makes a hissing noise and is irritating to the rat; consequently the resistance to jumping is broken. The condition of driving the rat to make a response to a card it has been trained to avoid was considered a conflict between doing and not doing, and it was the condition under which the violent seizures most frequently were produced.

These experiments raised two interesting questions: Was the seizure produced by the conflict, or by the sound of the air? Is the seizure akin to an epileptic attack and, therefore, an abnormality other than a neurosis? The implication of the second question is that the symptoms observed are too profound to be considered a neurosis.

Experimental studies concerning these and other points have been numerous. Our laboratory alone has contributed more than 25 studies, and a total of perhaps 150 studies have been published on some aspects of the rat's abnormal behavior. The studies include the effects of diet, drugs, heredity, emotionality, and brain injury on seizure susceptibility, as well as studies directed toward determining the nature of the abnormality.

At the present time it seems quite clear that the basic condition for producing the disturbance is conflict. The same auditory conditions, with and without the element of conflict, produce different results. The delay in settling this issue was due to the fact that auditory stimuli, such as the hiss of air, the sound of buzzers and bells, the jingling of keys, supersonic tones, and pure tones of low pitch all produce seizures in some animals. To explain these seizures it was necessary to show that these conditions also produce conflict. Certain sounds are irritants and arouse generalized escape behavior. However, when the animal is confined it is driven to escape, but at the same time its escape is blocked. Thus the animal is trapped in a situation which demands responses and yet inhibits those responses. It has been shown by Dr. Marcuse, of Cornell University, that seizures do not occur when the sound source is fastened to the animal. Under these conditions the escape behavior is permitted even though escape is not accomplished. It also has been shown that the type of confinement and the type of responses made during auditory stimulation influence the appearance of seizures. These facts indicate that auditory stimulation as mere sound stimulation is inadequate for producing seizures. Rather, other conditions must be present, and these other conditions determine whether behavior tensions are built up without permitting a release through some avenue of behavior. It is when these tensions become too great that they break forth as a seizure. The fact that smoke, water spray, and electric shock (applied during conflict) also produce seizures under proper conditions indicate that sound is not unique in its seizure-producing qualities. Since the expression of escape behavior prevents seizures, one is led to conclude that behavior must be blocked while irritants are applied.

The mere fact that conflict and unresolved tensions seem to be essential for producing seizures makes the seizure appear to be a form of neurosis rather than the epileptic attack of a defective organism. Perhaps Dr. Goldstein's classification, "catastrophic reaction," is more adequate than neurosis, since this term implies a form of disorganized behavior which occurs when the environment places demands on the organism that it is incapable of handling. Either "neurosis" or "catastrophic reaction," however, places the emphasis on the abnormality as being one that is situation-induced rather than the response of an injured or defective organism.

Because of the profound nature of the seizure, other aspects of the abnormality reported in our rats frequently have been overlooked. The conflict situation in the rat was highly frustrating and produced nervousness which extended outside the situation. Experimental rats become less likely to breed, and they develop a retiring nature. These behavior alterations are akin to personality changes, since they extend outside the test situation. Further, and more important, is the fact that the frustrating situation produced compulsive behavior in many of the rats, particularly those not showing seizures. Compulsive behavior commonly appears in neurosis and is one of the most difficult to explain. A classical illustration of compulsive behavior is Lady Macbeth's repeated handwashing, which is regarded as an effort to cleanse herself from guilt. Because compulsive behavior is a fundamental type of abnormality, it was selected for special study. Thus, from the outset, our studies of abnormal behavior in the rat have dealt with two distinct forms of abnormality.

When a rat is placed in the card-discrimination problem situation in which reward and punishment are applied in a random order, the animal is confronted with an insoluble problem. This fact is soon recognized by the animal, and it expresses its recognition of such a difficult problem by refusing to choose between cards. This refusal is so intense that hunger is not sufficient to cause the animal to take a 50–50 chance on happening to strike the reward card. In order to overcome this resistance, the animal is driven with a blast of air, as described earlier. Occasionally seizures are produced in this situation, but more commonly the animal jumps at one of the cards, and soon its choices follow a consistent pattern. Usually the rat chooses a card on a position basis, i.e., it chooses the card on the right (or left) side, regardless of which of the cards it is. Once the rat ceases trying out various possibilities and makes its choice on a position basis, this way of choosing becomes the response to the insoluble problem, and the animal never deviates from this procedure once it is established. In practicing the position response, the animal is punished on half its choices and rewarded on the other half, since these are applied in random order. Such a condition should not establish a preferred way of responding, yet under frustration a highly specific response becomes established.

Other animals can be *trained* to show similar position responses. This is accomplished by rewarding animals for choosing the cards on a position basis. Such animals are *motivated* to express position responses, whereas the animals in the insoluble problem situation express their position responses as a consequence of *frustration.*

The question now is, Are responses established under frustration different from those established through motivational training?

It is found that animals that acquire their responses under frustration cannot substitute them for other responses. In other words, they cannot learn new responses even when the situation ceases being insoluble. Not only are they unable to adopt new responses, but they are unable to drop their inadequate position responses. This is true even if they are punished each time they express their old responses. As a matter of fact, punishing them for making their former responses makes them *more* likely to repeat them in the future. Animals with such frustration-induced position responses will choose the punishment cards whenever they are placed on the side of the animals' position preferences. They will even refuse to jump to an open window in which food is clearly displayed when its position does not correspond with their position reaction. . . .

This rigid behavior is in contrast to that of animals that have acquired their position responses under conditions of motivation. These animals readily learn new responses when training conditions are changed, and they are constructively influenced when being punished for errors. If punished too severely, however, they, too, may become frustrated, and they then behave like the above-mentioned animals.

Because frustration makes behavior rigid and unchangeable, we have called the responses acquired under frustration "abnormal fixations" to distinguish them from normal habits. The adjective "abnormal" is used because the strength of the response does not follow the principles of learning in establishing or fixating habits.

Abnormal fixations not only are rigid but they have a compulsive character. This trait can be demonstrated in the following manner. Suppose that after a period of frustration a rat's jump to the card with the white circle is always rewarded, whereas a jump to the card with the black circle is always punished. In this situation a rat with a right-positional fixation will receive punishment whenever the card with the black circle is on the right side, and reward whenever the card with the white circle is on the right side. After a time in this situation, the rat begins to hesitate to jump whenever the punishment card is on the right, or position, side. When forced to jump it strikes the card with its rump to avoid a bump on the nose. When the reward card is on the right side, however, the animal jumps readily and hits the card with its nose and forepaws. It is evident that the animal knows which card punishes and which card rewards, and, although it expresses its knowledge of the difference in the cards by the way it jumps, it does not choose the card to jump to on this basis. The right-position fixation apparently prevents the rat from making an adaptive response to the situation, so it is forced to take punishment even though it knows better. This unadaptive behavior is in contrast to that of animals with normal position habits. As soon as they learn which card punishes and which card rewards, they abandon their position responses and, instead, follow the reward card from right to left.

Behavior similar to the abnormal fixations in rats has been demonstrated in college students by Dorothy Marquart, one of our graduate students. After mild frustration in any insoluble problem, the time required by students to learn a simple problem is greatly increased. Since all learning requires the acquisition of a new response, any resistance to change that is produced by frustration results in retarded learning. As might be expected, individual differences were apparent. Some of the students were not frustrated by the mild shock and learned at the normal rate. Those that were frustrated, however, required many more trials than the slowest of the normal learners.

The abnormal fixation is akin to rigid responses found in human beings. Accounts of compulsive behavior, such as is found in kleptomania, phobias, and alcoholism, are common in the literature of abnormality. So-called ritualistic behaviors, in which the person must repeat a senseless routine of activities, are further examples. The fact that some attitudes are rigid and not subject to modification, regardless of how senseless they are from a logical point of view, suggests that they are fixated. Of interest are the facts that rigid attitudes are emotionally loaded and are commonly associated with objects that are threats to a person's security. These observations support the suggestion that rigid attitudes have their basis in frustration. Thus, attitudes on socioeconomic topics, racial questions, and religious questions are least subject to modification, and these attitudes are most rigid during periods of frustration and stress.

The studies of abnormal behavior in the rat lead to a new theory of frustration. They demonstrate that behavior elicited during a state of frustration has certain unique properties, and that these properties make frustration-induced behavior different in kind from that produced in a motivated state. This basic separation between motivated and frustrated behavior is in contrast to the view which postulates that all behavior has a motive. When it is assumed that all behavior is motivated, it follows that any behavior expressed is a *means* to some *end*. Thus, one is led to assume that if a child steals he is doing it to achieve some goal, or end. It is said that he is solving the problem of satisfying his wants or needs, even though he may be going contrary to some other needs, such as being accepted by society. From this point of view it follows that if we make stealing unattractive (punishing for the act), such behavior will be deterred. If, on the other hand, we recognize that there are two different kinds of behavior, then it follows that there may be two kinds of stealing, one that is motivated and solves the problem of gratifying needs, and one that is frustration-instigated and compulsive in nature. The latter type of behavior solves no problem and has no goal to direct it. It may occur in children from broken homes in which the child has adequate spending money. This type of stealing may involve the theft of objects for which the child has no need or interest. Such behavior is similar to vandalism, in which objects are destroyed rather than taken. The fact that stealing increases with frustration indicates that we must distinguish between the various forms of stealing. The separation of behavior into frustration-instigated and goal-motivated behavior permits just such a distinction.

Once we accept the belief that behavior produced under frustration follows different principles from behavior motivated by goals, we can reorganize our knowledge of the subject of frustration. For example, it is known that destructive (aggressive or hateful) behavior is associated with frustration and that a frustrated person attacks his enemy. This behavior may appear to be problem-solving in nature, but difficulty is encountered in explaining why people who are frustrated so often strike out at innocent bystanders. One can see how the destruction of one's enemies would achieve objectives, but the fact is that frustrated persons do not always express their hates in such a manner as to solve problems. Instead, they create more problems by their hateful behavior. Thus, frustrated parents abuse their children and rationalize that they are training them. The children return the hatred or direct it toward society through delinquent behavior.

It seems useless to probe for problems which hate behavior solves. Instead, our theory suggests that frustration produces hate, and the hatred is directed toward anything that is convenient or is in the individual's attention during his frustration. Some of the animal experiments show that the type of behavior expressed in frustration is determined by its availability to the individual rather than by its effectiveness.

Another form of behavior associated with frustration is that of regression, which represents a type of behavior more childish than the individual's level of development warrants. Thus, bed-wetting in an eight-year-old is a sign of regression. A child that has learned to walk may temporarily revert to creeping when frustrated. Believers in the theory that all behavior is motivated have difficulty in explaining such senseless regressive behaviors. What problem is solved by this type of behavior? Frequently, it is said that the child desires attention. The attention he receives from bed-wetting, however, may be a spanking and degradation. Is this activity solving a problem for the child, or is it aggravating a condition that is already bad? If, however, we assume that frustration produces regression and that this simplification of behavior is a direct result of frustration, then our problem is to seek the source of frustration. The child that regresses may feel rejected. Punishment makes him feel more rejected. On the other hand, love and understanding reduce the state of frustration. It then follows that a child is most likely to be cured if he is given treatment that reduces his frustration, and this is frequently what the practicing psychiatrist recommends. He suggests love and attention because they work. Nevertheless, from a motivation point of view, rewarding a bad response with love should strengthen it. Yet both aggressive and regressive behaviors are reduced when treated with understanding and love.

From our point of view it follows that the behavior expressed gives no clue as to what the frustrated individual needs. A child that is insecure may develop a form of ritualistic behavior and so show signs of fixation; he may whine excessively, wet the bed, and have difficulty in learning, thereby showing signs of regression; he may become destructive with toys or be a bully in school, thereby showing aggressive symptoms; or he may show behaviors that are combinations of fixation, regression, and aggression. Regardless of which behaviors are expressed, however, the underlying cause may be the same. If the insecure or rejected child is to be made to feel secure, therapy is achieved in the same way, regardless of the specific symptoms that a given child exhibits.

To show more clearly the difference between motivated and frustrated behavior, we have listed in Table 1 those characteristics of each that seem to be sufficiently common to warrant inclusion (although there may be many others).

Table 1. Characteristics of Motivated and Frustrated Behavior

Motivation-Induced	*Frustration-Instigated*
Goal-oriented	Not directed toward a goal
Tensions reduced when goal is reached	Tensions reduced when behavior is expressed, but increased if behavior leads to more frustration
Punishment deters action	Punishment aggravates state of frustration
Behavior shows variability and resourcefulness in a problem situation	Behavior is stereotyped and rigid
Behavior is constructive	Behavior is nonconstructive or destructive
Behavior reflects choices influenced by consequences	Behavior is compulsive
Learning proceeds and makes for development and maturity	Learning is blocked and behavior regresses

The differences in behavior listed in the table are basic, and failure to make these distinctions seems only to lead to inconsistencies and confusion. If these differences are recognized it means that the first step in diagnosis is to determine which condition an individual is in when one attempts to correct behavior. The nonfrustrated person is subject to training because he is responsive to training methods, and he can be attracted to substitute goals.

The frustrated individual, however, needs relief from frustration. Can the situation be corrected? If so, then such correction is a form of therapy. Another possibility is to treat the *individual* rather than the *situation*. Can the state of frustration be relieved without making it necessary to change the situation? Actually the expression of a frustrated response reduces the state of frustration. An act of aggression such as writing a hateful letter achieves relief even if the letter is not mailed. Crying (a regressive response to frustration) reduces frustration and the person need not receive the concessions that tears sometimes attain. Rats which showed tendencies to have seizures when frustrated, had fewer seizures when they developed fixations. Thus the various frustration-induced responses seem to relieve the state of frustration, but it must not be supposed that the anticipation of such relief is an essential cause of the behavior. To make this supposition would deny the basic evidence which differentiates motivated and frustration-instigated behavior.

Unfortunately, the expression of frustration-instigated responses frequently leads to further frustration. When one strikes another or verbally abuses him, the other person strikes back and so creates a further problem. Thus the value of the relief gained through expression is offset by the fact that the end the expression has served is one which leads to new frustration. It is for this reason that therapy must permit harmless forms of aggression. Such harmless forms of aggression are encouraged in play therapy and in counselling situations. These permit children and adults to express hostility without having the behavior challenged.

We thus find that the experimentation with animals leads us to a theory of frustration which reorganizes the facts of human behavior and reinterprets the meaning and importance of certain forms of therapy. It has supplied us with certain basic principles which have a firm foundation in that the principles are experimentally derived. Whether the experimentation can proceed to aid us in answering many of our perplexing problems remains to be seen.

48. THE MAMMAL AND HIS ENVIRONMENT

D. O. HEBB

Hebb describes some of the provocative research with dogs, chimpanzees, and students that is being discussed currently. He concludes that perceptual restriction produces low intelligence and reports that dogs in an environment of low stimulation express their excitement in overactivity.

Dennis (selection 19), Spitz (selection 18), and Bowlby (selection 17) agree with these findings, and Bowlby's study reports similar results in experiments with children. Hebb, however, declares that such dogs do not become "neurotic" in the human or clinical sense.

The original intention in this paper was to discuss the significance of neurophysiological theory for psychiatry and psychology, and to show, by citing the work done by some of my colleagues, that the attempt to get at the neural mechanisms of behavior can stimulate and clarify purely behavioral—that is, psychiatric and psychological—thinking. The research to be described has, I think, a clear relevance to clinical problems; but its origin lay in efforts to learn how the functioning of individual neurons and synapses relates to the functions of the whole brain, and to understand the physiological nature of learning, emotion, thinking, or intelligence.

In the end, however, my paper has simply become a review of the research referred to, dealing with the relation of the mammal to his environment. The question concerns the normal variability of the sensory environment and this has been studied from two points of view. First, one may ask what the significance of perceptual activity is during growth; for this purpose one can rear an animal with a considerable degree of restriction, and see what effects there are upon mental development. Secondly, in normal animals whose development is complete, one can remove a good deal of the supporting action of the normal environment,

Reprinted from a paper read at the 110th annual meeting of the American Psychiatric Association (St. Louis, Mo., May 3–7, 1954) and published in *American Journal of Psychiatry*, CXI (1955), 826–831, by permission of the author and publisher.

to discover how far the animal continues to be dependent on it even after maturity.

THE ROLE OF THE ENVIRONMENT DURING GROWTH

The immediate background of our present research on the intelligence and personality of the dog is the work of Hymovitch (6) on the intelligence of rats. He reared laboratory rats in 2 ways: (1) in a psychologically restricted environment, a small cage, with food and water always at hand and plenty of opportunity for exercise (in an activity wheel), but with no problems to solve, no need of getting on with others, no pain; and (2) in a "free" environment, a large box with obstacles to pass, blind alleys to avoid, other rats to get on with, and thus ample opportunity for problem-solving and great need for learning during growth. Result: the rats brought up in a psychologically restricted (but biologically adequate) environment have a lasting inferiority in problem-solving. This does not mean, of course, that environment is everything, heredity nothing: here heredity was held constant, which prevents it from affecting the results. When the reverse experiment is done we find problem-solving varying with heredity instead. The *same* capacity for problem-solving is fully dependent on both variables for its development.

To take this further, Thompson and others have been applying similar methods to dogs (9). The same intellectual effect of an impoverished environment is found again, perhaps more marked in the higher species. But another kind of effect can be seen in dogs, which have clearly marked personalities. Personality—by which I mean complex individual differences of emotion and motivation—is again strongly affected by the infant environment. These effects, however, are hard to analyze, and I cannot at present give any rounded picture of them.

First, observations during the rearing itself are significant. A Scottish terrier is reared in a small cage, in isolation from other Scotties and from the human staff. Our animal man, William Ponman, is a dog lover and undertook the experiment with misgivings, which quickly disappeared. In a cage 30 by 30 inches, the dogs are "happy as larks," eat more than normally reared dogs, grow well, are physically vigorous: as Ponman says, "I never saw such healthy dogs—they're like bulls." If you put a normally-reared dog into such a cage, shut off from everything, his misery is unmistakable, and we have not been able to bring ourselves to continue such experiments. Not so the dog that has known nothing else. Ponman showed some of these at a dog show of national standing, winning first-prize ribbons with them.

Observations by Dr. Ronald Melzack on pain are extremely interesting. He reared 2 dogs, after early weaning, in complete isolation, taking care that there was little opportunity for experience of pain (unless the dog bit himself). At maturity, when the dogs were first taken out for study, they were extraordinarily excited, with random, rapid movement. As a result they got their tails or paws stepped on repeatedly—but paid no attention to an event that would elicit howls from a normally reared dog. After a few days, when their movements were calmer, they were tested with an object that gave electric shock, and paid little attention to it. Through 5 testing periods, the dog repeatedly thrust his nose into a lighted match; and months later, did the same thing several times with a lighted cigar.

A year and a half after coming out of restriction they are still hyperactive. Clipping and trimming one of them is a 2-man job; if the normal dog does not stand still, a cuff on the ear will remind him of his duty; but cuffing the experimental dog "has as much effect as if you patted him —except he pays no attention to it." It seems certain, especially in view of the related results reported by Nissen, Chow, and Semmes (7) for a chimpanzee, that the adult's perception of pain is essentially a function of pain experience during growth—and that what we call pain is not a single sensory quale but a complex mixture of a particular kind of synthesis with past learning and emotional disturbance.

Nothing bores the dogs reared in restriction. At an "open house," we put 2 restricted dogs in one enclosure, 2 normal ones in another, and asked the public to tell us which were the normal. Without exception, they picked out the 2 alert, lively, interested animals—not the lackadaisical pair lying in the corner, paying no attention to the visitors. The alert pair, actually, were the restricted; the normal dogs had seen all they wanted to see of the crowd in the first 2 minutes, and then went to sleep, thoroughly bored. The restricted dogs, so to speak, haven't the brains to be bored.

Emotionally, the dogs are "immature," but not in the human or clinical sense. They are little bothered by imaginative fears. Dogs suffer from irrational fears, like horses, porpoises, elephants, chimpanzees, and man; but it appears that this is a product of intellectual development, characteristic of the brighter, not the duller animal. Our dogs in restriction are not smart enough to fear strange objects. Things that cause fear in normal dogs produce only a generalized, undirected excitement in the restricted. If both normal and restricted dogs are exposed to the same noninjurious but exciting stimulus repeatedly, fear gradually develops in the restricted; but the normals, at first afraid, have by this time gone on to show a playful aggression instead. On the street, the restricted dogs "lead well," not bothered by what goes on around them, while those reared normally vary greatly in this respect. Analysis has a long way to go in these cases, but we can say now that dogs reared in isolation are not like ordinary dogs. They are both stupid and peculiar.

Such results clearly support the clinical evidence, and the animal experiments of others (1), showing that early environment has a lasting effect on the form of adjustment at maturity. We do not have a great body of evidence yet, and before we generalize too much it will be particularly important to repeat these observations with animals of different heredity. But I have been very surprised, personally, by the lack of evidence of emotional instability, neurotic tendency, or the like, when the dogs are suddenly plunged into a normal world. There is, in fact, just the opposite effect. This suggests caution in interpreting data with human children, such as those of Spitz (8) or Bowlby (3). Perceptual restriction in infancy certainly produces a low level of intelligence, but it may not, by itself, produce emotional disorder. The observed results seem to mean, not that the stimulus of another attentive organism (the mother) is necessary from the first but that it may become necessary only as psychological *dependence* on the mother develops. However, our limited data certainly cannot prove anything for man, though they may suggest other interpretations besides those that have been made.

THE ENVIRONMENT AT MATURITY

Another approach to the relation between the mammal and his environment is possible: that is, one can take the normally reared mammal and cut him off at maturity from his usual contact with the world. It seems clear that thought and personality characteristics develop as a function of the environment. Once developed, are they independent of it? This experiment is too cruel to do with animals, but not with college students. The first stage of the work was done by Bexton, Heron, and Scott (2). It follows up some work by Mackworth on the effects of monotony, in which he found extraordinary lapses of attention. Heron and his co-workers set out to make the monotony more prolonged and more complete.

The subject is paid to do nothing 24 hours a day. He lies on a comfortable bed in a small closed cubicle, is fed on request, goes to the toilet on request. Otherwise he does nothing. He wears frosted glass goggles that admit light but do not allow pattern vision. His ears are covered by a sponge-rubber pillow in which are embedded small speakers by which he can be communicated with, and a microphone hangs near to enable him to answer. His hands are covered with gloves, and cardboard cuffs extend from the upper forearm beyond his fingertips, permitting free joint movement but with little tactual perception.

The results are dramatic. During the stay in the cubicle, the experimental subject shows extensive loss, statistically significant, in solving simple problems. He complains subjectively that he cannot concentrate; his boredom is such that he looks forward eagerly to the next problem, but when it is presented he finds himself unwilling to make the effort to solve it.

On emergence from the cubicle the subject is given the same kind of intelligence tests as before entering, and shows significant loss. There is disturbance of motor control. Visual perception is changed in a way difficult to describe; it is as if the object looked at was exceptionally vivid, but impaired in its relation to other objects and the background—a disturbance perhaps of the larger organization of perception. This condition may last up to 12 or 24 hours.

Subjects reported some remarkable hallucinatory activity, some which resembled the effects of mescal, or the results produced by Grey Walter with flickering light. These hallucinations were primarily visual, perhaps only because the experimenters were able to control visual perception most effectively; however, some auditory and somesthetic hallucinations have been observed as well.

The nature of these phenomena is best conveyed by quoting one subject who reported over the microphone that he had just been asleep and had a very vivid dream and although he was awake, the dream was continuing. The study of dreams has a long history, and is clearly important theoretically, but is hampered by the impossibility of knowing how much the subject's report is distorted by memory. In many ways the hallucinatory activity of the present experiments is indistinguishable from what we know about dreams; if it is in essence the same process, but going on while the subject can describe it (not merely hot but still on the griddle), we have a new source of information, a means of direct attack, on the nature of the dream.

In its early stages the activity as it occurs in the experiment is probably not dream-like. The course of development is fairly consistent. First, when the eyes are closed the visual field is light rather than dark. Next there are reports of dots of light, lines, or simple geometrical patterns, so vivid that they are described as being a new experience. Nearly all experimental subjects reported such activity. (Many of course could not tolerate the experimental conditions very long, and left before the full course of development was seen.) The next stage is the occurrence of repetitive patterns, like a wallpaper design, reported by three-quarters of the subjects; next, the appearance of isolated objects, without background, seen by half the subjects; and finally, integrated scenes, involving action, usually containing dream-like distortions, and apparently with all the vividness of an animated cartoon, seen by about a quarter of the subjects. In general, these amused the subject, relieving his boredom, as he watched to see what the movie program would produce next. The subjects reported that the scenes seemed to be out in front of them. A few could, apparently, "look at" different parts of the scene in central vision, as one could with a movie; and up to a point could change its content by "trying." It was not, however, well under control. Usually, it would disappear if the subject were given an interesting task, but not when the subject described it, nor if he did physical exercises. Its persistence and vividness interfered with sleep for some subjects, and at this stage was irritating.

In their later stages the hallucinations were elaborated into everything from a peaceful rural scene to naked women diving and swimming in a woodland pool to prehistoric animals plunging through tropical forests. One man saw a pair of spectacles, which were then joined by a dozen more, without wearers, fixed intently on him; faces sometimes appeared behind the glasses, but with no eyes visible. The glasses sometimes moved in unison, as if marching in procession. Another man saw a field onto which a bathtub rolled: it moved slowly on rubber-tired wheels, with chrome hub caps. In it was seated an old man wearing a battle helmet. Another subject was highly entertained at seeing a row of squirrels marching single file across a snowy field, wearing snowshoes and carrying little bags over their shoulders.

Some of the scenes were in 3 dimensions, most in 2 (that is, as if projected on a screen). A most interesting feature was that some of the images were persistently tilted from the vertical, and a few reports were given of inverted scenes, completely upside down.

There were a few reports of auditory phenomena—one subject heard the people in his hallucination talking. There was also some somesthetic imagery, as when one saw a doorknob before him, and as he touched it felt an electric shock; or when another saw a miniature rocket ship maneuvering around him, and discharging pellets that he felt hitting his arm. But the most interesting of these phenomena the subject, apparently, lacked words to describe adequately. There were references to a feeling of "otherness," or bodily "strangeness." One said that his mind was like a ball of cottonwool floating in the air above him. Two independently reported that they perceived a second body, or second person, in the cubicle. One subject reported that he could not tell which of the 2 bodies was his own, and described the 2 bodies as overlapping in space—not like Siamese twins, but 2 complete bodies with an arm, shoulder, and side of each occupying the same space.

THEORETICAL SIGNIFICANCE

The theoretical interest of these results for us extends in 2 directions. On the one hand, they interlock with work using more physiological methods, of brain stimulation and recording, and especially much of the recent work on the relation of the brain stem to cortical "arousal." Points of correspondence between behavioral theory and knowledge of neural function are increasing, and each new point of correspondence provides both a corrective for theory and a stimulation for further research. A theory of thought and of consciousness in physiologically intelligible terms need no longer be completely fantastic.

On the other hand, the psychological data cast new light on the relation of man to his environment, including his social environment, and it is this that I should like to discuss a little further. To do so I must go back for a moment to some earlier experiments on chimpanzee emotion. They indicate that the higher mammal may be psychologically at the mercy of his environment to a much greater degree than we have been accustomed to think.

Studies in our laboratory of the role of the environment during infancy and a large body of work reviewed recently by Beach and Jaynes (1) make it clear that psychological development is fully dependent on stimulation from the environment. Without it, intelligence does not develop normally, and the personality is grossly atypical. The experiment with college students shows that a short period—even a day or so—of deprivation of a normal sensory input produces personality changes and a clear loss of capacity to solve problems. Even at maturity, then, the organism is still essentially dependent on a normal sensory environment for the maintenance of its psychological integrity.

The following data show yet another way in which the organism appears psychologically vulnerable. It has long been known that the chimpanzee may be frightened by representations of animals, such as a small toy donkey. An accidental observation of my own extended this to include representations of the chimpanzee himself, of man, and of parts of the chimpanzee or human body. A model of a chimpanzee head, in clay, produced terror in the colony of the Yerkes Laboratories, as did a lifelike representation of a human head, and a number of related objects such as an actual chimpanzee head, preserved in formalin, or a colored representation of a human eye and eyebrow. A deeply anesthetized chimpanzee, "dead" as far as the others were concerned, aroused fear in some animals and vicious attacks by others (4).

I shall not deal with this theoretically. What matters for our present purposes is the conclusion, rather well supported by the animal evidence, that the greater the development of intelligence the greater the vulnerability to emotional breakdown. The price of high intelligence is susceptibility to imaginative fears and unreasoning suspicion and other emotional weaknesses. The conclusion is not only supported by the animal data, but also agrees with the course of development in children, growing intelligence being accompanied by increased frequency and strength of emotional problems—up to the age of 5 years.

Then, apparently, the trend is reversed. Adult man, more intelligent than chimpanzee or 5-year-old child, seems not more subject to emotional disturbances but less. Does this then disprove the conclusion? It seemed a pity to abandon a principle that made sense of so many data that had not made sense before, and the kind of theory I was working with—neurophysiologically oriented—also pointed in the same direction.

The question then was, is it possible that something is concealing the adult human being's emotional weaknesses?

From this point of view it became evident that the concealing agency is man's culture, which acts as a protective cocoon. There are many indications that our emotional stability depends more on our successful avoidance of emotional provocation than on our essential characteristics: that urbanity depends on an urbane social and physical environment. Dr. Thompson and I (5) reviewed the evidence, and came to the conclusion that the development of what is called "civilization" is the progressive elimination of sources of acute fear, disgust, and anger; and that civilized man may not be less, but more, susceptible to such disturbance because of his success in protecting himself from disturbing situations so much of the time.

We may fool ourselves thoroughly in this matter. We are surprised that children are afraid of the dark, or afraid of being left alone, and congratulate ourselves on having got over such weakness. Ask anyone you know whether he is afraid of the dark, and he will either laugh at you or be insulted. This attitude is easy to maintain in a well-lighted, well-behaved suburb. But try being alone in complete darkness in the streets of a strange city, or alone at night in the deep woods, and see if you still feel the same way.

We read incredulously of the taboo rules of primitive societies; we laugh at the superstitious fear of the dead in primitive people. What is there about a dead body to produce disturbance? Sensible, educated people are not so affected. One can easily show that they are, however, and that we have developed an extraordinarily complete taboo system—not just moral prohibition, but full-fledged ambivalent taboo—to deal with the dead body. I took a poll of an undergraduate class of 198 persons, including some nurses and veterans, to see how many had encountered a dead body. Thirty-seven had never seen a dead body in any circumstances, and 91 had seen one only after an undertaker had prepared it for burial; making a total of 65% who had never seen a dead body in, so to speak, its natural state. It is quite clear that for some reason we protect society against sight of, contact with, the dead body. Why?

Again, the effect of moral education, and training in the rules of courtesy, and the compulsion to dress, talk and act as others do, adds up to ensuring that the individual member of society will not act in a way that is a provocation to others—will not, that is, be a source of strong emotional disturbance, except in highly ritualized circumstances approved by society. The social behavior of a group of civilized persons, then, makes up that protective cocoon which allows us to think of ourselves as being less emotional than the explosive 4-year-old or the equally explosive chimpanzee.

The well-adjusted adult therefore is not intrinsically less subject to emotional disturbance: he is well-adjusted, relatively unemotional, as long as he is in his cocoon. The problem of moral education, from this point of view, is not simply to produce a stable individual, but to produce an individual that will (1) be stable in the existing social environment, and (2) contribute to its protective uniformity. We think of some persons as being emotionally dependent, others not; but it looks as though we are all completely dependent on the environment in a way and to a degree that we have not suspected.

BIBLIOGRAPHY

1. BEACH, F. A., AND JAYNES, J. Psychol. Bull., 51:239, 1954.
2. BEXTON, W. H., HERON, W., AND SCOTT, T. H. Canad. J. Psychol., 8:70, 1954.
3. BOWLBY, J. Maternal Care and Mental Health. Geneva: WHO Monogr. #2, 1951.
4. HEBB, D. O. Psychol. Rev., 53:259, 1946.
5. HEBB, D. O., AND THOMPSON, W. R. in Lindzey, G. (Ed.), Handbook of Social Psychology. Cambridge: Addison-Wesley, 1954.
6. HYMOVITCH, B. J. Comp. Physiol. Psychol., 45:313, 1952.
7. NISSEN, H. W., CHOW, R. L., AND SEMMES, JOSEPHINE. Am. J. Psychol., 64:485, 1951.
8. SPITZ, R. A. Psychoanalytic Study of the Child, 2:113, 1946.
9. THOMPSON, W. R., AND HERON, W. Canad. J. Psychol., 8:17, 1954.

PART V

PLANNED
INTERVENTION

Parents usually assume that they know better than their children what the latter should become, and they usually also assume that they have the power and moral right to act as manipulators of their children's destinies. However, having decided just what they would like their children to become, they are still faced with the question of what methods to use in asserting their influence.

Although in its youth, the science of psychology has already produced a wealth of information and advice on influencing people, helping people in trouble, and teaching people. Numerous "schools"—from Freud and Watson to Rogers and Skinner—each with a body of practice and theory, compete in forming theories regarding successful personal influence.

This Part presents some theories which might be regarded as tools in skillful personal relationships. Experiments are described demonstrating the power of conditioned responses; the psychoanalytic, the client-centered, and group-work approaches; and the use of force and of freedom in bringing about desired changes in young people.

49. RETRAINING A CHILD TO EAT

ELIZABETH CADY AND EVELYN M. CARRINGTON

Experiments with animals and observations of children have shown that if they have learned that eating will result in punishment, they will refuse to eat, allowing themselves to starve to death even when food is present in the immediate environment. This study describes a child who would eat only through a tube until— by gentle handling, rocking and singing, and then by forced feeding—she was taught to accept oral feeding.

In February, 1956 when the senior writer first saw Sammie, she was a lethargic, pale four-year-old, swaying back and forth in her bed, gritting her teeth. . . . She had no speech, but at times made a mumbling sound. Occasionally, she smiled a lopsided grin.

The previous June, Sammie had entered the Children's Medical Center with the diagnosis of tubercular infection. Shortly thereafter, she developed meningitis, the encephalopathy being widespread with greatest dominance in the left posterior frontal region. She had difficulty in using her right leg, her right arm and hand were limp, and the left side of her face showed some paralysis.

. . . . .

During all this time, Sammie had been given through a tube a special formula which supplied her daily nutritional needs.

. . . . .

Since a psychologic evaluation in February showed Sammie's mental functioning to be at the eight-month level, the psychologist decided to treat her as an eight-month-old. When she rocked and sang to her, Sammie appeared relaxed and happily made humming noises. However, when her formula was given her in a bottle, the child was unable to suck and violently pushed it away. . . . Realizing that Sammie needed to be retrained to eat with her mouth, the dietetic intern took the case as a special project, working with the little girl from 30 min. to 1 hr. each day.

First Day. Sammie was rocked and an attempt was made to feed

Selections reprinted from the article in *Journal of the American Dietetic Association,* 33 (1957), 605–606, by permission of the authors and publisher.

her applesauce. She looked suspiciously at the spoon and cup of fruit, keeping her teeth clamped together. . . .

Third Day. It was decided to force feed Sammie, as she must taste food before she could conceive of what she was missing. Under protest, Sammie took some applesauce in her mouth. . . . She was laid on her back and her formula in a thickened form was spooned into her mouth. Several tablespoons were swallowed.

Fourth Day. . . . It was decided to use applesauce exclusively in the training sessions because it is easily swallowed, has a pleasant taste, and has enough fiber to induce chewing.

Fifth Day. Sammie voluntarily opened her mouth and took a teaspoon of applesauce which she chewed and swallowed. . . .

. . . . .

Ninth Day. The sugar was removed from Sammie's formula as she has vomited after her tube feedings for several days. This eliminated the vomiting. She also took one teaspoonful of applesauce.

Tenth Day. She was quite fussy today. She was fed some strained apricots, which were sent by mistake. The apricots seemed to interest her, but did not stay in her mouth well. She still showed no interest in learning to eat, batting at the spoon.

Thirteenth Day. After a half hour of encouragement, Sammie took a teaspoonful of applesauce. . . .

Seventeenth Day. All tube feedings have been discontinued and three times a day in spite of crying and flaying hands and feet, Sammie is given puréed vegetables, meat, and fruit. She tolerates the vegetables, regurgitates the meat, and takes the sweets with mild relaxation. Today she went into the kitchen, took out a box of dry cereal and played with it. However, she made no effort to eat any.

. . . . .

Twenty-Third Day. . . . All the food was taken orally and retained. Vomiting has stopped completely, and there has been no constipation. All strained foods are diluted with Protenum.

Twenty-Eighth Day. For the first time Sammie is eating while sitting in a high chair. She is still resistant to oral feedings and spits out any food she does not want. . . .

Thirty-Fifth Day. Sammie is no longer resistant to oral feedings. In fact, she not only eats her regular meal, but begs for additional food. . . . The accompanying personality changes are just this side of miraculous. The little girl is 100 per cent happier and more demonstrative. She is now on a regular diet, with puréed foods eliminated. Self-feeding will be the next training problem.

ANALYSIS OF THE PROBLEM

This feeding problem was complicated by several factors: (a) prolonged tube feeding, (b) paralysis of right facial muscles, and (c) mental regression due to severe illness. . . .

50. PREVENTING FAILURE BY
REMOVING RESISTANCE

PRESCOTT LECKY

What should be done about the child who is failing in his studies?
He may be forced to study, kept in after school until his work is
done. Or he may be bribed with promises of a dime, a dollar, or a
convertible if he passes.

The writings of the late Prescott Lecky, a brilliant theorist,
provide some indication of how ineffectual force or bribery can be.
Lecky contends that the individual fails because he expects himself
to fail; failure thus leads to expectation of renewed failure, in an
almost unbreakable cycle. Lecky suggests that the most effective
way to help the student, who, in failing, is actually resisting success,
is by altering his conception of self.

These findings have been confirmed in the editors' frequent
experiences as counselors to failing students. The students described
how their parents or teachers pressed them again and again to
study, to pass; eventually, it seemed that only by failing could the
students preserve their integrity. To pass would mean to surrender.

Ever so often, a child who has formerly been deficient in a certain subject suddenly seems to find himself, and rises toward the top of the class. Such cases present an interesting problem. Are we confronted by a miracle, or do these spontaneous changes only seem miraculous because their study has been neglected? More important still, assuming a clearer understanding of what takes place in these rare cases, is it possible to bring about similar results among large numbers of children? These are by no means idle questions. With approximately half of the pupils in our schools already below grade in either reading or mathematics, to say nothing of other subjects, the problem of what to do is an urgent one. Either we

Reprinted from *Self-Consistency: A Theory of Personality* (Island Press Co-operative, 1951), pp. 245–255, by permission of the publisher.

must devise some effective method of raising the level of accomplishment, or lower our educational standards.

Previous interpretations of spontaneous improvement have usually been stated in terms of increased interest or readiness. Since there seems to be nothing to do about readiness except to wait for it to develop, however, and since no practical method of increasing interest beyond the present level seems to be available, these diagnoses turn out to be little more than truisms which lead to no constructive action. This point is borne out by the fact that in the actual treatment of deficient pupils there seems to be no alternative except to send the child to remedial classes or recommend outside tutoring. These remedies are apparently based on the belief that children need additional instruction for some reason in order to help them to form the habits which they failed to form in the class room. But even if our present remedial methods were successful in every case, the expense of tutoring so many pupils would make this approach impracticable.

THE THEORY OF SELF-CONSISTENCY

The method described in this report is based on a different conception of the problem; namely, that the cause of most failures in school is not insufficient or inadequate instruction, but active resistance on the part of the child. To make this point clear, we must give a brief description of the theory of self-consistency, from which the method is derived.

The part of the theory which interests us here is the concept of the mind. According to self-consistency, the mind is a unit, an organized system of ideas. All of the ideas which belong to the system must seem to be consistent with one another. The center or nucleus of the mind is the individual's idea or conception of himself. If a new idea seems to be consistent with the ideas already present in the system, and particularly with the individual's conception of himself, it is accepted and assimilated easily. If it seems to be inconsistent, however, it meets with resistance and is likely to be rejected. This resistance is a natural phenomenon; it is essential for the maintenance of individuality.

Thus the acceptability of an idea to any particular pupil is determined by his needs as an individual. In order to understand the environment, he must keep his interpretations consistent with his experience, but in order to maintain his individuality, he must organize his interpretations to form a system of ideas which is internally consistent. This consistency is not objective, of course, but subjective, private, and wholly individual. It is difficult to understand resistance unless this point is borne in mind.

From this standpoint, learning cannot be understood as a process of forming separate habits, but only in terms of the development of the entire personality. It follows that no type of subject matter is interesting merely for its own sake. It is interesting only when an individual happens to be interested in it, because of the way he interprets it in relation to his problem. Indeed, though learning and resistance seem to point in opposite directions, they really serve the same purpose. In the one case we are supporting the system by the assimilation of consistent ideas, while in the other we are protecting the system from inconsistency and conflict. Both are necessary in order that the unity of the system may be preserved.

If the pupil shows resistance toward a certain type of material, this means that from his point of view it would be inconsistent for him to learn it. If we are able to change the self-conception which underlies this viewpoint, however, his attitude toward the material will change accordingly. With the resistance eliminated, he learns so rapidly that tutoring is often unnecessary.

Such a change in the pupil's attitude often results in improvement which is quite astonishing. A high school student who misspelled 55 words out of a hundred, and who failed so many subjects that he lost credit for a full year, became one of the best spellers in the school during the next year, and made a general average of 91. A student who was dropped from another college and was later admitted to Columbia was graduated with more than 70 points of "A" credits. A boy failing in English, who had been diagnosed by a testing bureau as lacking aptitude for this subject, won honorable mention a year later for the literary prize at a large preparatory school. A girl who had failed four times in Latin, with marks between 20 and 50, after three talks with the school counselor made a mark of 92 on the next test and finished with a grade of 84. She is now taking advanced Latin with grades above 80.

Two of the poorest spellers in the High School of Clifton, N.J., were used to demonstrate this method before a university class in psychology. Given twenty words to spell, one missed all twenty and the other nineteen. The school counselor, continuing the use of the method, reports that both are now excellent spellers and have taken up spelling as a sort of hobby. The results reported are taken from the work of three different counselors, showing that the method lends itself to general use in the school system.

These examples are selected to show how little we are justified in judging the future potentialities of the pupil by the record he has made in the past. In the majority of cases, of course, the improvement, if any, is much less spectacular. But the fact that such extraordinary results can be obtained at all, and by means of a method which is still in the experimental stage, show that an optimistic attitude in regard to the possibilities of the school population in general is not unreasonable. The greatest handicap to constructive action is the well-entrenched, though perhaps unconscious, dogma that learning is the direct result of teaching, a mechanical reaction to the school environment instead of a purposive achievement.

The methods that we use, in other words, reflect the theory that we accept. In psychology and education, theories are often accepted merely because they seem plausible. In the physical sciences, however, the value of a theory is judged by its ability to make predictions that are later verified by experience. Let us apply this test to the theory that learning is a process of habit formation.

Most of us have been taught that habits are fixed by exercise and the satisfaction obtained by practicing them, and that predictions based on this theory can be relied upon. Actually, however, such predictions often turn out to be highly unreliable. A good example is thumb-sucking. Certainly the child who sucks his thumb gives the act plenty of exercise and gets enough satisfaction from it to fix the act indelibly. Therefore if the habit theory is true, we should be able to predict absolutely that the child will continue to suck his thumb for the rest of his life. But what really happens? Every year millions of children who have industriously sucked their thumbs since birth, and who have successfully resisted every effort to force them to change their behavior, quit the practice spontaneously when they are five or six years old. The reason is that they are beginning at this age to think of themselves as big boys or girls, and they recognize that thumb-sucking is inconsistent with the effort to maintain this new idea. The changed conception of who they are, and the necessity of making good in the new role they have accepted, furnishes them with a new standard to which their behavior must now conform. If a child continues to think of himself as a baby, due perhaps to prolonged illness or overprotection by the parents, the necessary standard is lacking and the thumb-sucking will continue. Parents often invoke the "big boy" standard deliberately in the effort to change the child's behavior in many other situations.

The behavior of the child in the classroom must also be understood in terms of the standards he is trying to maintain. Let us take, for example, the well known fact that boys on the average are slower than girls in learning to read. Educational textbooks usually explain this by saying that girls have more native ability in respect to reading than boys. In terms of self-consistency, however, the explanation is that to most boys the reading material in elementary readers seems infantile and effeminate. The boy from six to eight years old, just beginning to learn to read, is mainly concerned with maintaining the conception of himself as manly. He likes to play cowboy, G-man and Indian. He tries not to cry when he gets a bump. The greatest possible insult would be to call him a sissy. Yet this boy, when the reading lesson begins, must stand up before his companions and read that "The little red hen says 'Cluck! Cluck! Cluck!'" —or something equally inconsistent with his standards of how he should behave. If a boy is trying to maintain a standard of manliness on the playground, he does not abandon that standard merely because he walks from the playground into the classroom. When boys are given books about railroads and airplanes, the resistance disappears, and they learn just as rapidly and have as much "native ability" as girls.

Thus the pupil's resistance to learning certain subjects is really resistance to behaving in a manner which is inconsistent with his personal standards. Eagerness to learn, on the other hand, is due to the pupil's effort to maintain and support his standards. But he is not conscious of these standards, and explains his failures and successes either in terms of ability, or as due to likes and dislikes over which he has no control.

STANDARDS RESPONSIBLE FOR FAILURE

Now suppose that a pupil thinks of himself as a poor speller or reader, or as one of those unfortunates who "just haven't got a mathematical mind." Is he merely lacking a standard to maintain? Not at all. This conception, so long as he believes it to be true, is just as definite as any other, and the standard is just as positive. Though he seems to be saying "I can't," he is really asserting "I won't try." Many people find it hard to believe that a person will defend and strive to maintain an idea which is not to his advantage. But the evidence allows of no other conclusion.

For example, if we examine the letters or themes written by a poor speller, we find that he seems to have a standard of how many words he should misspell per page. Often a word will be spelled both correctly and incorrectly in the same theme, but the average number of mistakes per page remains approximately constant. If we give him two spelling tests of the same length and equal difficulty, we find approximately the same number of errors on each of the tests. If we tutor him in spelling, the effect often wears off within a few weeks, and he returns to his characteristic level. As one student said, "I can remember how a word is spelled all right, but I can't remember whether it is the right way or the wrong way." The presence of a standard is also shown by the fact that many poor spellers in English have no more difficulty than others in spelling foreign languages.

In a study of remedial instruction in reading made in the New York schools last year, ten per cent of the pupils who were tutored actually retrogressed in reading ability, though their average I.Q. was slightly higher than that of the group which made normal progress. How could this be explained except in terms of the pupil's resistance to changing his standards?

Perhaps the most striking illustration of resistance is the complete inability to read which is known as congenital word-blindness. Word-blind pupils are suffering not from a visual handicap, but a mental one. They can see other things, including letters, but they cannot "see" words. In many cases they have I.Q.'s above normal, and often are proficient in non-reading subjects such as arithmetic. But they think of themselves as unable to read, and maintain this standard by rejecting the ideas necessary for reading, for these ideas are inconsistent with their self-conception and consequently cannot be assimilated. "None are so blind as those that will not see."

The reliability of a child's behavior, as indicated either by tests or by general observation, is thus explained by self-consistency as the outward expression of relatively fixed internal standards. It is often argued that the reliability of a test proves that the test is measuring the child's ability. All that any test can measure, however, is the level of performance which is characteristic of the child at the time when the test is given. It is not the test which is reliable, but the child. We cannot interpret the score simply as a measure of ability unless we disregard the problem of resistance entirely, and assume not only the presence of specific abilities, but also the motive to use them to the limit.

CHANGING STANDARDS BY AROUSING CONFLICTS

The problem of how to remove the deficiency, then, is really the problem of how to remove the standard responsible for it. We cannot remove it ourselves, of course, but if we can show the pupil that the standard in question is inconsistent with his other standards, and endangers the unity of the system as a whole, he will have to alter it himself. It can safely be taken for granted, in the majority of cases, that the "big boy" or "big girl" idea of childhood has developed and reached a more mature level, and hence that the pupil now thinks of himself as self-reliant and independent. Obviously, the childish standard which is causing the resistance does not belong in the same system with these mature standards. The pupil has not recognized the inconsistency, however, because he has always managed to keep the conflicting ideas apart. Reorganization is temporarily painful, and in order to avoid it he has resorted to private logic and rationalized the conflict away.

Our method must therefore aim to break down the structure of rationalization and bring the contradictory ideas into intimate relationship.

There is nothing novel in this plan. All of us use it frequently. But it has to be used with skill and understanding if we hope to circumvent the pupil's effort to preserve the status quo in spite of us.

A pupil whose unconscious standards are preventing his development in certain directions is really caught in a trap. He set up the standard originally as a means of avoiding conflict. By defining himself as unable or unwilling to master a subject which seemed to be difficult, he protected himself from the pain of contradiction by making it seem consistent to fail. As a result, he finds himself increasingly handicapped in the effort to maintain other standards whose preservation is imperative; for example, the ideas that he is normally intelligent and respected by others as an equal. But the longer he maintains the standard, and the greater the handicap becomes, the greater the difficulty he has in escaping from his own defenses.

To free himself, it would be necessary to set up a new and higher standard supported by consistency alone. This is by no means impossible, in spite of the influence of past experience. But he cannot make up his mind to this step because he is not clearly aware of the nature of the problem. The picture of himself as caught in a trap is hidden from his view. Hence he not only clings to the inhibiting idea, but defends it by rationalizing to the effect that since every one has his weaknesses, it is foolish to worry about them. The rationalization masks the problem so cleverly that the pupil sees no inconsistency to be corrected, and hence has no motive for changing his attitude. As long as they are protected by their parents and enjoy their customary social status, such pupils as a rule take an optimistic view of the future, anticipate a lenient and sympathetic attitude on the part of others, and expect to be successful in spite of their deficiency. Indeed, this attitude is necessary for defense.

In applying the method, we first explain to the pupil that his deficiency is not due to lack of ability, but to a standard which he created himself. We must make it clear that the standard is unconscious, since this explains why he has continued to maintain it. It is most important that the interpretation of his difficulty be offered in a friendly and uncritical manner. The attitude should be that this is not our problem, but his.

The next step is to demonstrate that the pupil also has other standards which likewise must be maintained; for example, the conception of himself as self-reliant, independent, socially acceptable, and able to solve his problems by his own effort.

Finally, we call attention without criticism to the inconsistency between mature and immature standards. We make the conflict as clear as possible. In this way we take advantage of the need for consistency and make it work in the pupil's favor instead of against him.

Many counselors make the mistake of trying to influence the pupil by appealing to practical or material motives, such as the need of arithmetic and spelling in business. Our experience has shown that these appeals have little or no effect. We can influence the pupil to change his behavior in order to preserve his mental integrity, but not in order to prepare himself to make a material success.

51. CASES ILLUSTRATING PSYCHOANALYTIC CONTRIBUTIONS TO THE PROBLEMS OF READING DISABILITIES

PHYLLIS BLANCHARD

Sometimes Johnny can't read because his father has told him over and over again he is a poor reader. Sometimes he can't read because the words remind him that his mother has left him; they remind him he is angry, or afraid or curious. Remedial reading often fails to help. Before he can learn to read he must resolve these underlying emotional problems.

This article discusses several cases in which the treatment of reading difficulties consisted of helping children understand their own feelings rather than tutoring them in the actual reading skills.

For purposes of brevity, the following illustrations will not be complete case summaries but will consist of material selected chiefly to clarify points made in the preceding general discussion. Since the selection has been made for research purposes and to illustrate theoretical concepts, no implications as to therapeutic methods and techniques are intended. In some instances, longer case reports have been published previously (in papers referred to in reviewing the literature on reading disabilities). Perhaps it should be stated that the children were seen at the clinics, appointments being once or twice weekly for varied periods of time. When the children were living in their own homes, case work with the parents was quite as important as psychotherapy for the children.

The first case illustrates a chronically unfavorable parent-child relationship in which the child was under constant emotional strain. For some

Reprinted from *Psychoanalytic Study of the Child*, Vol 11, (International Universities Press, Inc., 1946) by permission of the author and publisher.

three years prior to his referral to clinic, the boy had been the object of his father's anxiety and criticism, focused upon the subject of reading. Why the boy developed difficulty in reading and other neurotic symptoms should be self-evident from the case material presented below.

Case 1.   Matthew was a twelve-year-old boy who was repeating fifth grade and still failing the work. He was considered mentally deficient by parents, teachers and classmates but psychological examination showed that he actually was of superior intelligence, with an IQ of 133.

The boy's father had had considerable difficulty in his vocational adjustments and had often been unemployed. He displaced anxiety from himself onto worry about the boy's future, stressing success in school as a preparation for later vocational success. When the boy was in third grade, the father began to supervise his school work. Although Matthew's teachers gave him good marks in reading, his father decided that he was poor in this subject. The father came to this conclusion after asking Matthew to read matter that was far too advanced for a third grade pupil. From that time, however, the father centered his anxiety upon the boy's reading and began to tutor him in it. Invariably, he scolded and criticized the boy during these home lessons, so that they always ended with Matthew in tears and his father in a temper. It is not strange, therefore, that the boy made no further progress in reading between the third and fifth grades or that by the time he was in fifth grade, he had a serious reading disability. By then, also, he was so sensitive to criticism that he would burst into tears at the slightest reprimand from a teacher and would fight with any child who said a teasing word to him.

Neither remedial teaching nor psychotherapy helped in this case so long as the boy remained at home, for the father was unable to change in his relationship to the boy, continued to displace anxiety onto him, and could not be induced to forego tutoring him. When the boy went to a boarding school and was thus freed from his father's anxiety and criticisms, he was able to learn to read with the help of individual remedial teaching.

Unfavorable comparisons with a brother or sister have been mentioned in the literature as another type of chronic family situation leading to neurotic conflicts and trouble with reading, in some instances. In the next case, comparisons between a living child and brother who had died were intimately associated with the reading disability.

Case 2.   Patrick was a nine-year-old boy, of normal intelligence (IQ 105) but was unable to read. Remedial teaching provided at school was unsuccessful in helping him to learn reading. There had been three children in the family— a first son who had died, Patrick, and a younger sister.

In his interviews with the therapist, Patrick soon spoke of the death of his older brother as having occurred shortly before he himself started first grade. A little more than a year later, Patrick said, he received a book as a birthday gift but he had not liked it, for when the stories were read to him, they proved to be about people who were killed. He had hated the stories and cried whenever he saw the book. After hearing those stories, he felt that he never wanted to hear a book read again nor did he ever want to read one himself.

At first, during his interviews, he stressed his love for his mother and his dead brother and dwelt upon wishes always to be good and kind to people. However, he soon became jealous of other patients, was angry with them for coming and with the therapist for seeing them. He complained that the therapist was just like his teachers, preferring other boys to him. After awhile, he began to accuse his mother of never having loved him as much as his dead brother. He told how she often talked about the dead child, saying that he had learned to read very quickly and criticizing Patrick for not being as apt at reading. "I wouldn't want to be like my brother," Patrick asserted contemptuously, "maybe he could read but he couldn't stand up for himself with the other kids. I'm a good fighter. They don't dare pick on me."

Patrick also told of his mother's weekly visits to his brother's grave and the tears that she shed each time she went there. Discarding his desire to be good and kind, he went on to express his wishes to dig up the brother's body and bury it somewhere so far away that his mother would never be able to find the grave and visit it. Or better yet, he would burn the body, destroying it completely. He then told how he hated his mother when he believed that she was behaving as if she wished his brother had lived and he had died. Similarly, he hated his teachers and his therapist when he thought that they might prefer other boys to him.

The mother, in the above case, had brought the boy to the clinic at the insistence of the school; she rarely kept her appointments with the social worker but sent the boy alone for his interviews with the therapist; finally, she withdrew him from therapy before it was completed. The material is therefore of interest only in connection with the etiology of the boy's reading disability. Obviously, when he first came to therapy, his conflicts about his mother and brother had been unconscious and he had repressed his resentment and hostility. His wishes to be good and kind were defenses by which he maintained the repression. The book with stories about people being killed naturally stirred up the repressed aggressive drives and threatened to bring them into his conscious experience. In turn, this aroused feelings of guilt and anxiety (shown in his weeping whenever he saw the book) as he came closer to awareness of his hostility toward his mother and his dead brother. Thus another defense and way of maintaining the repressions was refusal to learn to read, for he feared that reading content might release aggressive impulses. Self-assertion through being different from his brother was indicated by his stating his preference for being a good fighter rather than a good reader and his desire not to be like his brother. This was another motive influencing his negative attitude toward reading. Again, not learning to read was a disguised expression of hostility toward the mother who wanted him to be clever in this respect. He identified the teachers who wanted him to read with the mother and also rebelled against learning to read to please them. Indeed he transferred his jealousy of his mother and brother to the teacher and other pupils at school, and to the therapist and other patients at the clinic, always neurotically recreating for himself the unpleasant and painful family situation which he was trying to repress from consciousness.

In the following case, we see how a later event may reactivate the unconscious feelings that surrounded an earlier traumatic one.

Case 3. Thomas was an eleven-year-old boy, failing fifth grade for the second time. He had made low ratings on group tests given at school. Individual tests showed that he had an IQ of 108 but was handicapped in doing both group tests and school work by a reading disability. He dated the start of his trouble with reading from the first part of third grade, when a teacher whom he liked very much had to go to the hospital for an operation. Since she did not return to school, Thomas assumed she had died. He explained that he was so worried over the teacher's absence and her supposed death that he could not keep his mind on his work and so fell behind in reading.

This preoccupation with the question of the teacher's possible death becomes more intelligible if we know that when the boy was five years old, his mother had been away in a hospital, for an operation. He did not recall these circumstances about his mother's hospitalization, even when they were mentioned to him; he only remembered about the teacher.

In some of his therapeutic interviews, Thomas wanted to read aloud. It then became obvious that the content of reading often brought up his unconscious emotional conflicts. He would be reading fairly well when suddenly he would begin to make many errors until he stopped and talked of personal matters suggested to him by something he had read. After speaking out what had come into his mind, he could resume reading without excessive mistakes. For example, in reading a story about a dog, Thomas began making errors and continued to do so until he had paused to talk about a dog he once had owned. He had loved his dog very much indeed, he said, but he had not been permitted to keep it. After his dog was given away, he was very lonely; he cried and cried because he wanted his dog back and because he did not know what might be happening to it. "I was afraid my dog might die without my knowing about it," he explained. "It is awful to be wondering whether someone you love is alive or dead."

By the time his therapy ended, he could read without breaking down as described above. According to follow-up reports, during the next two years, his school progress was satisfactory.

The circumstances of the teacher's going to a hospital for an operation evidently revived the boy's feelings about his mother's hospitalization even though he had repressed the memory of his mother's operation and his anxiety about it. Reactivation of the emotional trauma was not the only reason for his trouble with reading, however, for from his interviews it was evident that reading content too frequently tended to stir up his unconscious conflicts. It does not take a very vivid imagination to realize that his feelings about his dog, for instance, were like those he had experienced when his mother was in the hospital. These feelings quite obviously were brought closer to consciousness when he read the story about the dog, even though it was a very cheerful one, just because the content contained the word dog many times repeated.

Both case 2 and case 3 illustrate the statements in the preceding general theoretical formulation concerning the ease with which reading content becomes associated with a child's unconscious emotional conflicts, leading to a break-down in reading skill, or to an aversion to reading.

An immediate effect of an emotional trauma connected with separation from the mother at a time when the child is entering school is illustrated by the next case.

Case 4. When Ethel was nearly six years old, her mother was forced to place her in a boarding school. Ethel's father had died two years previously and now the mother had to go to work so that she could no longer keep the child with her. At the school, Ethel seemed to have little appetite and would refuse to eat very much except when her mother visited and brought her food, which she would eat heartily. She did not learn to read during two years in first grade. She was brought to the clinic at the age of eight years, unable to read, still refusing food and having lost weight to the point where she seemed weak and ill and had to be kept in bed for considerable periods. Medical examinations could detect no physical basis for her symptoms.

In her interviews at the clinic, both her refusal to eat and her failure in learning to read soon appeared as symptoms of her unconscious conflicts over being sent away to school by her mother. At first she spoke of how much she loved her mother but soon in her play she began to dramatize her other attitudes of anger and hostility. She portrayed a mother doll sending her little girl doll away to school. The little girl doll was then angry with the mother, would not let the mother have anything to eat because she wanted to starve her mother to death, a fate that would serve her right for sending the little girl away to school. Immediately afterward, however, the little girl was punished for being so bad to her mother and also was described as being unable to eat and feeling weak and ill. Another drama with the dolls showed the little girl refusing to study or to read at school. Her poor school reports were sent to the mother doll, who decided that the school was no good and came to take the little girl home.

After this play with the dolls, Ethel could talk about how she felt when her mother placed her in the boarding school. She became aware of her idea that if she became ill or did not do well in her school work, she could force her mother to take her home again. At this point, she went on to explain that in reality, her mother could not take her because she no longer had a home. Since her father was no longer alive to take care of her mother and herself, her mother had to work to support them. She worked hard to earn money to pay for Ethel's school and her clothing. Ethel then felt very sympathetic toward her mother, who was tired from her hard work, and she was sorry that she had worried her mother by not eating and not learning to read. She announced that she was eating all right now but she had not been able to learn to read at school and she wished she could have someone to help her with reading. This request was seen as indicative of a change in attitude toward reading and special teaching was provided. Ethel worked hard with her tutor. She learned to read and began to make regular progress in school. At the time of the last follow-up report she was in seventh grade. None of her symptoms had recurred.

We might ask why this girl reacted so much more violently to being placed in boarding school by her mother than to her father's death. We can only guess at the possible reasons. Many children have less conflict over the loss of a parent through death than over separation from a parent through placement. Apparently placement is often taken as an act of aggression and rejection from the parent and therefore stimulates anger and resentment as well as grief. When a parent dies, love and grief over the loss need not necessarily come into conflict with other attitudes of anger and resentment. Serious conflicts over the death of a parent of course do occur when there was so much hostility toward the parent that a child feels guilty because of the hostile wishes before the parent died, as if they were responsible for the event. Thus a parent's death may or may not be a source of conflict to a child, depending upon the relationship that preceded it. On the other hand, placement often arouses conflict because it engenders hostility toward the parent while at the same time love and wishes to be reunited with the parent still persist.

While the next case also involves a child's conflicts over placement by the mother, it was selected for presentation primarily because it illustrates how errors in reading may provide a disguised expression and gratification of repressed wishes and drives, as was suggested in the more theoretical explanations of reading difficulties.

Case 5. Benjamin was an eight-year-old boy who had remained for two years in the first half of first grade without learning to write or read words. His efforts to write them consisted of reversals of letters or sequence, seemingly meaningless combinations of letters, or a series of peculiar marks. Other symptoms were a solitary withdrawal from social relationships and wetting and soiling himself, although when still living with his own mother, he had established bladder and bowel control. Regression to wetting and soiling began when he was about three years of age after the mother placed him.

Repeated medical examinations revealed no physical basis for his symptoms. There was no left-handedness nor left or mixed eye-hand dominance connected with his tendency to reversals in writing words. At the age of three years, before his neurotic symptoms appeared, he achieved an IQ of 95. When tested by the same psychologist at five and seven years of age, he achieved IQ's of 75 and 74. At the end of therapy, after he had recovered from his severe neurosis, he was retested and his IQ then was 95.

Benjamin was placed in a foster home after the birth of a sister. Both children were illegitimate but the mother married the father of the second one. He did not wish to take the child by a former lover into their home, so the mother turned the boy over to a placement agency and then deserted him completely.

Benjamin was seen for nearly a year and a half, mostly twice a week. During these appointments, emotional conflicts about having been deserted by his mother were very evident. His feelings toward the mother were transferred to the therapist, whom he often reproached for sending him to live with strange people and causing his illness symptoms, saying, "I hate you for what you have done to me." He had various fantasy explanations of why his mother had deserted him. Since she placed him at the time of his sister's birth, he sometimes imagined that she had given him away because she loved girls better than boys. At other times, he suspected that she stopped loving him when she began to love the man she married, for it was after she had known this man that she gave up Benjamin. He hated his mother because he felt that placement was a proof of her ceasing to love him more than because of the placement per se. His hatred was expressed in certain fantasies associated with the symptoms of wetting and soiling; for example, he pictured burning up his mother with his hot urine or poisoning her by making her eat his feces. On the other hand, fantasies of being a baby, living with his mother and cared for tenderly by her, were also closely connected with his enuresis and soiling. Thus these symptoms concealed his love as well as his hostility and afforded gratification of ambivalent feelings toward his mother. Both his resentment toward his mother and his longing for her love had been repressed and were permitted an outlet only through his symptoms.

Benjamin regarded reading as evidence of being grown-up, but was blocked in his wishes to grow up because of fantasies that this could be achieved only by eating the father to gain his traits in magic manner. He was very guilty about such aggressive desires. But Benjamin's errors in writing words, like his other symptoms, were similarly disguised expressions of feelings toward his mother. He sometimes explained his mother's desertion as due to her not being Jewish, like himself, for he had heard that Christians were cruel to Jews. If his mother was not Jewish, the English language that they wanted him to write at school must be her language and he hated her so much that he did not want to learn it; instead, he wished to learn Hebrew, the language of Jewish people. He was unable to write Hebrew but he knew that it is written in the opposite direction to English; he explained that he tried to turn the English taught at school into Hebrew by writing it backwards. This was the reason for his reversals in writing words.

He called the peculiar marks that he sometimes made for words his "Chinese writing." He knew that the Chinese made peculiar marks to represent words; he had heard that Chinese tortured people whom they hated. When he hated his mother for deserting him, he elaborated, he felt like torturing her the way she had tortured him by letting him love her and then sending him away from her. His "Chinese writing" was a magic spell that would cause his mother to be tortured with sharp knives or in other ways and to be eaten by fierce animals.

These two types of errors in writing words—the reversals and the peculiar marks—were thus symbolic of his anger toward his mother, and his wish to hurt her. His other errors, in which he combined letters into what seemed nonsense, were symbolic of the love he still felt for his mother. For instance, he once wrote the following letter combinations—"As ur mor," which stood for the words, "Ask your mother." It developed that what he wanted to ask her (and the therapist, too) was to have a baby for him, as a proof that his love was returned. Then he need no longer fear that his mother loved the man she had married better than him.

It was only after he had produced all his imaginary explanations for his mother's having placed him and had become conscious of his repressed ambivalent feelings toward her, that he could realize there might be a different reason for the placement than those he had fantasied. Finally he accepted the reality that his mother had placed him because she could no longer take care of him. He then decided that he no longer needed to hate his mother, adding that this permitted him to love other women, too—his foster mother and his teachers at school. He explained that when he hated his own mother, he had hated all women, and so he had never wanted to do a single thing that his foster mother or his teachers asked of him. Now that he could love women, he wanted to do as they expected, so he would not have any more trouble with school work.

In thus describing how he felt about doing things for people because he loved them, this boy was confirming the psychoanalytic theory that the child first learns to please adults whom he loves. Of special interest was the fact that the reversals in writing words, often explained on a physical basis, in this instance were symbolic expressions of hostility and aggression. In two more recent clinic cases, reversals in reading and writing were similarly disguised forms of negative attitudes toward parents and teachers, accompanied by aggressive, destructive fantasies.

In reviewing the literature, there was a reference to a statement by Pearson and English concerning an inhibition of reading after a child had been forbidden peeping activities by parents. Our last case is that of a boy whose expressions of sexual curiosity and also of aggression had been stringently restricted. This case shows a reading disability developing from too severe limitations of instinctive drives.

Case 6.   Jonathan, eight years old when referred to the clinic, had been living in the same foster home since infancy. He had for some time been a tense, hyperactive child, hardly ever still. After two years in school, he had not learned to read. At first it was difficult to maintain contact with him or carry on any connected conversation because of his extreme motor restlessness. He was always running around the room and never continued any one play activity or topic of conversation for more than a few minutes. It was soon observed that he often hunted among the therapist's books, as if searching for something in particular, but he never would tell what he was looking for, saying that he did not know, which was probably quite true. One day as he rummaged through the books, he came upon *Growing Up*. He seized it with the exclamation, "That's what I wanted," but immediately replaced it upon the shelf, saying he could not read it. When asked if he would like it read to him, he hastily disclaimed any such wish.

For some time after this episode, the interviews were taken up with some of his conflicts about living in a foster home and having no parents of his own. At first he tried to protect himself from the anxiety aroused by the knowledge that his own parents had died when he was a small child, by fantasies that the foster parents were his own. After a while he gave up this defense and admitted the insecurity he felt at having no "real" parents like other children at school. Instead of running aimlessly around the room, he now began to do carpentry, liking to fashion swords, knives and guns out of wood. From his talk about these weapons, it was clear that they were symbols of both masculinity and aggressive tendencies, but he often had to leave them with the therapist because he was sure that his foster mother would object to his having them. Actually, when he did get courage to take home a sword he had made, his foster mother took it away from him. As he complained, she wanted him to act like a girl.

His complaint had foundation in the fact, for the foster mother told us that she had wanted the placement agency to give her a girl (although she had never mentioned this to the agency) and when receiving a boy instead, she had dressed him like a girl as long as he would tolerate it and still expected him to be feminine in his behavior.

After he had found some relief from the repression of aggression and masculinity imposed by the foster mother, he again sought out the book *Growing Up* and looked at the pictures, asking the therapist to read some of the pages. He was guilty about this until he had talked over how his foster father once read him this book—but behind locked doors and with a stern warning that Jonathan must never talk about these sex education matters with the foster mother or anyone else except the foster father himself. This was only one aspect of the foster father's need to assure himself the sole intimate relationship with the boy; he did not permit Jonathan to play after school with other children, visit them or invite them to his home. Once Jonathan had thrown aside the restriction his foster father had placed upon his speaking of sex matters to other people, his next interviews with the therapist were full of questions and talk about sex and babies, including repetition of all the slang words and phrases he had heard. He concluded this series of interviews by saying, "I wish I could have asked my mother these things and talked about them with her, but I didn't dare because it would have made my father so angry that maybe he wouldn't have kept me. I was afraid he would give me back to the agency." He also told how he had been eager to learn to read when he first went to school, so that he could read *Growing Up* by himself, only he was fearful that the foster father would not have liked his reading it, for he always kept the book locked in his desk.

After the therapy was completed, Jonathan was able to learn to read at school without remedial teaching. By then, too, he was ready for a move to another foster home where masculine and aggressive strivings were acceptable. Followup reports from the agency indicated that he was developing along normal masculine lines thereafter and when a young adolescent, he was seen for educational guidance tests and interview. At this later date, he could never have been recognized as the same repressed, effeminate boy who had come to the clinic years earlier.

It is interesting to raise a question as to whether this boy would have developed his reading disability as the result of limitation of sexual curiosity alone. To be sure, he was so guilty over wanting to read *Growing Up* and talk about it with his foster mother that he had to resist all reading, but it would seem that repression of aggression was also involved in his avoidance of reading. At least, it was plain in the therapeutic interviews that he could only admit his interest in sex questions, in defiance of his foster father's prohibitions, after relaxation of the repression of masculine, aggressive strivings. Apparently reading was not simply a way of acquiring knowledge but also was an activity that represented aggressive rebellion against the foster father's restrictions, and against his desire to keep the boy to himself. The boy realized that aggression of any kind would meet with disapproval from the foster mother, on whom he had been very dependent as a young child. He was afraid also that the foster father might punish rebellious resistance to his domination by refusing to give him a home any longer. Hence it is little wonder that the boy had to repress aggression so completely.

CONCLUSION

In the clinical cases just presented to illustrate reading disabilities of a psychogenic nature, it seems possible to interpret the material in the light of psychoanalytic theories of reading and learning. But it also appears that there is no single situation or personality maladjustment which can be isolated to explain the development of a reading disability as one of the child's neurotic symptoms. The background may be either traumatic or may reveal chronically unfavorable experiences; the personality difficulties may be severe (as in the case of Ethel who made herself ill by refusing food, or Benjamin who was withdrawn from social relationships and had other serious neurotic symptoms, or Jonathan who was inhibited, passive and effeminate); or maladjustments other than the trouble with reading may be mild enough to be masked from ordinary observation and may become fully apparent only to the professional eye in therapeutic work with the child. These statements might not seem warranted as generalizations on the basis of the comparatively small number of cases included in this paper or reported in previous ones, except for the fact that other investigators have arrived independently at the same conclusions by accumulating statistical data on large numbers of cases.

Both our individual case studies and the statistical findings of other psychologists suggest that a complexity of factors came together in a focal point around reading, particularly where the disability is of emotional origin. In this respect, the neurotic reading disability conforms to the psychoanalytic concept of neurotic symptoms generally as being overdetermined. It also conforms otherwise to psychoanalytic theories of symptom-formation: for the repression of instinctive drives and existence of emotional conflicts forms the setting for the reading disability as well as for other neurotic symptoms; errors in reading may serve as disguised ways of gratifying repressed impulses just as illness-symptoms serve this purpose; failure in reading may represent a hidden antagonism to adults expressed in passive resistance rather than in openly rebellious behavior, and thus may also conceal repressed attitudes. To be sure, at other times the failure may result from a wish to avoid reading because it has previously stirred up feelings of guilt or anxiety, but here, too, it closely resembles a well-known neurotic tendency toward avoidance of imaginary dangers.

In considering that reading disabilities tend to appear as a center of convergence for several emotional factors, we probably need to take into account the timing of this occurrence. It is reasonable to believe that reading is most apt to become involved in a child's emotional conflicts when these concur with the period of learning the fundamentals of the reading process in the early school grades. Once a firm foundation has been acquired, further proficiency in reading depends more upon enlarging the reading vocabulary than learning new processes so that disability for this subject is less likely to begin in higher grades, although it may have remained undetected until then. It is possible, therefore, that the time element may have a bearing on whether a special educational disability will be for reading or for some other subject. Since in many cases personality maladjustments of children begin by the time they enter school or soon afterward, this may be one reason why reading disabilities are more frequent than others. But an equally valid reason, already mentioned, is the ease with which reading content, either directly or symbolically, can become associated with unconscious emotional conflicts.

52. FAMILY PATHOLOGY, FAMILY DIAGNOSIS, AND FAMILY THERAPY WITH A CHILD WELFARE FOCUS

OTTO POLLAK

Theoretically it has long been accepted that a disturbed child is a symptom of a disturbed family. Pollak and his associates have been in the forefront of the attempts to apply this theoretical understanding practically—to focus treatment on the entire family unit rather than on only the child or only the mother and child.

In the following selections Pollak describes how his clinic analyzes and deals with the forces and personalities within the family—including, a family doctor who discouraged psychotherapy.

There seems to be very little recognition, and even less acceptance, in diagnostic and therapeutic emphasis, of the fact that the *family of procreation*—the biological and reproductive unit of the parents and

Selections reprinted from *Integrating Sociological and Psychoanalytic Concepts* (Russell Sage Foundation, 1956), pp. 31–34, 127–138, and from *Social Science and Psychotherapy for Children* (Russell Sage Foundation, 1952), pp. 42–43, by permission of the author and publisher.

child—need not be identical with the *family of orientation*—the sum total of persons who form continuing members of the household in which the child grows up, that is, the primary group at the home. There may be aunts and uncles, grandparents, or even boarders, who are in daily-living contact with the child for periods extending over the whole stretch of his formative years.

Perhaps the basic fact about the presence of "other persons" in the home is that they are not acceptable equally to all members of the family of procreation. They may be acceptable to the child, or to the parents, or to one parent and the child, and so on, but not to the other or others. The presence of an adult relative, particularly if childless, invariably means the presence of an active competitor with the parent of the same sex as the relative for the child's affection. This competition may be overt or it may be subtle or insidious. Or the adult relative is not included in the rules or regime which the parent imposes upon the others in the family; hence this adult, no matter how circumspect his behavior may be, appears to the child as a challenge to the parent's authority, or as a refuge or comfort which the child may seek. A good many domestic situations might be summarized in the statement that the presence of a younger adult in the family means a potential competitor for the affection of the child; and the presence of an older person, a potential competitor for his control. The problem, of course, is often less simple than such a summary suggests. Adults who live with other families tend often to be problem adults. A parent's brother or sister who is not married, or who has been married but not successfully, or who cannot get along with other people, or who is too sick or too feeble to live by himself—these constitute a good proportion of the adults who live with "their" families. Taking in a relative is often the assumption of a burden and a problem. Parents may assume such an obligation with the philosophy of maturity or the resignation of despair, but to the child the newcomer is as he is, without the comfort of compensating philosophy.[1]

This may arise particularly in situations where a member of the family of orientation, such as an old and feeble grandfather, competes with the child for the attention and care of the mother and thus actually starts something equivalent to sibling rivalry between himself and the grandchild.

Thus in psychodynamic terms all members of the family of orientation may become partners to emotionally significant interrelationships with the child and influence his growth process. Dynamic consideration of all persons living in the household in which the child grows up may give a now lacking measure of assurance that an important relationship is not overlooked, minimized, or perceived in its full impact only after considerable treatment time has been lost. Of course, treatment of the child's environment must admit the treatment needs of such persons as well as the treatment needs of the mother.

. . . . .

[1] James H. Bossard, *The Sociology of Child Development* (Harper and Bros., 1948), pp. 59–60.

It helped us to free ourselves from the perceptual trap presented by the dichotomy of patient and environment and actually to see the total family as a unit of diagnostic and therapeutic concern. It provided a permanent challenge to strive for a psychodynamic understanding of all the members of the family, to see the social interaction among them as based on these individual psychodynamic pictures, and to base therapeutic planning on such understanding. In essence, it helped us shift our orientation from child psychotherapy to family psychotherapy with child welfare focus and to experiment with procedures which such an orientation demanded. In response to this challenge of reorientation we attempted wherever possible to perform three tasks. First of all, we tried to formulate a clinical, a genetic, and a dynamic diagnosis of every family member in whom we encountered pathology. Essentially this was only an accumulation of individual diagnostic procedures which had been practiced before regularly as far the mother and the child were concerned. To be sure, the extension of this procedure to other members of the family as well was burdensome because of its demand on the worker's time. It also proved technically difficult because of the concern that such an extension of the diagnostic inquiry might on occasion interfere with the establishment of a relationship between the worker and the individual patient. Still, this was from the point of view of theory simply an additive process of gaining information.

The next step in our team thinking, however, presented theoretical difficulties which we did not fully overcome and which suggest a fruitful field of further research. To identify pathology in the various members of a family on an individual basis and even to gain an understanding of pathological interaction between two of them is one thing. To gain and formulate an understanding of pathological interaction patterns among three, four, or even more members of a household on which to base therapeutic planning on such an understanding is more difficult, because this presents problems of another order, namely, problems of formulating a family diagnosis and planning a family therapy. The solution of these problems requires specific conceptual tools and specific therapeutic practices which have been hardly yet developed, although the need for advance in that direction has been recognized and some promising beginnings have been made.

Thus, our own attempts at formulating a family diagnosis represent only one phase in a development of thought which apparently goes in this direction. They were characterized not only by an effort to keep a balance between our psychodynamic understanding of individuals and the observation of interactional patterns but by an effort to achieve an integration between these two orientations. We tried to see how the intrapsychic difficulties of the individuals involved determined their interaction patterns and how these interaction patterns in turn determined the development, persistence, or abating of their intrapsychic difficulties. Furthermore, we attempted to make these analyses not on a two-person but on a real family basis, which always involved more than two persons. Finally, we evaluated the nature and effect of the interaction patterns which we found operating in a family in terms of family functions and family tendencies as seen from an institutional angle.

Our third effort was concerned with the development of a family treatment plan. Owing to the very nature of our family diagnoses, these treatment plans had to express concern with pluralities greater than dualities. They had to be directed at the change of more than one interaction pattern. In consequence, frequently more than two persons had to be considered for treatment. Furthermore, because of trying to think in terms of families rather than in terms of two-person fragments thereof, we had to be reluctant about dividing cases. While it still may be possible to keep treatment procedures pursued by two workers integrated, the chances for maintaining such an integration where three workers are involved obviously are slight. In consequence, we found it fruitful to have the same worker see all the members of the family as actual or potential patients to be treated by herself until such time as special counterindications became apparent. The latter actually happened very infrequently.

Our attempts to treat families as totalities rather than only in terms of two-person fragments also strengthened our awareness of the limitation of goals. We became better aware of the fact that such limitations are determined not only by the intensity of intrapsychic difficulties in one or the other member of a family, but also by the nature and the level of common concern in the family unit. In this respect the child welfare focus of the agency proved to be helpful in keeping the various courses of therapy with the individual members of the family on a concerted plane.

It will be noticed that in this report the term "child focus" is replaced by the term "child welfare focus." This substitution of terms represents a postproject conceptualization. In our actual team discussions we had retained the term "child focus." In retrospect it appears, however, that the use of this term created a number of difficulties. It failed to express conceptually the reorientation which our situational approach implied. For this reason, it caused perceptual pitfalls and logical inconsistencies with which we had to struggle a great deal and against which the term "child welfare focus" promises to furnish a measure of protection.

By focusing upon the child as an individual, perception is likely to be restricted and the dynamic forces in his environment are likely to be blurred. Under the impact of such a terminology clinical consideration of the mother on an equal footing with the child is indeed an advance. By focusing on the welfare of a child, however, the perception of the plurality of factors involved is promoted and clinical emphasis upon the mother-child relationships as encountered in routinized practice appears to be fragmentation rather than comprehensiveness. Child welfare focus, furthermore, makes it difficult to single out one child from a number of siblings as the only receiver of clinical concern. It directs attention to the siblings rather than to a sibling. By doing so it is likely to enhance effectiveness in the prevention function of child guidance work. The concept of child welfare focus also promises to keep family therapy from disintegrating into a number of treatments which serve only the individuals involved for their own sake rather than gearing the therapeutic efforts to a common social interest. Thus, the concept may serve as an orchestrating principle in the management of the various individual lines of therapy which compose the family treatment, and it seems to anchor the clinical effort in a recognized area of social concern.

• • • • •

THE CASE OF EDWARD N.

PRESENTING SYMPTOMS

Edward's mother was referred to the Child Guidance Institute by a psychologist. He was an only child, described as destructive at home and aggressive to other children. He pulled at their genitals, threw rocks at girls, and pulled boys off bicycles. At other times he showed completely withdrawn behavior. As a result of these difficulties in relating to other children, he had no friends. He was also aggressive to his mother who, the psychologist reported, was overprotective toward the definite history of respiratory allergies, apparently accentuated at four years of age. He also complained frequently of abdominal distress. The family background showed a history of asthma in a maternal aunt. In the father's opinion, the boy was infantile, secretive, and had temper outbursts. The mother feared the boy's sexual interests. She worried lest he be "abnormal" like herself or a maternal aunt who had undergone psychiatric treatment.

Edward's health history revealed infantile colic, pneumonia at fifteen weeks, two and one-half years, and at three and one-half years, with frequent respiratory discomfort, eventually developing into known allergy at about the age of four. At six he had an ear infection with hearing difficulties, relieved by adenoidectomy. At nine, just before direct therapy, he developed a fourth attack of pneumonia. A number of medical specialists had been involved by consultation, and a general practitioner occupied the foremost role in caring for the boy's allergies, as well as advising the mother on matters of childrearing.

The mother suffered from recurrent depressions with obsessional thoughts and anxieties throughout her life history. An exacerbation of her depressions had occurred during and subsequent to her pregnancy, a further increase at the time of her menopause, which was prior to treatment at the Clinic. She had seen a psychiatrist twice during her post-partum depression, but had reacted with great apprehension and resisted psychiatric help for herself. She was the youngest of a large family, brought to the United States at the age of fifteen by an elder brother. She relied on the oldest sister in a very dependent way. As a child, she had been exposed to the rages of her father, and her pattern had been to withdraw from these scenes. The maternal grandmother was described as a frail, sweet-tempered woman who had tried to protect her daughters from the outbursts of their father by keeping them out of his way as much as possible.

Edward's father, an engineer, appeared to be more composed, and handled his wife's depressive moods with extreme patience. This served to increase guilt feelings and perpetuate her lack of effective effort. He recognized the difficulty of the mother-child relationship, was concerned about Edward's social adjustment and emotional attitudes, but had never taken any initiative in seeking professional help for the mother's difficulties. The contacts which the mother had attempted to make in this direction had been initiated by herself.

For many years it had been the stated policy of the Child Guidance Institute of the Jewish Board of Guardians not to accept children for psychotherapy if psychosomatic conditions were so severe that ambulatory medical treatment had to go on apace with psychotherapy. It was felt that such cases would best be served in hospital clinics where total treatment, providing close cooperation between the departments of psychiatry and those representing other medical specialties could be given to the patients. However, the appearance of severe emotional disturbance in the mother-child relationship, which the social work therapist readily perceives as important, plus the pressure of the initial referral source, plus the wishes of the medical practitioner himself, lead frequently to a decision for exploration in our Clinic. In many instances, this leads to dramatic supportive help, despite questions as to the effectiveness of the use of our time and personnel. In the case of Edward, these pressures had also exerted themselves.

AMBIVALENCE OF MOTHER

The mother was offered an interview shortly after application, but she was already away on summer vacation with her son. Intake was completed in the fall, and there then ensued another wait considerably longer than the first one because an assignment to a therapist could not be made. Throughout this time the mother, while ambivalent and depressed, had telephoned the Clinic on occasions and indicated her wish to keep the application open. When we informed her that we could offer a therapist, she reported that Edward had facial twitching and had suffered another siege of pneumonia which curtailed his summer vacation. The boy had responded well to a brief separation in the hospital, but had suffered recurrent colds thereafter. The mother realized that there was definite correlation between her own symptomatology and the boy's demanding behavior with her. Medical treatment consisted of periodic hypodermic injection of nonspecific vaccine to clear up his infectious bronchitis. The family physician had advised her not to send the boy to school because of his debilitated condition and had expressed also the opinion that Edward would not be ready to receive psychotherapy for four more months. The mother did not want the Clinic to close the case, however, and asked the worker to give her a month to decide.

AMBIVALENCE OF THE INTAKE WORKER

The long delay from first application to a second intake reevaluation in this case was contrary to practice. It was in part related to the problems of the Clinic and in part to the disturbed mother-child relationships. The mother always left a tentative line of approach open, but at times used the physician-child relationship to sustain her own mixed feelings. This seems to be more characteristic of mothers whose children have allergic discomforts than of mothers whose children show other types of maladjustments. As far as the Clinic was concerned there also seemed to have existed ambivalence on the part of the intake worker as to whether this case should be accepted for treatment or not. Apparently the worker's conflict between our general policy not to accept psychosomatic cases in which ambulatory medical treatment has to go on simultaneously and the pressure to offer some help in this severely disturbed situation had remained unresolved. When the case came up for discussion in the project seminar, the uncertainty underlying the original decision to take on Edward's case for exploration had again to be solved. The seminar group expressed the idea that previous indecision of the intake staff regarding acceptability had itself now become a factor in the mother's own hostile reactions toward Edward.

After we had decided to take on the case for research purposes and contact with the mother was planfully established, Mrs. N. appeared depressed, anxious, and easily threatened. She gave much detail of Edward's illnesses, but was protective about his behavioral disturbances. Although she did not conceal the boy's destructiveness, she tried to see in it only a way of self-expression. Admitting that he also showed other difficulties in his behavior at home, she was inclined to present things as improving in that area. She stated her chief concern to be not Edward's behavior at home but his rejection by other children. She indicated a deep sense of brooding responsibility rather than love for Edward. She was deeply dependent upon her husband's patience and devotion to the family to prevent worsening of her depressive moods, serious obsessional thoughts, and her anxiety. She felt "heavy," slept excessively during the daytime, retiring into her bedroom from the family activities. At these times she ate excessively, and her brooding and irritability were more marked toward Edward.

AMBIVALENCE OF THE FAMILY PHYSICIAN

Initially, Mrs. N. saw the Child Guidance Institute as a place for help with Edward's behavioral problems, apart from the physical factors. This definition of the situation on her part appeared to be influenced by the family physician who apparently wanted Edward to come to the Clinic for treatment but thought that his coming for help would have to wait until his physical distress was considerably lessened. The general practitioner had previously resisted suggestions by specialists for testing gastrointestinal factors in the allergic condition. The mother's utilization of the family physician seemed to serve her own need to infantilize the child by excessive physical care, occasioning long school absences and curtailment of his social activities. In addition, she satisfied her own dependency needs by the authoritative, guiding figure of the physician. On the other hand, the worker gained the impression that the mother herself had some questions as to whether Edward's problems could be strictly divided into physical and behavioral problems and whether his physical difficulties were not in part the result of his emotional difficulties.

At any rate, the mother's dependency on the judgment of the family physician required that considerable attention be paid to him in any attempt to establish a common frame of reference among all persons involved in the situation. The next problem on which the seminar discussion focused, therefore, was that of consulting the family physician. The values of such a contact were seen in his ability to clarify fully the medical history of the child and to help the mother cooperate in providing psychotherapy for the boy. It was agreed that the physician seemed to be a person of power in the situation. On the negative side, it was mentioned that the schedule of the doctor as well as that of the worker might prevent their getting together for a conference. The thought was also expressed that the mother might regard this contact as a criticism of her, with the result that her feelings of inadequacy and self-reproach might increase. In the discussion which ensued, the psychiatrist pointed out that it was dangerous to develop set attitudes against approaching another professional person. Such an attitude would in and by itself preclude any possibility of exploring potentially available opportunities of arriving at a common frame of reference in many situations. Doctors often had the notion that a physical condition should be cleared up first and that only afterward should a child receive psychotherapy. His opinion was that only an attempt to interchange experiences could offset this and particularly in this type of case.

Following seminar discussion, several interesting developments occurred. Instead of a possible heightening of the mother's feelings of inadequacy, the therapist's request to see the family doctor occasioned surprise and pleasure—proof of the therapist's interest in Edward. The mother also felt that it would be good for the doctor to gain an idea of the Clinic's treatment procedure inasmuch as he might then feel that it would not endanger Edward's physical status. In other words, the mother herself felt that the physician needed a new frame of reference within which to view the feasibility and potential of psychotherapy for Edward.

The doctor, finally reached by telephone after several unsuccessful calls, refused a conference. He could only talk over the telephone because of his lack of time. He said Edward had just had a really old-fashioned lobar pneumonia, and that his allergies had acted as a hindrance to his recovery. Psychotherapy should be postponed until February. He thought that Edward needed the Clinic's help for "environmental and behavioral reasons" and did not allow the therapist to explain the aims and nature of the psychotherapy. In our seminar discussions, it was felt that the physician by his advice to postpone therapy until February, a time when the boy's medical history indicated frequent recurrence of increased respiratory difficulties, might have revealed unconscious hostile trends toward psychotherapy.

AMBIVALENCE OF THE FATHER

Quite apart from our position that an integration of the concept of the family of orientation with psychodynamic concepts required contact with the father in principle, such a contact seemed particularly indicated in this situation. In some cases which we carried in our seminar, the correctness of our belief in the necessity of seeing the father was substantiated only after the contact has been established. In Edward's case, however, the need to make such a contact seemed to be factually determined before the worker even met Mr. N. First of all, there were the mother's serious condition of depression and the boy's physical distress which was likely to restrict the parental power of seeing his problems in their totality. There was further the doctor's attitude which would not be supportive. Finally, there were some remarks by the mother that Edward showed traits which reminded her of Mr. N. All these factors suggested that the father was a key figure in this situation and that without his support it was unlikely that we would be permitted to render meaningful services in this case. From the angle of preparing the case for treatment, it seemed imperative that we should find out what the father thought of the mother's depression, what he thought of the condition of the boy, how he viewed the position taken by the family physician, and what his ideas were regarding the treatment of his wife and son in the Clinic.

When the worker mentioned her interest in seeing Edward's father to Mrs. N., the latter accepted this without any trace of resistance and made an appointment for her husband. On the next day she confirmed the appointment by telephone. Mr. N., on his arrival, stated at first that he was on his way to his office and hard pressed for time. He could not stay more than five minutes. He said that he had come in only to tell us about his agreement with his wife that Edward should come to our Clinic for treatment. He was willing to give it a chance. His original attitude thus seemed to be one of submission to a proposition which he questioned and in which he did not see a reason for becoming personally involved. The worker, however, was able to convey to him interest in his personal thinking so effectively that Mr. N. quickly changed his mind and decided to stay for a discussion of the situation. In the course of this discussion, he was helped by the worker to reveal his true concerns and in doing so showed how justified we were in assuming that his cooperation would require an effort of the Clinic to give him an appropriate frame of reference within which to view the potential of our service.

First of all, Mr. N. gave expression to the idea that he might have been under a misapprehension as to the nature of our service. He had had the impression that the Clinic was intended to help only mentally dull children. He felt, however, that Edward was a bright boy and had wondered whether—if this was so—our Clinic was the right place for his son. After the worker cleared up with Mr. N. this misconception and had freed him from his concern in this respect, Mr. N. gave vent to another concern. He felt that his wife could use psychiatric treatment but he did not think that Edward needed it. In his understanding, Edward's troubles were essentially "health problems" and they were improving. He felt that if Edward's organic discomforts were removed, the boy would not need psychotherapy. As Mr. N. elaborated this theme he became increasingly aware of the fact that his boy's difficulties were not confined to the organic area. He began to mention the conflicts between Edward and his mother, his difficulties in getting along with other children, and particularly his physical aggressiveness. This development of his own train of thought apparently led Mr. N. to question his original position that Edward needed help only in the physical area, because he concluded his description of the boy's difficulties by asking how our Clinic operated. In reply to this question the worker used directness similar to the procedure followed in the preceding case. She explained to Mr. N. our efforts to build up a positive relationship between a child and his worker, our methods of gaining access to his ideas and problems by plan and discussion, and of coming to agreement with the child about the purpose of his therapy in terms which the child can understand and use. Finally, she clarified with Mr. N. the nature of the emotional learning and un-learning which children experience in therapy.

After having established a common frame of reference with the father along these lines, the worker engaged him in a discussion of

Edward's history of physical difficulties in the course of which the father himself broached the topic of the attitude of the family physician toward Edward's treatment. Mr. N. seemed to appreciate the physician's concern for Edward's physical condition, but showed signs of an increasing readiness to separate himself from the doctor's judgement. He felt there might be some reality in the doctor's wish to see psychotherapy for Edward postponed until he had built up his physical condition after his last bout with pneumonia. Mr. N. thought, however, that the boy had been well now for six weeks and that probably he had recovered sufficiently to start coming without further delay. When the worker suggested that she would want to discuss this again with the mother and the doctor, the father remarked that the physician was too busy to pay much attention to Edward beyond that required for giving him his injections. He thought it unlikely that the doctor would be able to tell the worker much about the boy's problems for that reason. With regard to his wife, he felt definitely that treatment at the Clinic would be helpful to her. Maybe she could find here some release from the emotional tension which made her so irritable at home and in turn affected the boy.

Toward the end of the interview, Mr. N. summed up the experience of his discussion with the worker by saying that at first he had not been convinced of the soundness of the idea of therapy for Edward. Now, however, and particularly in view of what the worker had told him about the type of child who received help here, he was in favor of Edward's coming to the Clinic for psychotherapy.

PLANNING A RESTRUCTURING OF THE SITUATION

When we reviewed our attempts at preparing this case for treatment up to this point, it became clear in our seminar discussions that again we had encountered extrafamilial as well as familial factors. Our identification of interpersonal relationships within the family of orientation, our appraisal of the relationships between the family physician and the parents, and our consideration of the physical manifestations of Edward's problems had suggested that three main factors in the situation had been dealt with so far.

The dependency needs of the mother which we had come to recognize in her use of the authoritarian attitude of the physician, in her beginning contacts with the worker, and in her relationship with her husband suggested that Mrs. N.'s narcissistic demands on the worker's patience and acceptance would be extreme. We had come to the decision, however, that these demands would have to be met if a positive relationship between Mrs. N. and the worker was to be established, and the existing pressures in the mother-child relationship were to be eased.

The father's misconception of therapy for the boy had been clarified. Since he had thought that therapy was only for dull children and since

Edward was obviously bright, it was apparent that it was chiefly his concern for his wife's depression that had led him even to consider psychotherapy for the boy. The clarification of a more appropriate frame of reference for Mr. N., therefore, was of great importance. Without it, he might easily have become a silent antagonist with a truly masochistic participation until his wife was helped. With clarification, however, the father seemed to lend support to the idea of psychotherapy for Edward —for Edward's sake. Secondly, he had also shown a measure of independence from the judgement of the family physician with regard to the start of this type of help for the boy.

Establishing a contact with the family doctor, while not assuring cooperation, was of great value to the family attitude and our planning. Interestingly enough, the negative character of the contact with the family physician proved to be one of the cornerstones of our plan. It is tempting in our cultural value system to expect that a contact between representatives of two different professional disciplines will produce teamwork. When this cultural expectation is not fulfilled, the contact is considered as having resulted in failure. In therapeutic situations such a failure is then considered as an obstacle to treatment. This tendency to view open conflict as essentially negative may well lead to a certain avoidance tendency on the part of psychotherapists with regard to organically oriented physicians. Our experience in this case suggested, however, that a negative outcome of an attempt to establish a common frame of reference with a family physcian and failure to enlist his cooperation can also be turned into constructive channels. Only the actual contact and the worker's personal experience of the attitude of the doctor toward psychotherapy gave an opportunity for a full appraisal of the force with which we had to deal in this physician. The comprehension of this force made it clear to us that we were faced with an impossibility of psychotherapy for Edward so long as the doctor's opposition maintained its dynamic power within the field of social realities in which we had to operate.

It had been clarified that an alignment of perception among all the persons who composed this field of forces was impossible. In order to provide a therapeutic milieu, this field of forces, therefore, had to be restructured in terms of a different composition rather than in terms of a different frame of reference for the persons who composed it originally. A beginning in that direction had been made by helping the father to visualize psychotherapy for Edward without complete dependence on the approval of the general practitioner. The mother, however, was not yet ready to view the situation independent of the physician's judgement. We felt, however, that the authoritative and magical meaning with which Mrs. N. had vested his opinion could be discussed by her and the therapist with a chance of developing some independence of judgement also on the mother's part. This required, of course, that the relationship between the mother and the worker be given a chance to develop. In consequence, we decided to initiate treatment first with the mother, emphasizing, however, from the start that this was done on the basis of her child's difficulties and with a view of working toward an improvement also of the latter.

The mother's treatment initially continued to reveal more and more her deep dependency needs and, the relationship with the worker provided great satisfaction of the needs on the basis of a "good mother" transference. Mrs. N. became less depressed after confiding to the worker her severe emotional difficulties of rage, overeating, and oversleeping. She recognized her infantilization of the boy, her concerns about his sexual interests, and her fears of his sadistic nature. She related her own family relationships, appreciated her resentment against her sister who had occupied an ambivalent mother role with her, and she was able to secure work as a professional person. This had coincided with the oft-expressed reassuring wish of her husband that when Edward would become older she would be able to spend less time with him. After four months of interviews, she was able to bring the boy in for treatment.

53. NON-DIRECTIVE PLAY THERAPY

VIRGINIA MAE AXLINE

The non-directive client-centered approach, is but one of the many methods of dealing with a child who is nervous, unmanageable, aggressive, or speechless. The excerpts from the book Play Therapy *discuss some of the major principles of the non-directive approach to disturbed children. The student may observe that some of the rules presented here appear to be violated by the writers of other articles in this section—yet those writers also claim successful therapeutic results.*

INTRODUCTION

BY CARL ROGERS

Some will read [these selections] and say, "It can't be true. Children are not like this. Bad children do not have within them the positive forces that are shown here. The whole thing is too good to be true!" To such

Selections reprinted from *Play Therapy: The Inner Dynamics of Childhood* (Houghton Mifflin Company, 1947) by permission of the author and publisher.

skeptics I can only say that results such as are portrayed in this book do occur when the principles which are set forth are faithfully followed. Not only can I vouch for the fact that Miss Axline achieves such results, but that many others without as much native tolerance, without such an intuitive understanding, can also achieve such outcomes. I might also suggest the final and conclusive test—that the skeptic try to put these principles into practice himself, and closely observe developments. Even though the therapy is carried on in blundering fashion because of the skepticism, there are likely to be highly rewarding experiences. School would become a very different institution, with markedly different effects upon the child, if even a few teachers undertook to deal with youngsters in the manner described in the chapters which follow.

NON-DIRECTIVE THERAPY

Non-directive therapy is based upon the assumption that the individual has within himself, not only the ability to solve his own problems satisfactorily, but also this growth impulse that makes mature behavior more satisfying than immature behavior.

PLAY THERAPY

Non-directive play therapy may be described as an opportunity that is offered to the child to experience growth under the most favorable conditions. Since play is his natural medium for self-expression, the child is given the opportunity to play out his accumulated feelings of tension, frustration, insecurity, aggression, fear, bewilderment, confusion.

By playing out these feelings he brings them to the surface, gets them out in the open, faces them, learns to control them, or abandon them. When he has achieved emotional relaxation, he begins to realize the power within himself to be an individual in his own right, to think for himself, to make his own decisions, to become psychologically more mature, and, by so doing, to realize selfhood.

The play-therapy room is good growing ground. In the security of this room where the child is the most important person, where he is in command of the situation and of himself, where no one tells him what to do, no one criticizes what he does, no one nags, or suggests, or goads him on, or pries into his private world, he suddenly feels that here he can unfold his wings; he can look squarely at himself, for he is accepted completely; he can test out his ideas; he can express himself fully; for this is his world, and he no longer has to compete with such other forces as adult authority or rival contemporaries or situations where he is a human pawn in a game between bickering parents, or where he is the butt of someone else's frustrations and aggressions. He is an individual in his own right. He is treated with dignity and respect. He can say anything that he feels like saying—and he is accepted completely. He can play with the toys in any way that he likes to—and he is accepted completely. He can hate and he can love and he can be as indifferent as the Great Stone Face—and he is still accepted completely. He can be as fast as a whirlwind or as slow as molasses in January—and he is neither restrained nor hurried.

Quotations of what children have actually said in describing the play-therapy experience as the remarks came out spontaneously are more indicative of what it means to the child than anything the therapist can say.

Three boys, aged eight, were experiencing group-therapy sessions. During the eighth interview, Herby suddenly asked the therapist, "Do you have to do this? Or do you like to do this?" Then he added, "I wouldn't know how to do this." Ronny asked, "What do you mean? You play. That's all. You just play." And Owen agreed with Ronny. "Why, sure you do," he said. But Herby continued the discussion. "I mean I wouldn't know how to do what she does. I don't even know what she does. She doesn't seem to do anything. Only all of a sudden, I'm free. Inside me, I'm free." (He flings his arms around.) "I'm Herb and Frankenstein and Tojo and a devil." (He laughs and pounds his chest.) "I'm a great giant and a hero. I'm wonderful and I'm terrible. I'm a dope and I'm so smart. I'm two, four, six, eight, ten people, and I fight and I kill!" The therapist said to Herby, "You're all kinds of people rolled up in one." Ronny added, "And you stink, too." Herby glared at Ronny, and replied, "I stink and you stink. Why, I'll mess you up." The therapist continued to speak to Herby—"You're all kinds of people in here. You're wonderful and you're terrible and you're dopey and you're smart." Herby interrupted exultantly, "I'm good and I'm bad and still I'm Herby. I tell you I'm wonderful. I can be anything I want to be!" Apparently Herby felt that during the therapy hour he could express fully all of the attitudes and feelings that were an expression of his personality. He felt the acceptance and permissiveness to be himself. He seemed to recognize the power of self-direction within himself.

Another boy, aged twelve, commented during a first therapy session: "This is all so different and so strange. In here you say I can do what I want to do. You don't tell me what to do. I can mess up a picture if I want to. I can make a clay model of my art teacher and let the crocodile eat her." He laughed. "I can do anything. I can be me!"

Feeling their way, testing themselves, unfolding their personalities, taking the responsibility for themselves—that is what happens during therapy.

. . . . .

Oscar had no sense of security at all. Some of the helpers mistreated him. He became one of the most maladjusted children imaginable. He was aggressive, belligerent, negative, insecure, defiant, dependent. He was a masterpiece of conflicting feelings. His mother, erratic and nervous, brought him to the psychologist. This is an excerpt from the initial contact.

MOTHER.   This is Oscar. Heaven only knows what you can do with him! But here he is.

THERAPIST.   Would you like to come over to the playroom with me?

OSCAR.   No! Shet up! [*Yells.*]

MOTHER [*also yelling*].   Oscar! Now you be polite. Stop that sass!

OSCAR [*louder than ever*].   No! No! No!

MOTHER.   Well, you are! What do you think I brought you up here for? The ride?

OSCAR [*whimpering*].   I don't wanta!

The beginning therapist asks herself at this point, "Now what?" Cajole him into the playroom? "We have such nice toys over in the playroom. You're such a nice big boy now. You come with me and I'll show you what there is to play with." That is not accepting Oscar exactly as he is. He doesn't want to come. Or should she say, with a note of regret in her voice, "Your mother brought you all the way up here and you don't want to come into the playroom with me!" That is a reflection of feeling, but it also carries subtle condemnation. There is an implied "My, aren't you an ungrateful little brute!" If the therapist wants to reflect his feeling only, what should she say? "You don't want to come with me." The therapist tries that.

THERAPIST.   You don't want to come with me.

OSCAR.   No! [*Makes face at therapist and folds up fists.*] Shet up!

MOTHER.   If you don't go over there, I'll leave you here forever.

OSCAR [*attaching self to mother, whimpering*].   Don't leave me. Don't leave me. [*Sobs hysterically.*]

THERAPIST.   Oscar is scared when Mother threatens to leave him here. [*This is a recognition of Oscar's feeling, but condemnation of Mother, who flares up.*]

MOTHER.   Well, I've got to do something. Honest to God, Oscar, if you don't shut up and go with this lady, I will leave you! Or give you away!

OSCAR.   You wait for me? [*Pitifully.*] You be here when I come back.

MOTHER.   Of course I will—if you behave.

OSCAR [*transferring death-like grip from Mother's skirt to therapist's skirt*].   You wait?

THERAPIST.   You want Mother to promise you that she will wait.

OSCAR.   You promise?

MOTHER.   I promise!

[*Therapist and Oscar go into the playroom. Therapist starts to close the door.*]

OSCAR [*screaming*].   Don't shet the door! Don't shet the door! [*Tears roll down his cheeks.*]

THERAPIST.   You don't want me to shut the door. You're afraid to stay here with me if I shut the door. Very well. We'll leave the door open and you close the door when you feel like it.

[*This leaves the responsibility up to Oscar. It is up to him to make the choice. Oscar looks around the playroom. As he thaws out, he becomes aggressive.*]

OSCAR.   I'll bust up everything in here!

What about limitations? Should the therapist say, "'You can play with the toys in here any way you want to, but you can't bust them up." Or, "Other children use these toys, too, so you can't bust them up." That is not responding to Oscar's expressed feeling. That is succumbing to the trap of responding to content rather than feeling back of content.

THERAPIST.   You're feeling tough now.

OSCAR [*glaring at therapist*].   I'll bust you up, too.

THERAPIST.   You're still feeling tough.

OSCAR.   I'll———— [*suddenly laughs*] I'll———— [*He wanders around the playroom and picks up the toy telephone.*] What's this?

ACCEPTING THE CHILD COMPLETELY

Jean is brought into the clinic by her mother. Jean, aged twelve, is getting completely out of hand. She shows no respect for her mother, quarrels with her younger brother, will not have anything to do with the other children in her class at school. After introductions, Jean goes to the playroom with the therapist. The therapist attempts to structure the situation verbally. "You may play with any of the toys in here any way that you want to, Jean. There are paints, clay, finger paints, puppets." The therapist smiles at Jean, who stares back at the therapist in obvious boredom. The therapist waits for a few moments. Jean sits down and maintains her stony silence. The therapist, anxious to get things moving, speaks again. "Don't you know just what to do first? Oh, and there is a family of dolls over in the doll house. Do you like to play with dolls?"

Jean shakes her head negatively. The therapist pursues her quarry. "You don't like to play with dolls. Don't you see anything in here that you would like to play with? You may play with any of these things in here in any way that you want to." Jean still maintains the icy silence. Then the therapist says, "You don't want to play. You just want to sit here." Jean nods agreement. "Very well," says the therapist. She, too, sits down and silence descends upon both of them. But the therapist is tense. "Would you rather just talk?" she asks hopefully. "No," says Jean. The therapist taps her pencil on her barren notebook. She taps her foot. She looks a little annoyed at Jean. This silence is maddening. There is a silent battle going on between the two, of which Jean is surely aware.

If the girl has been fighting for acceptance outside the clinic, why must she continue here? If it is obvious that she does not want to play or talk, why not be accepting and permissive to the extent of letting her sit there in silence? After explaining the situation clearly enough so that she understands that she might play with any of the things in the playroom, or use the hour any way she desires, the accepting therapist would go along with the child and, if silence was the order of the hour, then silence it would be. It would seem well to include in the preliminary explanation to the girl that it is her privilege either to play or not to play as she desires, to talk or not to talk, and, after the girl has made the decision, the therapist should abide by it. The therapist might busy herself with notes—or with doodling if she feels that she must do something. She should be on the alert to reflect any feeling the girl might express. A deep sigh, a longing glance out the window, might safely be reflected to her——"It is boring to just sit here with me. Perhaps you would rather be outside." At that understanding, Jean might relax a little.

ESTABLISHING A FEELING OF PERMISSIVENESS

During the first hour the child explores the materials and is very alert to the therapist's attitude. That is why words alone are not enough. Permissiveness is established by the therapist's attitude toward the child, by facial expressions, tone of voice, and actions.

If the child spills water deliberately and the therapist immediately wipes it up, the action more or less cancels the verbal expression of permissiveness.

If the therapist, thinking the child's problem is centered around family relationships, pushes the doll family toward the child with, "See the doll family? Wouldn't you like to play with them?" she is not granting permissiveness of choice to the child.

If the child picks up the ball of clay and rolls it idly between indecisive hands, the therapist will do well to refrain from commenting, "You don't know what to make." Such a remark might be taken by the child to indicate that the therapist is not satisfied to have the child roll the clay aimlessly back and forth. Permissiveness implies choice to use or not to use the materials according to the child's wishes.

There should be no attempt made to guide the actions or conversation of the child. That implies that there must be no probing questions directed toward the child.

For example, five-year-old May, who has been referred to the clinic for therapy because of a traumatic hospital experience, is playing with the family of dolls. She picks up the girl doll, places her in the toy wagon and pushes her across the floor. The therapist, thinking to capture the crucial experience says, "Is the little girl going to the hospital?" "Yes," says the child. "Is she afraid?" "Yes." "Then what happens?" asks the therapist. The child gets up, goes over to the window, turns her back on the therapist and doll family. "How much longer?" she asks. "Is the time up yet?" Thus the child wards off the probing. The child is not yet ready to explore the experience that has been so upsetting. She has not yet been accepted as she is. She has not been granted the permissiveness to open that door when she felt adequate to face what was beyond it.

When he feels so securely accepted by the therapist that he can beat up the mother doll, or bury the baby in the sand, or lie down on the floor and drink from a nursing bottle even though he is nine, ten, or eleven years old, and yet can do these things without a feeling of shame or guilt, then the therapist has established a feeling of permissiveness. The child is free to express his feelings. He gives vent to his most aggressive and destructive impulses. He screams, yells, throws the sand all over the place, spits water on the floor. He gets rid of his tensions. He becomes emotionally relaxed. Then, it seems, the groundwork for more constructive behavior has been laid.

RECOGNITION AND REFLECTION OF FEELINGS

One day Jack went home for a visit. He had been planning on this visit for a long time. He wanted to get his toys. He had been coming for play-therapy contacts for five weeks before the home visit. This was his first day back.

JACK. Well, I went home. [*He sat down at the paint table and drew a clean sheet of paper toward him, opened the box of paints, and began to paint, still grinning happily.*] I saw my father and my brother. And do you know why they hadn't come to see me?

THERAPIST. No.

JACK. Because they thought it would make me feel sad to see them and then have them leave me here. That's what my father said. And they took me on a picnic and we had ice cream and candy and a boat ride. I told my father I wanted to bring my toys back. I asked about my gun. And we went out in the country one day, too.

[*All the time Jack was relating the story of his visit back home, he was painting a tiny green spot in the middle of the paper and all round the green spot a growing expanse of black. Finally the paper was covered over with the black paint.*] Yep, I went home all right. But I didn't get my toys. And my brother had broken my gun. And he had lots of his own toys. He has fun all the time. He stays there.

THERAPIST. You went home, but you were disappointed in your visit.

[*This statement is interpretation. The therapist is drawing a conclusion from what Jack had said.*] You didn't get the toys you went after and your gun had been broken.

JACK.   Yes. [*He got up from the table and went over to the shelf and got the nursing bottle. He brought it back to the table and sat down across from the therapist.*] I told him a thing or two. I told him I wanted my toys. [*He seemed very close to tears. He looked at the therapist.*] Me baby [*sucking on the nursing bottle*].

THERAPIST.   Now you are a baby. You don't think they treated you very nice when you went home. [*This, too, is interpretation, going beyond what the child expressed. In reality, it seems to be what the therapist feels about the home situation, but it was close enough to Jack's feelings to be acceptable by him.*]

[*Jack filled his mouth with water. He leaned over and spat it on the floor.*]

JACK.   Look. I spit on my home.

THERAPIST.   You spit on your home.

[*Jack jerked off the nipple and filled his mouth again and once more spat on the floor.*]

JACK.   I spit on my brother. I spit on my father. I spit right in their very faces. They wouldn't give me my toys. He broke my gun. I'll show them. I'll spit on them. [*Again and again he filled his mouth with water and spat it on the floor.*]

THERAPIST.   You are very angry with your brother and your father. You would like to spit right in their faces because of the way they have treated you.

In this case the boy progresses from a polite verbalization about his trip home to a violent display of his true feelings. It is interesting to note how he releases his feelings with deeper significance as he receives recognition for each feeling that he does express.

.   .   .   .   .

No more fearful or inadequate child than Jerry ever came into the play-therapy room. He was four years old, mentally retarded, physically undersized. He could not talk, was very poorly co-ordinated, and seemed to be absolutely lacking in self-direction. He was brought in for play therapy because of his unreasonable fears, because he was a feeding problem, and because the mother thought that Jerry might learn how to talk as a result of this therapy experience.

When the therapist first met Jerry, she saw a whimpering, insecure, bewildered little fellow who didn't know what it was all about. He muttered and staggered around in circles when the therapist reached for his hand to take him into the playroom.

FIRST CONTACT

Jerry gazed around him at the toys in the playroom. Then he began to pick up the toys, look at them briefly, and drop them on the floor. He grunted and muttered, but said nothing intelligible. He picked out the army truck, smiled a very fleeting smile, dropped the truck on the floor. He lifted down the cardboard box containing the doll family. One by one he picked them up and dropped them down on the floor. Then he went to the box of blocks and repeated his activity, strewing the blocks aimlessly around the floor. During all this play, he grunted and muttered in a very subdued manner. His movements were nervous, quick, uncoordinated. Things fell out of his feeble grasp and he made no effort to pick them up again. Then he picked up the hammer and began to pound on the peg-board set, but he could not control the hammer. After a very short interval of hammering, he pushed it away and took the toy knives, forks, and spoons and strewed them across the floor. Finally, everything in the room that he could handle was on the floor. Jerry got the little wagon and pushed it across the floor.

During this play, whenever he laughed the therapist said, "Jerry likes to do that," or, "Jerry thinks that is funny." Occasionally he would hold up a toy truck or a doll and grunt at the therapist. She would name the object that he held up. Jerry seemed to get a great deal of satisfaction out of this. He began to center his actions around that type of activity. He would hold up the toy, look at the therapist, she would name it, he would smile, lay it down, and pick up something else.

After a while he began to select the truck every other time. The therapist continued to repeat the names of the toys, especially "truck," the toy which he intermittently held up. Finally, Jerry said "truck" himself as he held up the toy. He seemed to keep his eyes closed most of the time and to fumble among the toys rather than to attempt any real play with them.

Finally he went back to the wagon and pushed it. The therapist said, keeping up with his activity, "Jerry is pushing the wagon," "Jerry is shooting the gun," "Jerry is smashing the trucks together." Then Jerry began to yell. He banged the trucks together harder and harder and yelled something that sounded very much like "Truck smash!"

Then a fire engine went by the building. Jerry immediately dropped what he was doing, whimpered, ran over to the therapist, and took her hand. "Jerry is afraid of the noise," said the therapist. Jerry suddenly smiled.

Then Jerry took the therapist's hand and tried to convey some message to her. He said, "Do! Do!" very emphatically. "You want me to do something," said the therapist. Jerry pulled harder and repeated "Do!" He seemed to understand what the therapist said to him. Finally the therapist got up, Jerry led her over to the box of toys on the floor, and, by taking her hand, putting it down in the toy box and then putting a toy in her hand and guiding it over to his hand, finally conveyed the idea to the therapist that he wanted her to hand him the toys. The therapist did, one toy at a time, each of which he promptly dropped on the floor. He still tugged at the therapist's hand as though he wanted her to do something else. The therapist started to name the toys as she handed them to Jerry, and that was what he wanted. He began to smile. Finally he began to jabber and laugh and yell. Occasionally he would yell out "Truck!"

The mother reported a noticeable change in Jerry's behavior after the first contact. He had become more self-assertive in his non-verbal fashion. Previously he had been very docile, and stayed where he was put, doing nothing but crawling aimlessly around the baby pen that she kept him in. He now tried to climb out of the baby pen. The mother let him out. Then she noticed other improvements as time passed. He tried to talk. He said a few words that all could understand. He said "trucks," "streetcar," "ducks," and "cow."

54. ON EDUCATION

ALBERT EINSTEIN

Albert Einstein's was surely one of the greatest and liveliest minds of the ages. This statement of his views on education is filled with stimulating ideas. Particularly interesting are his remarks that intellectual work can be a source of pleasure.

A day of celebration generally is in the first place dedicated to retrospect, especially to the memory of personages who have gained special distinction for the development of the cultural life. This friendly service for our predecessors must indeed not be neglected, particularly as such a memory of the best of the past is proper to stimulate the well-disposed of today to a courageous effort. But this should be done by someone who, from his youth, has been connected with this State and is familiar with its past, not by one who like a gypsy has wandered about and gathered his experiences in all kinds of countries.

Translation by Lina Arronet of an address at the tercentenary celebration of higher education in America (Albany, New York, October 15, 1936), reprinted from *Out of My Later Years* (Philosophical Library, 1950), by permission of the Executor of the Estate of Albert Einstein.

Thus, there is nothing else left for me but to speak about such questions as, independently of space and time, always have been and will be connected with educational matters. In this attempt I cannot lay any claim to being an authority, especially as intelligent and well-meaning men of all times have dealt with educational problems and have certainly repeatedly expressed their views clearly about these matters. From what source shall I, as a partial layman in the realm of pedagogy, derive courage to expound opinions with no foundations except personal experience and personal conviction? If it were really a scientific matter, one would probably be tempted to silence by such considerations.

However, with the affairs of active human beings it is different. Here knowledge of truth alone does not suffice; on the contrary this knowledge must continually be renewed by ceaseless effort, if it is not to be lost. It resembles a statue of marble which stands in the desert and is continuously threatened with burial by the shifting sand. The hands of service must ever be at work, in order that the marble continue lastingly to shine in the sun. To these serving hands mine also shall belong.

The school has always been the most important means of transferring the wealth of tradition from one generation to the next. This applies today in an even higher degree than in former times, for through modern development of the economic life, the family as bearer of tradition and education has been weakened. The continuance and health of human society is therefore in a still higher degree dependent on the school than formerly.

Sometimes one sees in the school simply the instrument for transferring a certain maximum quantity of knowledge to the growing generation. But that is not right. Knowledge is dead; the school, however, serves the living. It should develop in the young individuals those qualities and capabilities which are of value for the welfare of the commonwealth. But that does not mean that individuality should be destroyed and the individual become a mere tool of the community, like a bee or an ant. For a community of standardized individuals without personal originality and personal aims would be a poor community without possibilities for development. On the contrary, the aim must be the training of independently acting and thinking individuals, who, however, see in the service of the community their highest life problem. So far as I can judge, the English school system comes nearest to the realization of this ideal.

But how shall one try to attain this ideal? Should one perhaps try to realize this aim by moralizing? Not at all. Words are and remain an empty sound, and the road to perdition has ever been accompanied by lip service to an ideal. But personalities are not formed by what is heard and said, but by labor and activity.

The most important method of education accordingly always has consisted of that in which the pupil was urged to actual performance.

This applies as well to the first attempts at writing of the primary boy as to the doctor's thesis on graduation from the university, or as to the mere memorizing of a poem, the writing of a composition, the interpretation and translation of a text, the solving of a mathematical problem or the practice of physical sport.

But behind every achievement exists the motivation which is at the foundation of it and which in turn is strengthened and nourished by the accomplishment of the undertaking. Here there are the greatest differences and they are of greatest importance to the educational value of the school. The same work may owe its origin to fear and compulsion, ambitious desire for authority and distinction, or loving interest in the object and a desire for truth and understanding, and thus to that divine curiosity which every healthy child possesses, but which so often is weakened early. The educational influence which is exercised upon the pupil by the accomplishment of one and the same work may be widely different, depending upon whether fear of hurt, egoistic passion, or desire for pleasure and satisfaction is at the bottom of this work. And nobody will maintain that the administration of the school and the attitude of the teachers do not have an influence upon the molding of the psychological foundation for pupils.

To me the worst thing seems to be for a school principally to work with methods of fear, force, and artificial authority. Such treatment destroys the sound sentiments, the sincerity, and the self-confidence of the pupil. It produces the submissive subject. It is no wonder that such schools are the rule in Germany and Russia. I know that the schools in this country are free from this worst evil; this also is so in Switzerland and probably in all democratically governed countries. It is comparatively simple to keep the school free from this worst of all evils. Give into the power of the teacher the fewest possible coercive measures, so that the only source of the pupil's respect for the teacher is the human and intellectual qualities of the latter.

The second-named motive, ambition or, in milder terms, the aiming at recognition and consideration, lies firmly fixed in human nature. With absence of mental stimulus of this kind, human cooperation would be entirely impossible; the desire for the approval of one's fellow-man certainly is one of the most important binding powers of society. In this complex of feelings, constructive and destructive forces lie closely together. Desire for approval and recognition is a healthy motive; but the desire to be acknowledged as better, stronger, or more intelligent than a fellow being or fellow scholar easily leads to an excessively egoistic psychological adjustment, which may become injurious for the individual and for the community. Therefore the school and the teacher must guard against employing the easy method of creating individual ambition, in order to induce the pupils to diligent work.

Darwin's theory of the struggle for existence and the selectivity connected with it has by many people been cited as authorization of the encouragement of the spirit of competition. Some people also in such a way have tried to prove pseudoscientifically the necessity of the destructive economic struggle of competition between individuals. But this is wrong, because man owes his strength in the struggle for existence to the fact that he is a socially living animal. As little as a battle between single ants of an ant hill is essential for survival, just so little is this the case with the individual members of a human community.

Therefore one should guard against preaching to the young man success in the customary sense as the aim of life. For a successful man is he who receives a great deal from his fellowmen, usually incomparably more than corresponds to his service to them. The value of a man, however, should be seen in what he gives and not in what he is able to receive.

The most important motive for work in the school and in life is the pleasure in work, pleasure in its result, and the knowledge of the value of the result to the community. In the awakening and strengthening of these psychological forces in the young man, I see the most important task given by the school. Such a psychological foundation alone leads to a joyous desire for the highest possessions of men, knowledge and artist-like workmanship.

The awakening of these productive psychological powers is certainly less easy than the practice of force or the awakening of individual ambition but is the more valuable for it. The point is to develop the childlike inclination for play and the childlike desire for recognition and to guide the child over to important fields for society; it is that education which in the main is founded upon the desire for successful activity and acknowledgment. If the school succeeds in working successfully from such points of view, it will be highly honored by the rising generation and the tasks given by the school will be submitted to as a sort of gift. I have known children who preferred school-time to vacation.

Such a school demands from the teacher that he be a kind of artist in his province. What can be done that this spirit be gained in the school? For this there is just as little a universal remedy as there is for an individual to remain well. But there are certain necessary conditions which can be met. First, teachers should grow up in such schools. Second, the teacher should be given extensive liberty in the selection of the material to be taught and the methods of teaching employed by him. For it is true also of him that pleasure in the shaping of his work is killed by force and exterior pressure.

If you have followed attentively my meditations up to this point, you will probably wonder about one thing. I have spoken fully about in what spirit, according to my opinion, youth should be instructed. But I have said nothing yet about the choice of subjects for instruction, nor about the method of teaching. Should language predominate or technical education in science?

To this I answer: in my opinion all this is of secondary importance. If a young man has trained his muscles and physical endurance by gymnastics and walking, he will later be fitted for every physical work. This is also analogous to the training of the mind and the exercising of the mental and manual skill. Thus the wit was not wrong who defined education in this way: "Education is that which remains, if one has forgotten everything he learned in school." For this reason I am not at all anxious to take sides in the struggle between the followers of the classical philologic-historical education and the education more devoted to natural science.

On the other hand, I want to oppose the idea that the school has to teach directly that special knowledge and those accomplishments which one has to use later directly in life. The demands of life are much too manifold to let such a specialized training in school appear possible. Apart from that, it seems to me, moreover, objectionable to treat the individual like a dead tool. The school should always have as its aim that the young man leave it as a harmonious personality, not as a specialist. This in my opinion is true in a certain sense even for technical schools, whose students will devote themselves to a quite definite profession. The development of general ability for independent thinking and judgment should always be placed foremost, not the acquisition of special knowledge. If a person masters the fundamentals of his subject and has learned to think and work independently, he will surely find his way and besides will better be able to adapt himself to progress and changes than the person whose training principally consists in the acquiring of detailed knowledge.

Finally, I wish to emphasize once more that what has been said here in a somewhat categorical form does not claim to mean more than the personal opinion of a man, which is founded upon *nothing but* his own personal experience, which he has gathered as a student and as a teacher.

55. MOBILE CHILDREN NEED HELP

WILLIAM W. WATTENBERG

Most of the data in this article were published twenty years ago, yet a study conducted in 1958 and 1959 by the editor and his students strongly confirmed them.

Two thousand pupils in a midwestern city were asked to fill

Selections reprinted from the article in *The Educational Forum* (March, 1948), 336–339, by permission of the author and Kappa Delta Pi.

out questionnaires telling how many schools they had attended and describing their problems in moving from school to school. The average sixth-grade child had attended about four schools; some had attended as many as fifteen, and very few, only one. The more frequently a child had moved, the lower were his reading and arithmetic achievement scores and the higher his age in a particular school grade; in some eighth-grade classes the average age was sixteen years and the average reading and arithmetic achievement only that of the third or fourth grade. These findings were more valid for working-class than for middle-class neighborhoods.

Among the problems in the actual moving, the children reported their difficulties in making new friends and understanding new teachers and stated that their parents tended to be disagreeable at moving time.

The sad reality is that, however clearly this article and the editor's study indicate that mobile children need help, they very probably will not get it in the near future.

In this article we shall deal with one, and it is only one, of the factors which may contribute directly or indirectly to maladjustments among children and, when those children reach adulthood, among adults. We shall try to indicate a few, and they are only a few, ways in which schools may help children to cope with that factor. The problem we have selected is mobility.

We know from extreme cases that when families move, when children are uprooted, the resultant events may lead to problems. These are most manifest in city areas where many families are transient. Such areas uniformly have high delinquency rates, and high insanity rates, symptoms of maladjustment.

Before going into greater detail on effects or possible counteracting measures, we first should appraise the scope of mobility affecting children. For a long time we have suspected that Americans' traditionally great mobility involved many children, but have had no accurate measures for the nation as a whole. How many children have to go through an adjustment, with their families, to a drastic change of setting, with all that means in terms of finding new friends and learning new neighborhood customs?

During the past year, the Census Bureau has released its statistics, gathered during the 1940 enumeration, of the number and ages of migrants. The census takers, in 1940, had to supply on their schedules, the answer to this question: "In what place did this person live on April 1, 1935?" If the 1940 address was in a different city or different county from the 1935 address, the individual was considered a migrant.

We are particularly interested in this 1935–40 period because it was a period of comparative normality, the pattern of which may be expected to be duplicated with comparatively minor variations in the immediate future. By 1935, the strong back-to-the-farm movement of the early 1930's had spent itself. The shifts to war plants and the post-war adjustment which uprooted 5,940,000 families, at least 3,600,000 of them containing children, between April, 1940, and February, 1946, had barely started.

During the period, 1935 to 1940, some 1,052,291 children of elementary school age (5 to 13) in 1940 were involved in migration and another 437,681 of high school age (14 to 17) had migrated. In percentage of the total population of their age groups, these young people represented eleven per cent of all children of elementary school age and nine per cent of all youth of high school age. That is, in a comparatively stable period, roughly one out of every ten young people of school age was involved in a migration and had to make an adjustment to strange surroundings, form new friendships and, if going to school, learn a more or less novel school routine. How many of these young people made more than one move we have no way of knowing.

The nature of the shift is indicated partially by the analysis, in Table I, of the type of community which the young people left and the type to which they went.

Table I.   Type of Migration, By Age Groups

Type of Migration	5 to 13 Year Group	14 to 17 Year Group
Urban to Urban	707,432	281,926
Urban to Non-Farm Rural	378,471	138,014
Urban to Farm Rural	152,477	69,438
Non-Farm Rural to Urban	198,783	87,636
Non-Farm Rural to Non-Farm Rural	214,532	78,338
Non-Farm Rural to Farm Rural	79,279	32,678
Farm Rural to Urban	104,804	49,521
Farm Rural to Non-Farm Rural	121,863	48,449
Farm Rural to Farm Rural	383,853	164,017

Two facts revealed by this table are striking: First, a very substantial number of these moves were between quite different types of community. This means that the young folks and their families had to undergo a marked change in patterns of living and recreation. Second, the number of urban children who had to adjust to rural settings was surprisingly great. In part, this represented a suburban trend. However, in some cases the moves to "non-farm rural" communities involved the growth of unorganized settlements, including trailer camps, on the fringe of metro-

politan areas. In other cases, the move to farm communities meant just
what it says: a child brought up in city streets had to learn the patterns
of farm life. In short, mobile children are not merely a problem of big
city schools; rural schools have an equal load in this respect.

Table II gives more complete statistics for the movement of young
people in and out of the ten largest cities of the United States.

Table II. Migration of Young People In and Out of Large Cities,
1935–40

City	5 to 13 Year Group	14 to 17 Year Group
New York City		
In-Migrants	19,029	9,346
Out-Migrants	49,778	18,260
Chicago		
In-Migrants	15,721	6,791
Out-Migrants	37,987	13,305
Philadelphia		
In-Migrants	7,841	3,089
Out-Migrants	15,607	6,359
Detroit		
In-Migrants	14,249	5,828
Out-Migrants	33,065	11,121
Los Angeles		
In-Migrants	30,385	13,827
Out-Migrants	30,259	11,822
Cleveland		
In-Migrants	4,620	1,994
Out-Migrants	15,933	6,266
Baltimore		
In-Migrants	5,206	2,088
Out-Migrants	7,352	3,127
St. Louis		
In-Migrants	6,275	2,754
Out-Migrants	15,144	5,749
Boston		
In-Migrants	4,346	1,678
Out-Migrants	10,718	3,269
Pittsburgh		
In-Migrants	3,427	1,486
Out-Migrants	9,693	3,968

It is clearly apparent that, although large city schools still had to
absorb considerable numbers of migrant children, the basic trend was
outward to smaller communities. To a child, the change from city life

to rural ways could involve as much confusion and as many problems as the adjustment to city patterns on the part of rural migrants.

In addition to change in patterns of living, many migrant children had to contend with sectional differences. As Table III shows, many of the moves were over long distances, and brought children in contact with somewhat different customs and patterns of climate.

Table III.   Distances of Migrations Affecting Young People, 1935–40

Distance of Migration	*5 to 13* Year Group	*14 to 17* Year Group
Within a state	1,553,608	639,520
Between contiguous states	494,683	195,951
Between noncontiguous states	434,665	175,647

Contrary to popular assumption, migration was not confined to poorly skilled laborers and dispossessed farmers. All economic levels were affected. In fact, the most mobile group during 1935–40 were professional people, some 25 per cent of whom had made at least one change of residence during the five-year period. Table IV gives the detailed figures on migration of the major occupational groups. We cite figures for men only, to give an indication of the economic status of families involved.

Table IV.   Occupational Level of Male Migrants, 1935–40

Occupational Group	Number	Number of Migrants	Per Cent
Professional and semiprofessional workers	1,875,387	476,162	25.4
Farmers and farm managers	4,991,715	410,793	8.2
Proprietors, managers and officials	3,325,767	511,235	15.4
Clerical, sales and kindred workers	4,360,648	690,950	15.8
Craftsmen, foremen and kindred workers	4,949,132	661,613	13.4
Operatives and kindred workers	6,205,898	784,476	12.6
Domestic service workers	142,231	24,798	17.4
Service workers, except domestic	2,196,695	393,239	17.9
Farm laborers and foremen	2,770,005	441,994	16.0
Laborers, except farm	3,210,427	383,825	12.0

Up to this point we have been dealing with migration between communities. To complete the picture, however, we must take into account the restlessness of city families which, until their movements were hampered temporarily by the housing shortage, frequently moved from house to house, and from neighborhood to neighborhood. No over-all figures on such intracity mobility are available.

However, a study of Rochester, New York gives a clue to the extensiveness of such movements. The city was divided into fourteen large areas and an analysis made of changes of residence between 1930 and 1940. In the median area, approximately one out of every five families had moved from one area to another, and an additional one out of seven families had changed addresses within the area. In the most stable area of the city, 77.0 per cent of the families had lived at the same address for ten years; in the most unstable area, only 48.5 per cent had stayed put for that long.

56. SUCCESS AND FAILURE IN THE CLASSROOM

ROGER G. BARKER

A number of studies have suggested that one way a child—or an adult—may respond to repeated failure is by dreaming he is successful. The mental hospitals are filled with victims of the more extreme forms of this dream.

Barker summarizes current research on the problems of failure and suggests some constructive ways of coping with them.

Of the numerous rôles which the classroom teacher plays, that of dispenser of success and failure is undoubtedly the most impressive and worrisome to the pupils, and one of the most crucial for their present and future adjustment. It is also the rôle in which many teachers meet their severest conflicts; to fail John or not to fail him, whichever is done, frequently leaves feelings of guilt and anxiety. Clearly an understanding of the conditions and effects of success and failure would be of greatest value to teachers.

When does a child experience success? When does he experience failure? In what ways do these experiences affect behavior? Do the schools make it possible for children to achieve a sufficient number of important success experiences? If not, what can be done about it? A small but very important body of verified knowledge is now available bearing upon these crucial questions. In this article only a very small segment of these data can be presented.

Professor Kurt Lewin, then at the University of Berlin, and his stu-

Reprinted from *Progressive Education*, 19 (1942), 221–224, by permission of the author and publisher.

dent Ferdinand Hoppe initiated an experimental approach to these questions in the late 1920's.[1] Hoppe first considered the fundamental problem of when a person experiences success and when failure. He presented his adult subjects with simple motor and intellectual tasks such as hanging 16 rings upon as many hooks as they passed upon a rapidly moving belt, and solving puzzles. During each trial with the tasks, Hoppe observed the subjects secretly and after the completion of each trial he interviewed them thoroughly in an effort to find out the circumstances under which they experienced success and failure. One result was clearly apparent: The experiences of success and failure were unrelated to the actual achievements of the individual. One subject might experience success when he placed 4 rings on the hooks; another experienced failure when he placed 15 correctly. In addition, for a particular person, the achievement experienced as success (or failure) continually changed; at one time a single ring correctly placed might give rise to an experience of success, while on a later occasion the placing of 6 rings would result in an experience of failure. These findings led Hoppe to a conclusion which seems very obvious once it is stated, but one that is so fundamental that it has very wide implications: The occurrence of success and failure experiences is independent of actual achievement; it is determined, rather, by the goals, expectations, and aspirations of the person at the time of the action. These expected achievements Hoppe called the level of aspiration.

It is obvious that the level of aspiration is important, for on it depends the occurrence of success and failure. Hoppe therefore directed his study to the effects of success and failure experiences on the level of aspiration. He found that after success the level of aspiration is usually raised (that is, a new and higher goal is set after a lower one is achieved), and that after failure of the level of aspiration is usually lowered (that is, a new and lower goal is set after a high one has not been achieved). He found, in other words, that the level of aspiration shifts in such a way that, whatever the actual achievement of the person, the frequency of his success and failure experiences remains fairly constant. This means that the level of aspiration operates as a mental hygiene factor of great significance. It constitutes a sort of governor; it protects the person against continual failure on the one hand, and against easy achievements which do not give the feeling of success, on the other hand. This fact is behind the frequent observation that feelings of success accompany the process of achieving but disappear after attainment.

Sometimes, however, this mechanism is thrown out of balance and it fails to perform this protective function. In some cases, aspirations are maintained consistently above achievement. The individual is then subjected to continual failure with its disastrous consequences for adjust-

---

[1] Hoppe, F., "Erfolg und Misserfolg," *Psychol. Forsch.*, 1930, *14*, 1–62.

ment and happiness. In other cases, aspirations are placed consistently below achievement with resulting lack of ambition, exaggerated caution, broken morale, cynicism, and so forth. In both instances very serious personal and social difficulties may develop. It is of the greatest importance, therefore, to determine why the level of aspiration does not function protectively for these persons.

Hoppe suggested that the level of aspiration is set as a compromise between two conflicting tendencies: (a) the desire to avoid the hurt accompanying failure, operating to force aspirations safely below the level of achievement; and (b) the desire to succeed at the highest possible level; operating to push goals above achievement levels. Subsequent investigations suggested that the latter tendency derives from social pressures to do what is most highly approved by society, irrespective of a realistic assessment of one's own capabilities. This conflict between fear of failure and desire to maintain goals that are socially approved results, usually, in a level of aspiration at or near the upper limit of one's ability range.

If this interpretation is correct, it would be expected that an increase in social pressure should alter the level of aspiration. This is, in fact, the case. Subsequent investigations have shown that pupils at the low end of the class achievement distribution aspire, on the average, above the level of their achievement possibilities (and therefore experience failure), while those at the upper end of the achievement distribution set their aspirations below their level of achievement (and therefore experience success).

Although the differences between aspiration and achievement are not great in a quantitative sense, they are psychologically very important. So far as success and failure are concerned, "a miss is as good as a mile." This difference in relation of aspiration to achievement appears to mean that the social pressures of the school situation may operate to throw off balance the protective mechanism of the level of aspiration, thus subjecting children to exaggerated failure and success experiences.

It is not difficult to understand why these pressures arise in many schools. Social acceptability in an intimate group such as a school class requires a high degree of conformity to group standards in all sorts of public behavior. The first step in achieving such acceptability is to set goals in accordance with the group standards. In schools where evaluation is largely on the basis of academic achievements this means that poor students are forced, by the social pressure of the classroom, to admit that they are mavericks; both are undesirable alternatives from a mental hygiene viewpoint. There is pressure upon bright students, also, to set their goals in conformity with the achievements of their roommates, rather than with their own.

Adults on the other hand are infrequently subjected to such pressures for long periods of time, for adults are able with considerable success to hide from others certain crucial symbols of their divergence from what is considered good or desirable (such as age, income, family background), and they are able to withdraw when the pressures become too great. Furthermore, achievement in most adult activities is not estimated with the precision that is attempted in many schools. Doctors, lawyers, plumbers, and bakers can vary within a considerable range of effectiveness and no one is wiser; they are still adequate. This gives a fundamental security which is denied to pupils who are frequently and publicly evaluated, that is, acclaimed or humiliated by an authority from whose decisions there is no recourse and in a group from which there is no escape.

Middle-class pupils are unusually sensitive to these pressures. They are, in effect, subjected to the demands of a single dominating institution, for the family supports the demands of the school. This means that the pressures, the demands, the rewards, the punishments, the successes, and the failures of the school are frequently of overwhelming importance to these children. No one with influence will question the righteousness of the school's verdicts or the correctness of its values. If the school is one in which the rewards are all centered about a very limited variety of achievements, for example, academic achievements, the child who is relatively dull or uninterested in academic activities must experience continual failure. He will fail even though he is kind, or good looking, or has a sense of humor, or has physical prowess, even though he is full of energy, graceful, courageous, friendly, or with mechanical abilities. He will fail in school even though these behavior characteristics are very highly valued by many other institutions, until in adolescence he becomes sufficiently independent to establish affiliations with other groups which do reward nonacademic achievement.

Compared with life outside school, many schools distribute success and failure in an extremely unrealistic way. Adults, for example, are inevitably influenced by various pressures, and rewarded according to conflicting values of a variety of institutions and social groups (family, vocation, clique, church, lodge, union, and so on), and these influences are likely to be of somewhat equal potency in their lives. This means that the adult can to some extent balance the failures in one region of his life by successes in other regions. The effects of vocational failures may be mitigated by successes in family and recreational relationships where quite different achievements are valued. In schools that emphasize academic achievement, this kind of balancing is impossible for middle-class children.

What is the consequence of the chronic failure and success that many schools enforce upon great numbers of pupils? We do not know a great amount from scientific experiment but what we do know is very suggestive.

Sears [2] studied the level of aspiration of a group of fifth grade children who had long histories of chronic school failure in reading and arithmetic, and another group with equally consistent histories of school success in reading and arithmetic. She found that the children who had experienced continual success set their aspirations at a realistic level, that is, at a level where success was frequently achieved. The children with a history of chronic failure, on the other hand, set their aspirations with little regard for their achievements. Of those in this latter group, some children apparently lived almost exclusively in terms of their aspirations, ignoring completely the fact that their achievements were entirely out of line with their expectations. In these cases the desire for respectability may have forced the children to an imaginary world where the mere gesture of achieving by setting high goals was accepted in lieu of real achievement. The seriousness of this behavior is sufficiently obvious to need no special emphasis. The institutionalized person for whom a gesture is sufficient to convince him he is Napoleon has traveled further along the same path.

The cases where the children failed to set goals even at the level of their poor achievement may involve withdrawal from the activity in any except a very peripheral sense; they may be cases of extreme caution or they may represent attempts to depreciate the importance of the activity by refusing to take it seriously. None of these outcomes of educational effort are desirable.

What can schools do to avoid throwing out of gear the protective mechanism of the level of aspiration with the resulting unfortunate consequences for the success and failure experiences of pupils? The answers are implied in the discussion, but they may be summarized as follows: (a) broaden the basis for evaluating pupils; (b) reduce to a minimum the prominence of the relative standing of the pupils; (c) allow maximum freedom to pupils to set their own goals and to alter them as their success and failure experiences require; that is, make success possible at all levels of achievement; (d) reduce the dominance of the teacher.

These conditions can be achieved in different ways. It is interesting to note, however, that they can hardly be avoided if democratic teaching procedures are used, if the interests of the child are followed, and if group undertakings are an important part of school activities.

[2] Sears, P. S., "Levels of Aspiration in Academically Successful and Unsuccessful Children," *Journal of Abnormal and Social Psychology*, 1940, 35, 498–536.

57. EXPERIMENTAL STUDIES OF FRUSTRATION IN YOUNG CHILDREN

ROGER G. BARKER, TAMARA DEMBO, KURT LEWIN, AND M. ERIK WRIGHT

What happens when young children are unable to get what they want or need? Anyone who has ever tried to maneuver a child who is tired or hungry, or who is angry because something he wants has just been taken away, knows how unreasonable the child can be, how unwilling he can be to adapt himself.

The experiments described here reveal that such frustrations result in impaired intellectual functioning, restlessness, destructiveness, increased intra-group unity (clannishness), and aggression against the out-group.

Frustration occurs when an episode of behavior is interrupted before its completion, i.e., before the goal appropriate to the motivating state of the individual is reached. It is well established that frustration has widely ramifying effects upon behavior; the behaving person is not like a rolling billiard ball that remains motionless when its movement is stopped. However, what these effects are and how they are produced have not yet been determined. To frustration has been attributed most of what is valued and deplored in individual and group behavior: delinquency, neurosis, war, art, character, religion. This, however, is speculation. It is of greatest importance that these questions be removed from the realm of speculation, that the conditions of frustration be conceptualized, that its degree and effects be measured and that systematic experimental studies be made. It is with these problems that the studies here reported are concerned. They constitute an effort to measure the degree of frustration and its effects upon intellectual and emotional behavior and social interaction.

This has been done by comparing the behavior of children in a non-frustrating play situation with their behavior in a frustrating play situation. Children were observed on two occasions: first, in a standardized playroom under conditions of unrestricted free play; second, in the same room with the same toys, but with a number of more attractive, but inaccessible, toys present. The latter were provided by replacing a wall of the original room with a wire-net partition through which the subjects could easily see the fine toys but through which they could not move. The subjects were children who attended the preschool laboratories of the Iowa Child Welfare Research Station. They ranged in age from 2 to 6 years.

Two series of experiments were performed. In the first series, by Barker, Dembo, and Lewin, 30 children were studied individually with the objective of determining some of the effects of frustration on intellectual and emotional behavior. In the second series, by Wright, 78 entirely different children were taken in pairs with the main emphasis upon the effects of frustration on social behavior. The second series of experiments served, also, as a check upon the first so far as effects on intelligence and emotion were concerned.

The Nonfrustrating Situation. On the floor of the experimental room in the nonfrustrating play situation there were three squares of paper, each 24 by 24 inches. A set of standardized play materials was placed on each square. After entering the experimental room with the child or pair of children, the experimenter demonstrated the toys and gave complete freedom to play. The child (or children) was left to play for a 30-minute period. During this time the experimenter, as if occupied with his own work, sat at his table in the corner and made records of the behavior occurring.

The Frustrating Situation. Three parts of the frustration experiment can be distinguished in the temporal order of their occurrence: the prefrustation period, the frustration period and the postfrustration period.

In the prefrustration period the dividing partition was lifted so that the room was twice the size it had been in the nonfrustrating situation. The squares were in their places, but all toys except the crayons and paper had been incorporated into an elaborate and attractive set of toys in the part of the room that had been behind the partition. In all cases the children showed great interest in the new toys and at once started to investigate them. Each child was left entirely free to explore and play as he wished. If, after several minutes, the child had played with only a limited number of toys, the experimenter demonstrated the others. The experimenter returned to his place and waited until the child had become thoroughly involved in play; this took from 5 to 15 minutes. The prefrustration period was designed to develop highly desirable goals for the child which he could later be prevented from reaching. This was a prerequisite to creating frustration.

The transition from prefrustration to frustration was made in the following way. The experimenter collected in a basket all the play materials which had been used in the nonfrustrating free-play session and distributed them, as before, on the squares of paper. He then approached the child and said, "Now let's play at the other end," pointing to the "old" part of the room. The child went or was led and the experimenter lowered the wire partition and fastened it by means of a large padlock. The part of the room containing the new toys was now physically inaccessible, but it was visible through the wire-net partition. With the lowering of the partition, the frustration period began. This part of the experiment was conducted exactly as was the nonfrustrating session. The experimenter wrote at his table, leaving the child completely free to play or not as he desired. The child's questions were answered, but the experimenter remained aloof from the situation in as natural a manner as possible.

Thirty minutes after the lowering of the partition, the experimenter suggested that it was time to leave. After the experimenter had made sure that the child was willing to leave, the partition was lifted. Usually the child was pleasantly surprised and, forgetting his desire to leave, joyfully hurried over to the fine toys. If the child did not return spontaneously, the experimenter suggested his doing so. The lifting of the partition at the end of the frustration period was designed to satisfy the desire of the child to play with the toys and to obviate any undesirable after-effects. The child was allowed to play until he was ready to leave.

Both the nonfrustrating and frustrating situations produced two general kinds of behavior: occupation with accessible goals, and activities in the direction of inaccessible goals. We shall call the first *free activities* and the second *barrier and escape behavior.* Playing with the available toys, turning on the light, and talking with each other or with the experimenter are examples of free activities. Trying to leave the experimental situation and attempting to reach the inaccessible toys behind the barrier or talking about them are examples of barrier and escape behavior.

A subject could be involved in more than one activity simultaneously, e.g., he might ask to have the barrier raised while swinging the fish line. In these cases we speak of *overlapping situations.* A type of overlapping situation of special importance occurred when play and nonplay activities took place simultaneously. We have called this *secondary play. Primary play*, on the other hand, occurred when the subject seemed to give play his complete attention.

Sample Record. A part of a record is given below to acquaint the reader with the sequence and content of the course of events. This is the type of material with which we had to work.

Subject #22 is a girl fifty-three months old. Her I.Q. is 122. Each unit of action is numbered consecutively. At the end of each unit the length in seconds and the constructiveness rating are given. Constructiveness rating is discussed in the section immediately following.

Nonfrustrating Situation

1. Subject: "Here," to the experimenter, "you make me something from this clay." She takes the clay to Square 1 and asks, "Where are the other

things?" (Referring to toys present in another experiment.) "I want you to play with me." The experimenter continues recording. (45; 2)

2. Subject throws clay onto Square 2. "This is an elephant." Then, finding a small peg on the floor, "Look what I found. I'll put it at his eyes." Looks at it. Makes elephant sit up. (70; 6)

3. Subject starts to draw. "I'm going to draw a picture. Do you know what I'm going to draw? That will be a house. That is where you go in." (45; 7)

4. Someone moves in another room. Subject: "Who is that?" (10)

5. Subject goes to Square 1, shakes phone, and examines it. Manipulates phone, pretends conversation but does not use words. "How do . . ." are the only words that experimenter can distinguish. (30; 5)

6. Subject sits on chair and looks around. "I guess I'll sit here and iron." Repeats, then says gaily, "See me iron." (45, 5)

Frustrating Situation

1. Subject watches experimenter lower the partition. She asks, "I will not play on the other side again?" Experimenter answers, "You can play here now." Subject faces the experimenter for about 15 seconds with hands behind her neck. (25)

2. Subject looks around. (5)

3. Subject goes to Square 3 and examines sailboat and fish pole. (15; 2)

4. Subject stands at Square 3 and looks at barrier. (5)

5. Turning to the play material on Square 3, Subject takes the fish line and dangles it about sailboat. (20; 2)

6. Subject goes to the barrier and reaches through the meshes of the screen. (5)

7. Subject turns around, looks at the experimenter, laughs as she does so. (15)

8. Subject goes to Square 3, takes the fish pole, and returns to the barrier. She asks, "When are we going to play on that side?" Experimenter does not answer. Then, in putting the fish pole through the barrier, Subject says, "I guess I'll just put this clear back." She laughs and says, "Out it comes!" Takes pole out again. (35; 2)

9. Subject walks to experimenter's table. (10)

10. Subject goes to Square 2 and manipulates clay. (10; 2)

11. From Square 2 she looks at the objects behind the barrier and says, "I do like the balloon." Then she asks, "Who put that house there?" Experimenter answers, "Some of my friends." (35)

Constructiveness of Play.   From this example, the reader will gain an impression of the richness of the play which occurred. It is possible to use such manifold material for many purposes. In the first experiments we were most interested in phases of the play related to the intellectual aspects of the child's behavior. For this purpose we made an analysis of the play activities on the basis of their constructiveness. One can distinguish variations in the type of play on a continuum ranging from rather primitive, simple, little-structured activities to elaborate, imaginative, highly developed play. We speak in the former case of low constructive-

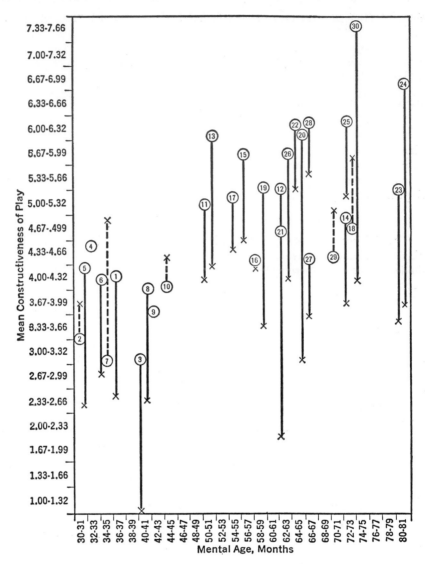

FIGURE 1. THE RELATION BETWEEN MEAN CONSTRUCTIVENESS OF PLAY AND MENTAL AGE IN THE NONFRUSTRATING AND THE FRUSTRATING PLAY SITUATIONS.

(1) The mean constructiveness of primary and secondary play in the nonfrustrating situation is indicated by circles. (2) The mean constructiveness of play in the frustrating situation is indicated by crosses. (c) Change in the constructiveness of play from the nonfrustrating to the frustrating situation is designated by solid lines when constructiveness decreases in frustration, and by broken lines when it increases. The absence of a cross indicates no change in constructiveness.

552

ness; in the latter, of high constructiveness. In our first experiment, constructiveness was rated on a 7-point scale (2 to 8) devised to be applicable to play with all the toys. Examples of its use are given in the preceding sample record. The mean constructiveness of play for an experimental session was determined by assigning the proper scale value to each play unit, multiplying by the duration of the unit, summing these values for the whole record, and dividing by the total time of play during the session. The mean constructiveness ratings had an estimated reliability cofficient of .88. Their validity as an indicator of intellectual level is indicated by a correlation with mental age of .73.

RESULTS

Average Constructiveness of Play in the Nonfrustrating and Frustrating Situations. The mean constructiveness of the play of each child in the nonfrustrating and frustrating situations is shown in the correlation chart. These data include all play, both primary and secondary. The mean constructiveness of play in the nonfrustrating situation is 4.99 and in the frustrating situation 3.94. The mean regression in constructiveness of play is 4.39 times its standard error. Stated in terms of mental-age equivalents, i.e., in terms of the regression of constructiveness upon mental age, the mean regression amounts to 17.3 months of mental age. Twenty-two of the subjects regressed in the constructiveness of their play, three did not change, and with five subjects the constructiveness of play increased in frustration.

These data establish rather definitely the fact that a frustrating situation of the kind considered here reduces, on the average, the constructiveness of play below the level upon which it normally occurs in a nonfrustrating, free-play situation. Further analysis showed that regression in the constructiveness of play occurred when only primary play and only play units of the same length in the nonfrustrating and frustrating situations were compared.

These results indicate that frustration not only affects actions involved in achieving inaccessible goals, such as attempts to find roundabout routes or aggression against physical or social barriers, but that it may also affect behavior not directly frustrated or involved in overcoming the frustration. The findings show the importance of the total situation for promoting or hindering a child's creative achievement, and they suggest that the level of intellectual functioning is dependent upon the immediately existing situation.

Measurement of Strength of Frustration. The technical arrangements of the experiment were planned to create frustration and nonfrustration. Inevitably, these results were not secured in all cases, inasmuch as we had control over only the immediate, experimental situation and not over the expectations and attitudes which the children brought to the experiment. In some instances frustration occurred in the nonfrustration situation and in others there was no frustration in the frustration situation. In addition, all degrees of strength of frustration occurred. Thus far in the analysis we have proceeded as if the technical arrangements had functioned with all subjects as was intended. The data have been classified according to the intention of the experimenters rather than according to the psychological realities of the situations for the subjects. We turn now to an analysis of some quantitative differences in the dynamic properties of the existing psychological situations.

We have taken as a measure of strength of frustration the proportion of the total experimental period occupied by barrier and escape behavior. Inasmuch as we are here concerned with the *changes* in strength of frustration from the nonfrustration to the frustration situations, we have limited ourselves to a consideration of the *difference* in the amount of time occupied with barrier and escape actions in the two settings. Using this difference as a measure of increase in frustration, it turned out that 20 subjects were relatively strongly frustrated and 10 subjects relatively weakly frustrated.

Considering these two groups of subjects, we find that there is a highly significant reduction in the constructiveness of play in the case of the strongly frustrated subjects amounting to 1.46 ± .15 constructiveness points when both primary and secondary play are considered, and 1.11 ± .15 constructiveness points when primary play alone is included. The first is equivalent to a regression of twenty-four months' mental age, the latter to a regression of nineteen months' mental age. With the weakly frustrated subjects, on the other hand, there is a small and not statistically significant reduction in constructiveness, amounting to 0.23 constructiveness points for primary and secondary play and 0.12 points for primary play. All subjects showing an increase in constructiveness of play in frustration fall in the weakly frustrated group.

From these results it is clear that regression in level of intellectual functioning is determined by dynamic situational factors that are subject to measurement.

EMOTION. *Pari passu* with the shift in constructiveness of play there occurred a change in emotional expression. In frustration there was a marked decrease in the happiness of the mood (e.g., less laughing, smiling and gleeful singing), there was an increase in motor restlessness and hypertension (e.g., more loud singing and talking, restless actions, stuttering, and thumb sucking); and there was an increase in aggressiveness (e.g., more hitting, kicking, breaking, and destroying). The changes were greater with the strongly frustrated than with the weakly frustrated subjects.

Social Interaction in the Nonfrustrating and Frustrating Situation. In order to describe the changes in social interaction from nonfrustration to frustration, it was first necessary to distinguish various types of social behavior. Five main categories of social interaction were differentiated: *Cooperative actions* included those in which both children strove towards a common goal and helped each other to achieve that goal. *Social parallel* behavior covered activities in which both children, separately, pursued almost the same goals but watched each other closely. *Sociable* actions were those in which the goal seemed to be maintenance of the social contact itself. *Social matter-of-fact* interactions were impersonal contacts made primarily for information about ownership or other property rights. *Conflict* actions occurred when children were aggressive toward each other; acts of aggression ranged in intensity from verbal teasing to physical violence.

The most typical form of social interaction in the nonfrustration situation was friendly in character; 67.2 percent of all social interaction was spent either in cooperative or sociable behavior. However, 14.9 percent of the time was spent in inter-child conflict.

There were two important shifts in social behavior from nonfrustration to frustration: Cooperative behavior increased from 38.2 percent to 50.4 percent of total interaction, and social conflict decreased from 14.9 percent to 6.9 percent. These changes are significant at the 2 percent and 1 percent levels, respectively. There were no statistically significant changes in the amount of time spent in sociable, social parallel, or matter-of-fact social interactions. The two shifts which occurred point toward increased interdependence and unity under the influence of frustration.

Table 1. **Percent of Hostile and Friendly Behavior toward the Experimenter Which Occurred as Social and Solitary Action**

SITUATION	HOSTILE		FRIENDLY	
	Social	Solitary	Social	Solitary
Nonfrustration	99	1	26	74
Frustration	82	18	51	49

Strength of Friendship and Social Interaction. On the basis of their behavior in the nursery school, 18 of the pairs of subjects were judged to be strong friends and 21 weak friends. The strong and weak friends resembled each other very closely in their social interaction in the nonfrustrating situation. However, the changes in social behavior in frustration were more marked for the strong friends than for the weak friends.

Cooperativeness increased and conflict decreased significantly for these subjects while they did not change significantly for the weak friends. When the weak and strong friends were compared with each other in the frustrating situation the strong friends were found to exhibit significantly more cooperative behavior and significantly less conflict behavior than the weak friends.

Under the relatively calm, stable conditions with low level of emotional tension that existed in the nonfrustrating situation, the social behavior of strong and weak friends was not observably different. When the environmental surroundings became precarious, however, when frustration occurred, and when there was a heightening of emotional tension, the influence of the pre-existing friendship relation became apparent. A greater cohesiveness and unity tended to occur under stress with the strong friends than with the weak friends.

In nonfrustration, the contacts with the experimenter were predominantly friendly: 80 percent of all experimenter-directed behavior was of this nature. A marked change took place in frustration. There was a 30 percent rise in the amount of hostile action toward the experimenter and a 34 percent decrease in friendly approaches. Although friendly contacts were still more frequent than hostile ones, the situation in frustration could no longer be characterized as predominantly friendly. It will be noted from the tabulation above that hostile actions against the experimenter were predominantly social in character in both nonfrustration and frustration, while friendly actions were not predominantly social. This suggests that the children may have felt more powerful and able to cope with hostile forces when in social contact than when alone. This interpretation is supported by the fact that in nonfrustration there was a great amount of solitary, friendly contact with the experimenter, while in the frustrating situation, where the power of the experimenter had become much stronger, the proportion of friendly, solitary actions toward the experimenter decreased, and the proportion of friendly social action increased. It appears that under frustration the children needed social support to make even a friendly approach to the powerful, implicitly hostile adult.

In general, only when the individuals combined did they feel strong enough to attack the superior adult power. We should expect that the stronger and more cohesive the group, the more capable they would feel of challenging the power of the experimenter. This interpretation is substantiated by the data on hostile actions toward the experimenter in the frustrating situation. The strong friends showed more hostile action against the experimenter than did the weak friends (47 percent and 31 percent respectively) and the difference was even more marked when direct physical attack on the experimenter was considered: 26 percent for the strong friends and 4 percent for the weak friends. Furthermore, only the strong friends went so far as to hit the experimenter with blocks, tear his records, throw him off his chair, scratch at him, etc. The weak friends stopped at touching the experimenter while calling him names.

DISCUSSION

The main findings of the studies reported may be summarized as follows: Frustration, as it operated in these experiments, resulted in an average regression in the level of intellectual functioning, in increased unhappiness, restlessness, and destructiveness, in increased intra-group unity, and in increased out-group aggression. The amount of intellectual regression and the amount of increase in negative emotionality were positively related to strength of frustration. The degree of intra-group unity and of out-group aggression were positively related to strength of friendship. These findings present important and difficult problems for social-psychological theories.

Theory in science has two main functions: to account for that which is known, and to point the way to new knowledge. It does this by formulating hypotheses as to the essential nature of the phenomenon under consideration. The fruitfulness of a theory lies in the unknown facts and relations it envisions which can then be tested, usually by experiments. A fruitful theory gives birth, as it were, to new knowledge which is then independent of its theoretical ancestry.

The main results of the present experiments were predicted on the basis of a theory. Originally the experiments were designed to test the hypothesis that strong frustration causes tension which leads to emotionality and restlessness, to de-differentiation of the person, and hence to behavioral regression. These results were obtained. It is probable that not only the changes in the constructiveness of play, but also the greater cohesiveness of the strong friends under frustration can be interpreted as regression. In the nonfrustrating situation the social interactions of the strong and the weak friends did not differ, but under the tensions created by frustration the previously existing, fundamental structure of interpersonal relations was revealed. De-differentiation of the person from diffusing tension would be expected to reduce the variety and complexity of both intellectual and social behavior and leave the strongest structures intact. In the case of the strong friends, this basic structure was one that led to a friendly, cooperative interrelation.

However, the experiments suggest that other factors probably enter also. In the frustrating situation, the subject's future time perspective and security were shattered by the superior power of the experimenter. This could easily have two results: first, to interfere with long-range planning, and this would certainly result in lowered constructiveness of play; second, to lead to a mobilization of power by the subject directed at increasing his security. Counter-aggression on the part of the subjects was clear in the shift toward hostility in their relations with the experimenter. It seems likely that the greater cohesiveness occurring in the frustrating situation is one aspect of the efforts of the subjects to increase their power *vis-à-vis* the experimenter. This is particularly likely in view of the predominantly social character of all hostile actions against the experimenter, and the greater hostility of the strong friends.

58. A STUDY OF CHILDREN'S REACTIONS TO FAILURE AND AN EXPERIMENTAL ATTEMPT TO MODIFY THEM

MARY E. KEISTER AND RUTH UPDEGRAFF

Although no human being is impervious to frustration, it undoubtedly has more destructive effects on some individuals than on others. How can those whose reactions to frustration are extreme be helped to respond more constructively?

This article describes the way in which two psychologists identified children whose responses to frustration were ineffective and then helped them to handle difficult problems in a more self-reliant manner.

Psychologists and educators believe that it is important for an individual to respond adequately in situations involving failure or great difficulty. After his first attempt meets failure, the individual's subsequent, possibly characteristic, reaction is related not only to his emotional adjustment but also to his ability to learn and to profit by experience.

It is natural for a young child to be confronted with many situations which are not readily resolved. Moreover, in his attempts to meet and overcome difficulties as they arise lie the child's opportunities to learn. In general, mental hygienists and educators have considered it desirable for a child to attack a difficult problem with composure, to try out one possibility after another in an attempt to reach a solution. It is usually

Reprinted from *Child Development,* 8 (1937), 241–248, by permission of the authors and the Society for Research in Child Development.

considered that he is not meeting the situation desirably if he retreats from the problem, if he rationalizes, if he leans heavily on an adult for assistance, if he attacks the problem with such emotional accompaniments as crying, sulking, and tantrums.

Even the most casual observation of young children reveals wide differences in such responses. In the face of a difficult situation, some children make attempts at their own solution, intently and without emotion. There are others, however, who under many circumstances, immediately ask for the help of an adult or another child; some retreat from the scene of action when they discover difficulty; some cry or become angry; some rationalize.

Given, then, a variability from child to child (and in some cases the occurrence of modes of behavior which are undesirable from the standpoint of the future as well as of the present), the problem becomes one of discovering the existence of an undesirable pattern and of modifying that pattern if possible. Such was the problem of this study, the purpose of which may be summarized as follows:

1. To devise tests by means of which one may discover what responses a child of preschool age gives when faced with failure.
2. To select a group of children evidencing undesirable models of response.
3. To attempt to modify, by special help or individual training, the responses of the children in this group.

Mental hygienists have employed the concept of failure in two ways. They have used it in connection with a situation which is ultimately impossible for the individual to overcome because of his own incapacity; under such circumstances it is important for him to realize this fact and adjust himself to the idea of the impossibility. In the second sense, failure has been thought of as a step in the process of solving a problem, as involved in the individual's working his way out of a difficulty. It is with behavior of the latter type that this study is concerned. Failure, as defined here, is the child's lack of immediate success following an attempt to contend with a situation, the situation being one in which he sees some relation to himself as an instrument of his own success or failure.

A preliminary survey of suitable approaches indicated the innapplicability of the observational method, at least in the beginning stages of the study. Not only did it become apparent that failure situations occurred in the nursery school with such infrequency that the time-sampling method was too extensive, but also controls of motivation and of the difficulty of the tasks were lacking. Accordingly, plans were made for presenting failure in experimental situations. The decision was made to confront the child with one situation somewhat in the form of a puzzle, with another which challenged his physical strength, and with a third which offered social obstacles. Among the criteria for setting up the experiments were the following:

1. They must be possible of accomplishment and yet of such difficulty that the child does not succeed immediately.
2. They must provide situations which are natural, in the sense that the difficulties are not obviously or forcibly imposed.
3. The average child should be able to see for himself that he has failed and to see in the situation some relation to himself as an instrument of his success or failure.

As a result of preliminary study, two test situations were believed adequate for use. The first, the puzzle box test, confronted the subject with a small, lidded, colored box, 9 by 7 by 1½ inches. The box being opened, it was found to have a false bottom within ¼ inch from the top.

Table 1.   Mean Number of Minutes During Which Responses Occurred During Puzzle Box Test (N = 81) [a]

Behavior	Mean	Standard Deviation
No overt attempt	2.2	3.2
Attempts to solve alone	11.1	4.2
Asks another to solve	1.2	2.3
Asks help	1.5	2.1
Destructive behavior	.1	.5
Rationalizes	1.2	1.8
Interest	10.2	4.7
No emotional manifestations	1.6	2.9
Indifference	.2	1.4
Smiles	.2	.9
Laughs	.1	.2
Sulks	.2	.6
Cries	.3	1.2
Whines	.8	2.0
Yells	.1	.4
Motor manifestations of anger	.04	.3

[a] Mean length of experimental period: 13.3 minutes.

On this lay ten small, colored figures, of irregular shape, ½ inch thick, representing various objects of interest to children, such as a sailboat and an engine. Because of their form they fitted rather closely into the available space. The experimenter then removed the figures and gave the test instructions which invited the child to put the blocks into the box so that the lid could go down again. In spite of the fact that there were several ways in which the blocks could be fitted into the space, the task was quite a difficult one to complete in the fifteen minutes allowed. There was no question of its being an interesting one to children.

The weighted box test consisted of a five-sided box, weighted at the ends and through the middle with from 60 to 90 pounds of iron weights. These weights were adjustable. The box was placed in the middle of a room upside down over a group of attractive toys. When the subject entered, the box was raised slightly, then lowered. Instructions indicated that the toys could be played with if the box could be lifted in order to obtain them. Ten minutes was the time allowed.

The same scheme for recording behavior, a system of controlled observation with time divisions of minutes, was used for both tests. The type of behavior observed is indicated in the tables.

Table 2.   Mean Number of Minutes During Which Responses Occurred During Weighted Box Test (N = 74) [a]

Behavior	Mean	Standard Deviation
No overt attempt	3.4	2.8
Attempts to solve alone	5.7	2.7
Asks another to solve	.4	3.6
Asks help	1.1	1.9
Rationalizes	1.0	1.5
Interest	5.7	3.2
No emotional manifestations	2.1	2.6
Indifference	.1	.9
Smiles	.3	.8
Laughs	.1	.4
Sulks	.2	1.0
Cries	.3	.9
Whines	.7	1.7

[a] Mean length of experimental period: 9.1 minutes.

The subjects in this study, 82 children (38 boys and 44 girls) aged three to six years, were enrolled in the preschool laboratories of the Iowa Child Welfare Research Station. The mean intelligence quotient was 122. Because the tests evidenced no statistically significant age differences, marked individual differences being apparent at all ages, the data have not been classified into age groups. Comparative frequency of various types of responses in the two tests is indicated in Tables 1 and 2. In each test the most frequent response of the group as a whole was "attempts to solve alone" although "interest" ran a close second. That requests for either partial or complete help and rationalizations were more common than disgruntled emotional responses proved to be the case.

Inasmuch as it was the purpose of these tests to differentiate between those subjects giving undesirable or immature responses and those responding more desirably, the extent to which this end was achieved was first to be determined. To describe the process briefly, certain objective criteria were set up in terms of test behavior. Five kinds of behavior occurring for at least a minimum amount of time were listed and definitely stated quantitatively. If a child's behavior fell into two or more of these classifications on either or both tests, he was judged to have given an immature response. In brief, these five types were as follows: (1) giving up attempts to solve the puzzle box in less than five minutes or to solve the weighted box in less than two minutes, (2) requesting help during more than one half the total time of the test, (3) manifesting destructive behavior, (4) making more than two rationalizations, (5) evidencing exaggerated emotional responses.

Analysis of the test records showed a total of fifteen children (18 per cent) who fell into the immature group.

The diagnostic value of the tests is illustrated by contrasting fre-

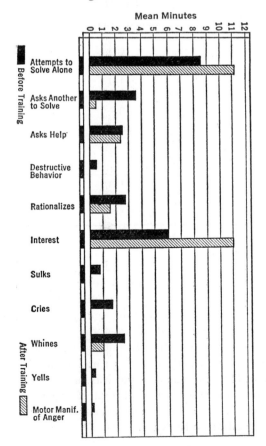

FIGURE 1.   RESPONSES OF TRAINED GROUP ON PUZZLE BOX TEST BEFORE AND AFTER TRAINING

quencies of behavior as shown in Tables 3 and 4, in which it is apparent that real differences do exist between the groups as classified by this means.

The next step in the study was the training program. In this, twelve out of the fifteen children participated.

Table 3. **Mean and Standard Deviation of Responses in Minutes for Two Groups of Subjects on Puzzle Box Test**

BEHAVIOR	GROUP SHOWING UNDESIRABLE OR IMMATURE RESPONSE (N = 15)		REMAINDER OF TOTAL GROUP (N = 54)	
	Mean	*Standard Deviation*	*Mean*	*Standard Deviation*
No overt attempt	6.0	3.7	1.6	2.3
Attempts to solve alone	8.5	4.2	13.0	3.0
Asks another to solve	3.6	3.4	.8	1.6
Asks help	2.5	2.4	1.5	2.1
Destructive behavior	.6	1.1		
Rationalizes	2.8	2.5	1.0	1.4
Interest	6.0	3.8	12.4	3.9
No emotional manifestations	2.5	2.4	1.7	3.2
Sulks	.8	1.3		
Cries	1.7	2.4		
Whines	2.6	2.9	.5	1.5
Yells	.3	.8		
Motor manifestations of anger	.2	.5		

The basic philosophy underlying the training assumed that children can learn to meet difficulty in a controlled manner and acceptably if they know from experience what type of behavior is most likely to bring success or satisfaction. It was the aim of the training program to raise the responses of the immature group nearer to the level of desirability. Specifically, in the training an attempt was made to teach the child to persist longer in the face of difficult tasks (which were, however, not impossible ones), to teach him to depend less upon an adult for help, and to attack a problem and see it through with some composure.

The method of training consisted in introducing the child to a series of problems which grew progressively more difficult as the program of training proceeded. The problem situations reflected the following criteria:

1. The tasks should be graded in difficulty so that the child experiences success in the earlier ones and gradually works up to problems which are difficult for him.
2. The later tasks must be of such difficulty that the child does not suc-

ceed immediately but is forced to persevere, to continue to try if he is to attain success.

3. The child must be able to see his progress and previous successes.

In describing the two training situations briefly [1] it may be said that they were similar in type but differed in the specific materials used. For the first, four picture-puzzle books were prepared, each one in the series more difficult than the one preceding and each one of graduated difficulty from beginning to end. For these, interesting, colorful and appropriate story books were cut up. The pictures were mounted on 4-ply wood, varnished, cut into puzzles, and the book was rebound on loose rings. The experimenter read the story to the child. As she reached a part illustrated by one of the pictures, she stopped for him to put the puzzle together before continuing the story. After the first picture was completed she covered it with cellophane, so that both she and the child could refer to it later, and resumed the story until the next picture. Each book contained four to six pictures.

Table 4. Mean and Standard Deviation of Responses in Minutes for Two Groups of Subjects on Weighted Box Test

BEHAVIOR	GROUP SHOWING UNDESIRABLE OR IMMATURE RESPONSE (N = 15)		REMAINDER OF TOTAL GROUP (N = 50)	
	Mean	*Standard Deviation*	*Mean*	*Standard Deviation*
No overt attempt	5.2	2.9	3.4	2.4
Attempts to solve alone	4.2	2.9	6.5	2.3
Asks another to solve	.7	1.6	.3	.9
Asks help	2.2	2.3	.9	1.7
Rationalizes	1.7	1.2	.8	1.5
Interest	3.5	3.0	6.8	2.9
Sulks	1.0	2.0		
Cries	1.0	1.6	.1	.4
Whines	2.3	2.3	.3	1.2

In the second situation a "block boy" was built. Copied from a drawn pattern hung on the wall, he was to be made of colored blocks placed upon each other so that having attained first feet, then legs, then trunk and arms, then head, he stood approximately three feet high, a somewhat precarious figure and a frequently exasperatingly unsteady one. Usually several attempts were necessary in order to complete him. After a successful production his builder had the task of devising a hat from a wide variety of materials provided.

[1] Detailed descriptions of all the materials used in this study may be obtained from the Iowa Child Welfare Research Station, Iowa City, Iowa.

The entire program of training was handled by one person. Training periods varied in length from eight to thirty-three minutes, depending largely upon the difficulty of the tasks and the child's behavior. To subject the twelve children to all of the training took approximately six weeks.

Behavior during the training program underwent a gradual improvement as is shown by both objective and subjective estimate. In order to study post-training behavior objectively, two approaches were utilized; first, retests by means of a similar but not identical puzzle box were given the trained subjects (Fig. 1); second, also retested were an equal number of children, not in the trained group, who during the initial tests had shown some undesirable behavior (Fig. 2).

It is evident from a study of Figure 1 that the behavior of the children after training was remarkably different from their behavior prior to training. Differences in the three items *attempts to solve alone, interest,* and *cries* are statistically significant. Excepting in the case of the item *asks help,* the remaining differences closely approximately significance.

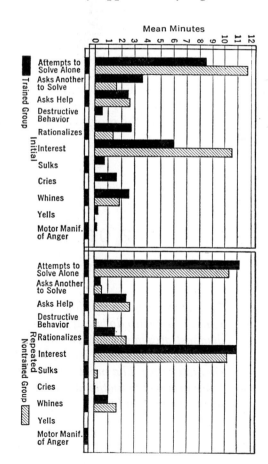

FIGURE 2. RESPONSES OF TRAINED AND UNTRAINED GROUPS ON PUZZLE BOX TEST

The differences were in form of the response given in the retest and indicate that a reasonable improvement was effected in the trained group. The exaggerated emotional responses of sulking and crying dropped out entirely in this group.

Figure 2 concerns responses of the trained and the compared non-trained group before and after training. The two groups differed in the responses *no overt attempt, attempts to solve alone, interest, sulks,* and *cries.* All of the differences were in favor of the trained subjects in spite of the fact that previous to training the difference lay in the opposite direction.

The results of this study, hopeful as they are, must be interpreted in the light of the specific conditions. The entire program was carried out by the experimenter, who also gave the retests. Further study, at present underway, must determine the extent to which the more desirable behavior occurs in other situations and with other persons. There is evidence that behavior of children in difficulties has been similar in two test situations; it would be valuable to make observations in other situations and under circumstances of a more social nature. Probably the most important contribution of the present study is its indication of the marked effect of this training program. After training, children tried longer, manifested more interest in solving problems themselves, and completely eliminated emotional behavior. Evidently this improvement was not a function of age or other training. Of particular interest to teachers and psychologists may be the fact that the program of training was neither arduous nor time-consuming.

59. A LABORATORY STUDY OF FEAR:
THE CASE OF PETER

MARY COVER JONES

This famous experiment followed the conditioning experiments of Ivan Pavlov with dogs and those of Watson with children. It demonstrates how a child developed fear of an object which never hurt him and how this fear spread to other objects with similar characteristics. The process followed in eventually "unconditioning" Peter provides valuable ideas of how children may be helped to overcome certain fears.

Reprinted from *Journal of Genetic Psychology,* XXXI (1924), 308–315, by permission of the author and The Journal Press.

As part of a genetic study of emotions, a number of children were observed in order to determine the most effective methods of removing fear responses.

The case of Peter illustrates how a fear may be removed under laboratory conditions. His case was selected from a number of others for the following reasons:

1. Progress in combating the fear reactions was so marked that many of the details of the process could be observed easily.
2. It was possible to continue the study over a period of more than three months.
3. The notes of a running diary show the characteristics of a healthy, normal, interesting child, well adjusted, except for his exaggerated fear reactions. A few descriptive notes show something of his personality:

> Remarkably active, easily interested, capable of prolonged endeavor. . . . A favorite with the children as well as with the nurses and matrons . . . Peter has a healthy passion for possessions. Everything that he lays his hands on is his. As this is frequently disputed by some other child, there are occasional violent scenes of protest. These disturbances are not more frequent than might be expected in a three-year-old, in view of the fact that he is continually forced to adjust to a large group of children, nor are they more marked in Peter's case than in others of his age. Peter's IQ at the age of 2 years and 10 months was 102 on the Kuhlmann Revision of the Binet. At the same time he passed 5 of the 3 year tests on the Stanford Revision. In initiative and constructive ability, however, he is superior to his companions of the same mental age.

4. This case is a sequel to one recently contributed by Dr. Watson and furnished supplementary material of interest in a genetic study of emotions. Dr. Watson's case illustrated how a fear could be produced experimentally under laboratory conditions. A brief review follows: Albert, eleven months of age, was an infant with a phlegmatic disposition, afraid of nothing "under the sun" except a loud sound made by striking a steel bar. This made him cry. By striking the bar at the same time that Albert touched a white rat, the fear was transferred to the white rat. After seven combined stimulations, rat and sound, Albert not only became greatly disturbed at the sight of a rat, but this fear had spread to include a white rabbit, cotton wool, a fur coat, and the experimenter's hair. It did not transfer to his wooden blocks and other objects very dissimilar to the rat.

In referring to this case, Dr. Watson says, "We have shown experimentally that when you condition a child to show fear of an animal, this fear transfers or spreads in such a way that without separate conditioning he becomes afraid of many animals. If you take any one of these objects producing fear and uncondition, will fear of the other objects in the series disappear at the same time? That is, will the unconditioning spread without further training to other stimuli?"

Dr. Watson intended to continue the study of Albert in an attempt to answer this question, but Albert was removed from the hospital and the series of observations was discontinued.

About three years later this case, which seemed almost to be Albert grown a bit older, was discovered in our laboratory.

Peter was 2 years and 10 months old when we began to study him. He was afraid of a white rat, and this fear extended to a rabbit, a fur coat, a feather, cotton wool, etc., but not to wooden blocks and similar toys. An abridgment of the first laboratory notes on Peter reads as follows:

> Peter was put in a crib in a play room and immediately became absorbed in his toys. A white rat was introduced into the crib from behind. (The experimenter was behind a screen.) At sight of the rat, Peter screamed and fell flat on his back in a paroxysm of fear. The stimulus was removed, and Peter was taken out of the crib and put into a chair. Barbara was brought to the crib and the white rat introduced as before. She exhibited no fear but picked the rat up in her hand. Peter sat quietly watching Barbara and the rat. A string of beads belonging to Peter had been left in the crib. Whenever the rat touched a part of the string he would say "my beads" in a complaining voice, although he made no objections when Barbara touched them. Invited to get down from the chair, he shook his head, fear not yet subsided. Twenty-five minutes elapsed before he was ready to play about freely.

The next day his reactions to the following situations and objects were noted:

Play room and crib	Selected toys, got into crib without protest
White ball rolled in	Picked it up and held it
Fur rug hung over crib	Cried until it was removed
Fur coat hung over crib	Cried until it was removed
Cotton	Whimpered, withdrew, cried
Hat with feathers	Cried
Blue woolly sweater	Looked, turned away, no fear
White toy rabbit of rough cloth . .	No interest, no fear
Wooden doll	No interest, no fear

This case made it possible for the experiment to continue where Dr. Watson had left off. The first problem was that of "unconditioning" a fear response to an animal, and the second, that of determining whether unconditioning to one stimulus spreads without further training to other stimuli.

From the test situations which were used to reveal fears, it was found that Peter showed even more marked fear responses to the rabbit than to the rat. It was decided to use the rabbit for unconditioning and to proceed as follows: Each day Peter and three other children were brought to the laboratory for a play period. The other children were selected carefully because of their entirely fearless attitude toward the rabbit and because of their satisfactory adjustments in general. The rabbit was always present during a part of the play period. From time to time Peter was brought in alone so that his reactions could be observed and progress noted.

From reading over the notes for each session it was apparent that there had been improvement by more or less regular steps from almost complete terror at sight of the rabbit to a completely positive response with no signs of disturbance. New situations requiring closer contact with the rabbit had been gradually introduced and the degree to which these situations were avoided, tolerated, or welcomed, at each experimental session, gave the measure of improvement. Analysis of the notes on Peter's reactions indicated the following progressive steps in his degrees of toleration:

A. Rabbit anywhere in the room in a cage causes fear reactions.
B.   "   12 feet away in cage tolerated.
C.   "   4   "   "   "   "   "
D.   "   3   "   "   "   "   "
E.   "   close   "   "   "
F.   "   free in room tolerated.
G.   "   touched when experimenter holds it.
H.   "   touched when free in room.
I.   "   defied by spitting at it, throwing things at it, imitating it.
J. Rabbit allowed on tray of high chair.
K. Squats in defenseless position beside rabbit.
L. Helps experimenter to carry rabbit to its cage.
M. Holds rabbit on lap.
N. Stays alone in room with rabbit.
O. Allows rabbit in play pen with him.
P. Fondles rabbit affectionately.
Q. Lets rabbit nibble his fingers.

These "degrees of toleration" merely represented the stages in which improvement occurred. They did not give any indications of the intervals between steps, nor of the plateaus, relapses, and sudden gains which were actually evident. To show these features a curve was drawn by using the seventeen steps given above as the Y axis of a chart [p. 570] and the experimental sessions as the X axis. The units are not equal on either axis, as the "degrees of toleration" have merely been set down as they appeared from consideration of the laboratory notes with no attempt to evaluate the steps. Likewise the experimental sessions were not equi-distant in time. Peter was seen twice daily for a period and thence only once a day. At one point illness and quarantine interrupted the experiments for two months. There is no indication of these irregularities on the chart. For

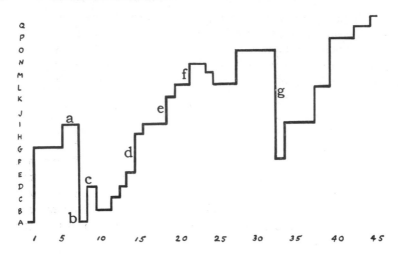

example, along the X axis, 1 represents the date December 4 when the observation began. Eleven and 12 represent the dates March 10 A. M. and P. M. (from December 17 to March 7, Peter was not available for study).

The question arose as to whether or not the points on the Y axis which indicated progress to the experimenter represented real advance and not merely idiosyncratic reactions to the subject. The "tolerance series" as indicated by the experimenter was presented in random order to six graduate students and instructors in psychology to be arranged so as to indicate increase in tolerance, in their judgment. An average correlation of 70 with the experimenter's arrangement was found for the six ratings. This indicates that the experimenter was justified from an *a priori* point of view in designating the steps to be progressive stages.

The first seven periods show how Peter progressed from a great fear of the rabbit to a tranquil indifference and even a voluntary pat on the rabbit's back when others were setting the example. The notes for the seventh period [see (a) on chart] read:

Laurel, Mary, Arthur, Peter playing together in the laboratory. Experimenter put rabbit down on floor. Arthur said, "Peter doesn't cry when he sees the rabbit come out." Peter, "No." He was a little concerned as to whether or not the rabbit would eat his kiddie car. Laurel and Mary stroked the rabbit and chattered away excitedly. Peter walked over, touched the rabbit on the back, exulting, "I touched him on the end."

At this period Peter was taken to the hospital with scarlet fever. He did not return for two months.

By referring to the chart at (b), it will be noted that the line shows a decided drop to the early level of fear reaction when he returned. This was easily explained by the nurse who brought Peter from the hospital. As they were entering a taxi at the door of the hospital, a large dog, running past, jumped at them. Both Peter and the nurse were very much frightened, Peter so much that he lay back in the taxi pale and quiet, and the nurse debated whether or not to return him to the hospital. This seemed reason enough for his precipitate descent back to the original fear level. Being threatened by a large dog when ill, and in a strange place and being with an adult who also showed fear, was a terrifying situation against which our training could not have fortified him.

At this point (b) we began another method of treatment, that of "direct conditioning." Peter was seated in a high chair and given food which he liked. The experimenter brought the rabbit in a wire cage as close as she could without arousing a response which would interfere with the eating. Through the presence of the pleasant stimulus (food) whenever the rabbit was shown, the fear was eliminated gradually in favor of a positive response. Occasionally also, other children were brought in to help with the "unconditioning." These facts are of interest in following the charted progress. The first decided rise at (c) was due to the presence of another child who influenced Peter's reaction. The notes for this day read:

Lawrence and Peter sitting near together in their high chairs eating candy. Rabbit in cage put down 12 feet away. Peter began to cry. Lawrence said, "Oh, rabbit." Clambered down, ran over and looked in the cage at him. Peter followed close and watched.

The next two decided rises at (d) and (e) occurred on the day when a student assistant, Dr. S., was present. Peter was very fond of Dr. S. whom he insisted was his "papa." Although Dr. S. did not directly influence Peter by any overt suggestions, it may be that having him there contributed to Peter's general feeling of well being and thus indirectly affected his reactions. The fourth rise on the chart at (f), was, like the first, due to the influence of another child. Notes for the 21st session read:

Peter with candy in high chair. Experimenter brought rabbit and sat down in front of the tray with it. Peter cried out, "I don't want him," and withdrew. Rabbit was given to another child sitting near to hold. His holding the rabbit served as a powerful suggestion; Peter wanted the rabbit on his lap, and held it for an instant.

The decided drop at (g) was caused by a slight scratch when Peter was helping to carry the rabbit to his cage. The rapid ascent following shows how quickly he regained lost ground.

In one of our last sessions, Peter showed no fear although another child was present who showed marked disturbance at sight of the rabbit.

An attempt was made from time to time to see what verbal organization accompanied this process of "unconditioning." Upon Peter's return from the hospital, the following conversation took place:

E.   [experimenter].   What do you do upstairs, Peter? [The laboratory was upstairs].

P.   I see my brother. Take me up to see my brother.

E.   What else will you see?

P.   Blocks.

Peter's reference to blocks indicated a definite memory as he played with blocks only in the laboratory. No further response of any significance could be elicited. In the laboratory two days later (he had seen the rabbit once in the meantime), he said suddenly, "Beads can't bite me, beads can only look at me." Toward the end of the training an occasional "I like the rabbit," was all the language he had to parallel the changed emotional organization.

Early in the experiment an attempt was made to get some measure of the visceral changes accompanying Peter's fear reactions. On one occasion Dr. S. determined Peter's blood pressure outside the laboratory and again later, in the laboratory while he was in a state of much anxiety caused by the rabbit's being held close to him by the experimenter. The diastolic blood pressure changed from 65 to 80 on this occasion. Peter was taken to the infirmary the next day for the routine physical examination and developed there a suspicion of medical instruments which made it inadvisable to proceed with this phase of the work.

Peter has gone home to a difficult environment but the experimenter is still in touch with him. He showed in the last interview, as on the later portions of the chart, a genuine fondness for the rabbit. What has happened to the fear of the other objects? The fear of the cotton, the fur coat, feathers, was entirely absent at our last interview. He looked at them, handled them, and immediately turned to something which interested him more. The reaction to the rats, and the fur rug with the stuffed head was greatly modified and improved. While he did not show the fondness for these that was apparent with the rabbit, he had made a fair adjustment. For example, Peter would pick up the tin box containing frogs or rats and carry it around the room. When requested, he picked up the fur rug and carried it to the experimenter.

What would Peter do if confronted by a strange animal? At the last interview the experimenter presented a mouse and a tangled mass of angleworms. At first sight, Peter showed slight distress reactions and moved away, but before the period was over he was carrying the worms about and watching the mouse with undisturbed interest. By "unconditioning" Peter to the rabbit, he has apparently been helped to overcome many superfluous fears, some completely, some to a less degree. His tolerance of strange animals and unfamiliar situations has apparently increased.

The study is still incomplete. Peter's fear of the animals which were shown him was probably not a directly conditioned fear. It is unlikely that he had ever had an experience with white rats, for example. Where the fear originated and with what stimulus, is not known. Nor is it known what Peter would do if he were again confronted with the original fear situation. All of the fears which were "unconditioned" were transferred fears, and it has not yet been learned whether or not the primary fear can be eliminated by training the transfers.

Another matter which must be left to speculation is the future welfare of the subject. His "home" consists of one furnished room which is occupied by his mother and father, a brother of nine years and himself. Since the death of an older sister, he is the recipient of most of the unwise affection of his parents. His brother appears to bear him a grudge because of this favoritism, as might be expected. Peter hears continually, "Ben is so bad and so dumb, but Peter is so good and so smart!" His mother is a highly emotional individual who can not get through an interview, however brief, without a display of tears. She is totally incapable of providing a home on the $25 a week which her husband steadily earns. In an attempt to control Peter she resorts to frequent fear suggestions. "Come in Peter, someone wants to steal you." To her erratic resorts to discipline, Peter reacts with temper tantrums. He was denied a summer in the country because his father "forgets he's tired when he has Peter around." Surely a discouraging outlook for Peter.

But the recent development of psychological studies of young children and the growing tendency to carry the knowledge gained in the psychological laboratories into the home and school induce us to predict a more wholesome treatment of a future generation of Peters.

60. BRAVE NEW WORLD

ALDOUS HUXLEY

If children can be conditioned to fear and not to fear, they can
also be conditioned to hate and love, to admire one kind of "ism"
and reject another. In fact, it might be possible for an entire society
to be so conditioned; perhaps many societies—possibly including our
own—have been.

Mr. Huxley imaginatively describes, in stark prose, the methods
which might be used for an almost totally effective conditioning
of a future society.

. . . The love of servitude cannot be established except as the result of a deep, personal revolution in human minds and bodies. To bring

Selections reprinted from *Brave New World* (Modern Library Edition), pp. 20–24, 27, 28–31, by permission of the author.

about that revolution we require, among others, the following discoveries and inventions. First, a greatly improved technique of suggestion—through infant conditioning and, later, with the aid of drugs, such as scopolamine. Second, a fully developed science of human differences, enabling government managers to assign any given individual to his or her proper place in the social and economic hierarchy. (Round pegs in square holes tend to have dangerous thoughts about the social system and to infect others with their discontents.) Third (since reality, however utopian, is something from which people feel the need of taking pretty frequent holidays), a substitute for alcohol and the other narcotics, something at once less harmful and more pleasure-giving than gin or heroin. And fourth (but this would be a long-term project, which it would take generations of totalitarian control to bring to a successful conclusion) a foolproof system of eugenics, designed to standardize the human product and so to facilitate the task of the managers. In *Brave New World* this standardization of the human product has been pushed to fantastic, though not perhaps impossible, extremes. Technically and ideologically we are still a long way from bottled babies and Bokanovsky groups of semi-morons. But by A.F. 600, who knows what may not be happening? Meanwhile the other characteristic features of the happier and more stable world—the equivalents of soma and hypnopaedia and the scientific caste system—are probably not more than three or four generations away. Nor does the sexual promiscuity of *Brave New World* seem so very distant. There are already certain American cities in which the number of divorces is equal to the number of marriages. In a few years, no doubt, marriage licenses will be sold like dog licenses, good for a period of twelve months, with no law against changing dogs or keeping more than one animal at a time. As political and economic freedom diminishes, sexual freedom tends compensatingly to increase. And the dictator (unless he needs cannon fodder and families with which to colonize empty or conquered territories) will do well to encourage that freedom. In conjunction with the freedom to daydream under the influence of dope and movies and the radio, it will help to reconcile his subjects to the servitude which is their fate.

All things considered it looks as though Utopia were far closer to us than anyone, only fifteen years ago, could have imagined.

. . . . .

INFANT NURSERIES. NEO-PAVLOVIAN CONDITIONING ROOMS, announced the notice board.

The Director opened a door. They were in a large bare room, very bright and sunny; for the whole of the southern wall was a single window. Half a dozen nurses, trousered and jacketed in the regulation white viscose-linen uniform, their hair aseptically hidden under white caps, were engaged in setting out bowls of roses in a long row across the floor. Big bowls, packed tight with blossom. Thousands of petals, ripe-blown and silkily smooth, like the cheeks of innumerable little cherubs, but of cherubs, in that bright light, not exclusively pink and Aryan, but also luminously Chinese, also Mexican, also apoplectic with too much blowing of celestial trumpets, also pale as death, pale with the posthumous whiteness of marble.

The nurses stiffened to attention as the D.H.C. came in.

"Set out the books," he said curtly.

In silence the nurses obeyed his command. Between the rose bowls the books were duly set out—a row of nursery quartos opened invitingly each at some gaily coloured image of beast or fish or bird.

"Now bring in the children."

They hurried out of the room and returned in a minute or two, each pushing a kind of tall dumbwaiter laden, on all its four wire-netted shelves, with eight-month-old babies, all exactly alike (a Bokanovsky Group, it was evident) and all (since their caste was Delta) dressed in khaki.

"Put them down on the floor."

The infants were unloaded.

"Now turn them so that they can see the flowers and books."

Turned, the babies at once fell silent, then began to crawl towards those clusters of sleek colours, those shapes so gay and brilliant on the white pages. As they approached, the sun came out of a momentary eclipse behind a cloud. The roses flamed up as though with a sudden passion from within; a new and profound significance seemed to suffuse the shining pages of the books. From the ranks of the crawling babies came little squeals of excitement, gurgles and twitterings of pleasure.

The Director rubbed his hands. "Excellent!" he said. "It might almost have been done on purpose."

The swiftest crawlers were already at their goal. Small hands reached out uncertainly, touched, grasped, unpetaling the transfigured roses, crumpling the illuminated pages of the books. The Director waited until all were happily busy. Then, "Watch carefully," he said. And, lifting his hand, he gave the signal.

The Head Nurse, who was standing by a switchboard at the other end of the room, pressed down a little lever.

There was a violent explosion. Shriller and even shriller, a siren shrieked. Alarm bells maddeningly sounded.

The children started, screamed, their faces were distorted with terror.

"And now," the Director shouted (for the noise was deafening), "now we proceed to rub in the lesson with a mild electric shock."

He waved his hand again, and the Head Nurse pressed a second lever. The screaming of the babies suddenly changed its tone. There was something desperate, almost insane, about the sharp spasmodic yelps to which they now gave utterance. Their little bodies twitched and stiffened; their limbs moved jerkily as if to the tug of unseen wires.

"We can electrify that whole strip of floor," bawled the Director in explanation. "But that's enough," he signalled to the nurse.

The explosions ceased, the bells stopped ringing, the shriek of the siren died down from tone to tone into silence. The stiffly twitching bodies relaxed, and what had become the sob and yelp of infant maniacs broadened out once more into a normal howl of ordinary terror.

"Offer them the flowers and the books again."

The nurses obeyed; but at the approach of the roses, at the mere sight of those gaily-coloured images of pussy and cock-a-doodle-doo and baa-baa black sheep, the infants shrank away in horror; the volume of their howling suddenly increased.

"Observe," said the Director triumphantly, "observe."

Books and loud noises, flowers and electric shocks—already in the infant mind these couples were compromisingly linked; and after two hundred repetitions of the same or a similar lesson would be wedded indissolubly. What man has joined, nature is powerless to put asunder.

"They'll grow up with what the psychologists used to call an "instinctive hatred of books and flowers. Reflexes unalterably conditioned. They'll be safe from books and botany all their lives." The Director turned to his nurses. "Take them away again."

Still yelling, the khaki babies were loaded on to their dumb-waiters and wheeled out, leaving behind them the smell of sour milk and a most welcome silence.

.   .   .   .   .

"The principle of sleep-teaching, or hypnopædia, had been discovered." The D.H.C. made an impressive pause.

The principle had been discovered; but many, many years were to elapse before that principle was usefully applied.

.   .   .   .   .

"These early experimenters," the D.H.C. was saying, "were on the wrong track. They thought that hypnopædia could be made an instrument of intellectual education . . ."

(A small boy asleep on his right side, the right arm stuck out, the right hand hanging limp over the edge of the bed. Through a round grating in the side of a box a voice speaks softly.

The Nile is the longest river in Africa and the second in length of all the rivers of the globe. Although falling short of the length of the

Mississippi-Missouri, the Nile is at the head of all rivers as regards the length of its basin, which extends through 35 degrees of latitude . . ."

At breakfast the next morning, "Tommy," some one says, "do you know which is the longest river in Africa?" A shaking of the head. "But don't you remember something that begins: The Nile is the . . ."

"The-Nile-is-the-longest-river-in-Africa-and-the-second-in-length-of-all-the-rivers-of-the-globe . . ." The words come rushing out. "Although-falling-short-of . . ."

"Well now, which is the longest river in Africa?"

The eyes are blank. "I don't know."

"But the Nile, Tommy."

"The-Nile-is-the-longest-river-in-Africa-and-second . . ."

"Then which river is the longest, Tommy?"

Tommy bursts into tears. "I don't know," he howls.)

That howl, the Director made it plain, discouraged the earliest investigators. The experiments were abandoned. No further attempt was made to teach children the length of the Nile in their sleep. Quite rightly. You can't learn a science unless you know what it's all about.

"Whereas, if they'd only started on *moral* education," said the Director, leading the way towards the door. The students followed him, desperately scribbling as they walked and all the way up in the lift. "Moral education, which ought never, in any circumstances, to be rational."

"Silence, silence," whispered a loud speaker as they stepped out at the fourteenth floor, and "Silence, silence," the trumpet mouths indefatigably repeated at intervals down every corridor. The students and even the Director himself rose automatically to the tips of their toes. They were Alphas, of course; but even Alphas have been well conditioned. . . .

Fifty yards of tiptoeing brought them to a door which the Director cautiously opened. They stepped over the threshold into the twilight of a shuttered dormitory. Eighty cots stood in a row against the wall. There was a sound of light regular breathing and a continuous murmur, as of very faint voices remotely whispering.

A nurse rose as they entered and came to attention before the Director.

"What's the lesson this afternoon?" he asked.

"We had Elementary Sex for the first forty minutes," she answered. "But now it's switched over to Elementary Class Consciousness."

The Director walked slowly down the long line of cots. Rosy and relaxed with sleep, eighty little boys and girls lay softly breathing. There was a whisper under every pillow. The D.H.C. halted and, bending over one of the little beds, listened attentively.

"Elementary Class Consciousness, did you say? Let's have it repeated a little louder by the trumpet."

At the end of the room a loud speaker projected from the wall. The Director walked up to it and pressed a switch.

". . . all wear green," said a soft but very distinct voice, beginning in the middle of a sentence, "and Delta children wear khaki. Oh no, I don't want to play with Delta children. And Epsilons are still worse. They're too stupid to be able to read or write. Besides they wear black, which is such a beastly colour. I'm *so* glad I'm a Beta."

There was a pause; then the voice began again.

"Alpha children wear grey. They work much harder than we do, because they're so frightfully clever. I'm really awfully glad I'm a Beta, because I don't work so hard. And then we are much better than the Gammas and Deltas. Gammas are stupid. They all wear green, and Delta children wear khaki. Oh, no, I *don't* want to play with Delta children. And Epsilons are still worse. They're too stupid to be able. . . ."

The Director pushed back the switch. The voice was silent. Only its thin ghosts continued to mutter from beneath the eighty pillows.

"They'll have that repeated forty or fifty times more before they wake; then again on Thursday, and again on Saturday. A hundred and twenty times three times a week for thirty months. After which they go on to a more advanced lesson."

Roses and electric shocks, the khaki of Deltas and a whiff of asafoetida—wedded indissolubly before the child can speak. But wordless conditioning is crude and wholesale; cannot bring home the finer distinction, cannot inculcate the more complex courses of behavior. For that there must be words, but words without reason. In brief, hypnopaedia.

"The greatest moralizing and socializing force of all time."

61. THE SCIENCE OF LEARNING AND THE ART OF TEACHING

B. F. SKINNER

If conditioning can be used to teach a dog to salivate or a child to fear rabbits, or to teach pigeons, cats, chickens, and other animals all kinds of complex tricks, why not use it to teach spelling or arithmetic?

Selections reprinted from the article in *Harvard Educational Review*, XXIV (1954), 86–87, and in *Current Trends in Psychology and the Behavior Sciences* (University of Pittsburgh Press, 1955), 38–58, by permission of the author and the University of Pittsburgh Press.

Professor Skinner has carefully examined two aspects of such teaching: determining what is to be taught and discovering adequate ways of rewarding (reinforcing) correct responses. Here he discusses the problem of reinforcement and describes a mechanical teaching device which he invented.

Perhaps the most serious criticism of the current classroom is the relative infrequency of reinforcement. Since the pupil is usually dependent upon the teacher for being right, and since many pupils are usually dependent upon the same teacher, the total number of contingencies which may be arranged during, say, the first four years, is of the order of only a few thousand. But a very rough estimate suggests that efficient mathematical behavior at this level requires something of the order of 25,000 contingencies. We may suppose that even in the brighter student a given contingency must be arranged several times to place the behavior well in hand. The responses to be set up are not simply the various items in tables of addition, subtraction, multiplication, and division; we have also to consider the alternative forms in which each item may be stated. To the learning of such material we should add hundreds of responses concerned with factoring, identifying primes, memorizing series, using short-cut techniques of calculation, constructing and using geometric representations or number forms, and so on. Over and above all this, the whole mathematical repertoire must be brought under the control of concrete problems of considerable variety. Perhaps 50,000 contingencies is a more conservative estimate. In this frame of reference the daily assignment in Arithmetic seems pitifully meagre.

The result of all this is, of course, well known. Even our best schools are under criticism for their inefficiency in the teaching of drill subjects such as arithmetic. The condition in the average school is a matter of wide-spread national concern. Modern children simply do not learn arithmetic quickly or well. Nor is the result simply incompetence. The very subjects in which modern techniques are weakest are those in which failure is most conspicuous, and in the wake of an ever-growing incompetence come the anxieties, uncertainties, and aggressions which in their turn present other problems to the school. Most pupils soon claim the asylum of not being "ready" for arithmetic at a given level or, eventually, of not having a mathematical mind. Such explanations are readily seized upon by defensive teachers and parents. Few pupils ever reach the stage at which automatic reinforcements follow as the natural consequences of mathematical behavior. On the contrary, the figures and symbols of mathematics have become standard emotional stimuli. The glimpse of a column of figures, not to say an algebraic symbol or an integral sign, is likely to set off—not mathematical behavior—but a reaction of anxiety, guilt, or fear.

The teacher is usually no happier about this than the pupil. Denied the opportunity to control via the birch rod, quite at sea as to the mode of operation of the few techniques at her disposal, she spends as little time as possible on drill subjects and eagerly subscribes to philosophies of education which emphasize material of greater inherent interest. . . .

There would be no point in urging these objections if improvement were impossible. But the advances which have recently been made in our control of the learning process suggest a thorough revision of classroom practices and, fortunately, they tell us how the revision can be brought about. This is not, of course, the first time that the results of an experimental science have been brought to bear upon the practical problems of education. The modern classroom does not, however, offer much evidence that research in the field of learning has been respected or used. This condition is no doubt partly due to the limitations of earlier research. But it has been encouraged by a too hasty conclusion that the laboratory study of learning is inherently limited because it cannot take into account the realities of the classroom. In the light of our increasing knowledge of the learning process we should, instead, insist upon dealing with those realities and forcing a substantial change in them. Education is perhaps the most important branch of scientific technology. It deeply affects the lives of all of us. We can no longer allow the exigencies of a practical situation to suppress the tremendous improvements which are within reach. The practical situation must be changed.

There are certain questions which have to be answered in turning to the study of any new organism. What behavior is to be set up? What reinforcers are at hand? What responses are available in embarking upon a program of progressive approximation which will lead to the final form of the behavior? How can reinforcements be most efficiently scheduled to maintain the behavior in strength? These questions are all relevant in considering the problem of the child in the lower grades.

In the first place, what reinforcements are available? What does the school have in its possession which will reinforce a child? We may look first to the material to be learned, for it is possible that this will provide considerable automatic reinforcement. Children play for hours with mechanical toys, paints, scissors and paper, noise-makers, puzzles—in short, with almost anything which feeds back significant changes in the environment and is reasonably free of aversive properties. The sheer control of nature is itself reinforcing. This effect is not evident in the modern school because it is masked by the emotional responses generated by aversive control. It is true that automatic reinforcement from the manipulation of the environment is probably only a mild reinforcer and may need to be carefully husbanded, but one of the most striking principles to emerge from recent research is that the *net* amount of reinforcement is of little significance. A very slight reinforcement may be tremendously effective in controlling behavior if it is wisely used.

If the natural reinforcement inherent in the subject matter is not enough, other reinforcers must be employed. Even in school the child is occasionally permitted to do "what he wants to do," and access to reinforcements of many sorts may be made contingent upon the more immediate consequences of the behavior to be established. Those who advocate competition as a useful social motive may wish to use the reinforcements which follow from excelling others, although there is the difficulty that in this case the reinforcement of one child is necessarily aversive to another. Next in order we might place the good will and affection of the teacher, and only when that has failed need we turn to the use of aversive stimulation.

. . . . .

. . . We have every reason to expect, that the most effective control of human learning will require instrumental aid. The simple fact is that, as a mere reinforcing mechanism, the teacher is out of date. This would be true even if a single teacher devoted all her time to a single child, but her inadequacy is multiplied many-fold when she must serve as a reinforcing device to many children at once. If the teacher is to take advantage of recent advances in the study of learning, she must have the help of mechanical devices.

The technical problem of providing the necessary instrumental aid is not particularly difficult. There are many ways in which the necessary contingencies may be arranged, either mechanically or electrically. An inexpensive device which solves most of the principal problems has already been constructed. It is still in the experimental stage, but a description will suggest the kind of instrument which seems to be required. The device consists of a small box about the size of a small record player. On the top surface is a window through which a question or problem printed on a paper tape may be seen. The child answers the question by moving one or more sliders upon which the digits 0 through 9 are printed. The answer appears in square holes punched in the paper upon which the question is printed. When the answer has been set, the child turns a knob. The operation is as simple as adjusting a television set. If the answer is right, the knob turns freely and can be made to ring a bell or provide some other conditioned reinforcement. If the answer is wrong, the knob will not turn. A counter may be added to tally wrong answers. The knob must then be reversed slightly and a second attempt at a right answer made. (Unlike the flash-card, the device reports a wrong answer without giving the right answer.) When the answer is right, a further turn of the knob engages a clutch which moves the next problem into place in the window. This movement cannot be completed, however, until the sliders have been returned to zero.

The important features of the device are these: Reinforcement for the right answer is immediate. The mere manipulation of the device will probably be reinforcing enough to keep the average pupil at work for a suitable period each day, provided traces of earlier aversive control can be wiped out. A teacher may supervise an entire class at work on such devices at the same time, yet each child may progress at his own rate, completing as many problems as possible within the class period. If forced to be away from school, he may return to pick up where he left off. The gifted child will advance rapidly, but can be kept from getting too far ahead either by being excused from arithmetic for a time or by being given special sets of problems which take him into some of the interesting by-paths of mathematics.

The device makes it possible to present carefully designed material in which one problem can depend upon the answer to the preceding and where, therefore, the most efficient progress to an eventually complex repertoire can be made. Provision has been made for recording the commonest mistakes so that the tapes can be modified as experience dictates. Additional steps can be inserted where pupils tend to have trouble, and ultimately the material will reach a point at which the answers of the average child will almost always be right.

If the material itself proves not to be sufficiently reinforcing, other reinforcers in the possession of the teacher or school may be made contingent upon the operation of the device or upon progress through a series of problems. Supplemental reinforcement would not sacrifice the advantages gained from immediate reinforcement and from the possibility of constructing an optimal series of steps which approach the complex repertoire of mathematical behavior most efficiently.

A similar device in which the sliders carry the letters of the alphabet has been designed to teach spelling. In addition to the advantages which can be gained from precise reinforcement and careful programming, the device will teach reading at the same time. It can also be used to establish the large and important repertoire of verbal relationships encountered in logic and science. In short, it can teach verbal thinking. As to content instruction, the device can be operated as a multiple-choice self-rater.

Some objections to the use of such devices in the classroom can easily be foreseen. The cry will be raised that the child is being treated as a mere animal and that an essentially human intellectual achievement is being analyzed in unduly mechanistic terms. Mathematical behavior is usually regarded, not as a repertoire of responses involving numbers and numerical operations, but as evidences of mathematical ability or the exercise of the power of reason. It is true that the techniques which are emerging from the experimental study of learning are not designed to "develop the mind" or to further some vague "understanding" of mathematical relationships. They are designed, on the contrary, to establish the very behaviors which are taken to be the evidences of such mental states or processes. This is only a special case of the general change which is under way in the interpretation of human affairs. An advancing science continues to offer more and more convincing alternatives to traditional formulations. The behavior in terms of which human thinking must eventually be defined is worth treating in its own right as the substantial goal of education.

Of course the teacher has a more important function than to say right or wrong. The changes proposed would free her for the effective exercise of that function. Marking a set of papers in arithmetic—"Yes, nine and six *are* fifteen; no, nine and seven *are not* eighteen"—is beneath the dignity of any intelligent individual. There is more important work to be done—in which the teacher's relations to the pupil cannot be duplicated by a mechanical device. Instrumental help would merely improve these relations. One might say that the main trouble with education in the lower grades today is that the child is obviously not competent and *knows it* and that the teacher is unable to do anything about it and *knows that too.* If the advances which have recently been made in our control of behavior can give the child a genuine competence in reading, writing, spelling, and arithmetic, then the teacher may begin to function, not in lieu of a cheap machine, but through intellectual, cultural, and emotional contacts of that distinctive sort which testify to her status as a human being.

Another possible objection is that mechanized instruction will mean technological unemployment. We need not worry about this until there are enough teachers to go around and until the hours and energy demanded of the teacher are comparable to those in other fields of employment. Mechanical devices will eliminate the more tiresome labors of the teacher but they will not necessarily shorten the time during which she remains in contact with the pupil.

A more practical objection: Can we afford to mechanize our schools? The answer is clearly yes. The device I have just described could be produced as cheaply as a small radio or phonograph. There would need to be far fewer devices than pupils, for they could be used in rotation. But even if we suppose that the instrument eventually found to be most effective would cost several hundred dollars and that large numbers of them would be required, our economy should be able to stand the strain. Once we have accepted the possibility and the necessity of mechanical help in the classroom, the economic problem can easily be surmounted. There is no reason why the school room should be any less mechanized than, for example, the kitchen. A country which annually produces millions of refrigerators, dish-washers, automatic washing-machines, automatic clothes-driers, and automatic garbage disposers can certainly afford the equipment necessary to educate its citizens to high standards of competence in the most effective way.

62. GROUP INTERVIEWING IN A CAMP FOR DISTURBED BOYS

WILLIAM C. MORSE AND DAVID WINEMAN

One of the functions of leadership is to maintain harmony within the group. This article describes how one discussion leader achieved this. Although the boys described are delinquents and their language is flashier than usual, the group processes demonstrated are the same as those in the home, at school, or at work: the individual who is being hurt by another person may try to hurt someone smaller than he; when attacked, the individual defends himself; and no group member "squeals" on another who is accused by an outsider.

When a camp plays host for the summer to ninety disturbed boys the staff must be fully aware of the potential volatility of this group. . . .

. . . . .

The problems that appear may range from periodic minor conflicts to sustained and painful disruptions which threaten to disintegrate the group. Since the staff aim is to maintain the group as an intact and relatively peaceful social unit, and since many of the individual personality difficulties appear most sharply when confronted with the challenges of group living, much time is spent in emergency interview sessions with the cabin groups. We have found that these interviews have been most effectively conducted by a staff member who embodies both administrative and therapeutic responsibility.

Naturally each group session runs its own course over a period of forty-five minutes to two hours and great flexibility must be used in working each one through. . . .

. . . . .

Let us turn to a sample of a group interview at the Fresh Air Camp. Although in dialogue form, this is not a transcript of an interview. It is

Selections reprinted from the article in *Journal of Social Issues*, XIII, No. 1 (1957), 23–31, by permission of the authors and publisher.

a post-situational recall of the essential material. It is very much condensed, since the particular interview ran about one and one-half hours, but many of the expressions are verbatim and we feel the style itself contains few, if any, distortions. The group represented in this interview were senior boys between the ages of twelve and fourteen. The following member by member thumbnail sketch may serve to identify them sufficiently to clarify the dialogue.

Tony. leader of the group—a slick, manipulative delinquent—detention home background—has a well-oiled, pleasant manner with adults except in moments of sudden negative rapport—can exert positive effect on the group when motivated to do so.

Rusty. overtly aggressive—a bully—distrustful—Tony's lieutenant —highly dependent upon him—at rare times betrays an almost infantile need for adult attention and affection which is usually under very expert concealment.

Jim. sole Negro in the group—detention home background—dangerously violent during outburst of rage—sadistic—once, before camp, beat a younger boy so badly with a lead pipe that he had to be hospitalized. In the cabin he is teased and scapegoated by Tony and Rusty; he in turn vents his fury on weaker members of the group.

"Ears". so called by the group because of the large size of the members referred to—ironically enough he has developed an ear infection, carrying around huge wads of cotton which he has stuffed in them—a compulsive stealer—dependent and insecure—he tries to avoid aggressive situations—scapegoated by Tony and Rusty when they are not attacking Jim.

Howie. a reserved, truculent boy—plays the role of an isolate in the group—jealous of Rusty's lieutenancy to, and intimacy with, Tony.

Chuck. an infantile, inept kid—the group stooge. Two other quiet boys who, together with Chuck and Ears, form a more subdued group in the cabin. As a group they are frequently scapegoated by Tony, Rusty, and Jim.

From these descriptions the reader can make an accurate guess about the nature of the problem facing this group. By the second week in camp the group is becoming progressively more disturbed because of Tony's corrupt leadership. Neighboring cabins are disturbed by the depredations of Tony and Rusty; these two, however, finagle events so that their innocent cabin-mates are the ones subjected to reprisal by the enraged victim. Due to progressive needling from Tony and Rusty, Jim has had severe blowups in which he recklessly tries to maim less powerful group members, such as Ears, with whatever weapon is at hand. As the group disturbance gains momentum the staff is alert for the appearance of a fresh incident which might serve as a basis for a group interview.

It should be emphasized that waiting for a typical episode which the group interview will seek to exploit is a deliberate strategy. It is not enough simply to know the general tenor and shape of group action in a cabin. The utmost concreteness and temporal immediacy is necessary or else the alibi experts in the group will quickly seize the opportunity to accuse you of being a fussy autocrat who wants only to bore them with discussion. If you say, "Yesterday there was some trouble," this is not enough. "Well what the hell are you talking about that for? Christ, that's over. Let's get outa this goddam joint," will inevitably greet you. And even the most miserably scapegoated and protection-hungry member of the group will be swayed by this lure and chime in, echoing, "Yeh, let's get out of here," turning his energies toward gaining acceptance from his tormentor by joining in the attack on the adult.

In this case an incident soon made its appearance. Before supper, between the time they come out of swimming and the actual serving of the meal (about 45 minutes), Jim has had one of his sadistic temper outbursts against Ears, cutting him by hurling a chunk of plaster at him. We learn from the counselor that during most of the day Tony and Rusty have been needling Jim. A contagious wave of unrest and impulsivity has spread even to the quiet youngsters in the group. Tony and Rusty are riding high on the crest of this choppy sea, finding it amenable to both their tastes and talents.

An interview is held in the evening after supper, the injury to Ears having been reported to the main lodge. The interview proceeds as follows:

DISCUSSION LEADER.   I called you guys together so we could talk over some of the things that are happening in the cabin. Today, for instance, there has been a lot of wild stuff and Ears [1] got hurt.

TONY [*immediately assuming the role as group spokesman*].   Yeh, Ears here got hurt, didn't you, Ears?

EARS [*excitedly*].   I'm sitting on my bunk reading a comic book and this boy [*pointing to Jim*] starts foolin' around.

TONY.   That's right.

JIM [*heatedly*].   Yeh, goddamit, them two bastards are always fussing around with me [*indicating, of course, Tony and Rusty*].

DISCUSSION LEADER.   What do you mean, Jim, fooling around with you? What do they do?

JIM.   Rusty started with me when we were in the boat—shoving me and grabbing my line and trying to throw my bait away. I ain't gonna take that, so I shoved back and then he beat the hell outa me. Boy, if they get my temper up I'll grind them so full of holes that they'll look like they was put through a sawmill.

[1] The discussion leader never refers to the camper as "Ears" although it is printed here for purposes of easy identification.

DISCUSSION LEADER.   How about it, Rusty?

RUSTY.   I don't have to say a goddamn thing.

DISCUSSION LEADER.   Look, you guys have got almost three more weeks out here at camp. The way things are going now, I don't think you can live with each other that long without working out some of the things that are bothering you.

Let us take our first brief recess from the interview at this point. The discussion leader is stressing as vividly as possible an elemental piece of social reality. In their present state of tension this has yet to penetrate the group's awareness. The keynote for the meeting is set: to survive together for the next three weeks we have to get down to the business of working out our problems. Let's return to our meeting and observe the impact of this on Rusty's defiant, clam-up mechanism.

RUSTY.   Well, that S.O.B. [*pointing to Jim*] doesn't have to insult me.

DISCUSSION LEADER.   How does he insult you?

RUSTY [*smiling in embarrassment*].   He keeps calling me "stale crusty."

JIM [*in great indignation*].   Oh, you bastard, how 'bout when Tony calls you that? I don't see you smacking him around and he even tells other guys to do it.

DISCUSSION LEADER.   How about that, Rusty?

RUSTY.   I can let whoever I want to call me that. I don't have to take it from Jim though.

DISCUSSION LEADER.   I don't mean that part of it. I agree with that. But how about the other thing that Jim said, that about Tony egging on the other guys to call you stale-crusty and then you turning around and pounding them for it?

TONY.   I suppose you're gonna tell us what we can say or not! Did you ever hear of freedom of speech?

Here we see Tony suddenly taking up the defense. For, trained as he is in the logic of group behavior, as befits a good delinquent leader, he sees the interviewer's last statement for what it is—a beginning attack on his manipulation of the group power structure.

DISCUSSION LEADER.   I'm only asking Rusty how he squares it with himself to pound other guys for what *you* seem to put them up to.

This is a feint by the discussion leader which has a double strategic purpose. It alludes to Tony's petty Machiavellianism while it confronts Rusty with something of a value issue: is it right to vent on other guys a fury which is really inspired by Tony? But Tony, not Rusty, carries on the counter-attack with a swift change in tactics.

TONY [*with menacing facial leers and yet, with a hint of childlike in-*

dignation]. Listen—I have moods. When I was in the detention home
I talked to the psychiatrist about them but I don't have to talk to you
about them, see. And when I have moods I do what I want, see!

Here we are beginning to obtain a picture of Tony's rationale. He is
a sick guy—certified as such by no less an authority than the psychiatrist
at the detention home. And he maneuvers himself away from guilt about
his acts as nimbly as he maneuvers the group into doing what he wishes.
He fights fire with fire. In this case the admission of sickness is turned
against the clinical invaders. When he has moods he can do what he
wants. And now, let us watch Rusty, who having been cued in by Tony,
springs alertly into the breech.

RUSTY.   Goddamit! He has moods and I have a brother who pounds
hell outa me at home and I'm not gonna take anything from anybody out
here. And I told it all to a visiting teacher at my school, whatever that
bag's name is, and I don't have to talk about it out here and I'm not.

JIM [*with a fine sarcastic fury*].   Oh, sure. HE [*pointing to Tony*]
has moods and HE [*designating Rusty*] has a brother who beats hell out
of him so he turns around and beats hell outa me and around and around
we go and where does that leave me?

Now we have one of the fascinating spectacles of the group interview. Here are these three tough, anti-verbal, casework-hardened youngsters one after another spitting out vital case history information. They
don't want to talk, least of all about themselves, but even when they use
their case histories to defeat our clinical effort, as Tony and Rusty are
doing, they bring a valuable piece of grist to our clinical mill. They confront us with the spectacle of their case histories clashing with one another. The scene they draw for themselves (better than a trained therapist
could) can now be turned into a tool for surgery on their group pathology.
Let's return to Jim, who, having so acidly etched out for us his plight in
the pincer of Tony's moods and Rusty's brother hatred, waits sardonically
for the discussion leader to reply.

DISCUSSION LEADER.   O.K. Jim, you're a good psychiatrist when it
comes to Tony and Rusty, let's see what you can do about yourself. Whom
do you turn around and pound?

JIM [*who knows his Fifth Amendment as well as the next one*].   I
don't have to talk a damn word.

DISCUSSION LEADER.   Yes, Jim, but how did the trouble start with Ears
today?

EARS.   Yeh, ask him, ask him. All I'm doing is reading my comic and
this guy Jim starts climbing up on my bunk and yanking at my feet and
yelling, "Hey Ears!" And when I say please get off and he don't, I push
him and then he blows his top and starts heaving around and I get hit.

DISCUSSION LEADER.   Isn't that part of the answer of where you're left, Jim? You turn around and pound Ears.

JIM [*angrily*].   Well, I'm not gonna take it from those bastards.

With this resistive remark Jim shows that he has understood our interpretive maneuver designed to clarify the chain of aggression between Tony, Rusty, himself, and Ears. What we will have to try to show him is that just as he shouldn't take it from them, he has a certain moral blindness in taking it out on Ears. This will be, perhaps, the topic of some of the post group-interview case work sessions we will have.

The interview continues:

DISCUSSION LEADER.   How about the stale-crusty crack?

HOWIE.   Aw, hell, Tony started that this morning.

DISCUSSION LEADER.   How about it, Tony?

TONY [*refuses to comment*].   The other group members look at Tony and remain silent.

DISCUSSION LEADER.   All the guys here seem to want to stay in good with you, Tony. They won't say anything.

TONY [*jeeringly*].   Because they're my friends, that's why.

DISCUSSION LEADER.   Well, Tony, I think that's swell, but it also seems like it's part of the trouble too. Let me tell you how it looks to me from what you have been saying. The guys like you; they want you to like them. O.K., then you have moods. Why you have them I don't know. But when you have them, for some reason you seem to get kind of mean. You have learned how to make guys fight with each other to stay in good with you. I guess when you have these mean moods you want them to do that.

TONY.   Who do you think you are, a psychiatrist or something? Hey, let's call him psycho, guys.

The interpretation threatens Tony. No leader wants his own psychology to be clearly understood by his submissive following. So what he does is to try to defame the discussion leader. For who is more to be feared and despised by the acting-out delinquent than a psychiatrist? Tony's subtle yet clear challenge to the group is: "Going to believe what he says—this imitation psycho?" It is now clearly the time to anoint Tony's wound and to take the pressure off while we simultaneously summarize the group problem as this part of the group interview has highlighted it:

DISCUSSION LEADER.   Look, Tony—this is not pleasant. I don't blame you for being a little sore. But let's be reasonable. It seems that you have a problem that we are going to have to work out if the guys in the cabin, including you, are going to have a decent time in camp. And you're not the only one with a problem either. Rusty here has a brother that pounds him so he is ramming around looking for a fight. Jim has a bad temper and he'd knock somebody silly if he wasn't stopped when he blows his top. Each guy is handing it out to another guy who either doesn't like to fight or who can't fight so well. Certainly you three guys —Tony, Rusty, and Jim—are going to have to work on that. Can anybody tell me why Ears has to take it from Jim, or Jim from Rusty, or Rusty be teased into fighting by Tony? [*no group comment*]

DISCUSSION LEADER.   My suggestion would be to talk it over with your counselor and also with some of the special people we have out here to help with your problems [*here the casework staff, whom they all know, are specified*]. Anytime you want to get together again as a group I'll be glad to talk to you.

We have tried to illustrate, through a synopsis of one type of group session at the Fresh Air Camp, the role of the group interview in the clinical management of the kind of boys who comprise a significant percentage of our clientele. Children with different pathologies of course react much differently than this group did. Some are quiet, some anxious and guilty. Some of the older boys seem to develop a fascination for the "round table" and ask for sessions on their own. There are times too when skilled adult leadership is needed to manage the intensity of emotional outbursts during the sessions. Seen in terms of the total clinical design of the camp, the group interview emerges as a valuable tool in coping with the problems these youngsters bring with them to the camp setting. It is seen as serving a variety of functions and as utilizing various processes that are specific to the group psychological scene. These processes serve to concretize individual pathologies which may become sources of conflict for the group. While it is a valuable tool, the group interview is still only one of many strategies that must be woven closely together for the most efficient clinical action against the pathology in these children. The most important aids to group interviewing are the followup by individual casework and the counselor handling of these issues when they arise again. The group interview seems to pave the way for an easy entré to these problems on future occasions, and the campers seem willing to use material from these meetings as a starting point for further discussion.

It should be recalled that each group session, and series of sessions with the same cabin, has its own characteristics. With the eight-year olds it is difficult to produce any problem-solving pattern while with the ten- and eleven-year olds there is discernible movement, during the session, from savage attack to workable solution. We are currently studying tape recordings of these group sessions to gain a fuller understanding of the shifting dynamics of the group in this situation. A particularly interesting phenomenon we have observed is the shift in content in the interviews following the discussion leader's understanding acceptance of guilt-producing behavior on the part of the boys. Hostility and tension seem to melt, and the campers reveal real empathy when, out of concern over the meaning of their own behavior, they discuss individual and group needs and problems. More needs to be known about how these defenses are penetrated and of the subsequent effect of such sessions on the group life.

63. TEACHER—ANNE SULLIVAN MACY

HELEN KELLER

Helen Keller's teacher, in helping the deaf, dumb, and blind child to make contact with the world, also found her own way back to society. What enabled this institutionalized orphan girl, herself plagued by poverty, isolation, prejudice, and half-blindness, to find the patience, kindness, strength, and persistence to provide both Helen's salvation and her own? Here Miss Keller herself describes this twofold miracle.

I

A daughter of Irish immigrants, at that time the most despised social group in the Northeast, Annie Sullivan was born in squalid poverty on April 4, 1866, in Feeding Hills, Massachusetts, and as far back as she could remember she had had trouble with her eyes. They still bothered her. Her mother died when she was eight years old, leaving two other children. Her father abandoned all three two years later and Annie never learned what became of him. Her younger sister Mary was placed with relatives and Annie and her seven-year-old brother Jimmie were sent to the State Infirmary, the almshouse, at Tewksbury, Annie because she was difficult to manage and too blind to be useful, Jimmie because he was becoming helplessly lame with a tubercular hip.

They entered the almshouse in February 1876 and Jimmie died in May. Annie stayed four years. No one outside was interested in her and she had no friends but her fellow paupers. It was one of them who told her that there were special schools for the blind and as time went on— she lost track of time in Tewksbury—her desire for an education grew. To escape from the pit of degradation and disease in which she lived seemed impossible until the stench from the almshouse rose so high that the State Board of Charities ordered an investigation. The investigators did not discover her. The inmates knew the name of the chairman and when the committee members arrived she flung herself towards them, unable to distinguish one from another, and cried out, "Mr. Sanborn, Mr. Sanborn, I want to go to school!"

She reached the Perkins Institution in October 1880 and there, at the age of fourteen, began her education by learning to read with her fingers. The school had no facilities for taking care of its pupils during vacations and when summer came she was put out to work in a rooming house in Boston. Through one of the lodgers she found her way to the Massachusetts Eye and Ear Infirmary and in August Dr. Bradford performed an operation on her left eye. The next August he attended to the right eye and when the operations were over Annie could see well enough to read in the ordinary way for limited periods of time, but not well enough to warrant transfer to a school for the seeing. She remained at Perkins for six years, graduating in 1886 as valedictorian of her class. The school had done what it could. The rest was up to her.

She recognized her handicaps—her meager years of education, her lack of contact with the amenities of gracious living, and, above all, her uncertain, precarious sight—but she had hoped for something more exciting than looking after a deaf-blind child. Captain Keller's offer was the best she had. After she had accepted it she spent some months reading Dr. Howe's reports on Laura Bridgman, a painful task because of her eyes. She already knew the manual alphabet. Like her schoolmates, she had learned it so as to talk with Laura, who was still cloistered at the Perkins Institution because she had never been able to adapt herself to any other kind of life. And yet Laura was the mark to aim at. No other deaf-blind person had come near the peak upon which she stood.

Red-eyed from another operation on her eyes and from crying with homesickness, Annie Sullivan arrived in Tuscumbia on March 3, 1887, a date that Helen has always cherished as her "soul's birthday." She began at once spelling into Helen's hand, suiting the word to the action, the action to the word, and the child responded by imitating the finger motions like a bright, inquisitive animal. It took a month to reach the human mind. On April 5, a date not second to March 3 in importance, the Phantom Helen made contact with reality. While Annie Sullivan pumped water over her hand it came to the child in a flash that water, wherever it was found, was water, and that the finger motions she had just felt on her palm meant water and nothing else. In that thrilling moment she found the key to her kingdom. Everything had a name and she had a way to learn the names. She formed a question by pointing to Annie Sullivan. "Teacher," Annie replied.

From that date Helen's progress was so rapid that educators soon became aware that a great teacher was at work, greater even than Dr. Howe. At the age of ten Helen announced that she was going to learn to talk with her mouth like other people instead of with her fingers like a deaf person, and when, after eleven lessons in oral speech she was able to say, however haltingly, "I-am-not-dumb-now," there seemed no limit to what she might achieve. But a fragmentation had occurred in public opinion. One segment pushed the teacher aside and called Helen a miracle. Another gave the whole credit to the teacher and called Helen an automaton. . . .

That hurt—it still hurts. But there were a few, notable among them Dr. Bell, who understood that it was the combination of gifted, intuitive teacher and eager, intelligent pupil that was producing the astonishing results. Helen and Teacher kept to their course, never apart, and Helen went on to Radcliffe College, entering in 1900 when she was twenty years old and coming out four years later with a *cum laude* degree won in open competition with girls who could see and hear. But even this was not enough. As long as Annie Sullivan lived, and she died in 1936, a question remained as to how much of what was called Helen Keller was in reality Annie Sullivan. The answer is not simple. During the creative years neither could have done without the other.

. . . . .

II

It was a bright, clear spark from Teacher's soul that beat back the sooty flames of thwarted desire and temper in little Helen's no-world. That spark was the word "water." Compassion in the old sense does not describe the springs of Teacher's motives. Her disbelief in nature as an unfailing friend of humanity lay back of her efforts to liberate Helen— "Phantom" I prefer to call the little being governed only by animal impulses, and not often those of a docile beast. Teacher's fight against her own blindness began in her childhood, and the partial restoration of her sight while she was in school at Perkins Institution for the Blind in Boston had not ended her struggle to maintain her ascendancy over nature. That struggle lasted as long as her earth-life.

Secretly or openly she always resented what seemed to her the purposeless evils that had marred her sight and laid waste the health, sanity, and happiness of millions throughout the world. How ruthless then was her assault upon the blindness, deafness, and muteness that bound her little pupil in triple dungeon of thwarted instincts. Boldly she resolved to put herself in the place of nature and topple it from its aimless supremacy over Helen by substituting love and inventive thought for the unconscious cruelty of the child's fate.

This is a period in Teacher's life which distresses me to remember. Naturally I wish that after the intoxicating tide of delight that swept over her when the operations made it possible for her to read with her eyes, she might have found a child responsive to her sympathetic touch. But, alas! Phantom had no sense of "natural" bonds with humanity. All the sweetness of childhood created by friendly voices and the light of smiling faces was dormant in her. She did not understand obedience or appreciate kindness. I remember her as plump, strong, reckless, and unafraid. She refused to be led, and had to be carried by force upstairs when she received her first lesson. Another time her table manners required correction. Phantom was in the habit of picking food out of her own plate and the plates of others with her fingers. Annie Sullivan would not put up with such behavior, and a fight followed during which the family left the room. Phantom acted like a demon, kicking, screaming, pinching her would-be deliverer and almost throwing her out of her chair, but Annie succeeded in compelling her to eat with a spoon and keep her hands out of the plate. Then Phantom threw her napkin on the floor, and after an hour's battle Annie made her pick it up and fold it. One morning Phantom would not sit down to learn words which meant nothing to her, and kicked over the table. When Annie put the table back in its place and insisted on continuing the lesson, Phantom's fist flew like lightning and knocked out two of Annie's teeth.

A sorrier situation never confronted a young woman on fire with a noble purpose. Phantom's parents were apt to interfere whenever attempts were made to discipline her. For this reason Annie won their consent to get her away to a quiet place, and, at their suggestion, took the child to a vine-covered annex near the homestead, Ivy Green. The furniture was changed so that Phantom would not recognize it—my smell memory too is different—and it was agreed that the family would come to them every day, without letting Helen know of their visits. From Teacher's later testimony I know that the two were, so to speak, caged in the annex, and I marvel that Annie dared to stay alone with such a menace to her personal safety.

Already I have referred to several fights between Annie and Phantom, not because I have any coherent or detailed remembrance of them, but because they indicate the grueling nature of the work Teacher had undertaken. In *The Story of My Life*, which I wrote with the carelessness of a happy, positive young girl, I failed to stress sufficiently the obstacles and hardships which confronted Teacher—and there are other defects in the book which my mature sense of her sacrifice will not permit to go uncorrected.

In my memory of the annex I am conscious of a Phantom lost in what seemed to her new surroundings. I perceive sudden jerks, pulls, and blows not dealt by Annie but by Phantom herself trying to escape restraining arms. How like a wild colt she was, plunging and kicking! Certainly it was a sturdy Phantom who belabored her supposed enemy. There comes back to me a scuffle round and round an object that my touch recollections represent as a bed, and a firm gesture of Annie to make her lie down or get up and dress.

Phantom had no sense of time, and it was years before she learned of the many exhausting hours which Annie spent trying to bring her under control without breaking her spirit. Even that was only partly accomplished when the two went home. Then Phantom grew angry over Annie's repeated attempts to impress upon her the difference between "water" and "mug." Tactually I recall quick footsteps in the room, a hand—my mother's—seizing Phantom and dragging her away for a sound spanking. After that Phantom began to improve, but still she lacked the normal child's love of praise. She was not aware that she had been punished because she did not distinguish between right and wrong. Her body was growing, but her mind was chained in darkness as the spirit of fire within the flint. But at last, on April 5, 1880, almost exactly a month after her arrival in Tuscumbia, Annie reached Phantom's consciousness with the word "water." This happened at the well-house. Phantom had a mug in her hand and while she held it under the spout Annie pumped water into it and as it gushed over the hand that held the mug she kept spelling w-a-t-e-r into the other hand. Suddenly Phantom understood the meaning of the word, and her mind began to flutter tiny wings of flame. Caught up in the first joy she had felt since her illness, she reached out eagerly to Annie's ever-ready hand, begging for new words to identify whatever objects she touched. Spark after spark of meaning flew through her mind until her heart was warmed and affection was born. From the well-house there walked two enraptured beings calling each other "Helen" and "Teacher." Surely such moments of delight contain a fuller life than an eternity of darkness.

64. THE DISCOVERY AND ENCOURAGEMENT OF EXCEPTIONAL TALENT

LEWIS M. TERMAN

After studying intelligence for over fifty years, Terman summarized in an address delivered in 1954, his research on children of high talent. Exploding the myths that genius is akin to insanity and that

Selections reprinted from *American Psychologist,* 9 (1954), 221–230, by permission of T. E. Terman, Executor of the Estate of Lewis M. Terman, and of the American Psychological Association.

talented children soon "burn themselves out," his studies revealed that superior children are healthier, better adjusted than average, and continue to be superior through adulthood.

I have often been asked how I happened to become interested in mental tests and gifted children. My first introduction to the scientific problems posed by intellectual differences occurred well over a half-century ago when I was a senior in psychology at Indiana University and was asked to prepare two reports for a seminar, one on mental deficiency and one on genius. Up to that time, despite the fact that I had graduated from a normal college as a Bachelor of Pedagogy and had taught school for five years, I had never so much as heard of a mental test. The reading for those two reports opened up a new world to me, the world of Galton, Binet, and their contemporaries. The following year my MA thesis on leadership among children (Terman, 1904) was based in part on tests used by Binet in his studies of suggestibility.

Then I entered Clark University, where I spent considerable time during the first year in reading on mental tests and precocious children. Child prodigies, I soon learned, were at that time in bad repute because of the prevailing belief that they were usually psychotic or otherwise abnormal and almost sure to burn themselves out quickly or to develop postadolescent stupidity. "Early ripe, early rot" was a slogan frequently encountered. By the time I reached my last graduate year, I decided to find out for myself how precocious children differ from the mentally backward, and accordingly chose as my doctoral dissertation an experimental study of the intellectual processes of fourteen boys, seven of them picked as the brightest and seven as the dullest in a large city school (Terman, 1906). These subjects I put through a great variety of intelligence tests, some of them borrowed from Binet and others, many of them new. The tests were given individually and required a total of 40 or 50 hours for each subject. The experiment contributed little or nothing to science, but it contributed a lot to my future thinking. Besides "selling" me completely on the value of mental tests as a research method, it offered an ideal escape from the kinds of laboratory work which I disliked and in which I was more than ordinarily inept. (Edward Thorndike confessed to me once that *his* lack of mechanical skill was partly responsible for turning *him* to mental tests and to the kinds of experiments on learning that required no apparatus.)

However, it was not until I got to Stanford in 1910 that I was able to pick up with mental tests where I had left off at Clark University. By that time Binet's 1905 and 1908 scales had been published, and the first thing I undertook at Stanford was a tentative revision of his 1908 scale. This, after further revisions, was published in 1916. The standardization of the scale was based on tests of a thousand children whose IQ's ranged from 60 to 145. The contrast in intellectual performance between the dullest and the brightest of a given age so intensified my earlier interest in the gifted that I decided to launch an ambitious study of such children at the earliest opportunity.

My dream was realized in the spring of 1921 when I obtained a generous grant from the Commonwealth Fund of New York City for the purpose of locating a thousand subjects of IQ 140 or higher. More than that number were selected by Stanford-Binet tests from the kindergarten through the eighth grade, and a group mental test given in 95 high schools provided nearly 400 additional subjects. The latter, plus those I had located before 1921, brought the number close to 1,500. The average IQ was approximately 150, and 80 were 170 or higher (Terman *et al.*, 1925).

The twofold purpose of the project was, first of all, to find what traits characterize children of high IQ, and secondly, to follow them for as many years as possible to see what kind of adults they might become. This meant that it was necessary to select a group representative of high-testing children in general. With the help of four field assistants, we canvassed a school population of nearly a quarter-million in the urban and semi-urban areas of California. Two careful checks on the methods used showed that not more than 10 or 12 per cent of the children who could have qualified for the group in the schools canvassed were missed. A sample of close to 90 per cent insured that whatever traits were typical of these children would be typical of high-testing children in any comparable school population.

Time does not permit me to describe the physical measurements, medical examinations, achievement tests, character and interest tests, or the trait ratings and other supplementary information obtained from parents and teachers. Nor can I here describe the comparative data we obtained for control groups of unselected children. The more important results, however, can be stated briefly: children of IQ 140 or higher are, in general, appreciably superior to unselected children in physique, health, and social adjustment; markedly superior in moral attitudes as measured either by character tests or by trait ratings; and vastly superior in their mastery of school subjects as shown by a three-hour battery of achievement tests. In fact, the typical child of the group had mastered the school subjects to a point about two grades beyond the one in which he was enrolled, some of them three or four grades beyond. Moreover, his ability as evidenced by achievement in the different school subjects is so general as to refute completely the traditional belief that gifted children are usually one-sided. I take some pride in the fact that not one of the major conclusions we drew in the early 1920's regarding the traits that are typical of gifted children has been overthrown in the three decades since then.

Results of thirty years' follow-up of these subjects by field studies in 1927–28, 1939–40, and 1951–52, and by mail follow-up at other dates, show that the incidence of mortality, ill health, insanity, and alcoholism is in each case below that for the generality of corresponding age, that the great majority are still well adjusted socially, and that the delinquency rate is but a fraction of what it is in the general population. Two forms of our difficult Concept Mastery Test, devised especially to reach into the stratosphere of adult intelligence, have been administered to all members of the group who could be visited by the field assistants, including some 950 tested in 1939–40 and more than 1,000 in 1951–52. On both tests they scored on the average about as far above the generality of adults as they had scored above the generality of children when we selected them. Moreover, as Dr. Bayley and Mrs. Oden have shown, in the twelve-year interval between the two tests, 90 per cent increased their intellectual stature as measured by this test. "Early ripe, early rot" simply does not hold for these subjects. So far, no one has developed postadolescent stupidity!

As for schooling, close to 90 per cent entered college and 70 per cent graduated. Of those graduating, 30 per cent were awarded honors and about two-thirds remained for graduate work. The educational record would have been still better but for the fact that a majority reached college age during the great depression. In their undergraduate years 40 per cent of the men and 20 per cent of the women earned half or more of their college expenses, and the total of undergraduate and graduate expenses earned amounted to $670,000, not counting stipends from scholarships and fellowships, which amounted to $350,000.

The cooperation of the subjects is indicated by the fact that we have been able to keep track of more than 98 per cent of the original group, thanks to the rapport fostered by the incomparable field and office assistants I have had from the beginning of the study to the present. I dislike to think how differently things could have gone with helpers even a little less competent.

The achievement of the group to midlife is best illustrated by the case histories of the 800 men, since only a minority of the women have gone out for professional careers (Terman, 1954). By 1950, when the men had an average age of 40 years, they had published 67 books (including 46 in the fields of science, arts, and the humanities, and 21 books of fiction). They had published more than 1,400 scientific, technical, and professional articles; over 200 short stories, novelettes, and plays; and 236 miscellaneous articles on a great variety of subjects. They had also authored more than 150 patents. The figures on publications do not include the hundreds of publications by journalists that classify as news stories, editorials, or newspaper columns; nor do they include the hundreds if not thousands of radio and TV scripts.

The 800 men include 78 who have taken a PhD degree or its equivalent, 48 with a medical degree, 85 with a law degree, 74 who are teaching or have taught in a four-year college or university, 51 who have done basic research in the physical sciences or engineering, and 104 who are engineers but have done only applied research or none. Of the scientists, 47 are listed in the 1949 edition of *American Men of Science*. Nearly all of these numbers are from 10 to 20 or 30 times as large as would be found for 800 men of corresponding age picked at random in the general population, and are sufficient answer to those who belittle the significance of IQ differences.

The follow-up of these gifted subjects has proved beyond question that tests of "general intelligence," given as early as six, eight, or ten years, tell a great deal about the ability to achieve either presently or 30 years hence. Such tests do not, however, enable us to predict what direction the achievement will take, and least of all do they tell us what personality factors or what accidents of fortune will affect the fruition of exceptional ability. Granting that both interest patterns and special aptitudes play important roles in the making of a gifted scientist, mathematician, mechanic, artist, poet, or musical composer, I am convinced that to achieve greatly in almost any field, the special talents have to be backed up by a lot of Spearman's g, by which is meant the kind of general intelligence that requires ability to form many sharply defined concepts, to manipulate them, and to perceive subtle relationships between them; in other words, the ability to engage in abstract thinking.

The study by Catharine Cox (1926) of the childhood traits of historical geniuses gives additional evidence regarding the role of general intelligence in exceptional achievement. That study was part of our original plan to investigate superior ability by two methods of approach: (a) by identifying and following living gifted subjects from childhood onward; and (b) by proceeding in the opposite direction and tracing the mature genius back to his childhood promise. With a second grant from the Commonwealth Fund, the latter approach got under way only a year later than the former and resulted in the magnum opus by Cox entitled *The Early Mental Traits of Three Hundred Geniuses* (1926). Her subjects represented an unbiased selection from the top 510 in Cattell's objectively compiled list of the 1,000 most eminent men of history. Cox and two able assistants then scanned some 3,000 biographies in search of information that would throw light on the early mental development of these subjects. The information thus obtained filled more than 6,000 typed pages. Next, three psychologists familiar with mental age norms read the documentary evidence on all the subjects and estimated for each the IQ that presumably would be necessary to account for the intellectual behavior recorded for given chronological ages. Average of the three IQ estimates was used as the index of intelligence. In fact two IQ's were estimated for each subject, one based on the evidence to age 17, and the other on evidence to the mid-twenties. The recorded evidence on development to age 17 varied from very little to an amount that yielded about as valid an IQ as a good intelligence test would give. Examples of the latter are Goethe, John Stuart Mill, and Francis Galton. It was the documentary information on Galton, which I summarized and published in 1917 (Terman, 1917), that decided me to prepare plans for the kind of study that was carried out by Cox. The average of estimated IQ's for her 300 geniuses was 155, with many going as high as 175 and several as high as 200. Estimates below 120 occurred only when there was little biographical evidence about the early years.

It is easy to scoff at these post-mortem IQ's, but as one of the three psychologists who examined the evidence and made the IQ ratings, I think the author's main conclusion is fully warranted; namely, that "the genius who achieves highest eminence is one whom intelligence tests would have identified as gifted in childhood."

Special attention was given the geniuses who had sometime or other been labeled as backward in childhood, and in every one of these cases the facts clearly contradicted the legend. One of them was Oliver Goldsmith, of whom his childhood teacher is said to have said "Never was so dull a boy." The fact is that little Oliver was writing clever verse at 7 years and at 8 was reading Ovid and Horace. Another was Sir Walter Scott, who at 7 not only read widely in poetry but was using correctly in his written prose such words as "melancholy" and exotic." Other alleged childhood dullards included a number who disliked the usual diet of Latin and Greek but had a natural talent for science. Among these were the celebrated German chemist Justus von Liebig, the great English anatomist John Hunter, and the naturalist Alexander von Humboldt, whose name is scattered so widely over the maps of the world.

In the cases just cited one notes a tendency for the direction of later achievement to be foreshadowed by the interests and preoccupations of childhood. I have tried to determine how frequently this was true of the 100 subjects in Cox's group whose childhood was best documented. Very marked foreshadowing was noted in the case of more than half of the group, none at all in less than a fourth. Macaulay, for example, began his career as historian at the age of 6 with what he called a "Compendium of Universal History," filling a quire of paper before he lost interest in the project. Ben Franklin before the age of 17 had displayed nearly all the traits that characterized him in middle life: scientific curiosity, religious heterodoxy, wit and buffoonery, political and business shrewdness, and ability to write. At 11 Pascal was so interested in mathematics that his father thought it best to deprive him of books on this subject until he had first mastered Latin and Greek. Pascal secretly proceeded to construct a geometry of his own and covered the ground as far as the 32nd proposition of Euclid. His father then relented. At 14 Leibnitz was writing on logic and philosophy and composing what he called "An Alphabet of Human

Thought." He relates that at this age he took a walk one afternoon to consider whether he should accept the "doctrine of substantial forms."

Similar foreshadowing is disclosed by the case histories of my gifted subjects. A recent study of the scientists and nonscientists among our 800 gifted men (Terman, 1954) showed many highly significant differences between the early interests and social attitudes of those who became physical scientists and those who majored in the social sciences, law, or the humanities. Those in medical or biological sciences usually rated on such variables somewhere between the physical scientists and the nonscientists.

What I especially want to emphasize, however, is that both the evidence on early mental development of historical geniuses and that obtained by follow-up of gifted subjects selected in childhood by mental tests point to the conclusion that capacity to achieve far beyond the average can be detected early in life by a well-constructed ability test that is heavily weighted with the g factor. It remains to be seen how much the prediction of future achievement can be made more specific as to field by getting, in addition, measures of ability factors that are largely independent of g. It would seem that a 20-year follow-up of the thousands of school children who have been given Thurstone's test of seven "primary mental abilities" would help to provide the answer. At present the factor analysts don't agree on how many "primary" mental abilities there are, nor exactly on what they are. The experts in this field are divided into two schools. The British school, represented by Thomson, Vernon, and Burt, usually stop with the identification of at most three or four group factors in addition to g, while some representing the American school feed the scores of 40 or 50 kinds of tests into a hopper and managed to extract from them what they believe to be a dozen or fifteen separate factors. Members of the British school are as a rule very skeptical about the realities underlying the minor group factors. There are also American psychologists, highly skilled in psychometrics, who share this skepticism. It is to be hoped that further research will give us more information than we now have about the predictive value of the group factors. Until such information is available, the scores on group factors can contribute little to vocational guidance beyond what a good test of general intelligence will provide.

I have always stressed the importance of *early* discovery of exceptional abilities. Its importance is now highlighted by the facts Harvey Lehman (1953) has disclosed in his monumental studies of the relation between age and creative achievement. The striking thing about his age curves is how early in life the period of maximum creativity is reached. In nearly all fields of science, the best work is done between ages 25 and 35, and rarely later than 40. The peak productivity for works of lesser merit is usually reached 5 to 20 years later; this is true in some twenty fields of science, in philosophy, in most kinds of musical composition, in art, and in literature of many varieties. The lesson for us from Lehman's statistics is that the youth of high achievement potential should be well trained for his life work before too many of his most creative years have been passed.

This raises the issue of educational acceleration for the gifted. It seems that the schools are more opposed to acceleration now than they were thirty years ago. The lockstep seems to have become more and more the fashion, notwithstanding the fact that practically everyone who has investigated the subject is against it. Of my gifted group, 29 per cent managed to graduate from high school before the age of 16½ years (62 of these before 15½), but I doubt if so many would be allowed to do so now. The other 71 per cent graduated between 16½ and 18½. We have compared the accelerated with the nonaccelerated on numerous case-history variables. The two groups differed very little in childhood IQ, their health records are equally good, and as adults they are equally well adjusted socially. More of the accelerates graduated from college, and on the average nearly a year and a half earlier than the nonaccelerates; they averaged high in college grades and more often remained for graduate work. Moreover, the accelerates on the average married .7 of a year earlier, have a trifle lower divorce rate, and score just a little higher on a test of marital happiness (Terman and Oden, 1947). So far as college records of accelerates and nonaccelerates are concerned, our data closely parallel those obtained by the late Noel Keys (1938) at the University of California and those by Pressey (1949) and his associates at Ohio State University.

The Ford Fund for the Advancement of Education (1953) has awarded annually since 1951 some 400 college scholarships to gifted students who are not over 16½ years old, are a year or even two years short of high school graduation, but show good evidence of ability to do college work. Three quarters of them are between 15½ and 16½ at the time of college entrance. A dozen colleges and universities accept these students and are keeping close track of their success. A summary of their records for the first year shows that they not only get higher grades than their classmates, who average about two years older, but that they are also equally well adjusted socially and participate in as many extracurricular activities. The main problem the boys have is in finding girls to date who are not too old for them! Some of them started a campaign to remedy the situation by urging that more of these scholarships be awarded to girls.

The facts I have given do not mean that all gifted children should be rushed through school just as rapidly as possible. If that were done, a majority with IQ of 140 could graduate from high school before the age of 15. I do believe, however, that such children should be promoted rapidly enough to permit college entrance by the age of 17 at latest, and that a majority would be better off to enter at 16. The exceptionally bright student who is kept with his age group finds little to challenge his intelligence and all too often develops habits of laziness that later wreck his college career. I could give you some choice examples of this in my gifted group. In the case of a college student who is preparing for a profession in science, medicine, law, or any field of advanced scholarship, graduation at 20 instead of the usual 22 means two years added to his professional career; or the two years saved could be used for additional training beyond the doctorate, if that were deemed preferable.

Learned and Wood (1938) have shown by objective achievement tests in some 40 Pennsylvania colleges how little correlation there is between the student's knowledge and the number of months or years of his college attendance. They found some beginning sophomores who had acquired more knowledge than some seniors near their graduation. They found similarly low correlations between the number of course units a student had in a given field and the amount he knew in that field. Some with only one year of Latin had learned more than others with three years. And, believe it or not, they even found boys just graduating from high school who had more knowledge of science than some college seniors who had majored in science and were about to begin teaching science in high schools! The sensible thing to do, it seems, would be to quit crediting the individual high school or the individual college and begin crediting the individual student. That, essentially, is what the Ford Fund scholarships are intended to encourage.

Instruments that permit the identification of gifted subjects are available in great variety and at nearly all levels from the primary grades to the graduate schools in universities.

. . . . .

I have discussed only tests of intelligence and of school achievement. There is time to mention only a few of the many kinds of personality tests that have been developed during the last thirty-five years: personality inventories, projective techniques by the dozen, attitude scales by the hundred, interest tests, tests of psychotic and predelinquent tendencies, tests of leadership, marital aptitude, masculinity-femininity, et cetera. The current output of research on personality tests probably equals or exceeds that on intelligence and achievement tests, and is even more exciting.

Along with the increasing use of tests, and perhaps largely as a result of it, there is a growing interest, both here and abroad, in improving educational methods for the gifted. Acceleration of a year or two or three, however desirable, is but a fraction of what is needed to keep the gifted child or youth working at his intellectual best. The method most often advocated is curriculum enrichment for the gifted without segregating them from the ordinary class. Under ideal conditions enrichment can accomplish much, but in these days of crowded schools, when so many teachers are overworked, underpaid, and inadequately trained, curriculum enrichment for a few gifted in a large mixed class cannot begin to solve the problem. The best survey of thought and action in this field of education is the book entitled *The Gifted Child*, written by many authors and published in 1951 (Witty). In planning for and sponsoring this book, The American Association for Gifted Children has rendered a great service to education.

But however efficient our tests may be in discovering exceptional talents, and whatever the schools may do to foster those discovered, it is the prevailing *Zeitgeist* that will decide, by the rewards it gives or withholds, what talents will come to flower. In Western Europe of the Middle Ages, the favored talents were those that served the Church by providing its priests, the architects of its cathedrals, and the painters of religious themes. A few centuries later the same countries had a renaissance that included science and literature as well as the arts. Although presumably there are as many potential composers of great music as there ever were, and as many potentially great artists as in the days of Leonardo da Vinci and Michaelangelo, I am reliably informed that in this country today it is almost impossible for a composer of *serious* music to earn his living except by teaching, and that the situation is much the same, though somewhat less critical, with respect to artists.

The talents most favored by the current *Zeitgeist* are those that can contribute to science and technology. If intelligence and achievement tests don't discover the potential scientist, there is a good chance that the annual Science Talent Search will, though not until the high school years. Since Westinghouse inaugurated in 1942 this annual search for the high school seniors most likely to become creative scientists, nearly 4,000 boys and girls have been picked for honors by Science Service out of the many thousands who have competed. As a result, "Science Clubs of America" now number 15,000 with a third of a million members—a twentyfold increase in a dozen years (Davis, 1953). As our need for more and better scientists is real and urgent, one can rejoice at what the talent search and the science clubs are accomplishing. One may regret, however, that the spirit of the times is not equally favorable to the discovery and encouragement of potential poets, prose writers, artists, statesmen, and social leaders.

But in addition to the over-all climates that reflect the *Zeitgeist*, there are localized climates that favor or hinder the encouragement of given talents in particular colleges and universities. I have in mind especially recent investigations of the differences among colleges in the later achievement of their graduates. One by Knapp and Goodrich (1952) dealt with the undergraduate origin of 18,000 scientists who got the bachelor's degree between 1924 and 1934 and were listed in the 1944 edition of *American Men of Science*. The list of 18,000 was composed chiefly of men who had taken a PhD degree, but included a few without a PhD who were starred scientists. The IBM cards of these men were then sorted according to the college from which they obtained the bachelor's degree, and an index of productivity was computed for each college in terms of the proportion of its male graduates who were in the list of 18,000. Some of the results were surprising, not to say sensational. The institutions that were most productive of future scientists between 1924 and 1934 were not the great universities, but the small liberal arts colleges. Reed College topped the list with an index of 132 per thousand male graduates. The California Institute of Technology was second with an index of 70. Kalamazoo College was third was 66, Earlham fourth with 57, and Oberlin fifth with 56. Only a half-dozen of the great universities were in the top fifty with a productivity index of 25 or more.

. . . .

The causes of these differences are not entirely clear. Scores on aptitude tests show that the intelligence of students in a given institution is by no means the sole factor, though it is an important one. Other important factors are the quality of the school's intellectual climate, the proportion of able and inspiring teachers on its faculty, and the amount of conscious effort that is made not only to discover but also to motivate the most highly gifted. The influence of motivation can hardly be exaggerated.

In this address I have twice alluded to the fact that achievement in school is influenced by many things other than the sum total of intellectual abilities. The same is true of success in life. In closing I will tell you briefly about an attempt we made a dozen years ago to identify some of the nonintellectual factors that have influenced life success among the men in my gifted group. Three judges, working independently, examined the records (to 1940) of the 730 men who were then 25 years or older, and rated each on life success. The criterion of "success" was the extent to which a subject had made use of his superior intellectual ability, little weight being given to earned income. The 150 men rated highest for success and the 150 rated lowest were then compared on some 200 items of information obtained from childhood onward (Terman and Oden, 1947). How did the two groups differ?

During the elementary school years, the A's and C's (as we call them) were almost equally successful. The average grades were about the same, and average scores on achievement tests were only a trifle higher for the A's. Early in high school the groups began to draw apart in scholarship, and by the end of high school the slump of the C's was quite marked. The slump could not be blamed on extracurricular activities, for these were almost twice as common among the A's. Nor was much of it due to difference in intelligence. Although the A's tested on the average a little higher than the C's both in 1922 and 1940, the average score made by the C's in 1940 was high enough to permit brilliant college work, in fact was equaled by only 15 per cent of our highly selected Stanford students. Of the A's, 97 per cent entered college and 90 per cent graduated; of the C's, 68 per cent entered but only 37 per cent graduated. Of those who graduated, 52 per cent of the A's but only 14 per cent of the C's graduated with honors. The A's were also more accelerated in school; on the average they were six months younger on completing the eighth grade, 10 months younger at high school graduation, and 15 months younger at graduation from college.

The differences between the educational histories of the A's and C's reflect to some degree the differences in their family backgrounds. Half of the A fathers but only 15 per cent of the C fathers were college graduates, and twice as many of A siblings as of C siblings graduated. The estimated number of books in the A homes was nearly 50 per cent greater than in the C homes. As of 1928, when the average age of the subjects was about 16 years, more than twice as many of the C parents as of A parents had been divorced.

Interesting differences between the groups were found in the childhood data on emotional stability, social adjustments, and various traits of personality. Of the 25 traits on which each child was rated by parent and teacher in 1922 (18 years before the A and C groups were made up), the only trait on which the C's averaged as high as the A's was general health. The superiority of the A's was especially marked in four volitional traits: prudence, self-confidence, perseverance, and desire to excel. The A's also rated significantly higher in 1922 on leadership, popularity, and sensitiveness to approval or disapproval. By 1940 the difference between the groups in social adjustment and all-round mental stability had greatly increased and showed itself in many ways. By that time four-fifths of the A's had married, but only two-thirds of the C's, and the divorce rate for those who had married was twice as high for the C's as for the A's. Moreover, the A's made better marriages; their wives on the average came from better homes, were better educated, and scored higher on intelligence tests.

But the most spectacular differences between the two groups came from three sets of ratings, made in 1940, on a dozen personality traits. Each man rated himself on all the traits, was rated on them by his wife if he had a wife, and by a parent if a parent was still living. Although the three sets of ratings were made independently, they agreed unanimously on the four traits in which the A and C groups differed most widely. These were "persistence in the accomplishment of ends," "integration toward goals, as contrasted with drifting," "self-confidence," and "freedom from inferiority feelings." For each trait three critical ratios were computed showing, respectively, the reliability of the A–C differences in average of self-ratings, ratings by wives, and ratings by parents. The average of the three critical ratios was 5.5 for perseverance, 5.6 for integration toward goals, 3.7 for self-confidence, and 3.1 for freedom from inferiority feelings. These closely parallel the traits that Cox (1926) found to be especially characteristic of the 100 leading geniuses in her group whom she rated on many aspects of personality; their three outstanding traits she defined as "persistence of motive and effort," "confidence in their abilities," and "strength or force of character."

There was one trait on which only the parents of our A and C men were asked to rate them; that trait was designated "common sense." As judged by parents, the A's are again reliably superior, the A–C difference in average rating having a critical ratio of 3.9. We are still wondering what self-ratings by the subjects and ratings of them by their wives on common sense would have shown if we had been impudent enough to ask for them!

Everything considered, there is nothing in which our A and C groups present a greater contrast than in drive to achieve and in all-round mental and social adjustment. Our data do not support the theory of Lange-Eichbaum (1932) that great achievement usually stems from emotional tensions that border on the abnormal. In our gifted group, success is associated with stability rather than instability, with absence rather than with presence of disturbing conflicts—in short with well-balance temperament and with freedom from excessive frustrations. The Lange-Eichbaum theory may explain a Hitler, but hardly a Churchill; the junior senator from Wisconsin, possibly, but not a Jefferson or a Washington.

At any rate, we have seen that intellect and achievement are far from perfectly correlated. To identify the internal and external factors that help or hinder the fruition of exceptional talent, and to measure the extent of their influences, are surely among the major problems of our time. These problems are not new; their existence has been recognized by countless men from Plato to Francis Galton. What is new is the general awareness of them caused by the manpower shortage of scientists, engineers, moral leaders, statesmen, scholars, and teachers that the country must have if it is to survive in a threatened world. These problems are now being investigated on a scale never before approached, and by a new generation of workers in several related fields. Within a couple of decades vastly more should be known than we know today about our resources of potential genius, the environmental circumstances that favor its expres‹ sion, the emotional compulsions that give it dynamic quality, and the personality distortions that can make it dangerous.

REFERENCES

1. COX, CATHARINE C. *The early mental traits of three hundred geniuses.* Vol. II of *Genetic studies of genius,* Terman, L. M. (Ed.) Stanford: Stanford Univer. Press, 1926.
2. DAVIS, W. Communicating science. *J. atomic Scientists,* 1953, 337–340.
3. KEYS, N. The underage student in high school and college. *Univer. Calif. Publ. Educ.,* 1938, 7, 145–272.
4. KNAPP, R. H., & GOODRICH, H. B. *Origins of American scientists.* Chicago: Univer. of Chicago Press, 1952.
5. KNAPP, R. H., & GREENBAUM, J. J. *The younger American scholar: his collegiate origins.* Chicago: Univer. of Chicago Press, 1953.
6. LANGE-EICHBAUM, W. *The problem of genius.* New York: Macmillan, 1932.
7. LEARNED, W. S., & WOOD, B. D. The student and his knowledge. *Carnegie Found. Adv. Teaching Bull.,* 1938, No. 29.
8. LEHMAN, H. C. *Age and achievement.* Princeton: Princeton Univer. Press, 1953.
9. PRESSEY, S. L. *Educational acceleration: appraisals and basic problems.* Columbus: Ohio State Univer. Press, 1949.
10. TERMAN, L. M. A preliminary study in the psychology and pedagogy of leadership. *Pedag. Sem.,* 1904, 11, 413–451.
11. TERMAN, L. M. Genius and stupidity: a study of some of the intellectual processes of seven "bright" and seven "dull" boys. *Pedag. Sem.,* 1906, 13, 307–373.
12. TERMAN, L. M. The intelligence quotient of Francis Galton in childhood. *Amer. J. Psychol.,* 1917, 28, 209–215.
13. TERMAN, L. M. (Ed.), *et al. Mental and physical traits of a thousand gifted children.* Vol. I of *Genetic studies of genius,* Terman, L. M. (Ed.) Stanford: Stanford Univer. Press, 1925.
14. TERMAN, L. M., & ODEN, M. H. *The gifted child grows up.* Vol. IV of *Genetic studies of genius,* Terman, L. M. (Ed.) Stanford: Stanford Univer. Press, 1947.
15. TERMAN, L. M. Scientists and nonscientists in a group of 800 gifted men. *Psychol. Monogr.,* 1954, 68, in press.
16. WITTY, P. (Ed.) *The gifted child.* Boston: Heath, 1951.
17. *Bridging the gap between school and college.* New York: The Fund for the Advancement of Education, 1953.

65. SOME CHARACTERISTICS OF
VERY SUPERIOR CHILDREN

W. DRAYTON LEWIS

The findings discussed here concur, in general, with those reported in selection 64, although, unlike Terman, Lewis contends that individuals with very high IQ's—over 145—tend to be maladjusted, and he finds all socio-economic levels represented in his superior group.

Popular opinion has long held the very superior individual to be some kind of freak, a very different and queer person who is likely to come to no good end, who can probably only look to a rather futile future at best. Psychologists have shown this popular belief to be erroneous, as they have done with so many popular ideas, but they have raised the question whether or not it is possible that very superior children may be too bright for their own good. The late Leta Hollingworth was quoted in the press on several occasions as having stated that the most desirable level of intelligence probably lies between *IQ*'s 125 and 145, that if one could choose his child's level of ability he should choose within this range since the best adjustment, educational, personal, and social, appears to be made by children whose ability falls within this range and since those who possess intelligence quotients above the level may be so bright, may be so superior, and thus different from the children with whom they must associate in school and on the playground, that adjustment may be very difficult in the ordinary school and social situation.

Dr. Hollingworth also expressed the belief in various articles that the adjustment of superior children becomes increasingly difficult as the *IQ*'s rise above 150. This study is concerned with very superior children and endeavors to throw some light upon the educational and personality adjustments of children of varying degrees of superiority with the hope of determining, in some measure, whether or not adjustments do become increasingly difficult as the *IQ* rises above 145 or 150.

Coördinated Studies in Education, Incorporated, was able to collect a large amount of data on some 45,000 elementary school children in grades four to eight, inclusive. These children were found in 455 schools

Reprinted from the *Journal of Genetic Psychology*, LXII (1943), 301–309, by permission of the author and The Journal Press.

and 310 communities in 36 states. The children included in this survey were given the Kuhlmann-Anderson Test and these test results were made the basis of selection for the subjects included in this study. Two methods of selection were used. For some phases of this study all those who obtained an *IQ* rating of 145 or more were selected and they are compared with those whose *IQ* ratings were between 125 and 144 in order to determine whether those of the latter group were making superior adjustments to those of the most superior group at the time the tests were given. The second method of selection used was to choose the 10 with the highest intelligence quotients in each grade since the intelligence quotients did not run as high in some grades as in others, indicating, perhaps, that the Kuhlmann-Anderson Tests are not of equal difficulty at all grade levels.

The writer feels that he is justified in stating that the children included in these two groups possess very superior ability since each child represents approximately one in a thousand in ability as measured by the Kuhlmann-Anderson Test. The purpose of this study is to investigate the home backgrounds and the personal and educational adjustments of these very superior children within the limits of the data available.

The methods of selection used in setting up the groups of superior children which have been publicized the most extensively in the literature have been such that some have expressed the opinion, which many have accepted almost without question, that superior children come from quite superior socio-economic levels. A socio-economic rating scale was set up for the purpose of investigating the origins of the very superior children included in this study. The socio-economic rating scale used takes account of the father's occupation, the presence in the home of a telephone, auto, radio, regular servant, and newspaper, and the room-per-person ratio. This scale gives a possible range of ratings from 0 to 18. The teachers also gave the home an economic rating of inferior, average, or superior—inferior to represent the lowest quarter and superior to represent the top quarter of the community economically.

The homes from which these very superior children come, that is, the children with *IQ* ratings of 145 and over, obtained ratings from 2 to 15, with a median rating of 8. The teachers were unable to give a rating relative to the economic status of many of the homes but 38 of the homes were rated. Seven were rated inferior, 27 average, and only four superior. This means that only four of the homes from which these very superior children came were judged to be on a par with the upper fourth of the community economically, whereas seven were rated as falling in the lower fourth economically, with approximately 70 per cent representing the middle half of the community economically. This means that some of the children come from homes where poverty is present, some from homes which are characterized by abundance, while the majority come from a wide range of middle class homes.

The highly significant finding, though, is that these very superior children can be expected in practically any type of home, as far as socio-economic rating is concerned. It is true that they tend to come from homes which have average ratings slightly higher than the average of the total population surveyed, but this fact can easily be over-emphasized and misinterpreted. It must be recognized that averages may be very misleading and that one gets an incorrect picture of the origins of these very superior children if emphasis is placed upon the average. The important finding is that these children can be expected in all kinds of homes, that the distribution of very superior ability is such that it might be termed a highly democratic distribution.

It is interesting to note that the median socio-economic rating for the group of superior children whose intelligence quotients range from 125 to 144 is slightly higher than that of the very superior group, 8.5 as compared with 8.0. Throughout this study the number of subjects, 930 for the 125 to 144 group and 50 for the very superior group, is too small to give statistically reliable results. For this reason, the writer does not believe that one is justified in interpreting the above results as indicating that the very superior group comes from homes which are inferior to those of the 125 to 144 group, but it does seem evident that they do not come from superior homes. The superiority of the homes of both of these groups is not very great when compared with the median rating for the entire population surveyed, which is 6.61.

The occupations of the fathers of the [very superior children] were listed. This listing, which is given in Table 1, emphasizes the fact that very superior ability may be expected in all types of homes.

One child was in an orphanage, and no information was available relative to the father, and the father of another child was an inmate of a state mental hospital.

A survey of the interests of this group of very superior children, as revealed by participation in the extra-curricular activities of the school and by their hobbies, gives no evidence of abnormality of interests for the group as a whole. They have, as a group, more extensive interests than average children and their interests in music and reading are very definitely superior to those of the total population surveyed. Three out of every five of these very superior children are designated as being interested in music, which is far greater than the interest of any other group in music. Equally significant is the fact that they have quite normal interests in all types of sports and games. The most significant finding here, we believe, is that the interests of this group of very superior children are quite normal in every sense of the term.

Most of the [very superior] children included in this study were given the *BPC Personal Inventory* and the scores obtained indicate that, as a group, their adjustment, as measured by this Inventory, is superior to that of any other group of children included in this survey [population of survey was approximately 45,000 children]. Their median score was 23.6, as compared with 27.8 for the group whose intelligence quotients lie between 125 and 144, 28.5 for the entire upper 10 per cent of this population, and 35 for an unselected group. This would appear to indicate that this

Table 1

Professional group—5	Skilled labor—16
High school principal	Farmer—6
Captain—United States Army	Barber
Doctor	Printer
Minister	Mechanic—3
Designer	Mason
	Mail carrier
Business and managerial group—18	Plumber
Merchant—2	Sign painter
Salesman—5	Sergeant in army
Fruit broker	
Grocer—2	Semi-skilled and unskilled labor—12
Pharmacist	Road work—2
Jeweler	Mill hand—2
Security exchange commission	Miner
Aviator	Logger—2
Clerk	Truck driver
Insurance	Common laborer—2
Postmaster	Factory worker—2
Assistant superintendent of railroad	

very superior group has achieved a type of emotional stability, as revealed by this Inventory, which is quite superior to that of the other groups.

The entire population included in this study was rated on the basis of a list of 70 personality traits. It was suggested to those doing the rating that they pick out not less than five or more than 12 traits which they deemed to be most characteristic of each child to be rated. These personality ratings indicate that, on the whole, these very superior children have achieved personalities which are far superior to those of average children, or even to those of the upper 10 per cent. The data appear to justify a statement to the effect that very superior children, at least those included in this study, have superior personalities.

The characteristic which appears to differentiate this very superior group most definitely is *adventuresome*. One in three of these children is rated as being adventuresome whereas only one in 6.5 of the upper 10 per cent, and one in 10 of the total population surveyed are so characterized. Other personality characteristics which the teachers who did the rating believed to be particularly characteristic of this group are ambitious, dependable, energetic, friendly, happy, honest, investigative, leader, likes jokes, original, polite, and tidy.

Most individuals who have given any thought to the matter will concede that the very superior child, as judged by intelligence tests, is the most promising material which comes to the schools. It is important, therefore, to note any information, available in the data at hand, relative to the adjustment of the very superior children to the school situation which they must face. It would appear, offhand, that any teacher should recognize as possessing exceptional ability a child who rates one in a thousand on an intelligence test. It certainly is not to be expected that any of these would be rated as dull or mentally sluggish. Neither of these expectations is realized, if we are to judge by the ratings made by the teachers.

Only one boy in five and two girls in five are characterized as being *precocious* or *mentally quick.* It must be recalled that these children rate as one in a thousand on tested mental ability. When children of such unusual ability do not stand out in the ordinary classroom one would appear to be justified in assuming that the school is failing to challenge the child of exceptional ability. It is to be noted that this is even more the case with the boys than with the girls. It is equally significant to note that two of this group have been designated as *dull* or *mentally sluggish* by their teachers. While this is not a large percentage, it is hardly to be expected that teachers would so designate such brilliant children. The fact that a higher percentage of the group whose intelligence quotients are above 144 are so designated than of those with intelligence quotients between 125 and 144 might be interpreted as indicating some greater maladjustment relative to the school situation for the very superior group, but the subjects are too few to justify anything more than a hazardous guess since it may be wholly a chance distribution. There is nothing in these characterizations, however, to indicate that the schools are doing much for these very exceptional children.

There is some evidence that those with the highest intelligence quotients are somewhat more maladjusted than those who are slightly below them in intelligence. Of the 10 children who attained intelligence quotients of 160 or more, seven appear to be somewhat maladjusted as far as personality traits or educational achievement are concerned. On the basis of personality traits which are assigned to them by their teachers, six of the 10 appear to be suffering from personality maladjustments. That is, they are listed by their teachers as possessing several traits which mental hygienists rate as undesirable. The traits referred to here are "goody-goody," cute, destructive, domineering, day-dreaming, cruel, immature, nervous, over-sensitive about self, over-critical of others, too easily frightened, stubborn, inattentive in class, slovenly, suggestible, quarrelsome, lack of interest in work, pouting, unhappy, moody, or depressed, and self-conscious. If only one of these traits was ascribed to a child it was not considered to be particularly significant. The child was only considered maladjusted when the teacher believed that several of these traits were characteristic of the child. The Personal Inventory only indicated maladjustment in about a third of these cases and it should be noted that whenever the Inventory indicated maladjustment the teachers' ratings also indicated maladjustment. This would appear to indicate that the Inventory is not sensitive enough to detect maladjustment in all cases. A seventh of the 10 children mentioned above appears to have had a well-adjusted personality but was quite retarded educationally. That is, the educational age achieved on a battery achievement test fell below the mental age as indicated by the intelligence test. Twelve children obtained intelligence quotients between 150 and 160, and there is evidence of maladjustment in the case of only two of these.

Few of these very superior children who are maladjusted give evidence of aggressive behavior. Rather, they are characterized by behavior of the withdrawing or egocentric type. The characteristics most frequently attributed to them, as noted above, are day-dreaming, nervous, moody, depressed, unhappy, over-sensitive about self, over-critical of others, suggestible, inattentive in class, lazy, self-conscious.

Unfavorable living conditions appear to react very powerfully, and even disastrously, upon these very superior children. Ten of the 50 were shown as having come from homes of poverty. All except one of the 10 appear to show the effects of this type of background and that one is well-adjusted both personally and educationally. . . .

Those with intelligence quotients above 145 show more educational maladjustment than those with intelligence quotients from 125 to 144. Sixty-four and five-tenths per cent of the former have educational ages which are below their mental ages whereas only 52.5 per cent of the latter have educational ages below their mental ages.

Decile scores were available for each grade of the total population on reading, geography, arithmetic problems, and language usage, the scores having been obtained from the *Unit Scales of Attainment Battery* which was administered to all of the children. In order to determine how these very superior children were achieving relative to the entire population surveyed, their scores were scattered in the various deciles in which they fell. No consideration is given here to the fact that these children, if working up to ability, should obtain scores which would fall in the extreme upper ranges of the highest decile since they are one in a thousand in ability. Rather they are treated as if they were one in 10 in ability.

It is striking, indeed, that so many of these very able children are doing so little in the way of achievement. As usual, they are doing better in reading than in other subjects, which again emphasizes that reading is more closely dependent upon intelligence than the other school subjects. It would appear to be a severe indictment of our present set up in the elementary school that less than half of these exceedingly able students, if we are to trust our measure of intelligence and achievement, are obtaining achievement scores which fall in the top decile and it is even more severe indictment that so many of them are so low in achievement that they earn scores which fall in the lowest five deciles. The comparisons shown in Table 2 indicate that the highest group, those with *IQ*'s of 145 or more, are achieving very little more than those with quotients from 125–144, in spite of their superior ability. It is evident from Table 2 that as large a percentage, except for reading, of the latter group obtain scores falling within the two highest deciles as there are of the former group.

Table 2. A Comparison of the Percentages of Children with *IQ*'s above 144 and Those with *IQ*'s from 125 to 144 Whose Scores on Designated Achievement Tests Fell in Various Deciles as Shown

	TENTH DECILES		NINTH AND TENTH DECILES		LOWEST FIVE DECILES	
	IQ		*IQ*		*IQ*	
	125–144	145 Up	125–144	145 Up	125–144	145 Up
Reading	40.2	46.7	56.2	63.9	14.5	9.6
Geography	32.9	42.0	49.6	51.7	15.6	19.3
Arithmetic problem	33.8	42.8	52.4	52.3	17.2	22.3
Language usage	34.5	35.0	50.2	49.2	19.7	19.0

The latter part of this study has stressed the maladjustments of the very superior group. Too much emphasis can be placed on this aspect of the study and there is a danger that the reader will conclude that these children represent a badly adjusted group. The writer believes, after a careful study of all cases, that the only conclusion which can be arrived at is that, as a group, they are by no means as badly adjusted as some previous studies might lead us to believe. Many, in fact the majority, have made excellent adjustments. The data at hand indicate, we believe, that the majority are very normal children making normal adjustments and there is no evidence here that abnormality or queerness is the typical characteristic. There is maladjustment to be sure, but it does appear to be evident that their very superior ability has enabled them to adjust, in the majority of cases, to an educational system which we know neglects them. When maladjustment is present, especially in the very superior group, it indicates great social waste, and there is maladjustment. This maladjustment appears to be slightly more prevalent in the very superior group as might well be anticipated. All of this calls for a readjustment of our elementary educational program in order to serve more adequately the most promising material which comes to our schools.

66. REACHING REJECTED YOUTH

RALPH DAVID FERTIG

This description of a street worker's prevention of delinquencies forces the editors to conclude that if Chicago had 200 such trained workers, and New York, 400, delinquency would be dealt a death blow in these cities. This is not a large number, considering that Chicago's 10,000 police and New York's 20,000 have failed to slow down the tragic increase in juvenile crime in those cities.

Hyde Park had become concerned about its hostile youth. Some young people did not "fit" into the *nice* church and community center programs. Most of them loitered threateningly on a street corner to which little bands drifted—or were pushed. In time a street corner would become the chief bond of these rejected youths; it would be their holding in the community and—their fort. Fear led to further confusion and rejection by the community, and this to further development of the street clubs in isolation from society and social values.

In 1955 the Welfare Council of Metropolitan Chicago, under a grant from the Wieboldt Foundation, set up the Hyde Park Youth Project. This agency was to test and demonstrate a bringing-together of various social work techniques and community forces for a neighborhood-centered attack on juvenile delinquency. In partnership with the Hyde Park Neighborhood Club, a local settlement house, Youth Project staff helped stimulate a public recognition of delinquency as a problem of the total community.

As part of this broad approach to a community and all of its young people, a worker was sent out to the street corners to meet with some of the clusters of anti-social youth. This Street Club Worker, identified as a Group worker from the Neighborhood Club, met with the staffs of both agencies. He would meet with the youth on the streets, come to know them, help them find new channels for expression which would reduce

Revised from the article in *Teleclass Study Guide in Child Psychology,* 1958, by permission of the author and the Chicago Board of Education.

or obviate anti-social behavior. In finding new opportunities and channels for his young clients, he would draw on every fibre and resource in the community before he was through. The help began as he met the youths where they were. This study follows some of his work.

The boys on the corners were 13 through 20 years of age; 90% of those past 16 had left school; less than 40% of them lived with their natural parents, over half lived in buildings slated for demolition for civic redevelopment. They were of American-Negro, Irish, Mexican, German, Scandinavian, Asiatic, Southern Mountain (white), Eastern European, and Italian backgrounds, in that order of frequency.

Many of these boys had common roots in their co-membership in a onetime "protective alliance." This alliance was in existence at the time the worker first established contact. It was formed by fifty-five teenaged American boys. This group included some Mexicans and Indians but excluded Negroes. These youths, whose delinquent tendencies may have had diverse origins, were provided with a focus for uniting themselves partly by the community's ambivalent reactions to the in-migration of Negroes. The movement of Negroes into the community so stimulated a conflict in the values of the dominant culture, that aggression directed against Negroes did not appear to be seriously disapproved of for the teen-agers in the groups which were encountered in the street club program. Community groups verbalized acceptance and brotherhood for the Negro newcomers, and local organizations passed resolutions supporting this point of view. However, the reactions of a substantial proportion of the adult community was the traditional pattern of whites moving out and raising the general level of rental to the newcomers moving in.

The boys interpreted these apparent inconsistencies as tacit approval by the adult community for resistance to and aggression against the Negroes who were moving in. However, the boys had to unite themselves outside of existing community agencies and institutions because they couldn't hope for approval of their aggressive behavior despite the opposition that was apparent to them. Antagonism toward the Negro newcomers was thus the chief focus of the alliance when the worker first encountered the boys considered here. An early job, then, was helping to set up a "peace club" which arbitrated disputes between white and Negro teenagers.

SPLITTING BY AGE GROUPS

Representatives from the rival, racially based street club met with the worker and the Director of the Neighborhood Club in the Neighborhood Club building. Over the course of several months, aggression between the two racial groups was diminished. The worker encouraged the group to split into two smaller groups, the "big guys" and the "little guys." The behavior of the "big guys" in social situations was directed, goal-oriented and reserved. In social situations the behaviors of the "little guys" was diffused, dis-oriented and conspicuous. The "big guys" formed the Cobras, and their twenty-four members were served both in the building-centered program of the Neighborhood Club and outside of it. They now spoke of being "free" from identification with the more ir-responsible "little guys" whose loud-mouthed and ostentatious activities helped focus police and community concern on them all. Furthermore, it was the "little guys" who started a disturbance and then came running to the "big guys" to help them "finish" the job.

On the other hand, the twenty-two "little guys" spoke of being happily relieved of the bullying "bigger guys." And now that they could not implicate the older fellows so easily, they tended to turn more to one another for other kinds of satisfactions within their own group, one which they called the Serpents.

FORMING AN AUTO-MECHANICS CLUB

As the Redevelopment moved many of the teenagers out of the area, some came to rely heavily upon means of transportation to retain their social lives. This, combined with the interest American adolescents have come to express in cars, suggested the formation of an auto-mechanics club. Seven of the Cobras, who had become proficient at socialized forms of organization combined with five of the working boys who, in the course of their semi-skilled means of employment, had picked up some knowl-edge of mechanics. At the worker's suggestion, five of the boys in lower status clubs were involved; these boys were especially responsive to the opportunity of moving up into this kind of association, and were willing to work hard. Still a fourth clique of four boys joined the group from among those in the Serpents who had not been involved in the building program at the Neighborhood Club; the young men were especially articulate and had helped talk around the idea of an auto-mechanics club for a long time before it got formed. When the group actually got under-way, the verbal abilities of these boys was put to use in a public relations program with the neighbors on the block in which the garage was located.

Out of their own organization, the 21 members raised money for garage rent and tools, fashioned a constitution and came to demand conformity to written group agreements. The specialized, functional cliques of "organizers," "mechanics," "workers," and "talkers" eventually gave way to a more integrated, comprehensive organization. Respon-sibility and safe driving practices were militantly demanded by the group, and by the fall of 1956, 4 months after the group was founded, 6 of the members were dropped from the organization. Of these 6, three were picked up in the less demanding group of Serpents who moved into the agency; 2 were helped in personalized plans; and one joined the Jr. Raiders.

THE RAIDERS

Until quite recently, there was a well known gang in the community with an almost 30 year tradition. Passed on from father to son, this organization remained isolated from the middle class intellectual dominant culture and often preyed upon it. This gang was known as the Raiders.

When some of those from the Serpents who did not move into the Neighborhood Club building cast about for identification with a street corner tradition, they picked up on the defunct Raiders and called themselves the Jr. Raiders. Altogether 19 boys gathered on the corner which had been dominated by their namesakes, though it had been abandoned to an almost all-Negro populace. They bought jackets with the name "Raiders" printed on them, and enjoyed the identities with which they were associated. Overnight, this device stimulated community concern and fear. Attracting attention to their control of this vital corner, the boys blocked the sidewalk, shouted vulgar language, and engaged in a great deal of conspicuous horseplay. Leaders of the group went a few steps further and burglarized stores and taverns.

THE ROLES OF THE STREET WORKER

These, then, are some of the groups with which the street club worker was engaged. The intent of his engagement was to present to each of these groups a person who, through his connection with a neighborhood agency, can represent the community's interest in the boys and concern for helping them find solutions for their needs. He shows his own sincere acceptance of them and at the same time communicates to them through his actions, the standards of mature behavior that he hopes they may take as a model for their own. This process of identification is mediated through the liking and respect that the boys develop for him, in response to the same attitude on his part towards them. As he gains their confidence and trust he is in a position to know ahead of time about crisis situations and to take preventive or, through his presence, protective action, while supporting the new and incompletely developed standards. Some examples of techniques used are provided below.

Shortly after first contact with the Cobras, the worker was still feeling his way in relationships with the boys and was less judgmental than he was to be at a later, more securely accepted stage. His responses to modify anti-social behavior were largely in terms of *appealing to the self interest* of the group or individual. The "Peace Club" was formed with this appeal, and the worker, in an encounter with a youth not a member of a street group, had this experience:

Encountered Ned Beaverman [1] in front of the hot dog stand and asked him how things were. He told me how his brother had been beaten up last night out on the West Side. Ned was going out there tonight to see his "girl-friend," but he was prepared, he affirmed, patting the chest of his black leather jacket. "What've you got there?" I asked. Ned showed me a lead pipe; "They ain't gonna' get me without a fight!" "You know what will happen to you if you're found with that on you," worker admonished Ned who had been in trouble with the police before. "Yeah, but I'll get a black eye or a bloody nose if I don't have this on me." "Which is worse," I asked, "a black eye or 6 months in 'Parental'?" "The six months," growled Ned, as he passed the lead pipe to the worker.

After a relationship of greater acceptance the worker tended to be more personally judgmental. Some months later, Lefty Leoni was discovered with a piece of rubber hose which suggested an attempt at siphoning gas from cars.

"That's a screwy damn thing . . . to do," worker asserted. "I know you talk big and tough but I always had you figured for a pretty straight guy, underneath it all," Lefty was embarrassed; he told of all the times he had felt temptation hot on his back but had kicked it off. "Cris', all the times I wanted to steal hub caps and it would've been so easy but I never once did it!" Lefty spoke of his economic needs; worker pointed out hazards of stealing as so much greater than those of gasoline poverty. This led to a discussion of money earning and Lefty's need for a job. Worker explained he couldn't recommend anyone for a job who could so easily go astray. Lefty asked for another chance to prove himself, but he needed a job in order to stay out of trouble. Worker reflected on how Lefty would have to avoid getting into trouble on the job, indicated we'd see how things went for the next week.

The inadequacy of this approach alone was discovered at an early point. Boys whose acting out behavior was part of a deep-seated emotional difficulty, had little concern for consequences. There was, for example, Guy Nelson, 17, who lives with his mother and two brothers, and mother's boy friend in a building slated for demolition. Guy's father is a chronic alcoholic, lives with another woman in a nearby tenement flat; mother and father have never formalized their separation by divorce and father occasionally returns to his wife. Neither parent accepts much responsibility for the children; father provides no support. Guy suffers from bad eyesight and chronic head-aches. He has quite a police record.

"You want to know how screwy I was? Last night I walked out on my back porch, I was going to jump. The headache drove me nuts! Went out in my shorts, too."

[1] Some names are fictitious.

Worker reassured Guy that the headaches could be cured. Guy wouldn't let the Neighborhood Club subsidize the clinical costs which would be involved, because the Club was keeping him out for a month as disciplinary action because of his drunken behavior at last Friday night's dance. He had scaled the roof of the building and perched there, threatening to jump before a grand audience that poured out from the gym and disrupted the dance. "I can't let the Club pay for curing my headaches, because I'm going to break into their dances!"

Why did Guy climb up onto the roof? "I like it up there; that's why I like steeplejack work. I like being up high, on top of everybody, where nobody can tell me what to do. Even if they came up after me, they couldn't get me down—they wouldn't push me down. Not even the cops would get me cause they wouldn't shoot at me as long as I was up there. Man, it's nice up there!"

He returned to suicide. "About 8 months ago, tried to hang myself—don't tell anybody—used an old raggedy suede belt and the damned thing broke. I've thought of it plenty of times. Nothing to do or think about at home, with my headaches killing me."

In another encounter with Guy, the worker had this experience:

Guy "tested" me by letting me know of a burglary he was going to pull in the company of Robert West and Jr. Sorillo (both of these latter are now in detention—the first at St. Charles and the second at Pontiac for subsequent acts). Guy told the others they could "trust" this worker even though this worker tried to talk the three out of this on the basis of it not being smart, the harshness of the consequences could far exceed the possible joy of the act. But the three boys went on, with the worker standing 10 feet or so away and tossed a rock through the window of a laundry around the corner from Hot Dog Haven; then, very much scared, the boys took rapid flight down 55th Street, urging the worker to come on along fast with them, before anyone got caught. Their fear had fortunately preceded their taking anything, but just to make sure this local laundry would not be robbed blind by the morning, I called in a complaint to the police station, stating an old man had just broken into the laundry —he was probably drunk, I told the law over the phone. Then a few minutes later, as I crouched in an alley-way with the boys in back of the infamous "Dorchester building," we heard the squad cars tear down to the laundry and the fellows allowed as maybe they hadn't been too wise, after all.

This somewhat-less-than-honest handling of the incident appears, in retrospect, to have been unwise; it could not but help to advance confusion around values. This was least helpful to Guy who so needed a consistent set of standards. Much later, when the worker was out of town and Guy got into some more trouble, he related it to the workers absence, saying,

"If you'd'a been around, this never would've happened, but I got to feeling that way and there was nobody else I could go to."

It was clear that Guy needed much more help, and efforts were made to reach him through his medical needs toward eventual involvement in case work services. The trouble reported above, however, intervened, and he is now incarcerated.

When group anti-social acts are anticipated, it would be most common for the worker to move in with *suggestions of socially acceptable alternatives.* For example, an incident with some Cobras:

> After they began necking I moved down to the corner on the steps of Frank's Movers caddy-cornered from Walgreen's. Here, were Eddie————, Ted Kinally, and another guy. The three fellows spent a great deal of time suggesting to one another what he would do with each I'll chick who hovered into view on any of the four corners. And they delighted in shouting out abusive suggestions to those too old, ugly, or harmless looking to resist remarks concerning their cars or persons. After picking up this drift, I was even further convinced that the one area of interest which would involve these kids is an objective discussion of sex and dating problems. These fellows want to, but just cannot relate in any personal or real terms. And they lack great knowledge in the procedures by which one gains entry to such relating.

This led to a discussion program and social events which did "involve" these otherwise lethargic youth and which led into making the Cobras a co-ed group at the Neighbor Club.

> . . . According to Claude there was going to be a fight against the Puerto Rican kids. The story I was able to put together went like this: Al Blinski had been walking down 55th St. with his girl-friend, Lila Lopez (of Filipine origin), when three Puerto Rican fellows marched out from the hot dog stand and grabbed Lila. Al threw the offending fellow off and threatened to fight him. This fellow along with his two friends ran down the street to Blackstone a block and a half east, saying that they would form their gang and be back to take care of Al. These fellows claimed that the Puerto Ricans, even now, were organizing themselves two blocks east on Blackstone and further down the block from me a group was huddling at the corner of Blackstone and 55th.
>
> The police came by and asked the mob to disperse. This gave me a chance to walk the two blocks to Blackstone where I encountered a group of 8 or 9 Puerto Rican fellows. I addressed the group partly in English, partly in Spanish, and they formed themselves in a semi-circle about me. I told them that I was a worker from the Hyde Park Neighborhood Club, mentioned its location, and said that I hoped that these fellows would be coming to the Neighborhood Club in the Fall at which time we will reopen once again in night time programs. I said that I understood, however, that some of the fellows from the Neighborhood Club planned to fight "you fellows" tonight and that I didn't think it was very smart to fight with our neighbors, that we all have to live in the same neighborhood, together, and certainly we ought to be able to be friends.
>
> These Puerto Rican fellows agreed that they wanted to be friends but proceeded to explain what their interpretation was of the incident between Al Blinski and Lila Lopez, and three of their group. They claimed as they left

Hot Dog Haven one of their group approached Lila for some matches. Al did not understand what he was saying and Al suddenly jumped on him from behind and shouted at them, they thought, because they are from Puerto Rico and they were not going to take this sort of persecution lying down. So they were going to run off and form their gang and properly put those persons who persecute Puerto Ricans in their place. They explained that they don't want to start a fight and they do not have many numbers in this neighborhood, but they could call friends from other neighborhoods who would get down here in a hurry to join them in any fight. Among those who represented this point of view worker spotted Luis Villareal. I asked him whether I had seen him at the Neighborhood Club. He said yes, and we went on to discuss some of the prejudices against the Puerto Ricans. I said that I agreed with them that there are some prejudices that other kids have that have to be gotten rid of, but the way we are going to get rid of these prejudices is by working together as friends and not fighting one another. They agreed to this and said if the other fellows wanted to have peace and call the fight off they would be willing to have peace and call the fight off. I asked if they would be willing to send two representatives to a truce meeting and they said they would. I asked them to wait for me while I returned to where the Cobras and the Copperheads were re-forming their ranks across 55th Street from Hot Dog Haven. I asked for two representatives from this conglomeration of kids for the purpose of talking things over with the other gang of Puerto Ricans. Lefty stepped forth and named Flash Berry to join him as representatives to the truce meeting. Lefty asked for Luis by name suggesting that he and one other fellow come from the Puerto Rican group. Lefty knows Luis well, being a next door neighbor to him, in the Dorchester building. Lefty and Flash headed toward Dorchester, the street which lay half way between the vantage points of each of the gangs. I ran ahead and then asked Luis and one other fellow to come forth. Luis willingly took position as spokesman for the group and was joined by Tony, last name unknown. Tony, Luis, Lefty, Flash and I met on the corner of Dorchester and 55th while gangs hovered awaiting our actions or decisions a block in either direction. Luis started it off saying, "We don't want to start any fights." Lefty held his hand out agreeing, saying, "We don't want to start a fight either, but if you guys are ready for one—." Luis went on to say, "Well we don't want to start it. If you're ready for one we'll fight you, but we don't want to start this one." There was a good deal of repetition of this point back and forth. Lefty agreed strongly that we have to live in the same neighborhood together, there is no point our fighting each other every night which is what we have to do if we were to get this thing started tonight.

At worker's suggestion hands were shaken all around and the delegates returned to their respective gangs. I could see Luis and Tony returning to their fellow Puerto Rican friends joyously and being greeted joyously. There were, however, mixed reactions from the Cobras. The fellows were somewhat quiet, saying, "Yea, I guess its a good thing as long as we are going to be living in the same neighborhood with those guys." The girls, however, notably Lea, Bootie, Joyce Anderson, and Minda Mayer were quite angry, and disappointed in the fact that there was no fight. They egged the fellows on suggesting that they were yellow, that they were cowards because they weren't willing to take on the Puerto Ricans.

These *mediating* techniques have specific application to inter-group conflicts; however the worker often must help mediate between the social standards for which he stands and the behavior of individuals who reject these standards. One way of doing this is by *example setting*. Without verbally imposing demands for the more desirable behavior, the worker communicates what he considers desirable by doing it . . . :

Went to Hot Dog Haven for a quick bite and encountered Harry who vilified worker's name as thoroughly as this worker has ever been cursed at. Basis for the swelling hostility was the worker's use of Liza's car for the Neighborhood Club. He suggested that it had all been a plot against him because he drives her car and ranted on about worker's nose, ears, etc., daring worker to take a punch at him. In the brief interludes in-between either Lem Wilcox or Alan O'Hanahan would slide up alongside worker who was seated on steps adjacent to Hot Dog Haven and reassure him that Harry was no good and worker was o.k. Alan asked "Why doesn't Harry like you," and worker explained about the loan of the car. Then Alan asked, "Do you dislike Harry?" to which worker said no, "Harry was o.k., he's just angry now but he'll get over it." Alan communicated that he very definitely disliked Harry and thought him no good. Worker reiterated some of Harry's sterling qualities. Then it came time for the meeting with the Copperheads and worker walked off slowly leaving a sputtering and signifying Harry.

On the following day:

Harry was present along with Alan O'Hanahan. Harry was sounding guilty for his behavior the night before and said in tone which made it clear he admired worker's reaction, "I tried to get you to fight me last night" and . . . he was glad there had been no fight.

.   .   .   .   .

Another technique is the *support and encouragement of tendencies toward socially acceptable behavior*. Doing this, the worker encourages those with the most socialized standards to take positions of leadership in the group. In one instance, the girl-friends of the Cobras were challenged and, egged on by the boys, a fight loomed. With the worker's support, Joan Anderson stepped forth and asserted that there was no basis for a fight. The girls concluded with a grumbling cold-war truce, but an immediate follow-up would be necessary to avoid further complications. The worker helped Joan formalize some leadership by having her bring the other girls together to set forth a new kind of club structure at the Neighborhood Club. The crafts teacher they met showed them jewelery making and started them toward the development of a group more independent of the boys and more socialized in its direction.

Shortly after the formation of the Serpents, misconduct by some of its members caused the entire group to be denied entry to a Friday night dance. The group responded by ejecting Junior, one of the more irresponsible members. As they were preparing to attend the next dance, Junior sought another chance; his story is told in the following diary excerpt:

Before the dance (which was scheduled for 8:00) many of the boys drifted into Hot Dog Haven, the Club, or waited on the street. Junior appeared in the Club building at 7:00 and I took him aside to explain what the group had decided last night: that he was no longer a member of the Serpents and hence could not, according to Club rules, be a member of the larger Club (having no other involvement) and could not be admitted to the dance. Junior was upset, at first denied the possibility of this decision, then asked me to overlook it. I interpreted to him that whatever decision the group would make, I would have to stick by and enforce.

He urged me then to not "see" him at the dance, to not look his way so that I wouldn't have to enforce the ruling. When he finally realized that this was impossible and that only the group as a whole could decide on this, he explained that the group had made a mistake. He claimed that they must have kicked him out because they thought he had put the egg in "Mr. Peeper's" (Joe's, a staff member) pocket; also he said he had been charged with putting an open match book in Joe's back pocket and lighting it. He insisted that he hadn't been the one to do it, saying he didn't want to squeal on the real culprit before, but he'll get that guy to admit it before the meeting. Also, he would tell Mr. Peepers. Now couldn't he come to the dance? Well, I explained, that would still be up to the group. "Then could the group decide tonight?" if he could get the guys together either at the Club or at Hot Dog Haven. I explained to him they could—if they so chose—let him come back temporarily until the next Thursday meeting at which they would have to make the final decision on his membership. So he dashed over to Hot Dog Haven to try to round up a sizeable group of the members. Junior got the group together and we met in the lobby of the Club. The group was made to understand how this decision could only be temporary if, and this was a matter of indifference, they chose to make any decision at all. They voted Junior in temporarily.

Wherever possible, we have tried to *work with the family* in helping the boy make a more sociable adjustment. When indicated, referral was made to the case work—and often into the treatment units of the Hyde Park Youth Project. However in many instances, the street club worker could adequately stimulate existing strengths of the family members to aid the child themselves. The following diary excerpt tells of an approach to parents whose son was in difficulty with the police. The father is a professor. The occasion was a party for the Kenwood Car Club.

The party took place at the Nye home. Shortly after it had begun the question of drinks came up. Richard assured the group that his parents wouldn't mind if they sent out for liquor. The pressure was on him since the group had been allowed to drink at the homes of two of the Adult Advisory Board members. The worker insisted that they must first have the expressed approval of the host—Richard's parents. Richard stuck to his story that his parents would approve it, and offered to go upstairs with the worker to ask them. Mr. Nye said, "No, I'd rather they did not have any drinking. Richard has been to a few parties where drinks were served and I've been disturbed about it." Worker accepted and supported this position, turned to leave with Richard. On the way down the stairs, worker asked Richard if he had a few decks of cards. He did. "Then get them" worker asserted and we re-entered the living room with cards in hand. "What'll it be?" asked worker shuffling like mad. About half the guys started emptying their pockets to announce their support for poker. Worker moved them into the dining room, set up the poker game, and returned to the living room to set up another poker game for chips—no money. Ray Nester was uncomfortable in either game so worker put him in charge of refreshments. After a short while Mr. Nye came downstairs and tried to busy himself with emptying ashtrays. Worker approached him, tried to interpret further what his position was on the drinking question. Pappa appeared somewhat unhappy, announced that earlier this day Richard had received his school grades and he had flunked all of his courses this semester. "I think its all due to that lousy car he's been spending all of his time on!" "Well, Mr. Nye, if it hadn't been the car, just what do you suppose it would have been?" worker asked Mr. Nye, suggesting a new concept on the role of the car. "You mean you think it was just a symptom of something—his working on the car?" "I don't know Mr. Nye, but I do think that Richard is a sensitive kid who finds it necessary to act out things that are disturbing him. Working on cars *could* serve that function." "That's interesting" mused the professor who was well acquainted, intellectually with these concepts, but had apparently never considered them in the light of his bringing up his own sons. Then he asked worker, "What do you think is wrong?" "That boy just won't do his school work. I've tried to talk with him and I've told him again and again that he's got to be reliable. He just won't listen to me, and he won't accept his responsibilities."

"Maybe" worker suggested, "you've been talking past Richard, not with him. He surely must feel a pretty unhappy relationship with his father; how more effectively could he reject you than to flunk in school, how could he more clearly bring shame upon himself than to fail where his home places greatest stress, in intellectual achievement?"

"Why would he want to do that? No, that boy is just plain unreliable, he just won't listen to me and he won't accept his responsibilities." "Take those automobile accidents, now. I tried to reason with him after that but he just wouldn't react." Mr. Nye spoke of two accidents just previous to Richard's joining the Car Club. "Maybe that's where the problem lies, Mr. Nye" suggested the worker, "maybe you were concerned with what to Richard was entirely the wrong thing. Did you ever try talking with Richard about what was on his mind at the time of the accident, what had occurred before it which he may associate with the whole mess that followed?" "You know, these kids tie up sudden crisis events like an accident with a lot of other things in their lives, and maybe you could help him untie the knot by helping him get at that underneath thing which may have led him into the accident, which may be forcing Richard into a lot of acting-out behavior, including his failure at school. You say Richard doesn't react to your talking with him, but Richard is a kid with a pretty overwhelming super-ego. He doesn't show it in the outward signs of shame, but he turns his guilt inward and has accidents, and flunks. . . ."

"Oh, I don't see why he just can't have an accident. All he did was push the shift into second instead of reverse; that was perfectly simple" said the professor. "Mr. Nye, how many thousands of times do you suppose Richard has made the same movement of the shift? No, you won't grant 'accidents' in your Laboratory, and I don't think I'll permit them to explain anything in mine," the worker asserted. "You may have something there, especially since there were *two* accidents right close to one another," Mr. Nye began to give in. Then recognizing that he was getting uncomfortably close to real life, he tried to dismiss the subject by saying, "Maybe he's just on the wrong track, he'll probably outgrow this behavior." "You've got yourself a sensitive, creative kid who's striking out against structures that are too tight for him." Worker pressed the point, "You're going to have to help him grow out of this behavior and in the right kind of direction." "What can I do?" Mr. Nye asked the worker. "Get in there and play with him" suggested the worker. "But I don't know how" said Mr. Nye. And then he reflected, "I can see what you mean; maybe that's at the root of this trouble."

"C'mon with me" worker then led the way and proceeded to show Mr. Nye how to play with his son. The game was poker, the no-money table. Worker turned to Richard saying "We've got an old codger here who wants to learn how to play poker. Think you can teach him?" Richard allowed as to how he could. From then on it was a continuous kidding.

As a figure more in touch with social agencies and processes, the street club worker is often called upon to *help in environmental problems.* We spent many weeks in setting up an odd jobs service with local agencies. Many clients and their families were counseled on their rights as tenants. Still others have been helped to find new quarters as their old apartments were vacated for demolition and redevelopment. We helped ten boys to receive hospital or medical services; another thirteen were aided in scholastic adjustments through conferences with teachers. Still others were given help on studies. Many boys were given support in their court appearances, all kinds of support: from cutting one lad's hair on the Sunday night before his appearance, to helping the court develop plans for the boy and/or family. In a number of cases, the case work unit of the Hyde Park Youth Project was given supervision of street club members in plans worked out with the court authorities.

The use and the effectiveness of each of these techniques depended heavily upon the kind of relationship that existed between the worker and the group. This relationship is based in part upon the worker's liking of the boys, but he must also show that he understands them and their problems for what they are. Though he likes the kids, this does not mean that he always likes or is willing to take part in all of their behavior. He never would conceal his identification with a welfare agency. He helps the boy who has committed a crime reach an adjustment with society, but he never suggests that committing the crime was unimportant or was excusable.

PART VI

ADOLESCENCE

INTRODUCTION

Adolescence is a period of rapid physical change affecting both the child's glands and bones and society's expectations regarding his behavior. It is a time for looking forward—to new purposes in life, to an occupation, to marriage, to independence from parents, and to a sense of self-identity.

In the selections in this Part, Kinsey and Jones discuss important physiological developments and some of their social and cultural consequences. Komarovsky analyzes family techniques in our society by which independence is inculcated in sons and dependence in daughters, providing meaning and significance for the term "sex role." Brodbeck and White offer different views of sex roles in their keen observations of Li'l Abner and his adventures in Dogpatch. Excerpts from the life of Mahatma Ghandi and from the biblical stories of Isaac, Jacob, and Joseph show how the family in other cultures and in other times may select bride and groom. Winch, Whiting, Terman, and Allen discuss physiological, sociological and psychological influences in choosing a career and a mate. Erikson's thoughtful analysis gives new meaning to the concept of self-identity.

67. THE ADOLESCENCE OF MAHATMA GANDHI

LOUIS FISCHER

Here the adolescence of a very remarkable man is described by himself with astonishing frankness. Particularly interesting is the constant juxtaposition in Gandhi's personality of a strong sense of duty, morality, personal integrity and denial of bodily wants with a natural lustiness, adventurousness, and interest in the forbidden. His relationship with his wife, whom he married when he was thirteen, is at the same time childish and mature.

In talking of his awkwardness on his wedding night and of his immoral activities "behind the barn" as a youth, Gandhi effectively denies the myth of the hero—"I am the great man, with only superior concerns"—and honestly affirms his inherent sense of brotherhood and humility—"I am like other common men in my awkwardness, my inconsiderateness, and my bungling."

THE BEGINNINGS OF AN EXTRAORDINARY MAN

Gandhi belonged to the Vaisya caste. In the old Hindu social scale, the Vaisyas stood third, far below the Brahmans who were the number one caste, and the Kshatriyas, or rulers and soldiers, who ranked second. The Vaisyas, in fact, were only a notch above the Sudras, the working class. Originally, they devoted themselves to trade and agriculture.

The Gandhis belonged to the Modh Bania subdivision of their caste. Bania is a synonym in India for a sharp, shrewd businessman. Far back, the Gandhi family were retail grocers: "Gandhi" means grocer. But the professional barriers between castes began to crumble generations ago, and Gandhi's grandfather Uttamchand served as prime minister to the princeling of Porbandar, a tiny state in the Kathiawar peninsula, western India, about halfway between the mouth of the Indus and the city of Bombay. Uttamchand handed the office down to his son Karamchand who passed it to his brother Tulsidas. The job had almost become the family's private property.

Karamchand was the father of Mohandas Karamchand Gandhi, the Mahatma.

Selections from *The Life of Mahatma Gandhi* (Harper & Brothers, 1950), pp. 12–23, 29, 35–37, by permission of the publisher. Copyright, 1950, by Louis Fischer.

The Gandhis apparently got into trouble often. Political intrigues forced grandfather Uttamchand out of the prime ministership of Porbandar and into exile in the nearby little state of Junagadh. There he once saluted the ruling Nawab with his left hand. Asked for an explanation, he said, "The right hand is already pledged to Porbandar." Mohandas was proud of such loyalty; "My grandfather," he wrote, "must have been a man of principle."

Gandhi's father likewise quit his position as prime minister to Rana Saheb Vikmatji, the ruler of Porbandar, and took the same office in Rajkot, another miniature Kathiawar principality 120 miles to the northwest. Once, the British Political Agent spoke disparagingly of Thakor Saheb Bawajiraj, Rajkot's native ruler. Karamchand sprang to the defense of his chief. The Agent ordered Karamchand to apologize. Karamchand refused and was forthwith arrested. But Gandhi's father stood his ground and was released after several hours. Subsequently he became prime minister of Wankaner.

In the 1872 census, Porbandar state had a population of 72,077, Rajkot 36,770 and Wankaner 28,750. Their rulers behaved like petty autocrats to their subjects and quaking sycophants before the British.

Karamchand Gandhi "had no education save that of experience," his son, Mohandas, wrote; he was likewise "innocent" of history and geography; "but he was incorruptible and had earned a reputation for strict impartiality in his family as well as outside." He "was a lover of his clan, truthful, brave and generous, but short-tempered. To a certain extent he might have been even given to carnal pleasures. For he married for the fourth time when he was over forty." The other three wives had died.

Mohandas Karamchand Gandhi was the fourth and last child of his father's fourth and last marriage. He was born at Porbandar on October 2, 1869. That year the Suez Canal was opened, Thomas A. Edison patented his first invention, France celebrated the hundredth anniversary of the birth of Napoleon Bonaparte, and Charles W. Eliot became president of Harvard University. Karl Marx had just published *Capital,* Bismarck was about to launch the Franco-Prussian War, and Victoria ruled over England and India.

Mohandas was born in the dark, right-hand corner of a room, 11 feet by 19½ feet and 10 feet high, in a three-story humble house on the border of town. The house is still standing.

The little town of Porbander, or Porbundar, rises straight out of the Arabian Sea and "becomes a vision of glory at sunrise and sunset when the slanting rays beat upon it, turning its turrets and pinnacles into gold," wrote Charles Freer Andrews, a British disciple of the Mahatma. It and Rajkot and Wankaner were quite remote, at the time of Gandhi's youth, from the European and Western influences which had invaded less isolated parts of India. Its landmarks were its temples.

Gandhi's home life was cultured and the family, by Indian standards, was well-to-do. There were books in the house; they dealt chiefly with religion and mythology. Mohandas played tunes on a concertina purchased especially for him. Karamchand wore a gold necklace and a brother of Mohandas had a heavy, solid gold armlet. Karamchand once owned a house in Porbandar, a second in Rajkot, and a third in Kutiana. But in his last three years of illness he lived modestly on a pension from the Rajkot prince. He left little property.

Gandhi's elder brother Laxmidas practiced law in Rajkot and later became a treasury official in the Porbander government. He spent money freely and married his daughters with a pomp worthy of petty Indian royalty. He owned two houses in Rajkot. Karsandas, the other brother, served as sub-inspector of police in Porbandar and ultimately of the princeling's harem. His income was small.

Both brothers died while Mohandas K. Gandhi was still alive. A sister, Raliatbehn, four years his senior, survived him. She remained resident in Rajkot.

Mohania, as the family affectionately called Mohandas, received the special treatment often accorded a youngest child. A nurse named Rambha was hired for him and he formed an attachment to her which continued into mature life. His warmest affection went to his mother Putlibai. He sometimes feared his father, but he loved his mother and always remembered her "saintliness" and her "deeply religious" nature. She never ate a meal without prayer, and attended temple services daily. Long fasts did not dismay her, and arduous vows, voluntarily made, were steadfastly performed. In the annual Chaturmas, a kind of Lent lasting through the four-month rainy season, she habitually lived on a single meal a day, and, one year, she observed, in addition, a complete fast on alternate days. Another Chaturmas, she vowed not to eat unless the sun appeared. Mohandas and his sister and brothers would watch for the sun, and when it showed through the clouds they would rush into the house and announce to Putlibai that now she could eat. But her vow required her to see the sun herself and so she would go outdoors and by then the sun was hidden again. "That does not matter," she would cheerfully comfort her children. "God does not want me to eat today."

As a boy, Mohandas amused himself with rubber balloons and revolving tops. He played tennis and cricket and also "gilli danda," a game, encountered in so many widely separated countries, which consists in striking a short, sharpened wooden peg with a long stick: "peggy" or "pussy" some call it.

Gandhi started school in Porbandar. He encountered more difficulty mastering the multiplication table than in learning naughty names for the teacher. "My intellect must have been sluggish, and my memory raw," the adult Mahatma charges against the child of six. In Rajkot, whither the family moved a year later, he was again a "mediocre student," but punctual. His sister recalls that rather than be late he would eat the food of the previous day if breakfast was not ready. He preferred walking to going to school by carriage. He was timid: "my books and lessons were my sole companions." At the end of the school day, he ran home. He could not bear to talk to anybody; "I was even afraid lest anyone should poke fun at me." When he grew older, however, he found some congenial mates and played in the streets. He also played by the sea.

In his first year at the Alfred High School in Rajkot, when Mohandas was twelve, a British educational inspector named Mr. Giles came to examine the pupils. They were asked to spell five English words. Gandhi misspelled "kettle." Walking up and down the aisles, the regular teacher saw the mistake and motioned Mohandas to copy from his neighbor's slate. Mohandas refused. Later the teacher chided him for this "stupidity" which spoiled the record of the class; everybody else had written all the words correctly.

The incident, however, did not diminish Gandhi's respect for his teacher. "I was by nature blind to the faults of elders. . . . I had learned to carry out the orders of elders, not to scan their actions." But obedience did not include cheating with teacher's permission.

Perhaps the refusal to cheat was a form of self-assertion or rebellion. In any case, compliance at school did not preclude revolt outside it. At the age of twelve, Gandhi began to smoke. And he stole from elders in the house to finance the transgression. His partner in the adventure was a young relative. Sometimes both were penniless; then they made cigarettes from the porous stalks of a wild plant. This interest in botany led to the discovery that the seeds of a jungle weed named dhatura were poisonous. Off they went to the jungle on the successful quest. Tired of life under parental supervision, they joined in a suicide pact. They would die, appropriately, in the temple of God.

Having made their obeisances, Mohandas and pal sought out a lonely corner for the final act. But maybe death would be long in coming, and meanwhile they might suffer pain. Maybe it was better to live in slavery. To salvage a vestige of self-respect they each swallowed two or three seeds.

Presently, serious matters claimed the juvenile's attention.

Mohandas K. Gandhi married when he was a high school sophomore —age thirteen. He had been engaged three times, of course without his knowledge. Bethrothals were compacts between parents, and the children rarely learned about them. Gandhi happened to hear that two girls to whom he had been engaged—probably as a toddler—had died. "I have a faint recollection," he reports, "that the third bethrothal took place in my seventh year," but he was not informed. He was told six years later, a short time before the wedding. The bride was Kasturbai, the daughter

of a Porbandar merchant named Gokuldas Nakanji. The marriage lasted
sixty-two years.

Writing about the wedding more than forty years later, Gandhi remembered all the details of the ceremony, as well as the trip to Porbandar where it took place. "And oh! that first night," he added. "Two
innocent children all unwittingly hurled themselves into the ocean of
life." Kasturbai, too, was thirteen. "My brother's wife had thoroughly
coached me about my behavior on the first night. I do not know who
had coached my wife." Both were nervous and "the coaching could
not carry me far," Gandhi wrote. "But no coaching is really necessary
in such matters. The impressions of the former birth are potent enough
to make all coaching superfluous." Presumably, they remembered their
experiences in an earlier incarnation.

The newlyweds, Gandhi confesses, were "married children" and
behaved accordingly. He was jealous and "therefore she could not go
anywhere without my permission" for "I took no time in assuming the
authority of a husband." So when the thirteen-year-old wife wanted to
go out to play she had to ask the thirteen-year-old Mohandas; he would
often say no. "The restraint was virtually a sort of imprisonment. And
Kasturbai was not the girl to brook any such thing. She made it a point
to go out whenever and wherever she liked." The little husband got
"more and more cross"; sometimes they did not speak to each other for
days.

He loved Kasturbai. His "passion was entirely centered on one
woman" and he wanted it reciprocated, but the woman was a child.
Sitting in the high school classroom he daydreamed about her. "I used
to keep her awake till late at night with my idle talk."

"The cruel custom of child marriage," as Gandhi subsequently casti-
gated it, would have been impossible but for the ancient Indian institution of the joint family: parents and their children and their sons'
wives and children, sometimes thirty or more persons altogether, lived
under one roof; newly wed adolescents therefore had no worry about
a home, furniture, or board. Later, British law, seconding Indian reformers, raised the minimum marriage age. In its time the evil was
mitigated by enforced separations for as much as six months per year
when the bride went to live with her parents. The first five years of
Gandhi's marriage—from thirteen to eighteen—included only three years
of common life.

The "shackles of lust" tormented Gandhi. They gave him a feeling
of guilt. The feeling grew when sex seemed to clash with the keen
sense of duty which developed in him at an early age. One instance of
such a conflict impressed itself indelibly. When Mohandas was sixteen
his father Karamchand became bedridden with a fistula. Gandhi helped
his mother and an old servant tend the patient; he dressed the wound

and mixed the medicines and administered them. He also massaged his father's legs every night until the sufferer fell asleep or asked his son to go to bed. "I loved to do this service," Gandhi recalls.

Kasturbai had become pregnant at fifteen and she was now in an advanced stage. Nevertheless, "every night whilst my hands were busy massaging my father's legs," Gandhi states in his autobiography, "my mind was hovering about [my wife's] bedroom—and that too at a time when religion, medical science, and common sense alike forbade sexual intercourse."

One evening, between ten and eleven, Gandhi's uncle relieved him at massaging Karamchand. Gandhi went quickly to his wife's bedroom and woke her. A few minutes later the servant knocked at the door and urgently summoned Gandhi. He jumped out of bed, but when he reached the sickroom his father was dead. "If passion had not blinded me," Gandhi ruminated forty years later, "I should have been spared the torture of separation from my father during his last moments. I should have been massaging him, and he would have died in my arms. But now it was my uncle who had had this privilege."

The "shame of my carnal desire at the critical moment of my father's death . . . is a blot I have never been able to efface or forget," Gandhi wrote when he was near sixty. Moreover, Kasturbai's baby died three days after birth, and Mohandas blamed the death on intercourse late in pregnancy. This doubled his sense of guilt.

Kasturbai was illiterate. Her husband had every intention of teaching her, but she disliked studies and he preferred lovemaking. Private tutors also got nowhere with her. Yet Gandhi took the blame upon himself and felt that if his affection "had been absolutely untainted with lust, she would be a learned lady today." She never learned to read or write anything but elementary Gujarati, her native language.

Gandhi himself lost a year at high school through getting married. Modestly he asserts he "was not regarded as a dunce." Every year he brought home a report on study progress and character; it was never bad. He even won some prizes but that, he says, was only because there were few competitors.

When Mohandas merited a teacher's rebuke it pained him and he sometimes cried. Once he was beaten at school. The punishment hurt less than being considered worthy of it; "I wept piteously."

Gandhi neglected penmanship and thought it unimportant. Geometry was taught in English, which was then a new language for him, and he had difficulty in following. But "when I reached the thirteenth proposition of Euclid the utter simplicity of the subject was suddenly revealed to me. A subject which only required a pure and simple use of one's reasoning powers could not be difficult. Ever since that time geometry has been both easy and interesting for me." He likewise had trouble with

Sanskrit, but after the teacher, Mr. Krishnashanker, reminded him that it was the language of Hinduism's sacred scriptures, the future Mahatma persevered and succeeded.

In the upper grades, gymnastics and cricket were compulsory. Gandhi disliked both. He was shy, and he thought physical exercises did not belong in education. But he had read that long walks in the open air were good for the health, and he formed the habit. "These walks gave me a fairly hardy constitution."

Mohandas envied the bigger, stronger boys. He was frail compared to his older brother and especially compared to a Moslem friend named Sheik Mehtab who could run great distances with incredible speed. Sheik Mehtab was spectacular in the broad and high jumps as well. These exploits dazzled Gandhi.

Gandhi regarded himself a coward. "I used to be haunted," he asserts, "by the fear of thieves, ghosts, and serpents. I did not dare to stir out of doors at night." He could not sleep without a light in his room; his wife had more courage than he and did not fear serpents or ghosts or darkness. "I felt ashamed of myself."

Sheik Mehtab played on this sentiment. He boasted that he could hold live snakes in his hand, feared no burglars, and did not believe in ghosts. Whence all this prowess and bravery? He ate meat. Gandhi ate no meat; it was forbidden by his religion.

The boys at school used to recite a poem which went:

> Behold the mighty Englishman,
> He rules the Indian small,
> Because being a meat-eater
> He is five cubits tall.

If all Indians ate meat they could expel the British and make India free. Besides, argued Shiek Mehtab, boys who ate meat did not get boils; many of their teachers and some of the most prominent citizens of Rajkot ate meat secretly, and drank wine, too.

Day in, day out, Shiek Mehtab propagandized Mohandas, whose older brother had already succumed. Finally, Mohandas yielded.

At the appointed hour the tempter and his victim met in a secluded spot on the river bank. Sheik Mehtab brought cooked goat's meat and bread. Gandhi rarely touched baker's bread (the substitute was chappatis, an unleavened dough cushion filled with air), and he had never even seen meat. The family was strictly vegetarian and so, in fact, were almost all the inhabitants of the Gujarat district in Kathiawar. But firm in the resolve to make himself an effective liberator of his country, Gandhi bit into the meat. It was tough as leather. He chewed and chewed and then swallowed. He became sick immediately.

That night he had a nightmare: a live goat was bleating in his stomach. However, "meat-eating was a duty," and, in the midst of the terrible dream, therefore, he decided to continue the experiment.

It continued for a whole year. Irregularly throughout that long period he met Sheik Mehtab at secret rendezvous to partake of meat dishes, now tastier than the first, and bread. Where Sheik got the money for these feasts Gandhi never knew.

The sin of consuming and liking meat was compounded by the sin of lying. In the end he could not stand the dishonesty and, though still convinced that meat-eating was "essential" for patriotic reasons, he vowed to abjure it until his parents' death enabled him to be a carnivore openly.

By now Gandhi developed an urge to reform Sheik Mehtab. This prolonged the relationship. But the naïve and younger Gandhi was no match for the shrewd, moneyed wastrel who offered revolt and adventure. Sheik also knew how to arrange things. Once he led Gandhi to the entrance of a brothel. The institution had been told and paid in advance. Gandhi went in. "I was almost struck blind and dumb in this den of vice. I sat near the woman on her bed, but I was tongue-tied. She naturally lost patience with me, and showed me the door, with abuses and insults." Providence, he explains, interceded and saved him despite himself.

About that time—Mohandas must have been fifteen—he pilfered a bit of gold from his older brother. This produced a moral crisis. He had gnawing pangs of conscience and resolved never to steal again. But he needed the cleansing effect of a confession: he would tell his father. He made a full, written statement of the crime, asked for due penalty, promised never to steal again, and, with emphasis, begged his father not to punish himself for his son's dereliction.

Karamchand sat up in his sickbed to read the letter. Tears filled his eyes and fell to his cheeks. Then he tore up the paper and lay down. Mohandas sat near him and wept.

Gandhi never forgot that silent scene. Sincere repentance and confession induced by love, rather than fear, won him his father's "sublime forgiveness" and affection.

Lest he give pain to his father, and especially his mother, Mohandas did not tell them that he absented himself from temple. He did not like the "glitter and pomp" of the Hindu temples. Religion to him meant irksome restrictions like vegetarianism which intensified his youthful protest against society and authority. And he had no "living faith in God." Who made the world; who directed it, he asked. Elders could not answer, and the sacred books were so unsatisfactory on such matters that he inclined "somewhat towards atheism." He even began to believe that it was quite moral, indeed a duty, to kill serpents and bugs.

Gandhi's anti-religious sentiments quickened his interest in religion, and he listened attentively to his father's frequent discussions with Moslem and Parsi friends on the differences between their faiths and Hinduism. He also learned much about the Jain religion. Jain monks often visited the house and went out of their way to accept food from the non-Jain Gandhis.

When Karamchand died, 1885, Mohandas's mother Putlibai took advice on family matters from a Jain monk named Becharji Swami, originally a Hindu of the Modh Bania sub-caste. Jain influence was strong in the Gujarat region. And Jainism prohibits the killing of any living creature, even insects. Jain priests wear white masks over their mouths lest they breathe in, and thus kill, an insect. They are not supposed to walk out at night lest they unwittingly step on a worm.

Gandhi was always a great absorber. Jainism, as well as Buddhism, perceptibly colored Gandhi's thoughts and shaped his works. Both were attempts to reform the Hindu religion, India's dominant faith; both originated in the sixth century B.C. in northeastern India, in what is now the province of Bihar.

The Jain monk, Becharji Swami, helped Gandhi go to England. After graduating from high school, Gandhi enrolled in Samaldas College, in Bhavnagar, a town on the inland side of the Kathiawar peninsula. But he found the studies difficult and the atmosphere distasteful. A friend of the family suggested that if Mohandas was to succeed his father as prime minister he had better hurry and become a lawyer; the quickest way was to take a three-year course in England. Gandhi was most eager to go. But he was afraid of law; could he pass the examinations? Might it not be preferable to study medicine? He was interested in medicine.

Mohandas's brother objected that their father was opposed to the dissection of dead bodies and intended Mohandas for the bar. A Brahman friend of the family did not take the same dark view of the medical profession; but could a doctor become prime minister?

Mother Putlibai disliked parting with her last-born. "What will uncle say? He is the head of the family, now that father is no more." And where will the money come from?

Mohandas had set his heart on England. He developed energy and unwonted courage. He hired a bullock cart for the five-day journey to Porbandar where his uncle lived. To save a day, he left the cart and rode on a camel; it was his first camel ride.

Uncle was not encouraging; European-trained lawyers forsook Indian tradition; cigars were never out of their mouths; they ate everything; they dressed "as shamelessly as Englishmen." But he would not stand in the way. If Putlibai agreed he would, too.

So Mohandas was back where he had started. His mother sent him to uncle and uncle passed to mother. Meanwhile, Gandhi tried to get a scholarship from the Porbandar government. Mr. Lely, the British administrator of the state, rebuffed him curtly without even letting him present his case.

Mohandas returned to Rajkot. Pawn his wife's jewels? They were valued at two to three thousand rupees. Finally, his brother promised to supply the funds, but there remained his mother's doubts about young men's morals in England. Here Becharji Swami, the Jain monk, came to the rescue. He administered an oath to Mohandas who then solemnly took three vows: not to touch wine, women, or meat. Therewith, Putlibai consented.

Joyfully, in June, 1888, Gandhi left for Bombay with his brother, who carried the money. That did not end his tribulations. People said the Arabian Sea was too rough during the summer monsoon season; one ship had sunk in a gale. Departure was delayed. Meanwhile, the Modh Banias of Bombay heard about the projected trip. They convened a meeting of the clan and summoned Mohandas to attend. No Modh Bania had ever been to England, the elders argued; their religion forbade voyages abroad because Hinduism could not be practiced there.

Gandhi told them he would go nevertheless. At this, the headman ostracized Mohandas. "This boy shall be treated as an outcaste from today," the elder declared.

Undaunted, Gandhi bought a steamer ticket, a necktie, a short jacket, and enough food, chiefly sweets and fruit, for the three weeks to Southampton. On September 4th, he sailed. He was not yet eighteen. Several months earlier, Kasturbai had borne him a male child, and they called it Harilal. Now the trip to England gave Gandhi "a long and healthy separation" from his wife.

GANDHI AND THE GITA

Gandhi first read the *Gita* in Sir Edwin Arnold's translation while he was a second-year law student in London. He admits it was shameful not to have read it until the age of twenty, for the *Gita* is as sacred to Hinduism as the *Koran* is to Islam, the Old Testament to Judaism, and the New Testament to Christianity.

Subsequently, however, Gandhi read the original Sanskrit of the *Gita* and many translations. In fact, he himself translated the *Gita* from Sanskrit, which he did not know very well, into Gujarati and annotated it with comments.

. . . . .

Soon after reading the *Gita,* and especially in South Africa, Gandhi began his strivings to become a Karma yogi. Later, defining a Karma yogi, Gandhi wrote, "He will have no relish for sensual pleasures and will keep himself occupied with such activity as ennobles the soul. That is the path of action. Karma yoga is the yoga [means] which will deliver the self [soul] from the bondage of the body, and in it there is no room for self-indulgence."

Krishna puts it in a nutshell couplet:

> For me, O Partha, there is naught to do in the
> three worlds, nothing worth gaining that I have
> not gained; yet I am ever in action.

In a notable comment on the *Gita*, Gandhi further elucidates the ideal man or the perfect Karma yogi: "He is a devotee who is jealous of none, who is a fount of mercy, who is without egotism, who is self-less, who treats alike cold and heat, happiness and misery, who is ever forgiving, who is always contented, whose resolutions are firm, who has dedicated mind and soul to God, who causes no dread, who is not afraid of others, who is free from exultation, sorrow and fear, who is pure, who is versed in action yet remains unaffected by it, who renounces all fruit, good or bad, who treats friend and foe alike, who is untouched by respect or disrespect, who is not puffed up by praise, who does not go under when people speak ill of him, who loves silence and solitude, who has a disciplined reason. Such devotion is inconsistent with the existence at the same time of strong attachments."

The *Gita* defines detachment precisely:

> Freedom from pride and pretentiousness; non-
> violence, forgiveness, uprightness, service of the
> Master, purity, steadfastness, self-restraint.
> Aversion from sense-objects, absence of conceit,
> realization of the painfulness and evil of birth,
> death, age and disease.
> Absence of attachment, refusal to be wrapped up
> in one's children, wife, home and family, even-
> mindedness whether good or evil befall. . . .

By practicing these virtues, the yogi will achieve "union with the Supreme" or Brahman, "disunion from all union with pain" and "an impartial eye, seeing Atman in all beings and all beings in Atman."

Gandhi summarized it in one word: "Desirelessness."

Desirelessness in its manifold aspects became Gandhi's goal and it created innumerable problems for his wife and children, his followers, and himself. Krishna declares,

> But there is a unique reward. The great yogis, the
> Mahatmas or Great souls having come to Me,
> reach the highest perfection; they come not
> again to birth, unlasting and abode of misery.

Thus the yogi's highest recompense is to become so firmly united with God that he need never again return to the status of migrating mortal man. Several times during his life Gandhi expressed the hope not to be born anew.

. . . . .

There are devout Hindus, and mystic Hindus, who sit and meditate and fast and go naked and live in Himalayan caves. But Gandhi aimed to be ever active, ever useful, and ever needless. This was the realization he craved. Like everybody else, Gandhi had attachments. He sought to slough them off.

Hindu detachment includes but also transcends unselfishness; it connotes the religious goal of auto-disembodiment or non-violent self-effacement whereby the devotee discards his physical being and becomes one with God. This is not death; it is Nirvana. The attainment of Nirvana is a mystic process which eludes most Western minds and is difficult of achievement even by Hindus who assume, however, that mortals like Buddha and some modern mystics have accomplished the transformation. Gandhi did not accomplish it.

Gandhi did, however, achieve the status of yogi. . . .

The *Gita* concentrates attention on the purpose of life. In the West a person may ponder the purpose of life after he has achieved maturity and material success. A Hindu, if moved by the *Gita*, ponders the purpose of life when he is still on its threshold. Gandhi was very much moved by the spirit of the *Gita*.

68. PRE-ADOLESCENTS—WHAT MAKES THEM TICK?

FRITZ REDL

The wild antics of some preadolescents are reported in this amusing article. Two possible explanations of such behavior are offered, along with some suggestions as to how parents can manage to live through this period of their children's metamorphosis.

The period of pre-adolescence is a stretch of no-man's land in child study work. By pre-adolescence I mean the phase when the nicest children begin to behave in a most awful way. This definition cannot exactly be called scientific, but those who have to live with children of that age

Reprinted from *Child Study*, 21 (1944), 44–48, 58–59, by permission of the author and the Child Study Association of America.

will immediately recognize whom I am talking about. This also happens
to be the age about which we know least. Most of our books are written
either about Children or about Adolescents. The phase I am talking
about lies somewhere between the two—crudely speaking, between about
nine and thirteen, in terms of chronological age, or between the fifth and
eight grade in terms of school classification.

It is surprising that we know so little about this age, but there certainly is no doubt that it is one of the most baffling phases of all. Most re-
ferrals to child guidance clinics occur around this age, and if you look for
volunteers to work on programs in recreation or child care, you will make
this peculiar discovery: you will have no trouble finding people who just
love to bathe little babies until they smell good and shine. You will have
a little more, but not too much, trouble finding people who are just waiting for a chance to "understand" adolescents who "have problems" and
long for a shoulder on which to cry. But the pre-adolescent youngster
offers neither of these satisfactions. You won't find many people who
will be very happy working with him.

Are they children? No. Of course, they still look like young children.
Practically no visible change has as yet taken place in their sex development. The voice is about as shrill and penetrating as it ever was, the personal picture which they represent as still highly reminiscent of a child—
of about the worst child you have met, however, definitely not of the
child they themselves were just a short time ago.

Are they adolescent? No. While filled with a collector's curiosity for
odd elements of information about human sex life at its worst, they are
not as yet really maturing sexually. While they occasionally like to brag
about precocity in their sex attitude, "the boy" or "the girl" of the other
sex is still something they really don't know what to do with if left alone
with it for any length of time. While impertinent in their wish to penetrate
the secrets of adult life, they have no concepts about the future, little
worry about what is going to happen to them, nothing they would like to
"talk over with you."

The reason why we know so little about this phase of development is
simple but significant: it is a phase which is especially disappointing for
the adult, and especially so for the adult who loves youth and is interested
in it. These youngsters are hard to live with even where there is the most
ideal child-parent relationship. They are not as much fun to love as when
they were younger, for they don't seem to appreciate what they get at
all. And they certainly aren't much to brag about, academically or otherwise. You can't play the "friendly helper" toward them either—they think
you are plain dumb if you try it; nor can you play the role of the proud
shaper of youthful wax—they stick to your fingers like putty and things
become messier and messier the more you try to "shape" that age. Nor
can you play the role of the proud and sacerdotal warden of the values

of society to be pointed out to eager youth. They think you are plain funny in that role.

So the parent is at a loss and ready for a desperate escape into either of two bad mistakes—defeatism or tough-guy-stubbornness. The teacher shrugs her shoulders and blames most of this pre-adolescent spook on the teacher the youngster had before her, or on lack of parental cooperation, and hopes that somehow or other these children will "snap out of it." Even the psychiatrist, otherwise so triumphantly cynical about other people's trouble with children, is in a fix. For with these children you can't use "play techniques" any longer. They giggle themselves to death about the mere idea of sitting in one room with an adult and playing a table game while that adult desperately pretends that this is all there is to it. And one can't use the usual "interview technique" either. They find it funny that they should talk about themselves and their life, that they should consider as a "problem" what has "just happened," that they should try and remember how they felt about things, and that they are constantly expected to have "worries" or "fears"—two emotions which they are most skillful at hiding from their own self-perception, even if they do occur. Most of these youngsters seriously think the adult himself is crazy if he introduces such talk, and they naively enjoy the troubles they make, rather than those they have, and would much rather bear the consequences of their troubles than talk about them, even though those consequences include frustration or a beating or two.

Research, too, with very few exceptions, has skipped this period. If you study adolescence, you certainly can have graphs and charts on the rate at which the growth of pubic hair increases, the timing between that and the change of voice, and the irrelevance of both in terms of psycho-sexual development. Unfortunately, at the age we are talking about little of all this seems to take place. No drastic body changes occur, and whatever may happen within the glands is certainly not dramatic enough to explain the undoubtedly dramatic behavior of that phase. For a while some Yale biologists tried to discover an increase in hormone production around the age of eight, long before there is any visible sex maturation. However, they had trouble in making their research results useful for practical purposes. It took them weeks for one specimen of urine to be boiled in the right way as to show up the existence or non-existence of these hormones, and in the meantime Johnny would probably have been kicked out of five more schools anyway. In short, research has discreetly left this phase alone, and has retired from it, as it always does from things which are either too hard to demonstrate by statistical methods, or too hot to talk about after they have been discovered.

Thus, the practitioner—the parent, the teacher, counsellor or group worker—is left to his own devices. Fortunately, most of the things which are characteristic symptoms of this phase are known to us all.

PRE-ADOLESCENT BEHAVIOR—BAD AND IMPROPER

Here are some of the most frequent complaints adults raise in connection with their attempts to handle pre-adolescents: Outwardly, the most striking thing about them is their extreme physical restlessness. They can hardly stand still, running is more natural to them than walking, the word sitting is a euphemism if applied to what they do with a table and a chair. Their hands seem to need constant occupational therapy—they will turn up the edges of any book they handle, will have to manipulate pencils, any objects near them, or any one of the dozen-odd things they carry in their pockets, or even parts of their own body, whether it be nose and ears, scratching their hair, or parts of the anatomy usually taboo in terms of infantile upbringing. The return to other infantile habits is surprisingly intensive in many areas: even otherwise well-drilled and very housebroken youngsters may again show symptoms like bed-wetting, soiling, nail-biting, or its substitutes, like skin-chewing, finger-drumming, etc. Funny gestures and antics seem to turn up overnight with little or no reason—such things as facial tics, odd gestures and jerky movements, long-outgrown speech disorders, and the like.

In other areas these youngsters do not return to exactly the same habits of their infancy, but they go back to typical problem areas of younger childhood and start again where they had left off. Thus their search for the facts of life which had temporarily subsided under the impact of partial parental explanations will be resumed with vehemence, and with the impudence and insistence of a news correspondent rather than with the credulity of an obedient young child. It is the oddity, the wild fantastic story and the gory detail which fascinate them more than parental attempts at well-organized explanations of propagation, which they find rather boring.

Their old interpretation of the difference of sexes is revived too. Girls seem obviously inferior to boys, who again interpret the difference in sex as that of a minus versus plus rather than of a difference in anatomical function. Thus girls are no good unless they are nearly like boys; and where the direct pride in masculine sexuality is subdued, indirect bragging about the size and strength of the biceps takes its place and becomes and sets the evaluation of anybody's worth. The girls go through somewhat the same phase, accept the interpretation of the boys all too eagerly and often wander through a period of frantic imitation of boyish behavior and negation of their female role. What sex manipulation does occur at this age usually happens in terms of experimentation and is on a highly organic level and very different from the masturbation of later adolescent years.

The fantasy life of youngsters of this age is something to look into, too. Wild day-dreams of the comic-strip type of adventure, on the one hand, long stages of staring into empty space with nothing going on in their conscious mind on the other, are the two poles between which their fantasy life moves rapidly back and forth. Often manipulative play with a piece of string or the appearance of listening to the radio cover long stretches of quickly changing flights of ideas, and youngsters who reply "nothing," when you ask them what they were thinking about, do not necessarily lie. This description really fits the content as far as it could possibly be stated in any acceptable logical order and grammatical form.

The most peculiar phenomena, though, are found in the area of adult-child relationships. Even youngsters who obviously love their parents and have reason to do so, will develop stretches of surprising irritability, distrust, and suspicion. Easily offended and constantly ready with accusations that adults don't understand them and treat them wrongly, they are yet very reckless and inconsiderate of other people's feelings and are quite surprised if people get hurt because of the way they behave. The concept of gratitude seems to be something stricken from the inventory of their emotions. The worst meal at the neighbors', at which they weren't even welcome, may be described more glowingly in its glory than the best-planned feast that you arranged for their birthday. The silliest antics, the most irrelevant possessions or skills of neighbors will be admired 'way beyond any well-rooted qualities and superior achievements of father and mother.

Daily life with Junior becomes a chain of little irritations about little things. The fight against the demands of obeying the rules of time and space is staged as vehemently as if the children were one or two years old again. Keeping appointed meal times, coming home, going to bed at a prearranged hour, starting work, stopping play when promised—all these demands seem to be as hard to get across and as badly resented, no matter how reasonable the parents try to be about them, as if they were the cruel and senseless torments of tyranny.

Lack of submission to parent-accepted manners becomes another source of conflict. If these youngsters would listen as attentively to what Webster has to say as they do the language of the worst ragamuffin on the street corner, their grades in English would be tops. Dressing properly, washing, keeping clean are demands which meet with obvious indignation or distrust. In a way, they seem to have lost all sense of shame and decency. Previously clean-minded youngsters will not mind telling the dirtiest jokes if they can get hold of them, and the most charming angels of last year can spend an hour giggling over the acrobatics which a youngster performs with his stomach gas and consider it the greatest joke.

And yet, while unashamed in so many ways, there are other areas of life where they become more sensitive rather than more crude: the idea of being undressed or bathed by their own parent may all of a sudden release vehement feelings of shame hitherto unknown to their elders, and the open display of affection before others makes them blush as though they had committed a crime. The idea of being called a sissy by somebody one's own age is the top of shamefulness and nearly intolerable because of the pain it involves.

One of the most interesting attitude changes during this period is that in boy-girl relationships. The boy has not only theoretical contempt for the girl but he has no place for her socially. Social parties which adults push so often because they find the clumsiness of their youngsters so cute, and because it is so safe to have boys and girls together at that age, such social dances are a pain in the neck to youngsters, who would obviously much rather have a good free-for-all or chase each other all over the place. The girls have little place in their lives for the same-age boys either. It is true that with them the transition through this pre-adolescent period usually is shorter than with the boys. But for a time their actual need for boy company is nil. The picture is different, though, if you watch the children within their own sex gangs. Then, all of a sudden, in talks under safe seclusion with their buddies, the boys or girls will display a trumped-up interest in the other sex, will brag about their sexual knowledge or precocity or about their success in dating. All this bragging, however, though it is about sex, is on an entirely unerotic level; the partner of the other sex only figures in it as the fish in the fisherman's story. The opposite sex, like the fish, serves only an indirect means for self-glorification.

WHAT MAKES THEM TICK?

The explanation of this peculiar phenomenon of human growth must, I think, move along two lines. One is of an *individualistic* nature, the second is a chapter in *group psychology.*

Explanation No. I: During pre-adolescence the well-knit pattern of a child's personality is broken up or loosened, so that adolescent changes can be built into it and so that it can be modified into the personality of an adult

Thus, the purpose of this developmental phase is not *improvement* but *disorganization;* not a permanent disorganization, of course, but a dis-organization for future growth. This disorganization must occur, or else the higher organization cannot be achieved. In short, a child does not become an adult by becoming bigger and better. Simple "improvement" of a child's personality into that of an adult would only produce an over-sized child, an infantile adult. "Growing" into an adult means leaving behind, or destroying some of what the child has been, and becoming something else in many ways.

The real growth occurs during adolescence: pre-adolescence is the period of preliminary loosening up of the personality pattern in order that the change may take place. It is comparable to soaking the beans before you cook them. If this explanation is true, then we can understand the following manifestations:

1. During this "breaking-up-of-child-personality" period, old, *long-forgotten or repressed* impulses of earlier childhood will come afloat again, for awhile, before they are discarded for good. This would explain all that we have described about the return to infantile habits, silly antics, irritating behavior, recurring naughty habits, etc.

2. During this period of the breaking up of an established pattern, we also find that *already developed standards and values* lose their power and become ineffectual. Therefore the surprising lack of self-control, the high degree of disorganization, the great trouble those youngsters have in keeping themselves in shape and continuing to live up to at least some of the expectations they had no difficulty living up to a short time ago. The individual conscience of the child seems to lose its power, and even the force of his intelligence and insight into his own impulses is obviously weakened. This would explain all we have said about their unreliability, the lowering of these standards of behavior, the disappearance of some of the barriers of shame and disgust they had established and their surprising immunity to guilt feelings in many areas of life.

3. During a period of loosening up of personality texture, we would expect that the whole individual will be full of conflict, and that the *natural accompaniments* of conflict will appear again, namely, *anxieties and fears,* on the one hand, and *compulsive mechanisms of symbolic reassurance,* on the other. This is why so many of these youngsters really show fears or compulsive tics which otherwise only neurotic children would show. Yet this behavior is perfectly normal and will be only temporary. This would explain the frequent occurrence of fantastic fears in the dark, of ghosts and burglars, and it would also explain the intensity with which some of these youngsters cling to protective mechanisms, like the possession of a flashlight or gun as a symbol of protection, or the display of nervous tics and peculiar antics which usually include magic tricks to fool destiny and assure protection from danger or guilt.

For a long time I thought that all this about finishes the picture of pre-adolescent development, until a closer observation of the group life of pre-adolescents showed me that such a theory leaves much unexplained. It seems to me that there is still another explanation for a host of pre-adolescent symptoms.

Explanation No. II: During pre-adolescence it is normal for young-sters to drop their identification with adult society and establish a strong identification with a group of their peers

This part of pre-adolescent development is of a group psychological nature, and is as important to the child's later functioning as a citizen in society as the first principle is for his personal mental and emotional health. This group phenomenon is surprisingly universal and explains much of the trouble we adults have with children of pre-adolescent age. To be sure that I am rightly understood, I want to emphasize that what happens during this age goes way beyond the personal relationship between Johnny and his father. Johnny's father now becomes for him more than his father: he becomes, all of a sudden, a representative of the value system of adult society versus the child, at least in certain moments of his life. The same is true the other way around. Johnny becomes more to his father than his child: at certain moments he isn't Johnny any more but the typical representative of Youth versus Adult. A great many of the "educational" things adults do to children, as well as many of the re-bellious acts of children toward adults, are not meant toward the other fellow at all; they are meant toward the general group of "Adults" or "Youth" which this other person represents. To disentangle personal in-volvement from this group psychological meaning of behavior is per-haps the most vital and so far least attempted problem of education in adolescence.

If this explanation is true, then it seems to me that the following phenomena of pre-adolescent behavior will be well understood:

1. In no other age do youngsters show such a deep need for *clique and gang formation* among themselves as in this one. From the adult angle this is usually met with much suspicion. Of course, it is true that youngsters will tend to choose their companions from among those who are rejected, rather than approved of, by their parents. Perhaps we can understand why the more unacceptable a youngster is on the basis of our adult behavior code, the more highly acceptable he will be in the society of his own peers. The clique formation of youngsters among themselves usually has some form of definitely "gang" char-acter: that means it is more thoroughly enjoyed by being somewhat "subversive" in terms of adult standards. Remember how youngsters often are magically fascinated by certain types of ring-leaders, even though this ring-leadership may involve rather harmless though irri-tating activities—such as smoking, special clothes, late hours, gang language, etc.

   From the angle of the adult and his anxieties, much of this seems highly objectionable. From the angle of the youngster and his normal development, most of it is highly important. For it is vital that he satisfy the wish for identification with his pals, even though or just because such identification is sometimes frowned upon by the powers that be. The courage to stick to his pal against you, no matter how much he loves you and otherwise admires your advice, is an important step forward in the youngster's social growth.

2. In all groups something like an *unspoken behavior code* develops, and it is this unwritten code on which the difference between "good" and "bad" depends. Up to now the youngster has lived within the psychological confines of the adult's own value system. Good and bad were defined entirely on the basis of adult tastes. Now he enters the magical ring of peer-codes. And the code of his friends differs essentially from that of adult society. In some items the two are diametrically opposed. In terms of the adult code, for instance, it is good if children bring home high grades, take pride in being much better than the neighbor's children, in being better liked by the teacher, and more submissive to the whims of the teaching adult than are other people's children. In terms of peer-standards things are directly reversed. Studying too much exposes you to the suspicion of being a sissy, aggressive pride against other children in suspiciously close to teacher-pet roles, and obedience to the adult in power often comes close to being a fifth columnist in terms of "the gang."

Some of the typically adult-fashioned values are clearly rejected by peer standards; others are potentially compatible at times, while conflicting at other times; some of them can be shared in common. Thus, a not too delinquent "gang" to which your youngster is proud to belong may be characterized by the following code-range: it is all right in this gang to study and work reasonably well in school. It is essential, though, that you dare to smoke, lie, even against your own father, if it means the protection of a pal in your gang, that you bear the brunt of scenes at home if really important gang activities are in question. At the same time this gang would not want you to steal, would be horrified if your sex activity went beyond the telling of dirty stories, and would oust you tacitly because they would think you too sophisticated for them. The actual group of pre-adolescents moves between hundreds of different shades of such gang-codes, and the degree to which we adults have omitted opening our eyes to this vital phase of child development is astounding.

3. The change from *adult-code* to *peer-code* is not an easy process for a youngster but full of conflict and often painful. For, while he would like to be admired by his pals on a peer-code basis, he still loves his parents personally and hates to see them misunderstand him or have them get unhappy about what he does. And, while he would love to please his family and be again accepted by them and

have them proud of him, he simply couldn't face being called a sissy or be suspected of being a coward or a teacher's pet by his friends. In most of those cases where we find a serious conflict between the two sets of standards, we will find the phenomenon of *social hysteria*. This applies to youngsters who so overdo their loyalty to either one of the two behavior standards that they then have to go far beyond a reasonable limit. Thus, you find youngsters so scared of being thought bad by their parents that they don't dare to mix happily with children of their own age; and you find others so keen to achieve peer status with friends of their own age that they begin to reject parental advice, every finer feeling of loyalty to the home, and accept all and any lure of gang prestige even if it involves delinquent and criminal activity. It is obvious that a clear analysis by the adult and the avoidance of counter-hysteria can do much to improve things.

HOW TO SURVIVE LIFE WITH JUNIOR?

If any of the above is true, then it should have an enormous impact on education. For then most of this pre-adolescent spook isn't merely a problem of things that shouldn't happen and ought to be squelched, but of things that should happen, but need to be regulated and channelized. Of course, you can't possibly just let Junior be as pre-adolescent as he would like without going crazy yourself, and you definitely shouldn't think of self-defense only and thus squelch the emotional and social development of your offspring. How to do both—survive and also channelize normal but tough growth periods without damage to later development —is too long a story to complete in a short article. But here are a few general hints:

1. AVOID COUNTER-HYSTERICS

It seems to me that ninety per cent of the more serious problems between children and parents or teachers on which I have ever been consulted could have been easily avoided. They were not inherent in the actual problems of growth. They were produced by the hysterical way in which the adults reacted to them. Most growth problems—even the more serious ones—can be outgrown eventually, though this may be a painful process—provided the adults don't use them as a springboard for this own over-emotional reactions. This does not mean that I advocate that you give up and let everything take its course. I do suggest you study the situation and decide where to allow things and where to interfere. The problem is: whichever you decide to do—the *way* you do it should be realistic, free from hysteric over-emotionalism. With this policy in mind you can enjoy all the fun of having problems with your child without producing a problem child.

2. DON'T FIGHT WINDMILLS

Let's not forget that pre-adolescents are much more expert in handling us than we ever can be in handling them. Their skill in sizing us up and using our emotions and weaknesses for their own ends has reached a peak at this age. It took them eight to ten years to learn, but they have learned by thorough observation. While we were worrying about them, they were not worried about us, and they had ample time and leisure to study our psychology. This means that if they now go out on the venture of proving to themselves how emancipated they are, they will choose exactly the trick which will irritate us most. They will develop pre-adolescent symptoms in accordance with their understanding of our psychology. Thus, some of them will smoke, curse, talk about sex, or stay out late. Some will stop being interested in their grades, get kicked out of school, or threaten to become the type of person who will never be acceptable in good society. Others again will develop vocational interests which we look down on, will choose the company we dread, talk language which makes us jump, or may even run away at intervals.

But whatever surface behavior they display—don't fall for it. Don't fight the behavior. Interpret the cause of it first, then judge how much and in what way you should interfere. Thus, Johnny's smoking may really mean he is sore that his father never takes him to a football match, or it may mean he thinks you don't appreciate how adult he already is, or it may mean he has become dependent on the class-clown. Mary's insistence upon late hours may mean she doesn't know how to control herself, or it may mean she is sore because her school pals think you are social snobs who live a life different from theirs, or it may mean she is so scared that her sex ignorance will be discovered that she has to run around with a crowd more sophisticated about staying up late, so as to hide her lack of sophistication in another respect.

In any case, all these things are not so hard to figure out. Instead of getting excited and disapproving of the strange behavior, just open your eyes for a while and keep them open without blinking.

3. PROVIDE A FRAME OF LIFE ADEQUATE FOR GROWTH

No matter how much you dislike it, every pre-adolescent youngster needs the chance to have some of his wild behavior come out in some place or other. It will make a lot of difference whether or not he has a frame of life adequate for such growth. For example: Johnny needs the experience of running up against some kind of adventurous situation where he can prove he is a regular guy and not just mother's boy. Cut him off from all life situations containing elements of unpredictability and he may have to go stealing from the grocery store to prove his point. Give him a free and experimental camp setting to be adventurous in and he will be happily pre-adolescent without getting himself or anybody else in trouble. All youngsters need some place where pre-adolescent traits can be exercised and even tolerated. It is your duty to plan for such places in their life as skillfully as you select their school or vocational opportunities.

4. WATCH OUT FOR PRE-ADOLESCENT CORNS

Most people don't mind their toes being stepped on occasionally. But if there is a corn there, that is a different matter. Well, all pre-adolescents have certain corns, places where they are hypersensitive. Avoid these as much as possible. One of the most important to avoid is harking back to their early childhood years. The one thing they don't want to be reminded of is of themselves as small children, yourself as the mother or father of the younger child. If you punish—don't repeat ways you used when they were little. If you praise—don't use arguments that would please a three-year-old but make a thirteen-year-old red with shame or fury. Whether you promise or reward, threaten or blackmail, appeal to their sense, morals, or anything else, always avoid doing it in the same way you used to do when they were little.

I have seen many pre-adolescents reject what their parents wanted, not because they felt that it was unreasonable or unjustified, but on account of the way in which the parents put the issue. There is something like a developmental level of parental control as well as developmental levels of child behavior. The two have to be matched or there will be fireworks.

5. IF IN DOUBT, MAKE A DIAGNOSTIC CHECK-UP

Not all the behavior forms we described above are always merely "pre-adolescent." Some of them are more than that. After all, there are such things as juvenile delinquents and psycho-neurotics, and we shouldn't pretend that everything is bound to come out in the wash.

Usually you can get a good hunch about dangerous areas if you check on these points: How deep is the pre-adolescent trait a youngster shows? If it is too vehement and impulsive, too unapproachable by even the most reasonable techniques, then the chances are that Johnny's antics are symptoms not only of growth but also of something being wrong somewhere and needing repair. Often this may be the case: Five of Johnny's antics are just pre-adolescent, pure and simple, and should not be interfered with too much. However, these five are tied up with five others which are definitely serious, hang-overs from old, never really solved problems, results of wrong handling, wrong environmental situations, or other causes. It will do no good to brush off the whole matter by calling it pre-adolescent. In that case the first five items need your protection and the other five need a repair job done. Whenever you are very much in doubt, it is wise to consult expert help for the checkup—just as you would in order to decide whether a heart murmur is due to too fast growth or to an organic disturbance.

69. GUIDING THE DEVELOPMENT OF THE PREADOLESCENT

A. W. BLAIR AND W. H. BURTON

The list presented here attempts to summarize the principles for guiding the development and growth of the preadolescent. The important assumptions on which many of the principles are based are unstated. It would be rewarding for the reader to list these.

A LIST OF GENERAL PRINCIPLES

The following principles and corollary practices are recommended for dealing with children [in later childhood]. They are drawn from those suggestions for guidance that have appeared throughout this study. Some of them are based upon the various investigators' interpretations of their own findings, others upon the interpretation of those findings by the present writers. All of these principles have had previous discussion in the body of this study.

I. The environment of children at this level should be so arranged as to provide for their increasing independence from adult domination.
  A. Children's basic emotional relations tend to have different degrees of importance at different developmental levels. *Security* in the family seems the greatest social need in infancy and early childhood. Self-expression and *self-development* become of primary importance in later childhood. *Social adjustment* takes the fore during adolescence and adulthood.
  B. Freedom for these children should be provided in such a way as to continue the security the child feels in his family relations. There is a tendency for adults to resent the natural conduct of later childhood.
    1. Parents and other adults should avoid the appearance of rejection as a result of the changing attitudes and behavior of

From *Growth and Development of the Preadolescent.* By Arthur Witt Blair and William H. Burton. Copyright, 1951, Appleton–Century–Crofts, Inc.

children at this level. The child who feels rejected is likely to exhibit extreme forms of behavior or delinquent conduct.

2. Adults must realize that the child is undergoing inner conflicts as a result of his efforts to live up to two sets of standards, those of his peers and those of his home and school. His feelings about each will fluctuate. The home and school must be available with the security they offer when the child seeks it.

3. Adults should remember that much of the behavior they expect of these children is related to maintaining their own social class status and that the child's concept of time is probably inadequate in understanding the long range implications of such status.

4. Adults should be able to accept without too great concern types of behavior that seem foolish and unreasonable and to take an interest in aspects of life they have long since rejected.

5. Children from nine to twelve are ready for a widening of social contacts, with guests in the home and visits to the homes of friends and play-mates.

6. Experiences should be provided so that the child can find expression of his desire for independence without harm (trips alone to relatives and friends, gang adventures, decisions about property, etc.).

7. Out-of-family experiences should be provided for these children in the community by means of club membership, activities with various community enterprises, and personal responsibilities.

8. Daily routines should be kept free of moral issues so that the observation or forgetting of them does not enter into the pattern of rebellion often exhibited by these children.

9. Family and school routines may be found more acceptable if the child of this age is allowed to make his own kind of arrangements.

10. What often appears to be irresponsibility, instability, disobedience, and restlessness may be due to the child's efforts to find an area for self-expression.

11. The immature and inadequate forms of expressing independence may be considered a desirable step in the direction of self-reliance.

C. Growth in independence appears to be one of the chief values accruing from membership in a gang.

1. Such membership may give the child psychological support for expressing himself in adult situations.

2. Gangs . . . make . . . demands upon the individual . . . cooperatively. . . .

3. For some children the gang provides an escape from over-solicitude.
4. The gang provides opportunity for wider expression of self.
5. Gang secrets and activities give a child a feeling of importance.
6. Ability or readiness to feel a part of the group depends upon the child's security in the home.
7. The tendency to assume or reject certain rôles in the group seems to depend upon the pattern of subordination, over-protection, or rejection found in the home.

D. The school and home have opportunity to help children at this age grow in independence from adult domination.

1. The interest these children have in setting up their own standards can be utilized in planning and participating in the activities of the school, and of the family.
2. The small spontaneously formed groups of age-sex mates may be a desirable basis for accomplishing some of the coöperative activities of the school and home.
3. These children are more likely to accept the purposes, decisions, and activities of school and home if they have had a part in the selection and planning of these activities. Adult-imposed activities in school or home are subject to the pattern of rebellion these children often exhibit toward adults.
4. Because of the child's disregard for adult standards, school success might better be achieved by more immediate forms of reward than the artificial rewards based on standards of achievement or the emphasis upon future values and status. Coöperation in the home follows the same pattern.
5. Since the task of winning peer recognition is such a powerful force in organizing the behavior and attitudes of these children, the school and home should make provision for individuals to gain success in group relations.
   a. A democratic school and family group with opportunities for coöperative planning on the part of children and teacher will help the rejected child find a place in the group as a valued individual.
   b. The teacher and parent may find in the children's success or failure in school work an indication of the achievement of individuals in winning status with their peers.
   c. The teacher or parent may help the child gain a place in peer group by giving him assistance in developing special interests of significance to the group.
   d. The school and home should provide recreational outlets for children in order that they may find satisfaction in additional group living.

6. Disabilities in academic subjects, particularly reading, may be used as a means of showing disregard for adult values.

   a. Extreme adult concern over reading disability at a time when the child's status with his gang is very important may result in an emotional conflict that further retards progress in reading.

   b. Efforts to improve reading or any of the other intellectual skills should probably not interfere with the opportunities the child has for establishing himself with children of his own age and sex.

   c. The child's security with adults should not rely heavily upon conformity to fixed school standards.

   d. Motivation for improving school skills during these years probably depends upon the extent to which these skills have functional value for the child in meeting situations of immediate concern to him.

E. Physically these children are capable of carrying on many activities that will give them increasing independent status.

   1. Opportunities should be made available for these children to take responsibilities commensurate with their new physical skill.

   2. Provisions should be made for children at this level to develop interests and activities in crafts and hobbies.

F. Intellectually these children are capable of many independent activities.

   1. Their interest in science, invention, and physical phenomena should be utilized in helping them gain a realistic conception of their environment.

   2. Opportunities should be provided for experimentation and problem solving involving causal relations.

   3. The skill in reading of the majority of these children should allow them to become less dependent upon adults for understanding their environment.

G. The success of this early striving for independence may in a large measure determine the child's reaction to further independence in adolescence and maturity.

II. The social and developmental status of later childhood should be utilized for the development of moral judgment.

A. These children should be allowed to make mistakes without causing undue excitement or evoking reference to moral values; they should experience some of the realities of cause and effect in human relationships.

   1. The child should learn to do things because of the satisfaction of doing them without worrying about such virtues as re-

sponsibility or regularity as expressions of his fluctuating feelings toward the people around him.

2. The standards set up by adults concerning private property, honesty, tidiness, and cleanliness are often put at a higher level than these children can normally attain, hence tensions and conflict result.

3. Immediate cause and effect relationships are probably more effective with this age group than discussion of the values and morals involved in their behavior.

4. Providing experiences which bring these children to grips with reality is an effective way to contribute to the development of desirable personal evaluations and relations with the environment.

5. The good habits and social conformity that have been acquired by imitation and the domination of adults in the immediately preceding years are being subjected to reality testing.

6. Most children of this level are ready for a program that gives them many opportunities to make their own decisions and to face the consequences of their mistakes where these consequences are not too serious.

B. The movement of the child away from almost complete dependence upon adult authority through the later childhood dependence upon the majority rule of his peers should be considered progress toward the capacity to "judge" situations for himself.

1. The child at this level is beginning to recognize that there may be more than one set of standards of right and wrong and to exercise some choice and judgment.

2. The child in his gang is learning to deal with others on an equal footing.

3. The gang teaches lessons that force consideration for others. These lessons are usually quite objective and impersonal. Faults are discussed openly and discipline is prompt and relentless.

4. As the child's capacity to identify himself with others and to be interested in others grows, his capacity to judge situations on a wider basis probably grows.

5. The guidance of gang activities will be more successful if it employs processes that are subtle and indirect. These children are likely to respond to spontaneous and affectionate interest.

   a. Individual competition and the control of behavior by authority does not recognize the basic attitude of these children toward each other and toward adults.

   b. There is need for regulation within the group but the adult's rôle is not one of restraint or too direct control.

      c. Failure to provide any supervision of the activities of the gang or the rejection of the child because of his gang activities may result in delinquent behavior.

  C. In schools where effort is made to reach a better understanding of the older child, less emphasis will be placed upon adult standards of behavior as such, and more upon the leads which the child gives as the means of guiding him toward desirable moral development.

    1. The center of instruction in the intermediate grades (fourth, fifth, and sixth) to develop social understanding should probably be organized around the problems and processes which are within the immediate experience of the child.

    2. School experiences should be selected so as to give these children an understanding of social realities.

III. Opportunities for adjusting to the proper sex rôle should be provided for the individual during these years.

  A. The group or gang life at this age provides almost the sole opportunity children have for imaginal or play activities in which they can express masculinity or femininity.

    1. A child whose growth pattern places him at the extremes either in size or functional maturity in his peer group—the accelerated or the delayed—may face grave difficulties of behavioral adjustments in his group.

    2. The ability to compete physically is closely associated with a child's achievement of confidence and his feeling of security in associating with his gang.

    3. Children at this level should be given help in developing those skills that will make them acceptable to their peers.

      a. Most of these skills are those requiring competence in games and manual activities.

      b. Some children will require guidance in assuming a more subordinating or a more dominating rôle.

      c. Others will need help in eliminating habits or characteristics that are more appropriate to the opposite sex.

      d. School, community, and home should make possible large amounts of physical activity. These children respond to organized games, self-testing activities, and athletic dances.

  B. In grouping these children for instruction the fact should be recognized that during later childhood girls are likely to have more mature social and intellectual interests because of their more rapid physical maturation.

    1. As a result of each sex identifying itself with those activities and attitudes which differentiate it from the other, there often develops antagonism between the sexes. This antagonism

might be lessened if the sexes were not placed together in highly competitive situations.

   a. The imposition by the schools of highly artificial standards upon all children of the same age, sex, or class group probably intensifies this antagonism.

   b. The more advanced language-skill of girls of the same age as boys probably makes much school comparison undesirable.

   c. There probably should be some differentiation between boys and girls at this level in the selection of materials (subject matter) and activities of instruction.

  2. The importance children of this age attach to gang membership and being among others of the same age and sex should be a factor in grouping these children for instruction.

   a. Physical skill and physical size are of primary importance in giving these children confidence among age-sex mates.

   b. The physical education programs for this level should recognize sex differences in interests and activities and provide a differing program for boys and girls.

   c. A measure of a child's social maturity is his imitation of others of the same age and sex and a disregard for the opposite sex.

C. Boys of this age range should have the opportunity of associating themselves closely with men to a greater extent than is common in the home and in the school. Some of their undesirable behavior appears to be an over-compensation for the lack of a realistic conception of the male rôle in society.

IV. The strains and conflicts of adolescent adjustment may be lessened by adequate provision for sound personal and social integration during later childhood.

A. The satisfaction the child receives from his relationships with adults as he tries out the new social contacts of later childhood are likely to affect the confidence he places in adults for help in achieving the social adjustments of adolescence.

B. The character of the independence the child achieves from adults during later childhood will probably help determine his development of independence during adolescence.

C. The child's success in finding the approval of his peers and security in the gang life of later childhood is likely to affect the confidence with which he attempts to adjust to the peer culture of adolescence.

D. The strength of the child's identification with members of his own sex during later childhood may largely determine his feelings of adequacy as he begins the heterosexual adjustments of adolescence.

E. During later childhood the individual should have access to that information which will help make sexual maturation and his relationships with the opposite sex realistic and free from anxiety.

   1. These children are likely to seek and understand this information more objectively than are adolescents.

   2. The variations in individual experiences and interests indicate that this information is probably best given in response to individual questions and to the extent of the child's personal interest.

   3. Questions about sexual matters may become personal and highly specific during these years but not necessarily emotional unless adults react emotionally to them.

SUGGESTIONS TO ENABLE PARENTS AND TEACHERS TO REACT TO THE EMOTIONAL AND SOCIAL DIFFICULTIES OF PREADOLESCENTS

1. *When children act like children, adults should act like adults.*

Children with emotional difficulties will "blow off steam," will be defiant, "sassy," or fresh. The adult often reverts to childish reactions and manifests emotional instability on a par with the developing child. Maturity should enable parents and teachers to "take it in stride," keep calm, or as the children themselves say, "keep their shirts on."

Let children "blow up" occasionally. Often expressing a "gripe" cures it. Sympathetic and understanding reception by parents and teachers gives the child confidence that he will be taken seriously and treated with respect. This is the first step in influencing the child toward more mature behavior. Eventually children can consider with adults the actual causes of their own behavior.

2. *Respect the developing individuality. Do not treat growing boys and girls like babies: do not treat them as adults.*

The type of restraint and punishment used with babies merely insults and antagonizes boys and girls who are achieving independence. Appeal to adult standards, ideals, or motives is meaningless to children, and merely convinces them further that adults are unreasonable and unfair.

3. *Use judgment in selecting occasions for discussion, restraint, or punishment.*

Taking note of every single noisy, boisterous, irritating action by children again convinces them that adults only "pick on them" unfairly. The child, however, cannot just run wild. Choice must be made of acts and occasions for discussion. Many everyday, routine disturbances may be overlooked, particularly those that are likely to change anyway. A small number of essential items may be selected for improvement through guidance.

4. *Take the time and trouble to provide opportunity for natural outlets in activity, preferably group activity.*

The basic change in the environment surrounding children has much to do with their so-called bad behavior and delinquency. An earlier rural environment provided ample natural activities, which the urban situation, with commercially provided amusement, with needs supplied through mass production of everyday goods, does not.

Encourage spontaneous group or gang activity, possibly redirecting these activities coöperatively if necessary. Indicate the opportunity for adult assistance and guidance without pressing the matter.

5. *Have and express faith in the children, confidence in their growing independence.*

Invite group participation in planning activities and in making decisions: in organizing learning activities, selecting and using subject matter and experiences. Encourage the assumption of independence and responsibility, provide opportunities for it. Allow for action to follow the group decisions and assumption of responsibility. Aid in picking up the pieces if mistakes occur, give guidance as one of the group, avoiding senseless censure for honest mistakes which are themselves a corrective and aid to further learning. Recognize and praise the successful completion of a child's planned project or learning experience.

Allow children to handle money, their own allowance or the treasury of the group with some independence. Plan together, in the family or the group, for the general uses of money but allow leeway for personal choice and decision. Children do not learn to spend money wisely by being told how, by being prevented from spending at all, but by buying what they want, to discover later that the purchase was not worth the cost.

6. *Act consistently, as fairly as you know how, and without betraying annoyance, or other emotional instability.*

There are causes for all behavior. Punishing the symptoms is futile. Punishing because of irritation and annoyance at the symptoms is worse than futile; it is actively detrimental. Patiently and honestly seek the cause, and often the behavior will seem natural and inevitable with resultant effect on adult reactions.

7. *Do not be fooled into neglecting the child who causes no trouble.*

The quiet, good children who "never cause a moment's trouble" are in fact those in far greater need of attention than those who irritate us with their noise and "bad behavior." These are the children who as adults have "breakdowns," who never achieve emotional stability, who "do not get along with people."

Aid these children in the area of human relations; in finding friends, in taking part in group processes, however simple. If the quiet child is academically advanced and socially retarded, give opportunities for developing balanced living. The same points hold for the "lonely" children also.

8. *Realize that, while possessing certain commonalties, children are different each from the other.*

Children cannot be expected to like the same things, books, or activities, not even when members of the same family. Patterns and rhythms of growth are basically different. Each can participate and learn only in his own way.

9. *Realize that children have feelings, and in this area, are under a double handicap.*

The feelings and emotions of childhood are not only strong, but mature controls have not yet developed. The child, in addition, is usually severely repressed by adults when emotional reactions appear. Children learn to hide or repress the overt behaviors of emotional expression but the frustration, antagonism, and tension cannot be dissipated. The bottled-up emotions find other outlets, usually with worse behavior than the original outburst.

10. *Recognize that children are members of a peer society, the aims, values, approvals, disapprovals, of which are far more potent with the child than the corresponding factors in the adult society surrounding the child.*

Neglect of the peer society of children is a tragic blunder by adults. The children are not only controlled more effectively by the organization of their own society, but they are, through that society, achieving standards and social habits which will later grow into necessary and desirable adult behavior.

11. *Provide opportunities for boys to have more association with men during these years.*

12. *Stop comparing boys with girls during these years when the girls' intellectual maturity is on the average about two years ahead of the boys:* Do not compare one child with another. Basic individual differences make this not only futile, but detrimental.

70. SEXUAL BEHAVIOR
IN THE HUMAN FEMALE

ALFRED C. KINSEY *et al.*

*Sexual relations before marriage are not sanctioned in our society.
Since young people mature sexually in their early teens, and since
most people marry in their early twenties, adolescents usually have
no socially acceptable outlets for their strong sexual urges for a
period of approximately ten years. Few societies in the world are as
sexually repressive as our own.*

*Kinsey deals with some of the sexual outlets which young
people discover for themselves. His comments raise a number of
questions which should be investigated further: Have laws,
punishment, and police action been effective in controlling sexual
activity? What are the problems here?*

SEXUAL PROBLEMS OF UNMARRIED YOUTH

As . . . [an] instance of the everyday need for a wider general
understanding of human sexual behavior, there are the sexual problems
of unmarried individuals in our social organization, and particularly of
unmarried youth. The problems are products of the fact that the human
female and male become biologically adults some years before our
social custom and the statute law recognize them as such, and of the
fact that our culture has increasingly insisted that sexual functions should
be confined to persons who are legally recognized as adults, and particularly to married adults.

This failure to recognize the mature capacities of teen-age youth is
relatively recent. Prior to the last century or so, it was well understood
that they were the ones who had the maximum sexual capacity, and
the great romances of literature turned around the love affairs of teen-
age boys and girls. Achilles' intrigue with Deidamia, by whom a son
was born, had occurred some time before he was fifteen. Acis had just
passed sixteen at the time of his love affair with Galatea. Chione was
reputed to have had "a thousand suitors when she reached the mar-
riageable age of fourteen." Narcissus had reached his sixteenth year

Selections reprinted from *Sexual Behavior in the Human Female* (W. B. Saunders
Co., 1953), pp. 13–21, 101–126, by permission of the publisher and the Institute for
Sex Research, Inc.

when "many youths and many maidens sought his love." Helen was twelve years old when Paris carried her off from Sparta. In one of the greatest of pastoral romances, Daphnis was fifteen and Chloe was thirteen. Heloise was eighteen when she fell in love with Abelard. Tristram was nineteen when he first met Isolde. Juliet was less than fourteen when Romeo made love to her. All of these youth, the great lovers of history, would be looked upon as immature adolescents and identified as juvenile delinquents if they were living today. It is the increasing inability of older persons to understand the sexual capacities of youth which is responsible for the opinion that there is a rise in juvenile delinquency, for there are few changes in the sexual behavior of the youth themselves.

There is an increasing opinion that these youths should ignore their sexual responses and should abstain from sexual activities prior to marriage—which means, for the average male and female in this country today, until they are somewhere between twenty-one and twenty-three years of age. But neither the law nor the custom can change the age of onset of adolescence, nor the development of the sexual capacities of teen-age youths. Consequently they continue to be aroused sexually, and to respond to the point of orgasm. There is no evidence that it is possible for any male who is adolescent, and not physically incapacitated, to get along without some kind of regular outlet until old age finally reduces his responsiveness and his capacity to function sexually. While there are many females who appear to get along without such an outlet during their teens, the chances that a female can adjust sexually after marriage seem to be materially improved if she has experienced orgasm at an earlier age. . . .

In actuality, the teen-age and twenty-year-old males respond more frequently than most older males; their responses are, on the whole, more intense than those of older males; and, in spite of their difficulty in finding socio-sexual outlets, they reach orgasm more frequently than most older males. Among unmarried males the frequency of orgasm is at a maximum somewhere between the ages of sixteen and eighteen. Similarly, among married males there is no age group in which sexual activity is, on an average, more frequent than it is among the males in their late teens and early twenties.

The attempt to ignore and suppress the physiologic needs of the sexually most capable segment of the population has led to more complications than most persons are willing to recognize. This is why so many of our American youth, both females and males, depend upon masturbation instead of coitus as a pre-marital outlet. Restraints on pre-marital heterosexual contacts appear to be primary factors in the development of homosexual activities among both females and males. . . . The considerable development of pre-marital petting, which many foreigners consider one of the unique aspects of the sexual pattern in this country, is similarly an outgrowth of this restraint on pre-marital coitus. . . . The law specifies the right of the married adult to have regular intercourse, but it makes no provision whatsoever for the approximately 40 per cent of the population which is sexually mature but unmarried. Many youths and older unmarried females and males are seriously disturbed because the only sources of sexual outlet available to them are either legally or socially disapproved.

Most unmarried males, and not a few of the unmarried females, would like to know how to resolve this conflict between their physiologic capacities and the legal and social codes. They would like to know whether masturbation will harm them physically or interfere with their subsequent responses to a marital partner; they would like to know whether they should or should not engage in petting; and, apart from the moral issues that may be involved, they would like to know what pre-marital petting experience may actually do to their marital adjustments. Should they or should they not have coitus before marriage? What effect will this sort of experience have on their subsequent marital adjustments? In any type of sexual activity, what things are normal and what things are abnormal? What has been the experience of other youth faced with these same problems? On all of these matters most youth are ready to consider the social and moral values, but they would also like to know what correlations the scientific data show between pre-marital and marital experience.

In an attempt to answer some of these questions, we have tried to discover the incidences and frequencies of non-marital activities among American females and males, and have attempted to discover what correlations there may be between pre-marital patterns of behavior and subsequent sexual adjustments in marriage. . . .

SEXUAL EDUCATION OF CHILDREN

Within the last thirty years, parents in increasing number have come to realize the importance of the early education of their children on matters of sex. But what things children should be taught, who should teach them, at what age they should be taught, and how the teaching should be conducted, are matters about which there has been much theory but few data on which to base any program of sex education. For some years we have, therefore, obtained information from our subjects in regard to the ages at which they acquired their first knowledge of various aspects of sex, the sources of their first knowledge, and the ages at which they first became involved in each type of sexual activity. In addition to obtaining this record from each adult, we have engaged in a more detailed study of younger children and particularly of children between two and five years of age. The study needs to be carried further before we are ready to report in detail, but some things already seem clear.

It is apparent that considerable factual knowledge about most sexual phenomena is acquired by most children before they become adolescent, but there is a considerable number who acquire their first information in their youngest years, as soon as they are able to talk. Although some persons insist that the sex education of the child should be undertaken only by the child's parents or religious mentors, not more than a few percent—perhaps not more than 5 per cent—of all the subjects in the present study recalled that they had received anything more than the most incidental sort of information from either of those sources. Most of the children had acquired their earliest information from other children. Whether it is more desirable, in terms of the ultimate effects upon their lives, that such information should come first from more experienced adults, or whether it is better that children should learn about sex from other children, is a question which we are not yet able to answer. At this stage in our study we are quite certain that no one has any sufficient information to evaluate objectively the relative merits of these diverse sources of sexual education.

It is apparent, however, that if parents or other adults are to be the sources of the child's first information on sex, they must give that information by the time the child is ten or twelve, and in many instances at some earlier age. Otherwise the child, whatever the parents may wish, will have previously acquired the information from its companions.

Our studies indicate, moreover, that the way in which a child reacts to the sexual information which it receives, and to the overt sexual activity in which it may become involved in later years, may depend upon attitudes which it develops while it is very young. Early attitudes in respect to nudity, to anatomic differences between the sexes, to the reproductive function, to verbal references to sex, to the qualities and prerequisites which our culture traditionally considers characteristic of females or males, and to still other aspects of sex are developed at very early ages. Emotional reactions on some of these matters have been discernible in some of the two-year-olds with which we have worked, and the three-year-old children have had pronounced reactions on most of these matters. When the child becomes older these early attitudes may influence its reactions to sexual manifestations in its own body, its capacity to meet sexual situations without serious disturbance, its acceptance or non-acceptance of socio-sexual contacts, and, as an adult, his or her capacity to adjust sexually in marriage. Because early training may be so significant, most parents would like to have information on the most effective methods of introducing the child to the realities of sex.

Most parents would like to know more about the significance of pre-adolescent sex play, about the sexual activities in which children actually engage, about the possibilities of their children becoming sexually involved with adults, and what effect such involvements may have upon a child's subsequent sexual adjustments. Most parents would like to know whether the sexual responses of a child are similar, physiologically, to those of an adult. They would like to know whether there are differences between the sexual problems of adolescent boys and those of adolescent girls; and if there are differences, they would like to know on what they depend. The data in the present volume will answer some of these questions.

In this study, we have had the excellent cooperation of a great many parents because they are concerned with the training of their children, and because they realize how few data there are on which to establish a sound program of sex education.

SOCIAL CONTROL OF SEXUAL BEHAVIOR

Most societies have recognized the necessity of protecting their members from those who impose sexual relationships on others by the use of force, and our own culture extends the same sort of restriction to those who use such intimidation as an adult may exercise over a child, or such undue influence as a social superior may exercise over an underling. In its encouragement of marriage society tries to provide a socially acceptable source of sexual outlet, and it considers that sexual activities which interfere with marriages and homes, and sexual activities which lead to the begetting of children outside of marriage, are socially undesirable. The social organization also tries to control persons who make nuisances of themselves, as the exhibitionist and voyeur may do, by departing from the generally approved custom. In addition our culture considers that social interests are involved when an individual departs from the Judeo-Christian sex codes by engaging in such sexual activities as masturbation, mouth-genital contacts, homosexual contacts, animal contacts, and other types of behavior which do not satisfy the procreative function of sex.

The Incidence of Sex Offenses.   Within the last decade, there has been a growing concern in this country over an apparent increase in the number of persons who engage in sexual activities which are contrary to our law and custom. Reports in the press and the information which is officially released often suggest that the number of sex offenders is steadily increasing.

Unfortunately, however, there has been no good measure of the actual extent of the problem that is involved. The conclusion that the incidences of sex offense have increased is based primarily upon an increase in the number of arrests on sex charges, but it is not sub-stantiated by our information on the incidences of various types of sexual activity among older and younger generations in the population as a whole. Statements concerning increasing incidences usually do not allow for the considerable increase in the total population of the country, the more complete reporting of sex crimes by the press and by the agencies which contribute to the official statistics, and the fact that the newer sex laws make felonies of some acts which were never penalized or which were treated as minor misdemeanors until a few years ago. Moreover, there has been no adequate recognition of the fact that fluctuations in the number of arrests may represent nothing more than fluctuations in the activities of law enforcement officers.

Preliminary analyses of our data indicate that only a minute fraction of one per cent of the persons who are involved in sexual behavior which is contrary to the law are ever apprehended, prosecuted, or convicted, and that there are many other factors besides the behavior of the apprehended individual which are responsible for the prosecu-tion of the particular persons who are brought to court. The prodding of some reform group, a newspaper-generated hysteria over some local sex crime, a vice drive which is put on by the local authorities to dis-tract attention from defects in their administration of the city govern-ment, or the addition to the law-enforcement group of a sadistic officer who is disturbed over his own sexual problems, may result in a doubling—a hundred percent increase—in the number of arrests on sex charges, even though there may have been no change in the actual behavior of the community, and even though the illicit sex acts that are apprehended and prosecuted may still represent no more than a fantastically minute part of the illicit activity which takes place every day in the community.

The Sex Offender.   A primary fault in most studies of sex offenders is the fact that they are confined to the study of sex offenders. Just as the laboratory scientist needs a control group to interpret what he finds in his experimental animals, so we need to understand the sexual behavior of persons who have never been involved with the law.

Psychologists, psychiatrists, sociologists, and criminologists have given us some understanding of the personalities of criminals, including some sex offenders, but the studies have rarely compared convicted individuals with persons involved in similar behavior in the population at large. It does not suffice to find that sex offenders were breast fed, or bottle fed, without knowing how many other persons who were similarly fed did not become sex offenders. It does not suffice to dis-cover that sex offenders come from disrupted homes without learning why so many other persons who come from similarly disrupted homes do not end up as sex offenders. It does not suffice to find that the homosexual offenders preferred their mothers to their fathers, when a survey of non-offenders shows that most children, for perfectly obvious reasons, are more closely associated with their mothers. We need to know why certain individuals, rather than all of those who engage in similar behavior, become involved with the law. We need to learn more about the circumstances of the particular activities which led to their apprehension, and about the way they were handled by the arresting police officer, the prosecutor, the court-attached psychiatrist, the judge, and the local press.

In the course of this present study we have secured the histories of some thirteen hundred persons who have been convicted and sentenced to penal institutions as sex offenders, but these histories would be difficult to interpret if we had not gathered the histories of more than fourteen thousand persons who have never been involved with the law.

We have been in a peculiarly favorable position to secure data from persons serving time in penal institutions as sex offenders. We have been able to guarantee the confidence of the record as no law enforcement officer, no clinician connected with the courts, and no institutional officer could guarantee. From coast to coast, the grapevine has spread the word that we have not violated the confidences which we have recorded in our histories, and that we have always refused to work in any institution in which the administration has not agreed to uphold our right to preserve such confidences. In addition to the information which we have secured directly from the prisoners, we have had access to the institutional files on each inmate, and in many instances we have had access to the court records, the probation records, and the records from the departments of public welfare or other agencies which had had contact with these cases.

Throughout our research, whether with persons who have been convicted as sex offenders or with our subjects in the population at large, we have tried to make it apparent that we wanted to understand their activities as they understood them. Consequently we have not found sex offenders prone to deny their guilt, or to rationalize their behavior. In actuality, most of them have given us a record of activity that far exceeded anything that had been brought out in the legal proceedings or in the records of the penal institution.

Effective Sex Law. Out of this study of sex offenders, and of the sexual behavior of females and males who have never been involved with the law, should come data which may some day be used by legislators in the development of a body of sex law that may provide society with more adequate protection against the more serious types of sex offenders. While we shall need to continue this part of our study before we are ready to summarize the data which we have been gathering, our present information seems to make it clear that the current sex laws are unenforced and are unenforceable because they are too completely out of accord with the realities of human behavior, and because they attempt too much in the way of social control. Such a high proportion of the females and males in our population is involved in sexual activities which are prohibited by the law of most of the states of the union, that it is inconceivable that the present laws could be administered in any fashion that even remotely approached systematic and complete enforcement. . . . The consequently capricious enforcement which these laws now receive offers an opportunity for mal-administration, for police and political graft, and for blackmail which is regularly imposed both by underworld groups and by the police them-selves.

The Protection of the Individual. Many people, perhaps fortu-nately, have no conception that their everyday sexual activities may, in actuality, be contrary to the law. On the other hand, many other persons live in constant fear that certain of their sexual activities, even though they are typical of those which occur in the histories of most females and males, may be discovered and lead to social or possibly legal difficulties. In its attempt to protect itself from serious sex offenders, society has threatened the security of most of its members who are old enough to perform sexually. The efficiency of many individuals and their integration into the social organization is, thereby, seriously impaired. While this is especially true of persons with histories of extra-marital coitus, with homosexual histories, and with histories of animal contacts on the farm, it is also true of some persons who have pre-marital coitus, of many of those who engage in mouth-genital con-tacts, and even of some of those who engage in pre-marital petting. Because of the social taboos there are many individuals who, even in this generation, are disturbed over their masturbatory histories.

In many instances the law, in the course of punishing the offender, does more damage to more persons than was ever done by the individ-ual in his illicit sexual activity. The histories which we have accumu-lated contain many such instances. The intoxicated male who acci-dentally exposes his genitalia before a child, may receive a prison sentence which leave his family destitute for some period of years, breaks up his marriage, and leaves three or four children wards of the state and without the sort of guidance which the parents might well have supplied. The older, unmarried women who prosecute the male whom they find swimming nude, may ruin his business or profes-sional career, bring his marriage to divorce, and do such damage to his children as the observation of his nudity could never have done to the women who prosecuted him. The child who has been raised in fear of all strangers and all physical manifestations of affection, may ruin the lives of the married couple who had lived as useful and honorable citizens through half or more of a century, by giving her parents and the police a distorted version of the old man's attempt to bestow grandfatherly affection upon her.

The male who is convicted because he has made homosexual advances to other males, may be penalized by being sent to an institution where anywhere from half to three-quarters of the inmates are regularly having homosexual activity within the institution. The laws penalizing homosexual approaches as well as homosexual activities, and which offer the possibility in some states of an individual being incarcerated for life because he "shows homosexual tendencies," have developed a breed of teen-age law-breakers who first seek satisfaction in sexual contacts with these males, and then blackmail and assault and murder, if necessary, and escape legal punishment on the specious plea that they were protecting themselves from "indecent sexual advances." Still more serious is the utilization of the same sort of blackmail and physical assault by the police in many of our larger cities. The pre-adolescent boy who is convicted of some offense may be sent to a juvenile institution where he turns adolescent and reaches the peak of his sexual capacity in a community which is exclusively male, and where he can find no socio-sexual outlet except with other males. If kept in such an institution until he reaches his middle teens, he may find it difficult to make social and socio-sexual adjustments with girls when he gets out of the institution, and may continue his homosexual activities for the rest of his life. Then he may be penalized for being what society has made him.

Somehow, in an age which calls itself scientific and Christian, we should be able to discover more intelligent ways of protecting social interests without doing such irreparable damage to so many individuals and to the total social organization to which they belong.

We began our research, as we have said, for the sake of increasing knowledge in an area in which knowledge was limited. We have continued the research through these years, in part because we have come to understand that the total social organization, and many individuals in it, may benefit by an increase in our understanding of human sexual behavior.

.   .   .   .   .

PRE-ADOLESCENT SEXUAL RESPONSE AND ORGASM

At least some newborn mammals, including some human infants, both female and male, are capable of being stimulated by and responding to tactile stimulation in a way which is sexual in the strictest sense of the term. We now understand that this capacity to respond depends upon the existence of end organs of touch in the body surfaces, nerves connecting these organs with the spinal cord and brain, nerves which extend from the cord to various muscles in the body, and the autonomic nervous system through which still other parts of the body are brought into action. . . . All of these structures are present at birth, and the record supplied by the recall of the adult females and males who have contributed to the present study, and direct observations made by a number of qualified observers, indicate that some children are quite capable of responding in a way which may show all of the essential physiologic changes which characterize the sexual responses of an adult.

Among both young children and adults, there appear to be differences in the capacity to be aroused sexually. Some individuals respond quickly and frequently to a wide variety of physical and psychologic stimuli. Others respond more slowly and infrequently. Even in a single individual the levels of response may vary from time to time as his general health, nutritional state, fatigue, and still other circumstances may affect his physiologic capacities. Levels of response may also depend on the age of the individual. Although all individuals may be born with the necessary anatomy and capacity to respond to tactile stimulation, the capacity to respond in a way which is specifically sexual seems to increase as the child develops physically, and in many children it does not appear until near the time of adolescence. In some females it may not appear until some years after the onset of adolescence. We do not understand all of the factors which are involved, but some of the capacity to respond sexually seems to depend on certain hormones which develop in the body of the growing boy and girl. . . .

Whether the late appearance of sexual responsiveness in some individuals means that they were actually not capable of responding at an earlier age, or whether it means that they had not previously been subjected to sexual stimuli which were sufficient to bring response, is a matter which it has not yet been possible to determine. It is possible that some younger children are not at all capable of responding sexually, or at least incapable of responding to the sorts of stimuli which would arouse an adult, but of this we are not certain. It is certain, however, that there are children, both female and male, who are quite capable of true sexual response.

Accumulative Incidence of Pre-Adolescent Response. What seem to be sexual responses have been observed in infants immediately at birth, and specifically sexual responses, involving the full display of physiologic changes which are typical of the responses of an adult, have been observed in both female and male infants as young as four months of age, and in infants and pre-adolescent children of every older age.

About one per cent of the older females who have contributed histories to the present study recalled that they were making specifically sexual responses to physical stimuli, and in some instances to psychologic stimuli, when they were as young as three years of age. . . . This, however, must represent only a portion of the children who were responding at that age, for many children would not recognize the sexual nature of their early responses.

About 4 per cent of the females in our sample thought they were responding sexually by five years of age. Nearly 16 per cent recalled such responses by ten years of age. All told, some 27 per cent recalled that they had been aroused erotically—sexually—at some time before the age of adolescence which, for the average female, occurs sometime between her twelfth and thirteenth birthdays. . . . However, the number of pre-adolescent girls who are ever aroused sexually must be much higher than this record indicates.

Comparisons of the records contributed by subjects who had terminated their schooling at the grade school, high school, college, and graduate school levels, indicate that pre-adolescent erotic responses may have occurred in a higher percentage of the groups which subsequently obtained the most extensive schooling . . . ; but this may simply reflect a greater capacity of the better educated females to recall their experience.

.   .   .   .   .

Accumulative Incidence of Pre-Adolescent Orgasm.   About 14 per cent of all the females in our sample—nearly half of those who had been erotically aroused before adolescence—recalled that they had reached orgasm either in masturbation or in their sexual contacts with other children or older persons (*i.e.,* in their *socio-sexual* contacts) prior to adolescence. It is not all impossible that a still higher percentage had actually had such experience without recognizing its nature.

On the basis of the adult recall and the observations which we have just recorded, we can report 4 cases of females under one year of age coming to orgasm, and a total of 23 cases of small girls three years of age or younger reaching orgasm. The incidences, based on our total female sample, show some 0.3 per cent (16 individuals) who recalled that they had reached orgasm by three years of age, 2 per cent by five years, 4 per cent by seven years, 9 per cent by eleven years, and 14 per cent by thirteen years of age. . . . Thus, there had been a slow but steady increase in the number of girls in the sample who had reached orgasm prior to adolescence. In the case of the male, the percentages of those who had reached orgasm also rose steadily through the early preadolescent years, but they began to rise more abruptly in the later preadolescent years.

Sources of Early Arousal and Orgasm.   One per cent of the females in our sample recalled that they were masturbating (in the strict sense of the term) by three years of age, and 13 per cent recalled masturbation by ten years of age. . . . The record does not show what percentage of the early masturbation had brought sexual arousal, but it does show 0.3 per cent of the females in the total sample masturbating to the point of orgasm by three years of age, and 8 per cent by ten years of age. . . .

Psychologic reactions or physical contacts with other girls were, in a few instances, the sources of sexual arousal at three years of age. About 3 per cent had been aroused by other girls by eleven years of age, and 6 per cent by thirteen years of age.

Reaction to or contacts with boys had brought similar arousal in a fraction of one per cent at three years of age, but in about 7 per cent of the sample by eleven, and in 12 per cent of the sample by thirteen years of age. . . .

Out of the 659 females in the sample who had experienced orgasm before they were adolescent, 86 per cent had had their first experience in masturbation, some 7 per cent had discovered it in sexual contacts with other girls, 2 per cent in petting, and 1 per cent in coitus with boys or older males. Interestingly enough, 2 per cent had had their first orgasm in physical contacts with dogs or cats. Some 2 per cent had first reached orgasm under other circumstances, including the climbing of a rope.

Orgasm had been discovered in self-masturbation more often by the girls than by the boys. In earlier pre-adolescence, the boy's first orgasms are frequently the product of physical and emotional situations which bring spontaneous sexual reactions; and although there is a great deal of incidental manipulation of genitalia among younger boys, it rarely brings orgasm. Among the adolescent boys in our sample, masturbation appears to have accounted for only 68 per cent of the first orgasms. . . .

. . . . .

The child's initial attempts at self-masturbation had been inspired in some instances by the observation of other children who were engaged in such activity, or through the more deliberate instruction given by some older child or adult. These were quite commonly the first sources of information for most of the males in the sample; but in the great majority of instances females learn to masturbate, both in pre-adolescent and later years, by discovering the possibilities of such activity entirely on their own. . . .

PRE-ADOLESCENT HETEROSEXUAL PLAY

Although 30 per cent of the females in the sample recalled pre-adolescent heterosexual play, and 33 per cent recalled pre-adolescent homosexual play, only 48 per cent recalled any sort of socio-sexual play before adolescence. This means that 15 per cent had had sex play only with boys, 18 per cent had had it only with girls, and another 15 per cent had had it with both boys and girls.

Accumulative Incidence of Heterosexual Play.   Our data on the incidence and frequency of sex play among pre-adolescent children are drawn in part from the studies we have made of children of very young ages, but they depend largely upon the recall of the adults who have contributed to the present study. It has been apparent, however, that the adults have recalled only a portion of their pre-adolescent experience, for even children forget a high proportion of their experience within a matter of weeks or months. This is due sometimes to the incidental nature of the sex play, and in some instances to the fact that the child was emotionally disturbed by the experience and blocked psychologically in recalling a taboo activity. But even though the child may not be able to recall its experience, it is possible that it has acquired information and attitudes which will affect its subsequent patterns of behavior. While the records show that 48 per cent of the adult females in the sample had recalled some sort of pre-adolescent sex play . . . , we are inclined to believe, for the above reasons, that a much higher percentage must have had sexual contacts as young children.

About equal numbers of the females recalled contacts with girls and with boys. There is no evidence that their interest in their own sex (the homosexual interest) had developed either before or after their interest in the opposite sex (the heterosexual interest). Freudian hypotheses of psychosexual development proceeding, as a rule, from narcissistic (masturbatory) interests and activities to interests in other individuals whose bodies are similar (the homosexual interests), and finally to interests in individuals who are physically different (the heterosexual interests), are not substantiated by the pre-adolescent or adolescent histories of either the females or the males in the sample.

Because of the restrictions which parents and our total social organization place upon the free intermingling of even small children of the opposite sex, it is not surprising to find that 52 per cent of the females in the sample had had more girls than boys as childhood companions, and that another 33 per cent had had boys and girls in about equal numbers as childhood companions. Only about 15 per cent had had more boys than girls as companions. This lesser significance of boys as the pre-adolescent companions of girls makes it all the more notable that the pre-adolescent sexual activities of the females in the sample were had with boys about as often as with girls. This had undoubtedly depended upon the fact that small boys are usually more aggressive than girls in their physical activities, and even at that age boys are more likely to initiate the sexual activities.

One per cent of the adult females in the sample recalled childhood sex play with boys when they were as young as three, but 8 per cent recalled such play by five, and 18 per cent by seven years of age. . . . All told, some 30 per cent recalled some play with boys before they turned adolescent. The figures differed for the various educational levels represented in the sample: among those females who had never gone beyond high school, some 24 per cent recalled sex play with boys, but 30 per cent of those who had gone on into college, and 36 per cent of those who had gone still further into graduate school, recalled such pre-adolescent play.

The data indicate that the percentage of children engaging in any kind of pre-adolescent sex play had increased in the course of three of the decades represented in the sample. In comparison with the females born before 1900, some 10 per cent more of those born between 1910 and 1919 recalled pre-adolescent sex play. . . .

. . . . .

Techniques of Heterosexual Play. Genital exhibition had occurred in 99 per cent of the pre-adolescent sex play. . . . In perhaps 40 per cent of the histories that was all that was involved.

Anatomic differences are of considerable interest to most children. Their curiosity is whetted by the fact that they have in many instances been forbidden to expose their own nude bodies and have not had the opportunity to see the nude bodies of other children. Their curiosity is especially stimulated by the fact that they have been cautioned not to expose their own genitalia, or to look at the genitalia of other children. The genital explorations often amount to nothing more than comparisons of anatomy, in much the same way that children compare their hands, their noses or mouths, their hair, their clothing, or any of their other possessions. As we have noted in regard to the boy, it is probable that a good deal of the emotional content which such play may have for the small girls is not sexual as often as it is a reaction to the mysterious, to the forbidden, and to the socially dangerous performance.

On the other hand, we have the histories of females who were raised in homes that accepted nudity within the family circle, or who attended nursery schools or summer camps or engaged in other group activities where boys and girls of young, pre-adolescent ages used common toilets and freely bathed and played together without clothing. In such groups the children were still interested in examining the bodies of the other children, although they soon came to accept the nudity as commonplace and did not react as emotionally as they would have if nudity were the unusual thing.

. . . . .

. . . In a goodly number of instances, these had amounted to nothing more than incidental touching. The heterosexual contacts had been specifically masturbatory in only a small number of cases. There had been mouth-genital contacts among only 2 per cent of the girls, and insertions of various objects (chiefly fingers) into the female vagina in only 3 per cent of the cases.

There had been some sort of coitus in 17 per cent of the cases for which any heterosexual play was reported, but it has been difficult to determine how much of the "coitus" of pre-adolescence involves the actual union of genitalia. In all instances recorded in the sample, there had been some apposition of the genitalia of the two children; and since erections frequently occur among even very young boys, penetrations may have been and certainly were effected in some of the pre-adolescent activity. However, the small size of the male genitalia at that age had usually limited the depth of penetration, and much of the childhood "coitus" had amounted to nothing more than genital apposition.

On the other hand, we have 29 cases of females who had had coitus as pre-adolescents with older boys or adult males with whom there had been complete genital union.

PRE-ADOLESCENT CONTACTS WITH ADULT MALES

There is a growing concern in our culture over the sexual contacts that pre-adolescent children sometimes have with adults. Most persons feel that all such contacts are undesirable because of the immediate disturbance they may cause the child, and because of the conditioning and possibly traumatic effects which they may have on the child's socio-sexual development and subsequent sexual adjustments in marriage. Press reports might lead one to conclude that an appreciable percentage of all children are subjected, and frequently subjected, to sexual approaches by adult males, and that physical injury is a frequent consequence of such contacts. But most of the published data are based on cases which come to the attention of physicians, the police, and other social agencies, and there has hitherto . . . been no opportunity to know what proportion of all children is ever involved.[1]

Incidence and Frequency of Contacts with Adults. We have data from 4441 of our female subjects which allow us to determine the incidence of pre-adolescent sexual contacts with adult males, and the frequency of such contacts. For the sake of the present calculations

[1] The following indicate the nature of the . . . concern over adult sexual approaches to children: Hoover, J. Edgar, "How Safe is Your Daughter?" American Magazine, July, 1947:32 ("depraved human beings, more savage than beasts, are permitted to roam America almost at will"). Wittels, "What Can We Do About Sex Crimes?" Saturday Evening Post Dec. 11, 1948:31 ("at least tens of thousands of them [sex killers] are loose in the country today"). Frankfurter, Justice Felix, dissenting in Maryland v. Baltimore Radio Show, 1950:338 U.S. 912.

we have defined an adult male as one who has turned adolescent and who is at least fifteen years of age; and, in order to eliminate experiences that amount to nothing more than adolescent sex play, we have considered only those cases in which the male was at least five years older than the female, while the female was still pre-adolescent. On this basis, we find that some 24 per cent (1075) of the females in the sample had been approached while they were pre-adolescent by adult males who appeared to be making sexual advances, or who had made sexual contacts with the child. Three-fourths of the females (76 per cent) had not recognized any such approach.

Approaches had occurred most frequently in poorer city communities where the population was densely crowded in tenement districts; and while many of the subjects covered by the present volume were raised in such communities, we would have found higher incidences of pre-adolescent contacts with adults if we had had more cases from lower educational groups, or if we had included the data which we have on females who had served penal sentences, and on Negro females. These latter groups, however, were excluded from the calculations in the present volume for reasons which we have already explained.

The frequencies of the pre-adolescent contacts with adults were actually low. Some 80 per cent of the females who were ever involved seem to have had only a lone experience in all of their pre-adolescent years. Another 12 per cent reported two such experiences, and 3 per cent reported something between three and six childhood experiences. On the other hand, 5 per cent of those who had been involved reported nine or more experiences during pre-adolescence. Repetition had most frequently occurred when the children were having their contacts with relatives who lived in the same household. In many instances, the experiences were repeated because the children had become interested in the sexual activity and had more or less actively sought repetitions of their experience.

Among the females who had been approached by adult males when they were pre-adolescent children, the ages at which they were approached were distributed as follows:

Ages of Females Having Adult Contacts

Age	Percent of Active Sample	Percent of Total Sample	Age	Percent of Active Sample	Percent of Total Sample
4	5	1	9	16	4
5	8	2	10	26	6
6	9	2	11	24	6
7	13	3	12	25	7
8	17	4	13	19	6
CASES				1039	4407

Adult Partners. The adult males who had approached these pre-adolescent children were identified as follows:

Adult Partners	Percent of Active Sample
Strangers	52
Friends and acquaintances	32
Uncles	9
Fathers	4
Brothers	3
Grandfathers	2
Other relatives	5
CASES REPORTING	609

Some 85 per cent of the subjects reported that only a single male had approached them when they were children. Some 13 per cent reported that two different males had made such approaches, 1 per cent reported three males, and another 1 per cent reported four or more males making such approaches.

Nature of Contacts with Adults. The early experiences which the 1075 females in the sample had had with adult males had involved the following types of approaches and contacts (numbers given are per cent): approach only, 9; exhibition, male genitalia, 52; exhibition, female genitalia, 1; fondling, no genital contact, 31; manipulation of female genitalia, 22; manipulation of male genitalia, 5; coitus, 3; other, 2.

. . . . .

Significance of Adult Contacts. There are as yet insufficient data, either in our own or in other studies, for reaching general conclusions on the significance of sexual contacts between children and adults. The females in the sample who had had pre-adolescent contacts with adults had been variously interested, curious, pleased, embarrassed, frightened, terrified, or disturbed with feelings of guilt. The adult contacts are a source of pleasure to some children, and sometimes may arouse the child erotically (5 per cent) and bring it to orgasm (1 per cent). The contacts had often involved considerable affection, and some of the older females in the sample felt that their pre-adolescent experience had contributed favorably to their later socio-sexual development.

On the other hand, some 80 per cent of the children had been emotionally upset or frightened by their contacts with adults. A small portion had been seriously disturbed; but in most instances the reported fright was nearer the level that children will show when they see insects, spiders, or other objects against which they have been adversely conditioned. If a child were not culturally conditioned, it is doubtful if it would be disturbed by sexual approaches of the sort which had usually been involved in these histories. It is difficult to understand why a child, except for its cultural conditioning, should be disturbed at having its genitalia touched, or disturbed at seeing the genitalia of other persons, or disturbed at even more specific sexual contacts. When children are constantly warned by parents and teachers against contacts with adults, and when they receive no explanation of the exact nature of the forbidden contacts, they are ready to become hysterical as soon as any older person approaches, or stops and speaks to them in the street, or fondles them, or proposes to do something for them, even though the adult may have had no sexual objective in mind. Some of the more experienced students of juvenile problems have come to believe that the emotional reactions of the parents, police officers, and other adults who discover that the child has had such a contact, may disturb the child more seriously than the sexual contacts themselves. The current hysteria over sex offenders may very well have serious effects on the ability of many of these children to work out sexual adjustments some years later in their marriages.

There are, of course, instances of adults who have done physical damage to children with whom they have attempted sexual contacts, and we have the histories of a few males who had been responsible for such damage. But these cases are in the minority, and the public should learn to distinguish such serious contacts from other adult contacts which are not likely to do the child any appreciable harm if the child's parents do not become disturbed. The exceedingly small number of cases in which physical harm is ever done the child is to be measured by the fact that among the 4441 females on whom we have data, we have only one clear-cut case of serious injury done to the child, and a very few instances of vaginal bleeding which, however, did not appear to do any appreciable damage.

ADOLESCENT DEVELOPMENT

Physical Development. Shortly after the end of the first decade, the female begins to develop physically at a faster rate than she had before, and acquires pubic hair, hair under the arms, more mature breasts, and a body form more nearly like that of an adult. During this period of development, she menstruates for the first time. It is during this period that her ovaries mature and, for the first time, begin to release eggs which are capable of being fertilized and developing into new individuals.

This period in which there is an increased rate of physical growth and the final development of reproductive function is the period which has come to be known as adolescence. Various physical developments are involved in this adolescent growth, and they do not all begin or reach their conclusion simultaneously. Consequently, there is no single

point at which adolescence may be said to begin, or any point at which
it may be said to stop, but from the onset of the first adolescent development to the completion of all adolescent development, the time
involved for the average (median) female is something between three
and four years.

Corresponding adolescent developments in the male usually do not
begin until a year or two after adolescence has begun in the female,
and they usually take four years or more to reach their conclusion. In
consequence, as far as physical development is concerned, the girl begins to "mature" at an earlier age, and reaches complete maturity before the average boy.

Exact studies of adolescent development should, of course, be based
upon the direct examination and measurement of developing children,
and our own data, based upon the recall of adults, cannot be as certain;
but the average ages at each stage of development, calculated from our
records, agree quite closely with those from the observational studies.
. . .

It has been customary, both in general thinking and in technical
studies, to consider that adolescence in the female begins at the time
of first menstruation (barring any unusual disturbance of normal menstrual development). This is an error, and for several reasons an unfortunate error; for considerable physical growth which should be
recognized as adolescent usually precedes the occurrence of the first
menstruation. Most of the females in our sample reported the appearance of pubic hair as the first of the adolescent developments. Some
of the females reported pubic hair development at ages as young as 8,
but others did not recall that pubic hair had developed until the age of
18. . . . For the median female in the sample, the hair had begun developing by 12.3 years of age.

Almost simultaneously with the appearance of pubic hair, breast
development became noticeable. The observational studies show that
the very first signs of breast development may actually precede the
appearance of the pubic hair. Among the females in our sample there
were some who recalled such development by the age of 8, and some
who did not recall breast development until the age of 25. . . . The
median age of breast development was 12.4 years for the females in the
sample.

Only a few of the adult females in the sample were able to recall
the age at which a marked increase in the rate of growth had first begun. It is difficult to notice the onset of a process which is as continuous
as this increase in rate of growth during adolescence. A much larger
number of the females in the sample thought they could recall the
ages at which they had completed their development in height. These
ages ranged from 9 to 25 years, but for the median female growth
seemed to have been completed by 15.8 years of age. . . .

The age of first menstruation had ranged from 9 to 25 years in the sample. . . . For the median female it had been 13.0 years. For the median female, there had been a lapse of 8.4 months between the onset of pubic hair and breast development, and the first menstruation. The first menstruation is such a specific event and, in many instances, such a dramatic event in the girl's history, that its appearance is recalled more often than any other adolescent development. It is, therefore, quite natural that since the time of ancient Jewish law, menstruation should have been taken as the best single sign of sexual maturity in the female. Unfortunately, menstruation is a phenomenon which is affected by a larger number of factors, chiefly hormonal, than most of the other biological developments at adolescence. In a few instances it may begin before there are any other adolescent developments. Not infrequently, however, it may be delayed for a considerable period of time, and in some instances for several years, after all of the other adolescent developments have been completed. It is customary today for parents to seek medical aid when first menstruation does not appear by the time the other adolescent developments are well under way; but among many of the older women in our histories, menstruation would have been a poor indicator of adolescent development.

It is popularly believed that the appearance of menstruation is an indication that a girl has become "sexually mature" enough to conceive and reproduce. On the basis of recent studies, it becomes clear, however, that the initial release of mature eggs from the ovaries is not always correlated with menstruation. There are known cases of fertile

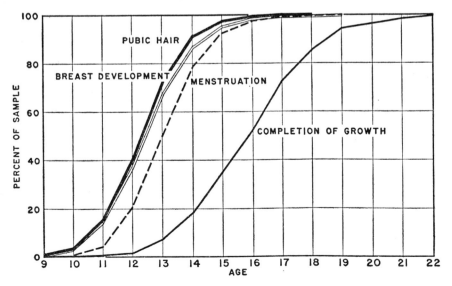

FIGURE 1. CUMULATED PERCENTS: ADOLESCENT PHYSICAL DEVELOPMENT IN THE FEMALE

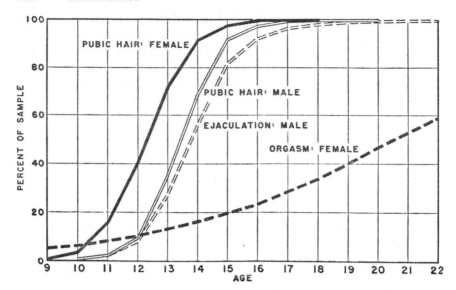

FIGURE 2.   CUMULATED PERCENTS, COMPARING FEMALE AND MALE: ON-
SET OF ADOLESCENCE AND SEXUAL RESPONSE

Taking appearance of pubic hair as first adolescent development, and
orgasm or ejaculation as specific evidence of erotic response.

eggs and pregnancy occurring before menstruation had ever begun;
and there is a considerable body of data indicating that the average
female releases mature eggs only sporadically, if at all, during the first
few years after she has begun to menstruate. This is the period of so-
called adolescent sterility. It is probable that the sterility is not complete, and more probable that eggs are occasionally released in that
period; but regular ovulation in each menstrual cycle probably does
not begin in the average female until she is sixteen to eighteen years
of age. Precise studies on this point are still to be made.

Psychosexual Development in Adolescence.   While these physical
changes at adolescence are a fundamental part of the process by which
the female becomes mature enough to reproduce, they seem to have
little relation to the development of sexual responsiveness in the female.
The steady increase in the accumulative incidence of erotic arousal and
response to orgasm which we have seen in the pre-adolescent data continues into adolescence and for some years beyond. There is a slight but
no marked upsurge in the incidence and frequency of arousal and orgasm
during adolescence, but they do not reach their maximum development
until the middle twenties or even thirties. . . .

In the case of the male, there is a sudden upsurge in sexual activity
which may begin a year or more before adolescence, and usually reaches
its peak within a year or two after the onset of adolescence. . . . From

that point the male's sexual responses and overt activity begin to drop and continue to drop steadily into old age. . . . These striking differences between female and male psychosexual development may depend upon basic hormonal differences between the sexes. . . .

Because of the earlier appearance of adolescence in the female, and because of her more rapid physical development in that period, the opinion is generally held that the girl matures sexually more rapidly than the boy. Mature reproductive cells may appear in the average female before they appear in the average male, but the capacity to reproduce is not synonymous with the capacity to be aroused erotically and to respond to the point of orgasm. The irregular release of mature eggs from the ovaries during the years of adolescent sterility makes it uncertain whether the capacity for reproduction develops earlier in one sex than in the other, and in regard to sexual responsiveness the female matures much later than the male. . . .

We have found that the human female is born with the nervous equipment on which sexual responses depend, but we have found that only a portion of the females respond before the onset of adolescence. The acquirement of any full capacity for response depends upon the sort of sexual experience that the female has in pre-adolescence, adolescence, and the later years, and on the variety of social factors which may condition her psychologically. . . .

71. FUNCTIONAL ANALYSIS OF SEX ROLES

MIRRA KOMAROVSKY

"A son is a son till he gets him a wife,
But a daughter's a daughter for all of her life."
It is often difficult to establish a truth from folk lore, because
for every proverb there is another which contradicts it. Here is one
proverb, however, which has been confirmed by social research.

The concept of social roles with special reference to sex and age roles has been the subject of increasing sociological interest. But the problem of sex roles in various segments of our society requires further systematic empirical study. This paper attempts to outline what is believed

Selections reprinted from *American Sociological Review*, 15, No. 4 (August, 1950), 508–516, by permission of the author and the American Sociological Society.

to constitute a fruitful theoretical orientation for such research and to illustrate the application of this theoretical approach in a pilot study, involving twenty intensive case histories of middle class urban married women, in the summer of 1949. The study was focused on the "problem" aspects of sex roles, and while the discussion will be thus delimited, the theoretical approach it advocates appears equally applicable to other aspects of this general subject.

That there exists a great deal of strain in women's roles among the urban middle classes is generally recognized but the description and analysis of this phenomenon remain to be developed. The mere diversity of roles that women must play at different ages or in different relations need not in itself create a problem. Many societies show such diversity without causing either social conflict or personal disorganization. Indeed in any society, age, sex, class, occupation, race, and ethnic background involve the individual in a variety of socially sanctioned patterns of interaction *vis-à-vis* different categories of persons. Why, then, to put the question most generally, do sex roles today present such an arena of social and mental conflict?

Probably the most influential and systematically developed answer to this question today is the one found in psychiatric literature. This answer centers upon two explanatory models. The orthodox analysts say with Freud: "Anatomy is her fate." They see women's problem in terms of the psychological dynamics arising out of some biologically determined sexual characteristic, i.e., penis envy or masochism. The individual life history is then taken as determining whether the development of this characteristic will follow normal or neurotic patterns. The other explanatory model takes more account of cultural factors. But, again, the root of the problem is seen in the clash between the biologically determined feminine impulses, on the one hand, and the social roles, on the other, which today, it is alleged, are peculiarly at variance with the biologically set needs of the feminine psyche.

In contrast to the psychiatric, the theoretical approach of this paper is sociological. It seeks to interpret social and mental conflict and the institutional malfunctioning which constitute the social problem in question, in terms of interrelation of elements within and between relevant social and cultural systems. It accepts the general premise that our culture is full of contradictions and inconsistencies with regard to women's roles, that new social goals have emerged without the parallel development of social machinery for their attainment, that norms persist which are no longer functionally appropriate to the social situations to which they apply, that the same social situations are subject to the jurisdiction of conflicting social codes, that behavior patterns useful at some stage become dysfunctional at another, and so on.

AN APPLICATION OF FUNCTIONAL ANALYSIS

It is well known that the family of procreation occupies a dominant position in our kinship system. This is evidenced in a large variety of ways. Typically, the family of procreation is residentially segregated from the family of orientation of either spouse which, of course, is not the case in the joint or stem family systems. The ties to ancestors which obtain in a clan society and the ties to siblings maintained in the consanguine family type are much weaker in our society. Furthermore, all social norms, from those expressed in the legal code to those expressed in the "advice to the lovelorn" column, reiterate the theme that the primary loyalty is to one's spouse and children as against parents or siblings. The legal expression of this theme is found in our inheritance and support laws. If a man dies intestate it is generally true that his wife and children get *all* his property. It is only in the absence of direct descendants that parents or collateral relatives share the inheritance with his widow. While statutes are fairly common requiring a son to contribute to the support of an indigent parent, his responsibility is more limited than it is toward his wife and children. These laws are deeply rooted in the mores. As an example, undergraduates have been observed by the writer to be shocked to learn that these cultural norms are far from being universal and that among the Arapaho, to take one instance, a dead man's brother has superior claim to his property even if the widow and his children are left destitute.

In fact, the priority of the marriage relationship over the parental family in our culture has in recent years found expression even in certain intellectual fields of inquiry. As the result of the diffusion of the psychiatric point of view, close ties to a parent are under suspicion as the "silver cord" and, conversely, the emancipation from the family of orientation is viewed as the touchstone of emotional maturity. These presuppositions often find their most explicit and unquestioned expression in textbooks. Thus, for example, a popular textbook on marriage states: "If there is a bona-fide in-law problem the young couple need first of all to be certain of their perspective. The success of their marriage should be put above everything else, even above attachment to parents. Husband and wife must come first. Otherwise the individual exhibits immaturity." Another textbook affirms: "Close attachments to members of the family, whether parents or siblings, accentuate the normal difficulties involved in achieving the response role expected in marriage." Again, ". . . there is a call for a new attitude, a subordinating of and to some extent an aloofness from the home of one's childhood." "Do not live with or in the neighborhood of your relatives and in-laws, and do not allow them to live with you."

Some recent research such as Morgan's and Dinkel's again testify to the extent to which the dominance of the family of procreation is rooted in our mores. Though these mores show some ethnic, religious and other variations, all available evidence points to the primacy of the family of procreation as the dominant American cultural pattern.

But although this pattern of the primacy of the family of procreation *vis-à-vis* the family of orientation has been abundantly recognized, it has not been systematically related to the wide range of its functional and dysfunctional consequences. From within this range we may mark out the problem of sociopsychological continuities and discontinuities in the kinship structure. More particularly, we wish to consider to what extent the training in the parental family makes for subsequent adjustment to the well-nigh exclusive loyalty to spouse and children. We are raising two specific problems. Which particular elements of role training in the parental family can be discerned to have by-products which affect later adjustment of the members in their own families of procreation? Which of the two sexes is enabled to make the shift from the parental family to marriage with the minimum of psychological hazards?

DIFFERENTIAL TRAINING OF THE SEXES IN THE PARENTAL FAMILY

Illuminating material bearing upon differential training of boys and girls in the parental family was collected by the writer in the form of 73 biographical documents prepared by women undergraduates. The documents reveal that despite increasing similarity in the upbringing of the sexes among middle-class families, some sex differences relevant to our problem still persist. The girls who had brothers testified that in various ways the parents *tended to speed up, most often unwittingly, but also deliberately, the emancipation of the boy from the family, while they retarded it in the case of his sister.*

Judging from these documents, there are three different mechanisms through which this is achieved. Interesting as these are in themselves, our main problem is to consider presently their further consequences for the operation of the kinship system. Among these mechanisms is, first of all, the pattern of providing sons with *earlier and more frequent opportunities for independent action.* The boys are freer to play away from home grounds, to return later, and to pick their own activities, movies and books. They are ordinarily allowed the first independent steps earlier than their sisters, such as the first walk to school without an adult, the first unaccompanied movie or baseball game, and later in life, the train trip or the job away from home.

A student writes:

It was thought to be a part of my brother's education to be sent away to school. I was expected to go to a local college so that I could live at home.

When my brother got his first job he got a room so that he would not have to commute too far. My sister, at 22, turned down several offers of jobs at a high salary and took a much less desirable one only because she could live at home. She continues to be as much under parental control as she was when in college. Frankly, if anything should happen to my parents, I would be at a complete loss while I know that my brothers could carry on alone very well.

The second mechanism through which the emancipation of sons is speeded up involves a *higher degree of privacy in personal affairs* allowed the boys. One girl writes:

My mother is very hurt if I don't let her read the letters I receive. After a telephone call she expects me to tell her who called and what was said. My brother could say "a friend" and she would not feel insulted.

And again:

My brother is 15, 3 years younger than I am. When he goes out after supper mother calls out: "Where are you going, Jimmy?" "Oh, out." Could I get away with this? Not on your life. I would have to tell in detail where to, with whom, and if I am half an hour late mother sits on the edge of the living-room sofa watching the door.

States another student:

I have a brother of 23, and a sister of 22, and a younger brother who is 16. My sister and I had a much more sheltered life than my brothers. My brothers come and go as they please. Even my younger brother feels that his current girl friend is his personal affair. No one knows who she is. But the family wants voluminous files on every boy my sister and I want to date. It is not easy for us to get the complete genealogy of a boy we want to go out with.

Thirdly, the *daughters* of the family *are held to a more exacting code of filial and kinship obligations.* When the grandmother needs somebody to do an errand for her, or Aunt Jane who doesn't hear well needs help, the girl is more likely to be called upon. The pressure to attend and observe birthdays, anniversaries, and other family festivals is apparently greater upon her than upon the boy.

These patterns of differential training of the sexes in the parental family are generally recognized to be functionally oriented to their respective adult roles. The role of the provider, on the one hand, and of the homemaker on the other, call for different attitudes and skills. Competitiveness, independence, dominance, aggressiveness, are all traits felt to be needed by the future head of the family. Although the girl can train for her adult role and rehearse it within the home, the boy prepares for *his* outside the home, by taking a "paper route" or a summer job away from home. Again, the greater sheltering of the girl may be functionally appropriate in the light of greater risks incurred by her in the case of sexual behavior and also in marriage since, for the woman, marriage is not only a choice of a mate but also of a station in life.

The parents at times explicitly recognize this functional character of their training. One girl, for example, reports that both her parents were more indulgent to her. With a little pleading she could usually get what she wanted. Her brother, on the other hand, was expected to earn money for his little luxuries because "boys need that kind of training." In a couple of cases the girls testified that their brothers were expected to work their way through college, while the girls were supported. A student writes:

> My brother is two years younger than I am. When we started going to school my father would always say as he saw us off in the morning, "Now, Buddy, you are the man and you must take good care of your sister." It amused me because it was I who always had to take care of him.

Another student recollects that when her brother refused to help her with her "math" on the ground that no one was allowed to help *him*, her mother replied: "Well, she is a girl, and it isn't as important for her to know 'math' and to learn how to get along without help."

More often, however, the proximate ground for enforcing the proper roles is expressed in terms of what constitutes manly or unmanly behavior or just "the right thing to do." The degree to which the recognition of functional implications is explicit is in itself an important problem bearing upon social change.

But if the differential upbringing of the sexes thus constitutes a preparation for their adult roles, it also has unintended consequences. This role training or, more specifically, the greater sheltering of the girl, has, as unintended by-products, further consequences for kinship roles which are not perceived. And it is to this that we now address ourselves. We are now prepared to advance a hypothesis that the greater sheltering of the girl has what Merton terms a "latent dysfunction" for the woman and for marriage in general. More specifically, we suggest that the major unintended consequence of this greater sheltering of the girl is to create in her such ties to the family of orientation that she is handicapped in making the psycho-social shift to the family of procreation which our culture demands. Our problem is not merely to demonstrate the fact of discontinuities in role training so perceptively discerned in other spheres by Benedict and others. These discontinuities must be related to their structural contexts. We shall show how tendencies created within one social structure react back upon the operation of another structure within the same kinship system without the intention or, indeed, the awareness of the participants.

The hypothesis just set forth requires us to examine the actual mechanisms through which these postulated consequences follow. Essentially it is assumed that to the extent that the woman remains more "infantile," less able to make her own decisions, more dependent upon one or both parents for initiating or channeling behavior and attitudes, more closely attached to them so as to find it difficult to part from them or to face their disapproval in case of any conflict between her family and spouse, or shows any other indices of lack of emotional emancipation—to that extent she may find it more difficult than the man to conform to the cultural norm of primary loyalty to the family she establishes later, the family of procreation. It is possible, of course, that the only effect of the greater sheltering is to create in women a generalized dependency which will then be transferred to the husband and which will enable her all the more readily to accept the role of wife in a family which still has many patriarchal features. In contrast to this, we shall explore the hypothesis that this dependency is specific; it is a dependency upon and attachment to the family of orientation.

For the purposes of testing, this hypothesis may be restated in two steps: first, the alleged greater attachment of the girl to her family of orientation and, second, the resulting difficulties for marriage.

Turning to family studies in the search for data bearing crucially upon this hypothesis, we find the data to be scanty indeed. The comparative absence of materials suggests that the hypothesis requiring this material was not at hand. With regard to the first step, the greater attachment to and dependence of the woman upon her family of orientation, the evidence, though scanty, is consistent and confirming.

SEX DIFFERENCES IN ATTACHMENT TO AND DEPENDENCE UPON THE FAMILY OF ORIENTATION

In a recent study, Winch discovers a contrast between the sexes with respect to attachment and submissiveness to parents. Among the 435 college males included in the study, age correlated negatively with love for both parents and submissiveness to them, whereas among the 502 college women neither of these correlations is significant. The author puts forth and is inclined to support the hypothesis that, at least while in college, women do not become emancipated from their families to the same degree or in the same manner as men do.

Another set of data, . . . from the same study, of 936 college men and women also tends to support our hypothesis. It suggests that the college women are somewhat more attached to parents, less likely to make decisions contrary to the wishes of the parents, more frequently experience homesickness than is the case with the male undergraduates. No sex differences were found in feelings that parents have attempted to dominate their lives.

Another confirming datum concerning undergraduates is found in a study of some 1500 students at the University of Minnesota. The author observes: "In two widely separated surveys of the total group, the frequency and type of family problems were found to be related to several other descriptive factors: girls, for example, had family problems more often than boys, especially such problems as 'difficulty in achieving independence.'"

The relative attachment to parents on the part of older men and women is revealed by Burgess and Cottrell. The authors studied a sample of 526 couples, the majority of whom had been married from two to four years. Two tables record the extent of attachment to parents derived from the statements made by the respondents themselves. Four degrees of attachment were distinguished: little or none, moderate, a good deal, and very close. The tables show that a slightly greater proportion of wives than of husbands characterized their own attachment to parents as "very close." The difference is greater in attitudes towards the father than towards the mother (to whom both sexes were, incidentally, more attached).

	Husbands (526 cases)	*Wives* (526 cases)
Attachment to Father		
Very close	21%	30%
Attachment to Mother		
Very close	35%	42%

Terman's findings are on the whole similar. The figures are as follows:

	Husbands (734 cases)	*Wives* (721 cases)
Attachment to Father		
Greatest	16.7%	20.1%
Attachment to Mother		
Greatest	28.9%	35.1%

To sum up, when asked to characterize their own attachment to parents, somewhat more women than men give the response, "Very close." The size of the difference is small but the pattern is consistent. The sex difference is greater with regard to the father.

These studies were cited because they are almost the only ones available. It should be noted that they all depend upon the direct testimony of respondents. Except when the verbally expressed attitude is precisely what is wanted, all such studies raise the question of the relation of the verbal index to the phenomenon it allegedly represents. Failures of memory, of honesty, of self-knowledge often stand between the verbal index and the phenomenon studied. The next datum bearing upon our hypothesis has the advantage of having been derived from the study of behavior rather than from verbal attitudes alone though it would have been given added meaning had it also included the latter.

The Women's Bureau (Bulletin No. 138) made a study of two communities widely different in employment offered to women: City of Cleveland and the State of Utah. The report concludes:

> In families with unmarried sons and daughters, daughters supply more of the family supporting income than sons supply, though earning less than their brothers earn (p. 13). In Cleveland twice the proportion of boys as of girls contributed nothing to the family support. With working sons and daughters under 21 years, about a third of the girls compared with a fourth of the boys turn over *all* their earnings to their families.

It would be important to determine whether such a pattern of greater contribution of single daughters to family support is generally true. For if it is, it would have bearing upon a more general problem. It would represent a standardized pattern of behavior *which is not directly called for by social norms, but is a by-product of social roles.* In other words, it would mean that differential training of boys and girls in anticipation of adult sex roles has had, as an unintended by-product, a closer identification of the girl with her family and her greater responsibility for family support. Tracing this by-product brings out anew how interrelations of institutional patterns operate to produce other ramified patterns which are below the threshold of recognition.

So much for the first step of our hypothesis: the lesser emancipation of the daughter in the middle class kinship structure from the family of orientation. In so far as it is valid, we may expect that the transition from the role of the daughter to that of the spouse will be more difficult for her than for the son. She might find it more difficult, as was suggested earlier, to face parental disapproval in case of conflict between parents and spouse and, in general, to sever ties to her parents and to attain the degree of maturity demanded of a wife in our culture.

WOMAN'S LESSER EMANCIPATION FROM HER FAMILY OF ORIENTATION AS A FACTOR IN MARITAL DISCORD

That marriage difficulties arise as a result of the attachment of the wife to her family was amply illustrated in the pilot study conducted by the writer. In some cases the problem took the form of a mental conflict over the claims of parents and husband. For example, one woman said:

> When I was single, I always helped my family. Now I have just heard that my father isn't well and should have a week's vacation. If only I had some money of my own I wouldn't hesitate a minute to send him a check. As it is, even if my husband would agree to give me the money, have I the right to ask him to deny himself the new radio for the sake of my family?

In other cases, the relation of the wife to her family caused marital conflict. The overt conflicts were sometimes about the excessive (in the husband's view) concern of the wife over her younger siblings. One husband accused his wife of neglecting their children in her preoccupation with the problems of her adolescent brother and sister whom, he maintained, she "babied too much." She telephoned them daily, waiting, however, for the husband to leave for work because the telephone conversations irritated him. The relation of the wife to her mother was the focal point of marriage conflict in still other cases. The husband objected to the frequent visits of the wife to her mother, the mother-in-law's excessive help with the housework ("You are shirking your duties as a wife"), the wife's dependence upon her mother for opinions, the mother-in-law's interference, and so on.

If our hypothesis is valid, we should find that such in-law problems in marriage more frequently involve the wife's parents than the husband's parents.

Given this theoretical expectation we examined the body of relevant opinion and data contained in some twenty texts and other books on the family. Of those examined, the bulk were written by sociologists, a few by psychiatrists and psychologists. As far as the sociologists were concerned, the field is virtually barren of data bearing crucially upon our hypothesis. The reason is simple—the problem was never posed. Several writers suggested that the mother-in-law constitutes a greater hazard to marriage than the father-in-law *but they do not raise the question of the side from which the in-law problem is more likely to arise.*

This gap reveals vividly the decisive role of theory in empirical studies. Evidently the sociologists were concerned with the explicit and acknowledged cultural norms which assert the structural symmetry of our bilateral family with identical relations to both families of orientation on the part of the spouses. Deviations from the norm of symmetry, then, tend to be interpreted in terms of individual pathologies. It was the failure to perceive that deviations from the norm of symmetry may themselves be induced by other workings of the kinship structure and not merely by individual abnormality that resulted in the observed gap. Indeed, the illustrations used in books were inadvertently misleading. While the text implied a symmetrical relation to the two sets of in-laws as the norm, the illustrations of deviance cited more frequently a "mother's boy." Illustrations frequently come from clinical sources which are selective. Furthermore, in-law trouble which is due to the husband's dependence upon his parents, although rarer, may be more acute and, therefore, more obvious.

The psychiatrists, represented by Hamilton and Dreikurs, have passing references to the problem which are contrary to our hypothesis, but with no supporting data. Dreikurs asserts that the husband's family is more disturbing in marriage. Hamilton considers that the male "mother love victim" is the greater threat to marriage because "fathers seldom get a chance to absorb their daughters' emotions so much that they never love any other man."

It may be suggested that whatever the merits of the case, a certain theoretical bias has predisposed the psychoanalyst to this position. The psychoanalysts have been absorbed in the childhood drama of emotional development. The Oedipus complex has been more prominent in the orthodox theory than the Electra complex. In speculating about the in-law problem, the fixation of the son upon the mother would naturally loom important. The writers have not explored the possibility that the cultural definitions of sex roles may have differential consequences for the adjustment at issue.

An indirect but confirming bit of evidence comes from Burgess and Cottrell. The authors cite a result for which they offer no explanation. They find that "closeness of attachment . . . in the association of parents and son show a consistent though small positive relation to marital adjustment." No such consistent pattern appears in the association between parents and daughter, although "no" attachment to the father and "little" or "no" attachment to the mother appear to work against a high marital adjustment score. In terms of our hypothesis, it is possible that *more* women than men who checked "a good deal of attachment" represented cases of "over-attachment" with its inimical influence upon marriage happiness.

Terman studied the same relationship. He cites the mean happiness scores of husbands and wives according to the degree of parent-child attachment and also correlations of happiness scores with parent-child attachment. In contrast to Burgess and Cottrell he finds a positive correlation between attachment and happiness for *both* men and women. He does not state in the text what appears in the figures, however, that the correlation is lower for women. Again it is possible that the favorable features in good relations with parents are counterbalanced in the case of women by the too close a tie which is sometimes hidden in the response "very close attachment."

If future research is to bear crucially upon the hypothesis that the "overattachment" of the wife to her family of orientation creates marriage conflict as evidenced by "in-law" trouble, it must be so designed as to disentangle various contradictory tendencies. It is possible, for example, that such marriage conflict is much more frequent among women whereas among men, though rarer, it may be experienced more acutely. Excessive ties to parents would be even more dysfunctional for the male role of the family head than for the housewife. Our culture is less permissive towards unusually close son-parent ties. Consequently, the "silver cord" may be more socially visible and better reported even if (and because?) it is a rare occurrence as compared with the daughter-mother ties.

Another refinement suggests itself. The role of in-laws as sources of tension may vary with the stages of the family cycle. We have hitherto stressed the attitudes of the spouses towards their parents as the source of in-law trouble. But the parents contribute their share. And here it is possible that during engagement and perhaps even in the first year of marriage it is the husband's family which creates more trouble for the young couple. As a rule, the girl's family may be more favorably disposed to marriage because a reasonably early marriage is more advantageous to the woman. Furthermore, the very attachment of the girl to her family means, as the folklore has it, that "when your son marries, you lose a son, when your daughter marries, you gain one," or, "your son is your son till he takes him a wife, your daughter is your daughter all her life." Again, the greater control exercised over the choice of mates by the girl's family may mean that the prospective son-in-law is more acceptable than the prospective daughter-in-law . . . But whereas in the engagement period the husband's family may figure more prominently in in-law conflicts, it is assumed, in the light of this paper, that as the marriage continues, the basic dependence of the woman upon her family tends to make her parents the principal actors in the in-law drama.

72. THE FUNCTION OF MALE INITIATION CEREMONIES AT PUBERTY

JOHN W. M. WHITING, RICHARD KLUCKHOHN, AND ALBERT ANTHONY

Describing the manner in which teenagers are initiated into adulthood in various cultures, this remarkable study indicates the influence of the general values in each culture on its attitude toward children. Strangely enough, it suggests that a society's behavior toward its adolescents is precisely the reverse of that toward its infants. If it indulges one, it is strict toward the other.

Contemporary American society seems to fit into the category of cultures which deprive infants and indulge teenagers. Individual parents may feel that they are deciding for themselves how they will treat their children, but when cultures are compared around the world, it appears that parents in each culture tend to treat their children just like most of the other parents in that culture treat theirs.

Reprinted from *Readings in Social Psychology*, Third Edition, by Eleanor E. Maccoby, Theodore M. Newcomb, and Eugene L. Hartley. By permission of Henry Holt and Company, Inc., Copyright 1958.

Our society gives little formal recognition of the physiological and social changes a boy undergoes at puberty. He may be teased a little when his voice changes or when he shaves for the first time. Changes in his social status from childhood to adulthood are marked by a number of minor events rather than by any single dramatic ceremonial observance. Graduation from grammar school and subsequently from high school are steps to adulthood, but neither can be considered as a *rite de passage*. Nor may the accomplishment of having obtained a driver's license, which for many boys is the most important indication of having grown up, be classed as one. Legally the twenty-first birthday is the time at which a boy becomes a man; but, except for a somewhat more elaborate birthday party this occasion is not ceremonially marked and, therefore, cannot be thought of as a *rite de passage*. Neither physiologically, socially, nor legally is there a clear demarcation between boyhood and manhood in our society.

Such a gradual transition from boyhood to manhood is by no means universal. Among the Thonga, a tribe in South Africa, every boy must go through a very elaborate ceremony in order to become a man. When a boy is somewhere between ten and 16 years of age, he is sent by his parents to a "circumcision school" which is held every four or five years. Here in company with his age-mates he undergoes severe hazing by the adult males of the society. The initiation begins when each boy runs the gauntlet between two rows of men who beat him with clubs. At the end of this experience he is stripped of his clothes and his hair is cut. He is next met by a man covered with lion manes and is seated upon a stone facing this "lion man." Someone then strikes him from behind and when he turns his head to see who has struck him, his foreskin is seized and in two movements cut off by the "lion man." Afterwards he is secluded for three months in the "yards of mysteries," where he can be seen only by the initiated. It is especially taboo for a woman to approach these boys during their seclusion, and if a woman should glance at the leaves with which the circumcised covers his wound and which form his only clothing, she must be killed.

During the course of his initiation, the boy undergoes six major trials: beatings, exposure to cold, thirst, eating of unsavory foods, punishment, and the threat of death. On the slightest pretext he may be severely beaten by one of the newly initiated men who is assigned to the task by the older men of the tribe. He sleeps without covering and suffers bitterly from the winter cold. He is forbidden to drink a drop of water during the whole three months. Meals are often made nauseating by the half-digested grass from the stomach of an antelope which is poured over his food. If he is caught breaking any important rule governing the ceremony, he is severely punished. For example, in one of these punishments, sticks are placed between the fingers of the offender, then a strong man closes his hand around that of the novice practically crushing his fingers. He is frightened into submission by being told that in former times boys who had tried to escape or who revealed the secrets to women or to the un-initiated were hanged and their bodies burnt to ashes.

Although the Thonga are extreme in the severity of this sort of initia-tion, many other societies have rites which have one or more of the main features of the Thonga ceremony. Of a sample of 55 societies chosen for this study, 18 have one or more of the four salient features of the Thonga ceremony, e.g., painful hazing by adult males, genital operations, seclu-sion from women, and tests of endurance and manliness, the remaining 37 societies either have no ceremony at all or one which does not have any of the above features.

HYPOTHESIS

It is the purpose of this paper to develop a set of hypotheses concern-ing the function of male initiation rites which accounts for the presence of these rites in some societies and the absence of them in others. The theory that we have chosen to test has been suggested by previous ex-planations for the rites, particularly those of psychoanalytic origin. These explanations were modified to fit the problem of this research in two re-spects. First, certain of the concepts and hypotheses were restated or re-defined so as to be coherent with the growing general behavioral theory of personality development, and second, they were restated in such a way as to be amenable to cross-cultural test, i.e., cultural indices were specified for each variable.

We assume that boys tend to be initiated at puberty in those societies in which they are particularly hostile toward their fathers and dependent upon their mothers. The hazing of the candidates, as well as the genital operations, suggests that one function of the rites is to prevent open and violent revolt against parental authority at a time when physical maturity would make such revolt dangerous and socially disruptive. Isolation from women and tests of manliness suggest that another function of the rites is to break an excessively strong dependence upon the mother and to ensure identification with adult males and acceptance of the male role.

It is to be noted here that the educational and disciplinary functions of the initiation are not limited in time to the actual period of initiation. The boy knows all during childhood and latency about the initiation which he will face at puberty. While he is overtly not supposed to know any of the secrets of the rite, he actually knows almost everything that will happen to him. He is both afraid of what he knows will happen and also envious of the kudos and added status which his older friends have acquired through having successfully gone through this rite. Thus, through the boy's whole life the initiation ceremony serves as a conditioner of his behavior and his attitudes towards male authority, while at the same time emphasizing the advantages of becoming a member of the male group through initiation.

We assume that a long and exclusive relationship between mother and son provides the conditions which should lead to an exceptionally strong dependence upon the mother. Also, we assume that if the father terminates this relationship and replaces his son, there should be strong envy and hostility engendered in the boy which, although held in check during childhood, may dangerously manifest itself with the onset of puberty, unless measures are taken to prevent it.

As we indicated above, the hypothesis is derived from psychoanalytic theory. However, it should be noted that there are some modifications which may be important. First, no assumption is being made that the envy is exclusively sexual in character. We are making the more general assumption that if the mother for a prolonged period devotes herself to the satisfaction of all the child's needs—including hunger, warmth, safety, freedom from pain, as well as sex—he will become strongly dependent upon her. In accordance with this we believe rivalry may be based upon a competition for the fulfillment of any of these needs. Second, we do not propose, as most psychoanalysts do, that Oedipal rivalry is a universal, but rather we claim it is a variable which may be strong or weak depending upon specific relationships between father, mother, and son. Thus, we assume father-son rivalry may range from a value of zero to such high intensities that the whole society may be required to adjust to it.

An illustration of cultural conditions which should intensify the dependency of a boy on his mother and rivalry with his father is found in the following case.

Kwoma Dependency. The Kwoma, a tribe living about 200 miles up the Sepik River in New Guinea, have initiation rites similar to those of the Thonga. Examination of the differences in the relationship of a mother to her infant during the first years of his life reveals some strong contrasts between the Kwoma and our own society. While in our society an infant sleeps in his own crib and the mother shares her bed with the father, the Kwoma infant sleeps cuddled in his mother's arms until he is old enough to be weaned, which is generally when he is two or three years old. The father, in the meantime, sleeps apart on his own bark slab bed. Furthermore during this period, the Kwoma mother abstains from sexual intercourse with her husband in order to avoid having to care for two dependent children at the same time. Since the Kwoma are polygynous and discreet extramarital philandering is permitted, this taboo is not too hard on the husband. In addition, it is possible that the mother obtains some substitute sexual gratification from nursing and caring for her infant. If this be the case, it is not unlikely that she should show more warmth and affection toward her infant than if she were obtaining sexual gratification from her husband. Whether or not the custom can be attributed to this sex taboo, the Kwoma mother, while her co-wife does the housework, not only sleeps with her infant all night but holds it in her lap all day without apparent frustration. Such a close relationship between a mother and child in our society would seem not only unbearably difficult to the mother, but also somewhat improper.

When the Kwoma child is weaned, a number of drastic things happen all at once. He is suddenly moved from his mother's bed to one of his own. His father resumes sexual relations with his mother. Although the couple wait until their children are asleep, the intercourse takes place in the same room. Thus, the child may truly become aware of his replacement. He is now told that he can no longer have his mother's milk because some supernatural being needs it. This is vividly communicated to him by his mother when she puts a slug on her breasts and daubs the blood-colored sap of the breadfruit tree over her nipples. Finally he is no longer permitted to sit on his mother's lap. She resumes her work and goes to the garden to weed or to the swamp to gather sago flour leaving him behind for the first time in his life. That these events are traumatic to the child is not surprising. He varies between sadness and anger, weeping and violent temper tantrums.

It is our hypothesis that it is this series of events that makes it necessary, when the boy reaches adolescence, for the society to have an initiation rite of the type we have already described. It is necessary to put a final stop to (1) his wish to return to his mother's arms and lap, (2) to prevent an open revolt against his father who has displaced him from his mother's bed, and (3) to ensure identification with the adult males of the society. In other words, Kwoma infancy so magnifies the conditions which should produce Oedipus rivalry that the special cultural adjustment of ceremonial hazing, isolation from women, and symbolic castration, etc., must be made to resolve it.

If our analysis of the psychodynamics in Kwoma society is correct, societies with initiation rites should have similar child-rearing practices, whereas societies lacking the rite should also lack the exclusive mother-son sleeping arrangements and *post-partum* sexual taboo of the Kwoma.

TESTING THE HYPOTHESIS

To test this hypothesis a sample of 56 societies was selected. First, the ethnographic material on more than 150 societies was checked to determine whether or not there was an adequate description of our variables e.g., sleeping arrangements, *post-partum* sex taboo, and initiation rites at puberty. Only half of the societies reviewed fulfilled these conditions. Although we had initially endeavored to select our cases so as to have maximum distribution throughout the world, we found that some areas were represented by several societies, while others were not represented by any. To correct for any bias that might result from this sample, we made a further search of the ethnographic literature in order to fill in the gaps, and we thereby added several societies from areas previously not represented. Finally, to maximize diversity and to minimize duplication through selection of closely related societies, whenever there were two or more societies from any one culture area which had the same values on all our variables, we chose only one of them. Using these criteria, our final sample consisted of 56 societies representing 45 of the 60 culture areas designated by Murdock.

The societies comprising our final sample range in size and type from small, simple, tribal groups to segments of large, complex civilizations such as the United States or Japan. In the latter case, our information has been drawn from ethnographic reports on a single delineated community.

When this sample had finally been chosen, the material relevant to our variables was first abstracted, and then judgments were made for each society as to the nature of the transition from boyhood to manhood, the sleeping arrangements, and the duration of the *post-partum* sex taboo. To prevent contamination, the judgments on each variable were made at different times and the name of the society disguised by a code. All judgments were made by at least two persons and in every case where there was a disagreement (less than 15 percent of the cases for any given variable), the data were checked by one of the authors, whose judgment was accepted as final. Our findings with respect to initiation rites have been tabulated in Table 1 below.

We discovered that only five societies out of the total number had sleeping arrangements similar to our own, that is, where the father and mother share a bed and the baby sleeps alone. In only three societies did the mother, the father, and the baby each have his or her own bed. In the remaining 48, the baby slept with his mother until he was at least a year old and generally until he was weaned. In 24 of the latter, however, the father also shared the bed, the baby generally sleeping between the mother and father. The remaining 24 societies had sleeping arrangements like the Kwoma in which the mother and child sleep in one bed and the father in another. Often the father's bed was not even in the same house. He either slept in a men's club house or in the hut of one of his other wives leaving mother and infant not only alone in the same bed but alone in the sleeping room.

Similarly, the societies of our sample were split on the rules regulating the resumption of sexual intercourse following parturition. Twenty-nine, like our own, have a brief taboo of a few weeks to permit the mother to recover from her delivery. In the remaining 27, the mother did not resume sexual intercourse for at least nine months after the birth of her child, and in one instance, the Cheyenne, the ideal period adhered to

Table 1.   The Relationship between Exclusive Mother-Son Sleeping Arrangements and a *Post-partum* Sex Taboo * and the Occurrence of Initiation Ceremonies at Puberty

CUSTOMS IN INFANCY		CUSTOMS AT ADOLESCENT INITIATION CEREMONIES	
Exclusive Mother-Son Sleeping Arrangements	*Post-partum Sex-Taboo*	*Absent*	*Present*
Long	Long		Azande *hgs* †
			Camayura *hs*
			Chagga *hgs*
			Cheyenne *ht*
			Chiricahua *ht*
			Dahomeans *hgs*
			Fijians *gs*
			Jivaro *ht*
		Ganda	Kwoma *hgs*
		Khalapur (Rajput)	Lesu *gs*
		Nyakyusa	Nuer *hs*
		Tepoztlan	Samoans *g*
		Trobrianders	Thonga *hgs*
		Yapese	Tiv *hgs*
	Short	Ashanti	
		Malaita	Cagaba *ht*
		Siriono	
Short	Long	Araucanians	Kwakiutl *s*
		Pilaga	Ojibwa *t*
		Pondo	Ooldea *hgs*
		Tallensi	
	Short	Alorese	Hopi *hs*
		Balinese	Timbira *hst*
		Druz	
		Egyptians (Silwa)	
		Eskimos (Copper)	
		French	
		Igorot (Bontoc)	
		Japanese (Suye Mura)	
		Koryak (Maritime)	
		Lakher	
		Lamba	

* Both of a year or more duration.
† The letters following the tribal designations in the right-hand column indicate the nature of the ceremony—*h* = painful hazing, *g* = genital operations, *s* = seclusion from women, and *t* = tests of manliness.

Table 1. The Relationship between Exclusive Mother-Son Sleeping Arrangements and a *Post-partum* Sex Taboo and the Occurrence of Initiation Ceremonies at Puberty (*Continued*)

CUSTOMS IN INFANCY		CUSTOMS AT ADOLESCENT INITIATION CEREMONIES	
Exclusive Mother-Son Sleeping Arrangements	*Post-partum Sex-Taboo*	*Absent*	*Present*
		Lapps	
		Lepcha	
		Maori	
		Mixtecans	
		Navaho	
		Ontong Javanese	
		Papago	
		Serbs	
		Tanala (Menabe)	
		Trukese	
		United States (Homestead)	
		Yagua	

was reported as ten years. The duration of the taboo generally corresponded to the nursing period and in many cases was reinforced by the belief that sexual intercourse curdles or sours the mother's milk, thus making it harmful for the infant. In other societies, like the Kwoma, the taboo is explicitly for the purpose of ensuring a desired interval between children where adequate means of contraception are lacking. In these societies the taboo is terminated when the infant reaches some maturational stage, e.g., "until the child can crawl," "until the child can walk," or "until he can take care of himself." For the 27 societies that have this taboo, more than a few weeks long, the average duration is slightly more than two years.

RESULTS AT THE CULTURAL LEVEL

Our hypothesis may now be restated in cultural terms as follows: *Societies which have sleeping arrangements in which the mother and baby share the same bed for at least a year to the exclusion of the father and societies which have a taboo restricting the mother's sexual behavior for at least a year after childbirth will be more likely to have a ceremony of transition from boyhood to manhood than those societies where these conditions do not occur (or occur for briefer periods).* For the purposes of this hypothesis, transition ceremonies include only those ceremonies characterized by at least one of the following events: painful hazing of the initiates, isolation from females, tests of manliness, and genital operations.

The test of this hypothesis is presented in Table 1. It will be observed from this table that of the 20 societies where both antecedent variables are present, 14 have initiation ceremonies and only six do not. Where both antecedent variables are absent only two of the 25 societies have the ceremonies. Thus, over 80 per-cent of the 45 pure cases correspond with the prediction. Though our hypothesis was not designed for predicting the mixed cases, that is, where only one of the antecedent variables is present, it seems that they tended not to have the transition ceremonies.

Although the eight cases which are exceptional to our theory, the six in the upper left-hand column and the two in the lower right-hand column may be simply misclassified through error of measurement, re-examination uncovers some other unanticipated factor which may account for their placement. This analysis turns out to be enlightening.

Reviewing, first the six cases in the upper left-hand column, that is, the societies which have both exclusive mother-son sleeping arrangements and a *post-partum* sex taboo but no initiation, we found that four of them (Khalapur, Trobrianders, Nyakusa, and Yapese) have an adjustment at adolescence which may serve as a psychological substitute for the initiation ceremony. The boys at this time leave the parental home and move to a men's house or a boys' village where they live until they are married. Malinowski observed this type of adjustment amongst the Trobrianders in 1927. He wrote:

> But the most important change, and the one which interests us most is the partial break-up of the family at the time when the adolescent boys and girls cease to be permanent inmates of the parental home . . . a special institution . . . special houses inhabited by groups of adolescent boys and girls. A boy as he reaches puberty will join such a house. . . . Thus the parent home is drained completely of its adolescent males, though until the boy's marriage he will always come back for food, and will also continue to work for his household to some extent. . . .
>
> At this stage, however, when the adolescent has to learn his duties, to be instructed in traditions and to study his magic, his arts and crafts, his interest in his mother's brother, who is his teacher and tutor, is greatest and their relations are at their best.

This account suggests that this change of residence serves the same functions that we have posited for initiation ceremonies, for example, by establishing male authority, breaking the bond with the mother, and ensuring acceptance of the male role. It is important for our hypothesis, also, that there are only two other societies in our sample where such a change of residence occurs. One of these is the Malaita which has one but not both of our antecedent variables; the other is the Ashanti where the boy may move to the village of his mother's brother at or before puberty, but this is not mandatory and only half the boys do so. Thus, if we were to revise our hypothesis such that a change of residence was considered to be equivalent to initiation, the four societies mentioned should be moved over to the right-hand column and the exceptional cases would be reduced from eight to four.

Some comment should be made on the two remaining cases in the upper left-hand column. The Ganda are reported to have an interesting method of child rearing which may or may not be relevant to our theory. For the first three years of his life, a Ganda child sleeps exclusively with his mother and she is subject to a sexual taboo. At this point the boy is reported to be weaned and transferred to the household of his father's brother by whom he is brought up from then on. It might be assumed that this event would obviate the need for later ceremonial initiation into manhood. Since several other societies that do have initiation also have a change of residence at weaning, however, this simple explanation cannot be accepted and the Ganda must remain an unexplained exception. Finally Lewis reports for the Tepoztlan that there was some disagreement among his informants as to the length of the taboo and exclusive sleeping arrangements. Since again there were other equally equivocal cases, we shall have to accept the verdict of our judges and let this case also remain an exception.

A reconsideration of the two exceptions in the lower right-hand column, the Hopi and the Timbira, which have the type of initiation into manhood required by our theory but have neither exclusive sleeping arrangements nor a prolonged *post-partum* sex taboo, also turns out to be fruitful. In neither of these societies does the father have authority over the children. This is vested in the mother's brother who lives in another household. That these societies should have an initiation rite, again, does not seem to contradict our general theory, even though it does contradict our specific hypothesis. From clinical studies in our own society it is clear that even with the lack of exclusive sleeping arrangements and a minimal *post-partum* sex taboo, an appreciable degree of dependence upon the mother and rivalry with the father is generated. The cases here suggest that, although these motives are not strong enough to require ceremonial initiation into manhood if the father is present in the household and has authority over the child, this may be required if he lacks such authority.

But what of the cases which have but one of the antecedent variables? Taking into account the societies with exclusive sleeping arrangements but no *post-partum* sex taboo, our theory predicts that these conditions should produce dependency and rivalry. However, since the mother is receiving sexual satisfaction from her husband, she has less need to obtain substitute gratification from nurturing her infant, so that the dependency she produces in her child would be less intense and the need for initiation should be attenuated. Three of the four cases with exclusive sleeping arrangements but no taboo appear to fulfill these conditions. As we have reported above, the Ashanti and the Malaita practice a change of residence which, it could be argued, is somewhat less drastic than initiation. In any case this is permissive and not required for the Ashanti. When the Cagaba boy reaches adolescence, he is given instruction in sexual intercourse by a priest and then sent to practise these instructions with a widow who lives with him temporarily in a specially built small hut. The boy is not allowed to leave this hut until he succeeds in having sexual intercourse with her. This trial is reported to be terrifying to the boy and it is often several days before he does succeed. This type of initiation, however, does not seem to compare with other societies which like the Thonga have a full-fledged ceremony. The Siriono, on the other hand, do not have any ceremonial recognition of the shift from boyhood to manhood and they must be regarded as an exception to our theory.

The final group of cases to consider are those that have a long *post-partum* sex taboo but not exclusive mother-son sleeping arrangements. For these, our theory would also predict an attenuated need for initiation ceremonies. Although the mothers of this group are presumed to gain substitute sexual gratification from being especially nurturant and loving toward their infants, they have less opportunity to do so than with those of societies where there are also exclusive sleeping arrangements.

As in the previous group of societies the ceremonies are, except for the Ooldea which will be discussed below, mild. The Kwakiutl have a ceremony which consists of a potlach given by the father for the son. There the boys undergo no hazing or genital operations but are secluded and expected to perform a dance. For the Ojibwa, the boy is expected to obtain a guardian spirit in a vision before he reaches maturity. Thus, generally when he is 11 or 12 years old, he goes alone into the forest where he stays often for several days without food, water, and generally without sleep until he either has a vision or returns home to recuperate before trying again. Again neither hazing or genital operations are involved.

The Ooldea, a tribe situated in southwestern Australia do, however, have a full-fledged initiation rite with hazing, isolation, and a very painful genital operation. This apparently runs counter to our assumption that the rites should be mild if only one determinant is present.

Radcliffe-Brown, however, reports that in many Australian tribes

. . . the discipline of very young children is left to the mother and the other women of the horde. A father does not punish and may not even scold his infant children, but if they misbehave he will scold the mother and perhaps give her a blow with a stick. He regards the mother as responsible for misbehavior by very young children. When they are a little older, the father undertakes the education of the boys but leaves the education of the girls to the mother and the women of the horde. But the father behaves affectionately and is very little of a disciplinarian. Discipline for a boy begins when he approaches puberty and is exercised by the men of the horde. The big change comes with the initiation ceremonies when, in some tribes, the father, by a ceremonial (symbolic) action, hands over his son to the men who will carry out the initiation rites. During the initiation period of several years the boy is subjected to rigid and frequently painful discipline by men other than his father.

If the Ooldea be one of those Australian tribes described above, they fall, along with the Trobrianders, Hopi, and Timbira, into the class of societies where the function of initiation is to make up for the lack of discipline exercised by a father over the boy during childhood.

A study of those societies without exclusive sleeping arrangements and with a long *post-partum* sex taboo which do not have the rites is interesting. In the first place both the Pondo and the Araucanians are reported to have had initiation ceremonies in the recent past, indicating that they are perhaps near the threshold of needing them. The Tallensi also are interesting. An observer notes that the Tallensi should have invented the Oedipus-conflict theory since they are quite open and conscious of the strong rivalry and hostility between father and son, a conflict which remains strong and dangerous, guarded only by ritualized forms of etiquette, until the father dies and the son takes his place. Furthermore, family fissions are reported to occur frequently and the oldest son often leaves the family to establish a new lineage of his own.

Thus, the presence of a *post-partum* sex taboo alone seems to produce tension, which these societies commonly seek to resolve through initiation ceremonies. Societies in this group which do not have ceremonies either had them recently or show evidence of unresolved tension.

Summary. The cross-cultural evidence indicates that:

1. A close relationship is established between mother and son during infancy as a consequence of either (a) their sleeping together for at least a year to the exclusion of the father or (b) the mother being prohibited from sexual intercourse for at least a year after the birth of her child or (c) both of these together have measurable consequences which are manifested in cultural adjustments at adolescence.
2. The cultural adjustments to the presence of the above factors are made when the boy approaches or reaches sexual maturity. These adjustments are either (a) a ceremony of initiation into manhood involving at least one and generally several of the following factors; painful *hazing* by the adult males of the society, tests of endurance and manliness, seclusion from women, and genital operations, or (b) a change of residence which involves separation of the boy from his mother and sisters and may also include some formal means for establishing male authority such as receiving instructions from and being required to be respectful to the mother's brother or the members of the men's house.

3. If both the factors specified in (1) are present, the consequences at adolescence tend to be more elaborate and severe than if only one is present.
4. The cultural adjustments specified in (2) also occur in societies where the father does not have the right to discipline his son, whether or not the conditions specified in (1) are present.

The evidence for these statements is summarized in Table 2.

Table 2. The Relationship of Infancy Factors to Cultural Adjustments at Adolescence

CUSTOMS IN INFANCY AND CHILDHOOD			CULTURAL ADJUSTMENT AT ADOLESCENCE		
Authority of Father over Son	*Exclusive Mother-Son Sleeping Arrangement*	*Post-partum Sex Taboo*	*None*	*Change of Residence*	*Initiation Ceremony*
Present	Long	Long	2	3	14
		Short	1	2	1
	Short	Long	4	0	2
		Short	23	0	0
Absent			0	1	3

THE SOCIOPSYCHOLOGICAL IMPLICATIONS

So much for the manifest results at the cultural level. But what is the most reasonable sociopsychological interpretation of these relationships? What are the psychodynamics involved? We are not concerned with the bizarre rites of the Thonga or the peculiar life of a Kwoma infant, for their own sakes, but rather in discovering some general truth about human nature. We, therefore, wish to state what we believe to be the underlying processes that are involved. These are processes that we have not directly observed and which must be accepted or rejected on the grounds of their plausibility or, more important, on the basis of further research implied by our theory.

We believe that six sociopsychological assumptions are supported by our findings:

1. The more exclusive the relationship between a son and his mother during the first years of his life, the greater will be his emotional dependence upon her.
2. The more intensely a mother nurtures (loves) an infant during the early years of his life, the more emotionally dependent he will be upon her.

3. The greater the emotional dependence of a child upon a mother, the more hostile and envious he will be toward anyone whom he perceives as replacing him in her affection.[1]

4. If a child develops a strong emotional dependence upon his mother during infancy, and hostility toward and envy of his father in early childhood at the time of weaning and the onset of independence training, these feelings (although latent during childhood) will manifest themselves when he reaches physiological maturity in (a) open rivalry with his father and (b) incestuous approaches to his mother, unless measures are taken to prevent such manifestations.

5. Painful hazing, enforced isolation from women, trials of endurance or manliness, genital operations, and change of residence are effective means for preventing the dangerous manifestation of rivalry and incest.

6. Even a moderate or weak amount of emotional dependence upon the mother and rivalry with the father will be dangerous at adolescence if the father has no right to (or does not in fact) exercise authority over his son during childhood.

If these sociopsychological hypotheses are true, they have some interesting implications for individual differences in our own society.[2] It has long been known that there is an association between certain types of juvenile delinquency and broken homes. We would predict that the probability of a boy becoming delinquent in such instances would be highest where the separation of the mother and father occurred during the early infancy of the boy and where she remarried when he was two or three years old.

We would further predict that insofar as there has been an increase in juvenile delinquency in our society, it probably has been accompanied by an increase in the exclusiveness of mother-child relationships and/or a decrease in the authority of the father. It is not unreasonable that industrialization and urbanization have done just this, but, of course, this matter should be investigated before such an interpretation is accepted.

Finally, if further research shows that juvenile delinquency in our society is in part a function of the early childhood factors that have been described in this paper, then it can be countered either by decreasing the

---

[1] If, however, the mother herself is perceived by the child as the one responsible for terminating the early intense relationship, this should lead the boy to both envy her and identify with her. This should produce conflict with respect to his sex role identity, which initiation rites would serve to resolve.

[2] In a study of infant training William Sewell reports that "the children who slept with their mothers during infancy made significantly poorer showings on the self-adjustment, personal freedom, and family relations components of the California Test of Personality and suffered more sleep disturbances than did those who slept alone." W. H. Sewell, "Infant Training and the Personality of the Child," *Am. J. Sociol.*, 1953, LVIII, 157.

exclusiveness of the early mother-child relationship, increasing the authority of the father during childhood, or instituting a formal means of coping with adolescent boys functionally equivalent to those described in this paper. Change of residence would seem more compatible with the values of our society than an initiation ceremony. The Civilian Conservation Corps camps of the 1930's were an experiment which should provide useful data in this regard. The present institution of selective service would perhaps serve this purpose were the boys to be drafted at an earlier age and exposed to the authority of responsible adult males.

73. THE LATER CAREERS OF BOYS WHO WERE EARLY- OR LATE-MATURING

MARY COVER JONES

Physical changes in adolescence have tremendous social and psychological significance for the individual. For example, a boy who matures early gains social status among his peers and elders, and his own self-esteem is probably enhanced as well.

Mary Cover Jones compared a group of early- and late-maturing boys to reveal the superior social-emotional adjustment of the early-maturers. Here she traces the boys into manhood and discovers that the advantages of the early-maturers, elaborated in more successful careers, have been maintained into adult life.

Similar studies of girls show the reverse to be true: early maturation is a handicap.

A previous study (6) compared two groups of boys who had been classified as physically accelerated or retarded, in terms of skeletal age. These groups represented approximately the 20 per cent at each extreme of a normal public school sample. The comparison showed differences in physical growth, sexual maturing, and in a number of psychological measures, and led to the conclusion that ". . . those who are physically accelerated are usually accepted and treated by adults and other children as more mature. They appear to have relatively little need to strive for status. From their ranks come the outstanding student body

Selections reprinted from the article in *Child Development*, 28, No. 1 (March, 1957), 113–128, by permission of the author and the Society for Research in Child Development.

leaders in senior high school. In contrast, the physically retarded boys exhibit many forms of relatively immature behavior: this may be in part because others tend to treat them as the little boys they appear to be. Furthermore, a fair proportion of these give evidence of needing to counteract their physical disadvantages in some way—usually by greater activity and striving for attention, although in some cases by withdrawal."

It is clear that early- or late-maturing may have a considerable bearing upon the social life and personal adjustment of some individuals during the middle years of their adolescence. Perhaps of greater importance, however, is the inquiry as to longer-term effects or relationships in adult life, and on this point no evidence has previously been offered.

The subjects who participated in the original study are now in their early thirties. Contacts have been maintained with many of the group during the intervening years; in a systematic follow-up study beginning in 1954 current data have been obtained for 20 of the early- and late-maturing boys, out of an original sample of 32.

ADOLESCENT DIFFERENCES

Figures 1, 2, 3, 4, and 5 present data from the adolescent period for the original groups, and for the subsamples available in the present study. Figure 1 shows the distribution of skeletal ages (at around chronological age 17) for the early- and late-maturing. Each circle represents an individual case: the black circles those included in the follow-up and the open circles those who have dropped out. It can be seen that the new selection has not substantially altered the maturity differential of the two groups.

Figures 2 and 3 present cumulative records for height and weight in terms of standard scores at ages 12 to 17. Standard scores (in which 50 is taken as the mean and 10 as the SD) are indicated on the left vertical

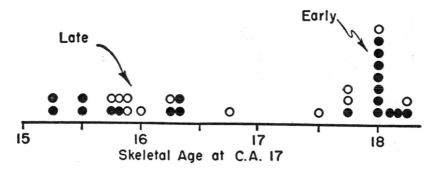

FIGURE 1. SKELETAL AGES AT 17 YEARS, OF THE LATE- AND EARLY-MATURING

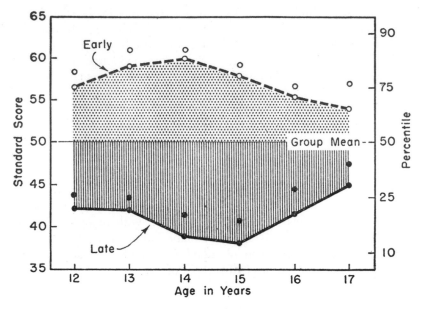

FIGURE 2. HEIGHT COMPARISONS FOR TWO CONTRASTING GROUPS OF BOYS

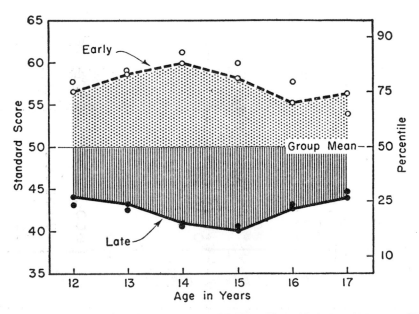

FIGURE 3. WEIGHT COMPARISONS FOR TWO CONTRASTING GROUPS OF BOYS

axis, and percentiles on the right. In these and the following figures, the points on connecting lines represent averages for the follow-up group, consisting of 11 early- and 9 late-maturing individuals. The adjacent points denote averages for the original 16 early- and 16 late-maturing.

The early-maturing tend to fall at the 75 percentile or above, and the late-maturing at the 25 percentile or below, with differences which are at a maximum at around 14 years, when the early-maturing are on the average approximately 8 inches taller and 34 pounds heavier.

In these physical measures the adolescent data for the follow-up sample are similar to those of the original sample, and this is also shown in Figure 4, based on a measure of static dynamometer strength (right grip).

Other physical comparisons included Greulich's (5) 5-point standards of maturity (rated by physicians from pubic hair and external genitalia) and Bayley's ratings of androgeny (1). On the Greulich scale the late-maturing boys at age 14 averaged only 2.0, well below the norm; while the early-maturing averaged 4.5, or close to the scale maximum. In the androgeny assessments, the early-maturing were nearly all in the "masculine" or "hyper-masculine" zone, while approximately half of the late-maturing were classified as "asexual," "bisexual," "hypo-bisexual," or physically "disharmonious." In these as in other respects the follow-up samples yielded distributions similar to those of the original study.

With such marked adolescent differences in size, strength, masculine conformation, and associated athletic abilities, we might also predict, in

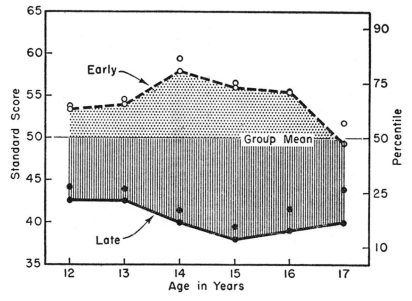

FIGURE 4.   STRENGTH COMPARISONS: RIGHT GRIP OF BOYS

our culture, average differences in reputational status and in some aspects of self-acceptance. In the original study comparisons were presented, at an average age of 16, for a series of ratings made in "free play" situations. The early-maturing were judged to be more attractive in physique and as showing more attention to grooming. They tended to be more relaxed, more matter-of-fact and less affected in their behavior. Differences were significant at the .05 level for each of these traits; for a number of other characteristics, such as interest in the opposite sex, and "good-naturedness," quite consistent differences were obtained over nine semesters of observation. The late-maturing were significantly more expressive, but their small-boy eagerness was also associated with greater tenseness and more affected attention-seeking mannerisms.

. . . The early-maturing are centered close to the average in this characteristic [physical attractiveness and expressive behavior] while the late-maturing are judged to be more juvenile and less poised in their expressiveness, especially in the middle years of adolescence. Similar results were found for such characteristics as "animated," "talkative," and "uninhibited."

On behavior items suggesting a large component of self-acceptance (being relaxed, unaffected and matter-of-fact) the early-maturing were rated higher at the end of the study, with the late-maturing becoming increasingly "tense" and "affected" in the high school years. Figure 5 illustrates this for the characteristic which we have called "matter-of-fact." Both groups fluctuate around the average in this trait until age 16 when

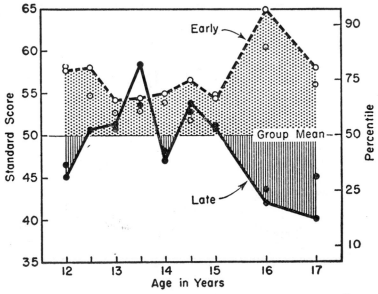

FIGURE 5.   COMPARATIVE RATINGS OF "MATTER-OF-FACTNESS" OF BOYS

they separate noticeably, the early-maturing falling on the favorable or well-adjusted side, and the late-maturing on the attention-seeking or showoff side of the scale. Similar wide separation at ages 16 and 17 has been found for the trait "unaffected-affected" and for "relaxed-tense." In these, as in other relevant psychological measures, the follow-up groups had adolescent records similar to those of the original study; the loss of cases has not substantially changed the selection.

ADULT DIFFERENCES

We may now consider the adult characteristics of the early- and late-maturing, as observed at an average age of 33 years. As was predicted at age 17, the differences in gross size tend to disappear. The early-maturing average only half an inch taller, at 5 feet 10 inches; and 7 pounds heavier, at 172 pounds. These differences are not significant. In body build, the prediction is that the early-maturing would be more mesomorphic. The tendency is in this direction, but the differences are not significant. The chief thing to note is the wide range of physiques within each group (both in adolescence and in adulthood) and the marked consistency over the years. A slight change is apparent in the direction of greater mesomorphy in eight of the nine late-maturing and they now present a somewhat more developed and sturdy appearance.

Some differences would be expected in constitutional indices of masculinity. Among the late-maturing, the majority of the original study and of those included in the follow-up were rated as having a deficiency in masculine development, at age 17. At age 33, however, Sheldon ratings of gynandromorphy (7) in the two groups showed considerable overlap and only a small and nonsignificant difference in favor of the early-maturing.

Personality differences in adult life have been examined with reference to a number of criteria. Two sources of data to be considered here are Gough's California Psychological Inventory and the Edwards Personal Preference Schedule. The first of these, the C.P.I., attempts to appraise aspects of character and temperament which are significant for social living and interpersonal behavior and which are related to personal maturity and creative achievement. Eighteen scales are available which describe individuals in terms of social responsibility, tolerance, flexibility, academic motivation, self-control and the like (3).

Most of the above scales did not show significant differences between the groups. One outstanding exception is the scale entitled "good impression," (interest in, and capacity for, creating a "good impression" on others) (4). Differences here favored the early-maturing with a significance at the .006 level.

Some of the interpretative phrases associated with high scores on this scale include: "is turned to for advice and reassurance; fatherly; is concerned with making a good impression; is persistent in working toward his goal." High scorers on this "Gi" scale are also designated as responsible, cooperative, enterprising, sociable and warm.

In our groups the early-maturing tend in addition to obtain higher scores on the C.P.I. scales for socialization, dominance, self-control and responsibility. Although none of these shows differences at a significance level better than .07, it is true that the early-maturing have high average scores and present a consistently favorable personality picture with regard to these important social variables.

The phrases and adjectives associated with high scores on these five scales (good impression, socialization, dominance, self-control, and responsibility) remind us strikingly of the social behavior and personal traits attributed, by their peers and by adults, to the early-maturing boys in adolescence. For the total group of 43 boys thus far included in the follow-up, a correlation of .50 (significant at the .01 level) was found between the "good impression" score on the C.P.I., and their level of skeletal maturity 18 years earlier. The corresponding Pearson r for the socialization score at age 33, and skeletal maturity at age 15, was .40, significant at the .01 level. For these correlations skeletal quotients were computed (skeletal age over chronological age), to make allowance for slight differences in the age at which the skeletal X-rays were obtained.

One other scale yields an interesting difference, significant at the .05 level. This is the scale for what has been termed "flexibility." Those who score high on this scale are described by Gough as tending to be rebellious, touchy, impulsive, self-indulgent, assertive, and also insightful. Low scorers are described as deliberate, methodical, and industrious, rigid, mannerly, overly-controlling of impulses, compliant. In these terms, the late-maturers tend to be more "flexible" than the early-maturers.

We might hazard the guess that some of the little boy behavior— the impulsiveness, playfulness and also the "touchiness" repeatedly noted in late-maturing adolescents is mirrored in the description of high scorers on this scale. We might speculate further that in the course of having to adapt to difficult status problems, the late-maturers have gained some insights and are indeed more flexible, while the early-maturing, capitalizing on their ability to make a good impression, may have clung to their earlier success pattern to the extent of becoming somewhat rigid or over-controlled.

The Edwards Personal Preference test shows relatively few significant differences between the two groups. This is a self-report device which measures 15 variables named from Murray's list of needs (2).

On the Edwards test, two of the scales are discriminating for our groups at the 4 and 5 per cent levels respectively. The early-maturing group scores high on the *dominance* scale: "to be a leader, persuade, argue for a point of view," while the late-maturing score high in *succorance:* "to seek encouragement, to be helped by others, to have a fuss made over one when hurt." For the total group of 40 who took the Edwards test at around age 33, skeletal maturing at age 17 correlated .40 with dominance, and —.48 with succorance (both significant at the .01 level). Table 1 summarizes the statistical findings for the follow-up comparisons.

Table 1. Summary of Statistical Findings for the Follow-up Comparisons

	Physical Measures: Means			
	EARLY		LATE	
	Age 14	*Age 33*	*Age 14*	*Age 33*
Height	5 ft. 8 in.	5 ft. 10 in.	5 ft.	5 ft. 9½ in.
Weight	126.9 lb.	172 lb.	93.2 lb.	165 lb.
Endomorphy *	2.6	3.1	3.1	3.3
Mesomorphy *	4.5	4.6	3.9	4.3
Ectomorphy *	3.4	3.4	3.7	3.7

	Psychological Scales				
	MEANS		*Signif. of Difference* †	*r* ‡	*Signif. Level*
	Early	*Late*			
California Psychological Inventory					
Good Impression	25.6	15.7	.006	.50	<.01
Flexibility	9.7	13.8	.05	—.23	
Delinquency §	13.9	20.3	.07	—.40	<.01
Impulsivity	17.1	23.4	.13	—.31	<.05
Dominance	31.7	27.4	.17	.26	
Responsibility	32.9	30.0	.19	.35	<.05
Edwards Personal Preference Schedule					
Dominance	19.4	12.6	.04	.40	<.01
Succorance	7.1	12.4	.05	—.48	<.01

* Rating on 7-point scale; 7 is high.
† Significance level, Wilcoxon Rank Test.
‡ Pearson product-moment correlation with skeletal age/chronological age, at 15 years.
§ A low score indicates "socialization."

To those of us who have known these young men for over 20 years, some of the most interesting questions remain to be answered. What have been their successes and failures in achieving occupational and personal goals? All are married, and in each group the present number of children averages 2.3. Socio-economic ratings, based on homes and neighborhoods, show no differences for the two groups. There are no significant differences in average educational level, although a slightly higher proportion of the later-maturing have college degrees and the only college teacher is in this group.

There is some indication that more of the early-maturing have attained vocational goals which are satisfying and status-conferring. Among this group five are in professional careers; four are executives; one is a skilled mechanic and one in a clerical position. Of the executives, three are in positions of somewhat impressive status.

Among the late-maturing, four are in professions, two are still university students, two are salesmen, and one is a carpenter. None has attained an important managerial position and several, by their own account and the nature of their work, seem somewhat precariously unsettled.

. . . . .

SUMMARY AND CONCLUSION

Boys who had been classified as physically accelerated or retarded in terms of skeletal age during adolescence were compared as young adults at age 33, to determine the long-term effects of rate of maturing upon personality.

Although some cases were lost from the original sample, the data for the follow-up group as reconstituted showed no substantial alteration in the adolescent differentials of the early- and late-maturing.

For the original sample and for the subsample available in the present study, analysis of ratings by adults and classmates indicated that the early-maturing boys were significantly more attractive in physique, more relaxed, poised and matter-of-fact. Consistent differences in other characteristics, such as interest in the opposite sex and "good-naturedness," were obtained over nine semesters of observation. Late-maturing boys were described as more expressive, active, talkative, eager, attention-getting.

The physical differences noted for these boys at adolescence have tended to disappear in adulthood. Personality characteristics as appraised by the California Psychological Inventory and the Edwards Personal Preference Schedule have shown a number of significant differences on the various scales for which the tests are scored (e.g., higher scores for the early-maturing on measures of "good impression" and "socialization.") Where such differences were found, they tended to describe the young adults much as they had been described in adolescence.

No differences were found between the early- and late-maturing in present marital status, family size or educational level. A few of the early-maturing have made exceptionally rapid progress as junior executives and a few of the late-maturing are still somewhat unsettled, vocationally.

The foregoing presentation of data and the case summaries remind us again of the conclusions to the original study which stressed individual differences within each group, resulting from the complex interplay of factors. During the adolescent period late-maturing is a handicap for many boys and can rarely be found to offer special advantages. Early-maturing carries both advantages and disadvantages. In our culture it frequently gives competitive status, but sometimes also involves handicaps in the necessity for rapid readjustments and in requiring the adolescent to meet adult expectations which are more appropriate to size and appearance than to other aspects of maturing. The adolescent handicaps and advantages associated with late- or early-maturing appear to carry over into adulthood to some extent, and perhaps to a greater extent in psychological than in physical characteristics.

REFERENCES

1. BAYLEY, NANCY, & BAYER, LEONA M. The assessment of somatic androgyny. *Amer. J. phys. Anthrop.*, 1946, 4, 433–462.
2. EDWARDS, A. L. *Edwards Personal Preference Schedule*. New York: Psychological Corporation, 1954.
3. GOUGH, H. G. *The California Psychological Inventory*. Stanford: Consulting Psychologists' Press, Copyright, 1951.
4. GOUGH, H. G. On making a good impression. *J. educ. Res.*, 1952, 46, 33–42.
5. GREULICH, W. W., *et al.* Somatic and endocrine studies of puberal and adolescent boys. *Monogr. Soc. Res. Child Develpm.*, 1942, 7, No. 3.
6. JONES, MARY C., & BAYLEY, NANCY. Physical maturing among boys as related to behavior. *J. educ. Psychol.*, 1950, 41, 129–148.
7. SHELDON, W. H., STEVENS, S. S., & TUCKER, W. B. *The varieties of human physique*. New York: Harper, 1940.

74. JOSEPH AND HIS BROTHERS:

SIBLING RELATIONS

GENESIS 37–46, 49–50

Once again utilizing the Bible as a source of sociological and psychological insights, here is the story of a favorite son who is hated by his brothers and sold by them into exile in Egypt. Joseph

is falsely accused by his master's wife, imprisoned, then released
to interpret Pharaoh's dreams. He rises to power, and finds both
vengeance and forgiveness for his brothers, in a story of family life
that is as moving today as when it was first told.

And Jacob dwelt in the land wherein his father was a stranger, in
the land of Canaan. These are the generations of Jacob. Joseph, being
seventeen years old, was feeding the flock with his brethren; and the
lad was with the sons of Bilhah, and with the sons of Zilpah, his father's
wives: and Joseph brought unto his father their evil report. Now Israel
loved Joseph more than all his children, because he was the son of his
old age: and he made him a coat of many colours. And when his brethren
saw that their father loved him more than all his brethren, they hated
him, and could not speak peaceably unto him.

And Joseph dreamed a dream, and he told it his brethren: and
they hated him yet the more. And he said unto them, Hear, I pray you,
this dream which I have dreamed: For, behold, we were binding sheaves
in the field, and, lo, my sheaf arose, and also stood upright; and, behold,
your sheaves stood round about, and made obeisance to my sheaf. And
his brethren said to him, Shalt thou indeed reign over us? or shalt thou
indeed have dominion over us? And they hated him yet the more for his
dreams, and for his words.

And he dreamed yet another dream, and told it his brethren, and
said, Behold, I have dreamed a dream more; and, behold, the sun and
the moon and the eleven stars made obeisance to me. And he told it to
his father, and to his brethren: and his father rebuked him, and said
unto him, What is this dream that thou hast dreamed? Shall I and thy
mother and thy brethren indeed come to bow down ourselves to thee
to the earth? And his brethren envied him; but his father observed the
saying.

.   .   .   .   .

. . . And when they saw him afar off, even before he came near
unto them, they conspired against him to slay him. And they said one
to another, Behold, this dreamer cometh. Come now therefore, and let
us slay him, and cast him into some pit, and we will say, Some evil
beast hath devoured him: and we shall see what will become of his
dreams. And Reuben heard it, and he delivered him out of their hands;
and said, Let us not kill him. And Reuben said unto them, Shed no
blood, but cast him into this pit that is in the wilderness, and lay no
hand upon him; that he might rid him out of their hands, to deliver
him to his father again.

And it came to pass, when Joseph was come unto his brethren,
that they stript Joseph out of his coat, his coat of many colours that

was on him; And they took him, and cast him into a pit: and the pit was empty, there was no water in it. And they sat down to eat bread: and they lifted up their eyes and looked, and, behold, a company of Ishmeelites came from Gilead with their camels bearing spicery and balm and myrrh, going to carry it down to Egypt. And Judah said unto his brethren, What profit is it if we slay our brother, and conceal his blood? Come, and let us sell him to the Ishmeelites, and let not our hand be upon him; for he is our brother and our flesh. And his brethren were content. Then there passed by Midianites merchantmen; and they drew and lifted up Joseph out of the pit, and sold Joseph to the Ishmeelites for twenty pieces of silver: and they brought Joseph into Egypt.

And Reuben returned unto the pit; and, behold, Joseph was not in the pit; and he rent his clothes. And he returned unto his brethren, and said, The child is not; and I, whither shall I go? And they took Joseph's coat, and killed a kid of the goats, and dipped the coat in the blood; And they sent the coat of many colours, and they brought it to their father; and said, This have we found: know now whether it be thy son's coat or no. And he knew it, and said, It is my son's coat; an evil beast hath devoured him; Joseph is without doubt rent in pieces. And Jacob rent his clothes, and put sackcloth upon his loins, and mourned for his son many days. And all his sons and all his daughters rose up to comfort him; but he refused to be comforted; and he said, For I will go down into the grave unto my son mourning. Thus his father wept for him. And the Midianites sold him into Egypt unto Potiphar, an officer of Pharaoh's, and captain of the guard.

. . . . .

And Joseph was brought down to Egypt; and Potiphar, an officer of Pharaoh, captain of the guard, an Egyptian, bought him of the hands of the Ishmeelites, which had brought him down thither. . . . And his master saw that the LORD was with him, and that the LORD made all that he did to prosper in his hand. And Joseph found grace in his sight, and he served him: and he made him overseer over his house, and all that he had he put into his hand. And he left all that he had in Joseph's hand; and he knew not ought he had, save the bread which he did eat. And Joseph was a goodly person, and well favoured.

And it came to pass after these things, that his master's wife cast her eyes upon Joseph; and she said, Lie with me. But he refused, and said unto his master's wife, Behold, my master wotteth not what is with me in the house, and he hath committed all that he hath to my hand; There is none greater in this house than I; neither hath he kept back any thing from me but thee, because thou art his wife: how then can I do this great wickedness, and sin against God? And it came to pass, as she spake to Joseph day by day, that he hearkened not unto her, to lie by her, or to be with her. And it came to pass about this time, that Joseph went into the house to do his business; and there was none of the men of the house there within. And she caught him by his garment, saying, Lie with me: and he left his garment in her hand, and fled, and got him out. And it came to pass, when she saw that he had left his garment in her hand, and was fled forth, That she called unto the men of her house, and spake unto them, saying, See, he hath brought in an Hebrew unto us to mock us; he came in unto me to lie with me, and I cried with a loud voice: And it came to pass, when he heard that I lifted up my voice and cried, that he left his garment with me, and fled, and got him out. . . . And Joseph's master took him, and put him into the prison, a place where the king's prisoners were bound: and he was there in the prison.

But the LORD was with Joseph, and shewed him mercy, and gave him favour in the sight of the keeper of the prison. And the keeper of the prison committed to Joseph's hand all the prisoners that were in the prison; and whatsoever they did there, he was the doer of it. . . .

And it came to pass after these things, that the butler of the king of Egypt and his baker had offended their lord the king of Egypt. And Pharaoh was wroth against two of his officers, against the chief of the butlers, and against the chief of the bakers. And he put them in ward in the house of the captain of the guard, into the prison, the place where Joseph was bound. And the captain of the guard charged Joseph with them, and he served them: and they continued a season in ward.

And they dreamed a dream both of them, each man his dream in one night, each man according to the interpretation of his dream, the butler and the baker of the king of Egypt, which were bound in the prison. And Joseph came in unto them in the morning, and looked upon them, and, behold, they were sad. And he asked Pharaoh's officers that were with him in the ward of his lord's house, saying, Wherefore look ye so sadly to day? And they said unto him, We have dreamed a dream, and there is no interpreter of it. And Joseph said unto them, Do not interpretations belong to God? tell me them, I pray you. And the chief butler told his dream to Joseph, and said to him, In my dream, behold, a vine was before me; And in the vine were three branches: and it was as though it budded, and her blossoms shot forth; and the clusters thereof brought forth ripe grapes: And Pharaoh's cup was in my hand: and I took the grapes, and pressed them into Pharaoh's cup, and I gave the cup into Pharaoh's hand. And Joseph said unto him, This is the interpretation of it: The three branches are three days: Yet within three days shall Pharaoh lift up thine head, and restore thee unto thy place: and thou shalt deliver Pharaoh's cup into his hand, after the former manner when thou wast his butler. But think on me when it shall be well with thee, and shew kindness, I pray thee, unto me, and make mention of me unto Pharaoh, and bring me out of this house: For indeed I was stolen away out of the land of the Hebrews: and here also have I done nothing that they should put me into the dungeon. When the chief baker saw that the interpretation was good, he said unto Joseph, I also was in my dream, and, behold, I had three white baskets on my head: And in the uppermost basket there was of all manner of bakemeats for Pharaoh; and the birds did eat them out of the basket upon my head. And Joseph answered and said, This is the interpretation thereof: The three baskets are three days: Yet within three days shall Pharaoh lift up thy head from off thee, and shall hang thee on a tree; and the birds shall eat thy flesh from off thee.

And it came to pass the third day, which was Pharaoh's birthday, that he made a feast unto all his servants: and he lifted up the head of the chief butler and of the chief baker among his servants. And he restored the chief butler unto his butlership again; and he gave the cup into Pharaoh's hand: But he hanged the chief baker: as Joseph had interpreted to them. Yet did not the chief butler remember Joseph, but forgat him.

And it came to pass at the end of two full years, that Pharaoh dreamed: and, behold, he stood by the river. And, behold, there came up out of the river seven well favoured kine and fatfleshed; and they fed in a meadow. And, behold, seven other kine came up after them out of the river, ill favoured and leanfleshed; and stood by the other kine upon the brink of the river. And the ill favoured and leanfleshed kine did eat up the seven well favoured and fat kine. So Pharaoh awoke. And he slept and dreamed the second time: and, behold, seven ears of corn came up upon one stalk, rank and good. And, behold, seven thin ears and blasted with the east wind sprung up after them. And the seven thin ears devoured the seven rank and full ears. And Pharaoh awoke, and, behold, it was a dream. And it came to pass in the morning that his spirit was troubled; and he sent and called for all the magicians of Egypt, and all the wise men thereof: and Pharaoh told them his dream; but there was none that could interpret them unto Pharaoh.

Then spake the chief butler unto Pharaoh, saying, I do remember my faults this day: Pharaoh was wroth with his servants, and put me in ward in the captain of the guard's house, both me and the chief baker: And we dreamed a dream in one night, I and he; we dreamed each man according to the interpretation of his dream. And there was there with us a young man, an Hebrew, servant to the captain of the guard; and we told him, and he interpreted to us our dreams; to each man according to his dream he did interpret. And it came to pass, as he interpreted to us, so it was; me he restored unto mine office, and him he hanged.

Then Pharaoh sent and called Joseph, and they brought him hastily out of the dungeon: and he shaved himself, and changed his raiment, and came in unto Pharaoh. And Pharaoh said unto Joseph, I have dreamed a dream, and there is none that can interpret it: and I have heard say of thee, that thou canst understand a dream to interpret it. And Joseph answered Pharaoh, saying, It is not in me: God shall give Pharaoh an answer of peace. And Pharaoh said unto Joseph, In my dream, behold, I stood upon the bank of the river: And, behold, there came up out of the river seven kine, fatfleshed and well favoured; and they fed in a meadow: And, behold, seven other kine came up after them, poor and very ill favoured and leanfleshed, such as I never saw in all the land of Egypt for badness: And the lean and the ill favoured kine did eat up the first seven fat kine: And when they had eaten them up, it could not be known that they had eaten them; but they were still ill favoured, as at the beginning. So I awoke. And I saw in my dream, and, behold, seven ears came up in one stalk, full and good: And, behold, seven ears, withered, thin, and blasted with the east wind, sprung up after them: And the thin ears devoured the seven good ears: and I told this unto the magicians; but there was none that could declare it to me.

And Joseph said unto Pharaoh, The dream of Pharaoh is one: God hath shewed Pharaoh what he is about to do.

The seven good kine are seven years; and the seven good ears are seven years: the dream is one. And the seven thin and ill favoured kine that came up after them are seven years; and the seven empty ears blasted with the east wind shall be seven years of famine. This is the thing which I have spoken unto Pharaoh: What God is about to do he sheweth unto Pharaoh. Behold, there come seven years of great plenty throughout all the land of Egypt: And there shall arise after them seven years of famine; and all the plenty shall be forgotten in the land of Egypt; and the famine shall consume the land; And the plenty shall not be known in the land by reason of that famine following; for it shall be very grievous. And for that the dream was doubled unto Pharaoh twice; it is because the thing is established by God, and God will shortly bring it to pass. Now therefore let Pharaoh look out a man discreet and wise, and set him over the land of Egypt. Let Pharaoh do this, and let him appoint officers over the land, and take up the fifth part of the land of Egypt in the seven plenteous years. And let them gather all the food of those good years that come, and lay up corn under the hand of Pharaoh, and let them keep food in the cities. And that food shall be for store to the land against the seven years of famine, which shall be in the land of Egypt; that the land perish not through the famine.

And the thing was good in the eyes of Pharaoh, and in the eyes of all his servants. And Pharaoh said unto his servants, Can we find such a one as this is, a man in whom the Spirit of God is? And Pharaoh said unto Joseph, Forasmuch as God hath shewed thee all this, there is none so discreet and wise as thou art: Thou shalt be over my house, and according unto thy word shall all my people be ruled: only in the throne will I be greater than thou. And Pharaoh said unto Joseph, See, I have set thee over all the land of Egypt. And Pharaoh took off his ring from his hand, and put it upon Joseph's hand, and arrayed him in vestures of fine linen, and put a gold chain about his neck; . . . .

And Joseph was thirty years old when he stood before Pharaoh king of Egypt. And Joseph went out from the presence of Pharaoh, and went throughout all the land of Egypt. And in the seven plenteous years the earth brought forth by handfuls. And he gathered up all the food of the seven years, which were in the land of Egypt, and laid up the food in the cities: the food of the field, which was round about every city, laid he up in the same. . . .

And the seven years of plenteousness, that was in the land of Egypt, were ended. And the seven years of dearth began to come, according as Joseph had said: and the dearth was in all lands; but in all the land of Egypt there was bread. . . .

Now when Jacob saw that there was corn in Egypt, Jacob said unto his sons, Why do ye look one upon another? And he said, Behold, I have heard that there is corn in Egypt: get you down thither, and buy for us from thence; that we may live, and not die.

And Joseph's ten brethren went down to buy corn in Egypt. But Benjamin, Joseph's brother, Jacob sent not with his brethren; for he said, Lest peradventure mischief befall him. And the sons of Israel came to buy corn among those that came: for the famine was in the land of Canaan. And Joseph was the governor over the land, and he it was that sold to all the people of the land: and Joseph's brethren came, and bowed down themselves before him with their faces to the earth. And Joseph saw his brethren, and he knew them, but made himself strange unto them, and spake roughly unto them; and he said unto them, Whence come ye? And they said, From the land of Canaan to buy food. And Joseph knew his brethren, but they knew not him. And Joseph remembered the dreams which he dreamed of them, and said unto them, Ye are spies; to see the nakedness of the land ye are come. And they said unto him, Nay, my lord, but to buy food are thy servants come. We are all one man's sons; we are true men, thy servants are no spies. And he said unto them, Nay, but to see the nakedness of the land ye are come. And they said, Thy servants are twelve brethren, the sons of one man in the land of Canaan; and, behold, the youngest is this day with our father, and one is not. Joseph said unto them, That is it that I spake unto you, saying, Ye are spies: Hereby ye shall be proved: By the life of Pharaoh ye shall not go forth hence, except your youngest brother come hither. Send one of you, and let him fetch your brother, and ye shall be kept in prison, that your words may be proved, whether there be any truth in you: or else by the life of Pharaoh surely ye are spies. And he put them all together into ward three days. And Joseph said unto them the third day, This do, and live; for I fear God: If ye be true men, let one of your brethren be bound in the house of your prison: go ye, carry corn for the famine of your houses: But bring your youngest brother unto me; so shall your words be verified, and ye shall not die. And they did so.

And they said one to another, We are verily guilty concerning our brother, in that we saw the anguish of his soul, when he besought us, and we would not hear; therefore is this distress come upon us. And Reuben answered them, saying, Spake I not unto you, saying, Do not sin against the child; and ye would not hear? therefore, behold, also his blood is required. And they knew not that Joseph understood them; for he spake unto them by an interpreter. And he turned himself about from them, and wept; and returned to them again, and communed with them, and took from them Simeon, and bound him before their eyes.

Then Joseph commanded to fill their sacks with corn, and to restore every man's money into his sack, and to give them provision for the way: and thus did he unto them. And they laded their asses with the corn, and departed thence. And as one of them opened his sack to give his ass provender in the inn, he espied his money; for, behold, it was in his sack's mouth. And he said unto his brethren, My money is restored; and, lo, it is even in my sack: and their heart failed them, and they were afraid, saying one to another, What is this that God hath done unto us?

And they came unto Jacob their father unto the land of Canaan, and told him all that befell unto them; saying, . . .

And it came to pass as they emptied their sacks, that, behold, every man's bundle of money was in his sack: and when both they and their father saw the bundles of money, they were afraid. And Jacob their father said unto them, Me have ye bereaved of my children: Joseph is not, and Simeon is not, and ye will take Benjamin away: all these things are against me. And Reuben spake unto his father, saying, Slay my two sons, if I bring him not to thee: deliver him into my hand, and I will bring him to thee again. And he said, My son shall not go down with you; for his brother is dead, and he is left alone: if mischief befall him by the way in the which ye go, then shall ye bring down my gray hairs with sorrow to the grave.

And the famine was sore in the land. And it came to pass when they had eaten up the corn which they had brought out of Egypt, their father said unto them, Go again, buy us a little food. And Judah spake unto him, saying, The man did solemnly protest unto us, saying, Ye shall not see my face, except your brother be with you. If thou wilt send our brother with us, we will go down and buy thee food: But if thou wilt not send him, we will not go down: for the man said unto us, Ye shall not see my face, except your brother be with you. And Israel said, Wherefore dealt ye so ill with me, as to tell the man whether ye had yet a brother? And they said, The man asked us straitly of our state, and of our kindred, saying, is your father yet alive? have ye another brother? and we told him according to the tenor of these words: could we certainly know that he would say, Bring your brother down? And Judah said unto Israel his father, Send the lad with me, and we will arise and go; that we may live, and not die, both we, and thou, and also our little ones. I will be surety for him; of my hand shalt thou require him: if I bring him not unto thee, and set him before thee, then let me bear the blame for ever: For except we had lingered, surely now we had returned this second time. And their father Israel said unto them, If it must be so now, do this; take of the best fruits in the land in your vessels, and carry down the man a present, a little balm, and a little honey, spices, and myrrh, nuts, and almonds: And take double money in your hand; and the money that was brought again in the mouth of your sacks, carry it again in your hand; peradventure it was an oversight: Take also your brother, and arise, go again unto the man: And God Almighty give you mercy before the man, that he may send away your other brother, and Benjamin. If I be bereaved of my children, I am bereaved.

And the men took that present, and they took double money in their hand, and Benjamin; and rose up, and went down to Egypt, and stood before Joseph. And when Joseph saw Benjamin with them, he said to the ruler of his house, Bring these men home, and slay, and make ready; for these men shall dine with me at noon. And the man did as Joseph bade; and the man brought the men into Joseph's house. And the men were afraid, because they were brought into Joseph's house; and they said, Because of the money that was returned in our sacks at the first time are we brought in; that he may seek occasion against us, and fall upon us, and take us for bondmen, and our asses. And they came near to the steward of Joseph's house, and they communed with him at the door of the house, And said, O sir, we came indeed down at the first time to buy food: And it came to pass, when we came to the inn, that we opened our sacks, and, behold, every man's money was in the mouth of his sack, our money in full weight: and we have brought it again in our hand. And other money have we brought down in our hands to buy food: we cannot tell who put our money in our sacks. And he said, Peace be to you, fear not: your God, and the God of your father, hath given you treasure in your sacks: I had your money. And he brought Simeon out unto them. And the man brought the men into Joseph's house, and gave them water, and they washed their feet; and he gave their asses provender. And they made ready the present against Joseph came at noon: for they heard that they should eat bread there.

And when Joseph came home, they brought him the present which was in their hand into the house, and bowed themselves to him to the earth. And he asked them of their welfare, and said, Is your father well, the old man of whom ye spake? Is he yet alive? And they answered, Thy servant our father is in good health, he is yet alive. And they bowed down their heads, and made obeisance. And he lifted up his eyes, and saw his brother Benjamin, his mother's son, and said, Is this your younger brother, of whom ye spake unto me? And he said, God be gracious unto thee, my son. And Joseph made haste; for his bowels did yearn upon his brother: and he sought where to weep; and he entered into his chamber, and wept there. And he washed his face, and went out, and refrained himself, and said, Set on bread. And they set on for him by himself, and for them by themselves, and for the Egyptians, which did eat with him, by themselves: because the Egyptians might not eat bread with the Hebrews; for that is an abomination unto the Egyptians. And they sat before him, the firstborn according to his birthright, and the youngest according to his youth: and the men marvelled one at another. And he took and sent messes unto them from before him: but Benjamin's mess was five times so much as any of theirs. And they drank, and were merry with him.

And he commanded the steward of his house, saying, Fill the men's sacks with food, as much as they can carry, and put every man's money in his sack's mouth. And put my cup, the silver cup, in the sack's mouth of the youngest, and his corn money. And he did according to the word that Joseph had spoken. As soon as the morning was light, the men were sent away, they and their asses. And when they were gone out of the city, and not yet far off, Joseph said unto his steward, Up, follow after the men; and when thou dost overtake them, say unto them, Wherefore have ye rewarded evil for good? Is not this it in which my lord drinketh, and whereby indeed he divineth? ye have done evil in so doing.

And he overtook them, and he spake unto them these same words. And they said unto him, Wherefore saith my lord these words? God forbid that thy servants should do according to this thing: Behold, the money, which we found in our sacks' mouths, we brought again unto thee out of the land of Canaan: how then should we steal out of thy lord's house silver or gold? With whomsoever of thy servants it be found, both let him die, and we also will be my lord's bondmen. And he said, Now also let it be according unto your words: he with whom it is found shall be my servant; and ye shall be blameless. Then they speedily took down every man his sack to the ground, and opened every man his sack. And he searched, and began at the eldest, and left at the youngest: and the cup was found in Benjamin's sack. Then they rent their clothes, and laded every man his ass, and returned to the city.

And Judah and his brethren came to Joseph's house; for he was yet there: and they fell before him on the ground. And Joseph said unto them, What deed is this that ye have done? wot ye not that such a man as I can certainly divine? And Judah said, What shall we say unto my lord? What shall we speak? or how shall we clear ourselves? God hath found out the iniquity of thy servants: behold, we are my lord's servants, both we, and he also with whom the cup is found. And he said, God forbid that I should do so: but the man in whose hand the cup is found, he shall be my servant; and as for you, get you up in peace unto your father.

Then Judah came near unto him, and said, Oh my lord, let thy servant, I pray thee, speak a word in my lord's ears, and let not thine anger burn against thy servant: for thou art even as Pharaoh. My lord asked his servants, saying, Have ye a father, or a brother? And we said unto my lord, We have a father, an old man, and a child of his old age, a little one; and his brother is dead, and he alone is left of his mother, and his father loveth him. And thou saidst unto thy servants, Bring him down unto me, that I may set mine eyes upon him. And we said unto my lord, The lad cannot leave his father: for if he should leave his father, his father would die. And thou saidst unto thy servants, Except your youngest brother come down with you, ye shall see my face no more. And it came to pass when we came up unto thy servant my father, we told him the words of my lord. And our father said, Go again, and buy us a little food. And we said, We cannot go down: if our youngest brother be with us, then will we go down: for we may not see the man's face, except our youngest brother be with us. And thy servant my father said unto us, Ye know that my wife bare me two sons: And the one went out from me, and I said, Surely he is torn in pieces; and I saw him not since: And if ye take this also from me, and mischief befall him, ye shall bring down my gray hairs with sorrow to the grave. Now therefore when I come to thy servant my father, and the lad be not with us; seeing that his life is bound up in the lad's life; It shall come to pass, when he seeth that the lad is not with us, that he will die: and thy servants shall bring down the gray hairs of thy servant our father with sorrow to the grave. For thy servant became surety for the lad unto my father, saying, If I bring him not unto thee, then I shall bear the blame to my father for ever. Now therefore, I pray thee, let thy servant abide instead of the lad a bondman to my lord; and let the lad go up with his brethren. For how shall I go up to my father, and the lad be not with me? lest peradventure I see the evil that shall come on my father.

Then Joseph could not refrain himself before all them that stood by him; and he cried, Cause every man to go out from me. And there stood no man with him, while Joseph made himself known unto his brethren. And he wept aloud: and the Egyptians and the house of Pharaoh heard. And Joseph said unto his brethren, I am Joseph; doth my father yet live? And his brethren could not answer him; for they were troubled at his presence. And Joseph said unto his brethren, Come near to me, I pray you. And they came near. And he said, I am Joseph your brother, whom

ye sold into Egypt. Now therefore be not grieved, nor angry with yourselves, that ye sold me hither: for God did send me before you to preserve life. For these two years hath the famine been in the land: and
yet there are five years, in the which there shall neither be earing nor
harvest. And God sent me before you to preserve you a posterity in the
earth, and to save your lives by a great deliverance. So now it was not
you that sent me hither, but God: and he hath made me a father to
Pharaoh, and lord of all his house, and a ruler throughout all the land of
Egypt. Haste ye, and go up to my father, and say unto him, Thus saith
thy son Joseph, God hath made me lord of all Egypt: come down unto
me, tarry not: And thou shalt dwell in the land of Goshen, and thou shalt
be near unto me, thou, and thy children, and thy children's children, and
thy flocks, and thy herds, and all that thou hast: And there will I nourish
thee; for yet there are five years of famine; lest thou, and thy household,
and all that thou hast, come to poverty. And, behold, your eyes see, and
the eyes of my brother Benjamin, that it is my mouth that speaketh unto
you. And ye shall tell my father of all my glory in Egypt, and of all that
ye have seen; and ye shall haste and bring down my father hither. And
he fell upon his brother Benjamin's neck, and wept; and Benjamin wept
upon his neck. Moreover he kissed all his brethren, and wept upon them:
and after that his brethren talked with him.

And the fame thereof was heard in Pharaoh's house, saying, Joseph's
brethren are come: and it pleased Pharaoh well, and his servants. And
Pharaoh said unto Joseph, Say unto thy brethren, This do ye; lade your
beasts, and go, get you unto the land of Canaan; And take your father
and your households, and come unto me: and I will give you the good of
the land of Egypt, and ye shall eat the fat of the land. Now thou art
commanded, this do ye; take you wagons out of the land of Egypt for
your little ones, and for your wives, and bring your father, and come.
Also regard not your stuff; for the good of all the land of Egypt is
yours. And the children of Israel did so: and Joseph gave them wagons,
according to the commandment of Pharaoh, and gave them provision
for the way. To all of them he gave each man changes of raiment; but
to Benjamin he gave three hundred pieces of silver, and five changes of
raiment. And to his father he sent after this manner; ten asses laden
with the good things of Egypt, and ten she asses laden with corn and
bread and meat for his father by the way. So he sent his brethren away,
and they departed: and he said unto them, See that ye fall not out by the
way.

And they went up out of Egypt, and came into the land of Canaan
unto Jacob their father, And told him, saying, Joseph is yet alive, and he
is governor over all the land of Egypt. And Jacob's heart fainted, for he
believed them not. And they told him all the words of Joseph, which he

had said unto them: and when he saw the wagons which Joseph had sent to carry him, the spirit of Jacob their father revived: And Israel said, It is enough; Joseph my son is yet alive: I will go and see him before I die.

And Israel took his journey with all that he had, and came to Beer-sheba, and offered sacrifices unto the God of his father Isaac. And God spake unto Israel in the visions of the night, and said, Jacob, Jacob. And he said, Here am I. And he said, I am God, the God of thy father: fear not to go down into Egypt; for I will there make of thee a great nation: I will go down with thee into Egypt; and I will also surely bring thee up again: and Joseph shall put his hand upon thine eyes. And Jacob rose up from Beer-sheba: and the sons of Israel carried Jacob their father, and their little ones, and their wives, in the wagons which Pharaoh had sent to carry him. And they took their cattle, and their goods, which they had gotten in the land of Canaan, and came into Egypt, Jacob, and all his seed with him: His sons, and his sons' sons with him, his daughters, and his sons' daughters, and all his seed brought he with him into Egypt.

. . . . .

. . . All the souls that came with Jacob . . . were three score and six. . . .

And he sent Judah before him unto Joseph. . . . And Joseph made ready his chariot, and went up to meet Israel his father . . . ; and he fell on his neck, and wept on his neck a good while. And Israel said unto Joseph, Now let me die, since I have seen thy face, because thou art yet alive. And Joseph said unto his brethren . . . , I will go up and shew Pharaoh, and say unto him, My brethren, and my father's house, . . . have come unto me: And the men are shepherds, for their trade hath been to feed cattle; and they have brought their flocks, and their herds, and all that they have. And it shall come to pass, when Pharaoh shall call you, and shall say, What is your occupation? That ye shall say, Thy servants' trade hath been about cattle from our youth . . . : that ye may dwell in the land of Goshen; for every shepherd is an abomination unto the Egyptians.

. . . . .

. . . And . . . Jacob . . . gathered up his feet into the bed, and yielded up the ghost. . . . And when Joseph's brethren saw that their father was dead, they said, Joseph will peradventure hate us, and will certainly requite us all the evil which we did unto him. And they sent a messenger unto Joseph [to ask forgiveness]. . . . And Joseph said unto them, Fear not. . . . : I will nourish you, and your little ones. And he . . . spake kindly unto them.

75. REBEKAH AND ISAAC;
JACOB AND ESAU

GENESIS 24–28

The story of Isaac's family illustrates how one man got a wife, sibling rivalry, primogeniture, exogamy, and multiple marriage in a series of dramatic events.

And Abraham was old and well stricken in age: and the LORD had blessed Abraham in all things. And Abraham said unto his eldest servant of his house, that ruled over all that he had, Put, I pray thee, thy hand under my thigh: And I will make thee swear by the LORD, the God of heaven, and the God of the earth, that thou shalt not take a wife unto my son of the daughters of the Canaanites, among whom I dwell: But thou shalt go unto my country, and to my kindred, and take a wife unto my son Isaac. And the servant said unto him, Peradventure the woman will not be willing to follow me unto this land: must I needs bring thy son again unto the land from whence thou camest? And Abraham said unto him, Beware thou that thou bring not my son thither again.

The LORD God of heaven, which took me from my father's house, and from the land of my kindred, and which spake unto me, and that sware unto me, saying, Unto thy seed will I give this land; he shall send his angel before thee, and thou shalt take a wife unto my son from thence.

And if the woman will not be willing to follow thee, then thou shalt be clear from this my oath: only bring not my son thither again. And the servant put his hand under the thigh of Abraham his master, and sware to him concerning that matter.

And the servant took ten camels of the camels of his master, and departed; for all the goods of his master were in his hand: and he arose, and went to Mesopotamia, unto the city of Nahor. And he made his camels to kneel down without the city by a well of water at the time of the evening, even the time that women go out to draw water. And he said, O LORD God of my master Abraham, I pray thee, send me good speed this day, and shew kindness unto my master Abraham. Behold, I stand here by the well of water; and the daughters of the men of the city come out to draw water: And let it come to pass, that the damsel to whom I shall say, Let down thy pitcher, I pray thee, that I may drink; and she shall say, Drink, and I will give thy camels drink also: let the same be she that thou hast appointed for thy servant Isaac; and thereby shall I know that thou hast shewed kindness unto my master.

And it came to pass, before he had done speaking, that, behold, Rebekah came out, who was born to Bethuel, son of Milcah, the wife of Nahor, Abraham's brother, with her pitcher upon her shoulder. And the damsel was very fair to look upon, a virgin, neither had any man known her: and she went down to the well, and filled her pitcher, and came up. And the servant ran to meet her, and said, Let me, I pray thee, drink a little water of thy pitcher. And she said, Drink, my lord: and she hasted, and let down her pitcher upon her hand, and gave him drink. And when she had done giving him drink, she said, I will draw water for thy camels also, until they have done drinking. And she hasted, and emptied her pitcher into the trough, and ran again unto the well to draw water, and drew for all his camels. And the man wondering at her held his peace, to wit whether the Lord had made his journey prosperous or not. And it came to pass, as the camels had done drinking, that the man took a golden earring of half a shekel weight, and two bracelets for her hands of ten shekels weight of gold; And said, Whose daughter art thou? tell me, I pray thee: is there room in thy father's house for us to lodge in? And she said unto him, I am the daughter of Bethuel the son of Milcah, which she bare unto Nahor. She said moreover unto him, We have both straw and provender enough, and room to lodge in. And the man bowed down his head, and worshipped the Lord. And he said, Blessed be the Lord God of my master Abraham, who hath not left destitute my master of his mercy and his truth: I being in the way, the Lord led me to the house of my master's brethren. And the damsel ran, and told them of her mother's house these things.

And Rebekah had a brother, and his name was Laban: and Laban ran out unto the man, unto the well. And it came to pass, when he saw the earring and bracelets upon his sister's hands, and when he heard the words of Rebekah his sister, saying, Thus spake the man unto me; that he came unto the man; and, behold, he stood by the camels at the well. And he said, Come in, thou blessed of the Lord; wherefore standest thou without? for I have prepared the house, and room for the camels.

And the man came into the house: and he ungirded his camels, and gave straw and provender for the camels, and water to wash his feet, and the men's feet that were with him. And there was set meat before him to eat: but he said, I will not eat, until I have told mine errand. And he said, Speak on. And he said, I am Abraham's servant. And the Lord hath blessed my master greatly; and he is become great: and he hath given him flocks, and herds, and silver, and gold, and menservants, and maidservants, and camels, and asses. And Sarah my master's wife bare a son to my master when she was old: and unto him hath he given all that he hath. And my master made me swear, saying, Thou shalt not take a wife to my son of the daughters of the Canaanites, in whose land I dwell: But thou shalt go unto my father's house, and to my kindred, and take a wife unto my son. And I said unto my master, Peradventure the woman will not follow me. And he said unto me, The Lord, before whom I walk, will send his angel with thee, and prosper thy way; and thou shalt take a wife for my son of my kindred, and of my father's house: Then shalt thou be clear from this my oath, when thou comest to my kindred; and if they give not thee one, thou shalt be clear from my oath. And I came this day unto the well, and said, O Lord God of my master Abraham, if now thou do prosper my way which I go: Behold, I stand by the well of water; and it shall come to pass, that when the virgin cometh forth to draw water, and I say to her, Give me, I pray thee, a little water of thy pitcher to drink; And she say to me, Both drink thou, and I will also draw for thy camels: let the same be the woman whom the Lord hath appointed out for my master's son. And before I had done speaking in mine heart, behold, Rebekah came forth with her pitcher on her shoulder; and she went down unto the well, and drew water: and I said unto her, Let me drink, I pray thee. And she made haste, and let down her pitcher from her shoulder, and said, Drink, and I will give thy camels drink also: so I drank, and she made the camels drink also. And I asked her, and said, Whose daughter art thou? And she said, The daughter of Bethuel, Nahor's son, whom Milcah bare unto him: and I put the earring upon her face, and the bracelets upon her hands. And I bowed down my head, and worshipped the Lord, and blessed the Lord God of my master Abraham, which had led me in the right way to take my master's brother's daughter unto his son. And now if ye will deal kindly and truly with my master, tell me: and if not, tell me; that I may turn to the right hand, or to the left. Then Laban and Bethuel answered and said, The thing proceedeth from the Lord: we cannot speak unto thee bad or good. Behold, Rebekah is before thee, take her, and go, and let her be thy master's son's wife, as the Lord hath spoken. And it came to pass, that, when Abraham's servant heard their words, he worshipped the Lord, bowing himself to the earth. And the servant brought forth jewels of silver, and jewels of gold, and raiment, and gave them to Rebekah: he gave also to her brother and to her mother precious things. And they did eat and drink, he and the men that were with him, and tarried all night; and they rose up in the morning, and he said, Send me away unto my master. And her brother and her mother said, Let the damsel abide with us a few days, at the least ten; after that she shall go. And he said unto them, Hinder me not, seeing the Lord hath prospered my way; send me away that I may go to my master. And they said, We will call the damsel, and inquire at her mouth. And they called Rebekah, and said unto her, Wilt thou go with this man? And she said, I will go. And they sent away Rebekah their sister, and her nurse, and Abraham's servant, and his men.

And they blessed Rebekah, and said unto her, Thou art our sister, be thou the mother of thousands of millions, and let thy seed possess the gate of those which hate them.

And Rebekah arose, and her damsels, and they rode upon the camels, and followed the man: and the servant took Rebekah, and went his way. And Isaac came from the way of the well Lahai-roi; for he dwelt in the south country. And Isaac went out to meditate in the field at the eventide: and he lifted up his eyes, and saw, and, behold, the camels were coming. And Rebekah lifted up her eyes, and when she saw Isaac, she lighted off the camel. For she had said unto the servant, What man is this that walketh in the field to meet us? And the servant had said, It is my master: therefore she took a vail, and covered herself. And the servant told Isaac all things that he had done. And Isaac brought her into his mother Sarah's tent, and took Rebekah, and she became his wife; and he loved her: and Isaac was comforted after his mother's death.

. . . And Isaac intreated the Lord for his wife, because she was barren: and the Lord was intreated of him, and Rebekah his wife conceived. And the children struggled together within her; and she said, If it be so, why am I thus? And she went to inquire of the Lord. And the Lord said unto her, Two nations are in thy womb, and two manner of people shall be separated from thy bowels; and the one people shall be stronger than the other people; and the elder shall serve the younger.

And when her days to be delivered were fulfilled, behold, there were twins in her womb. And the first came out red, all over like an hairy garment; and they called his name Esau. And after that came his brother out, and his hand took hold on Esau's heel; and his name was called Jacob: and Isaac was three-score years old when she bare them. And the boys grew: and Esau was a cunning hunter, a man of the field; and Jacob was a plain man, dwelling in tents. And Isaac loved Esau, because he did eat of his venison: but Rebekah loved Jacob.

And Jacob sod pottage: and Esau came from the field, and he was faint: And Esau said to Jacob, Feed me, I pray thee, with that same red pottage; for I am faint: therefore was his name called Edom. And Jacob said, Sell me this day thy birthright. And Esau said, Behold, I am at the point to die: and what profit shall this birthright do to me? And Jacob said, Swear to me this day; and he sware unto him: and he sold his birthright unto Jacob. Then Jacob gave Esau bread and pottage of lentiles; and he did eat and drink, and rose up, and went his way: thus Esau despised his birthright.

•   •   •   •   •

And it came to pass, that when Isaac was old, and his eyes were dim, so that he could not see, he called Esau his eldest son, and said unto him, My son: and he said unto him, Behold, here am I. And he said,

Behold now, I am old, I know not the day of my death: Now therefore take, I pray thee, thy weapons, thy quiver and thy bow, and go out to the field, and take me some venison; And make me savoury meat, such as I love, and bring it to me, that I may eat; that my soul may bless thee before I die. And Rebekah heard when Isaac spake to Esau his son. And Esau went to the field to hunt for venison, and to bring it.

And Rebekah spake unto Jacob her son, saying, Behold, I heard thy father speak unto Esau thy brother, saying, Bring me venison, and make me savoury meat, that I may eat, and bless thee before the Lord before my death. Now therefore, my son, obey my voice according to that which I command thee. Go now to the flock, and fetch me from thence two good kids of the goats; and I will make them savoury meat for thy father, such as he loveth: And thou shalt bring it to thy father, that he may eat, and that he may bless thee before his death. And Jacob said to Rebekah his mother, Behold, Esau my brother is a hairy man, and I am a smooth man: My father peradventure will feel me, and I shall seem to him as a deceiver; and I shall bring a curse upon me, and not a blessing. And his mother said unto him, Upon me be thy curse, my son: only obey my voice, and go fetch me them. And he went, and fetched, and brought them to his mother: and his mother made savoury meat, such as his father loved. And Rebekah took goodly raiment of her eldest son Esau, which were with her in the house, and put them upon Jacob her younger son: And she put the skins of the kids of the goats upon his hands, and upon the smooth of his neck: And she gave the savoury meat and the bread, which she had prepared, into the hand of her son Jacob.

And he came unto his father, and said, My father: and he said, Here am I; who art thou, my son? And Jacob said unto his father, I am Esau thy firstborn; I have done according as thou badest me: arise, I pray thee, sit and eat of my venison, that thy soul may bless me. And Isaac said unto his son, How is it that thou has found it so quickly, my son? And he said, Because the Lord thy God brought it to me. And Isaac said unto Jacob, Come near, I pray thee, that I may feel thee, my son, whether thou be my very son Esau or not. And Jacob went near unto Isaac his father; and he felt him, and said, The voice is Jacob's voice, but the hands are the hands of Esau. And he discerned him not, because his hands were hairy, as his brother Esau's hands: so he blessed him. And he said, Art thou my very son Esau? And he said, I am. And he said, Bring it near to me, and I will eat of my son's venison, that my soul may bless thee. And he brought it near to him, and he did eat: and he brought him wine, and he drank. And his father Isaac said unto him, Come near now, and kiss me, my son. And he came near, and kissed him: and he smelled the smell of his raiment, and blessed him, and said, See, the smell of my son is as the smell of a field which the Lord hath blessed: Therefore God give thee of the dew of heaven, and the fatness of the earth, and plenty of corn and wine: Let people serve thee, and nations bow down to thee: be lord over thy brethren, and let thy mother's sons bow down to thee: cursed be every one that curseth thee, and blessed be he that blesseth thee.

And it came to pass, as soon as Isaac had made an end of blessing Jacob, and Jacob was yet scarce gone out from the presence of Isaac his father, that Esau his brother came in from hunting. And he also had made savoury meat, and brought it unto his father, and said unto his father, Let my father arise, and eat of his son's venison, that thy soul may bless me. And Isaac his father said unto him, Who art thou? And he said, I am thy son, thy firstborn Esau. And Isaac trembled very exceedingly, and said, Who? where is he that hath taken venison, and brought it me, and I have eaten of all before thou camest, and have blessed him? yea, and he shall be blessed. And when Esau heard the words of his father, he cried with a great and exceeding bitter cry, and said unto his father, Bless me, even me also, O my father. And he said, Thy brother came with subtilty, and hath taken away thy blessing. And he said, Is not he rightly named Jacob? for he hath supplanted me these two times: he took away my birthright; and, behold, now he hath taken away my blessing. And he said, Hast thou not reserved a blessing for me? And Isaac answered and said unto Esau, Behold, I have made him thy lord, and all his brethren have I given to him for servants; and with corn and wine have I sustained him: and what shall I do now unto thee, my son? And Esau said unto his father, Hast thou but one blessing, my father? bless me, even me also, O my father. And Esau lifted up his voice and wept. And Isaac his father answered and said unto him, Behold, thy dwelling shall be the fatness of the earth, and of the dew of heaven from above; And by thy sword shalt thou live, and shalt serve thy brother; and it shall come to pass when thou shalt have the dominion, that thou shalt break his yoke from off thy neck.

And Esau hated Jacob because of the blessing wherewith his father blessed him: and Esau said in his heart, The days of mourning for my father are at hand; then will I slay my brother Jacob. And these words of Esau her elder son were told to Rebekah: and she sent and called Jacob her younger son, and said unto him, Behold, thy brother Esau, as touching thee, doth comfort himself, purposing to kill thee. Now therefore, my son, obey my voice; and arise, flee thou to Laban my brother to Haran; And tarry with him a few days, until thy brother's fury turn away; Until thy brother's anger turn away from thee, and he forget that which thou hast done to him: then I will send, and fetch thee from thence: why should I be deprived also of you both in one day? And Rebekah said to Isaac, I am weary of my life because of the daughters of Heth: If Jacob take a wife of the daughters of Heth, such as these which are of the daughters of the land, what good shall my life do me?

And Isaac called Jacob, and blessed him, and charged him, and said unto him, Thou shalt not take a wife of the daughters of Canaan. Arise, go to Padan-aram, to the house of Bethuel thy mother's father; and take thee a wife from thence of the daughters of Laban thy mother's brother. And God Almighty bless thee, and make thee fruitful, and multiply thee, that thou mayest be a multitude of people; And give thee the blessing of Abraham, to thee, and to thy seed with thee; that thou mayest inherit the land wherein thou art a stranger, which God gave unto Abraham.

. . . . .

When Esau saw that Isaac had blessed Jacob, and sent him away to Padan-aram, to take him a wife from thence; and that as he blessed him he gave him a charge, saying, Thou shalt not take a wife of the daughters of Canaan; And that Jacob obeyed his father and his mother, and was gone to Padan-aram; And Esau seeing that the daughters of Canaan pleased not Isaac his father; Then went Esau unto Ishmael, and took unto the wives which he had Mahalath the daughter of Ishmael Abraham's son, the sister of Nebajoth, to be his wife.

. . . . . .

76. CHILDHOOD BACKGROUND OF SUCCESS IN A PROFESSION

PHILIP J. ALLEN

Where is the self-made man, the one who pulls himself up by his bootstraps by personal qualities alone, in true Horatio Alger style? The more evidence we have from social science the more the image fades. The following study presents some statistical and sociological data about the person who succeeds in one profession, the Methodist ministry. He is from a large city; he attended a large school; he is an only child of a mother and father who were only children. His father and mother are well educated and happily married. If one matches the pattern, his chances are good in any profession.

Selections reprinted from the article in the *American Sociological Review,* 20, No. 2 (April, 1955), 186–190, by permission of the author and the American Sociological Society.

The general run of vertical mobility studies seem to constitute an attempt to delineate occupational movement along a vertical axis between two or more male generations. However valuable some of these studies may be, they do not seem to throw much light upon vertical movement within a given occupation group.

Does anyone know what makes for success within any occupation?

. . . . .

Several investigators have attempted to relate background factors to *general* achievement. What seem to be needed are studies of *specific* achievement within specific occupations, relating such achievement to background factors in the life history. If a large enough number of independent variables among background factors could be discovered associated with success within a given occupation, vocational counseling could be done with greater confidence.

The difficulties confronting an investigator of success, or upward mobility, within an occupation are numerous. Some of these are related to the construction of an accurate and valid scale for measuring status as well as vertical movement within a given occupation. The present investigator utilized what seems to be a fruitful method for studying vertical mobility within a profession.

The profession studied is the Methodist ministry, and the measurement of status within the professional group is, with qualifications, annual salary. This occupational group was selected because it seems to possess certain desirable features: (1) its status system seems to be reflected in annual salary, (2) the salary is available in annual publications, and (3) upward mobility within this profession seems greatly determined by publicly demonstrated and evaluated performance in a field of clearly defined values to be achieved.

Upward mobility is a consequence of successful face-to-face social interaction with laymen and fellow ministers. One's salary is commensurate with his desirability as pastor and preacher, a desirability based upon his reputation and observed performance. In such performance, whether from the pulpit or in small group interaction, there is something revealed, not merely in the nature of professional skills which can be learned by the average person through formal education and years of professional experience, but particularly in the nature of crucial factors related to personality structure which, although known, cannot be readily learned, factors possibly explained through childhood social interaction. One's testing is continuous and status must be continuously validated by current performance.

A minister's social skills, repeatedly demonstrated, become a favorite topic of conversation among church members. His unusual accomplishments, as well as his unfortunate blunders, very rapidly are passed around the church community by the few who were there to the many, via grape-vine. This gossip has the effect of raising or lowering the minister's prestige, influencing subsequent attendance at church services by members as well as by non-members who are potential members or who, at any rate, currently contribute to the church. Status is continuously validated through social interaction, and there is no escape from the process.

The social selection of those who move upward in this profession requires of them an insight into the nature of human motivation, social organization, sources of social power, as well as channels through which such power flows. It requires not only the knowledge but, what is equally important, an ability to utilize it, applying it strategically at appropriate times in social interaction. This, it seems, is crucial for upward mobility. Many appear to have the knowledge of and insight into factors indicated above. But relatively few seem able to use such knowledge and insight to achieve deliberately sought results.

SELECTION OF SAMPLE

The sample was drawn from a sub-universe within a universe of over 20,000 Methodist ministers. The sub-universe comprised only those who had been in the active ministry between 20 and 26 years. It had been found in an earlier pilot study that the highest status attainable within the Methodist clergy, that of bishop, takes on an average of 20 to 26 years to reach. On the other hand, some downward mobility, except in the case of bishops, tends to occur during the last decade or so of professional life. Since present salary was to be used as the present status differentiating measure, the sample was selected from those who had been in the profession from 20 to 26 years. Only white subjects were included in the sample, in order to avoid an important variable. All 44 white bishops were arbitrarily included. In all, the original sample included 608 persons.

METHOD

After 17 case histories were secured through interviews with a cross-sectional sample and with 3 bishops, a detailed questionnaire was constructed, calling for data on the life history, particularly on childhood background. Together with a personally typed letter, this questionnaire was sent to all 608 in the "gross" sample. Adding deaths of subjects in the sample of questionnaires returned by the post office, stamped "Address Unknown," a total of 60 had to be discarded from the original sample of 608, leaving 548. Of these, 332 returned questionnaires, including 24 bishops. Only 316 of those returned were usable.

The 316 subjects represented in the usable returned questionnaires were ranked according to salary, with qualifications. Each subject was first ranked within his own geographic area, the Annual Conference area, of which there are 106. Of these, 93 are white Annual Conference areas, of which 77 are represented in the sample.

In the ranking of subjects, a salary frequency distribution was first made for each Annual Conference area, and each subject was ranked within his own area on salary, a percentile rank score being calculated for him. Then, all 316 subjects were ranked with each other, the order of rank being determined by the numerical value of the rank score of each. This, it is believed, neutralized the regional variation in annual salary. Bishops were arbitrarily assigned the topmost rank.

In the analysis, the sample was stratified into quarters of 79 each, and comparisons were made of the upper with the lower parts of the distribution. Chi-square was used to test for difference. Only those differences between the more successful and less successful subjects which could have occurred by chance less than 5 times out of 100 are being presented here.

Table 1. Correlates of Success of Methodist Ministers with a Level of Significance below .01

Correlate	Direction of Association
Size of community of residence, age 6–12	Q_1 resided in largest communities and Q_4 in smallest
Size of school subject attended, age 6–12	Q_1 attended the largest and Q_4 the smallest
Age when subject started high school	Q_1 started earliest and Q_4 latest
Age when subject felt himself accepted as equal by mother	Q_1 felt accepted at earliest age and Q_4 at latest
Age when subject *first* got idea of entering ministry	Q_1 got idea at earliest age and Q_4 latest
How favorably mother of subject viewed ministers during subject's childhood	Q_1 mothers viewed ministers most favorably and mothers of Q_4 least favorably
How often subject's mother's counsel was sought by friends and neighbors	Counsel of Q_1 mothers was sought most often and that of Q_4 mothers least often
Number of children in subject's childhood family	Q_1 had smallest and Q_4 largest
Subject's major field in college:	
Social Sciences	Q_1 had largest number and Q_4 smallest
Philosophy	Q_1 had largest number and Q_4 smallest
Religion	Q_1 had smallest number and Q_4 largest

FINDINGS

No special effort is here made to relate the findings to each other. They are being merely listed in the following tables, where Q_1 and Q_4 represent the highest-ranking and lowest-ranking quartiles, respectively. Table 1 lists those correlates of success which could have occurred by chance less than one time out of 100. Table 2 lists those with a probability between .01 and .05.

DISCUSSION

A number of the above correlates suggest relatively stable culturally defined patterns of social interaction involving familiar roles, child-father, child-mother, older sibling-younger sibling, social-class role, school role, community role, and the like. . . . No detailed analysis of roles, social, cultural, or situational, is being attempted, here. What is being suggested is that roles provide ready-made molds for channeling and gratifying impulse, as well as for habitual patterning of responses. Indeed, culture seems to be internalized largely through assumption of roles in group living, or through covert internal rehearsal of observed roles in anticipation of enacting them overtly sometime in the future. Through role-playing one internalizes basic responses which seem to persist tenaciously into adulthood and which seem to be related to success within this profession under analysis.

Although the correlates listed here focus largely upon the external situation, it is realized that roles have both objective and subjective components. . . .

. . . . .

. . . The roles which seem to leave the deepest imprint are those which, of the many tried, have been found satisfying or necessary to the social interaction in which one must participate, particularly those roles with which one has become most deeply ego-involved. These roles may have emerged from trial-and-error or they may have been adopted by way of one's identification with an admired other. Roles adopted may be found already tailored and may be put on as a ready-made suit or they may be personally tailored by one for his own individual use. In any case, once adopted, roles provide a mold for the deposit of current experience, on the one hand, and a ready vehicle for entering the parade, or drama, of social interaction, on the other.

CONCLUSIONS

Among the correlates of success in the professional listed above, about a half-dozen or so may be found to comprise independent variables around which others are clustered. For example, size of community

Table 2. Correlates of Success of Methodist Ministers with a
Level of Significance between .01 and .05

Correlate	Direction of Association
Size of community of residence of subject:	
age 0–5	Largest for Q_1 and smallest for Q_4
age 13–college	Largest for Q_1 and smallest for Q_4
Size of school attended, aged 13 to college age	Largest for Q_1 and smallest for Q_4
Age when subject started school (except bishops)	Q_1 earliest and Q_4 latest
Number of times subject moved from one community to another before high school graduation	Q_1 greatest number and Q_4 smallest
Subject's sibling position: Only child	Q_1 greatest number and Q_4 smallest
Mother's sibling position: Only child	Q_1 greatest number and Q_4 had *none*
Father's sibling position: Only child	Q_1 greatest number and Q_4 had *none*
Older or oldest	Q_1 greatest number and Q_4 smallest
Younger or youngest	Q_4 greatest number and Q_1 smallest
Age-interval between subject and next older sibling, in months	Interval between Q_1 and sibling was greatest, and interval between Q_4 and sibling was smallest
Number of children subject's mother ever had	Q_4 had greatest number and Q_1 smallest
father ever had.*	Q_4 had greatest number and Q_1 smallest
Occupation of subject's father:	
Professional	Q_1 had greatest number and Q_4 smallest
Proprietors, Managers and Officials	Q_1 had greatest number and Q_4 smallest
Farmers (including owners and laborers)	Q_4 had greatest number and Q_1 smallest
Years of education for:	
father	Q_1 had greatest number and Q_4 smallest
mother	Q_1 had greatest number and Q_4 smallest
subject	Q_1 had greatest number and Q_4 smallest
Age when subject felt himself accepted as equal by father (except bishops)	Q_1 at lowest age and Q_4 at highest
How happily married father was	Q_1 most happily and Q_4 least

* Some remarried parents had children with two or more mates, hence the necessity for indicating separately the number of children for each parent.

of residence may represent an independent variable around which are clustered such factors as size of school, intercommunity residential mobility and, possibly, number of children parents had. On the other hand, this latter factor of number of children may also be related to what appears to be another independent variable, occupation of father. Clearly, some statistical device should be applied to the above correlates, such as multiple correlation, in an effort to interrelate what appear to be the more important variables. But the task of designing this project, of selecting the sample, of constructing the questionnaire, of securing the cooperation of respondents and, finally, of isolating the above correlates was so enormous that it was decided to postpone further analysis. Meanwhile, it was believed desirable to publish results so far, in the interest of suggesting to other potential investigators in this field what seems to be a fruitful methodological procedure for studying upward mobility within a single vocational group.

The present investigator believes that, after a large enough number of independent variables have been isolated for a given occupation, it may be possible to construct an aptitude test for that occupation, of sufficient validity and reliability to permit vocational counselors to advise high school and college students.

77. THE EVIL EYE: FEAR OF SUCCESS

MORRIS L. HAIMOWITZ AND
NATALIE READER HAIMOWITZ

There has been much discussion of the fear of failure, but very little of the fear of success. The general prevalence of failure throughout the world may, however, indicate that more people fear success than fear failure. This study describes how children and adults unconsciously strive to avoid the terrifying consequences of success.

The evil eye is the fear that calamity will fall in the hour of success and rejoicing, that afflictions will harass the fortunate and prosperous. Among the Italians it is called jettatura; among the Jews, nehurrah. Among American Indians and prerevolutionary New Englanders, the evil eye (the power to afflict) was attributed to witches. Those accused of

Revised from the article in *Teleclass Study Guide in Child Psychology,* 1958, pp. 84–91, by permission of the Chicago Board of Education.

being witches were usually poor, miserable, elderly, crippled—persons with less than their neighbors. The evil eye is obviously the envious eye. It appears among people everywhere from time immemorial that the poor envy the rich, the lame envy the strong, the ugly envy the beautiful, and those who are blessed with desirable attributes or possessions expect to be envied. For the rich empathize with the poor, hating themselves as they are hated, and cursing the poor for this vicarious misery.

SOME EXAMPLES OF THE EVIL EYE AMONG PRELITERATES [1]

When Sumner wrote his study of *Folkways* in 1906 he described the evil eye among primitive people. In Bornu, for example, when a horse is sold, if it is a fine one, it is delivered by night, for fear of the evil eyes (covetous and envious eyes) of bystanders (one of whom might lose his self-control and steal it?) In the Sudan food is usually covered with a conical straw cover to prevent the evil eye (of hungry people who might admire and long for it?) Customs of eating and drinking in private belong here (in many societies children and parents must not see each other eating). At Katanga, Central Africa, only the initiated may watch the smelting of copper, for fear of the evil eye, which would spoil the process (or lay bare the secrets of the trade). The cloistering and veiling of women was intended to protect them, especially if they were beautiful, from the covetous eye. The admiration they would attract would be fatal (or would steal them away). The notion of the evil eye led to covering some parts of the body and so to notions of decency. Shells, fig leaves, strips of leather, clothing, etc. catch attention to divert the evil eye from the organs which are valued.

PROTECTIONS AGAINST THE EVIL EYE

Certain customs seem to be an attempt of the successful to hide their success, or protect themselves from the retaliation it provokes. Sumner observed this in many groups. In the East Indies the phallus, or the symbol of it, is a charm against the evil eye. Roman boys wore such a symbol. In India they used teeth or claws or obscene symbols or strings of shells. Whatever dangles and flutters attracts attention to itself away from the thing to be protected. Mohammed believed in the evil eye. Children, horses and asses were disfigured amongst Moslems to protect them from the risk they would suffer if beautiful. Homer's heroes were taught as a life policy to avert envy; self-disparagement was an approved pose. Soldiers of Rome followed the chariot of the triumphant general and shouted derisive and sarcastic verses while the

[1] William Graham Sumner, *Folkways* (Ginn & Co., 1906), pp. 515–19.

populace showered him with small stones and garbage. (As we shower a bride with rice or an old shoe.) Modern Egyptians leave their children ragged and dirty especially when out of doors for fear of admiration and envy. Boys are greatly envied. They are kept long in the harem and dressed in girls clothes for the same protection. In Cairo as part of the marriage ritual fancy chandeliers are hung before the bridegroom's house. If a crowd gathers to look at it, a jar is broken to distract attention from it, lest an envious eye should cause it to fall. In China, children are often given ugly names: "dog," "hog," "flea." In Southern Europe one does not permit his children to be praised or caressed. If someone does admire a child, he should then spit on it three times or say "What an ugly child." If someone asks "How are you feeling" one says "Knock on wood, I'm fine." The knocking on wood diverts the evil eye. When a young girl first menstruates her mother may slap her or spit on her.[2]

The fear of success, the need to hide or to deny assets, or in some instances the need to fail, is, an expression of the evil eye syndrome. It is difficult to find any society, in any period of history, where this phenomena has been absent. It is the purpose of this article to explore the ways in which the evil eye, which is an ancient heritage, actively influences us today. Let us look at our own tradition.

THE EVIL EYE IN OUR OWN TRADITION (OR SECRET FORCES FOR THE PREVENTION OF SUCCESS)

The Holy Bible eloquently describes the Fall as the consequence of success. Adam and Eve discovered and ate the sweet fruit of the tree of knowledge. How were they rewarded for this example of initiative, curiosity, exploration, (and disobedience)? Their eyes were opened so they could see, learn, and be ashamed.

Unto the woman, God said, I will greatly multiply thy sorrow and thy conception; in sorrow thou shalt bring forth children . . . and unto Adam, He said, cursed is the ground for thy sake; in sorrow shalt thou eat of it all the days of thy life. In the sweat of thy face shalt thou eat, till thou return unto the ground; for dust thou art and unto dust shalt thou return.

The moral? If you discover something new, if you taste the good fruit of the tree of knowledge, or the sweet taste of freedom or success, you may be punished. If you violate the norms, if you disobey the rules, you will suffer severely. Be safe. Conform. A similar theme is repeated in the story of Eve's children. Cain, a poor farmer, was envious of his successful brother Abel, and killed him. The moral? If you do too well, your brother may kill you.

In recent literature the evil eye has been rediscovered, renamed

[2] *Ibid.*

(Riesman's "other directed" man, Whyte's "organization man"), and erroneously regarded as a modern phenomenon.

Many persons own jewelry they never wear, or if they don't own the gems, want them but do not buy them. Some women, after buying a fur coat, fear to wear it lest it become soiled or torn or stolen, at least that's what they say. But if they are questioned somewhat more closely it often turns out they fear the envious glances of their sisters without fur coats, just as they themselves had been envious previously.

Some feel that if they only could have a baby they would be happy. Having a baby would mean success to them. Once pregnant however, they develop fears: perhaps the baby will be a monster, have two heads, be born ugly, have scars, be defective.

Some men can never wear their best pants or the tie they really like, or their new coat or hat or can't use their new watch or fountain pen. Or they can't use their new broom or hammer or even a new nail. They may have new ones, but would rather use the old, until the new ones get rusty. Sometimes this is "thrift," sometimes it is the "Secret Society" we are describing—that part of our customs which says one must not boast, one must not show off one's success. To many this means one must not have success.

What often passes for modesty or humility, benevolence or altruism, or even miserliness may have the same underlying feeling: if I do well or show that I am doing well or take what I want, others who want as much as I will hate me (as I used to hate those who had what I wanted).

A blind man reported that he had had the opportunity to have his sight restored by a cornea replacement, but that he preferred not to have the operation. The reason he gave is interesting. He might have said he feared the operation, or that it cost too much, but he didn't. He said "They could use that cornea for other blind people who are not as well off as I. I have a business selling Christmas cards; I have a lovely wife. We have been married fourteen years and are getting along fine. Give the sight to a man who needs it worse, or who is younger than I." It is noteworthy that he compared himself not with seeing persons but with other blind persons, persons younger or weaker than himself, persons who might envy his vision.

The humble kinds of success may also be fraught with anxiety. To the obese, a successful self is not so heavy. The obese person who wants to reduce sometimes suffers from fantasies of dying of starvation, of looking like a skeleton, of becoming ill, nauseous or weak if he should reduce to a normal weight. Although it is well known that food may be a source of gratification when interpersonal gratifications are disappointing, and that people may feel hungry when they are disappointed in not receiving something for which they long (love, approval, consideration), it is suggested here that an important aspect of the body weight is the value placed upon it.

Similarly with the underweight. His humble goal in life is to gain a few pounds and be like others. He diets and exercises too, and eats a lot of butter and milk and becomes panicky after he has gained a few pounds, catches a cold, has nightmares, or feels nervous and places the cause for his distress on the butter or other special foods. "A doctor told me to eat yellow corn meal with butter to help me gain weight. It is not expensive and I like it. But when I have gained a couple of pounds I catch a bad cold, lose my appetite and go back to where I was before I started gaining."

Success has many meanings:—it may mean winning a tennis match, or getting married, or going swimming, or painting a picture or changing a tire or building a home or having a child or getting a job or gaining weight or making a million or having a birthday party. Specific fantasies of success are thus highly idiosyncratic, specific for each individual. The fears and penalties associated with achieving success, however, appear to be an age-old phenomena which few entirely escape.

Success may also mean, "I am my brother's keeper." If one is successful, one must take care of those less successful, which may be something of a burden. At family reunions there is talk of the successes and failures of relatives. If everyone has been healthy and prosperous, the meeting is pleasureable. If, however, one has not been successful, or has been ill, the success of his brothers irritates him, even as his failure casts a shadow on the gathering. If his ill fortune continues others will have to take care of him. It is only when such responsibility is felt strongly that people adopt extreme behavior to avoid helping the unfortunate. A common example of this is the miser who has lots of money but pretends to be poor. Similarly, persons who are strongly tempted to help a beggar and feel enormous guilt when they pass him by, nourish the fantasy that this beggar may really be a wealthy man whose Cadillac brings him to the corner each day and picks him up in the evening. This idea appeared in one of the adventures of Sherlock Holmes. We have found it in many clients who feel pursued by the evil eye. The non-giver is thus exonerated. Many men who achieve, who acquire, have freed themselves partially as compared with their brothers who have been more timid, but they pay a certain price for their success in their inner psychological state. They are haunted by guilt, shame, or fear of coming face to face with their unwillingness to share.

One of the ideals of our society is the rugged individualist. He is productive, creative; he uses initiative, he gets ahead, he is aggressive, fights for the things he feels are right regardless of where the crowd is heading. Although such vigor is ideal, most people experience considerable ambivalence about achieving it; there is both desire for it and fearful avoidance of it.

Below is an account of an experiment conducted to study some of the forces described above, as they operate in people at a less conscious level.

THE ASSOCIATIONS OF 100 STUDENTS TO SYMBOLS OF SUCCESS

PROBLEM

It is well known that many people function at a level much lower than their potential, and it is often difficult for them to increase their ability up to their potential.

HYPOTHESIS

Success is associated with anxiety. One reason some persons are not fully productive is their anxiety regarding success.

METHOD OF TESTING THE HYPOTHESIS

Assumptions.

1. In our society, certain words and phrases such as *promotion, new car, graduation, best in class,* and *a lovely marriage* would symbolize success to college students.
2. Other words and phrases such as *open air, wood, crayon, billboard, here and now,* would not symbolize success to college students.
3. Students asked to associate to the words above will write down whatever comes to mind.
4. If more words and phrases suggesting anxiety or blocking behaviors occur with the success words than with the non-success words, our hypothesis is supported.

Procedure. One hundred college freshmen were read the following instructions:

This is an exercise to show how different words bring forth different associations or responses. I am going to write some words on the blackboard and ask that you write down on a sheet of paper whatever comes to your mind. You will have 20 seconds for each. Write down as many words or phrases as you can think of, and write down every one that comes to your mind. If you don't think of any word or phrase, don't write down anything. For example: if I say "green," what does it make you think of? (red, grass, park, sky, blue, dress, etc.) Don't say anything out loud. It will disturb the others. Here is the first word. You have 20 seconds. Copy the word first: (Write on blackboard "open air." Twenty seconds later, "billboard," and so on with this list: promotion, wood, new car, crayon, graduation, here and now, best in class, a lovely marriage.)

Since each of the 100 students associated to ten expressions, there were a total of 1,000 sets of associations. Since most students associated more than once to each expression, the total number of associations came to approximately 3,000.

The 3,000 associations were read and those judged to be symbolic of anxiety, displeasure, or negation were tabulated. It is assumed that crossing out or misspelling simple words, or blocking (inability to associate to a word) may also symbolize, connote, reveal or be an expression of some inner anxiety. Approximately 300 or 10 per cent of the expressions were judged to express anxiety.

Table 1. The Number of Persons Responding with Anxiety to Non-Success and to Success Words

STIMULUS WORD	ANXIETY ASSOCIATIONS			
NON-SUCCESS	*Unpleasant*	*Blocking*	*Crossed-out Misspelled*	*Total*
1. open air	3	0	0	3
2. billboard	6	0	0	6
4. wood	4	0	0	4
6. crayon	3	0	0	3
8. here and now	4	2	0	6
Totals	20	2	0	22
SUCCESS				
3. promotion	9	1	1	11
5. new car	18	3	0	21
7. graduation	9	0	3	12
9. best in class	14	7	3	24
10. a lovely marriage	17	2	4	23
Totals	67	13	11	91

Table 1 lists the stimulus words and the number of persons responding with unpleasant, blocking, or crossed-out and misspelled words in response to each. Thus three students gave one or more unpleasant associations to the stimulus word "open air;" nine students gave one or more unpleasant associations to the stimulus word "promotion." (See Table 2.) The totals 20 and 67 do not indicate the number of different students because some students had anxiety expressions for several words. The average number of students expressing anxiety for the non-success words was four; the average number of students expressing anxiety for the success words was thirteen—three times as many. If we compare blocking, we find thirteen blocking responses to the success words compared to only two for non-success words. And if we compare crossed out and misspelled words, we find eleven to zero. (Only misspelling of one-syllable words was included.)

Table 2.   A List of the Stimulus Words in the Order Presented with the Words or Phrases Judged to Be Unpleasant or Negative, or Symbolic of Anxiety. (Comma Separates Responses of Different Subjects, Hyphen Separates Responses of the Same Subjects)

Open air:	air raid, lust, fall - hurt
Billboard:	pain in the neck - waste of wood, train wreck, sloppy - gaudy, nuisance, hard sleep - tension, obnoxious
Promotion:	big shot, longer hours to work, test, grey hair, con-man, fight, flunk - sad, me - never - damm (sic), top floor - mess
Wood:	floods, knife, knife, boo
New car:	big payments but nice, increased budget, monthly payments (4), show-off, expensive, scratches, traffic ticket, too much chrome, too-big, too expensive, accident, accident, junk, unhappiness, unemployment-recession
Crayon:	problems, kids-wall-scolding, defacing property
Graduation:	sadness, never, look for job, me - bottom, mistakes, phoney, bad grades, work, joy and tears
Here and now:	boring class, anxiety, tired, fight
Best in class:	stupid bum, teacher's pet, apple polisher, exam, time for nothing but study - no friends - showoff, hard work, brown noser, con-man, no one, wrong emphasis, odd ball - non-socialistic, me - no - I want, worst (2)
A lovely marriage:	far, far away, selfish, divorce, quick divorce, struggle, unlikely, one of few, never, hard to find, arguments - children - difficulty - mother-in-law, no mother-in-law, is over, - too bad, - good, - too short, stopped, no fights, nuts - no such thing, sorrow, worry - tired - impossible - people are not grown up

Conclusion. The hypothesis is supported. Approximately thirteen per cent of our sample of 100 students associated to success words with anxiety, while only four per cent associated to non-success words with anxiety.

DISCUSSION

Having experimentally demonstrated the ambivalence about success, let us proceed to examine some of the manifestations of ambivalence in more complex situations. The cost to our society of this ambivalance is inestimable in terms of dollars, human creativity, and maximum use of individual capacities. Take, for example, the following incidents.

A soldier told us this experience:

During the war we were stationed on an island in the Pacific. The only lumber available was in the army lumberyard. The army was burning tons of scrap lumber every week. Occasionally natives would ask for a piece of lumber, or request that the scrap lumber be set aside and given or sold to the natives. The Commanding General would not hear of this. "We must burn the lumber," he said, "Otherwise if we let people come in and get some, they might stumble over it, hurt themselves and sue us."

A commuter reported:

A bus was held up for several minutes while cars slipped and spun in the snow in front of it. While waiting for a car to dislodge itself, several passengers of the bus, very impatient at being late for work, went to the driver of the bus and said we want to go out and help that car. We'll be right back. The driver said, "If you go out, I'll have to charge you another fare." "That's crazy," the passenger said. "That man is holding up the bus and traffic for blocks while his wheels are spinning in the snow and we could push him out in just a minute." The driver said "If I let you out of the bus to push that car, and if you slipped and broke a leg, I'd get sued."

A student told us he wanted to use some tools in the school workshop:

Students were not permitted to use the huge workshop, "Because," the engineer seriously related, "a student once cut off his finger." Today the workshop stands idle most of the time, used only by the engineers.

A beautiful swimming pool in a public school is closed most of the time because "Once someone drowned in the pool."

We find such conflicts often heightened in specific crisis situations in which the individual, confronted with a problem to be solved, or an opportunity to be grasped, either initiates effective activity in response to it, or retires passively to "safe," "well-tested" ground.

In these four examples there were strong psychological factors preventing the individual decision-maker from extending himself, from "going out on a limb," or from showing initiative by improvising better solutions to problems. What are these factors? Are we all equally bound by them? Are there some factors in our life experience which intensify fear of success, intensify inhibition, and are there other factors that reduce it?

The common element to these apparently diverse phenomena, wearing clothing to distract attention from the genitals, knocking on wood when admitting success, fear of abandoning "usual" inadequate procedures of problem solving to explore new, untested ones, appears to be the expectation of loss ("bad luck"). The expectation of loss or punishment is accompanied by rationalizations to justify the feelings. The reasons given in the four examples above are good reasons (sometimes bad reasons) but they are not the primary reasons. The fear apparently originates unconsciously from childhood experiences and is reinforced during adult life.

CHILDHOOD ORIGINS OF THE EVIL EYE: SOME HYPOTHESES

We may understand the evil eye as originating in the early life experience of each individual. For some, the significant early experiences are so severe that the fear of success, the need to conform, establishes rigid limits of living. Any temptation to compete, to strive, to create, to own, brings with it such severe anxiety that the individual withdraws within the area of the safe status quo. A conflict appears when, as part of general mobility, those individuals who are fearful of success must achieve in order to conform to a group in which everybody else is achieving, graduating, getting married, having a baby, buying a car, a home, getting a better job or giving a superior performance on whatever job he has. In such circumstances the individual must achieve just to conform, a situation which requires him to surpass others in order to be inconspicuous in his intimate social group, and one which may arouse continuous anxiety.

What are some of these significant early experiences which influence later freedom? First is the universal experience of envy. Everyone has wanted what someone else owned. This is often first experienced in the Oedipus Complex and in sibling rivalry. One child in the family gets admiration or new clothing, and the other children may get none. When a less-favored child envies, he wishes to harm or to destroy his more fortunate brother (as with Cain and Abel, Jacob and Esau, and with Joseph and his brothers). Apparently, then, a most significant factor in later life is the extent to which envy is aroused in the early family life. If we have envied greatly and hated intensely, throughout our lives we are alerted to these feelings, in ourselves and in others (or imagine them). Similarly, if we have been greatly envied and hated by other members of the family, the discomfort of this experience makes us highly ambivalent about being in this special position again. It may be that where children feel loved and appreciated, and where no child is continually favored, envy is reduced. Children who feel loved can tolerate the experience of another child's getting some needed clothing or food or attention without intense hatred. Conversely, where a child seriously doubts parental affection, "buying one for everybody" brings little comfort for him, for he suspects that "his brother's is better, or bigger or in some way more desirable," and his envy (really envy of parental love) is aroused anyway.

A second feature is the extent to which parents can tolerate strength and adequacy in their children. Many parents are able to be protective and tender when their children are docile and weak and helpless; but when the children begin to show signs of strength or skill, the parents may become anxious. When parents feel inadequate, and unable to compete with their contemporaries, they may be driven to compete with their children. Such parents being, at least for a while, stronger, older, more skillful, defeat the child, whose early attempts to develop strength and initiative thus result in pain and punishment, as well as with the subtle threat of the loss of parental love and the loss of the necessities of life. It follows then that feelings of adequacy on the part of parents, in comparison with their contemporaries, is one factor in their tolerance of initiative, skillfulness and aggressiveness in their children.

A young man we know was thinking about making a fireplace screen. He planned to cut the screen, pound, twist and polish the wrought iron. He thought not only of how beautiful his handiwork would be, but also of the danger. He might hurt himself. "I keep thinking of the saw blade slipping and cutting off a hand and the pliers slipping and nipping a finger." Such fears were associated with his father, who he scorned as being a weak braggart, but whose strength and power he also envied. A constant fantasy was that his father envied him. As a child, each time he was successful in some task his father would compete, to prove that the father was better. On the chinning bar the boy chinned three times. He ran proudly to tell his father. That's nothing, the father chided, and to prove it he went to the bar and chinned *six* times. One day, when he hit a home run while playing baseball, he ran to tell his father, who replied, "That's not bad, but when I was your age I was hitting *two* home runs." The son felt the father was weak in having to prove his superiority, because he was not successful with men his own age. But the father was also strong in that each time, he was able to better his son. This strength the son envied and hated. His fear was that if he bettered his father, the father would then envy him as he previously had envied and hated his father. The fact that his father had been dead for years made little difference until the young man understood why he feared being cut, and in psychotherapy worked through his Oedipal problem.

There are several factors related to unexpected, unavoidable tragedies. As a child grows, and becomes aggressive, death or illness of a sibling or parent may constitute a severe shock to the child, leading him to the conclusion that it was his aggressiveness that caused the damage. Children are not logical in their cause-and-effect reasoning, and they cannot realistically assess their own strength. When early beginnings of assertiveness occur simultaneously with painful losses, the child may associate these and feel one to be the consequence of the other, making him forever fearful of his own initiative.

Similarly, a child may regard the birth of younger children as parental retaliation for assertiveness. Very often, in a family where parents feel burdened by several young children, any show of strength or adequacy (ability to walk, dress oneself, carry a package) is met with the strain of parental expectation that the new achievement is to be repeated "from now on." The more adequate the child reveals himself to be, the more is expected of him. He not only gives up the pleasure of parental doting and assistance, but is expected to take on additional duties in the care of younger children. He may regard this as punishment for accomplishment. "You're a big boy now. You have to walk. The baby rides in the buggy." So who wants to be big? One may expect loss of support when one demonstrates strength.

A boy reports:

I was translating Latin. The teacher had called on me and I knew the lesson well. But suddenly I felt everyone was watching me; they usually did not know the lesson. If I knew the lesson and no one else did, the kids would make fun of me. Suddenly I was stumbling. I pretended to labor over every word. The teacher said something sharp and my turn was over. I felt a little relieved that it was over, and a little ashamed at my failure.

Older girls say they must not finish college. "If I finish college I can't get a husband because boys don't like girls with too much education; so I'm quitting this semester, before I graduate."

A similar argument is used by fathers who tell their sons: "Why should you stay in school and learn all that malarky. I never went to school and look at me." A father in trouble with the truant officer because he kept his son out of school recently told us, "I don't see why he has to go to school. That boy can already read and write." The father could not read or write. And in a few minutes, we found out all the boy could write was his name. He told us, "School ain't for me. You won't have no friends if you go to school."

Some people fear such common acts as asking for a job, asking for a date, asking for a loan, seeking information on the highway, information on how to operate a machine in a factory. For some people to ask for help means to put oneself in an inferior position, in a vulnerable position. It is an acknowledgement of weakness. Or is it a fear of being punished for being aggressive, for getting ahead?

"My brother is a year younger than I. We attended the same grammar school. He had some of the same teachers that I had the year before. He was not as obedient as I had been. He made poorer marks. All through school his teachers would say, 'Why can't you behave like your sister?' There was always a little bitterness in the way he felt towards me which disturbed me a great deal. Because of this we went to different high schools."

"I and several of my friends were in a contest for homecoming queen. As the day for selection approached, tension among us rose. Nobody would talk to anyone else. And after I was elected queen, my best friend wouldn't talk to me anymore." Her best friend was the lady-in-waiting to her majesty.

Many students will not run for office because they fear the crowd won't like them if they win, and they will hate themselves if they lose.

One boy we were counseling who got many gold stars in spelling suddenly could not spell any more. After some rambling he told us "Someone stole my gold stars, so I got the idea the other kids didn't like me for having too many gold stars so I missed words the rest of the year."

78. HOW TO READ LI'L ABNER

INTELLIGENTLY

ARTHUR J. BRODBECK AND DAVID M. WHITE

This study analyzes one typically American comic strip, suggesting that it presents in caricature some of the general values and problems of our culture—particularly those of family life and social roles. In Mammy Yokum we see the all-powerful American mother, and in Li'l Abner, the maternally overprotected American boy. Humor almost always contains elements of courage and resignation, and in looking at the doings in Dogpatch, Americans may be bravely resigning themselves to their fate.

It is a common misbelief that American comic strips consist of little more than "wish-fulfillment," slick attempts to provide 100 million readers with daily dreams of adventure and happiness, power and glory, the stuff of which dreams are made. Of course, "Li'l Abner," like other comic strips and popular art forms, *does* deal with wishes, for what are "wishes" but another name for "problems"? However, those who ap-

Reprinted from *Mass Culture: The Popular Arts in America*, edited by Bernard Rosenberg (The Free Press, The Falcon's Wing Press, 1957), chapter 10, by permission of the publisher.

proach "Li'l Abner" as merely an excursion up the river toward the fulfillment of wishes will take back only a minor part of what it contains. For Al Capp's creation deals with some very painful parts of reality and, while it deals with wishes, it does not invariably fulfill them.

All art teaches us something—usually under conditions where we *think* we are being entertained. The secret of much art is that it tries to keep us off guard, subtly relaxing our shopworn critical senses, by *pretending* to be flattering our egos, while it nevertheless educates us. Art, whether in a play by Congreve or in the newer form utilized by a Harriman, a Walt Kelly or Capp, coaxes our minds to move out of their established conceptual grooves and liberates them for a fresh, creative look at reality. It tries to get us to practice a new kind of response to ourselves and the world. Yet all the while it keeps our fears down low enough by a certain amount of reassurance that things will all work out all right at the end.

"Li'l Abner" tries to do this. It may not always succeed, yet for more than two decades it has been telling millions of Americans each day something about the nature of our contemporary existence—and if we accept the "message" more easily because it is *only* a comic strip, that does not negate the artistic force of the strip.

We often go away from our daily visit to Dogpatch with renewed courage to tackle our own quarrels with urban living, deprivations to our social status and much else of the same kind. For "Li'l Abner" stresses how far from perfect we and our real world are. But through its art it enables us simultaneously to laugh at the discrepancy, to see our human condition humbly but bravely. The ability to laugh at ourselves always has an element of bravery in it.

Although "Li'l Abner" is concerned with a multitude of the facts of American culture, from a Liberace fad to our fantastic needs to "belong" (like the rejected member of the Gourmet Club), there is nonetheless one central problem on which it hinges: *the maternally overprotected boy*, the boy with an overpowering mother.

Some years ago a British anthropologist came over to view Americans as he might view a primitive tribe, reaching conclusions which were not too different from those of Al Capp about the central American problem. Geoffrey Gorer, in *The American People*, tried to compress in a short volume the structure of American culture, the problems and pains in it, as well as the satisfactions and joys it embodied.

His conclusions have been deeply resisted by Americans, since it is seldom pleasant to have to take a good frank look at ourselves. (The Irishman, for instance, who behaves exactly like Barry Fitzgerald is most likely to look upon him as "caricaturing" the Irish personality.) Yet, there are many who believe that Gorer was not too far from the truth about us, although still more remains to be said.

Gorer tried to show first that every "red-blooded" American boy is expected to be "better" than his parents; in fact, he's supposed to "outgrow" them. It is interesting that "Li'l Abner," when it first began in 1934, started off with Mammy and Pappy Yokum as tall as their son. But within a few months a curious thing happened. Mammy and Pappy began to shrink. It was a period of great conflict, perhaps second only to Li'l Abner's marriage. For the parents never remained "shrunken." They rose—first one, then the other—back to full initial stature again, or very near it, continuing to shrink and grow unpredictably. Finally, they were permanently "dwarfed" as they are now.

It was almost as if, as Al Capp made his way toward success (as every red-blooded American boy is supposed to do) he could "afford" to shrink the parent figures, to feel it was artistically right. In order to feel one's own sense of self-esteem, we Americans more frequently than not set, as a condition of that, some signs of tangible success—a better home, more money, wider acclaim, etc.—that "prove" we have risen "above" our parents. Change between generations is built into the structure of our society. And it is sometimes hard on us indeed. "Li'l Abner" symbolizes all of this wish for social mobility by a mere picture.

But this is to oversimplify what the strip tells us. For Mammy Yokum—small, wizened and masculinized as she is—is endowed with magical powers. She is par excellence the overprotecting mother. Or at least, she is her son's childlike conception of such a type of mother, the *way* in which he believes in her and imagines her to be. She can handle the "monsters" four times her size by "wrasslin' Dogpatch style"—which knowledge *she*, not Pappy, imparts to her son. She is the leader of her community, ready to impress by force if necessary her and her offspring's importance upon all others. When not using her "fisks," she divines truth by supernatural incantations and brings about justice in mysterious ways. Her famous duel with "Evil Eye" Fleegle (who symbolizes the "sinfulness" of city life), in which rays of "goodness" emerge from her eyes, casts Mammy Yokum in the heroic mold. Anything you can do she can do better. What woman could compare with her? The feminine Daisy Mae is weak and helpless. The city women are designing, shallow and seething with lust. (Basically, says the strip, all American women, unlike Mammy, are constantly trying to put a man's potency to test, when they are not engaged in destroying his independence and innocence through such devices as "Sadie Hawkins Days.") Beside Mammy, Li'l Abner's father is the merest caricature of a man—and to accentuate this feature, by a twist of Capp's special use of irony, Pappy is called "Lucifer," while Mammy is named "Pansy," which connotes inappropriately a shrinking, timid woman of delicate design and presents a denial of the masculinity and power of American mothers by the magic words juxtaposed against what is so graphically otherwise.

As a matter of fact, what we are looking at is nothing but the American version of the Oedipus complex set in a mother–dominated family. To identify with Mother is to become a "Pansy"; yet, the source of strength lies nowhere else, since the protection and guidance of the son is all generated from the mother figure. Indeed, "Lucifer" is almost a cry of protest, comically contrived, against a father who is not there in any important sense.

In the early days of the strip, when Li'l Abner put on the wedding suit of his father, as he starts out to the big city and symbolically up the social ladder, the usual Oedipal feeling would demand that the suit be oversized. Instead, it is comically small and shrunken and leads the "sassiety" people into gales of laughter when they see it. Li'l Abner succeeds through his family connections on Mammy's side (her sister) and despite the inadequacy of Pappy's bequest to him.

But the Oedipus complex comes out fully and strongly in the traditional way—feelings of active possessiveness toward the mother and competitive feelings toward the father for her favors—as Abner moves among "high sassiety" people or aristocratic foreigners from the "old country." As Malinowski discovered, just as the uncle occupies the father's position in the Oedipus triangle among the Trobrianders, so the people above oneself in the social scale, as one moves out of the family, brings out one's true, not inverted, Oedipus feelings. One's masculinity is suddenly aroused as one moves up the social ladder. The "high sassiety" women are constantly acting out their sexual feelings toward Li'l Abner, and the "bosses" and the other male aristocrats of mass society vent their spleen on Li'l Abner, and sometimes compete with him for the favors of the women. A count who courts Li'l Abner's "high sassiety" aunt, and is continually frustrated in the courtship by Li'l Abner, finally delivers a blow (below the belt) to him, explaining that it's an "old custom" in his own land (the European land of patriarchy where the real Oedipus complex exists, instead of the American land of matriarchy where boys find their fathers nonentities). Dumpington Van Lump, a cruel, selfish and slobbish "high sassiety" creature, tries to wrench Daisy Mae away from Abner and to destroy all of Dogpatch—the primary ego—in the process.

Gorer has tried to show that it is the overprotective, all-powerful American mother who is the source of the strengths *and* weaknesses of American men. This contributes in subtle ways to their fears of being effeminate—since they identify with and get their source of strength and self-esteem from their mothers more than their fathers. It leads them to feel "guilty" about sex which is not "idealistic" and which does not partake of the noble and passive relationship the American male has had with his own Mother. But it makes him strong enough to be sympathetic and kind to the weak, as Mother was. And it makes him able to endure stress, although sometimes complaining as one would to Mother, and to blind himself to the harm the others can (and sometimes do) cause him, because of the optimistic *weltanschauung* that mother bequeathed him.

Food, Gorer has pointed out, is the way in which American mothers and sons express their love for each other: the mother by filling the child with it and the child by passively allowing himself to be filled. Food themes abound everywhere in "Li'l Abner." At crucial moments in his life, moments of crisis and danger, Abner calls for his "Po'k chops." He is calling for Mother-Love, and attempting to assuage his anxiety by recalling the strength he has gotten from Mother. He is engaged in a magical act—and we laugh at the magic of it, the palpable absurdity— and yet, it is the type of magic that operates in both high and low places in the lives of American men. The "monsters" and "high society" people often deprive Abner of his food indulgences. The world is not like the nursery, even though Abner frequently expects it to be bountiful in the food of Mother-Love.

There is a Henry James complexity to the strip. Each episode, depending on which character's eyes you see it from, takes on a slightly different meaning. In this way, Li'l Abner's personality is seen from a multitude of viewpoints that exist in American society, viewpoints that condemn the results of maternal overprotection and viewpoints which beam on it. In general, however, it is the problems which the over-protected boy causes for other people with whom he must constantly interact that is stressed. The complexity of the strip thus makes us see its most exaggerated consequences. And to repeat, it does this and makes us like it—whereas, when Geoffrey Gorer did it, we were repelled.

At no time does the strip allow us to examine the themes with complete pessimism or complete optimism. Li'l Abner's courage often seems incomprehensible and his pessimistic fears seem ridiculous. True, we always tend to feel that things will really work out for the best in the end, but never without a certain amount of "comic" pain and misery first. (Watch the way Li'l Abner "sweats" unremittingly on his way through life!) Nothing comes easy, except Mammy Yokum's strength and her willingness to use it for her son.

We can never be sure about endings in "Li'l Abner." All the shmoos were killed—and the shmoo was a sort of truncated symbol for the very concept of wish-fulfillment. And Truth, masquerading as the Bald Iggle, must be silenced in the end, even if it has to be by a female impersonator of Mother. And Abner does marry and so loses his boyish innocence.

No, "Li'l Abner" does not run away from reality, even when it is most fantastic; it doesn't hestitate to frustrate wishes, even when it ironically denies reality in ways in which many Americans deny it in their everyday lives. In fact, by *exaggerating* our own defenses against the painful parts of our American reality, especially those concerned with the pain in social mobility, it shows how absurd those defenses really are. It speaks in reverse English directly to our unconscious knowledge about ourselves and the world by overdoing the kind of flattery we treat ourselves to as we march through life. In his ironic "Did I say that?" type of artlessness, which is practiced as a high art, Capp gets us to see what hypocrites we are, and yet doesn't force us to hate ourselves for it. It is done so tactfully, so gently, as though we were all good friends. Indeed, there is a warmness for people in "Li'l Abner," an affectionate streak and a kind one, even though the sentiment is always firmly but fantastically married to realism. The eyes of the strip do not wear rose-colored glasses.

Even the style of the strip is completely American in its fierce "individualism," which it is constantly redefining. It never quite allows us to hate or love any one character or movement wholeheartedly. It sees imperfection everywhere. No one, not even Li'l Abner, is exempt from a savage honesty of appraisal, except again Mammy Yokum—and there have even been times when the strip, perhaps without knowing what it was doing, and getting carried away by its own style, took a fast-running, critical side-glance at her. The style permits of no whole-hearted sentimentalization of any person, idea or organization. Yet, though there is no *unqualified* love and adoration expressed toward anyone, there remains *warmth* and *compassion*. And is this not, truly, an American style of feeling, part of what we have come to mean by "individualism"? The very best we have in American Life? The very heart of the complexity of our spiritual quality existing among our technological and materialistic way of living?

Without plunging into the pros and cons of popular culture and mass society, let us not forget that Shakespeare was once an element in Elizabethan popular culture and that it took dozens of decades before the guardians of high literary standards allowed him to rise in respectability and permitted us to see his permanent worth. Any art, no matter how popular, which has the kind of complexity that is the substance of "Li'l Abner," and has learned to communicate the complexity to us so simply, so matter of factly, is bound to have a certain amount of lastingness, even though it is embodied in a particular time and place, even though it makes concessions to the "mass mind."

Does Capp altogether know what he is saying through his comic strip? Is it perhaps a case, more than with Shakespeare, of one person's unconscious speaking through a large circulation to millions of others? The answer is bound to be moot. Writers often learn an astonishing amount from their critics about what they have written. Since "Li'l

Abner" depicts so much of the unconscious and unrecognized forces at work in American life, some of it is bound to well from Capp's own unconscious itself.

But reading "Li'l Abner" is much different than listening to the free associations of a single gifted exponent of American culture. These associations have become, through Capp's artistic talents, transformed and universalized. He is not talking to an analyst, but he is communicating with twenty to thirty million fellow American citizens. The artistic transformation means that whatever is unique in one's associations must be communicated by more universal symbols or else it can not be shared. The artist need not be ashamed of the sources of his inspirations and we do not need to know what they are in order to judge the quality of his finished product.

It is often said that our "mass society" has produced a greater leisure than ever before for the general run of mankind; but the people have turned away from "the higher art" and "the better culture" to indulge themselves in the tawdry *kitsch* of the mass-media industry. Surely, the gulf between the higher and the popular arts is not quite so wide, and some of the elements of "good" art are present in Capp's comic-strip fantasies.

But may the public have turned away from the "higher art" because it is so full of pessimism and unhappy ending and no resolutions to the problems of life? It may be not so much that people want to be flattered, as they may want some *help* and *guidance* in finding solutions to the problems that confront them. The "higher art," many times, only reiterates the conflicts which they already feel and leaves them at the same, or even worse, impasse than that at which they were already. Hollywood takes over precisely because the most gifted and complex of artists share a grotesque form of pessimism about life's problems and present only masochistic reveries for people.

It is indeed fortunate that there is someone like Capp to fill the gap, until the "higher art" begins to offer solutions again to the woebegotten state of life it depicts. If anything, Capp should not be criticized too much for the pleasantness of his comic reveries. Instead, like the "higher art," he frequently in his more recent work destroys hope and courage and becomes more devoid of solutions to the American dilemmas. One might wish him to be more optimistic, without losing his complexity. There never was a time when Americans, Mass or Elite, needed it more, if there are some realistic grounds on which it can be maintained.

79. MATE SELECTION: THE "H" CASE

ROBERT F. WINCH

*This article deals with dating and mating; who likes whom
and why. Long before—though perhaps especially since—
Freud elaborated his theory of the Oedipus Complex, people
noticed that a young man was usually attracted to a girl
"just like the girl who married dear old dad." The case histories
and conclusions in the book* Mate Selection *support the general
notion of determinism: the individual is shown as driven by
his early experiences to seek a mate with whom he can
continue certain behavior patterns begun in his own immediate
family.*

*The selection below summarizes the "complementary needs"
hypothesis and illustrates it with the "H" Case.*

CHILD DEVELOPMENT AND COMPLEMENTARY NEEDS

. . . Observations on child development in the American middle
class have centered about: (1) incorporation of parental disciplines and
the formation of the super-ego, (2) the nature of the ideal self as formed
by the setting up and abandoning of successive ego-models, and (3) the
hypothesis that self-doubt is at the base of our cult of personality. My
purpose in selecting these points in the total picture of child development is that they seem to suggest the lines along which will develop
needs which the individual will seek to gratify in the love relationship
of marriage. From (1) we can see the possibility of inhibitions, conflicts,
and doubts about the expression of aggression and of sex, and also
about the converse—passivity. From (2) it appears that certain phenomena in mate-selection can be understood when we compare a person's concept of his actual self and of his ideal self on the one hand
with his percept of the spouse on the other. From (3) we can see that
the fact of being married carries a connotation of self-affirmation (and
thus tends to neutralize self-doubt) for it is evidence that at least one
person—the spouse—thinks the self is "acceptable" even if no one else
does.

.   .   .   .   .

Selections reprinted from *Mate Selection* (Harper & Brothers, 1958), pp. 86–87,
194–201, by permission of the publisher.

To tie these ideas together, let us dream up a little boy, Herbert, whose mother demanded "model" behavior and gave him to understand that neither she nor anyone else would ever have anything to do with him unless he did as she said. Let us imagine that little Herbert was frightened and conformed but realized that occasionally he had impulses to be "bad." Let us assume that he was worried about those impulses and subsequently became a very "good" and "controlled" boy—a bit of a sissy and not very popular. One of his ego-models—taken up, cherished, and abandoned—would probably be a swashbuckling exemplar of derring-do, mobilized at all times to run his sword through anyone who might cross his path. And as Herbert became an adult, we might expect that he would be attracted to expressive people, to people who talk back and don't take nonsense from others. This is something we might feel sure that he would wish he could do—just feel some aggression well up in his veins. We might expect him to draw vicarious gratification from seeing other people "blow their tops." We might even expect that he would marry a girl who would blow her top regularly. As we shall see . . . Herbert did just that.

. . . . .

THE "H" CASE

Herb is a quiet and modest-appearing fellow. In a group he is friendly and coöperative but seldom appears assertive. He is a bit shy about revealing much of himself to others, and he does not make close friends easily. He spends much of his time preparing for his occupational future and is rather optimistic about his prospects, but occasionally he becomes depressed over the conviction that he has not done a good enough job or that he doesn't have all that it takes to get there.

. . . Herb does not seem to have much anger. "Sometimes," he says, "I simulate anger because that's what people expect more or less. [*Laughs.*] That's the best way to do it, and it also makes you feel better if you aren't angry and you let on that you are. I am so big that I look awfully tough, but I'm really not."

From his earliest memories the anger of others has frightened Herb. "Even with a smaller person—a person I'm not afraid of—when that person gets mad, unless I consciously say to myself that there's nothing to be scared about, I get scared. I know now that the only way to counteract someone else's show of violent temper is to flare up a little bit yourself. It took me a long time to be certain and to be able to do that."

On the basis of what we have seen in previous cases and from what little we know of Herb thus far we can make a few educated guesses. (1) We might surmise that Herb has been subjected to expressions of anger—indeed to violent outbursts—which have frightened him. It seems likely that such violence was expressed by one of his parents. (As of the moment we have no information to lead us to conjecture whether it might have been Herb's father or his mother, or conceivably both.) Furthermore, the expressive parent was probably quite dominant, and we can sense that Herb has come to feel some resentment about this dominance. (2) On the other hand it seems plausible that Herb has patterned his own behavior after that of one of his parents, and accordingly one might surmise that one of the parents is, like Herb, quiet, nonassertive, unexplosive. (3) We might expect that Herb, . . . would be attracted to and select as a wife a woman who could express her anger readily just so long as the anger was not directed at him. From just observing such venting of anger it would appear that Herb would feel better. Well, let's see.

What about Herb's mother? "If she got angry," Herb states, "she got angry and let fly, whereas Dad just shut up. She would never throw anything. She just talked in a loud voice. She talked fast, and she'd say pretty strong things."

Herbert's father had been reared in a home wherein children were required to be quiet and where the father was unquestioned master. Early in the marriage Herb's father tried to establish his mastery in his own house, i.e., over Herb's mother. As Herb reports it, however, "at that age Mother had a strong personality herself, and she changed Dad's ideas about ruling the house." Both Herb and his father are quiet. His father would rather read the paper than talk. Both are self-critical, serious, not self-assertive, easygoing, and mild tempered—too mild at times, Herb opines. Herb says that his mother imposes on his father and has him do more of the domestic chores than he should. Herb does not plan to help with the dishes every night as his father does.

It turns out that Herb's mother is an extraordinarily dominant woman who has supervised the lives of Herb and his father. Herb spent the first twenty years of his life in an effort to please her and to win her favor. As he approached adulthood, he rebelled at her domination. But when he was free of both her orders and those of the military, as we shall see, he was without direction and energy. It seems, then, that Herb's mother was the more dominant and the more violently expressive of the two parents; we cannot be absolutely certain that she was the agent of his fearfulness, but this is a plausible conjecture.

And so as far as our relevant evidence goes, it *is* consistent with— but falls short of substantiating in their entirety—our first two conjectures: (1) that Herb had one dominant, explosive parent who frightened him and (2) that he had one nondominant, unexplosive parent after whom Herb patterned his own behavior. What about our third conjecture?

On the third point we find that Harriet, Herb's wife, is energetic, frank, and open in the display of her feelings. "Enthusiastic" is her term. She loves to talk about herself and to be the center of attention. She is dramatic in speech and gesture. Whenever feeling hostile, which is not infrequently, Harriet can be counted on to express it. She is one who "gets things off her chest." And here is the way Herb sees it: "When I came out of the navy, I didn't have much of a purpose, you know, or goal to work for. I just wanted a pretty easy life if I could, you know, just relax and take it easy. I didn't think particularly about getting married or anything like that at all. And then I met Harriet. In the first place she has a very wonderful quality of enthusiasm. I never had much enthusiasm. Probably it was in me really, but I had a sort of idealization of blaséness, you know. She is very warm, enthusiastic, vivacious. I like that. I suppose that is why I love her." Just once in a while he is bothered by the fact that her readiness to express her feelings causes other people to feel injured, for he does not want to hurt anyone. When this happens, he is a bit self-conscious. This self-consciousness represents one error in our surmises. It is true that Herb feels great admiration for (and presumably participates vicariously in) Harriet's expressiveness in general, but when it causes offense, he becomes uncomfortable at the conscious level. (At deeper levels there is evidence that Herb turns a good deal of his hostility in on himself and suffers from feelings of depression.) Herb feels that he needed direction and energy. Harriet has provided these essentials and has Herb organized for what promises to be a productive career.

As one would expect, Herb is a fellow who approaches a problem with caution, looks at it from all angles, and then is reluctant to come to a decision. He does not wish to be this way. He has always wanted to be "the kind of man who would definitely make decisions and then stick with them and wouldn't be afraid to go ahead on the basis of his decision—like General Patton, for instance. You've got to take risks. Once you've made a decision, don't renege on it. I want to be a person who is decisive." Being impulsive, Harriet jumps into the middle of a problem. She is not one to wait for all the evidence to come in. She is ready with a decision—perhaps not thought out, but it is a decision. This appeals to Herb.

. . . . .

Thus Herb has replaced his expressive, decisive, and dominant mother with an expressive, decisive, and dominant wife. Just how clearly Herb sees this emotional equivalence I do not know. In view of the fact that he sees his mother as a very difficult person, whereas there is relatively little conflict in his relation with Harriet, it would not be astonishing if Herb were to deny stoutly that Harriet was like his mother. (As we shall see, Harriet is explicit in seeing some resemblance between Herb and her father.)

It does appear, however, that there are some qualifications on this equivalence which seem to have importance for Herb. In the first place, although he recognizes that Harriet is a bit bossy, he is able to control this tendency in her. He has only to tell her to "stop nagging," and because she so resented the way her mother treated her father, she is filled with remorse and stops immediately. The second feature is that Harriet is changing somewhat. From time to time Herb has let her know when he has felt that she has unnecessarily hurt someone's feelings. He thinks that as a consequence she has become a bit more restrained. Thirdly, Herb is at work trying to become less mouse and more lion, and he feels that he is making progress at becoming more leonine.

Let me offer the following schematic outline of what has happened to Herb. In childhood he observed the pattern of quietly submissive father and expressively dominant mother. Presumably he learned that since he was a male like his father he should use his father as a model for his own behavior. This involved giving up the expressive role, which thereupon became an "abandoned self." This abandonment of expressiveness was probably reinforced by the dominant mother, who, one would suspect, rewarded Herb for being "nice" and "quiet" and made her disapproval unmistakable on the occasion of any deviations from this pattern. Then Harriet entered the scene and reënacted the expressive role. Because of this she became doubly attractive to Herb. First, he cherished her as a representation of his expressive "abandoned self." (Or as he phrases it, he likes "lively" people.) Second, he cherished her because she gave new life to his ambition that he too might become expressive and that—now that he is no longer under his mother's supervision—he may do so without fear of punishment. (In his words she has "rekindled" his "enthusiasm.") In conclusion, I am suggesting that the kernel of Herb's love for Harriet is that she represents for him (1) an abandoned self and (2) an ego-model.

. . . . .

In their marital interaction Herb plays the role of the respectful, admiring father who soothes her taut and frayed nerves. "There is something about Herbie," Harriet relates, "that takes all the nerves out of a person. You're with him a while and pretty soon you cease to be nervous about things. He has such a wonderfully calm way about him."

And Herb seems to be getting the orientation and the "energizing" which he says he needs, and he seems to feel that he is getting these emotional goods in a much less unpleasant and "bitchy" way than his mother had offered them.

Thus it appears that both Herb and Harriet learned the same conception of sex roles in their respective parental homes—that women are assertive and dominant, that men are quiet and submissive. On the other hand, since both rejected the degree of submissiveness which their fathers revealed, it appears that both had some conflict with respect to these role-definitions. It appears that both are reiterating salient features of these sex roles in their own marriage. The conflict in each of them tends to temper the degree to which each reënacts the respective parental roles: Herb sees himself as more rebellious than his father, as tending to curb Harriet when she gets too far out of line, and as tending for the long haul to become a more generally expressive and assertive man. Whenever Herb points up the parallel between Harriet and her mother, Harriet is horrified with herself and sets about consciously to play the feminine role in its more traditional conception—more quiet and less directive.

80. IDENTITY VERSUS SELF-DIFFUSION

ERIK H. ERIKSON

Adolescent behavior is frequently dictated by the individual's desire to develop a sense of identity. He strives to know what he is and what he is not; he sees himself as others see him and yet wishes to be himself openly and undefensively. Erikson analyzes several aspects of this search for personal "integrity."

With the establishment of a good relationship to the world of skills and to those who teach and share the new skills, childhood proper comes to an end. Youth begins. But in puberty and adolescence all samenesses and continuities relied on earlier are questioned again because of a rapidity of body growth which equals that of early childhood and because of the entirely new addition of physical genital maturity. The growing and developing youths, faced with this physiological revolution within them, are now primarily concerned with attempts at consolidating their social roles. They are sometimes morbidly, often curiously, preoccupied with what they appear to be in the eyes of others as compared with what they feel they are and with the question of how to connect the earlier cultivated roles and skills with the ideal prototypes of the day. In

Selections reprinted from "Growth and Crises" in *Symposium on the Healthy Personality,* edited by Milton J. Senn (Josiah Macy Jr. Foundation, 1950), pp. 134–143, by permission of the author and publisher.

their search for a new sense of continuity and sameness, some adolescents have to refight many of the crises of earlier years, and they are ever ready to install lasting idols and ideals as guardians of a final identity.

The integration now taking place in the form of an ego identity is more than the sum of the childhood identifications. It is the inner capital accrued from all the experiences of each successive stage, when successful identifications led to a successful alignment of the individual's *basic drives* with his *endowment* and his *opportunities*. In psychoanalysis we ascribe such successful alignments to "ego synthesis"; this writer has tried to demonstrate that the ego values accrued in childhood culminate in what he has called a sense of ego identity. The sense of ego identity, then, is the accrued confidence that one's ability to maintain inner sameness and continuity (one's ego in the psychological sense) is matched by the sameness and continuity of one's meaning for others.

. . . . .

In general it is primarily the inability to settle on an occupational identity which disturbs young people. To keep themselves together they temporarily overidentify, to the point of apparent complete loss of identity, with the heroes of cliques and crowds. On the other hand, they become remarkably clannish, intolerant, and cruel in their exclusion of others who are "different," in skin color or cultural background, in tastes and gifts, and often in entirely petty aspects of dress and gesture arbitrarily selected as *the* signs of an in-grouper or out-grouper. It is important to understand (which does not mean condone or participate in) such intolerance as the necessary *defense against a sense of self-diffusion,* which is unavoidable at a time of life when the body changes its proportions radically, when genital maturity floods body and imagination with all manner of drives, when intimacy with the other sex approaches and is, on occasion, forced on the youngster, and when life lies before one with a variety of conflicting possibilities and choices. Adolescents help one another temporarily through such discomfort by forming cliques and by stereotyping themselves and their ideals.

It is important to understand this because it makes clear the appeal which simple totalitarian doctrines have on the minds of the youth of such countries and classes as have lost or are losing their group identities (feudal, agrarian, national, and so forth) in these times of world-wide industrialization. The dynamic quality of the tempestuous adolescence lived through in patriarchal and agrarian countries (countries which face the most radical changes in political structure and in economy) explains the fact that their youths find convincing and satisfactory identities in the simple totalitarian doctrines of race, class, or nation. Even though we may be forced to win wars against their leaders, we still are faced with the job of winning the peace with these grim youths by convincingly demonstrating to them (by living it) a democratic identity which can be strong and yet tolerant, judicious and still determined.

But it is equally important to understand this in order to treat the intolerances of our adolescents at home with understanding and guidance rather than with verbal stereotypes or prohibitions. It is difficult to be tolerant if deep down you are not quite sure that you are a man (or a woman), that you will ever grow together again and be attractive, that you will be able to master your drives, that you really know who you are, that you know what you want to be, that you know what you look like to others, and that you will know how to make the right decisions without, once for all, committing yourself to the wrong friend, girl, or career.

Religions help the integration of such identity with "confirmations" of a clearly defined way of life. In many countries, nationalism supports a sense of identity. In primitive tribes puberty rites help to standardize the new identity, often with horrifying impressive rituals.

. . . . .

Here childhood and youth come to an end; life, so the saying goes, begins: by which we mean work or study for a specified career, sociability with the other sex, and in time, marriage and a family of one's own. But it is only after a reasonable sense of identity has been established that real *intimacy* with the other sex (or, for that matter, with any other person or even with oneself) is possible. Sexual intimacy is only part of what I have in mind, for it is obvious that sexual intimacies do not always wait for the ability to develop a true and mutual psychological intimacy with another person. What I have in mind is that late-adolescent need for a kind of fusion with the essence of other people. The youth who is not sure of his identity shies away from interpersonal intimacy; but the surer he becomes of himself, the more he seeks it in the forms of friendship, combat, leadership, love, and inspiration. There is a kind of adolescent attachment between boy and girl which is often mistaken either for sexual attraction or for love. Except where the mores demand heterosexual behavior, such attachment is often devoted to an attempt at arriving at a definition of one's identity by talking things over endlessly, by confessing what one feels like and what the other seems like, and by discussing plans, wishes, and expectations. Where a youth does not accomplish such intimate relation with others—and, I would add, with his own inner resources—in late adolescence or early adulthood, he may either isolate himself and find, at best, highly stereotyped and formal interpersonal relations (formal in the sense of lacking in spontaneity, warmth, and real exchange of fellowship), or he must seek them in repeated attempts and repeated failures. Unfortunately, many young people marry under such circumstances, hoping to find themselves in finding one another; but alas, the early obligation to act in a defined way, as mates and as parents, disturbs them in the completion of this work on themselves. Obviously, a change of mate is rarely the answer, but rather some wisely guided insight into the fact that the condition of a true twoness is that one must first become oneself.

. . . . .

The problem of genitality is intimately related to the seventh criterion of mental health, which concerns parenthood. Sexual mates who find, or on the way to finding, true genitality in their relations will soon wish (if, indeed, developments wait for the express wish) to combine their energies in the care of common offspring. This wish I have termed the desire for generativity, because it concerns the establishment (by way of genitality and genes) of the next generation. No other fashionable term, such as creativity or productivity, seems to me to convey the necessary idea. Generativity is primarily the interest in establishing and guiding the next generation, although there are people who, from misfortune or because of special and genuine gifts in other directions, do not apply this drive to offspring but to other formal creativity, which may absorb their kind of parental responsibility. The principal thing is to realize that this is a stage of the growth of the healthy personality and that where such enrichment fails altogether, regression from generativity to an obsessive need for pseudointimacy takes place, often with a pervading sense of stagnation and interpersonal impoverishment. Individuals who do not develop generativity often begin to indulge themselves as if they were their own one and only child. The mere fact of having or even wanting children does not, of course, involve generativity; in fact the majority of young parents seen in child-guidance work suffer, it seems, from the inability to develop this stage. The reasons are often to be found in early childhood impressions; in faulty identifications with parents; in excessive self-love based on a too strenuously self-made personality; and finally (and here we return to the beginnings) in the lack of some faith, some "belief in the species," which would make a child a welcome trust of the community.

Only he who in some way has taken care of things and people and has adapted himself to the triumphs and disappointments adherent to being, by necessity, the originator of others and the generator of things and ideas—only he may gradually grow the fruit of the seven stages. I know no better word for it than integrity. Lacking a clear definition, I shall point to a few attributes of this state of mind. It is the acceptance of one's one and only life cycle and of the people who have become significant to it as something that has to be and that, by necessity, permitted of no substitutions. It thus means a new, a different love of one's parents, free of the wish that they should have been different, and an acceptance of the fact that one's life is one's own responsibility. It is a sense of comradeship with men and women of distant times and of different pursuits, who have created orders and objects and sayings conveying human dignity and love. Although aware of the relativity of all the various life styles which have given meaning to human striving, the possessor of integrity is ready to defend the dignity of his own life style against all physical and economic threats. For he knows that an individual life is the accidental coincidence of but one life cycle with but one segment of history; and that for him all human integrity stands or falls with the one style of integrity of which he partakes.

Correlation of This Book with Standard Texts

Almy CHILD DEVELOPMENT Holt, 1955	*Baldwin* BEHAVIOR AND DEVELOP- MENT IN CHILDHOOD Dryden Press, 1955	*Cole* PSYCHOLOGY OF ADOLES- CENCE, 5TH ED. Rinehart, 1959
Text *chs. Related Articles*	*Text* *chs. Related Articles*	*Text* *parts Related Articles*
1. 14, 67	1. 25, 80	Part I 1–5, 15, 16, 68
2. 15, 17–20	2. 3, 4	Part II 29, 54–58, 60, 61,
3. 23, 25–27, 16, 59	3. 14, 67	63–65
4. 24	4. 20–21, 59	Part III 17–20, 25–27, 34,
5. 17–19, 21, 22, 23	5. 56–58	42, 44–46, 51, 53,
6. 5, 7	6. 31, 63	59
7. 10, 11, 13, 28, 49	7. 48, 59	Part IV 7–14, 28–33, 35–
8. 34, 53, 57, 58	8. 15–21, 42–43, 74–75	41, 66–69
9. 29, 30–33, 52, 56, 60– 63	9. 1, 3, 4, 8–13, 23	Part V 62, 63, 70–78
10. 36, 38, 40–41, 42, 43, 51	10. 24–27, 36, 57–58	Part VI 49–63, 79–80
11. 67–76	11. 63–65	
12. 35, 37–39, 64–66, 77, 78–80	12.	
13. 1–4, 6	13. 27, 28, 34	
	14. 35, 36, 37	
	15.	
	16. 17–20	
	17. 59–61	
	18. 5, 23, 31	
	19. 20, 47	
	20. 37, 39	
	21. 38, 40–42, 44, 45, 46	
	22. 21, 23–27	
	23. 29, 30, 49–55, 77–80	
	24. 7	

Correlation of This Book with Standard Texts (*Continued*)

English CHILD PSYCHOLOGY Holt, 1951	*Garrison* PSYCHOLOGY OF ADOLES- CENCE, 5TH ED. Prentice Hall, 1956	*Jenkins, Schacter, Bauer* THESE ARE YOUR CHILDREN Scott, Foresman, 1953
Text *chs. Related Articles*	*Text* *chs. Related Articles*	*Text* *chs. Related Articles*
1. 11, 13	1. 14, 67	1. 15, 16, 44, 64, 65
2. 24	2. 15–21, 70	2. 17, 18, 19, 21, 22
3. 5, 9, 23	3.	3. 25, 28, 40
4. 35, 36, 37, 38, 66	4. 7, 29, 45–46, 50, 61,	4. 11, 34, 57, 58
5. 26, 27, 28	63–65	5. 7, 27, 37, 38
6. 29, 30	5. 7, 25–28, 30, 34, 47,	6. 26, 45, 46, 55
7. 20, 21	48	7. 51, 53, 56
8. 17, 18, 19, 22, 56, 57,	6. 74, 75, 77, 78	8. 6, 7, 13
58	7. 31–33, 40–44, 60	9. 1, 5, 8, 10, 14
9. 50, 51, 52, 53	8. 1–4, 9–14	10. 12, 68, 69, 73
10. 15, 16	9. 37, 68, 69, 72, 73	11. 67, 72, 76, 78
11. 42, 44, 49	10. 54–59, 70–71	12. 34, 40, 41, 42, 43
12. 7, 64	11. 69	13. 30, 31, 32, 33
13. 61, 63	12. 8–14, 37–41, 50–53	14. 39, 70, 71, 80
14. 31, 32, 33, 62	13. 31–33, 70, 71, 72	
15. 1, 2, 3, 4, 29	14. 6–7, 60, 62, 66, 77, 76	
16. 6, 21, 38, 39, 40, 41	15. 29, 30, 50, 51	
17. 14, 34	16. 53–56, 61, 63, 76	
	17. 9, 17, 23, 35, 36, 37,	
	38, 40–41, 47, 66, 75	
	18. 1, 76, 77–80	

Correlation of This Book with Standard Texts (*Continued*)

Jersild CHILD PSYCHOLOGY, 4TH ED. Prentice Hall, 1954	*Mc Donald* EDUCATIONAL PSYCHOLOGY Wadsworth Publishing Co., 1959	*Martin and Stendler* CHILD BEHAVIOR AND DE- VELOPMENT Harcourt, Brace, 1959
Text *chs. Related Articles*	*Text* *chs. Related Articles*	*Text* *chs. Related Articles*
1. 24	1. 1, 2, 3, 4, 15, 16	1. 20, 22
2. 15, 16	2. 31, 33, 54, 63	2. 21, 24, 25, 26, 49, 59
3. pp. 121–124	3. 24, 34	3.
4. 17–19, 22	4. 25, 26, 27, 28	4. 16
5. pp. 121–124	5. 51, 52	5. 15
6. 26–27	6. 45, 46, 61	6. 1, 3, 4, 8, 9, 11, 13, 28
7. 32	7. 36–44	7. 26, 27, 34
8. 28, 31, 33, 43	8. 29, 30, 32	8. 23, 29, 30, 35, 36, 40,
9. 20–21, 70–72	9. 36–47	41
10. 45–47, 59, 77	10. 23, 56, 57, 58	9. 17, 18, 19
11. 36, 42, 74–75	11. 17, 18, 19, 20, 21, 25	10. 37–42
12. 50, 51, 53, 61, 63	12. 14, 35, 50, 77, 80	11. 46, 50, 54, 55, 56, 57,
13. 34	13. 28, 59–63, 66	58, 61, 63
14. 51	14. 5, 6, 7	12. 31, 32, 33, 66, 75
15. 51–52	15. 64, 76	13. 35, 43, 62, 71, 72
16. 25–28, 34, 51, 53	16. 65, 73	14. 70, 73
17. 1–5, 10–14, 29, 30,	17. 67, 68, 69	15. 51, 63, 64, 65
40–42	18. 14, 54	16. 5, 6, 76, 77
18. 44, 64, 65		
19. 6, 7, 53, 48, 68, 69		

Correlation of This Book with Standard Texts (*Continued*)

Merry and Merry THE FIRST TWO DECADES OF LIFE, 2ND ED. Harper, 1958	*Mussen and Conger* CHILD DEVELOPMENT AND PERSONALITY Harper, 1956	*Sawrey & Telford* EDUCATIONAL PSYCHOLOGY Allyn & Bacon, 1958
Text *chs. Related Articles*	*Text* *chs. Related Articles*	*Text* *chs. Related Articles*
1. 1, 24, 70–73	1. 1, 2, 3, 4, 7, 24	1. 25, 26, 27
2. 15, 16	2. 15, 16	2. 30, 59, 63
3. 17, 18, 19	3. 15, 16	3. 60, 61
4. 20–22	4. 21, 59	4. 72, 73
5. pp. 121–124	5. 46, 54, 61	5. 28, 29, 34
6. 26, 27, 34, 51	6. 17–22	6. 1, 2, 3, 4, 6, 7
7. 45, 46, 54–58, 63–65	7. 19, 21, 23	7. 15, 16, 20
8. 47, 49, 51, 59–61	8. 26, 27, 28, 34, 42, 49	8. 44, 69, 70
9. 23, 25, 49–53, 56–58	9. 34, 51, 52, 53, 57, 58	9. 63, 64, 65
10. 6–13, 28, 31–33, 35, 48, 55	10. 37, 38, 39, 40, 49, 73	10. 68, 71
11. 17–19, 23, 25, 28–30, 45–47	11. 6, 28–33, 50, 54, 56, 60–65	11. 20, 21, 45, 46, 55, 56, 57, 58
12. 1–5, 14, 35–41, 62, 66–70	12. 35, 36, 40–47, 66, 68, 77	12. 5, 6, 9, 35–41, 74, 75, 77
13. 26–28, 51, 78	13. 9, 70, 71, 72, 73, 74, 75	13. 30, 31, 32, 33, 53, 61
14. 5–7, 14, 28, 31–33, 54, 73, 77, 80	14. 14, 78, 79, 80	14. 62, 63, 66, 69, 71
		15. 34, 53, 51, 52, 79

774

Correlation of This Book with Standard Texts (*Continued*)

Stone and Church CHILDHOOD AND ADOLES- CENCE Random House, 1957	*Thompson* CHILD PSYCHOLOGY Houghton Mifflin, 1952	*Robert I. Watson* PSYCHOLOGY OF THE CHILD Wiley, 1959
Text *chs. Related Articles*	*Text* *chs. Related Articles*	*Text* *chs. Related Articles*
1. 15	1. 24, 27, 34, 45, 47, 56, 57, 58, 59	1. 1, 2, 3, 9, 24
2. 16, pp. 121–124	2. 15, 20, 22	2. 5, 7, 13, 24, 32
3. 17–22	3. 16, 17, 18	3. 15, 16
4. 25–27, 10–13	4. 46, 50, 51, 54, 59, 60, 61	4. 4, 8, 10, 11, 12, 23
5. 9, 74, 75	5. 38, 40, 41, 42, 44, 56, 57, 58, 62, 66	5. 23, 25, 26, 27, 28, 34, 36, 51
6. 23, 28, 59, 63	6. 6, 32, 48, 63	6. 18, 19, 20, 21, 59
7. 34, 49, 51, 53, 57, 58	7. 16, 19, 47	7. 17, 25, 38
8. 8, 9, 33, 35–38	8. 20, 21, 26, 42, 45, 46	8. 17, 18, 19
9. 1–5, 29, 30, 51, 53	9. 51, 53	9. 21, 23, 26, 42
10. 66, 68, 69, 72	10. 6, 15, 64, 65	10. 23, 38, 57, 58
11. 14, 67, 70, 71	11. 27, 30, 31, 33, 38	11. 63, 64, 65, Part VI
12. 6, 73–76, 80	12. 11, 12, 13, 29, 35, 43	12. 6, 29, 30–33, 41–47, 70, 77
13. 34–48	13. 1, 3, 4, 13, 25, 36	13. Part IV, 49, 51, 52, 53
14. 7, 49–66	14. 5, 6, 7, 76, 77, 80	

INDEX

I

Date Due